Collins
Gage

Canadian
Intermediate
Thesaurus

Collins

THOMSON
NELSON

HarperCollins Publishers
Westerhill Road
Bishopbriggs
Glasgow
G64 2LP
Great Britain

© HarperCollins Publishers 2006

Collins ® is a registered trademark of
HarperCollins Publishers Limited
www.collins.co.uk

Gage ® is a registered trademark of Nelson,
a division of Thomson Canada Limited

school distribution by
Nelson, a division of
Thomson Canada Limited
1120 Birchmount Road,
Toronto, ON M1K 5G4
www.nelson.com

trade distribution by
HarperCollins Canada
2 Bloor Street East,
Toronto, ON M4W 1A8
www.harpercollins.ca

ISBN 0-00-639580-5

National Library of Canada
Cataloguing in Publication
Collins Gage Canadian Intermediate Thesaurus.

1. English language—Canada—Synonyms and
antonyms—Dictionaries, Juvenile.
2. English language—Synonyms and antonyms—
Dictionaries, Juvenile.
3. Canadianisms (English)
PE3233.C65 2005   j423'.12
C2005-906667-9

Typeset by Wordcraft
Printed in Canada by Webcom Limited

Project Management
Morven Dooner, Ann Downar, David Friend,
Elaine Higgleton

Editors
Lorna Gilmour, Dan Liebman, Sandy Manley,
Lisa Peterson, Anne Robertson

Series Editor, Collins
Lorna Knight

**Director of Literacy and Reference Publishing,
Nelson**
Joe Banel

**General Manager, Literacy, Reference, and
International, Nelson**
Kevin Martindale

Introduction and Activities
James Coulter
Middle Years Adolescent Literacy Project
Toronto District School Board
Ontario

Reviewed by the Following Educators
Maria Carty
Annapolis Valley Regional School Board
Nova Scotia

James Coulter
Toronto District School Board
Ontario

Ingrid Fawcett
Nadine Naughton
Greater Victoria School District #61
British Columbia

Irene Heffel
Edmonton Public Schools
Alberta

Gale May
York Region District School Board
Ontario

Collins Gage Canadian reference resources
combine the strengths of the Collins and
Gage reference lines. They contain the most
accurate and up-to-date information, prepared
in consultation with Canadian educators for
Canadian students.

Collins is one of the world's leading reference
publishers. The Collins Word Web contains 125
million words of Canadian English and grows
at over 1.5 million words per month.

Gage represents a 40-year tradition of
Canadian dictionary making. Today, Gage is
the reference division of Thomson Nelson,
Canada's foremost educational publisher.

Contents

Introduction

LOOK FOR WORD STUDIES ON THESE PAGES

	Page		Page		Page
bad	46	fat	189	new	323
badly	45	good	218	nice	325
best	55	great	223	old	334
better	55	happy	231	say	423
big	57	high	238	short	438
break	66	hit	240	small	447
call	75	laugh	279	strong	470
close	90	little	289	thin	491
cry	120	long	292	walk	527
cut	123	look	293	wide	535
eat	159	mark	304		
end	165	move	317		

WHAT IS A THESAURUS?

A thesaurus is an important writing resource. It can help you replace an ordinary word with one that is more **interesting**. It can also help you find substitutes for words you think you use to often in your writing.

interesting: **absorbing**
                       compelling
                       entertaining
                       gripping
                       intriguing
                       stimulating

Thesaurus is from the Greek word *thesauros*, which means "treasure house." In what ways is a thesaurus like a treasure house?

Not a Dictionary!

As you know, a dictionary contains words and their definitions. A thesaurus, even though it is organized alphabetically like a dictionary, is quite different. It contains words and their synonyms (words that have similar meanings), allowing you to choose the most appropriate word for your writing task. When you use words that are richer or more precise than common or overused words, the people who read your writing will think "Hey, this person really knows how to write!"

Thesaurus	Dictionary
✔ Shows words in alphabetical order	✔ Shows words in alphabetical order
✔ Gives the part of speech of the word	✔ Gives the part of speech of the word
✔ Focuses on **synonyms**	✔ Focuses on **definitions**
✔ Sometimes gives brief descriptions	✔ Sometimes provides synonyms
✔ Gives antonyms when appropriate	✔ Gives pronunciations, word histories, etc.
✔ Is a useful resource for any writer!	✔ Is a useful resource for any writer!

This Thesaurus Is Special

The entry words in the *Collins Gage Canadian Intermediate Thesaurus* are the words that you use most often in your schoolwork and personal writing. Each entry word has a brief definition, then a list of several of the most useful synonyms. If a word has more than one meaning, there are synonyms for each meaning. There are almost 30 000 entry words and synonyms in total. That's a lot of words! In addition to the synonyms, many entries also give the best antonym (word with the opposite meaning) for one or more of the meanings.

WHY USE A THESAURUS?

You don't need to use a thesaurus every time you write something, but when you are working on a piece of writing that has to make a strong impression on your readers, a thesaurus is an excellent tool to have close at hand.

Better Writing!

Whether you are an experienced writer of English or someone new to the language, a thesaurus is a vital part of your "writer's toolkit." A thesaurus can help you to improve your writing in many ways. It can help you to:

✔ find that "just right" word that expresses exactly what you want to say

✔ select alternatives to overused words (such as **bad**, **good**, and **say**)

✔ choose words that will reflect the tone that you want to convey (e.g., a formal, informal, persuasive, or sarcastic tone)

✔ build up your vocabulary so that you have lots of great words to choose from when you write

Better Reading!

When you choose words carefully and creatively, you make your readers' job much more enjoyable. Your readers will find it easy to understand what you're saying, and they'll also want to keep reading because your words are holding their interest.

Remember that a good writer always writes with readers in mind. Different readers have different reasons for reading, and your writing should meet those needs. Thinking about your readers and your purpose for writing will help you to decide what form of writing you will use and the tone that will work best.

Readers	Writing Purpose	Type of Writing	Readers' Needs
• Friend	• To tell about an experience	• Friendly e-mail	• Informal tone, entertaining language
• Mayor	• To request information	• Formal letter	• Formal and respectful tone, brief and clear message
• Peers	• To capture an emotion	• Poem	• Vivid, imaginative language

HOW TO USE THIS THESAURUS

This thesaurus has been designed to be both informative and user-friendly. Say you want to look up the word **clean**. Flip to the C words and look at the guide words at the top of each page. The guide word on the left is the first full entry on the page, and the one on the right is the last entry on the page.

guide words

class **clear**

Clean falls between **class** and **clear** alphabetically, so you know you've found the right page.

Each entry follows the same format, so you can easily locate the information you need. Here is the entry for **dark**:

entry word •—— **dark**
part of speech •——— ▷ *ADJECTIVE*
definition of one meaning of the entry word • **1** lacking light: *It was too dark to see what was happening.*
cloudy *a cloudy sky*
dim *the dim outline of a small boat*
synonyms and examples • **dingy** *a dingy basement*
murky *the murky waters of the swamp*
overcast *a cold, windy, overcast afternoon*
shadowy *a shadowy corner*
antonym •——— *ANTONYM* **light**
definition of another meaning of the entry word • **2** dull in colour: *a dark suit*
black *a black leather coat*
swarthy *a swarthy complexion*
▷ *NOUN*
3 lack of light: *I've always been afraid of the dark.*
darkness *The room was plunged into darkness.*
dimness *I squinted to adjust my eyes to the dimness.*
dusk *She disappeared into the dusk.*
gloom *the gloom of a foggy November morning*
cross-reference • *ANTONYM* **light**
See also **dim, gloomy**

On the Right Track

Sometimes you will look up a word and it will tell you to go to another word. This feature is called a **cross-reference**. For example, here is what you will find if you look up the word **regain**:

regain *See* **recover**

When you go to **recover**, you'll find other words you might use instead of **regain**, such **as get back**, **recapture**, or **retrieve**.

FEATURE BOXES

There are special features in this thesaurus that are designed to help you with some of the more troublesome aspects of the English language: overused words, informal expressions, and words that are easily confused.

Overused Words

Some words are so overused that they require in-depth coverage. The **WORD STUDY** feature gives you a broad range of more interesting and precise words to replace words that are used so often they aren't very effective (like **bad**):

WORD STUDY: BAD

Bad is such a commonly used word that it has come to lose much of its effectiveness. There are more expressive substitutes that can be used instead.

• **having a harmful effect**
Stress can be **damaging** healthwise.
Which chemicals have a **destructive** effect on the ozone layer?
This could have a **detrimental** impact on the environment.
There are **harmful** effects of radiation.
Illnesses can be caused by an **unhealthy** lifestyle.
The side effects of this drug are **unpleasant**.

• **lacking skill**
Incompetent managers will be fired.
The actor gave an **inept** performance.
She's a **poor** judge of character and is easily fooled.
He is **useless** at all sports.

• **having an evil character**
The rebels fought to defeat a **corrupt** government.

Informal Expressions

Some words are used in informal expressions that have their own unique meaning. For example, the word **cold**, meaning "having a low temperature" is used in the expression **cold feet**, meaning "loss of nerve or courage." The **INFORMALLY SPEAKING** feature highlights different informal expressions and defines them.

INFORMALLY SPEAKING

cold feet: loss of nerve or courage
out cold: unconscious
out in the cold: alone or neglected

Easily Confused Words

In the English language there are many words that tend to be misused in writing because they are easily confused with similar words. For example, many people mix up **to, too,** and **two** in their writing, especially when they are in a hurry. The **CONFUSABLES** feature warns you about some of these writing pitfalls.

CONFUSABLES

loose means **not tight**
lose usually means **misplace** or **fail to keep**

Category Lists

Sometimes it's best to use a *specific* word to replace a word that is very general. For example, you might replace the general word **boat** with an appropriate specific term such as **dinghy, kayak,** or **motorboat**. Boxes with headings such as **TYPES OF...** and **NAMES OF...** provide lists of specific words in different categories, such as a particular colour or geographical feature. A maple leaf beside a word in one of these boxes means that the word either started in Canada, or is used here in a special way.

TYPES OF ... *FOREST*	
bush ❧	thicket
grove	woodland
jungle	woods
rainforest	

Top Five Thesaurus Tips

1. When you are editing a draft, **underline words** that are repeats. Using this thesaurus can help you find ways to avoid repetition.

2. Look at the **list of Word Studies** on page 3. You can use the Word Studies to find replacements for overused words you have spotted in your writing.

3. **Ask a classmate** to read your draft and **point out words** that could be replaced with more effective language. Use this thesaurus to help you find the new words.

4. Before you replace a word, **make sure you have a good idea of what the synonym means.** In this thesaurus, look carefully at the example sentence or phrase that shows how the synonym is used. If you're still not sure whether the meaning is right, look up the word in a dictionary, or choose a different synonym that you know will fit.

5. If you look up a word and don't find a good synonym, **check for a "See also" list** at the end of the entry. If you look up the words in the "See also" list, you'll find other entries with synonyms that might work.

THESAURUS ACTIVITIES

Try this with a partner.

Thesaurus Scavenger Hunt

This Scavenger Hunt is designed to help you become more familiar with the features and content of the *Collins Gage Canadian Intermediate Thesaurus*.

Use this book to answer the following questions. Write your answers in your notebook or on a separate piece of paper.

1. Which part of speech is the word **rowdy**?

2. What does the word **whim** mean?

3. How many different meanings are given for the word **near**?

4. What is the antonym listed for the word **agile**?

5. How many synonyms are provided for the word **fast**?

6. List three synonyms for the word **soft**.

7. List four alternatives for the overused word **say**.

8. Find two informal expressions that contain the word **part**.

9. Explain the difference between the confusable words **affect** and **effect**.

10. List five different types of boat.

THESAURUS ACTIVITIES

Try this with a partner.

Text Rescue!

The passage below has correct spelling and grammar, but it could use your help to make it more interesting. Use the *Collins Gage Canadian Intermediate Thesaurus* to replace the underlined words with more colourful alternatives. Record your word choices in your workbook or on a piece of paper.

Make this passage pop!

Lost

The <u>tired</u> hiker climbed the ridge to get a better view of the whole valley. He covered his eyes against the <u>bright</u> sun.

"Oh no!" he <u>said</u> to himself. "It's official. I am lost!"

He looked for a familiar landmark. Sadly, he couldn't <u>see</u> anything helpful. With a sigh, the hiker picked what he thought was a <u>good</u> direction and started walking.

After a couple of hours, the hiker really began to worry. The sun was <u>really</u> hot. He could feel his <u>uncovered</u> skin beginning to sunburn. His shirt was <u>wet</u> with sweat and was <u>sticking</u> to his skin.

Just when he began to lose hope, he saw a <u>green</u> truck coming over a hill. Help at last! A woman in a ranger's uniform stopped her truck near the hiker.

"I thought that you could use some <u>help</u>," she said. "Have you been out here long?"

"Yes! I mean thanks!" the hiker <u>said</u> as he jumped into the truck. "I'm so <u>happy</u> you found me."

"I'll take you back to headquarters, where we can give you some water and a lesson in how to <u>read</u> a map!" the woman <u>laughed</u> as they drove away.

THESAURUS ACTIVITIES

Try this with a partner.

Revising Gone Wrong

A thesaurus provides many different and interesting synonyms for words that you may wish to replace in your writing. You have to be careful, though, about which synonym you choose. Some synonyms have meanings that won't match with what you want to express in your writing. For example, one synonym for the word **nice** is **polite**, but you would never tell someone "Have a polite day!"

The students who created the poster below used a thesaurus to try to make the language more exciting. Unfortunately, they didn't choose suitable synonyms, and now the poster makes no sense! Use the *Collins Gage Canadian Intermediate Thesaurus* to find better synonyms for the underlined words. Record your choices in your workbook or on a piece of paper.

<u>Vast</u> Bake Sale Today!

— 12:00 in the Lunchroom —

- Help us <u>shelter</u> the animals!

- There is a <u>menace</u> that hundreds of species will <u>fade</u>!

- Buy our <u>palatable</u> baked goods! Win <u>remarkable</u> prizes!

- Help a <u>magnanimous</u> cause. You'll be <u>contented</u> that you did!

ANSWERS

Thesaurus Scavenger Hunt

1. **Rowdy** is an adjective.
2. **Whim** means "a sudden idea or wish to do something."
3. **Near** is given 3 different meanings.
4. The antonym listed for **agile** is **clumsy**.
5. There are 14 synonyms provided for **fast**.
6. The synonyms listed for **soft** are (choose any 3 of the following): **flexible, pliable, squashy, supple, yielding; gentle, low, mellow, muted, quiet, subdued; dim, faint, light, mellow, pale, pastel.**
7. The alternatives listed for **say** are (choose any 4 of the following): **utter, comment, remark, state, mention, note, observe, point out, announce, assert, affirm, declare, add, interrupt, chat, converse, gossip, explain, ask, inquire, query, question, answer, reply, respond, riposte, retort, chatter, gabble, prattle, ramble, breathe, whisper, hiss, mumble, murmur, mutter, croak, grunt, rasp, wheeze, gasp, pant, groan, moan, growl, snarl, snap.**
8. Informal expressions that contain the word **part** are (choose any 2 of the following): **for my part, for the most part, in part, part and parcel, part with, play a part.**
9. **Affect** means "influence" and is a verb. **Effect** means "result," and is usually a noun.
10. The types of boat listed are (choose any 5 of the following): **barge, canoe, coracle, dinghy, dugout, ferry, gondola, houseboat, iceboat, junk, kayak, ketch, longliner, motorboat, punt, rowboat, sailboat, speedboat, umiak, yacht.**

Text Rescue!

Answers will vary. Here are some appropriate synonyms for each of the underlined words in the passage: **tired** exhausted, weary, worn out; **bright** brilliant, dazzling; **said** remarked, announced, declared, muttered, groaned; **see** discern, observe, perceive, spot; **good** beneficial, favourable; **really** truly, extremely, terribly; **uncovered** bare, exposed; **wet** drenched, saturated, soaked, sodden; **sticking** adhering, clinging; **green** (any of the green colour words is acceptable); **help** aid, assistance, support; **said** answered, replied, responded; **happy** delighted, ecstatic, glad, overjoyed, thrilled; **read** decipher, interpret; **laughed** chuckled, chortled.

Revising Gone Wrong

Answers will vary. Here are some of the appropriate synonyms for each of the underlined words in the passage: **vast** colossal, enormous, gigantic, huge, mammoth; **shelter** protect, safeguard, defend; **menace** danger, risk, threat; **fade** die out, disappear, vanish, become extinct, cease to exist; **palatable** tasty, delicious; **remarkable** excellent, great, marvellous, superb, wonderful, amazing, incredible, magnificent; **magnanimous** noble, worthy; **contented** delighted, glad, happy.

Aa

abandon

▷ VERB

1 to leave someone or something: *He abandoned the car and walked home.*
desert *The street was deserted at night.*
jilt *She was jilted by her first fiancé.*
leave *She has left home to go to university.*
leave behind *He walked out and left behind unfinished work.*

▷ NOUN

2 lack of restraint: *He began to laugh with abandon.*
recklessness *the headstrong recklessness of youth*
wildness *Their wildness just needed to be channelled properly.*
ANTONYM **control**
See also **cancel, leave**

abandoned   See **derelict**

abate

▷ VERB

to become less: *The four-day flood at last abated.*
decrease *The pain had decreased considerably.*
diminish *The media attention to the political scandal has not diminished.*
ebb *Her strength was ebbing fast.*
lessen *After a while, the cramps lessened.*
subside *Their enthusiasm was beginning to subside.*
wane *His popularity shows no sign of waning.*
See also **ease, lessen, moderate**

abbreviate   See **shorten**

abdicate   See **resign**

abduct   See **kidnap**

abhor   See **dislike, hate**

abhorrence   See **horror**

abhorrent   See **hateful**

abide   See **bear, put up with**

abide by   See **obey**

abiding   See **permanent**

ability

▷ NOUN

the skill needed to do something: *the ability to get along with others*
capability *We have the capability of going out and winning.*
competence *Professional athletes have a high level of competence.*
expertise *legal expertise*
skill *the skill to play at a higher level*
talent *a talent for music*
ANTONYM **inability**
See also **capacity, gift, potential, qualification, skill, talent**

able

▷ ADJECTIVE

good at doing something: *She proved herself to be an able politician.*
accomplished *an accomplished pianist*
capable *a very capable manager*
efficient *a team of efficient workers*
expert *My brother is an expert baker.*
first-rate *This run is suitable only for first-rate skiers.*
skilled *a skilled technician*
talented *a talented actor*
See also **capable, expert, proficient, skilful, skilled**

ably   See **well**

abnormal   See **strange**

abode   See **home, house**

abolish

▷ VERB

to do away with something: *Their objective was to abolish the new tax.*
annul *The marriage was annulled after one month.*
do away with *the proposal to do away with nuclear weapons*
overturn *criminals seeking to overturn their convictions*
put an end to *efforts to put an end to the famine*

abortive   See **futile, vain**

about

▷ PREPOSITION

1 of or concerning: *anxiety about his sick son*
concerning *statistics concerning the hockey season*
on *his book on Wilfrid Laurier*
regarding *strict rules regarding the disposal of hazardous waste*
relating to *the rules relating to competitive figure skating*

▷ ADVERB

2 not exactly: *The procedure takes about 30 minutes.*
almost *Their wages have almost doubled.*
approximately *The lynx was approximately three times the size of a domestic cat.*

around *The crowd here is around 12 000.*
nearly *a tradition going back nearly
20 centuries*
roughly *One litre is roughly equivalent to a
quart.*
See also **almost**

above

▷ PREPOSITION

1 over or higher than something: *above the
clouds*
higher than *There are many hotels higher
than 20 storeys.*
over *the picture over the fireplace*
ANTONYM **below**
2 greater than a certain level or amount: *The
temperature is above 30°.*
beyond *I expect to live way beyond 100.*
exceeding *an area exceeding 200 km².*
See also **over**

abrasion *See* **graze**

abrupt

▷ ADJECTIVE

1 sudden or unexpected: *the abrupt
resignation of the prime minister*
sudden *this week's sudden blizzard*
unexpected *Her career came to an
unexpected end.*
unforeseen *unforeseen difficulties*
2 unfriendly and impolite: *He was taken
aback by her abrupt manner.*
curt *"The matter is closed," was the curt
reply.*
rude *He was frequently rude to servers.*
short *She seemed tense and was definitely
short with me.*
terse *He received a terse one-line e-mail
after the job interview.*
ANTONYM **polite**
See also **rude, sharp, sudden**

absence *See* **lack, want**

absent

▷ ADJECTIVE

not present: *absent from work*
away *She is away on a business trip.*
elsewhere *Four witnesses can testify he was
elsewhere at the time.*
gone *I'll be gone for only ten minutes.*
missing *Another 44 passengers are still
missing.*
ANTONYM **present**

absent-minded

▷ ADJECTIVE

forgetful or not paying attention: *Her absent-
minded stepfather left the camera in the taxi.*
distracted *He seems distracted, giving the*
impression of not listening.
forgetful *The patient is getting rather
forgetful, and living mostly in the past.*

absolute

▷ ADJECTIVE

1 total and complete: *He is talking absolute
nonsense.*
complete *The operation was a complete
success.*
total *total silence*
downright *That's a downright lie!*
pure *a work of pure genius*
sheer *It would be sheer madness to go out in
this weather.*
thorough *He has a thorough knowledge of
the subject.*
utter *She stared at me in utter disbelief.*
2 having total power: *an absolute ruler*
dictatorial *a dictatorial system of
government*
supreme *He made a supreme effort to
control his temper.*
tyrannical *uprisings against tyrannical
rulers*
See also **complete, final, perfect, pure,
rank, sheer, total, utter**

absolutely *See* **exactly, quite, really**

absolutely not *See* **no**

absolve *See* **clear, forgive**

absorb

▷ VERB

to soak up or take in something: *Plants
absorb carbon dioxide.*
digest *Fats are hard to digest.*
soak up *Leave until the dried fruit has
soaked up all the water.*
take in *Leaves take in light and process it
for food.*
See also **busy, fascinate, grasp, take in**

absorbed *See* **preoccupied**

absorbing *See* **interesting**

abstain

▷ VERB

to choose not to do something: *The patient
had to abstain from food for several hours.*
avoid *Heartburn sufferers should try to
avoid fatty foods.*
deny oneself *I won't deny myself some
dessert tonight.*
forgo *Our family had to forgo a vacation
this year.*
give up *She gave up smoking last year.*
refrain *Please refrain from talking in the
theatre.*
See also **decline, refuse**

absurd

▷ ADJECTIVE

ridiculous or nonsensical: *an absurd waste of money*
crazy INFORMAL *It would be crazy to change coaches now.*
illogical *completely illogical arguments*
ludicrous *It was ludicrous to suggest that the visit could be kept secret.*
nonsensical *Many diets are harmful and nonsensical.*
ridiculous *The plan is too ridiculous to take seriously.*
See also **impossible, incredible, irrational, ridiculous, silly, stupid**

absurdity *See* **stupidity**

abundance

▷ NOUN

a great amount of something: *an abundance of wildlife*
affluence *Areas of affluence co-exist with areas of poverty.*
bounty *summer's bounty of fruit*
plenty *Allow plenty of time to get home.*
ANTONYM **shortage**
See also **lot** or **lots, wealth**

abundant

▷ ADJECTIVE

present in large quantities: *an abundant supply of fuel*
ample *ample space for a good-sized kitchen*
copious *copious amounts of water*
full *a full tank of gas*
plentiful *a plentiful supply of vegetables*
ANTONYM **scarce**
See also **ample, generous, plentiful, rich**

abuse

▷ NOUN

1 cruel treatment of a person or an animal: *the prevention of animal abuse*
exploitation *The exploitation of the workers is unforgivable.*
harm *the harm smokers willingly do to their own health*
hurt *The cruel treatment caused lasting hurt.*
ill-treatment *the ill-treatment of political prisoners*
oppression *the oppression of certain religions throughout history*
2 unkind remarks directed toward someone: *I was left shouting abuse as the car sped off.*
censure *a controversial policy that has attracted international censure*
derision *He was greeted with shouts of derision.*
insults *They traded insults with each other.*
invective *A stranger on the bus hurled racist*

invective at the family.
▷ VERB

3 to speak insultingly to someone: *The baseball umpire was verbally abused by the hometown fans.*
curse *We started cursing the bad weather under our breath.*
insult *I did not mean to insult you.*
scold *They scolded their daughter for having talked like that.*
See also **impose on, harm, insult, mistreat, wrong**

abused *See* **oppressed**

abusive

▷ ADJECTIVE

rude and unkind: *abusive language*
disparaging *He made some disparaging remarks about the team.*
insulting *The language in the book is insulting to many readers.*
offensive *There's no excuse for your offensive remarks.*
rude *He is rude to her friends.*
scathing *The critic made some particularly scathing comments about the play.*
See also **offensive**

abysmal *See* **terrible**

abyss

▷ NOUN

a very deep hole: *He crawled forward to peer over the edge of the abyss.*
chasm *The climbers strung a rope across the chasm.*
fissure *The earthquake opened large fissures in the ground.*
gorge *The valley narrowed to a gorge.*
pit *I lost my footing and began to slide into the pit.*
void *As he sat at the edge of the cliff, his feet dangled in the void.*
See also **hell**

academic *See* **learned**

accelerate

▷ VERB

to go faster: *She accelerated away from the curb.*
hurry *He shouted at me to hurry.*
quicken *My pulse quickened in alarm.*
speed up *The new technology is designed to speed up credit-card transactions.*
See also **hurry**

accelerated *See* **fast**

accent *See* **emphasis, emphasize**

accentuate *See* **emphasize, stress**

accept

▷ *VERB*

to receive or agree to something: *All those invited to next week's conference have accepted.*

acknowledge *He was willing to acknowledge their complaints.*

agree to *Hours before the deadline, the officials agreed to the prisoners' demands.*

concur with *I concur with her opinion.*

consent to *The leaders consented to the peace treaty.*

take *He took the job.*

ANTONYM **refuse**

See also **resign oneself, admit, assume, believe, grant, receive, tolerate**

acceptable

▷ *ADJECTIVE*

good enough to be accepted: *an acceptable standard of living*

adequate *a lack of adequate facilities*

all right *The meal was all right for the price.*

fair *He is a fair player, but not outstanding.*

good enough *I'm afraid that excuse just isn't good enough.*

passable *I speak fluent Spanish and passable Italian.*

satisfactory *The workers have done a satisfactory job.*

tolerable *a tolerable level of noise*

See also **adequate, all right, correct, okay, right, satisfactory, suitable, tolerable**

accepted *See* **general, proper, standard**

access *See* **entrance**

accessible *See* **available, ready**

accessory *See* **attachment, extra, fitting**

accident *See* **chance, crash, luck**

accidental

▷ *ADJECTIVE*

happening by chance: *The fire was accidental.*

casual *a casual remark*

chance *a chance meeting*

inadvertent *The inadvertent pun made us laugh.*

random *the random chance of winning the lottery*

ANTONYM **deliberate**

See also **casual**

accolade *See* **honour, praise, prize, tribute**

accommodate

▷ *VERB*

to provide someone with a place to stay: *a hotel built to accommodate many guests*

house *The dormitory houses many students.*

put up *I wanted to know if she could put me up for a few days.*

shelter *sheltered from the storm*

accommodating

▷ *ADJECTIVE*

willing to help: *his polite, accommodating manner*

considerate *I try to be considerate to those who are still sleeping.*

helpful *The staff members in the Toronto office are very helpful.*

hospitable *She was very hospitable when I went to New York.*

kind *It was very kind of you to visit.*

obliging *an extremely pleasant and obliging person*

See also **helpful**

accommodation

▷ *NOUN*

a house or room for living in: *Travel and overnight accommodation are included in the price.*

digs INFORMAL *living in student digs*

house *They sold their house in the suburbs and moved downtown.*

housing *a serious housing shortage*

lodgings *The student lodgings were comfortable but not luxurious.*

quarters *the officers' quarters*

See also **space**

accompany

▷ *VERB*

1 to go somewhere with someone: *Children must be accompanied by an adult.*

conduct FORMAL *He asked if he might conduct us to the gala dinner.*

escort *They were escorted by the police to their plane.*

go with *I haven't asked my friend to go with me yet.*

usher *I ushered him into the office.*

2 to occur with something: *severe pain accompanied by fever*

come with *Stress comes with this job.*

go together with *Too little sleep and a lack of exercise go together with exhaustion.*

See also **guide**

accomplish

▷ *VERB*

to manage to do something: *We could*

accomplish a lot by working together.
achieve *Achieving our goals makes us feel good.*
bring about *the only way to bring about political change*
complete *She has just completed her first novel.*
do *Have you done the dishes yet?*
fulfill *All the necessary conditions were fulfilled.*
manage *We managed to complete the difficult project.*
See also **achieve, carry out, fulfill**

accomplished *See* **able, capable, practical, proficient, skilful, skilled**

accomplishment *See* **achievement, act, action, qualification**

accord *See* **agree, understanding**

account *See* **bill, note, record, report, statement, story**

accountability *See* **blame**

accumulate *See* **collect, concentrate, gather, stockpile**

accurate
▷ ADJECTIVE
correct to a detailed level: *Quartz watches are very accurate.*
correct *The correct answers can be found at the bottom of the page.*
exact *an exact copy*
faithful *a faithful translation*
precise *precise sales figures*
right *That clock never tells the right time.*
strict *He has never been a workaholic in the strict sense of the word.*
true *a true account of what happened*
ANTONYM **inaccurate**
See also **correct, exact, faithful, precise, right, strict, true**

accurately *See* **exactly**

accuse
▷ VERB
to charge someone with doing something wrong: *He accused me of cheating.*
blame *They blamed me for giving away the secret.*
censure *The government took the unusual step of censuring the politician.*
charge *The police have charged him with theft.*
cite *He was banned for 30 days after being cited for foul play.*
denounce *She publicly denounced their nuclear policy.*
See also **blame**

A

accustomed
▷ ADJECTIVE
used to something: *I've become accustomed to his poor performance.*
adapted *The camel's feet, well adapted for dry sand, are useless in mud.*
familiar *He was very familiar with classical music.*
used *I'm used to having my sleep interrupted.*
ANTONYM **unaccustomed**
See also **usual**

ace *See* **expert**

ache *See* **long, pain**

ache for *See* **be dying for**

achieve
▷ VERB
to gain by hard work or ability: *She has achieved her best tournament result yet.*
accomplish *halfway toward accomplishing an important career goal*
carry out *They debated about how such reforms should be carried out.*
complete *I completed the course last year.*
do *I have done what I came here to do.*
fulfill *He has fulfilled his obligations.*
perform *He performed his duties under pressure.*
See also **accomplish, carry out, fulfill, gain, win**

achievement
▷ NOUN
something that someone has succeeded in doing: *His presence here is an achievement in itself.*
accomplishment *The list of her accomplishments is staggering.*
deed *Her heroic deeds were celebrated all over the world.*
exploit *His wartime exploits were later made into a TV series.*
feat *A racing car is an extraordinary feat of engineering.*
See also **act, action, qualification**

aching *See* **painful, tender**

acid *See* **bitter, sour**

acknowledge *See* **accept, admit, confess, grant, recognize**

acknowledgment *See* **confession, reaction**

acquaintance *See* **contact**

acquainted with *See* **aware of, familiar**

acquire

▷ VERB

to get something: *I have recently acquired a digital camera.*

attain *Students who attain the required grades will graduate.*

gain *He gained valuable experience from the job.*

get *My DVD player is broken — I'll have to get a new one.*

obtain *I couldn't obtain a ticket at any price.*

pick up *You can pick up some real bargains at the Boxing Day sales.*

procure *It was difficult to procure food and fuel.*

secure *The team has secured a place in the quarterfinals.*

See also **buy, earn, gain, get, obtain, possess, secure**

acquit See **clear**

acquittal See **forgiveness**

acrid See **bitter**

acrimonious See **bitter**

act

▷ VERB

1 to do something: *The bank acted properly in the best interests of the depositors.*

function *All the computer systems functioned properly.*

operate *He temporarily operated in the positions of director and treasurer.*

perform *He performed well in the World Cup.*

work *All sides will work toward a practical solution.*

2 to perform in a play, movie, or television program: *He acted at the Stratford Festival in Ontario.*

act out *Puppets acted out the scene.*

perform *She performed the role on television.*

play *She played Marilla in* Anne of Green Gables.

play the part of *She agreed to play the part of Juliet.*

portray *His moody looks are perfect for the character he portrays.*

▷ NOUN

3 a single thing someone does: *an act of disloyalty to the king*

accomplishment *Winning the tournament would be an incredible accomplishment.*

achievement *She was honoured for her achievements as a novelist.*

deed *forgotten deeds of heroism*

feat *an outstanding feat of strength*

undertaking *Organizing the show has been a massive undertaking.*

See also **appear, behave, conduct yourself, law, perform**

act against See **counteract**

act on See **affect**

act out See **act**

act toward See **treat**

action

▷ NOUN

1 the process of doing something: *He had to take evasive action to avoid being hit.*

activity *the electrical activity of the brain*

operation *It is quite a tricky operation.*

process *the peace process*

2 something that is done: *He did not like his actions questioned.*

accomplishment *her many accomplishments in the sports world*

achievement *If we can win the title, it will be a great team achievement.*

deed *daring and heroic deeds*

exploit *the stories of his heroic exploits*

feat *extraordinary feats of engineering*

See also **activity, case, fight**

active

▷ ADJECTIVE

1 full of energy: *Having an active child around the house can be exhausting.*

energetic *an energetic, happy youngster*

lively *a lively teenager*

restless *The kids will be too restless to sleep since we begin our vacation tomorrow.*

sprightly *a sprightly elf*

vivacious *She was very vivacious and great fun to work with.*

2 busy and hardworking: *people who are active in local politics*

busy *My grandfather lived a full and busy life.*

engaged *The candidates are now fully engaged in their campaigns.*

enthusiastic *an enthusiastic member of the audience*

hard-working *a team of hard-working and dedicated volunteers*

industrious *industrious bees*

involved *They are heavily involved in local projects.*

occupied *A busy social life will keep you fully occupied in February.*

See also **alive, busy, healthy, lively, vital**

activist *See* **fanatic**

activity

▷ NOUN

1 a situation in which lots of things are happening: *There is an extraordinary level of activity in the office.*
action *a movie full of action and excitement*
bustle *the hustle and bustle of a busy hospital*
energy *I love the energy in big cities.*
liveliness *a restaurant with a wonderful atmosphere of liveliness*
2 something you do for pleasure: *sports and other leisure activities*
hobby *My hobby is road cycling.*
interest *Among his many interests are reading and painting.*
pastime *You need a more active pastime than playing computer games.*
pursuit *I like fishing and other outdoor pursuits.*
See also **action, bustle, excitement, exercise, interest, pastime**

actual

▷ ADJECTIVE

real, rather than imaginary or guessed at: *That is the estimated figure. The actual figure is much higher.*
authentic *music played on authentic medieval instruments*
genuine *a genuine diamond*
realistic *a realistic picture of life in 19th century Québec*
true *The movie is based on a true story.*
verified *verified reports of a major archaeological discovery*
See also **precise, real**

actually *See* **really**

acute

▷ ADJECTIVE

1 severe or intense: *an acute shortage of supplies*
critical *suffering from a critical illness*
extreme *a disease that causes extreme pain*
grave *His country faces grave problems.*
great *a feeling of great discomfort*
intense *I felt an intense loneliness.*
serious *Reckless driving increases the risk of serious injuries.*
severe *Nuts can trigger a severe allergic reaction.*
2 very intelligent: *an acute mind*
alert *Our cat is old, but he's quick and alert.*
astute *He has a remarkably astute brain.*
bright *You don't need a bright mind to figure that one out.*

A

keen *a competent economist with a keen intellect*
perceptive *a perceptive analysis of the situation*
quick *a child with a quick mind*
sharp *Her vagueness disguised a sharp mind.*
shrewd *He demonstrated a shrewd understanding of human nature.*
See also **brilliant, extreme, grave, intelligent, intense, perceptive, serious, severe, uncommon, violent**

ad *See* **advertisement**

adage *See* **saying**

adamant *See* **firm**

adapt

▷ VERB

to alter for a new use: *The TV series was adapted from a movie.*
adjust *He had to adjust the seat.*
alter *The government has altered the rules.*
change *The law needs to be changed.*
convert *The table can be converted into an ironing board.*
modify *The car was modified for Canadian weather conditions.*
See also **fit**

adaptable *See* **flexible**

adapted *See* **accustomed**

add

▷ VERB

1 to put something with something else: *Add the grated cheese to the sauce.*
attach *Don't forget to attach the completed entry form.*
augment *A second job helped to augment the family income.*
supplement *I suggest supplementing your diet with vitamin A.*
2 to combine numbers or quantities: *Banks add all the interest and other charges together.*
add up *adding up calories on a calculator*
count up *They counted up all the hours we worked.*
total *The restaurant bill totalled $100.*
ANTONYM **subtract**

INFORMALLY SPEAKING

add up: make sense
add up to: amount to

add to *See* **augment, enlarge, extend, supplement**

add up *See* **add, count**

add up to *See* **total**

added *See* **extra, more**

addiction *See* **habit**

addition

▷ NOUN

something that has been added to something else: *recent additions to their CD collection*
increase *a substantial increase in his workload*
supplement *a supplement to their basic pension*
See also **extra, supplement**

additional *See* **extra, more**

address *See* **lecture, speech, talk**

adept *See* **capable, expert, proficient, skilful**

adequate

▷ ADJECTIVE

enough in amount or quality for a purpose: *an adequate diet*
acceptable *a company that offers an acceptable number of benefits*
ample *You've had ample time to discuss this matter.*
enough *enough money to live on*
satisfactory *a satisfactory bid to host the games*
sufficient *About 5 mL of salt should be sufficient.*
ANTONYM **insufficient**
See also **acceptable, all right, decent, satisfactory, sufficient, tolerable**

adequately *See* **well**

adhere *See* **stick**

adhere to *See* **obey**

adherent *See* **fan, supporter**

adhesive *See* **sticky**

adjacent *See* **near, next**

adjacent to *See* **beside, near**

adjoining *See* **near, next**

adjourn *See* **postpone**

adjust *See* **adapt**

adjustment *See* **correction**

administer

▷ VERB

I to be responsible for managing something: *people who administer large companies*
be in charge of *Who is in charge of this department?*
command *Who would command the troops in the event of war?*
control *She controls the largest construction company in the city.*
direct *The new manager will direct day-to-day operations.*
manage *Within two years, he was managing the store.*
run *This is no way to run a business.*
supervise *the men and women who supervised the project*
2 to inflict or impose something on someone: *He administered most of the punishment.*
carry out *I didn't expect him to carry out his threat.*
deal *to be dealt a severe penalty*
dispense *The court dispensed swift justice.*
execute *The skater executed a perfect jump.*
impose *The judge had no choice but to impose a stiff penalty.*
inflict *to inflict us with his awful jokes*
perform *She had to perform emergency surgery.*
See also **control, handle, rule, run**

administration *See* **bureaucracy, management**

admirable *See* **fine**

admirably *See* **well**

admiration

▷ NOUN

a feeling of great liking and respect: *I have always had the greatest admiration for him.*
appreciation *gifts presented to them in appreciation of their work*
approval *He had a need to gain everyone's approval.*
esteem *Their public esteem has never been lower.*
regard *She has always been held in high regard.*
respect *We all have so much respect for her.*
See also **approval, esteem, respect, worship**

admire

▷ VERB

to like and respect someone or something: *All those who knew him admired his work.*
appreciate *to appreciate all the time involved in putting out the yearbook*
look up to *A lot of the younger players look up to you.*
respect *I want him to respect me as a career woman.*
value *She genuinely values his opinion.*
ANTONYM **scorn**

See also **appreciate, approve, praise, respect**

admirer See **fan**

admission See **confession, entrance**

admit
▷ VERB
I to agree that something is true: *The driver admitted to falling asleep at the wheel.*
accept *I accepted his reasons for missing the test.*
acknowledge *Eventually, the government acknowledged the problem.*
grant *The lawyer granted that the case had merit.*
ANTONYM **deny**
2 to allow to enter: *He was admitted to university.*
accept *The puppy was immediately accepted into the family.*
let in *He was accused of letting in fans without tickets.*
receive *The prime minister received the visiting president.*
take in *They took in students to help pay the rent.*
ANTONYM **exclude**
See also **confess, grant**

adolescent See **young**

adorable See **lovable**

adoration See **love, worship**

adore See **like, love, worship**

adored See **beloved**

adoring See **fond**

adorn See **decorate**

adornment See **ornament**

adrift See **lost**

adulation See **flattery, worship**

adult
▷ NOUN
a grown-up person: *I'd like tickets for three children and two adults.*
grown-up *Both kids and grown-ups liked the movie.*
man *He is now a man of 42.*
woman *She is now a woman of 42.*
ANTONYM **child**
See also **mature**

adulterous See **unfaithful**

advance
▷ VERB
I to move forward or develop: *Rebel forces are advancing on the capital.*

make inroads *They have made impressive inroads in the movie business.*
press on *The country pressed on with economic reform.*
proceed *He proceeded down the spiral stairway.*
progress *the ability to progress from one step to the next*
▷ NOUN
2 progress in something: *a scientific advance*
breakthrough *a breakthrough in cancer treatment*
development *the development of new computer technology*
gain *a gain of nearly ten percent*
progress *signs of progress in his reading*
step *the first step toward peace*
See also **develop, early, gain, go, improve, improvement, loan, payment, proceed, produce, progress, raise**

advance warning See **notice**

advanced See **sophisticated**

advantage
▷ NOUN
a more favourable position or state: *We have a competitive advantage.*
ascendancy *The opponents are gaining ascendancy.*
benefit *For maximum benefit, take the vitamins every day.*
dominance *the battle for dominance in the soccer league*
superiority *military superiority*
ANTONYM **disadvantage**
See also **beauty, benefit, merit, value, virtue**

advantageous See **beneficial, favourable, helpful**

advent See **appearance**

adventure See **excitement, experience**

adventurous See **bold, daring**

adversary See **competitor, enemy, rival**

adversity See **hardship, misfortune**

advertise
▷ VERB
to present something to the public in order to sell it: *They advertise their products on television.*
plug INFORMAL *If I hear another actor plugging his latest book, I will scream!*

promote *What are you doing to promote your new movie?*
publicize *He never publicized his plans.*
push *a publisher who knows how to push a product*
See also **announce, promote, publicize**

advertisement

▷ NOUN
a public announcement to sell or publicize something: *She recently placed an advertisement in the local newspaper.*
ad INFORMAL *an ad for the new pizza store*
commercial *She has turned down an opportunity to do TV commercials.*
notice *The information is published in notices in today's newspapers.*
plug INFORMAL *a shameless plug for his new movie*
See also **announcement, notice**

advertising See **publicity**

advice

▷ NOUN
a suggestion about what to do: *Take my advice and stay away from him!*
counsel FORMAL *He had always been able to count on her wise counsel.*
guidance *The nation looks to them for guidance.*
opinion *You should seek a medical opinion.*
suggestion *She made suggestions about how I could improve my diet.*
See also **help, hint**

advise

▷ VERB
1 to offer advice to someone: *They advised him to leave as soon as possible.*
caution *The researchers cautioned against drawing general conclusions from this study.*
counsel *My lawyer counselled me to say nothing.*
recommend *We strongly recommend reporting the incident to the police.*
suggest *He suggested a visit to the Group of Seven exhibition.*
urge *We urge that vigorous action be taken immediately.*
2 to notify someone: *I think it best that I advise you of my decision to quit.*
inform *He informed us that the arena would be closed on the weekend.*
make known *The details will be made known by the end of August.*
notify *We notified everyone that the date was wrong.*

See also **brief, inform, notify, suggest**

adviser

▷ NOUN
a person whose job is to give advice: *The premier and her advisers spent the day in meetings.*
aide *a former aide to the mayor*
consultant *a management consultant*
guru *He became Canada's modern design guru.*
mentor *He is my friend and musical mentor.*
tutor *my math tutor*

advocate

▷ VERB
to publicly support a plan or course of action: *She advocates better conditions for prisoners.*
back *The newspaper is backing the residents' campaign.*
champion *He passionately champions our cause.*
endorse *We are reluctant to endorse such drastic measures.*
favour *coaches who favour stricter penalties*
promote *He promoted the idea of free concerts.*
recommend *I can't recommend such a course of action.*
support *people who supported his policies*
uphold *We uphold the principles of free speech.*
See also **back, champion, defender, lawyer, suggest, supporter**

afar See **far**

affable See **pleasant**

affair

▷ NOUN
1 an event or series of events: *The funeral was a sad affair.*
business *This business has really upset me.*
event *A wedding should be a joyous event.*
issue *a major political issue*
matter *I never interfere in these business matters.*
question *the difficult question of unemployment*
situation *The whole situation is now under control.*
subject *a subject that had worried him for some time*
2 a secret and romantic relationship: *He had an affair with someone he met on vacation.*

fling *We had a brief fling, but it was nothing serious.*
liaison *They denied that they had had a liaison.*
relationship *She went public about her relationship with a Hollywood star.*
romance *Our company discourages office romances.*
See also **business, concern, event, experience, matter, occasion, relationship, undertaking**

affect
▷ *VERB*
to influence something or someone: *More than 7 million people have been affected by the drought.*
act on *This drug acts very fast on the central nervous system.*
alter *The earth's climate appears to have been altered by pollution.*
change *It was to change the course of my life.*
impinge on *My private life does not impinge on my professional life.*
See also **concern, infect, influence, move, touch**

CONFUSABLES
Affect means **influence**, and is a verb.
Effect means **result**, and is usually a noun.

affected *See* **pretentious**

affecting *See* **moving, touching**

affection
▷ *NOUN*
a feeling of fondness for someone or something: *She thought of him with affection.*
attachment *Parents and children form a close attachment.*
fondness *his fondness for cats*
liking *a liking for flashy cars*
love *My love for all my children is unconditional.*
warmth *He greeted us with warmth and affection.*
ANTONYM **dislike**
See also **attachment, friendship, love**

affectionate
▷ *ADJECTIVE*
full of fondness for someone: *She gave me a long and affectionate hug.*
caring *a loving, caring husband*
fond *He gave her a fond smile.*
loving *The children were very loving to me.*
tender *a tender kiss*
ANTONYM **cold**

See also **fond, friendly, loving, tender, warm**

affiliation *See* **association, connection, link, tie**

affinity *See* **relationship, tie**

affirm *See* **declare, state**

affirmation *See* **declaration**

affirmative *See* **favourable**

affix *See* **attach, connect**

affliction *See* **disorder, evil, illness**

affluence *See* **abundance, luxury, wealth**

affluent *See* **rich, wealthy**

afford *See* **spare**

affront *See* **insult, offend**

afraid
▷ *ADJECTIVE*
scared of something unpleasant happening: *I was afraid of the large dog.*
apprehensive *People are still terribly apprehensive about the future.*
fearful *Bankers were fearful of a world banking crisis.*
frightened *I used to be frightened of flying.*
nervous *He's nervous because he thinks something bad will happen.*
scared *The last scene in the movie really scared me.*
ANTONYM **unafraid**
See also **frightened**

afresh *See* **again**

after
▷ *ADVERB*
at a later time: *Shortly after, police arrested five suspects.*
afterwards *He was taken to hospital but was released soon afterwards.*
following *We shared so much, not only during university, but also in the many years following.*
later *He resigned ten years later.*
subsequently *She subsequently became coach of the curling team.*
ANTONYM **before**

afterwards *See* **after, next**

again
▷ *ADVERB*
happening one more time: *He told the story again.*

afresh *The couple moved abroad to start life afresh.*
anew *She's ready to start anew.*
once more *Anger overcame him once more.*

against

▷ *PREPOSITION*

I in opposition to: *I am against animal cruelty.*
averse to *He's not averse to your idea.*
hostile to *hostile to the opposing army*
in opposition to *Your idea of relaxation is in direct opposition to mine.*
versus *the Maple Leafs versus the Flyers*
2 in preparation for or in case of something: *precautions against fire*
in anticipation of *His school was one of several that closed in anticipation of the blizzard.*
in expectation of *The hotel was being renovated in expectation of a tourist boom.*
in preparation for *She got her passport in preparation for a trip to the United States.*

agenda *See* **program**

agent *See* **representative**

aggregate *See* **total, whole**

aggressive

▷ *ADJECTIVE*

tending to attack: *These fish are very aggressive.*
hostile *The prisoner eyed him in a hostile silence.*
quarrelsome *a quarrelsome young man*
ANTONYM **peaceful**
See also **fierce, pushy**

aggrieved *See* **hurt, resentful**

agile

▷ *ADJECTIVE*

able to move quickly and easily: *as agile as a cat*
lithe *a lithe young gymnast*
nimble *A boxer needs quick reflexes and nimble footwork.*
sprightly *Our dog is alert and sprightly for his age.*
supple *as supple as a dancer*
ANTONYM **clumsy**

agitate

▷ *VERB*

I to campaign energetically for something: *They began to agitate for better conditions.*
campaign *an organization that campaigns for better consumer rights*
demonstrate *marchers demonstrating for political reform*

protest *farmers who were protesting against the proposed airport*
push *Some board members are pushing for the merger.*
2 to worry or distress someone: *Everything she said was beginning to agitate me.*
bother *It really bothers me when you talk like that.*
distress *sudden noises that distressed the animals*
disturb *These dreams disturb me for days afterwards.*
faze INFORMAL *Nothing seems to faze him.*
perturb *She didn't appear perturbed by the changes at work.*
trouble *Are you troubled by thoughts of the future?*
upset *The whole incident upset me dreadfully.*
worry *I didn't want to worry you with my own problems.*
See also **disturb, excite, shake, trouble, upset**

agitate for *See* **incite**

agitated *See* **excited, uneasy, upset**

agitation *See* **excitement, frenzy, fuss**

agony *See* **hell, pain**

agree

▷ *VERB*

I to have the same opinion as someone: *So we both agree there's a problem?*
assent *The council assented to the neighbourhood proposal.*
be of the same opinion *All the other players are of the same opinion.*
concur *Four other judges concurred.*
see eye to eye *He has not always seen eye to eye with his brother.*
ANTONYM **disagree**
2 to match or be the same as something: *Her second statement agrees with facts as stated by the other witnesses.*
accord *I cannot support policies that do not accord with my principles.*
conform *The new deck doesn't conform with current building regulations.*
jibe INFORMAL *His story did not jibe with what really happened.*
match *Attendances do not match the ticket sales.*
square *Does that explanation square with the facts?*
tally *The figures don't seem to tally.*
See also **correspond, match, settle, submit, suit**

agree to *See* **accept**

agree with *See* **side with**

agreeable

▷ ADJECTIVE

1 pleasant or enjoyable: *I found it a most agreeable experience.*

delightful *I've had a delightful time.*

enjoyable *an enjoyable meal*

lovely *I hope you have a lovely holiday.*

nice *It would be very nice to get away for a few days.*

pleasant *This restaurant offers good food in pleasant surroundings.*

pleasurable *the pleasurable task of deciding where to go this summer*

ANTONYM **disagreeable**

2 willing to allow or do something: *She said she was agreeable to this plan.*

game *Are you game to try something a little bit different?*

happy *I'm happy to go along with what everyone else thinks.*

prepared *Would you be prepared to line up for hours for a ticket?*

ready *I'm ready to take over if she resigns.*

willing *Are you willing to take part in a survey?*

See also **pleasant, ready, willing**

agreement

▷ NOUN

a decision reached by two or more people: *The two countries have signed agreements on fishing and oil rights.*

arrangement *Eventually we came to an arrangement that suited us both.*

contract *She has signed an exclusive contract with the music company.*

deal INFORMAL *The company recently won a five-year deal to repave highways.*

pact *They ruled out any formal pact between their two countries.*

settlement *She accepted an out-of-court settlement of $10 000.*

treaty *negotiations over a 1992 treaty on global warming*

See also **approval, bond, understanding**

ahead *See* **in front**

ahead of time *See* **early**

aid *See* **benefit, encourage, help**

aide *See* **adviser, assistant, helper**

ailing *See* **ill, sick, unhealthy, unwell**

ailment *See* **illness**

aim

▷ VERB

1 to plan to do something: *The company aims to sign up at least a million customers within the next five years.*

aspire *people who aspire to public office*

attempt *He will attempt to win the title for the second year running.*

intend *I intend to try out for the debate team.*

plan *The passenger was planning to sue over injuries he received.*

propose *Where do you propose to stay when you visit?*

strive *He strives hard to keep himself very fit.*

▷ NOUN

2 what someone intends to achieve: *Our main aim is to offer a superior product.*

ambition *Her ambition is to sail around the world.*

goal *I have to keep setting goals for myself.*

intention *It was always my intention to visit my cousin.*

objective *Her objective was to improve her batting average.*

plan *His plan was to get a job after school.*

target *His target is to get 20 goals this season.*

See also **cause, focus, goal, intend, intention, mean, object, point, purpose, seek**

aimed *See* **calculated**

aimless *See* **random**

aimlessly *See* **at random**

air *See* **look, show**

aisle *See* **passage**

ajar *See* **open**

akin *See* **like**

alarm

▷ NOUN

1 a feeling of fear: *The cat sprang back in alarm.*

anxiety *anxiety about crime*

apprehension *I tensed every muscle in my body in apprehension.*

fright *The puppy barked in fright.*

nervousness *I smiled warmly so she wouldn't see my nervousness.*

panic *There was panic in the streets when the fire broke out.*

scare *You gave us a scare when you fell.*

ANTONYM **calm**

2 a device used to warn people of something: *a burglar alarm*

distress signal *The captain was trying to send a distress signal when the boat crashed.*

siren *a police siren*

A

warning *The warning signalled the computer was about to crash.*

▷ VERB

3 to fill with fear: *We could not see what had alarmed him.*

distress *He is very distressed by what happened.*

frighten *The future frightens me.*

panic *They panicked when the fire broke out.*

scare *Horses scare me.*

startle *startled by a sudden loud noise*

unnerve *The skater was unnerved when he fell on the triple jump.*

ANTONYM **calm**

See also **fear, frighten, horror, panic, scare, warning**

alarmed See **frightened**

alarming See **frightening, scary, serious**

alcohol

▷ NOUN

a drink that can make you drunk: *There wasn't any alcohol at the party.*

booze INFORMAL *a bottle of booze*

drink *Too much drink is bad for you.*

liquor *I could smell liquor on his breath.*

spirits *a ban on advertising spirits*

alcoholic See **drunk**

alert

▷ ADJECTIVE

1 paying full attention: *apprehended by alert security staff*

attentive *an attentive audience*

observant *an observant police officer*

on guard *on guard against the threat of invasion*

vigilant *vigilant against computer viruses*

wary *He kept a wary eye on the dog as he passed the gate.*

ANTONYM **unaware**

▷ VERB

2 to warn of danger: *I was hoping she'd alert the police.*

forewarn *The guide had forewarned me what to expect.*

inform *The patient was not properly informed of the risks.*

notify *The passengers were notified of the delay.*

warn *They warned him of the dangers of sailing alone.*

See also **acute, alive, astute, scare, sharp, warn, warning**

alien See **strange, unfamiliar**

alight See **land**

alike

▷ ADJECTIVE

1 similar in some way: *You and your father are so alike.*

analogous *Your hands and feet are analogous to a dog's paws.*

close *a creature close in appearance to a panther*

identical *Nearly all the houses were identical.*

similar *These two beverages are very similar in taste.*

the same *products that are almost the same in every respect*

ANTONYM **different**

▷ ADVERB

2 in a similar way: *I punish all players alike who break the rules.*

equally *Democracy calls for all people to be treated equally.*

in the same way *He speaks in the same way to his boss as to co-workers.*

similarly *All the children were dressed similarly.*

uniformly *The rules apply uniformly to everyone.*

See also **like, same, similar**

alive

▷ ADJECTIVE

1 having life: *The lost skier was found alive.*

animate *animate beings*

breathing *The dog was barely breathing when rescued.*

living *The blue whale is the largest living thing on the planet.*

ANTONYM **dead**

2 lively and active: *I never expected to feel so alive in my life again.*

active *An active lifestyle will keep you healthy.*

alert *A brisk walk will make you feel more alert.*

animated *He becomes animated when talking about his work.*

energetic *a vital and energetic person*

full of life *She was so chatty and full of life.*

lively *The lively child is a handful.*

vivacious *a vivacious personality*

ANTONYM **dull**

See also **live**

all

▷ PRONOUN

the whole of something: *Why did you have to say all that?*

each *Each of us received a free gift.*

every one *Every one of you must take a share of the blame.*

everything *Sit down and tell me everything.*
the whole amount *Have you paid the whole amount of the fine?*
the (whole) lot INFORMAL *The whole lot of you will be punished.*
See also **whole**

INFORMALLY SPEAKING

all but: almost; nearly
all in: very tired
go all out: use all your resources

allegation *See* **claim**

allege *See* **claim**

alleged *See* **supposed**

alliance *See* **party**

allocate *See* **allow, distribute, grant**

allocation *See* **grant**

allot *See* **allow, distribute**

allotment *See* **share**

allow
▷ *VERB*
1 to permit someone to do something: *Talking will not be allowed during the exam.*
approve *The principal approved our plans for the School Fair.*
authorize *authorized to sign the agreement*
let *They won't let us join the club.*
permit *Unauthorized personnel are not permitted to enter.*
stand for *We won't stand for it any longer.*
tolerate *I won't tolerate sloppiness.*
ANTONYM **forbid**
2 to set aside for a particular purpose: *Allow four hours for the paint to dry.*
allocate *an efficient method of allocating resources*
allot *Each contestant was allotted 30 seconds.*
assign *the budget assigned for the year*
grant *Funding had been granted for the project.*
set aside *money set aside for education*
See also **grant, let, permit, sanction**

allowance *See* **grant**

alloy *See* **blend, mixture**

all right
▷ *ADJECTIVE*
acceptable: *It was all right, but nothing special.*
acceptable *We've made an acceptable start, but it could have been better.*
adequate *Our accommodation was adequate, but not special.*

A

average *average height*
fair *The overall standard of the entries was fair.*
OK INFORMAL *The prices here are OK.*
See also **acceptable, okay, safe, satisfactory, sound**

allude to *See* **mention**

allure *See* **charm**

allusion *See* **mention**

ally *See* **assistant, connect, supporter**

almost
▷ *ADVERB*
very nearly: *Over the past decade their salaries have almost doubled.*
about *I was about nine at the time.*
approximately *He's approximately twice my age.*
close to *They lived in PEI for close to 30 years.*
nearly *The beach was nearly empty.*
not quite *It's more than a hill, but not quite a mountain.*
practically *I've known him practically all my life.*
See also **about, barely, nearly**

alone
▷ *ADJECTIVE*
not with other people or things: *He was all alone in the middle of the hall.*
detached *The detached house stands alone.*
isolated *Talking things over in a group meant none of us felt isolated.*
separate *They were kept separate from the other prisoners.*
single *One brother is single and the other is married.*
See also **lonely, on your own**

alongside *See* **beside, near**

aloof *See* **cold, distant, impersonal, remote, unfriendly**

aloud
▷ *ADVERB*
out loud: *Our father reads aloud to us.*
audibly *He sighed audibly.*
out loud *I tried not to laugh out loud.*

also
▷ *ADVERB*
in addition: *The artist is also a well-known writer.*
as well *She published historical novels as well.*
besides *You get to have dinner and take home leftovers besides.*

furthermore *Furthermore, they claim that any such interference is completely ineffective.*
into the bargain *We got two pizzas for the price of one, and free pop into the bargain.*
moreover *They have accused the government of corruption. Moreover, they have named names.*
too *I was there, too.*

alter *See* **adapt, affect, change, transform, vary**

alteration *See* **change, variation**

altercation *See* **disagreement, row, squabble**

alternate *See* **vary**

alternative *See* **choice**

although *See* **but**

always
▷ ADVERB
all the time or forever: *You're always moaning.*
continually *My cousin was continually changing his mind.*
every time *You can't get it right every time.*
forever *He was forever attempting to arrange deals.*
invariably *Their teamwork was invariably good.*
perpetually *The two groups are perpetually arguing.*

amalgamate *See* **combine, mix**

amalgamation *See* **blend, combination, mixture, union**

amass *See* **gather, stockpile**

amaze
▷ VERB
to surprise greatly: *He amazed us by his knowledge of sports history.*
astonish *I was astonished by his vocabulary.*
astound *I am astounded at the incorrect comments made by the mayor.*
shock *She was shocked by the appalling news.*
stagger *He was staggered by the sheer size of the crowd.*
stun *Many moviegoers were stunned by the picture's tragic ending.*
surprise *We'll solve the case ourselves and surprise everyone.*
See also **surprise**

amazement
▷ NOUN
complete surprise: *Much to my amazement,*

he arrived on time for once.
astonishment *They looked at each other in astonishment.*
shock *I am still getting over the shock of winning.*
surprise *To my surprise, I found I liked it.*
wonder *He simply shook his head in wonder.*
See also **surprise**

amazing
▷ ADJECTIVE
very surprising or remarkable: *some of the most amazing stunts you're ever likely to see*
astonishing *an astonishing display of physical strength*
astounding *The results are quite astounding.*
staggering *There was a staggering 17 percent jump in sales.*
startling *startling new evidence*
stunning *a stunning piece of news*
surprising *A surprising number of customers order the same sandwich every day.*
See also **extraordinary, incredible, wonderful**

ambiguous *See* **uncertain, unclear**

ambition *See* **aim, dream, drive, hope**

ambitious *See* **forceful**

amble *See* **ramble**

amend *See* **correct, reform, revise**

amendment *See* **correction, reform**

amends *See* **compensation**

amiable *See* **friendly, pleasant, warm**

amicable *See* **favourable**

amid *See* **among**

amidst *See* **among**

amok *See* **on the rampage**

among
▷ PREPOSITION
1 surrounded by: *The bike lay among piles of chains and pedals.*
amid *a tiny cottage amid clusters of trees*
amidst *They found the box of photos amidst the wreckage.*
in the middle of *a tiny island in the middle of the Pacific*
in the thick of *a visitors' centre found in the thick of the woods*
surrounded by *surrounded by bodyguards*
2 between more than two: *The money will be divided among seven charities.*
to each of *a thousand dollars to each of the five winners*

amorous *See* **romantic**

amount
▷ *NOUN*
how much there is of something: *I still do a certain amount of work for them.*
expanse *a vast expanse of lawn*
quantity *vast quantities of food*
volume *the sheer volume of traffic on a Friday afternoon*
See also **figure, measure, price, quantity**

amount to *See* **total**

ample
▷ *ADJECTIVE*
of an amount: more than enough: *There is ample space for a good-sized kitchen.*
abundant *providing abundant food for local wildlife*
enough *Do you have enough money for a taxi home?*
plenty of *You've had plenty of time to make up your mind.*
sufficient *The police have sufficient evidence to charge them.*
See also **abundant, adequate, generous, handsome, plentiful, spacious, sufficient**

amply *See* **well**

amuse *See* **delight, entertain, please**

amuse oneself *See* **play**

amusement *See* **entertainment, fun, pleasure**

amusing *See* **funny, witty**

analogous *See* **alike, like, similar**

analogy *See* **resemblance, similarity**

analyze *See* **examine, research**

analysis *See* **examination, research, review**

anarchy *See* **riot**

ancestor
▷ *NOUN*
a person from whom someone is descended: *He could trace his ancestors back 700 years.*
forebear *our immigrant forebears*
parent *music from my parents' generation*
predecessor *Our predecessors were pioneers.*

ancestry *See* **origin, stock**

ancient *See* **former, past**

anecdote *See* **story**

anew *See* **again**

angel *See* **dear**

anger
▷ *NOUN*
1 extreme annoyance: *We vented our anger at the umpire.*
fury *He flew into a fury because he didn't get what he wanted.*
outrage *The decisions provoked outrage from human rights groups.*
rage *An intense rage was burning inside me.*
wrath *He incurred the wrath of the referee.*
▷ *VERB*
2 to make someone angry: *remarks that will anger his critics*
enrage *He enraged the actors with a nasty review of the play.*
infuriate *Your mean comments infuriated me.*
outrage *Customers are outraged by the price of gasoline.*
ANTONYM **calm**
See also **irritate, provoke, rage, resentment**

angle *See* **tilt**

angry
▷ *ADJECTIVE*
very annoyed: *She gets angry with me if I'm late.*
cross *He was cross because I ate the last butter tart.*
enraged *The wolf became enraged when her cubs were attacked.*
furious *He was furious when the less qualified person was promoted.*
mad INFORMAL *I'm pretty mad about it, I can tell you.*
See also **cross, mad, resentful**

anguish *See* **hell, pain**

animal
▷ *NOUN*
a living creature: *attacked by wild animals*
beast *wild beasts*
creature *sea creatures*

animate *See* **alive, excite, live**

animated *See* **alive, energetic, lively**

animation *See* **spirit**

animosity
▷ *NOUN*
a feeling of strong dislike toward someone: *There is no animosity between these two players.*
antagonism *a history of antagonism between the two sides*
antipathy *antipathy toward snakes*

dislike *my extreme dislike of broccoli*
hatred *He didn't conceal his hatred of the evil deed.*
hostility *unacceptable hostility toward the new employee*
ill will *He didn't bear anyone any ill will.*
malice *There was no malice in her voice.*
resentment *There is growing resentment toward newcomers.*
See also **dislike, hate, hatred, hostility, resentment**

annex *See* **seize**

annihilate *See* **destroy**

annihilation *See* **destruction**

anniversary *See* **festival**

announce
▷ *VERB*
to make known publicly: *He will announce tonight that he is resigning from office.*
advertise *I did not want to advertise my presence in the town.*
make known *Details will be made known tomorrow.*
proclaim *She loudly proclaimed her innocence.*
reveal *They were now free to reveal the secret.*
tell *He finally told the full story.*
See also **declare, reveal**

announcement
▷ *NOUN*
a statement giving information about something: *There has been no formal announcement by either government.*
advertisement *an advertisement placed in the local newspaper*
broadcast *a live broadcast from the scene of the crime*
bulletin *At noon, a bulletin was released announcing the decision.*
declaration *a public declaration of support*
report *News reports estimate that 5000 people were at the concert.*
statement *a short statement by her lawyers*
See also **statement, word**

annoy
▷ *VERB*
to irritate or displease someone: *Try making a note of the things that annoy you.*
bother *I didn't think it would bother me to see my ex-boyfriend again.*
displease *Not wishing to displease her, he avoided answering the question.*
get on someone's nerves *INFORMAL*
That song gets on my nerves!
hassle *INFORMAL Stop hassling me for money.*
irritate *The flippancy in her voice seemed to irritate him.*
plague *We were plagued by mosquitoes.*
vex *I was vexed at not having noticed it myself.*
See also **bother, irritate, pester, provoke**

annoyance
▷ *NOUN*
1 a feeling of irritation: *He made no secret of his annoyance.*
displeasure *She voiced her displeasure at her treatment.*
irritation *He tried not to let his irritation show.*
2 something that causes irritation: *Snoring can be more than an annoyance.*
bore *His speech was a bore.*
drag *INFORMAL Waiting for the game to start was a drag.*
nuisance *He can be a bit of a nuisance when he asks for favours.*
pain *INFORMAL It's a pain to stand in line for so long.*
pain in the neck *INFORMAL Traffic jams are a pain in the neck.*
pest *She's a pest when she doesn't get her own way.*
See also **bother, nuisance**

annoyed *See* **cross**

annul *See* **abolish, cancel**

anoint *See* **bless**

another *See* **different**

answer
▷ *VERB*
1 to reply to someone: *I knew he was lying when he answered me.*
reply *He replied that this was absolutely impossible.*
respond *He responded promptly to my e-mail request.*
retort *I asked him if he was afraid. "Afraid of what?" he retorted.*
ANTONYM **ask**
▷ *NOUN*
2 a reply given to someone: *Without waiting for an answer, he left the room.*
reply *I called out a challenge, but there was no reply.*
response *There has been no response to yesterday's e-mail.*
retort *His sharp retort clearly made an impact.*
ANTONYM **question**

INFORMALLY SPEAKING

answer back: reply disrespectfully
answer for: bear the consequences of

antagonism See **animosity, conflict, hostility**

antagonist See **enemy, rival**

antagonistic See **hostile, unfriendly**

anticipate See **expect**

anticipated See **likely**

antipathy See **animosity, dislike, hatred**

antiquated See **old-fashioned, out of date**

antiquity See **the past**

antiseptic See **clean, sterile**

antithesis See **foil, opposite**

anxiety
▷ NOUN
nervousness or worry: *our growing anxiety about their safety*
apprehension *a feeling of apprehension about the future*
concern *growing concern about the environment*
fear *His fears might be groundless.*
misgiving *She had some misgivings about what she had been asked to do.*
nervousness *I smiled, trying to hide my nervousness.*
unease *a sense of unease about the upcoming job*
worry *a major source of worry to us all*
See also **alarm, burden, care, concern, strain, stress, worry**

anxious
▷ ADJECTIVE
nervous or worried: *He admitted he was still anxious about the situation.*
apprehensive *Their families are apprehensive about the trip.*
bothered *I'm still bothered about what she's going to say.*
concerned *a phone call from a concerned neighbour*
fearful *We are all fearful for the security of our jobs.*
nervous *I still get nervous before a visit to the dentist.*
troubled *He was troubled about his son's lifestyle.*
uneasy *an uneasy feeling that something*

was wrong with the plan
worried *Her parents are worried about her lack of progress.*
See also **eager, nervous, tense, uneasy, worried**

any minute now See **soon**

apart from See **except**

apartment
▷ NOUN
a set of rooms for living in: *a two-bedroom apartment*
flat *a huge flat overlooking the lake*
rooms *They shared rooms when they were at college.*

apathetic
▷ ADJECTIVE
not interested in anything: *apathetic about politics*
cool *The idea met with a cool response.*
indifferent *People have become indifferent to the suffering of others.*
passive *His passive attitude made things easier for me.*
uninterested *unhelpful and uninterested salespeople*
ANTONYM **enthusiastic**
See also **uninterested**

apathy See **boredom**

ape See **copy, imitate**

apex See **top**

aplomb See **confidence**

apologetic See **sorry**

apologize
▷ VERB
to say sorry for something: *I apologize for being late.*
ask forgiveness *He fell to his knees asking for forgiveness.*
beg someone's pardon *I was impolite and I do beg your pardon.*
express regret *I expressed regret that I couldn't attend the play.*
say sorry *He didn't even say sorry for breaking the window.*

appal See **horrify, shock**

appalling See **awful, dreadful, horrible, terrible**

apparatus See **equipment, machine, stuff**

apparent See **clear, conspicuous, evident, obvious, probable, visible**

apparition *See* **ghost, spirit, vision**

appeal
▷ *VERB*
1 to make an urgent request for something: *The police appealed for witnesses to come forward.*
beg *I begged him to leave me alone.*
call upon *Frequently he was called upon to resolve conflicts.*
plead *I pleaded to be allowed to go.*
request *She had requested that the door to her room be left open.*
2 to attract or interest: *The idea appealed to him.*
attract *What attracted you to this hobby?*
fascinate *Classical music had fascinated him since the age of three.*
interest *It was the garden that really interested me.*
please *It pleased him to talk to her.*
▷ *NOUN*
3 a formal request for something: *an appeal for peace*
petition *The court rejected their petition.*
plea *an urgent plea for help*
request *a request to send help to flood victims*
See also **ask, charm, interest, plead, request**

appeal to *See* **attract**

appealing *See* **attractive, cute**

appear
▷ *VERB*
1 to become visible or present: *A woman appeared at the far end of the street.*
come into view *At last a train came into view.*
crop up INFORMAL *Problems will crop up so be ready to deal with them.*
emerge *He emerged soaking wet from the shower.*
show up INFORMAL *He failed to show up at the ceremony.*
surface *This problem will surface again.*
turn up *This is like waiting for a bus that never turns up.*
ANTONYM **disappear**
2 to begin to exist: *small white flowers that appear in the spring*
become available *The DVD will become available next week.*
be invented *Basketball was invented by James Naismith in 1891.*
come into being *That law came into being last year.*

come into existence *before our solar system came into existence*
come out *The first movie in the series came out in 2004.*
3 to take part in a movie, play, or television program: *He is soon to appear in two more episodes.*
act *She has also been acting in a sitcom.*
perform *He is currently performing in the new musical.*
play *She played Lady Macbeth to packed houses.*
play a part *His ambition is to play the part of Dracula.*
See also **come, look, occur, seem**

appearance
▷ *NOUN*
1 the time when something begins to exist: *the appearance of modern technology*
advent *the advent of the computer*
arrival *the arrival of the space age*
coming *the coming of the railways*
dawn *the dawn of the Ice Age*
debut *the debut of the new channel*
emergence *the emergence of pay-per-view TV*
introduction *the introduction of the cellphone*
2 the way that a person looks: *I used to be so fussy about my appearance.*
bearing *a person of aristocratic bearing*
image *He urged the rest of the band to update their image.*
look *She is so much happier with her new look.*
looks *wholesome good looks*
See also **entrance, entry, front, look**

appease *See* **pacify**

appendix *See* **supplement**

appetite *See* **desire, taste**

appetizing *See* **delicious, tasty**

applaud *See* **praise**

appliance *See* **gadget, machine**

applicable *See* **relevant**

applicant *See* **candidate**

application *See* **effort, request, use**

applied *See* **practical**

apply *See* **spread, use**

apply to *See* **concern**

appoint *See* **employ, hire**

appointment
▷ *NOUN*
1 an arrangement to meet someone: *She has*

an appointment with her accountant.
date *I have a date with my new girlfriend.*
interview *a job interview*
meeting *Can we arrange a meeting to discuss that?*
rendezvous *They arranged a secret rendezvous.*
2 the choosing of a person to do a job: *his appointment as manager*
election *a provincial election*
naming *the naming of the new captain*
nomination *She accepted the nomination as class president.*
selection *his selection as a candidate*
3 a job: *He applied for a diplomatic appointment.*
assignment *my first assignment for the CBC*
job *He's trying for a job at the mall.*
place *I won a place on the executive committee.*
position *She took up a position at the arts council.*
post *I have held several senior military posts.*

apposite *See* **relevant**

appraisal *See* **estimate, judgment**

appraise *See* **judge, rate, value**

appreciable *See* **respectable**

appreciate
▷ VERB
1 to value something highly: *I appreciate fine food.*
admire *All those who know him admire him for his work.*
prize *Toy cars are prized by collectors.*
rate highly *The four-year-old mare is rated highly by her trainer.*
respect *I respect her talent as a pianist.*
treasure *She treasures her memories of those joyous days.*
value *I value the work she gives me.*
ANTONYM **scorn**
2 to understand a situation or problem: *I didn't appreciate the seriousness of it at the time.*
be aware of *I am well aware of the arguments on the other side.*
perceive *I perceive some tension between the two brothers.*
realize *People don't realize how serious this is.*
recognize *They have been slow to recognize it as a problem.*
understand *They are too young to understand what is going on.*
See also **admire, comprehend, enjoy,**
grasp, like, love, realize, recognize, see, take in, understand, value

appreciation *See* **admiration, gratitude, understanding**

appreciative *See* **grateful**

apprehend *See* **arrest, capture, catch, know**

apprehension *See* **alarm, anxiety, arrest, concern, worry**

apprehensive *See* **afraid, anxious, nervous, suspicious**

apprentice *See* **beginner**

approach *See* **contact, method, style, way**

approaching *See* **future, near**

appropriate
▷ ADJECTIVE
suitable or acceptable for a given situation: *Jeans are not appropriate clothing for some jobs.*
apt *an apt title for his book*
correct *The wedding toast she made was correct for the occasion.*
fitting *a fitting tribute to a great teacher*
proper *the proper course for the court to take*
suitable *a suitable location*
ANTONYM **inappropriate**
See also **correct, fitting, proper, relevant, right, seize, steal, suitable**

approval
▷ NOUN
1 agreement given to something: *The plan will require approval from those in charge.*
agreement *The players and the league finally reached an agreement.*
authorization *We didn't have authorization to go by ourselves.*
blessing *She gave her blessing to the proposed change.*
endorsement *His endorsement of the candidate meant a great deal.*
green light INFORMAL *The producer gave the script the green light.*
permission *They cannot leave the country without permission.*
sanction *This law cannot be enacted without the sanction of Parliament.*
2 liking and admiration of a person or thing: *He wanted to gain his parents' approval.*
admiration *a strategy that is winning*

admiration from around the world

esteem Their public esteem has never been lower.

favour He has won favour with a wide range of groups.

praise She is full of praise for the range of excellent services available.

respect We all have so much respect for the coach.

ANTONYM **disapproval**

See also **admiration, blessing, favour, permission, praise, sanction**

approve

▷ VERB

1 to think something or someone is good: Not everyone approves of his idea.

admire I admire her for her work.

favour The opposition parties favour reform.

praise He praised the fans for their continued support.

respect I want him to respect me as a career woman.

think highly of He thought highly of his sister.

ANTONYM **disapprove**

2 to agree formally to something: The court approved the compensation plan.

authorize He authorized the bank to invest his money.

consent to His parents consented to let him stay out late.

endorse I can endorse their opinion wholeheartedly.

permit You are not permitted to enter this area.

sanction He may now be ready to sanction the use of force.

ANTONYM **veto**

See also **allow, praise, sanction**

approved See **formal**

approving See **favourable**

approximate

▷ ADJECTIVE

close but not exact: We believe that an approximate figure of 20 percent is more accurate.

estimated Our estimated time of arrival is 3:30.

inexact Forecasting is an inexact science.

loose a loose translation

rough a rough estimate

ANTONYM **exact**

See also **broad, rough**

approximately See **about, almost**

apt See **appropriate, proper, relevant, suitable**

aptitude See **gift, head, potential, talent**

arbitrary See **random**

arbitrate See **intervene**

arc See **bend, curve**

arcane See **mysterious, obscure**

arch See **bend, curve**

archaic See **old-fashioned, out of date**

archives See **record**

arctic See **cold, frozen**

ardent

▷ ADJECTIVE

full of enthusiasm and passion: an ardent supporter of animal rights

avid an avid follower of the team

devoted surrounded by devoted fans

enthusiastic enthusiastic collectors of Elvis memorabilia

fervent a fervent admirer of hers

intense his intense love of basketball

keen a keen supporter of the cause

passionate She developed a passionate interest in skiing.

See also **eager, enthusiastic, fervent, intense, keen, passionate**

ardour See **love**

arduous See **difficult, hard, stiff, tough**

area

▷ NOUN

1 a particular part of a place: a built-up area of the city

district I drove around the business district.

locality There are three restaurants and a supermarket in our immediate locality.

neighbourhood evening strolls around the neighbourhood

region a remote mountainous region of Afghanistan

zone a war zone

2 the size of a two-dimensional surface: The islands cover a total area of 625 square kilometres.

expanse a huge expanse of blue-green sea

extent the extent of the rainforest

range a driver's range of vision

size Québec is about three times the size of France.

See also **field, place, region, stretch, territory**

arena See **scene**

argue

▷ VERB

1 to disagree with someone in an angry way: *They argued over the cost of the taxi fare.*

bicker *They bickered endlessly about which route to take.*

disagree *They can communicate even when they strongly disagree.*

fall out INFORMAL *I fell out with my friend after he revealed my secret.*

feud *feuding neighbours*

fight *We're always fighting about money.*

quarrel *My brother quarrelled with my cousin.*

squabble *The children were squabbling over the computer game.*

wrangle *Delegates wrangled over the future of the organization.*

2 to try to prove: *She argued that her client had been wrongly accused.*

assert *The defendants continued to assert their innocence.*

claim *Geologists claim that the land contains gold.*

debate *Parliament will debate the issue today.*

maintain *He had always maintained his innocence.*

reason *I reasoned that if he could do it, so could I.*

See also **quarrel, squabble**

argument

▷ NOUN

1 an angry disagreement: *She got into an argument with the referee.*

clash *clashes between police and demonstrators*

dispute *a dispute over who was responsible for the damage*

feud *a two-year feud between neighbours*

fight *We had another fight about money.*

row *My cousin and I had a terrible row.*

squabble *a family squabble over Sunday lunch*

2 a set of reasons presented for something: *There's a strong argument for lowering the price.*

case *The lawyer's case is weak.*

grounds *grounds for the employee's dismissal*

logic *The logic is that, without more employment, the deficit will rise.*

reasoning *the reasoning behind the decision*

See also **defence, disagreement, dispute, fight, quarrel, row, squabble**

arid See **barren, dry**

arise See **occur, result, start**

aristocrat See **noble**

aristocratic

▷ ADJECTIVE

upper-class: *He loves talking about his aristocratic family.*

genteel *genteel behaviour*

arm See **equip**

armistice See **peace**

aroma See **fragrance, smell**

aromatic See **fragrant, sweet**

around See **about**

arouse See **excite**

arrange

▷ VERB

1 to make plans to do something: *Why don't you arrange to meet him later?*

organize *She organized the trip to the museum.*

plan *She planned to leave in August.*

schedule *Our appointment is scheduled for Tuesday.*

2 to set things out in a particular order: *He started to arrange the CDs in alphabetical order.*

classify *Meteorologists classify clouds into several different groups.*

fix up *We fixed up the room to make the guests feel comfortable.*

group *The fact sheet is grouped into seven sections.*

order *The way a person orders his or her priorities says a lot about that person.*

organize *He began to organize his materials.*

sort *The cards were sorted into three stacks.*

See also **classify, determine, fit, group, lay, organize, plan, position, set up, settle, sort, stage**

arranged See **set**

arrangement See **agreement, layout, sequence, structure, system**

array See **variety**

arrest

▷ VERB

1 to take someone into custody: *Police arrested five men in connection with the attack.*

apprehend *Police have not apprehended the thief.*

capture *Her accomplice was captured by the RCMP.*

seize *Two military observers were seized at*

gunpoint by rebels yesterday.
take prisoner *He was taken prisoner during the war.*
▷ NOUN
2 the act of arresting someone: *The police made two arrests.*
apprehension *information leading to the apprehension of the killer*
capture *He was trying to evade capture by security forces.*
seizure *the mass seizure of terrorists*
See also **capture, catch, stop**

arrival *See* **appearance, entrance, entry**

arrive *See* **come**

arrive at *See* **reach**

arrogance *See* **pride**

arrogant *See* **bossy, haughty, pompous, stuck-up**

arsenal *See* **stockpile**

artful *See* **crafty, cunning**

article
▷ NOUN
1 a piece of writing in a newspaper or magazine: *There's an article about it in today's paper.*
feature *a travel feature about the Bay of Fundy*
item *I read an item about this only last week.*
piece *I disagree with the journalist's recent piece about our city.*
story *Most newspapers had a story about the playoffs.*
2 a particular item: *household articles*
item *Various items have gone missing from my desk.*
object *everyday objects such as pens and pencils*
thing *I have a few things to buy for the trip.*
See also **feature, item, object, piece, thing**

articulate *See* **fluent, state**

artificial *See* **fake, false, mock**

as *See* **because**

as a result *See* **therefore**

as a result of *See* **by virtue of**

as a rule *See* **on average**

as good as *See* **nearly**

as one *See* **together**

as well *See* **also, too**

ascend *See* **climb, rise**

ascendancy *See* **advantage, power**

ascertain *See* **determine, hear, learn, prove, see**

ashamed
▷ ADJECTIVE
feeling embarrassed or guilty: *He was not even ashamed of what he had done.*
embarrassed *I'm not embarrassed to admit I cried.*
guilty *When she realized I was watching, she looked guilty.*
humiliated *I felt humiliated at the scene he was causing.*
sheepish *"I'm afraid it was my idea," he admitted, looking sheepish.*
sorry *She's really sorry for all the trouble she's caused.*
ANTONYM **proud**
See also **embarrassed, guilty**

ashen *See* **pale**

ask
▷ VERB
1 to put a question to someone: *She asked me if I'd enjoyed my dinner.*
inquire *I called to inquire about the time of arrival.*
interrogate *I interrogated everyone even slightly involved.*
query *He queried several statements that I made in the first draft.*
question *They were questioned by the police.*
quiz *I was quizzed about where I had been.*
ANTONYM **answer**
2 to make a request to someone: *We had to ask him to leave.*
appeal *The police appealed for witnesses to come forward.*
beg *I begged him to leave me alone.*
demand *I demanded an explanation from him.*
implore *I implored him to visit his sick friend.*
plead *She pleaded to be allowed to go.*
seek *Always seek legal advice before signing a contract.*
3 to invite someone: *Not everybody had been asked to the wedding.*
bid LITERARY *They all smiled at him and bade him eat.*
invite *She invited him to her birthday party.*
See also **plead, pose, request**

ask (for) *See* **charge**

ask for advice *See* **consult**

ask forgiveness *See* **apologize**

ask oneself *See* **wonder**

asleep *See* **unconscious**

aspect

▷ NOUN

a feature of something: *Test results are only one aspect of a school's success.*
consideration *The cost involved will be a chief consideration in our choice.*
element *Fitness is now an important element in our lives.*
factor *an important factor in a child's development*
feature *the most interesting feature of her personality*
part *Respect is an important part of any relationship.*
point *There is another point to remember when making your decision.*
side *He had an unpleasant side to his character.*
See also **detail, face, factor, feature, quality, view**

aspiration *See* **dream**

aspire *See* **aim**

aspire to *See* **seek**

assassinate *See* **kill, murder**

assassination *See* **murder**

assault *See* **attack, raid**

assemble

▷ VERB

1 to gather together in a group: *a convenient place for students to assemble between classes*
collect *We all collected around him to listen.*
come together *a room where we can come together and relax*
congregate *Kids love to congregate here in the evenings.*
convene *A committee has convened to gather information.*
gather *We all gathered in the boardroom.*
mass *Troops were massing on both sides of the border.*
2 to fit the parts of something together: *Workers were assembling planes.*
build *A carpenter built the shelves for us.*
construct *He had constructed a crude explosive device.*
erect *to erect a building*
make *I like making model planes.*
put together *You can buy the parts and put it together yourself.*
See also **build, collect, construct, form, gather, make, manufacture, mass, meet, piece together**

assembly *See* **company, convention, council, gathering, making, manufacture**

assent *See* **agree, permission**

assert *See* **argue, claim, declare, state**

assertion *See* **claim**

assertive *See* **forceful**

assess *See* **judge, test, value**

assessment *See* **estimate, judgment, opinion, test**

asset *See* **beauty, benefit, merit, virtue**

assets *See* **possessions, property**

assign *See* **allow**

assignation *See* **meeting**

assignment *See* **appointment, duty, task, work**

assimilate *See* **grasp, take in**

assist *See* **benefit, help**

assistance *See* **help**

assistant

▷ NOUN

a person who helps someone: *His assistant took over while he was out of town.*
aide *The prime minister's aide set up a meeting.*
ally *She was supported by her political allies.*
colleague *a business colleague*
deputy *When the minister is away, her deputy will chair all meetings.*
helper *a group of volunteer helpers*
right-hand person *the resignation of the manager's right-hand person*
See also **helper**

associate

▷ VERB

1 to connect one thing with another: *Poverty is sometimes associated with old age.*
connect *a common problem directly connected with stress*
couple *Coupled with unsanitary conditions, the earthquake was a major disaster.*
identify *Candidates want to identify themselves with reform.*
link *Lung cancer is linked to smoking.*
2 to spend time with a person: *I began associating with different crowds of people.*
hang out INFORMAL *People want to hang out with you for the wrong reasons.*
mingle *reporters who mingled freely with the crowd*

mix *She mixed well with the crowd at the party.*

run around INFORMAL *What's he doing running around with criminals?*

socialize *She made little effort to socialize with other staff members.*

▷ NOUN

3 a person known through work: *the restaurant owner's business associates*

colleague *learning from more experienced colleagues*

co-worker *Their co-workers often worked long days.*

See also **colleague, connect**

associate with *See* **identify with**

association

▷ NOUN

1 an organization: *a research association*

body *the student body*

club *the local chess club*

company *a major auto-parts company*

confederation *the Confederation of Bakers*

group *an environmental group*

institution *a member of various financial institutions*

league *the National Hockey League*

society *the Humane Society*

syndicate *a syndicate of international banks*

2 a connection or involvement with a person or group: *his association with an animal rights group*

affiliation *He has no affiliation with any political party.*

attachment *Bears and their cubs form a close attachment.*

bond *There is a special bond between us.*

connection *He has denied any connection with the organization.*

relationship *Ours was strictly a professional relationship.*

tie *I had very close ties with the family.*

See also **body, club, connection, fellowship, link, organization, relationship, society, union**

assorted *See* **several, various**

assortment *See* **collection, range, variety**

assume

▷ VERB

1 to accept that something is true: *I assumed that he would turn up.*

believe *I believe she'll be back next week.*

guess INFORMAL *I guess she thought that was pretty smart.*

imagine *I imagine he'll be late again.*

suppose *I see no reason to suppose that it isn't working.*

think *They thought that they had won.*

2 to take responsibility for something: *She will assume the position of chief executive officer.*

accept *He accepted the role of player-captain.*

shoulder *He has had to shoulder the responsibility of his boss's mistakes.*

take on *Don't take on more responsibilities than you can handle.*

undertake *He undertook to edit the yearbook.*

See also **believe, expect, gather, imagine, reckon, suppose**

assumed *See* **supposed**

assurance *See* **confidence, guarantee, promise, word**

assure *See* **convince, promise**

assured *See* **confident, definite**

astonish *See* **amaze, surprise**

astonishing *See* **amazing, incredible, unexpected**

astonishment *See* **amazement, surprise**

astound *See* **amaze, surprise**

astounding *See* **amazing, incredible, wonderful**

astray *See* **lost**

astringent *See* **bitter**

astute

▷ ADJECTIVE

very intelligent or perceptive: *an astute judge of character*

alert *The alert cat is aware of every sound.*

clever *a clever business move*

keen *a keen understanding of politics*

perceptive *his perceptive analysis of the situation*

quick *He has a quick wit.*

sharp *His casual manner disguised a sharp mind.*

shrewd *He demonstrated a shrewd understanding of human nature.*

smart *a very smart move*

See also **acute, keen, perceptive, sharp, shrewd, smart**

asylum *See* **refuge, shelter**

asymmetrical *See* **irregular**

at an end *See* **over**

at ease *See* **comfortable, relaxed**

at fault _See_ **responsible**

at hand _See_ **available, handy, present**

at home _See_ **comfortable**

at large _See_ **free**

at last _See_ **finally**

at liberty _See_ **free**

at no time _See_ **never**

at once _See_ **immediately, now, together**

at someone's disposal _See_ **available**

at the last moment _See_ **finally**

at times _See_ **sometimes**

at your fingertips _See_ **handy**

atone _See_ **compensate**

atonement _See_ **compensation**

atrocious _See_ **dreadful, wicked**

attach

▷ _VERB_

to join or fasten things together: _The gadget can be attached to any surface._

affix _His name was affixed to the door of his office._

connect _Connect the pipe to the tap._

couple _The engine is coupled to a gearbox._

fasten _The shelves are fastened to the wall with screws._

join _two sticks joined by a chain_

link _tree houses linked by ropes_

tie _He tied the tent to the posts._

ANTONYM **separate**

See also **add, connect, fasten, fix, hang, join, link, secure, stick**

attachment

▷ _NOUN_

1 a feeling of love and affection: _The puppies formed a close attachment to each other._

affection _the affection between a pet and its owner_

bond _There has always been a strong bond between us._

fondness _I have a great fondness for all animals._

liking _He has never shown any liking for his colleagues._

love _A deep love gradually developed between them._

2 a part attached to something else: _The drill comes with a wide range of attachments._

accessory _a range of accessories for your cellphone_

component _Additional components are available as listed._

fitting _pipe fittings_

fixture _light fixtures_

part _Extra parts can be added later._

unit _The unit plugs into any TV set._

See also **affection, association, bond, fitting, friendship, link**

attack

▷ _VERB_

1 to use violence against someone or something: _I thought the dog was going to attack me._

assault _The victim was assaulted with this weapon._

charge _She ordered the soldiers to charge._

invade _The army invaded the enemy town._

raid _a police raid on the drug dealers_

set upon _As the bus drove east, it was set upon by bandits._

storm _The attackers stormed the embassy._

2 to criticize someone strongly: _She attacked the government's economic policies._

blast _He blasted the referee for his inconsistency._

censure _The bank has been censured and fined by the government._

criticize _The regime has been harshly criticized._

put down INFORMAL _He was always putting me down in front of others._

vilify FORMAL _He was vilified, hounded, and forced into exile._

▷ _NOUN_

3 violent physical action against someone or something: _a vicious attack on an unarmed person_

assault _The rebels are poised for a new assault._

charge _a bayonet charge_

invasion _the Roman invasion of Britain_

offensive _the government's military offensive against the rebels_

onslaught _civilians trying to flee the military onslaught_

raid _a raid on a house by armed police_

See also **bomb, invade, raid, savage**

attain _See_ **acquire, earn, reach, win**

attainable _See_ **possible**

attempt

▷ _VERB_

1 to try to do something: _They attempted to escape._

endeavour _I will endeavour to arrange a meeting._

seek _We have never sought to impose our views._

strive *The school strives to treat students as individuals.*
try *I tried hard to persuade him to stay.*
try your hand at *He'd always wanted to try his hand at writing.*
▷ NOUN
2 an act of trying to do something: *one of his rare attempts at humour*
bid *a bid to save the newspaper*
crack INFORMAL *his third crack at the world heavyweight title*
go INFORMAL *My friend suggested I should have a go at becoming a jockey.*
shot INFORMAL *We'd like a shot at competing in the Olympics.*
stab INFORMAL *Several tennis stars have taken a stab at acting.*
try *That makes the plan worth a try.*
See also **aim, effort, go, seek, strive, try**

attend See **frequent, listen**

attend to See **deal, take care of**

attention See **care, consideration, heed, interest**

attentive See **alert, observant, thoughtful**

attire See **clothes, dress**

attitude
▷ NOUN
someone's way of thinking and behaving: *negative attitudes to work*
outlook *behaviour that seems contrary to his whole outlook*
perspective *The experience gave me a new perspective on life.*
point of view *Try to look at this from my point of view.*
position *What's your position on this issue?*
stance *the government's stance on capital punishment*
See also **conduct, outlook, view, viewpoint**

attorney See **lawyer**

attract
▷ VERB
to appeal to or interest: *The championship has attracted many leading skaters.*
appeal to *The idea appealed to him.*
draw *The tennis match drew a large crowd.*
entice *She resisted attempts to entice her into politics.*
lure *They were being lured into a trap.*
pull INFORMAL *They have to employ performers to pull in a crowd.*
tempt *Can I tempt you with some cake?*

ANTONYM **repel**
See also **appeal, lure**

attraction See **beauty, charm, lure, pull**

attractive
▷ ADJECTIVE
pleasant, especially to look at: *an attractive woman*
appealing *an appealing smile*
charming *a charming little village*
fetching *a fetching outfit*
handsome *a handsome man*
lovely *a lovely island*
pretty *What a pretty picture!*
ANTONYM **unattractive**
See also **beautiful, cute, handsome, lovely, pretty**

attractiveness See **beauty**

attribute
▷ NOUN
a quality or feature: *a normal attribute of human behaviour*
characteristic *their physical characteristics*
feature *the most striking feature of his music*
property *the magnetic properties of iron*
quality *His humility is one of his most endearing qualities.*
trait *personality traits*
See also **characteristic, feature, point, property, virtue**

audacious See **daring**

audacity See **daring, impudence**

audibly See **aloud**

audience See **meeting**

augment
▷ VERB
to add something to something else: *a good way to augment your income*
add to *An updated kitchen adds to the value of your house.*
boost *people who boost their earnings by working part-time from home*
complement *a benefits package that complements her salary*
increase *He is eager to increase his income.*
reinforce *measures that will reinforce the current trend*
supplement *I suggest supplementing your diet with vitamin A.*
top up *contributions to top up pension plans*
See also **add, supplement**

austere See **harsh, plain**

authentic
▷ ADJECTIVE
real and genuine: *an authentic French recipe*

bona fide *We are happy to donate to bona fide charities.*
genuine *Experts are convinced the manuscript is genuine.*
real *It's a real Emily Carr painting.*
true *Of course he's not a true prince.*
ANTONYM **fake**
See also **actual, exact, genuine, real, realistic, true**

authenticity *See* **reality**

authoritarian *See* **bossy, strict**

authority *See* **control, expert, influence, power**

authorization *See* **approval, permission, permit, power, sanction**

authorize *See* **allow, approve, permit, sanction**

authorized *See* **legal, official**

automated *See* **automatic**

automatic
▷ *ADJECTIVE*
1 operating mechanically by itself: *An ATM is an automatic teller machine.*
automated *highly automated production lines*
mechanical *the oldest working mechanical clock in the world*
robotic *a robotic arm for the space station*
self-propelled *a self-propelled torpedo*
2 without conscious thought: *automatic body functions*
instinctive *an instinctive reaction*
involuntary *involuntary muscle movements*
natural *the insect's natural instinct to feed*
reflex *Blushing is a reflex action linked to the nervous system.*

automobile
▷ *NOUN*
a vehicle for carrying a few people: *the Japanese automobile manufacturer*
car *We traded in our old car.*
vehicle *We waved down a passing vehicle.*
See also **car**

autonomous *See* **independent**

available
▷ *ADJECTIVE*
ready for use: *There are three campsites still available for the long weekend.*
accessible *This information is accessible on the Internet.*
at someone's disposal *Do you have all the facts at your disposal?*
free *There was only one seat free on the train.*

handy *Keep your keys handy so you can get into your car quickly.*
on hand *Having the right equipment on hand will be enormously useful.*
ANTONYM **unavailable**
See also **ready**

avenge *See* **revenge**

average
▷ *ADJECTIVE*
standard or normal: *the average Canadian teenager*
normal *I am now back to leading a perfectly normal life.*
regular *He's just a regular guy.*
standard *the standard price of a CD*
typical *A typical day begins at 8:30.*
usual *This isn't the usual kind of weather for July.*

on average
▷ *ADVERB*
for the most part: *Men are, on average, taller than women.*
as a rule *As a rule, performances begin at 8 p.m.*
generally *Fresh-squeezed orange juice is generally more expensive than the frozen kind.*
normally *Normally, the subway system carries 50 000 passengers a day.*
typically *It's a typically hot summer day.*
usually *He's usually late, but today he was early.*
See also **all right, common, medium, moderate, normal, typical**

averse to *See* **against, reluctant, unwilling**

aversion *See* **dislike, hate, hatred, horror**

avert *See* **prevent**

avid *See* **ardent, eager, enthusiastic, keen**

avoid
▷ *VERB*
1 to make an effort not to do something: *He avoids talking about unpleasant things.*
dodge *She dodged the question by changing the subject.*
duck out of INFORMAL *ducking out of the post-game press conference*
refrain from *I refrained from making any comment.*
shirk *We won't shirk our responsibility.*
2 to keep away from someone or something: *She thought he was trying to avoid her.*

dodge *He refuses to dodge his critics.*
elude *an attempt to elude photographers*
eschew FORMAL *The celebrity eschewed publicity and avoided nightclubs.*
evade *He managed to evade the police.*
shun *Everybody shunned him.*
sidestep *Rarely does he sidestep a question.*
steer clear of *It would be best to steer clear of that subject.*
See also **abstain, dodge, escape**

awake *See* **wake**

award *See* **give, grant, present, prize**

award-winning *See* **prize**

aware of
▷ ADJECTIVE
I conscious of something: *She was acutely aware of the noise of the city.*
acquainted with *He was well acquainted with Shakespeare's works.*
conscious of *I was conscious of them staring at me.*
familiar with *I am not familiar with your work.*
mindful of *Everyone should be mindful of the dangers.*
ANTONYM **unaware**
2 knowing about something: *Keep me aware of any developments.*
informed *the importance of keeping the public properly informed*
in the picture *He's always kept me in the picture.*
knowledgeable *He's very knowledgeable about new technology.*
See also **perceptive**

awareness *See* **grasp**

away *See* **absent**

awe *See* **fear**

awesome *See* **impressive**

awful
▷ ADJECTIVE
very unpleasant or very bad: *the same awful jokes*
appalling *living under the most appalling conditions*
dreadful *They told us the dreadful news.*
frightful *a frightful ordeal*
ghastly *The unruly child's behaviour was ghastly.*
horrendous *The death toll was horrendous.*
terrible *My French is terrible!*
See also **dreadful, horrible, terrible**

awkward *See* **clumsy, embarrassed, uncomfortable**

awkwardness *See* **clumsiness, embarrassment**

axiom *See* **principle, saying**

aye *See* **yes**

Bb

B

babble
▷ VERB
to talk in an excited way: *He babbled on and on.*
burble *He burbled on about his new video game.*
chatter *The child chattered about the kittens.*
gabble *I started to gabble in the interview.*
jabber *I jabbered when I started talking to the principal.*
prattle *Oh, no. He's prattling on again.*
See also **ramble, rave**

babies See **young**

baby
▷ NOUN
a very young child: *I've had a dimple since I was a baby.*
infant *young parents with infants in strollers*
tot *tots in a playground*
See also **child**

back
▷ NOUN
1 the part that is behind the front: *the back of a postcard*
end *the end of the corridor*
rear *the rear of the building*
reverse *Please sign the reverse of this form.*
stern *the stern of a boat*
ANTONYM **front**
▷ VERB
2 to support a person or organization: *His friends are backing him.*
advocate *Doctors advocate prevention rather than cure.*
encourage *The government is encouraging better child care.*
endorse *Do you endorse his opinion?*
favour *I favour a different approach.*
promote *Thanks for promoting my ideas.*
support *We supported her campaign for class president.*
ANTONYM **oppose**
See also **advocate, finance, gamble, promote, sanction, support**

back away See **retreat**

back off See **retreat**

back out See **withdraw**

background
▷ NOUN
where you come from: *What is your family's background?*

culture *people from different cultures*
environment *the environment I grew up in*
history *She has an interesting history.*
upbringing *a strict upbringing*
See also **foil, record, surroundings**

backing See **blessing, sanction**

backlash See **reaction**

backside See **buttocks**

bad
▷ ADJECTIVE
1 harmful, unpleasant, or upsetting: *I have some bad news.*
ANTONYM **good**
2 of poor quality: *bad roads*
ANTONYM **satisfactory**
3 evil in character: *a bad person*
ANTONYM **good**
See WORD STUDY **bad** on next page
See also **evil, naughty, rotten, serious, unpleasant, wicked, wrong**

INFORMALLY SPEAKING

bad for you: unhealthy
bad luck: misfortune

badger See **hassle, pester**

badly
▷ ADVERB
in an inferior way: *This essay is badly written.*
ANTONYM **well**
See WORD STUDY **badly**

WORD STUDY: BADLY

Badly can be avoided in favour of a more expressive alternative.

• **in an inferior way**
The volunteers are **inadequately** trained.
The event was **poorly** organized.

• **seriously**
She was **deeply** hurt by what you said.
He looked **desperately** depressed.

• **cruelly**
He was **savagely** beaten by thugs.
This cat has been **viciously** treated.

badness See **evil**

bad-tempered See **irritable**

baffle See **confuse, puzzle**

Bad is such a commonly used word that it has come to lose much of its effectiveness. There are more expressive substitutes that can be used instead.

• **having a harmful effect**
Stress can be **damaging** healthwise.
Which chemicals have a **destructive** effect on the ozone layer?
This could have a **detrimental** impact on the environment.
There are **harmful** effects of radiation.
Illnesses can be caused by an **unhealthy** lifestyle.
The side effects of this drug are **unpleasant**.

• **making someone feel upset or uneasy**
She was shocked at the **distressing** images shown in the film.
We have just had some **disturbing** news.
He's been having a **grim** time of it lately.
That sight evokes **painful** memories.
She is just recovering from a **traumatic** period in her life.
The atmosphere in the room was **unsettling**.
It was an **upsetting** experience.

• **causing physical pain**
She had an **acute** attack of appendicitis.
What an **agonizing** way to die!
I got an **intense** cramp in my leg while running.
A **painful** back stops me working out.
He suffers from **serious** knee problems.
After lunch, she had **severe** stomach pains.
I have a **terrible** headache.

• **of poor quality**
This product is **defective** and caused a serious injury.
Poor health can result from a **deficient** diet.
Customers are asked to return **faulty** goods to the manufacturer.
Imperfect work will not be accepted.
The committee protested about the **inadequate** working conditions.
I was disappointed by the **inferior** quality of the recording.
What a **pathetic** excuse!
This area has **poor** housing and high unemployment.
We complained about the **unsatisfactory** service in the restaurant.

• **lacking skill**
Incompetent managers will be fired.
The actor gave an **inept** performance.
She's a **poor** judge of character and is easily fooled.
He is **useless** at all sports.

• **having an evil character**
The rebels fought to defeat a **corrupt** government.
Do not blame all of us for the **criminal** actions of a few individuals.
The accused was a **depraved** criminal.
Who is the most **evil** person in history?
Many people believe gambling is **immoral**.
Such behaviour is considered **sinful** by society.
She played a **villainous** character in her last movie.
Tell the children the story of the good prince and his **wicked** twin brother.
If you do something **wrong**, you must take the consequences.

• **of children, misbehaving**
They don't believe in punishing **disobedient** children.
He was **mischievous** when he was younger.
She is **naughty** and teases her brother.
There were a few **undisciplined** students disrupting the class.
Should there be laws to penalize the parents of **unruly** children?

• **of food**
This bread is **mouldy**.
One of the eggs is **rotten**.
The milk was **sour**.

• **of language**
The song lyrics are **obscene**.
I don't like to hear **offensive** language.
The little boy said a **rude** word and ran off.
How can you use such a **vulgar** expression?

baffled *See* **confused**

baffling *See* **confusing, hard, mysterious**

baggy *See* **full, loose**

bait

▷ *NOUN*

something used to tempt someone: *He isn't taking the bait.*

bribe *a dishonest police officer who took bribes*

decoy *He acted as a decoy to trap the robber.*

inducement *financial inducements to talk to the newspapers*

lure *the lure of a huge salary*

temptation *the temptation of easy money*

See also **incentive, lure, pick on**

bake *See* **cook, harden**

balance

▷ *VERB*

1 to make or remain steady: *Balancing on one leg is difficult.*

level *House prices have levelled off.*

stabilize *attempts to stabilize the economy*

steady *She steadied herself before kicking the ball.*

▷ *NOUN*

2 a stable relationship between things: *the chemical balance of the brain*

equilibrium *I'm unable to maintain my equilibrium because of dizziness.*

equity *plans for greater equity among Canada's provinces*

parity *She won pay parity with male colleagues.*

See also **compensate, difference, remainder, rest**

ball

▷ *NOUN*

a round object: *a soccer ball*

drop *a drop of blood*

globe *the globe of the world*

pellet *food pellets for a rabbit*

sphere *a sphere the size of a tennis ball*

See also **lump**

ballot *See* **vote**

balmy *See* **calm, mild, warm**

ban

▷ *VERB*

1 to disallow something: *The coach was banned from the game.*

bar *The press will be barred from the trial.*

disqualify *He was disqualified from the playoffs.*

exclude *They were excluded from math class.*

forbid *The rules forbid the use of oversize goalie pads.*

outlaw *regulations outlawing child labour*

prohibit *a law that prohibits the sale of alcohol*

ANTONYM **permit**

▷ *NOUN*

2 a rule disallowing something: *a ban on smoking*

disqualification *The disqualification was due to a technicality.*

embargo *an embargo on trade with the country*

prohibition *a prohibition on smoking in restaurants*

suppression *the suppression of antigovernment protests*

ANTONYM **permit**

See also **exclude, forbid, prohibit, sanctions, veto**

banal *See* **corny, hackneyed**

band

▷ *NOUN*

1 a group of musicians who play together: *a singer in a rock band*

group *They formed the group while they were still at school.*

orchestra *the Toronto Symphony Orchestra*

2 a group of people who share a common purpose: *a band of thugs*

bunch *A bunch of friends get together to play hockey.*

company *a professional acting company*

crowd *A small crowd of onlookers had gathered.*

gang *a street gang*

party *A party of eight arrived at the restaurant.*

troupe *She toured with a professional dance troupe.*

See also **body, bunch, company, group, party, ring, team**

bandit *See* **thug**

bane *See* **pest**

bang

▷ *VERB*

1 to hit or put something down hard, with a loud noise: *a toddler banging a saucepan with a wooden spoon*

beat *They sat in a circle, beating small drums.*

hammer *They hammered on the window to get our attention.*

B

hit *They were hitting the sides of the van with sticks.*
knock *I knocked on the door for ages, but nobody answered.*
pound *We pounded on the walls.*
slam *I slammed down the receiver.*
thump *The students cheered and thumped on their desks.*
▷ *NOUN*
2 a sudden, short, loud noise: *The balloon exploded with a bang.*
blast *the ear-splitting blast of a trumpet*
boom *There was a boom and a cloud of smoke.*
crack *the crack of a whip*
detonation *We heard several loud detonations coming from the building.*
explosion *the deafening explosion of gunshots*
thump *I dropped the suitcase to the floor with a loud thump.*
▷ *NOUN*
3 a hard or painful bump against something: *a nasty bang on the elbow*
blow *a blow to the side of the head*
knock *The knock to my head caused quite a bump.*
thump *a thump on the chest*
whack *She gave the rug several whacks with a brush.*
See also **blow, bump, crash, explosion**

INFORMALLY SPEAKING

bang for your buck: value for your money
bang into: hit
with a bang: with great success

---

bang into *See* **hit**

banish
▷ *VERB*
1 to exile someone: *banished to a distant island*
deport *The criminal was deported from Canada.*
eject *He was ejected from the club.*
evict *evicted for non-payment of rent*
exile *The prince was exiled from his land.*
expel *expelled from school*
2 to get rid of something or someone: *to banish illness*
discard *Read the instructions before discarding the box.*
dismiss *I dismissed the idea from my mind.*
dispel *The myths are being dispelled.*
eliminate *They eliminated us from the contest.*

eradicate *Scientists have made efforts to eradicate certain diseases.*
remove *They removed several requirements from the players' agreements.*

bank
▷ *NOUN*
1 a store of something: *a blood bank*
fund *a pension fund*
hoard *a hoard of treasure*
reserve *the world's oil reserves*
stock *How many printers are in stock?*
store *a secret store of candy*
2 the edge of a river: *He sat fishing on the bank.*
brink *trees near the brink of the cliffs*
edge *The child stood too close to the edge of the river.*
shore *He swam toward the shore.*
side *a picnic by the side of the river*
See also **row**

bank on *See* **depend**

banking *See* **finance**

bankruptcy *See* **crash**

banned *See* **illegal**

banquet *See* **meal**

banter *See* **joke**

baptize *See* **name**

bar
▷ *NOUN*
1 a piece of metal: *bars across the windows*
pole *a flag pole*
rail *the rail in front of the balcony*
rod *a fishing rod*
shaft *the shaft of a spear*
▷ *VERB*
2 to stop someone: *His bodyguards barred the way.*
obstruct *Vehicles have obstructed the entrance.*
prevent *A locked gate prevents people from entering the property.*
See also **ban, block, close, exclude, obstruct**

barbarian *See* **savage**

barbaric *See* **savage**

barbarity *See* **cruelty**

barbarous *See* **cruel, savage**

barbecue *See* **cook**

barbed *See* **jagged**

bare
▷ *ADJECTIVE*
1 not covered: *bare legs*

exposed *His chest was exposed.*
naked *a naked body*
nude *a nude artist's model*
uncovered *His arms were uncovered.*
undressed *I got undressed in the bathroom.*
ANTONYM **covered**
2 unoccupied or with with nothing inside: *a small bare office*
empty *an empty room*
open *open country*
spartan *spartan accommodation*
vacant *a vacant chair*
See also **blank, empty, naked, plain**

barefaced See **shameless**

barely
▷ ADVERB
only just: *She is barely sixteen.*
almost *I almost didn't make it.*
hardly *I could hardly believe it.*
just *I won by just three votes.*
scarcely *I can scarcely hear him.*
See also **hardly**

bargain See **cheap**

barge See **burst**

bark See **bay**

barrage See **hail**

barren
▷ ADJECTIVE
with nothing growing on it: *a barren desert*
arid *the arid Badlands of Alberta*
desert *desert regions*
desolate *a desolate place*
dry *poor, dry countries*
empty *the empty stretch of land*
unproductive *40 hectares of unproductive land*
waste *waste land*
ANTONYM **fertile**

barricade See **barrier**

barrier
▷ NOUN
1 something preventing entry: *The eager fans broke through the barriers.*
barricade *a barricade of vehicles*
fence *a garden fence*
obstacle *The accident at the intersection was an obstacle to traffic.*
obstruction *Check that the exhaust pipe is clear of obstructions.*
wall *the walls of Québec City*
2 something that prevents progress: *trade barriers between Canada and the United States*
handicap *It is a handicap not knowing a second language.*

B

hindrance *a potential hindrance to the peace process*
hurdle *the first hurdle in a job search*
impediment *a serious impediment to economic growth*
obstacle *the main obstacle to the takeover*
See also **disadvantage, obstacle, protection, safeguard**

barter See **change, exchange, swap**

base
▷ NOUN
1 the lowest part of something: *the base of the cliffs*
bed *the river bed*
bottom *the bottom of the ladder*
foot *the foot of the mountain*
foundation *They have laid the foundations for the new building.*
pedestal *The statue is back on its pedestal.*
stand *a microphone stand*
ANTONYM **top**
2 the place you work from: *a military base*
camp *refugee camps*
centre *a health centre*
headquarters *company headquarters in Winnipeg*
post *a diplomatic post in Paris*
station *the police station*
▷ VERB
3 to use as a foundation: *The movie is based on a true story.*
build *a reputation built on lies*
derive *The name is derived from a Greek word.*
found *My hopes were founded on a mistake.*
ground *I like a movie to be grounded in reality.*
hinge *The entire play hinges on one character.*
See also **bottom**

CONFUSABLES

A **base** supports something physical, like a statue.
A **basis** supports a belief or opinion.

basement See **bottom**

bash See **club**

bashful See **shy, timid**

bashfulness See **embarrassment**

basic
▷ ADJECTIVE
most necessary: *the basic requirements for the job*

central *What is the central point of your essay?*
elementary *elementary computer training*
essential *essential reading and writing skills*
fundamental *fundamental rights and freedoms*
key *key skills such as communication and teamwork*
necessary *They lack the necessary resources.*
vital *vital supplies*
See also **essential, straightforward**

basics *See* **essentials**

basis
▷ *NOUN*
the main principle of something: *The same theme is the basis of several poems.*
core *the core of the country's problems*
fundamental *the fundamentals of road safety*
heart *the heart of the matter*
premise *the premise of his argument*
principle *the principles of a belief*
See also **cause, grounds**

bass *See* **deep**

bat *See* **club, stick**

batch *See* **bunch, lot, set**

bathe *See* **soak, wash**

batter *See* **beat, club**

battle *See* **clash, conflict, contest, fight, war**

batty *See* **mad**

bauble *See* **ornament**

bawdy *See* **obscene**

bawl *See* **shout**

bay
▷ *NOUN*
l a curve in a coastline: *the Bay of Fundy*
cove *a sandy cove with white cliffs*
gulf *the Gulf of St. Lawrence*
inlet *a deep inlet on the Newfoundland coast*
sound *streams that run into Nootka Sound*
▷ *VERB*
2 to make a howling noise: *wolves baying in the moonlight*
bark *a small dog barking at a seagull*
cry *the cry of a loon*
howl *distant coyotes howling in the night*
yelp *A dog snapped and yelped at them.*
See also **compartment**

bazaar *See* **fair, market**

be advantageous *See* **pay**

be afraid *See* **fear**

be after *See* **seek**

be alert *See* **watch out**

be aware of *See* **appreciate, know, sense**

beach
▷ *NOUN*
an area beside the sea: *building sandcastles on the beach*
coast *a day at the coast*
sands *the sands along the Lake Huron coast*
seashore *walks along the seashore*
seaside *a hotel at the seaside*
shore *a trip to the New Brunswick shore*
See also **coast**

beacon *See* **signal**

bead *See* **blob, drip, drop**

beam *See* **shine, smile**

bear
▷ *VERB*
l to carry something: *The ice wasn't thick enough to bear their weight.*
carry *She always carried a newspaper.*
convey *The limousine conveyed us to the prom.*
shoulder *He had to shoulder the blame for the mistake.*
support *Thick wooden posts support the ceiling.*
take *You'd better take an umbrella.*
2 to have or show something: *The room bore the signs of a party.*
exhibit *He began to exhibit symptoms of the disease.*
harbour *They still harbour feelings of resentment.*
have *I have a grudge against her.*
3 to accept something: *He can't bear to talk about it.*
abide *I can't abide selfish people.*
endure *The pain was hard to endure.*
stomach *He could not stomach violence.*
suffer *I had to suffer his company all day.*
tolerate *Some people tolerate pain better than others.*
See also **bring, carry, put up with, suffer, take, tolerate**

bear a resemblance to *See* **resemble**

bear in mind *See* **consider**

bear out *See* **confirm**

bearable *See* **tolerable**

bearing *See* **appearance, look, manner, relation**

beat

▷ VERB

1 to hit someone or something hard: *He started to beat the poor dog.*

batter *The waves kept battering the life raft.*

buffet *Their plane was buffeted by storms.*

hit *She hit the ball with the bat.*

pound *Someone was pounding on the door.*

strike *struck across the mouth*

thrash *He threatened to thrash the poor creature.*

2 to defeat: *She was easily beaten in the race.*

defeat *The team hasn't been defeated all year.*

outdo *One comedian was trying to outdo the other.*

outstrip *The company is outstripping its rivals in sales.*

overcome *My cousin overcame his fear of flying.*

overwhelm *The first attack overwhelmed the enemy.*

vanquish *the man who helped vanquish Napoleon*

▷ NOUN

3 a rhythm: *the thumping beat of the music*

cadence *the pulsing cadences of his music*

metre *the metre of the poem*

rhythm *His foot tapped a rhythm on the floor.*

stress *differences of stress in speech*

time *a song written in waltz time*

See also **bang, club, defeat, rhythm, top, vanquish**

beautiful

▷ ADJECTIVE

attractive or pleasing: *beautiful music*

attractive *an attractive room*

delightful *The perfume is delightful.*

exquisite *an exquisite view of the Rockies*

fine *a fine summer's day*

gorgeous *a gorgeous painting*

lovely *You look lovely!*

pleasing *a pleasing appearance*

ANTONYM **ugly**

See also **fine, lovely, pretty**

beauty

▷ NOUN

1 the quality of being beautiful: *a scene of outstanding beauty*

attractiveness *the attractiveness of the region*

charm *a person of elegance and charm*

elegance *the elegance of the overall design*

loveliness *the loveliness of the scene*

ANTONYM **ugliness**

2 a good-looking person: *a dark-haired*

B

beauty with a great smile

hunk INFORMAL *That actor is such a hunk!*

stunner INFORMAL *the 23-year-old stunner*

3 an attractive feature: *The beauty of the deal is that everyone makes money.*

advantage *the advantages of the new system over the old one*

asset *Honesty is one of her greatest assets.*

attraction *The main attraction of the place is the monument.*

benefit *Every age has its benefits.*

because

▷ CONJUNCTION

for the reason that: *I went home because I was tired.*

as *Don't cook for me as I'll be home late.*

due to *The train's late arrival was due to bad weather.*

owing to *Owing to the storm, the game was postponed.*

since *Since you didn't listen, I'll repeat that.*

because of *See* **by virtue of**

beckon *See* **lure, signal**

become *See* **get, grow**

bed *See* **base, bottom**

bedraggled *See* **untidy**

beefy *See* **plump**

before

▷ ADVERB

at a previous time: *Have you been to Greece before?*

earlier *Here is a cake I made earlier.*

formerly *He had formerly been a mechanic.*

in advance *We booked the concert tickets well in advance.*

previously *Previously she had little time to exercise.*

sooner *I wish I'd arrived sooner.*

ANTONYM **after**

See also **in front**

before long *See* **soon**

beforehand *See* **early, first**

beg

▷ VERB

to ask anxiously for something: *I begged him to come to the party.*

beseech FORMAL *I beseech you to show mercy.*

implore *I implore you not to say anything.*

petition *He petitioned the court for a new trial.*

plead *They were pleading with me to stay.*

See also **appeal, ask, implore, plead, press, request, scrounge, urge**

beg someone's pardon See **apologize**

begin

▷ *VERB*

to start or cause to start: *She began to move around the room.*

commence FORMAL *He commenced his journey.*

inaugurate *The committee was inaugurated ten days ago.*

initiate *They wanted to initiate a discussion.*

institute *The school instituted an advanced swimmers' program.*

originate *The idea originated when I was daydreaming.*

set about *He set about tackling his problems.*

start *The meeting starts at 10 o'clock.*

ANTONYM **end**

See also **proceed, start**

begin again See **renew**

beginner

▷ *NOUN*

someone learning to do something: *a course for beginners*

apprentice *an apprentice in a trade*

intern *an intern at the hospital*

learner *young learners of the language*

novice *Many of us are novices on the computer.*

trainee *a trainee in a newspaper office*

ANTONYM **expert**

See also **recruit**

beginning

▷ *NOUN*

where something starts: *the beginning of the city*

birth *the birth of modern art*

commencement FORMAL *a date for the commencement of talks*

onset *the onset of the storm*

opening *the opening of the trial*

origin *the origins of civilization*

outset *This was a problem from the outset.*

start *the start of the chapter*

ANTONYM **end**

See also **head, opening, source, start**

begrudge See **envy**

begrudging See **bitter**

behave

▷ *VERB*

to act in a certain way: *They were behaving like small children.*

act *He is acting like a spoiled child.*

function *They are functioning as a team.*

operate *I know how the other team operates.*

work *My mind is working well today.*

See also **conduct yourself**

behave toward See **treat**

behaviour See **conduct, manner**

behind time See **late**

behold See **see**

belated See **late**

belief

▷ *NOUN*

1 the certainty something is true: *belief in reincarnation*

confidence *I have every confidence that you'll do well.*

conviction *She speaks with conviction.*

judgment *My judgment is that he should leave.*

opinion *My cousin has strong opinions.*

trust *She has complete trust that you'll help her.*

view *In my view, he is wrong.*

2 a principle of a religion or system: *the culture and beliefs of ancient times*

creed *people of different nationalities and creeds*

doctrine *church doctrine*

dogma *religious dogma*

faith *Do you practise any faith?*

ideology *different political ideologies*

principle *the principles of the Jewish faith*

tenet *the fundamental tenets of Islam*

See also **confidence, faith, idea, opinion, view, viewpoint**

believable

▷ *ADJECTIVE*

possible or likely to be the case: *The book is full of believable characters.*

credible *credible witnesses*

imaginable *It is scarcely imaginable that it happened here.*

likely *It's more likely that she forgot.*

plausible *a plausible explanation*

possible *It's quite possible that I'm wrong.*

probable *the most probable outcome*

ANTONYM **unbelievable**

believe

▷ *VERB*

to accept something is true: *Don't believe everything you read in the papers.*

accept *He can't accept that he is wrong.*

assume *I assume these eggs are fresh.*

presume *I presume you know what you're talking about.*

swallow INFORMAL *I found their story hard to swallow.*

trust *I trust that you will manage.*

ANTONYM **doubt**

See also **assume, consider, expect, feel, imagine, reckon, suppose, suspect, think, understand**

believed *See* **supposed**

believer *See* **follower**

belittle

▷ VERB

to make someone or something seem less important: *He belittles my opinions.*

deride *He is derided as weak and incompetent.*

detract from *The flower's odd smell detracts from its beauty.*

downgrade *Don't downgrade the importance of your contribution.*

minimize *Don't minimize the amount of work required.*

scorn *Don't scorn the work of others.*

undervalue *We must never undervalue freedom.*

ANTONYM **praise**

See also **put down**

belligerent *See* **hostile**

bellow *See* **shout**

belly *See* **stomach**

belong *See* **fit**

belongings *See* **possessions, property, stuff, things**

beloved

▷ ADJECTIVE

dearly loved: *His beloved pet died last year.*

adored *an adored father*

cherished *his most cherished possession*

darling *our darling child*

dearest *my dearest friend*

precious *I love my precious cat.*

treasured *treasured memories*

ANTONYM **despised**

See also **dear**

below

▷ PREPOSITION or ADVERB

lower down: *about 6 cm below sea level*

beneath *I hid the letter beneath the mattress.*

down *I fell down to the bottom.*

lower *The price will fall lower than this.*

under *tunnels under the ground*

underneath *He crawled underneath the table.*

ANTONYM **above**

See also **under**

bench *See* **court**

bend

▷ VERB

1 to make or become curved: *Bend the bar into a horseshoe.*

buckle *The pavement buckled in the heat.*

curve *The wall curves to the left.*

turn *The road turns right at the end.*

twist *glass twisted into elaborate patterns*

warp *The wood had started to warp.*

2 to move forward and downward: *I bent over and picked up the loonie.*

arch *Don't arch your back!*

bow *He turned and bowed to her.*

crouch *We were crouching in the bushes.*

incline *He inclined his head to one side.*

lean *She leaned out the window.*

stoop *Stooping down, he picked up a stone.*

▷ NOUN

3 a curve in something: *a bend in the road*

arc *the full arc of a rainbow*

corner *He drove around the corner.*

curve *the curve of the stream*

loop *The river curves in a loop.*

turn *a turn in the path*

See also **curve, fold, twist**

bend down *See* **crouch**

beneath *See* **below, under**

beneficial

▷ ADJECTIVE

giving some benefit: *Calcium is beneficial to the bones.*

advantageous *an advantageous arrangement*

good for you *Regular exercise is good for you.*

healthy *trying to switch to a healthy lifestyle*

helpful *This treatment is particularly helpful to hay fever sufferers.*

useful *a useful kitchen gadget*

wholesome *food made with good, wholesome ingredients*

See also **favourable, helpful, useful, valuable**

benefit

▷ NOUN

1 an advantage: *the benefits of relaxation*

advantage *The advantages of the new system far outweigh its disadvantages.*

asset *A second language is an asset in this job.*

boon *The new software is a great boon for users.*

gain *He used the knowledge for his personal gain.*

good *Study for your own good!*

help *It's no help to know I was right.*

profit *the profits of working hard*

use *His training was of no use to him.*

ANTONYM **disadvantage**

▷ VERB

2 to help in something: *The experience will benefit you.*

aid *measures to aid new sports programs*

assist *The extra money will assist you.*

enhance *His injury does not enhance our chances.*

further *His support will further our cause.*

help *The new laws won't help the environment.*

profit *It won't profit us to complain.*

ANTONYM **harm**

See also **advantage, beauty, blessing, gain, value**

benevolence See **generosity, goodwill, kindness**

benevolent

▷ ADJECTIVE

kind and helpful: *a benevolent ruler*

benign *a benign and lovable man*

charitable *charitable organizations*

compassionate *my compassionate friends*

humane *humane treatment of animals*

kind *You have been kind and helpful to us.*

See also **humane, kind**

benign See **benevolent, gentle, kind**

bent See **crooked, determined**

bent on See **determined**

bequeath See **hand down, will**

bequest See **gift, inheritance, legacy**

berserk

▷ ADVERB

enraged, in a wild and violent way: *The protester went berserk and started attacking the crowd.*

amok *The wild animal ran amok and injured several people.*

on the rampage *a bull on the rampage through the streets*

wild *They just went wild after he left.*

beseech See **beg, implore, plead, urge**

beside

▷ PREPOSITION

next to: *In the photo, I'm standing beside my father and my uncle.*

adjacent to *a hotel adjacent to the beach*

alongside *a house alongside the river*

close to *The restaurant is close to their home.*

near *He stood very near the front door.*

next to *She sat down next to him.*

besides See **also, too**

best

▷ ADJECTIVE

1 of the highest standard: *the best TV series I have seen in a long time*

ANTONYM **worst**

▷ NOUN

2 the preferred thing: *Of all my presents, this is the best.*

ANTONYM **worst**

See WORD STUDY **best** on next page

See also **foremost, prime, senior, top**

best part See **majority**

best-loved See **favourite**

bestow See **present**

bet See **gamble**

betray

▷ VERB

1 to do someone harm: *I was betrayed by someone I had thought was a friend.*

be unfaithful *He's been unfaithful to the people who trusted him.*

break your promise *I broke my promise to her.*

double-cross INFORMAL *I was angry that he double-crossed me.*

inform on *people who inform on their colleagues*

2 to show feelings: *My voice betrayed little emotion.*

expose *She never exposed her hostile feelings.*

manifest *Fear can manifest itself in many ways.*

reveal *His expression revealed nothing.*

show *His eyes showed his unhappiness.*

See also **inform on**

better

▷ ADJECTIVE

1 of more worth than another: *Today was much better than yesterday.*

ANTONYM **inferior**

2 well after being ill: *I hope you feel better soon.*

ANTONYM **worse**

See WORD STUDY **better** on next page

See also **improve, reform, senior, superior, top**

better part See **majority**

WORD STUDY: BEST

There are a number of alternatives for the word **best** that will make your writing more interesting.

• **of the highest standard**
This shop sells the **choicest** fruit from local farms.
Our local hospital provides the **finest** available health care.
The critics agreed that it was a **first-rate** musical performance.
She was the **foremost** writer of her generation.
It's probably the **greatest** movie ever made.
What's the **highest** mark you ever got for a report?
He has established himself as one of Canada's **leading** actors.
Our hockey team was **outstanding** in the tournament.
She is considered to be today's **pre-eminent** pop singer.
We plan to visit Vancouver's **principal** tourist attractions.
The company claimed to offer the **superlative** deal on cellphones.

This novel is the **supreme** achievement of his career.
She's one of Canada's **top** swimmers.
His time for the sprint is **unequalled**.

• **most desirable**
Keeping silent was the **correct** thing to do, under the circumstances.
What do you think is the **most desirable** location for the picnic?
This sounds like the **most fitting** solution to the problem.
I believe I am the **right** person for this job.

• **the preferred thing**
The exhibition was set up as a showcase for the **cream** of the local artists.
The **elite** of the sports world will be at the banquet.
Is that the **finest** you have to offer?
Congratulations! You have chosen the **pick** of the litter.
I will do my **utmost** to help you.

WORD STUDY: BETTER

Better can be avoided in favour of a more expressive alternative.

• **of higher quality or worth**
There is no **finer** place to live.
We're moving to a much **grander** neighbourhood.
His hopes are now set on a **greater** prize.
My dad thinks that owning a car is **preferable** to leasing one.
Your last essay was **superior** to this one.
This software is of **surpassing** quality.
Save your energy for a **worthier** cause.

• **of greater skill**
She is generally acknowledged to be the **greater** writer.
This slope is suitable for **more advanced** skiers.
He is **more expert** at some things than others.

You are a **more skilful** player than the others on the team.
There are lots of actors **more talented** than she is.

• **in improved health**
I used to have insomnia, but now I'm **cured**.
I'm a lot **fitter** now that I've started biking to school.
He had a back injury, but now he's fully **recovered**.
She's much **healthier** since she started exercising.
My health is much **improved**, thank you.
He's slowly getting **stronger** after the accident.
I hope you'll be feeling **well** again soon.

between *See* **among**

beware
▷ *VERB*
to be cautious: *Beware of the dog.*

be careful *Be careful what you say to him.*
be cautious *Doctors are cautious about using the treatment.*
be wary *I'm wary of driving at night.*

guard against *We have to guard against car thieves.*
look out *Look out! There's a train coming!*
watch out *Watch out for ice.*

bewilder *See* **confuse, puzzle**

bewildered *See* **confused, dazed**

bewildering *See* **confusing**

bewitch *See* **charm, entrance, fascinate**

bewitching *See* **magical**

beyond *See* **above, past**

bias
▷ *NOUN*
prejudice for or against a person or group: *Some employers show bias against younger workers.*
bigotry *religious bigotry*
favouritism *His promotion was due to favouritism.*
prejudice *racial prejudice*
See also **colour, favouritism, injustice, prejudice**

biased
▷ *ADJECTIVE*
showing prejudice: *biased attitudes*
one-sided *a one-sided argument*
partial *I'm partial to cake rather than pie.*
prejudiced *Don't be prejudiced by what you read.*
slanted *a slanted newspaper article*
weighted *The decision is weighted in favour of the developers.*
ANTONYM **neutral**
See also **narrow-minded**

bicker *See* **argue, quarrel, squabble**

bid *See* **ask, attempt, command, effort, tender**

bidding *See* **command**

big
▷ *ADJECTIVE*
1 of a large size: *a big house*
ANTONYM **small**
2 of great importance: *a big name in the world of hockey*
ANTONYM **unimportant**
See WORD STUDY **big** *on next page*
See also **large**

big name *See* **celebrity, personality**

bigmouth *See* **braggart**

bigoted *See* **narrow-minded**

bigotry *See* **bias, prejudice**

bill
▷ *NOUN*
a statement of how much is owed: *a huge restaurant bill*
account *Please charge it to my account.*
charge *What's the admission charge?*
invoice *They sent an invoice for the damage.*
statement *a credit-card statement*
See also **notice**

billow *See* **cloud**

bind *See* **bond, fix, secure, tie**

birth *See* **beginning, start**

bisect *See* **divide**

bit
▷ *NOUN*
a small amount: *a bit of bread*
crumb *a crumb of comfort*
fragment *glittering fragments of broken glass*
grain *His story contains a grain of truth.*
part *part of the problem*
piece *The vase was smashed to pieces.*
scrap *a scrap of evidence*
speck *a speck of dust*
See also **part, piece, portion**

bitchy *See* **spiteful**

bite
▷ *VERB*
to cut into something with your teeth: *His cat bit me when I tried to pat it.*
chew *You make so much noise when you chew gum!*
gnaw *The bones had been gnawed by wild animals.*
nibble *She nibbled at the cookie.*
nip *The puppy nipped at my heels.*
See also **savage, taste**

INFORMALLY SPEAKING

bite someone's head off: be sharply angry with someone
bite your tongue: keep from saying something
put the bite on: demand money from
take a bite out of: use up a large part of

biting *See* **cold**

bitter
▷ *ADJECTIVE*
1 angry and resentful: *a bitter argument*
acrimonious *an acrimonious discussion*
begrudging *He gave me begrudging thanks.*
embittered *an embittered employee who had never received a promotion*
rancorous *the issue that has led to rancorous disputes*

WORD STUDY: BIG

There are an enormous number of substitutes for the word **big** that will make your writing livelier.

• in size

The village square was dominated by a **colossal** statue.

An **enormous** building sat where the parking lot used be.

Tyrannosaurus rex was a **gigantic** dinosaur.

Her arrival caused a **great** commotion.

It was my job to bake a **huge** birthday cake.

Sorting out all my notes will be an **immense** task.

There is to be a **massive** fireworks display on Canada Day.

She worked hard to make a **significant** improvement in her grades this year.

It will take more than 60 000 people to fill the **vast** stadium.

• in importance

Sir John A. Macdonald was an **eminent** politician.

My teachers had an **important** influence on me.

Is she an **influential** figure in the government?

Margaret Atwood is one of Canada's **leading** novelists.

I have a **major** role in the school play.

The villain of the story is a **powerful** executive in a multinational company.

• of an issue or problem

The country was passing through a **grave** crisis.

Much discussion was needed before making the **momentous** decision to go to war.

He hadn't raced in competition for a long time, and so was at a **serious** disadvantage.

There is an **urgent** need for more investment in education.

Whenever I have a **weighty** problem to solve, I talk it over with a friend.

---

resentful *He is resentful of others' success.*
sour *a sour expression*
2 tasting or smelling unpleasant or sharp: *the pill has a bitter taste*
acid *the acid smell of sweat*
acrid *clouds of acrid smoke*
astringent *astringent chemicals*
sharp *a grapefruit's clean, sharp taste*
sour *sour lemons*
tart *a crisp, tart apple*
ANTONYM **sweet**
See also **cold, resentful, sour**

bitterness *See* **resentment**

bizarre
▷ *ADJECTIVE*
very strange or eccentric: *He has some bizarre ideas about gardening.*
curious *a curious mixture of ancient and modern*
eccentric *Your eccentric behaviour is beginning to attract attention.*
extraordinary *What an extraordinary character he is!*
odd *a series of very odd coincidences*
outlandish *an outlandish style of dressing*
peculiar *a peculiar combination of flavours*
queer *A very queer thing happened to me tonight.*
strange *I've noticed you've been behaving in*

a very strange way lately.
weird *his weird theories about UFOs*
ANTONYM **ordinary**
See also **curious, eccentric, extraordinary, odd, peculiar, strange, weird**

SHADES OF ... *BLACK*

ebony	pitch black
inky	raven
jet	sable
jet black	

blackout *See* **faint**

blacklist *See* **boycott**

blame
▷ *VERB*
1 to believe someone caused something: *Don't blame me for this trouble.*
accuse *She accused him of causing the fire.*
charge *He will be charged for the crime.*
hold responsible *I hold you responsible for this mess.*
▷ *NOUN*
2 the responsibility for something bad: *I'm not going to take the blame for that!*
accountability *He escaped accountability for his crimes.*

fault *The fault was all yours.*
liability *He admitted liability for the crash.*
responsibility *responsibility for the crime*
See also **accuse, censure, condemn, fault, responsibility**

blameless See **innocent**

bland See **tasteless**

blank

▷ *ADJECTIVE*
1 with nothing on it: *a blank sheet of paper*
bare *bare walls*
clean *a clean sheet of paper*
clear *a clear desk*
empty *an empty page*
plain *a plain envelope*
unmarked *an unmarked board*
2 showing no feeling: *a blank expression on his face*
deadpan *the card player's deadpan expression*
dull *a dull stare*
empty *She saw the empty look in his eyes.*
impassive *an impassive smile*
vacant *a vacant stare*
See also **empty, ignore, space**

blanket See **layer**

blaring See **loud**

blast See **attack, bang, explosion**

blatant See **clear, conspicuous, naked, obvious**

blaze See **burn, fire, glare**

bleached See **light**

bleak See **cold**

blemish See **fault, flaw, spot**

blend

▷ *VERB*
1 to mix things so as to form a single item or substance: *Blend the butter with the sugar.*
combine *Combine the ingredients in a large bowl.*
merge *how to merge the graphics with the text*
mingle *the mingled smells of flowers and coffee*
mix *Mix the two liquids together with a fork.*
ANTONYM **separate**
2 to combine in a pleasing way: *The colours blend with the rest of the decor.*
complement *The flavours complement each other perfectly.*
coordinate *Choose shoes that coordinate with your outfit.*

go well *Milk goes well with chocolate cake.*
harmonize *shades of colours that harmonize rather than clash*
match *Those shoes don't match that dress.*
suit *glasses that suit the shape of your face*
▷ *NOUN*
3 a mixture or combination of things: *a blend of juice and sparkling water*
alloy *an alloy of copper and tin*
amalgamation *the amalgamation of several towns into a single municipality*
combination *a fantastic combination of colours*
compound *a compound of water, sugar, and enzymes*
fusion *a fusion of cooking styles*
mix *a delicious mix of exotic spices*
mixture *a sticky mixture of flour and water*
See also **combination, combine, cross, mix, mixture, union**

bless

▷ *VERB*
to make holy or ask for religious protection: *The priest blessed the congregation.*
consecrate *ground that has been consecrated*
dedicate *to dedicate a new temple*
hallow *A building could be hallowed by prayer.*
ANTONYM **curse**

blessed See **holy, lucky**

blessing

▷ *NOUN*
1 something good: *Good health is a blessing.*
benefit *the benefits of technology*
boon *The Meals on Wheels service is a boon to the elderly.*
gift *A cheerful nature is a gift.*
godsend *The extra twenty dollars was a godsend.*
help *My new laptop is a real help in my work.*
ANTONYM **disadvantage**
2 approval or permission to do something: *They got married with their parents' blessing.*
approval *Does this plan have your approval?*
backing *We can't do anything without his backing.*
consent *He gave his consent to the article.*
leave *a two-week leave of absence from work*
permission *You have my permission to go.*
support *The manager has given full support to her project.*
ANTONYM **disapproval**
See also **approval, sanction**

blight See **infect, pest**

bliss *See* **ecstasy, heaven, joy**

blister *See* **boil**

blob

▷ *NOUN*

a small amount of a thick or sticky substance: *He had a blob of pudding on his tie.*

bead *beads of sweat on my forehead*
dab *You've got a dab of glue on your nose.*
drop *a few thick drops of maple syrup*
droplet *droplets of the medication*

block

▷ *NOUN*

1 a large piece: *a block of wood*
bar *a bar of soap*
brick *concrete bricks*
chunk *chunks of stewing beef*
ingot *a gold ingot*
lump *lumps of metal*
piece *a big piece of cake*

▷ *VERB*

2 to close by putting something across: *Mud blocked the river.*
choke *The town was choked with cars.*
clog *Hair clogged the drain.*
obstruct *The accident obstructed the road.*
plug *Have you plugged the leaks?*
ANTONYM **unblock**

▷ *VERB*

3 to prevent something happening: *The committee blocked his plans.*
bar *He was barred from entering the arena.*
check *a policy to check immigration*
halt *attempts to halt the spread of disease*
obstruct *Lack of funding obstructed our progress.*
stop *measures to stop the rising crime rate*
thwart *My plans for the ski trip were thwarted by warm weather.*
See also **blockage, close, frustrate, hinder, impede, obstruct, plug**

blockage

▷ *NOUN*

a thing that clogs something: *a blockage in the pipe*
block *I have a mental block and can't think of your name.*
obstruction *an obstruction on the track*

blond *See* **fair, light**

blonde *See* **fair, light**

bloodshed *See* **violence**

bloodthirsty *See* **violent**

bloom *See* **flourish**

blooming *See* **well**

B

blossom *See* **progress**

blot *See* **spot, stain**

blotch *See* **spot**

blot out

▷ *VERB*

to cover and prevent from being seen: *The heavy smoke blotted out the sky.*
eclipse *The moon eclipsed the sun.*
obliterate *Our view was obliterated by mist.*
obscure *The view was obscured by fog.*
shadow *The brim of the cap shadowed his face.*

blow

▷ *VERB*

1 to move or cause to move in the wind: *The wind blew his papers away.*
buffet *The ship was buffeted by gales.*
drive *The strong wind drove us forward.*
flutter *The flags are fluttering.*
sweep *A sudden blast swept away my scarf.*
waft *His hair wafted in the breeze.*
whirl *The autumn leaves whirled about.*

▷ *NOUN*

2 a hit from something: *a blow to the head*
bang *He suffered some bangs and bumps.*
knock *a nasty knock on the elbow*
smack *She gave the puppy a gentle smack on the nose.*
thump *a thump on the chest*
whack *I got a whack on the head from the falling branch.*

▷ *NOUN*

3 something disappointing or upsetting: *Our third loss in overtime was a major financial blow.*
bombshell *His unexpected departure was a bombshell for the team.*
disappointment *My results on the chemistry test were a real disappointment.*
misfortune *a series of misfortunes*
setback *Each step forward seemed to be followed by a setback.*
shock *The news came as a shock.*
upset *The defeat caused an upset.*
See also **bang, disappointment, hit, shock, sound**

INFORMALLY SPEAKING

blow away: astonish
blow over: pass by or be forgotten
blow your mind: amaze you

---

blow up *See* **bomb, explode**

bludgeon See **club**

SHADES OF ... BLUE	
aqua	lapis lazuli
aquamarine	midnight blue
azure	navy
cerulean	peacock blue
cobalt	periwinkle
cyan	royal blue
robin's-egg blue	sapphire
electric blue	sky blue
gentian	teal
indigo	turquoise

blueprint See **plan**

bluff See **con**

blunder See **err, error, mistake, slip**

blunt
▷ ADJECTIVE
1 having rounded edges: *blunt scissors*
dull *a dull knife*
rounded *rounded edges*
unsharpened *an unsharpened pencil*
ANTONYM **sharp**
2 saying what you think: *a blunt speaker*
brusque *His response was brusque.*
forthright *a forthright reply*
frank *I'll be frank with you.*
outspoken *an outspoken critic*
straightforward *She has a straightforward manner.*
ANTONYM **tactful**
See also **candid, direct, frank, straight**

blush
▷ VERB
to go red in the face: *I felt myself blushing.*
flush *I saw her face flush.*
go red *His face went red as a beet.*
turn red *He turned red with embarrassment.*

board See **council, management, sign**

boast
▷ VERB
to talk proudly: *He boasted about his high marks.*
brag *I don't mind bragging about my talents.*
crow *Stop crowing about your success.*
See also **brag**

boaster See **braggart**

boastful
▷ ADJECTIVE
tending to brag about things: *a boastful skateboarder*

cocky *The young tennis star is cocky and brash.*
conceited *You really have nothing to be conceited about.*
crowing *crowing remarks*
egotistical *You're so egotistical — only thinking about yourself.*
swaggering *He has a swaggering manner.*
ANTONYM **modest**

TYPES OF ... BOAT	
barge	kayak ✖
canoe	ketch
coracle	longliner ✖
dinghy	motorboat
dugout ✖	punt
ferry	rowboat
gondola	sailboat
houseboat	speedboat
iceboat ✖	umiak ✖
junk	yacht

bob See **bounce, float**

body
▷ NOUN
1 all your physical parts: *My whole body hurts!*
build *He is of medium build.*
figure *The model has a nice figure.*
form *clothes that flatter your form*
frame *their bony frames*
physique *a powerful physique*
shape *his trim shape*
2 a dead body: *a body buried in the forest*
carcass *a sheep's carcass*
corpse *The investigators dug up and examined the corpse.*
dead body *He'd never seen a dead body.*
remains *human remains*
3 an organized group of people: *local voluntary bodies*
association *the Canadian Soccer Association*
band *a band of rebels*
company *the Canadian Opera Company*
confederation *a confederation of states*
corporation *the Canadian Broadcasting Corporation*
organization *student organizations*
society *I joined the local photographers' society.*
See also **association, build, figure, organization**

boggle See **wonder**

bogus See **false, phony**

boil
▷ VERB
1 to bubble: *The water is boiling.*

bubble *Soup bubbled in the pot.*
fizz *The liquid fizzed and bubbled.*
foam *When the butter foams, add the onions.*
froth *The milk frothed over the top of the pan.*
▷ NOUN
2 a swelling on the skin: *a boil on my neck*
blister *a blister on my index finger*
swelling *a swelling under the eye*
tumour *The surgeon removed the tumour.*
See also **cook**

INFORMALLY SPEAKING

boil down: reduce to essentials
boil over: let excitement or anger show

---

boiling See **hot**

boisterous See **rowdy, wild**

bold
▷ ADJECTIVE
1 confident and not shy: *a bold question*
brash *a brash young officer*
brazen *a brazen young motorcyclist*
cheeky *a cheeky grin*
confident *I felt confident confronting him.*
forward *It was forward of you to ask such a personal question.*
impudent *an impudent child*
ANTONYM **shy**
2 unafraid of risk or danger: *a bold attempt*
adventurous *an adventurous spirit*
brave *a brave police officer*
courageous *courageous firefighters*
daring *daring feats*
fearless *a fearless warrior*
intrepid *an intrepid explorer*
valiant *a valiant knight*
ANTONYM **cowardly**
3 clear and noticeable: *bold colours*
bright *bright light*
flashy *flashy clothes*
loud *a loud tie*
striking *a striking design on the scarf*
strong *dressed in strong reds and yellows*
vivid *vivid green and purple*
ANTONYM **dull**
See also **brave, daring**

boldness See **bravery, daring, impudence**

bolster See **reassure, strengthen, support**

bolt
▷ VERB
to escape or run away: *I bolted toward the exit.*
dash *He dashed out of the room in a panic.*
escape *They escaped from the boring concert.*

flee *They fled before the police arrived.*
fly *The actor flew down the stairs with the photographers in hot pursuit.*
run away *I called to him, but he just ran away.*
run off *He ran off when he spotted me.*
rush *They all rushed away as we approached.*
See also **catch, dash, flee, run**

bomb
▷ NOUN
1 an explosive device: *The bomb exploded near the city.*
device *Experts defused the device.*
explosive *The explosive was set to go off after one hour.*
missile *long-range missiles*
rocket *a rocket launcher*
shell *Shells began to fall.*
torpedo *The torpedo struck the ship.*
▷ VERB
2 to attack with bombs: *London, England, was heavily bombed during World War II.*
attack *We are being attacked!*
blow up *They tried to blow up the building.*
bombard *Warships began to bombard the coast.*
destroy *Helicopters destroyed the village.*
shell *They shelled the troops heavily.*
torpedo *The ship was torpedoed in the Atlantic Ocean.*

bombard See **bomb**

bombardment See **hail**

bombshell See **blow, shock, surprise**

bona fide See **authentic, genuine, real, true**

bond
▷ NOUN
1 a close relationship: *a special bond between us*
affinity *an affinity between the two countries*
attachment *Parents and children form close attachments.*
connection *a family connection*
link *the links of friendship*
relationship *the relationship between husband and wife*
tie *the ties of blood*
union *the union of father and son*
2 an obligation to do something: *the bonds of marriage*
agreement *He has broken our agreement.*
contract *He signed a two-year contract.*
obligation *your obligation to your family*
pledge *a pledge of support*
promise *You must keep your promises.*
word *I give you my word.*

▷ VERB
3 to attach separate things: *strips of wood bonded together*
bind *pages bound in a book*
fasten *I fastened the picture to the wall.*
fuse *The pieces to be joined are fused together.*
glue *Glue the pieces together.*
paste *We pasted the photos in our scrapbook.*
tape *He taped the poster to the wall.*
See also **association, attachment, connection, link, relation, relationship, stick, tie**

bonds *See* **stock**

bonus *See* **extra, reward**

bony *See* **skinny**

book
▷ NOUN
I a number of pages bound between covers: *I'm reading a great book.*
publication *publications about summer jobs*
textbook *He wrote a textbook on Canadian history.*
title *We publish a range of titles.*
tome FORMAL *a heavy tome*
volume *small volumes of poetry*
work *my favourite work by Alice Munro*

TYPES OF ... BOOK

anthology	guidebook
atlas	handbook
autobiography	manual
biography	nonfiction
dictionary	novel
directory	phrasebook
encyclopedia	short stories
fiction	textbook
gazetteer	thesaurus
glossary	

Parts of a book

acknowledgments	heading
appendix	illustration
bibliography	index
blurb	introduction
caption	layout
chapter	line
cover	page
dust jacket	preface
footnote	table of contents
foreword	title
glossary	

▷ VERB
2 to arrange to have or use: *The tickets for the cruise are booked.*
charter *A plane was chartered for them.*
engage *We engaged the services of a plumber.*
organize *I have organized the trip to my grandparents' home.*
reserve *Hotel rooms have been reserved.*
schedule *A meeting is scheduled for Monday.*

INFORMALLY SPEAKING
by the book: according to the rules
in my book: in my opinion
throw the book at: punish as severely as the law allows

booklet *See* **brochure**

boom *See* **bang, flourish**

boon *See* **benefit, blessing**

boost *See* **augment, encourage**

booty *See* **loot**

booze *See* **alcohol, drink**

border
▷ NOUN
I a dividing line between things or places: *the border between two countries*
borderline *the borderline between health and sickness*
boundary *national boundaries*
frontier *The next frontier is outer space.*
line *the line between fact and fiction*
2 an edge of something: *plain tiles with a bright border*
bounds *the bounds of good taste*
edge *the edge of town*
limits *the city limits*
margin *the western margins of the island*
rim *the rim of the lake*
▷ VERB
3 to form an edge: *Tall trees bordered the fields.*
edge *the woods that edge the lake*
fringe *Street lights fringe the bay.*
rim *the restaurants rimming the harbour*
trim *coats trimmed with leather collars*
See also **coast, edge**

borderline *See* **border**

bore *See* **annoyance, pest, pierce**

bored
▷ ADJECTIVE
impatient and not interested in something: *I am bored with this movie.*
fed up *He is fed up with his job.*
tired *I am tired of this music.*

uninterested *He seems uninterested in politics.*
wearied *He spoke in a wearied voice.*
ANTONYM **interested**
See also **sick of, uninterested**

boredom

▷ NOUN
a lack of interest: *the boredom of long trips*
apathy *political apathy*
dullness *a period of dullness*
flatness *the flatness of the speaker's voice*
monotony *the monotony of winter*
tedium *the tedium of unemployment*
weariness *a sense of weariness*
ANTONYM **interest**

boring

▷ ADJECTIVE
dull and uninteresting: *a boring job*
dull *dull tasks*
flat *Her flat performance put me to sleep.*
humdrum *humdrum lives*
monotonous *the monotonous prison routine*
tedious *The factory work is tedious.*
tiresome *a tiresome comedian*
ANTONYM **interesting**
See also **dreary, dull, flat**

CONFUSABLES

Borrow means **get**.
Lend means **give**.

boss

▷ NOUN
a person in charge of something: *His boss insisted he get to work on time.*
chief *the police chief*
director *the directors of the bank*
employer *He was sent to Montréal by his employer.*
head *Heads of government met in Edmonton.*
leader *The party's leader has resigned.*
manager *the company's marketing manager*
See also **chief, employer, head, leader, manager, superior**

bosses *See* **management**

bossy

▷ ADJECTIVE
telling people what to do: *a rather bossy little child*
arrogant *arrogant behaviour*
authoritarian *He takes an authoritarian approach to politics.*
dictatorial *a dictatorial management style*
domineering *My grandmother was a*

domineering and ruthless individual.
imperious *He has an imperious manner.*
overbearing *an overbearing skating coach*
See also **pushy**

botch

▷ VERB
to do something badly: *a botched operation*
bungle *inefficient people who bungled the job*
mar *The billboard marred the lovely scenery.*
mess up *He nearly messed up his life.*

botch up *See* **mess**

bother

▷ VERB
1 to cause worry or concern: *His lack of money bothers him.*
annoy *the irritating things that annoy me*
concern *The future concerns me.*
disturb *It disturbs me to see you unhappy.*
get on someone's nerves INFORMAL *His whistling gets on my nerves.*
trouble *Are you troubled by nightmares?*
worry *I'm worried that I won't get a summer job.*
▷ NOUN
2 trouble and difficulty: *I hate the bother of shopping.*
annoyance *Snoring can be an annoyance.*
difficulty *The detours are causing difficulties for commuters.*
inconvenience *a minor inconvenience*
irritation *Noise is an irritation.*
trouble *You've caused me a lot of trouble.*
worry *It was a time of worry for us.*
See also **agitate, annoy, concern, distress, disturb, fuss, hassle, irritate, nuisance, pester, trouble, upset, worry**

bothered *See* **anxious, worried**

bottom

▷ NOUN
1 the lowest part of something: *the bottom of the stairs*
base *the base of the spine*
bed *The bed of the river was soft and muddy.*
depths *the depths of the ocean*
floor *the ocean floor*
foot *the foot of the bed*
ANTONYM **top**
See also **buttocks**
▷ ADJECTIVE
2 in the lowest place or position: *the bottom drawer*
basement *a basement apartment*
ground *ground level*
lowest *the lowest part of the brain*

ANTONYM **highest**
See also **base**

bottomless *See* **deep**

bounce

▷ *VERB*

to spring back or move up and down: *I bounced a ball against the wall.*
bob *The raft bobbed along.*
bound *He bounded up the stairway.*
bump *My bicycle bumped along the rough ground.*
jump *They jumped up and down to keep warm.*
ricochet *The little stones ricocheted off the waves.*
See also **glance, leap**

bound *See* **bounce, jump, leap**

boundary *See* **border, edge, extreme**

boundless *See* **infinite**

bounds *See* **border, limit, range**

bountiful *See* **plentiful**

bounty *See* **abundance, reward, wealth**

bouquet *See* **bunch, fragrance**

bout *See* **event, fight**

boutique *See* **store**

bovine *See* **cow**

bow *See* **resign oneself, bend, submit**

box

▷ *NOUN*

a container with a firm base and sides: *All her possessions were packed in boxes.*
carton *cartons full of books*
case *It is still in its original case.*
chest *She kept her treasures in a carved wooden chest.*
container *substances kept in heavy metal containers*
trunk *a trunk full of toys*
See also **case**

boy

▷ *NOUN*

a male child: *I knew him several years ago, when he was a boy.*
fellow *a nice young fellow*
lad *I remember being a lad of his age.*
schoolboy *a group of schoolboys*

boycott

▷ *VERB*

to refuse to have anything to do with: *Some voters are boycotting the election.*

blacklist *He has been blacklisted by the committee.*
embargo *Imports of fruit and meat were embargoed.*
exclude *I exclude animal products from my diet.*
reject *She rejected my ideas.*
spurn *You spurned his last offer.*
See also **sanctions**

brace *See* **refresh, steady, strengthen, support**

brag

▷ *VERB*

to boast about something: *They never stop bragging about their achievements.*
boast *He kept boasting about his rich friends.*
crow *Stop crowing about your victory.*
See also **boast**

braggart

▷ *NOUN*

a person who boasts: *He's a braggart and a liar.*
bigmouth SLANG *He's nothing but a bigmouth.*
boaster *an idle boaster looking for an audience*
bragger *He was quite a bragger.*
show-off *The peacock is quite a show-off.*

bragger *See* **braggart**

bragging *See* **boastful**

brain *See* **genius, head, mind**

brains *See* **genius, sense**

brainteaser *See* **puzzle**

brainy *See* **bright, brilliant, intelligent**

brake *See* **curb**

brand *See* **kind, make, sort, type**

brandish *See* **flourish, shake, wave**

brash *See* **bold, cocky**

brave

▷ *ADJECTIVE*

1 willing to do dangerous things: *a brave attempt to stop the attack*
bold *a bold explorer*
courageous *a courageous decision*
daring *a daring escape*
fearless *his fearless campaigning for justice*
heroic *The heroic police sergeant risked her life.*
intrepid *an intrepid traveller*
plucky *The plucky child amazed the doctors.*
valiant *a valiant attempt to keep going*
ANTONYM **cowardly**

▷ VERB
2 to face something without fear: *Fans braved the rain to hear him sing.*
face *I can't face another three years of this.*
stand up to *I stand up to bullies.*
See also **bold, daring**

bravery
▷ NOUN
the quality of being courageous: *He deserves praise for his bravery.*
boldness *an outward display of boldness*
courage *They do not have the courage to apologize.*
fortitude *The patient suffered with tremendous fortitude.*
heroism *acts of heroism*
pluck *He has pluck to stand up to the bullies.*
valour *He won a medal for valour.*
ANTONYM **cowardice**
See also **courage, daring**

brawl *See* fight

brawn *See* power, strength

brazen *See* bold, shameless

breach
▷ NOUN
I a breaking of an agreement or law: *a breach of confidence*
infringement *an infringement of the rules*
offence *criminal offences*
violation *a violation of the peace agreement*
2 a gap in something: *the breach in the wall*
crack *a large crack in the ice*
gap *a narrow gap between the two houses*
hole *We cut holes in the fabric.*
opening *an narrow opening in the tent*
rift *The earthquake caused a deep rift in the ground.*
split *There's a split in this piece of wood.*
See also **break, division, split**

TYPES OF ... BREAD	
bannock ✹	pita
brioche	nan
chapati	roti
croissant	tortilla
fry bread ✹	

break
▷ VERB
I to separate into pieces: *I broke a plate.*
See WORD STUDY **break** *on next page*
2 to fail to keep a rule or promise: *He broke his promise to attend.*
breach *Discipline was breached.*
contravene *Your behaviour contravenes our code of conduct.*
infringe *The umpire agreed that the tennis*

player had infringed no rules.
violate *They violated the peace agreement.*
▷ NOUN
3 a short period of rest or change: *I took a five-minute break from work.*
interlude *a happy interlude in my life*
intermission *The second act began after a brief intermission.*
interval *a long interval when nobody spoke*
pause *After a pause, the actor spoke.*
recess *The court adjourned for a recess.*
respite *Theere is no respite from bad news.*
rest *I'll start again after a rest.*
See also **burst, crack, dash, disobey, gap, holiday, interrupt, interval, pause, rest, ruin**

INFORMALLY SPEAKING
break down: stop functioning
break even: gain nothing and lose nothing
break off: stop suddenly

break free *See* escape

break into *See* raid

break out *See* escape

break up *See* disintegrate, separate

break your promise *See* betray

breakable *See* fragile

breakdown *See* failure

breaker *See* wave

breakfast *See* eat

break-in *See* raid

breakneck *See* furious

breakthrough *See* advance, progress

breakup *See* split

breathing *See* alive

breathtaking *See* superb

breed
▷ NOUN
I a type of animal: *What breed of dog shall we get?*
kind *What kind of horse is that?*
species *Pandas are an endangered species.*
stock *cattle of poor stock*
strain *a special strain of rat*
type *different types of pets*
variety *many varieties of birds*
▷ VERB
2 to produce and look after: *They breed dogs at the farm.*

B

WORD STUDY: BREAK

The word **break** is often over-used. There are lots of more descriptive words that you can use to give additional information about how something breaks, so try to choose one of them instead.

- If something hard **cracks**, or you **crack** it, it becomes slightly damaged, with lines appearing on its surface.
A gas main had **cracked** under my garden.
To get at the coconut flesh, **crack** the shell with a hammer.

- If something **fractures**, or you **fracture** it, it gets a slight crack in it.
One of the beams in the floor had **fractured** and had to be repaired.
You've **fractured** a rib.

- If something **snaps**, or you **snap** it, it breaks suddenly, with a sharp cracking noise.
A twig **snapped** under his foot.
She gripped the pipe in both hands, trying to **snap** it in half.

- If something **splits**, or you **split** it, it breaks into two or more parts.
In the severe gale, the ship **split** in two.
We **split** the board down the middle.

- If something **splinters**, or you **splinter** it, it breaks into thin, sharp pieces.
The ruler **splintered** into pieces.
The stone hit the glass, **splintering** it.

- If something **fragments**, or is **fragmented**, it breaks or separates into small parts.
The rock began to **fragment** and crumble under the heavy hammer blows.

- If something **crumbles**, or you **crumble** it, it breaks into small pieces.
Under the pressure of the flood, the wall **crumbled** into fragments.
Crumble the cheese into a bowl.

- If something **disintegrates**, it breaks into many pieces and is destroyed.
The car's windscreen **disintegrated** with the impact of the crash.

- If you **smash** something, or it **smashes**, it breaks into many small pieces, often because it has been hit or dropped.
Someone had **smashed** a bottle against the fence.
Two glasses fell off the table and **smashed** into pieces.

- If you **wreck** or **demolish** something, you completely destroy it.
The bridge was **wrecked** by the storm.
The hurricane **demolished** houses across a wide area.

---

cultivate *She cultivates fruit and vegetables.*
develop *A new variety of potato is being developed.*
keep *He keeps guinea pigs.*
nurture *trimming and nurturing plants and saplings*
raise *He raises chickens as a hobby.*
rear *the difficulties of rearing children*
▷ VERB
3 to produce offspring: *Frogs can breed in most ponds.*
multiply *Rats multiply quickly.*
produce *They went on to produce a large family.*
propagate *This plant is difficult to propagate.*
reproduce *the natural desire to reproduce*
See also **kind, type**

bribe *See* **bait, corrupt**

bribery *See* **corruption**

brick *See* **block**

brief
▷ ADJECTIVE
I lasting for a short time: *a brief appearance on television*
fleeting *a fleeting glimpse*
momentary *There was a momentary silence.*
quick *a quick look at the newspaper*
short *a short holiday*
swift *a swift glance at the opponent's face*
ANTONYM **long**
▷ VERB
2 to give necessary information: *The press secretary briefed reporters.*
advise *I must advise you of my decision to retire.*
fill in *Can you fill me in on what I missed when I was sick?*

inform *They will inform him of their progress.*
instruct *He instructed us in first aid.*
prepare *I'll try to prepare you for their visit.*
prime *They primed him for his interview.*
See also **concise, quick, short**

bright
▷ ADJECTIVE
I strong and startling: *a bright light*
brilliant *brilliant green eyes*
dazzling *a dazzling white shirt*
glowing *the glowing windows of the city hall*
luminous *a luminous star*
radiant *eyes as radiant as sapphires*
vivid *strong, vivid colours*
ANTONYM **dull**
2 clever and alert: *my brightest student*
brainy *I don't consider myself brainy.*
brilliant *She has a brilliant mind.*
clever *a clever child*
ingenious *an ingenious idea*
intelligent *Dolphins are an intelligent species.*
smart *He thinks he's as smart as I am.*
ANTONYM **dim**
3 cheerful and lively: *a bright smile*
cheerful *She sounded quite cheerful about the idea.*
happy *a confident, happy child*
jolly *a jolly nature*
light-hearted *They are light-hearted and enjoy life.*
lively *He has a lively personality.*
merry *bursts of merry laughter*
See also **acute, astute, bold, brilliant, cheerful, clever, colourful, gaudy, glossy, intelligent, sharp, shining, smart**

brighten *See* **light**

brightness *See* **light**

brilliance *See* **genius, gloss, light**

brilliant
▷ ADJECTIVE
I very bright: *a brilliant light*
bright *a bright star*
dazzling *a dazzling smile*
gleaming *gleaming headlights*
glowing *glowing colours*
luminous *luminous orange paint*
radiant *a radiant ring around the moon*
sparkling *a necklace of sparkling jewels*
vivid *the vivid hues of tropical flowers*
ANTONYM **dull**

2 very smart: *a brilliant student*
acute *His relaxed exterior hides an acute mind.*
bright *an exceptionally bright child who is fond of reading*
clever *What a clever idea!*
intelligent *Poodles are highly intelligent dogs.*
perceptive *a perceptive analysis of the situation*
sharp *a sharp intellect*
smart *He's the smartest student we've ever had.*
ANTONYM **stupid**
See also **bright, colourful, glossy, keen, shining, witty**

brim *See* **edge**

bring
▷ VERB
I to take somewhere: *Bring a friend to the party.*
carry *She carried her son to the car and buckled him into the car seat.*
convey *Emergency supplies were conveyed by truck.*
lead *She led him into the house.*
take *He took brownies to the party.*
transport *They transported the apples to the market in the city.*
2 to cause to happen: *Bring the water to a boil.*
cause *My mistake caused me some concern.*
create *The new factory will create more jobs.*
inflict *The attack inflicted heavy casualties.*
produce *The drug produces side effects.*
result in *Many accidents result in serious injuries.*
wreak *Violent storms wreaked havoc on the islands.*
See also **take**

bring about
▷ VERB
to cause something to happen: *Her suggestions brought about several big improvements.*
cause *This may cause delays.*
create *The new law will create even more confusion.*
generate *the excitement generated by the latest digital camera*
make happen *If you want change, you have to make it happen yourself.*
produce *His comments produced an enthusiastic response.*

provoke *a move that has provoked a storm of protest*
See also **accomplish, cause, create, result in**

bring back to *See* **remind**

bring down *See* **overthrow**

bring forward *See* **produce**

bring in *See* **earn**

bring out *See* **publish**

bring around *See* **persuade, reason**

bring to a standstill *See* **cripple**

bring to an end *See* **end**

bring to bear *See* **employ**

bring to light *See* **expose, produce, reveal, uncover**

bring up *See* **mention, raise, refer, vomit**

brink *See* **bank**

briny *See* **salty**

brisk *See* **hasty, quick, swift**

bristling *See* **thick**

broach *See* **mention, raise**

broad
▷ ADJECTIVE
I large, especially from side to side: *His shoulders were broad and his waist narrow.*
expansive *expansive lawns at the front of the house*
extensive *Extensive grounds surrounded the castle.*
large *a large dog with a gentle nature*
thick *a finger as thick as a sausage*
vast *rich families who own vast stretches of land*
wide *a wide highway*
ANTONYM **narrow**
2 including or affecting many different things or people: *A broad range of issues was discussed.*
comprehensive *a comprehensive history of the Prairie provinces*
extensive *extensive research into my family history*
general *The project should raise general awareness about poverty.*
sweeping *sweeping economic reforms*
universal *the universal problem of pollution*
wide *a major event that brought together a wide range of groups*
wide-ranging *wide-ranging ideas for fighting pollution*
3 general, rather than detailed: *a broad outline of Canadian politics*
approximate *They did not have even an approximate idea of what the word meant.*
general *the general decline in the student population*
non-specific *I intend to use these terms in a deliberately non-specific way.*
rough *I have a rough idea of what he looks like.*
sweeping *a sweeping statement about young drivers*
vague *They have only a vague idea of the amount of water available.*
See also **extensive, general, spacious, widespread**

broadcast *See* **announcement, program, send**

broad-minded *See* **tolerant**

brochure
▷ NOUN
a pamphlet or small booklet with information about a subject: *a travel brochure*
booklet *a booklet outlining the rules of the game*
circular *A circular was sent out to the neighbours.*
flyer *a supermarket flyer listing the week's specials*
leaflet *Protesters were handing out leaflets.*
pamphlet *a pamphlet on animal rights*

broke *See* **poor**

broken
▷ ADJECTIVE
I in pieces: *a broken window*
burst *a burst pipe*
demolished *a demolished building*
fractured *a fractured rib*
fragmented *fragmented images*
shattered *shattered glass*
smashed *smashed dishes*
2 not kept: *a broken promise*
infringed *a case of infringed human rights*
violated *a series of violated agreements*
See also **imperfect**

broken-down *See* **worn out**

broker *See* **trader**

brood *See* **ponder, worry, young**

brotherhood See **camaraderie**

SHADES OF ... *BROWN*	
auburn	khaki
beige	mahogany
bronze	mocha
buff	oatmeal
burnt sienna	ochre
burnt umber	putty
café au lait	russet
camel	rust
chestnut	sandy
chocolate	sepia
cinnamon	tan
coffee	taupe
dun	tawny
fawn	terracotta
ginger	umber
hazel	

bruised See **tender**

brush See **glance, touch**

brush up See **polish**

brusque See **blunt, impatient**

brutal See **cruel, savage, violent**

brutality See **cruelty, violence**

brute See **oaf, savage**

bubble See **boil, foam**

bubbles See **foam**

buckle See **bend, clasp, give**

budding See **in the making**

buddy
▷ NOUN
INFORMAL a friend: *We've been buddies since we were kids.*
chum INFORMAL *He went on vacation with his two best chums.*
crony OLD-FASHIONED *They are always surrounded by their cronies.*
friend *lifelong friends*
pal INFORMAL *She'd never let a pal down.*
See also **friend**

budgetary See **economic**

budgeting See **finance**

buff See **expert, polish**

buffer See **protection**

buffet See **beat, blow**

bug See **pester**

B

build
▷ VERB
1 to make something: *The house was built last year.*
assemble *We assemble model planes.*
construct *plans to construct a stadium on the site*
erect *The building was erected in 1900.*
fabricate *The tools are fabricated from steel.*
form *a sculpture formed from clay*
make *a wall made of bricks*
ANTONYM **dismantle**
2 to develop gradually: *I want to build a relationship with them.*
develop *Battles can develop into war.*
extend *The company is planning to extend its range of products.*
increase *The population continues to increase.*
intensify *The conflict is bound to intensify.*
strengthen *Cycling strengthens the muscles.*
▷ NOUN
3 the size of a body: *He is of medium build.*
body *a body of average size*
figure *You see all sorts of figures at the beach.*
form *clothes that flatter your form*
frame *their bony frames*
physique *a powerful physique*
shape *his trim shape*
See also **assemble, base, body, construct, figure, make**

build up See **reconstruct**

building
▷ NOUN
a structure with walls: *a glass building*
edifice *historic edifices in the area*
structure *The museum is an impressive structure.*
See also **house, making, structure**

bulge
▷ VERB
1 to swell out: *He bulges out of his black T-shirt.*
expand *The pipes expanded in the heat.*
protrude *His blue eyes protruded from his head.*
stick out *My stomach stuck out under my jacket.*
swell *My ankles swelled.*
▷ NOUN
2 a lump in something: *My wallet made a bulge in my pocket.*
bump *a bump in the road*
hump *a camel's hump*

lump *He wound up with a lump on his head.*
protrusion *a strange protrusion on his forehead*
swelling *a swelling on my foot*
See also **bump, lump**

bulk *See* **majority, size**

bulky *See* **heavy**

bull *See* **nonsense**

bulletin *See* **announcement, message, news, statement, word**

bully
▷ NOUN
I someone who deliberately frightens or hurts others: *the class bully*
oppressor *They were powerless against their oppressors.*
persecutor *Eventually he stood up to his persecutors.*
▷ VERB
2 to frighten or hurt someone deliberately and repeatedly: *I wasn't going to let him bully me.*
intimidate *He set out to intimidate all the smaller children.*
oppress *The oppressed people finally rebelled.*
persecute *They were persecuted because of their beliefs.*
pick on *I don't like to see you pick on younger children.*
tease *Stop teasing the poor dog and leave him alone.*
torment *My older brother and sister used to torment me.*
▷ VERB
3 to make someone do something, sometimes by using force: *bullied into doing his work for him*
force *I cannot force you to do anything. You must decide.*
intimidate *attempts to intimidate people into voting for the governing party*
pressure *Do not feel pressured to make your decision immediately.*

bump
▷ VERB
I to hit something: *He bumped his head on the wall.*
bang *I banged my shin on the edge of the table.*
collide *The car collided with a tree.*
hit *She hit the last barrier and fell.*
jolt *We hit the wall with a jolt.*
knock *He knocked on the door.*
strike *His head struck the windshield.*

▷ NOUN
2 a dull noise: *He heard a bump outside.*
bang *I heard four or five loud bangs.*
knock *They heard a knock at the door.*
thud *She tripped and fell with a thud.*
thump *There was a loud thump against the house.*
▷ NOUN
3 a raised part of something: *a bump in the road*
bulge *My wallet made a bulge in my pocket.*
hump *a camel's hump*
knob *a door with a brass knob*
lump *a nasty lump on the head*
swelling *a swelling on my foot*
See also **bounce, bulge, crash, hit, lump**

bump into *See* **meet**

bumpy *See* **irregular, rough, uneven**

bunch
▷ NOUN
I a group of people: *The players were a great bunch.*
band *Bands of criminals have been roaming some neighbourhoods.*
crowd *Many people from the old crowd have come out for this occasion.*
gaggle *A gaggle of journalists were waiting in the hotel lobby.*
gang *Come on over — we've got most of the old gang here.*
group *a close group of friends*
lot *Future generations are going to think that we were a pretty boring lot.*
multitude *surrounded by a noisy multitude*
2 several cut flowers held together: *There was a huge bunch of flowers in the hotel room.*
bouquet *She laid a bouquet on the grave.*
posy *a posy of wildflowers*
spray *a small spray of violets*
3 a group of things: *He took out a bunch of keys.*
batch *She brought a large batch of newspaper clippings.*
bundle *a bundle of sticks tied together with string*
cluster *a cluster of stores, restaurants, and motels*
heap *a heap of old boxes for the bonfire*
load *My cousin came up with a load of embarrassing stories.*
pile *I've got a pile of questions for you.*
set *a complete set of keys to the building*
See also **band, group, lot**

bundle *See* **bunch**

bungle *See* **botch, mess**

bungling *See* **incompetent**

buoyant *See* **cheerful, optimistic**

burble *See* **babble**

burden

▷ *NOUN*

1 a load that is carried: *My wet clothes were an added burden.*
load *a load of hay*
weight *straining to lift heavy weights*
2 something that worries you: *the burden of looking after a sick parent*
anxiety *He expressed his anxieties to me.*
care *Forget all the cares of the day.*
strain *I find travelling a strain.*
stress *the stress of the playoffs*
trouble *I think they have money troubles.*
worry *My new job is a worry to me.*
See also **handicap**

bureaucracy

▷ *NOUN*

complex rules and procedures: *Is there too much bureaucracy in government?*
administration *high administration costs*
officialdom *Officialdom is against us.*
red tape *Our application was delayed by red tape.*
regulations *absurd regulations about closing times*

burglar *See* **thief**

burgle *See* **rob**

burly *See* **plump**

burn

▷ *VERB*

1 to be on fire: *a fire burning in the fireplace*
be ablaze *The houses were ablaze.*
be on fire *The ship was on fire.*
blaze *The wreckage blazed.*
flame *We watched as the barn flamed in the night.*
flare *The match flared in the dark.*
flicker *The fire flickered and crackled.*
2 to destroy with fire: *The old house burned down.*
char *charred hamburgers*
incinerate *Hospitals incinerate waste.*
scorch *The bonfire scorched the grass.*
shrivel *The grapes shrivelled in the sun.*
singe *singed hair*

INFORMALLY SPEAKING

burn out: wear out through much use
burn up: make angry or annoyed

burrow *See* **dig**

burst

▷ *VERB*

1 to split apart: *The balloon burst.*

B

break *The dish broke in half.*
crack *The vase was cracked.*
explode *The gas pipe exploded.*
puncture *The nail punctured the tire.*
rupture *His appendix ruptured.*
split *My pants split when I bent over.*
2 to happen or appear suddenly: *to burst into flames*
barge *He barged into the room.*
break *Her face broke into a smile.*
erupt *Violence could erupt soon.*
gush *Water gushed out of the broken tap.*
rush *Water rushed out of the hose.*
▷ *NOUN*
3 a short period of something: *a burst of energy*
fit *a fit of rage*
outbreak *an outbreak of chicken pox*
rush *a sudden rush of excitement*
spate *a spate of traffic accidents*
surge *a surge of emotion*
torrent *a torrent of words*
See also **broken, explode, flash, split**

bush *See* **country**

business

▷ *NOUN*

1 the buying and selling of goods: *a career in business*
commerce *commerce between Canada and China*
dealings *All dealings with the company were suspended.*
industry *the Canadian movie industry*
trade *U.S. trade with Canada*
trading *trading between the two countries*
transaction *We settled the transaction over lunch.*
2 an organization selling goods or services: *a family business*
company *the world's largest shoe company*
corporation *international corporations*
enterprise *small industrial enterprises*
establishment *stores and other commercial establishments*
firm *a firm of engineers*
organization *a well-run organization*
3 any event or situation: *This business has upset me.*
affair *He handled the affair badly.*
issue *What is your view on this issue?*
matter *This is a matter for the police.*
problem *solutions to the smuggling problem*
question *the whole question of TV censorship*
subject *He raised the subject of money.*
See also **affair, company, concern,**

enterprise, event, firm, matter, profession, scene, trade, undertaking, work

businesslike See efficient

bustle
▷ VERB
I to move hurriedly: *Salespeople bustled about the store.*
dash *We dashed to catch the train.*
fuss *Servers were fussing around the table.*
hurry *She hurried to catch up to us.*
rush *I'm rushing to finish the dinner.*
scurry *rats scurrying about*
scuttle *Crabs scuttle along the bank.*
▷ NOUN
2 busy and noisy activity: *the bustle of modern life*
activity *a burst of activity in the building*
commotion *He heard a commotion outside.*
excitement *The news created great excitement.*
flurry *a flurry of activity*
fuss *He works without any fuss.*
hurry *the hurry and excitement of the city*
ANTONYM **peace**
See also **activity, fuss, rush**

busy
▷ ADJECTIVE
I doing something: *What is it? I'm busy.*
active *He is active in school organizations.*
employed *He was employed helping me.*
engaged *He was engaged in conversation.*
engrossed *She is engrossed in her work.*
occupied *He is occupied with the school play.*
working *I am working on a novel.*
ANTONYM **idle**
2 full of activity: *Halifax is a busy port.*
active *My grandparents are active and independent.*
full *a full life*
hectic *my hectic school and work schedule*
lively *a lively concert*
restless *a restless mind*
▷ VERB
3 to occupy or keep busy: *We busied ourselves in the kitchen.*
absorb *Her job absorbed her completely.*
employ *You'd be better employed helping me.*
engage *He was engaged in a meeting when I called.*
immerse *She immersed herself in her book.*
occupy *Try to occupy yourself with something.*

See also **active, industrious**

busybody
▷ NOUN
a person who interferes in other people's business: *the neighbourhood busybody*
meddler *a meddler in everyone's business*

but
▷ CONJUNCTION
I although: *Heat the cider until it is very hot but not boiling.*
although *He was in love with her, although he had not yet admitted it to himself.*
though *He's very attractive, though not exactly handsome.*
while *The first two CDs are free, while the third one costs $20.*
yet *It is completely waterproof, yet light and comfortable.*
▷ PREPOSITION
2 with the exception of: *The crew gave them nothing but bread to eat.*
except *Everyone except my mother was at the barbecue.*
except for *Nobody has complained except for you.*
save *The people had no water at all save that brought up from the well.*
other than *This route is not recommended to anyone other than the most experienced cyclist.*
See also **except**

butcher See kill

butt in See interfere, interrupt, intrude

buttocks
▷ PLURAL NOUN
the part of the body that you sit on: *exercises for your buttocks*
backside *the muscles in your backside*
behind *He kicked me on the behind.*
bottom *Sit on your bottom!*
posterior *She fell on her posterior.*
rear *I was thrown out on my rear.*

buy
▷ VERB
to obtain with money: *I'd like to buy him lunch.*
acquire *I have acquired a new DVD player.*
invest in *I invested in a laptop.*
obtain *She went to obtain a ticket.*
pay for *He let me pay for his ticket.*
procure *attempts to procure more food for the flood victims*
purchase *He purchased a sandwich for lunch.*
ANTONYM **sell**

CONFUSABLES

Buy means **purchase**.
By means **beside**.

buy off *See* **corrupt**

buyer *See* **customer**

by *See* **past**

by degrees *See* **slowly**

by design *See* **on purpose**

by dint of *See* **by virtue of**

by oneself *See* **on your own**

bygone *See* **former, past**

bystander *See* **spectator, witness**

B

Cc

cache *See* **hide, hoard, reserve, stockpile, store, supply**

cadence *See* **beat**

cadge *See* **scrounge**

cagey *See* **secretive**

cajole *See* **coax**

cake *See* **harden, lump**

calamitous *See* **fatal**

calamity *See* **disaster**

calculate
▷ *VERB*
to work out a number or amount: *how to calculate the cost of setting up a business*
count *Voters are counting the ballots.*
determine *calculations to determine the rate of tax*
reckon *to reckon the price of each meal*
work out *Work out the distance of the return trip.*
See also **count, reckon, work out**

calculated
▷ *ADJECTIVE*
deliberately planned: *Everything they said was calculated to hurt his feelings.*
aimed *The restructuring is aimed at reducing costs.*
designed *a plan designed to help improve the environment*
intended *the intended effect of the revised guidelines*
planned *a carefully planned campaign*
ANTONYM **unplanned**
See also **deliberate**

calculating *See* **devious**

calculation *See* **count**

calibre *See* **quality, standard**

call
▷ *VERB*
1 to give a name: *We called our dog Bandit.*
2 to telephone: *He called me at my office.*
3 to say loudly: *Did someone call my name?*
See WORD STUDY **call** *on next page*
▷ *NOUN*
4 an instance of someone shouting out: *a call for help*
cry *the cry of a seagull*
shout *I heard a distant shout.*
yell *He let out a yell.*
See also **cry, name, request, shout, visit**

call off *See* **cancel**

call on *See* **visit**

call to mind *See* **remember**

call upon *See* **appeal**

callous
▷ *ADJECTIVE*
not concerned about other people: *his callous disregard for other people's safety*
cold *What a cold, unfeeling woman she was.*
heartless *It was a heartless thing to do.*
indifferent *indifferent to the suffering of others*
insensitive *insensitive remarks*
ANTONYM **caring**
See also **cruel, merciless**

callousness *See* **cruelty**

calm
▷ *ADJECTIVE*
1 not worried or excited: *Try to keep calm.*
collected *I was cool and collected during the interview.*
composed *a very composed debater*
cool *We have to keep a cool head in this situation.*
impassive *He remained impassive as his sentence was passed.*
relaxed *a relaxed manner*
ANTONYM **worried**
2 still because there is no wind: *Tuesday was a clear and calm day.*
balmy *balmy summer evenings*
mild *a mild winter climate*
still *The air was still.*
tranquil *a tranquil lake*
ANTONYM **rough**
▷ *NOUN*
3 the state of being peaceful: *He liked the calm of the evening.*
calmness *an aura of calmness*
peace *a wonderful feeling of peace*
peacefulness *the peacefulness of the gardens*
quiet *a quiet, relaxing holiday*
serenity *the serenity of a tropical sunset*
stillness *the stillness of the summer night*
▷ *VERB*
4 to make less upset or excited: *We were trying to calm the puppy.*
relax *This music is supposed to relax you.*
soothe *I think a bath may soothe me.*
See also **cool, ease, pacify, patient, peace, peaceful, quiet, relaxed, silence, still**

WORD STUDY: CALL

Depending on which sense of **call** you are thinking of, there are a number of words that you can substitute to make your language more interesting.

• **to give a name**
The forest was **designated** an "area of natural beauty."
The man **dubbed** "the world's greatest living explorer!" is on television tonight.
They **named** their child Anthony.

• **to describe as**
I **consider** myself an artist.
I'm not what you'd **describe** as an emotional person.
Do you **judge** this result a success?
He **referred** to her as a genius.
The ruler of that country was widely **regarded** as a tyrant.
This building is for prisoners **termed** "political."
People will **think** us very foolish.

• **to telephone**
Contact us immediately if you have any new information.
Phone me as soon as you get home.
I'll **ring** you tomorrow.
Please **telephone** to make an appointment.

• **to say loudly**
"Dinner is served," **announced** the waiter.

"Run, Forrest!" she **cried**.
He **cried out** to us as he disappeared from view.
She **shouted** to me from across the room.
"Ahoy there!" the captain **yelled**.

• **to send for someone**
Can someone please **fetch** a nurse?
The manager **sent** for the police at once.
I was **summoned** to the principal's office.

• **to bring together**
They **assembled** the group for the closing ceremony.
The chief has **convened** a council of elders.
He **gathered** us together in a small circle.
They **mustered** an army of over 10 000 soldiers.
We have been **summoned** to a meeting this afternoon.

• **to pay a visit** (informal)
I hate it when people just **drop in** without any warning.
Do **pop in** any time you're in the area.
I just thought I'd **stop by** on my way home.

---

calmness *See* **calm, patience, quiet**

camaraderie *See* **fellowship**

camp *See* **base, side**

campaign
▷ *NOUN*
actions planned to get a certain result: *a campaign to educate people*
crusade *the crusade for human rights*
movement *the human rights movement*
operation *a full-scale military operation*
push *an all-out push to promote the school show*
See also **agitate, movement**

cancel
▷ *VERB*
1 to stop something from happening: *We're going to have to cancel our picnic.*
abandon *They had to abandon their vacation plans.*
call off *The union has called off the strike.*
2 to stop something from being valid: *They*

were forced to cancel their contract.
annul *The marriage was annulled.*
quash *His jail sentence was quashed when new evidence came to light.*
repeal *The new law was repealed within the year.*
revoke *His licence was immediately revoked.*
See also **lift**

cancel out *See* **compensate**

candid
▷ *ADJECTIVE*
honest and frank: *a candid interview*
blunt *She is blunt about his faults.*
frank *They had a frank discussion about the issue.*
honest *What is your honest opinion?*
open *He had always been open with her, and she would know if he lied.*
truthful *We've all learned to be truthful about our personal lives.*
straightforward *I was impressed by his straightforward manner.*

See also **direct, frank, natural, open, straight, straightforward**

candidate
▷ NOUN

a person being considered for a position: *a candidate for the presidency of the debating team*
applicant *one of thirty applicants for the manager's position*
competitor *several competitors for the contract*
contender *a strong contender for the championship*

candy
▷ NOUN

a sweet-tasting snack: *I ate too many candies and I feel sick.*
confectionery *This store sells confectionery from all over the world.*
sweets *Don't eat sweets before supper.*

cane *See* **stick**

canine *See* **dog**

canny *See* **shrewd, smart**

canon *See* **principle**

cantankerous *See* **irritable**

cap *See* **top**

capability *See* **ability, capacity, potential, qualification**

capable
▷ ADJECTIVE

able to do something well: *a capable leader*
able *a very able carpenter*
accomplished *an accomplished painter*
adept *an adept juggler*
competent *a competent and careful driver*
efficient *efficient organizers*
proficient *proficient with computers*
skilful *Canada's most skilful politician*
ANTONYM **incompetent**
See also **able, proficient**

capable of *See* **equal to**

capacity
▷ NOUN

1 the maximum amount that something holds or produces: *the vehicle's fuel capacity*
dimensions *the dimensions of the car's trunk*
room *There wasn't enough room in the trunk for all the baggage.*
size *My bedroom is half the size of yours.*

space *There is space in the back for two people.*
volume *a container with a volume of two litres*
2 a person's power or ability to do something: *Our capacity for giving care, love, and attention is limited.*
ability *The public never had faith in his ability to handle the job.*
capability *a country with the capability of launching a nuclear attack*
facility *She has a facility for picking up languages.*
gift *As a youth he discovered a gift for making people laugh.*
potential *the potential to be a top goalie*
power *The coach has the power to suspend players.*
See also **part, potential, room, space, talent**

capital *See* **fund, money**

capitalize on *See* **profit**

capitulate *See* **give in, submit, surrender**

capitulation *See* **surrender**

capsize *See* **overturn, upset**

captain *See* **leader**

captivate *See* **charm, delight, entrance, fascinate, interest**

captive *See* **prisoner**

capture
▷ VERB

1 to take prisoner: *captured by rebels*
apprehend *Police have not yet apprehended the killer.*
arrest *Seven people were arrested.*
catch *The thief was caught, and the money was returned.*
seize *seized by armed police*
take *An army unit took the village.*
ANTONYM **release**
▷ NOUN

2 the act of capturing: *She evaded capture for eight years.*
arrest *Police made two arrests.*
seizure *the seizure of territory*
taking *the taking of hostages*
trapping *The trapping of these animals is illegal.*
See also **arrest, catch, kidnap**

car
▷ NOUN

a vehicle for carrying a few people: *I finally left the car at the garage.*

automobile *My father works at an automobile plant.*
vehicle *Get out of the vehicle.*
See also **automobile**

carcass *See* **body**

cardinal *See* **essential, main**

care
▷ VERB
1 to be concerned about something: *a company that cares about the environment*
be bothered *I am not bothered about what others think of me.*
be concerned *We are concerned about the problem.*
be interested *He's not interested in what anyone else says.*
mind *I don't mind if you arrive a little late.*
▷ NOUN
2 something that causes you worry: *without a care in the world*
anxiety *anxieties about money*
concern *Their main concern is unemployment.*
stress *the stresses of modern life*
trouble *She has had her share of troubles.*
woe *They blame the government for all their woes.*
worry *My biggest worry is how I will cope on my own.*
▷ NOUN
3 close attention when doing something: *We took great care in choosing a location.*
attention *medical attention*
caution *Proceed with caution.*
pains *to take great pains with your appearance*
See also **burden, caution, mind**

care for *See* **keep, look after, take care of, tend, treat**

career *See* **profession, record, speed**

carefree *See* **easy**

careful
▷ ADJECTIVE
1 acting with care: *Be careful what you say to him.*
cautious *a cautious approach*
prudent *prudent management*
ANTONYM **careless**
2 complete and well done: *It needs careful planning.*
meticulous *meticulous attention to detail*
painstaking *a painstaking search*
precise *precise instructions*
thorough *a thorough examination*
ANTONYM **careless**

See also **cautious, deliberate, economical, thrifty**

careless
▷ ADJECTIVE
1 not taking enough care: *careless driving*
irresponsible *an irresponsible attitude*
neglectful *neglectful pet owners*
sloppy INFORMAL *sloppy work*
ANTONYM **careful**
2 relaxed and unconcerned: *careless laughter*
casual *a casual remark*
nonchalant *a nonchalant attitude*
offhand *his usual offhand way*
See also **casual, irresponsible**

cargo *See* **load**

caring *See* **affectionate, compassionate, humane, tender, thoughtful**

carnal *See* **lustful**

carnival *See* **fair, festival**

carp *See* **complain, grumble**

carping *See* **critical**

carriage *See* **compartment, walk**

carry
▷ VERB
to hold and take something somewhere: *She was carrying a briefcase.*
bear *He arrived bearing gifts.*
convey FORMAL *The limousine conveyed them to the dance.*
lug *lugging boxes of books around*
take *Don't forget to take your camera.*
transport *goods being transported across the province*
See also **bear, bring, hold, take, transport**

carry on *See* **continue, last, proceed**

carry out
▷ VERB
to do and complete something: *the surgeon who carried out the operation*
accomplish *the desire to accomplish a task*
achieve *We have achieved our objective.*
fulfill *to fulfill a promise*
perform *to perform an act of bravery*
See also **achieve, administer, commit, conduct, do, fulfill, keep, perform**

carton *See* **box**

carve
▷ VERB
to make something by cutting: *He always*

carves his figures from pine.
chisel the sculptor chiselling her stone
cut a figure cut from marble
engrave initials engraved on the watch
inscribe the words inscribed on the monument
sculpt a sculpted clay figure
See also **model**

case

▷ NOUN

1 a particular situation or example: a case of mistaken identity
example an example of what can go wrong
illustration a clear illustration of the point I'm trying to make
instance a serious instance of corruption
occasion the last occasion on which he appeared
occurrence a frequent occurrence
2 a container for holding something: an eyeglass case
box a box of chocolates
container a huge plastic container
3 a trial or legal inquiry: a libel case
action a civil action for damages
lawsuit The judge dismissed their lawsuit.
proceedings criminal proceedings against the former leader
trial The witness testified at the trial.
See also **argument, box, cover, patient, situation**

cash See **money**

cast See **throw**

cast a vote See **vote**

cast aside See **discard**

castle See **fort**

casual

▷ ADJECTIVE

1 happening by chance: a casual remark
accidental a verdict of accidental death
chance a chance meeting
incidental an incidental problem not likely to happen again
ANTONYM **deliberate**
2 showing no concern or interest: a casual look over his shoulder
careless careless remarks
cursory a cursory glance
nonchalant I was surprised by his nonchalant attitude to the situation.
offhand a deceptively offhand style
relaxed a relaxed manner

ANTONYM **concerned**
See also **accidental, careless, informal, relaxed**

cat

▷ NOUN

a small animal kept as a pet: sharing his apartment with four cats
feline Even the most cuddly feline has claws.
kitty a kitty stuck up a tree
pussy, puss, or **pussycat** INFORMAL a fluffy little pussycat

catalogue See **list**

catastrophe See **disaster**

catastrophic See **fatal**

catch

▷ VERB

1 to capture someone or something: another technique for catching criminals
apprehend the force necessary to apprehend a suspect
arrest Police arrested the armed robber.
capture Poachers had captured a gorilla.
snare a plan to snare the thief
trap to trap a mouse
▷ NOUN
2 a device that fastens something: windows fitted with safety catches
bolt the sound of a bolt being slid open
clasp the clasp of her handbag
clip She took the clip out of her hair.
latch You left the latch off the gate.
▷ NOUN
3 a hidden difficulty: The catch is that you have to change planes twice.
disadvantage The disadvantage is that this plant needs frequent watering.
drawback The apartment's only drawback was its size.
snag The snag is that you have to pay in advance.
See also **capture, clasp, develop, hear, snag, stick, tangle, trap**

INFORMALLY SPEAKING

catch it: be scolded or punished
catch on: understand; be popular

catch on See **understand**

catching See **infectious**

catchy See **memorable**

categorize See **class, classify, sort**

category

▷ NOUN

a set of things with something in common:

The items were organized into six different categories.

class *dividing the stars into six classes of brightness*

classification *There are various classifications of genres, or types, of book.*

group *She is one of the most promising players in her age group.*

set *She tries to be part of the celebrity set.*

sort *What sort of school did you go to?*

type *The majority of complaints received are of this type.*

See also **class, kind, sort, variety**

cattle *See* **cow**

catty *See* **spiteful**

cause
▷ NOUN
1 what makes something happen: *the most common cause of back pain*

origin *They couldn't even remember the origin of their feud.*

root *We need to get to the root of the problem.*

source *the source of the leak*

2 an aim supported by a group: *dedication to the cause of peace*

aim *political aims*

ideal *democratic ideals*

movement *the animal rights' movement*

3 the reason for something: *They gave us no cause to believe that.*

basis *There is no basis for this assumption.*

grounds *discrimination on the grounds of race or religion*

justification *There was no justification for what he was doing.*

motivation *the motivation for his actions*

motive *Police have ruled out robbery as a motive.*

reason *You have every reason to be upset.*

▷ VERB
4 to make something happen: *This may cause delays.*

bring about *We must try to bring about a better world.*

create *The plan may create even more confusion.*

generate *the excitement generated by this movie*

produce *His comments produced an immediate response.*

provoke *a move that has provoked a storm of protest*

See also **bring, bring about, create, factor, grounds, lead to, prompt, provoke, reason, result in, source**

caustic *See* **sarcastic**

C

caution
▷ NOUN
1 great care taken in order to avoid danger: *Drivers are urged to exercise extreme caution in icy weather.*

care *Scissors can be safe for young children if used with care.*

prudence *A lack of prudence may lead to problems.*

▷ VERB
2 to scold or warn someone against doing something: *The two men were cautioned, but police say they will not be charged.*

reprimand *He was reprimanded for sending personal e-mails.*

warn *They were warned not to talk to strangers.*

See also **advise, care, warn, warning**

cautious
▷ ADJECTIVE
acting very carefully to avoid danger: *a cautious approach*

careful *Be extremely careful when travelling alone.*

guarded *a guarded response*

tentative *a tentative approach*

wary *Small companies should be wary of expanding too quickly.*

ANTONYM **daring**
See also **careful, deliberate, wary**

cavalcade *See* **parade**

cave in *See* **give**

cease
▷ VERB
1 to stop happening: *Almost miraculously, the noise ceased.*

be over *The audience applauded when the play was over.*

come to an end *The players' strike came to an end.*

die away *The sound died away and silence returned.*

end *The school year ends in June.*

finish *The teaching day finished at about four o'clock.*

stop *The rain had stopped.*

ANTONYM **begin**
2 to stop doing something: *A small number of companies have ceased doing business.*

desist from *His friends never desisted from trying to change his mind.*

discontinue *Do not discontinue the treatment without consulting your doctor.*

finish *As soon as he'd finished eating, he excused himself.*

give up *She gave up drinking coffee at night.*
stop *Stop throwing those stones!*
suspend *to be suspended from school for a week*
ANTONYM **start**
See also **disappear, end, fail, halt, stop, vanish**

cede *See* **surrender**

ceiling *See* **maximum**

celebrate

▷ *VERB*

to do something special to mark an event: *I was in a mood to celebrate.*
commemorate *The anniversary of the composer's death was commemorated with a concert.*
party *It's your birthday — let's have a party!*
rejoice *My family rejoiced at the happy news.*
ANTONYM **mourn**
See also **commemorate, rejoice**

celebrated *See* **famous**

celebration

▷ *NOUN*

an event in honour of a special occasion: *his eighteenth birthday celebration*
festival *a religious festival*
festivity *the wedding festivities*
gala *the Olympics' opening gala*
party *a housewarming party*
See also **party**

TYPES OF ... *CELEBRATION*	
Buddhist	**Jewish**
Wesak	Hannukkah
Christian	Passover
Advent	Purim
Christmas	Rosh Hashana
Easter	Shavuot
Good Friday	Succoth
Lent	Yom Kippur
Palm Sunday	**Muslim**
Pentecost	Bairam
Hindu	Eid-ul-Adha
Diwali	Eid-ul-Fitr
Durga Puja	Ramadan
Holi	**Sikh**
	Baisakhi

celebrity

▷ *NOUN*

a famous person: *At the age of twelve, he was already a celebrity.*

big name *all the big names in rock music*
name *some of the most famous names in popular music*
personality *a well-known television personality*
star *Many movie stars turned out for the benefit.*
superstar *a Hollywood superstar*
VIP *such VIPs as the Governor General*
See also **personality, star, success**

censure

▷ *NOUN*

1 strong disapproval: *a controversial policy that has attracted international censure*
blame *I'm the one who'll get the blame if things go wrong.*
condemnation *There was widespread condemnation of the violence.*
criticism *This policy has repeatedly come under strong criticism.*
disapproval *His action had been greeted with almost universal disapproval.*
reproach *People in public life should be beyond reproach.*
▷ *VERB*

2 to criticize severely: *He should not have been censured for his personal opinions.*
condemn *The critics condemned the movie for its pointless violence.*
criticize *The company has been harshly criticized for its poor working conditions.*
denounce *to denounce the country's human rights violations*
pan INFORMAL *The play was panned by the critics and closed after a week.*
reproach *reproached for breaking a promise*
See also **abuse, accuse, attack, condemn, criticism, criticize, disapproval, fault**

CONFUSABLES
Censure means **criticize severely**. **Censor** means **delete something considered unsuitable**.

central *See* **crucial, middle, vital**

centre

▷ *NOUN*

1 the middle of something: *the centre of the room*
core *the Earth's core*
focus *World peace is the focus of my speech.*
heart *the heart of the problem*
hub *The kitchen is the hub of most households.*
middle *in the middle of the back row*
ANTONYM **edge**

▷ VERB

2 to have as the main subject: *All his thoughts were centred around himself.*
concentrate *Scientists are concentrating their efforts on finding a cure.*
focus *Attention is likely to focus on sales growth.*
revolve *Since childhood, her life has revolved around tennis.*
See also **base, focus, middle**

ceremony

▷ NOUN

1 formal actions done for a special occasion: *The awards ceremony was followed by a banquet.*
observance *a Remembrance Day observance*
pomp *The princess's arrival was celebrated with suitable pomp.*
rite *marriage rites*
ritual *The Canada Day picnic is a family ritual.*
service *The prime minister attended the memorial service.*
2 formal and polite behaviour: *He hung up without ceremony.*
decorum *a responsibility to behave with decorum*
etiquette *the rules of etiquette*
formality *his lack of formality*
niceties *social niceties*
protocol *minor breaches of protocol*

certain

▷ ADJECTIVE

1 definite or reliable: *One thing is certain — they respect each other.*
definite *It's too soon to give a definite answer.*
definitive *The definitive descriptions are found in the encyclopedia.*
established *an established medical fact*
guaranteed *Success is not guaranteed.*
inevitable *If she wins her case, it is inevitable that other people will sue the company.*
known *It is not known when my grandparents came to Canada.*
sure *When my ankle starts to ache, it's a sure sign of rain.*
undeniable *undeniable proof of guilt*
ANTONYM **uncertain**
2 having no doubt in your mind: *She's absolutely certain she's going to win.*
clear *It is important to be clear about what you are doing.*
confident *I am confident that everything will come out right.*
convinced *He was convinced that I was*

part of the problem.
definite *My sister is very definite about this fact.*
sure *She was no longer sure how she felt about him.*
positive *I'm as positive as I can be about it.*
satisfied *People must be satisfied that the treatment is safe.*
ANTONYM **uncertain**
See also **confident, definite, necessary, positive, sure**

certainly

▷ ADVERB

without any doubt: *I'll certainly do all I can to help.*
definitely *Something should definitely be done.*
undeniably *Bringing up a baby is undeniably hard work.*
undoubtedly *She is undoubtedly a great player.*
unquestionably *He is unquestionably a star.*
without doubt *Without doubt, that is my final answer.*
See also **really**

certainly not See **no**

certainty See **fact**

certified See **official**

certify See **declare**

chaff See **joke**

chain See **sequence, series**

challenge

▷ NOUN

1 a suggestion to try something: *They issued a challenge to their rivals.*
dare *He'd do almost anything on a dare.*
▷ VERB
2 to give someone a challenge: *He challenged his rival to a duel.*
dare *I dare you to ask him.*
defy *I defy you not to smile at this joke.*
▷ VERB
3 to question the truth or value of something: *challenging the authority of the government*
dispute *He disputed the charge.*
question *questioning the jury's verdict*
See also **contest, dare, dispute, query, question**

challenger See **competitor, rival**

challenging See **formidable**

chamber *See* **compartment, room**

champion

▷ *NOUN*

1 a person who wins a competition: *the world chess champion*
hero *the hero of the playoffs*
title holder *He became the youngest world title holder at the age of 22.*
victor *the Stanley Cup victors*
winner *The winner was a horse called Baby Face.*
2 someone who supports a group, cause, or principle: *He received acclaim as a champion of the oppressed.*
advocate *She is a strong advocate of free trade.*
defender *a strong defender of human rights*
guardian *The political party wants to be seen as a guardian of free speech.*
protector *a protector of human rights*
▷ *VERB*
3 to support a group, cause, or principle: *He passionately championed the poor.*
defend *her courage in defending human rights*
fight for *fighting for an end to child labour*
promote *You don't have to sacrifice the environment to promote economic growth.*
stick up for INFORMAL *She has shown courage in sticking up for the rights of children.*
support *The fishing industry has the government's support.*
uphold *upholding the artist's right to creative freedom*
See also **advocate, defender, support, supporter, winner**

championship *See* **competition**

chance

▷ *NOUN*

1 a possibility of something happening: *a good chance of success*
likelihood *the likelihood of infection*
odds *What are the odds of that happening?*
possibility *the possibility of pay cuts*
probability *a probability of victory*
prospect *There is little prospect of peace.*
2 an opportunity to do something: *He didn't give me a chance to explain.*
occasion *I had no occasion to speak to her that day.*
opening *an opening for a person with the right qualifications*
opportunity *an opportunity to travel across Canada*

time *There was no time to think.*
3 the way things happen without being planned: *events that were merely the result of chance*
accident *a strange accident of fate*
coincidence *It was no coincidence that she arrived just then.*
fortune *a change of fortune*
luck *His injury was just bad luck.*
See also **accidental, casual, fate, gamble, luck, occasion, possibility, risk, turn, unexpected, unpredictable**

chances *See* **probability**

change

▷ *NOUN*

1 an alteration in something: *a change in her attitude*
alteration *You must make some alterations in your diet for better nutrition.*
difference *a noticeable difference in his behaviour*
modification *Some minor modifications were required.*
transformation *the transformation of a wilderness into a garden*
▷ *VERB*
2 to make or become different: *My views have changed since I began working here.*
alter *They won't alter their decision.*
convert *a plan to convert the spare room into an office*
moderate *They persuaded him to moderate his views.*
modify *He refused to modify his behaviour.*
reform *The finance minister plans to reform the economy.*
transform *The landscape has been transformed.*
▷ *VERB*
3 to exchange one thing for another: *Can I change this sweater for one a size bigger?*
barter *bartering wheat for cotton and timber*
exchange *We exchanged the gift for something more suitable.*
interchange *Beans and rice can be interchanged with meat as a source of protein.*
replace *His smile was replaced by a frown.*
substitute *You can substitute honey for the sugar.*
swap *Let's swap places.*
trade *They traded baseball cards.*
See also **adapt, affect, exchange, reverse, transform, turn, variation, vary**

changeable

▷ ADJECTIVE

likely to change all the time: *changeable weather*

erratic *erratic driving*
fickle *Fashion is a fickle business.*
irregular *an irregular heartbeat*
unpredictable *unpredictable behaviour*
unstable *The government of that country is unstable.*
variable *a variable rate of interest*
volatile *a volatile political situation*
ANTONYM **constant**

channel *See* **medium, passage, route, way**

chaos *See* **confusion, disorder, mess, muddle**

chaotic *See* **confused, untidy**

chap *See* **man**

char *See* **burn**

character

▷ NOUN

1 the qualities of a person: *He has a dark side to his character.*
makeup *Determination has always been a part of her makeup.*
nature *a sunny nature*
personality *an outgoing personality*
temperament *his impulsive temperament*
2 an honourable nature: *She showed real character in her attempt to win over the crowd.*
honour *He has acted with honour.*
integrity *a person of integrity*
strength *He had the strength to turn down the offer.*
See also **eccentric, figure, individual, name, nature, personality, reputation, sign**

characteristic

▷ NOUN

1 a typical quality: *His chief characteristic is honesty.*
attribute *a normal attribute of human behaviour*
feature *a feature of the Saskatchewan landscape*
property *This liquid has many unique properties.*
quality *leadership qualities*
trait *personality traits*
▷ ADJECTIVE

2 typical of a person or thing: *She responded with characteristic generosity.*
distinctive *a distinctive voice*
distinguishing *no distinguishing marks*

typical *his typical Canadian generosity*
ANTONYM **uncharacteristic**
See also **attribute, feature, individual, point, property, quality, representative, special, typical**

charge

▷ VERB

1 to ask someone for money as a payment: *Most electricians charge a fair price.*
ask (for) *The artist was asking $6000 for each painting.*
bill *Are you going to bill me for this?*
levy *Should taxes be levied without the authority of Parliament?*
2 to rush forward, often to attack someone: *He charged into the room.*
dash *She dashed in from the garden.*
rush *She rushed into the burning building to save the child.*
stampede *The crowd stampeded out of the arena.*
storm *He stormed into the store, demanding to see the manager.*
▷ NOUN

3 the price you have to pay for something: *We can arrange this for a small charge.*
cost *Programs are available at a cost of $5.*
fee *Pay your legal fees.*
payment *I'll do it for a small payment.*
price *We negotiated a price for the service.*
See also **accuse, attack, blame, cost, direction, price, rate, tear**

charges *See* **bill**

charitable *See* **benevolent, generous, humane, kind**

charity *See* **generosity, kindness, pity**

charlatan *See* **fraud**

charm

▷ NOUN

1 an attractive quality: *a man of great charm*
allure *the allure of foreign lands*
appeal *I don't understand the appeal of that movie.*
attraction *the attractions of living by a lake*
fascination *It is hard to explain the fascination of this place.*
magnetism *an individual of enormous magnetism*
▷ VERB

2 to use charm to please someone: *He charmed the entire audience.*
bewitch *bewitched by his sparkling eyes*
captivate *The crowd was captivated by her performance.*

delight *a style of music that has delighted audiences*
entrance *entranced by her smile*
See also **beauty, delight, entertain, entrance, please**

charmed *See* **lucky**

charming *See* **attractive, cute, lovable, pleasant**

charter *See* **book, hire, law**

chase
▷ VERB
1 to try to catch someone or something: *She chased the thief until he surrendered.*
hunt *He fled the country after being hunted by police.*
pursue *He pursued the man who had snatched the laptop.*
2 to force to go somewhere: *Angry protestors chased him away.*
drive *The troops drove the rebels into the forest.*
hound *He was hounded out of his job.*

chasm *See* **abyss, pit**

chat
▷ NOUN
1 a friendly talk: *We sat around and had a chat.*
conversation *a telephone conversation*
talk *We will have a talk about it later.*
▷ VERB
2 to talk in a friendly way: *He was chatting to his father.*
gossip *We gossiped into the night.*
talk *She's very easy to talk to.*
See also **talk, word**

chatter *See* **babble, ramble, talk**

chatty *See* **talkative**

chauvinism *See* **prejudice**

cheap
▷ ADJECTIVE
1 costing very little: *Cheap flights are available.*
bargain *selling at bargain prices*
economical *These cars are very economical to run.*
inexpensive *an inexpensive wine*
reasonable *His rates were quite reasonable.*
ANTONYM **expensive**
2 inexpensive but of poor quality: *a suit made of some cheap material*
inferior *an inferior imitation*
second-rate *second-rate equipment*

tacky *tacky souvenirs*
See also **economical, petty, reasonable**

cheat
▷ VERB
to get something from someone dishonestly: *the people he cheated out of their life savings*
con INFORMAL *He conned his way into a job.*
deceive *Investors were deceived by a scam.*
defraud *charges of conspiracy to defraud the government*
dupe *Stamp collectors were duped into buying fakes.*
fleece *He fleeced them out of thousands of dollars.*
rip off SLANG *They really ripped off those workers.*
swindle *two executives who swindled their employer*
See also **con, crook, dupe, fraud**

cheating *See* **dishonesty**

check
▷ VERB
1 to examine something: *Check all the details first.*
check out INFORMAL *Check out the financial figures.*
examine *She examined my passport and stamped it.*
inspect *the right to inspect company files*
test *The drug must be tested in clinical trials.*
2 to reduce or stop something: *a policy to check the inflation rate*
control *a measure to control illegal sales*
curb *reforms that aim to curb spending*
halt *an attempt to halt the spread of the disease*
inhibit *factors that inhibit growth*
restrain *the need to restrain the guard dog*
stop *measures to stop the trade in ivory*
▷ NOUN
3 an examination: *a thorough check of the equipment*
examination *a medical examination*
inspection *a routine inspection of the premises*
test *I passed the driving test.*
See also **block, curb, delay, examination, examine, foil, frustrate, halt, hinder, inspect, slow (down), stop, test**

check out *See* **check, try**

checkup *See* **examination**

cheek *See* **nerve**

cheeky *See* **disrespectful**

cheer *See* **comfort, encourage**

cheer up *See* **reassure**

cheerful
▷ ADJECTIVE
in a happy mood: *She was very cheerful despite her illness.*
bright *"May I help you?" asked a bright voice.*
buoyant *in a buoyant mood*
cheery *a cheery nature*
happy *a confident, happy child*
jaunty *a jaunty tune*
jolly *a jolly, easygoing man*
light-hearted *They were light-hearted and enjoyed life.*
merry *a burst of merry laughter*
ANTONYM **miserable**
See also **bright, cheery**

cheery
▷ ADJECTIVE
happy and cheerful: *He is loved by everyone for his cheery disposition.*
cheerful *They are both very cheerful in spite of their circumstances.*
chirpy *She sounded quite chirpy on the phone.*
good-humoured *My brother is consistently good-humoured.*
happy *a confident, happy child*
jolly *a jolly, kind-hearted individual*
sunny *a nice young woman with a sunny disposition*
upbeat *His colleagues said he was in a joking, upbeat mood.*
See also **cheerful**

cherish *See* **love, prize, treasure, value**

cherished *See* **beloved, dear**

chest *See* **box**

chew
▷ VERB
to break food up with the teeth: *Eat slowly and chew your food properly.*
chomp *He chomped loudly on the apple.*
crunch *She crunched the ice cube loudly.*
gnaw *He sat and gnawed at a chicken leg.*
munch *Deer were munching the leaves.*
See also **bite**

INFORMALLY SPEAKING
chew out: scold
chew the fat: chat

chic *See* **exclusive, smart, style**

chicken *See* **coward, cowardly**

C

chide *See* **scold**

chief
▷ NOUN
1 the leader of a group or organization: *the chief of the fire department*
boss *He cannot stand his boss.*
chieftain *the legendary British chieftain, King Arthur*
director *the financial director of the company*
head *heads of government from 100 countries*
leader *the leader of the Conservative Party*
manager *a retired bank manager*
warden *The incident was reported to the prison warden.*
▷ ADJECTIVE
2 most important: *The job went to one of her chief rivals.*
foremost *one of the world's foremost scholars of ancient Mexican culture*
key *He is expected to be the key witness at the trial.*
main *one of the main tourist areas of Montréal*
prevailing *the prevailing attitude toward women in this society*
primary *Your health is my primary concern.*
prime *The police will see me as the prime suspect!*
principal *What is the principal reason for your change of mind?*
See also **boss, first, foremost, head, leader, leading, main, prime, principal, supreme, top**

chiefly *See* **mainly**

chieftain *See* **chief**

child
▷ NOUN
a young person: *I lived in Manitoba as a child.*
baby *She took care of me when I was a baby.*
infant *young parents with infants in strollers*
juvenile *a court for juveniles*
kid INFORMAL *They've got three kids.*
minor *charged with selling cigarettes to minors*
offspring *parents choosing shoes for their offspring*
toddler *The toddler just started walking by himself.*
tot *The tot was too young to know what was happening.*

youngster *I was only a youngster when she was born.*
ANTONYM **adult**
See also **baby**

childish

▷ *ADJECTIVE*
immature and foolish: *I don't have time for this childish behaviour.*
immature *He is emotionally immature.*
infantile *infantile jokes*
juvenile *juvenile behaviour*
puerile *a puerile sense of humour*
ANTONYM **mature**

childlike *See* **innocent**

CONFUSABLES

Childish means **immature**, like a child.
Childlike means **innocent**, like a child.

---

chill *See* **cool**

chilled *See* **cool, frozen**

chilling *See* **scary**

chilly *See* **cold, cool**

chime *See* **ring, sound**

chink *See* **gap, leak, opening**

chirpy *See* **cheery**

chisel *See* **carve**

choice

▷ *NOUN*
1 a range of things to choose from: *available in a choice of colours*
range *a range of dairy products*
selection *an interesting selection of recipes*
variety *a variety of candidates from which to choose*
2 the power to choose: *They had little choice in the matter.*
alternative *He said he could not see any alternative.*
option *He was given the option of going to jail or paying a fine.*
say *We don't have a say in the company's decisions.*
See also **prime, select, superior, will**

choke *See* **block, gasp, obstruct**

choose

▷ *VERB*
to decide to have or do something: *a number of foods from which to choose*
opt for *He opted for early retirement.*
pick *She was picked for the debating team.*

select *She paused to select another cookie from the box.*
take *She took the option they offered to her.*
See also **decide, determine, pick, select**

choosy *See* **fussy, particular**

chop

▷ *VERB*
to cut down or into pieces: *I heard him chopping wood in the yard.*
cut *Cut the vegetables up.*
fell *A large number of trees are felled each year.*
hack *They hacked away at the undergrowth.*
lop *Somebody had lopped the heads off our tulips.*

chore *See* **task, work**

chortle *See* **laugh**

christen *See* **name**

chubby *See* **plump**

chuck *See* **throw**

chuckle *See* **laugh**

chunk *See* **block, lump, piece, portion**

chunky *See* **stocky**

chutzpah *See* **impudence**

circle *See* **club, company, ring, society**

circular *See* **leaflet, round**

circulate

▷ *VERB*
to pass around: *He circulated rumours about everyone.*
distribute *distributing leaflets*
propagate *They propagated their political ideas.*
spread *spreading malicious gossip*
See also **distribute, flow, spread**

circumstance *See* **event, incident**

circumstances *See* **situation, state**

citadel *See* **fort**

cite *See* **accuse, quote, refer**

citizen *See* **inhabitant**

citizens *See* **people**

city

▷ *NOUN*
a large urban community: *the city of Regina*
metropolis *a busy metropolis*
municipality *a sprawling municipality*
town *the oldest town in the province*

civic *See* **public**

civil *See* **polite**

civility *See* **courtesy, politeness**

civilization *See* **society**

civilized

▷ ADJECTIVE
having an advanced society: *a highly civilized society*
cultured *a cultured environment*
enlightened *this enlightened century*
See also **refined**

claim

▷ VERB
1 to say something is the case: *He claims to have lived here all his life.*
allege *He is alleged to have killed someone.*
assert *The defendants continued to assert their innocence.*
hold *She holds that these requirements are unnecessary.*
insist *They insisted that they had no money.*
maintain *I still maintain that I am not guilty.*
profess *She professed to know nothing about the incident.*
▷ NOUN
2 a statement that something is the case: *He rejected claims that he had taken bribes.*
allegation *allegations of theft*
assertion *his assertion that he did not plan to remarry*
See also **argue**

clamber *See* **climb**

clammy *See* **damp, humid**

clamour *See* **racket**

clandestine *See* **private**

clang *See* **ring, sound**

clarification *See* **explanation**

clash

▷ VERB
1 to fight or argue with another person: *A group of 400 demonstrators clashed with police.*
battle *Conservationists battled with the developers.*
fight *two rival gangs fighting in the streets*
quarrel *My brother quarrelled with his best friend.*
wrangle *Delegates wrangled over the future of the organization.*
2 of two things: to be so different that they do not go together: *Their decisions clashed with company policy.*
conflict *She held opinions that sometimes*

conflicted with my own.
contradict *Cutbacks like these contradict the government's commitment to education.*
differ *The two leaders differed on several issues.*
disagree *Our managers disagreed on several matters.*
go against *Changes are being made that go against my principles.*
jar *They had always been good together, and their temperaments seldom jarred.*
▷ NOUN
3 a fight or argument: *a number of clashes between rival parties*
battle *the battle on the Plains of Abraham*
conflict *attempts to prevent a conflict between workers and management*
confrontation *This issue could lead to a military confrontation.*
fight *I broke up the fight between the children.*
skirmish INFORMAL *Border skirmishes between the two countries were common.*
squabble *There have been minor squabbles between the neighbours.*
struggle *a struggle between good and evil forces*
See also **argument, conflict, crash, dispute, game, quarrel, war**

clasp

▷ VERB
1 to hold someone or something tightly: *I clasped the winning ticket tightly.*
clutch *She was clutching a photograph.*
embrace *People were crying for joy and embracing each other.*
grip *He gripped her hand when they were introduced.*
hold *He carefully held the two cups of coffee.*
hug *She hugged him tenderly.*
press *I pressed the child closer to my chest.*
squeeze *They squeezed hands.*
▷ NOUN
2 a fastening such as a hook or catch: *She undid the clasp of her necklace.*
buckle *He wore a belt with a large brass buckle.*
catch *She fiddled with the catch of her briefcase.*
clip *She took the clip out of her hair.*
fastener *nails, screws, and various other fasteners*
fastening *The fastening on this bracelet is difficult to open.*
See also **catch, grasp, grip, hold, hug**

class

▷ *NOUN*

1 a group of a particular type: *a new class of SUV*

category *different categories of movies*
genre *books of the horror genre*
grade *the lowest grade of apple*
group *a plan to help people in this group*
kind *the biggest prize of its kind in the world*
set *The celebrity set all go to this restaurant.*
sort *several articles of this sort*
type *various types of vegetables*

▷ *VERB*

2 to regard as being in a particular group: *He is classed as a comedian.*

categorize *Her books are hard to categorize.*
classify *Rhubarb is classified as a vegetable.*
designate *The house is designated as a national monument.*
grade *This ski run is graded as easy.*
rank *She is ranked in the world's top 50 players.*
rate *He rates the film highly.*

See also **category, family, form, grade, group, kind, lesson, polish, range, rank, rate, sort, type, variety**

classes See course

classic See ideal, simple

classification See category, family, kind

classify

▷ *VERB*

to arrange similar things in groups: *We can classify frogs according to family.*

arrange *Arrange the books in neat piles.*
categorize *This movie is hard to categorize.*
grade *musical pieces graded according to difficulty*
rank *ranked among Canada's wealthiest families*
sort *sorting the computer files into folders*
See also **arrange, class, grade, group, sort**

classy See exclusive, posh

clay See earth, soil

clean

▷ *ADJECTIVE*

1 free from dirt or marks: *clean shoes*
immaculate *immaculate white sheets*
impeccable *dressed in an impeccable manner*
laundered *freshly laundered shirts*

spotless *The kitchen was spotless.*
washed *newly washed hair*
ANTONYM **dirty**

2 free from germs or infection: *a lack of clean water and sanitation*
antiseptic *an antiseptic hospital room*
hygienic *a hygienic kitchen*
purified *Only purified water is used.*
sterilized *a sterilized bottle for the baby*
uncontaminated *uncontaminated air*
unpolluted *unpolluted beaches*
ANTONYM **contaminated**

▷ *VERB*

3 to remove dirt from: *We cleaned the house from top to bottom.*
cleanse *a lotion to cleanse the skin*
dust *I dusted the furniture.*
scour *He scoured the sink.*
scrub *I started to scrub off the dirt.*
sponge *Sponge the counter.*
swab *The janitor was swabbing the floor.*
wash *He got a job washing dishes in a restaurant.*
wipe *He wiped the perspiration from his face.*
ANTONYM **soil**
See also **blank, pure, simple**

cleanliness See hygiene

cleanse See clean, wash

clear

▷ *ADJECTIVE*

1 easy to see or understand: *He made it clear that he did not want to talk.*
apparent *There is no apparent reason for the crime.*
blatant *a blatant piece of cheating*
conspicuous *one conspicuous difference*
definite *a definite advantage*
evident *He ate with evident enjoyment.*
explicit *He was very explicit about his intentions.*
manifest *his manifest dislike of authority figures*
obvious *There are obvious dangers.*
palpable *The tension between them was palpable.*
plain *The results are plain to see.*
unequivocal *She gave me an unequivocal answer.*

2 easy to see through: *a clear liquid*
crystalline *crystalline green waters*
glassy *The water was a deep glassy blue.*
translucent *I can see only shapes through the translucent glass.*
transparent *transparent glass walls*
ANTONYM **cloudy**

▷ *VERB*

3 to prove someone is not guilty: *She was cleared of all suspicion.*
absolve *He was absolved of all charges.*
acquit *acquitted of disorderly conduct*
ANTONYM **convict**
See also **blank, certain, definite, empty, evident, innocent, jump, manifest, obvious, plain, positive, sure, transparent, visible**

clear up *See* **resolve, settle, solve**

clear-cut *See* **positive**

cleft *See* **crack, fissure, opening**

clever
▷ *ADJECTIVE*
very intelligent: *Today's contestants are all quite clever.*
brainy INFORMAL *I don't consider myself to be especially brainy.*
bright *an exceptionally bright child*
intelligent *Dolphins are intelligent.*
shrewd *a shrewd businessperson*
smart *a very smart move*
See also **astute, bright, brilliant, intelligent, smart, witty**

cleverness *See* **intelligence**

clichéd *See* **hackneyed**

client *See* **customer**

climax *See* **peak**

climb
▷ *VERB*
to move upward over something: *Climbing the first hill took half an hour.*
ascend *He ascended the ladder into the loft.*
clamber *They clambered up the stone walls.*
mount *He mounted the steps.*
scale *the first person to scale Mount Everest*
See also **rise**

climb to *See* **reach**

clinch *See* **hug**

cling *See* **stick**

clip *See* **catch, clasp**

clique *See* **party, ring**

cloak *See* **cover, obscure**

clog *See* **block, obstruct**

C

close
▷ *VERB*
1 to shut something: *Close the gate behind you.*
secure *The shed was secured by a padlock.*
shut *Someone had forgotten to shut the door.*
ANTONYM **open**
2 to block so that nothing can pass: *The northbound road is closed due to an accident.*
bar *Protesters barred the way to his car.*
block *The road was blocked by garbage.*
obstruct *The parade obstructed traffic.*
seal *Soldiers had sealed the border.*
▷ *ADJECTIVE*
3 near to something: *a restaurant close to their home*
ANTONYM **distant**
▷ *ADJECTIVE*
4 friendly and loving: *We became close friends.*
ANTONYM **distant**
See WORD STUDY **close** on next page
See also **alike, conclude, conclusion, finish, friendly, halt, handy, immediate, imminent, near, shut, stuffy**

close to *See* **almost, beside, near**

closed *See* **shut**

closely *See* **immediately, well**

closeness *See* **friendship**

closest *See* **next**

closet *See* **secret**

closing *See* **final, last**

clot *See* **thicken**

cloth
▷ *NOUN*
woven or knitted fabric: *a piece of red cloth*
fabric *waterproof fabric*
material *This material shrinks badly.*
textiles *silk, cotton, linen, and other textiles*
See also **material**

clothe *See* **dress**

clothes
▷ *PLURAL NOUN*
the things people wear: *They spend too much money on clothes.*
attire *formal attire*
clothing *men's clothing*
costume *national costume*
dress *traditional dress*
garments *winter garments*

Close is another overused word. Depending on whether you are talking about people or things that are close (in distance or in time), the closeness of personal relationships, a closeness in resemblance between two things, or you are referring to a description or translation, you can use various other words as substitutes.

• in distance
Don't worry, help is **at hand**.
The fire spread to **adjacent** buildings.
The smell of hamburgers from the **adjoining** yard was making us feel hungry.
Keep a pencil and paper **handy**.
The bus stop is quite **near**.
I dashed into a **nearby** store.
Who was sitting at the **neighbouring** table?

• in relationship
We've become very **attached** to one another over the years.
His dog was a **dear** companion to him.
My parents are a deeply **devoted** couple.
I don't like people who try to get too **familiar**.
We gradually became very **friendly**.
You are one of my most **intimate** friends.
They forged a **loving** relationship.

• in time
My birthday is **approaching**.
The time is **at hand** when we must take action.
Sunrise is **coming**.

They now reckon a deal is **imminent**.
I feel a sense of **impending** disaster.
The day of reckoning is **near**.

• of a resemblance
This vehicle has a **distinct** resemblance to a lunar buggy.
There is a **marked** similarity between him and his brother.
We need to use a metal with **pronounced** similarities to copper.
What is the name of a prehistoric animal that bore a **strong** resemblance to a horse?

• of a description or translation
She gave an **accurate** description of her attacker.
I can't give an **exact** translation of the phrase.
He gave a **faithful** rendition of the classic song.
You should begin with a **literal** interpretation of the words.
Specify your requirements in **precise** detail.
The witness gave a **strict** account of the events.

---

gear INFORMAL *trendy gear*
outfit *a stunning scarlet outfit*
wardrobe *next summer's wardrobe*
wear *evening wear*
See also **dress**

clothing See **clothes, dress**

clotted See **thick**

cloud
▷ NOUN
1 a mass of vapour or smoke: *The sky was dark with clouds.*
billow *Smoke billowed from the engine.*
fog *fog over Lake Louise*
haze *a haze of exhaust fumes*
mist *The valley was wrapped in thick mist.*
vapour *warm vapour rising from the ground*
▷ VERB
2 to make something confusing: *Anger has clouded his judgment.*
confuse *You're just confusing the story by bringing my friends into it.*

distort *a distorted memory*
muddle *The question muddles up two separate matters.*
See also **obscure**

cloudy
▷ ADJECTIVE
1 full of clouds: *a cloudy sky*
dull *It's always dull and wet here.*
gloomy *gloomy weather*
leaden *leaden skies*
overcast *a damp, overcast morning*
ANTONYM **clear**
2 difficult to see through: *a glass of cloudy liquid*
muddy *a muddy pond*
murky *murky waters*
opaque *an opaque glass jar*
ANTONYM **clear**
See also **dark, dull**

clout See **bang, blow**

cloying See **sweet**

club

▷ NOUN

1 an organization for people with a special interest: *a swimming club*
association *the Canadian Library Association*
circle *a local painting circle*
group *an environmental group*
guild *the Guild of Canadian Film Composers*
society *a historical society*
union *the Canadian Union of Public Employees*
2 a heavy stick: *pictures of cave dwellers armed with clubs*
bat *a baseball bat*
stick *a hockey stick*

▷ VERB

3 to hit with a heavy object: *Two thugs clubbed him with baseball bats.*
bash *He bashed his forehead when he tripped and fell.*
batter *An enormous wave battered the ship.*
beat *beaten with bare fists*
bludgeon *The victim had been brutally bludgeoned.*
See also **association, fellowship, society**

clue   See **hint, idea, indication, lead, sign**

clumsiness

▷ NOUN

awkwardness of movement: *The accident was entirely the result of his own clumsiness.*
awkwardness *They moved with the awkwardness of robots.*
ungainliness *physical ungainliness*

clumsy

▷ ADJECTIVE

moving awkwardly: *He is big and clumsy in his movements.*
awkward *an awkward gesture*
gauche *He tries to make me feel uneducated and gauche.*
lumbering *a big, lumbering man*
uncoordinated *an uncoordinated dancer*
ungainly *As an adolescent, he was lanky and ungainly.*
ANTONYM **graceful**

cluster   See **bunch**

clutch   See **clasp, grab, grasp, grip, hold**

clutches   See **grip**

clutter   See **disorder, junk**

cluttered   See **untidy**

coach   See **instruct, teach, teacher, train**

coaching   See **education, lesson**

coalition   See **party, union**

coarse   See **common, crude, vulgar**

coast

▷ NOUN

the land next to a sea or ocean: *a holiday by the coast*
beach *a beautiful sandy beach*
border *the border of Lake Superior*
coastline *the stunning coastline of the Gaspé Peninsula*
seaside *a day at the seaside*
shore *a bleak and rocky shore*
See also **beach**

coastline   See **coast**

coat

▷ NOUN

an animal's fur or hair: *She gave the dog's coat a brush.*
fleece *a blanket of lamb's fleece*
fur *a kitten with black fur*
hair *He's allergic to cat hair.*
hide *rhino hide*
pelt *a wolf pelt*
skin *convicted of attempting to sell the skin of an endangered animal*
wool *Lanolin comes from sheep's wool.*
See also **coating, cover, layer, spread**

coating

▷ NOUN

a layer of something: *a thin coating of ice*
coat *a coat of paint*
covering *a covering of dust*
layer *a layer of dead leaves*
See also **cover, layer**

coax

▷ VERB

to persuade gently: *We coaxed her into coming with us.*
cajole *Her sister cajoled her into playing euchre.*
persuade *My cousin persuaded me to visit.*
talk into *They've talked him into getting a new car.*
See also **persuade, prompt**

cocky

▷ ADJECTIVE

too self-confident: *He was a bit cocky because he was winning all the time.*
arrogant *an air of arrogant indifference*
brash *On stage, the actors appeared hard and brash.*
conceited *I thought him conceited.*
overconfident *The overconfident actor*

missed his cue and forgot his lines.
See also **boastful, conceited**

code   *See* **convention, law**

coil
▷ *VERB*
to wind in loops: *a coiled spring*
curl *dark, curling hair*
loop *A rope was looped between his hands.*
spiral *vines spiralling up toward the roof*
twine *This lily produces twining stems.*
twist *She twisted her hair into a bun.*
wind *winding the thread around the spool*

coin   *See* **create, invent**

coincide   *See* **correspond**

coincidence   *See* **chance**

cold
▷ *ADJECTIVE*
1 having a low temperature: *the coldest winter in ten years*
arctic *arctic conditions*
biting *a biting wind*
bitter *driven inside by the bitter cold*
bleak *The weather can be bleak on the coast.*
chilly *It's chilly for June.*
freezing *This house is freezing!*
icy *the icy north wind*
raw *a raw December morning*
wintry *wintry showers*
ANTONYM **hot**
2 not showing affection: *a cold, unfeeling individual*
aloof *He seemed aloof and detached.*
distant *She was polite but distant.*
frigid *a frigid smile*
lukewarm *a lukewarm response*
reserved *emotionally reserved*
stony *He gave me a stony look.*
ANTONYM **warm**
See also **callous, cool, impersonal, remote, stiff, unfriendly**

INFORMALLY SPEAKING

cold feet: loss of nerve or courage
out cold: unconscious
out in the cold: alone or neglected

cold-blooded   *See* **cruel**

collaborate   *See* **cooperate, team, unite**

collapse
▷ *VERB*
1 to fall down: *The whole building is about to collapse.*

fall down *The ceiling fell down.*
give way *The bridge gave way beneath him.*
2 to fail: *Thousands of small businesses collapsed last year.*
fail *His software business has failed.*
fold *We were laid off when the company folded.*
founder *a foundering radio station*
▷ *NOUN*
3 the failure of something: *the collapse of their marriage*
downfall *the downfall of the government*
failure *the failure of their business empire*
See also **crash, downfall, faint, fall, give**

colleague
▷ *NOUN*
a person someone works with: *I'll have to consult my colleagues.*
associate *business associates*
fellow worker *I get along well with my fellow workers.*
partner *her business partner*
workmate *the nickname his workmates gave him*
See also **assistant, associate**

collect
▷ *VERB*
to gather together: *collecting signatures for a petition*
accumulate *Most children enjoy accumulating knowledge.*
assemble *trying to assemble a team*
gather *gathering information*
raise *We are raising money for the school play.*
ANTONYM **scatter**
See also **assemble, concentrate, gather, stockpile**

collected   *See* **calm, cool**

collection
▷ *NOUN*
a group of things collected together: *my CD collection*
assortment *an assortment of candy*
group *a group of songs*
store *a vast store of knowledge*
See also **group, number, variety**

collectively   *See* **together**

collide   *See* **bump, crash**

collide with   *See* **hit**

collision   *See* **crash**

colloquial
▷ *ADJECTIVE*
used in conversation: *a colloquial expression*

conversational *a conversational style*
everyday *He used plain, everyday English.*
informal *an informal expression*
See also **informal**

colony

▷ *NOUN*

I a land controlled by another country: *a former British colony*
dependency *Greenland is a Danish dependency*
dominion *The Constitution Act, 1867 established the Dominion of Canada.*
territory *Canada's provinces and territories*
2 a collected group of people in a place: *an artists' colony*
community *the British community in Canada*
outpost *a remote outpost*
settlement *an isolated settlement*

colossal

▷ *ADJECTIVE*

very large: *a colossal statue*
enormous *The main bedroom is enormous.*
gigantic *a gigantic task*
huge *They are making huge profits.*
immense *an immense cloud of smoke*
mammoth *This mammoth undertaking was completed in 18 months.*
massive *a massive steamboat*
vast *farmers who own vast stretches of land*
ANTONYM **tiny**
See also **enormous, huge, immense, large, unbelievable, vast**

colour

▷ *NOUN*

I a shade or hue: *Her favourite colour is blue.*
hue *delicate pastel hues*
pigmentation *skin pigmentation*
shade *walls painted in two shades of green*
tint *a distinct orange tint*
2 a substance used to give colour: *food colour*
dye *hair dye*
paint *a can of red paint*
pigment *a layer of blue pigment*
▷ *VERB*
3 to give something a colour: *men and women who colour their hair*
dye *She dyed the shoes to match her dress.*
paint *She paints her toenails red.*
stain *Some foods can stain the teeth.*
tint *tinted glass*
▷ *VERB*
4 to affect the way you think: *The experience coloured his opinion of lawyers.*
bias *a biased opinion*
distort *The newspaper article distorted*

some of the facts of the matter.
prejudice *His rough speech prejudiced people against him.*
slant *deliberately slanted news coverage*
See also **blush**

colourful

▷ *ADJECTIVE*

I full of colour: *colourful clothes*
bright *a bright green dress*
brilliant *brilliant wild flowers throughout the field*
intense *an intense shade of blue*
jazzy INFORMAL *a jazzy new tie*
rich *a rich blue glass bowl*
vibrant *vibrant orange shades*
vivid *vivid hues*
ANTONYM **dull**
2 interesting or exciting: *a colourful character*
graphic *a graphic account of his career*
interesting *She has led an interesting life.*
lively *a lively imagination*
rich *the rich history of the island*
vivid *a vivid description*
ANTONYM **dull**

colourless See **pale**

column See **feature, line, rank, row**

comb See **search**

combat See **conflict, fight, war**

combination

▷ *NOUN*

a mixture of things: *a combination of charm and skill*
amalgamation *an amalgamation of two organizations*
blend *The play is a blend of comedy and drama.*
mix *a mix of fantasy and reality*
mixture *a mixture of horror, envy, and awe*
See also **blend, cross, mixture, union**

combine

▷ *VERB*

to join or mix together: *trying to combine business with pleasure*
amalgamate *a plan to amalgamate the two communities*
blend *The band blends jazz and rock music.*
fuse *a performer who fuses magic and dance*
integrate *integrating various styles of art*
merge *The two leagues have merged into one.*
mix *mixing business with pleasure*

unite *people uniting to fight racism*
ANTONYM **separate**
See also **blend, mix, unite**

combustion *See* **fire**

come
▷ *VERB*

1 to move or arrive somewhere: *Two young children came into the room.*
appear *He appeared out of nowhere.*
arrive *My brother has just arrived.*
enter *The class fell silent as the teacher entered.*
materialize *The car seemed to materialize from nowhere.*
show up INFORMAL *He showed up more than an hour late.*
turn up INFORMAL *I'll call you when she turns up.*
2 to happen or take place: *It's too bad that birthdays come only once a year.*
fall *Canada Day falls on a Thursday this year.*
happen *Nothing ever happens on a Sunday.*
occur *How did the accident occur?*
take place *The meeting never took place.*

come about *See* **happen, take place**

come across *See* **discover, find, meet**

come after *See* **follow**

come apart *See* **split**

come back *See* **return**

come between *See* **divide**

come first *See* **win**

come on *See* **flourish**

come out *See* **appear**

come to *See* **cost, total, wake**

come together *See* **assemble**

come up with *See* **invent**

come upon *See* **meet**

come with *See* **accompany**

comedy *See* **humour, play**

comfort
▷ *NOUN*

1 a state of ease: *I settled back in comfort.*
ease *a life of ease*
luxury *brought up in an atmosphere of luxury*
well-being *a wonderful sense of well-being*
2 relief from worry or unhappiness: *Her words gave him some comfort.*
consolation *He knew he was right, but it was no consolation.*
help *Just talking to you has been a great help.*
relief *temporary relief from the pain*
satisfaction *At least I have the satisfaction of knowing I tried.*
support *His relatives were a great support to him.*
▷ *VERB*

3 to give someone comfort: *trying to comfort the upset child*
cheer *The thought did nothing to cheer him.*
console *"Never mind," he consoled me.*
reassure *He did his best to reassure her.*
soothe *I soothed the frightened dog by petting him gently.*
See also **reassure**

comfortable
▷ *ADJECTIVE*

1 physically relaxing: *a comfortable chair*
cosy *a cosy living room*
easy *You've had an easy time of it.*
homey *a homey atmosphere*
relaxing *a relaxing holiday*
restful *a restful scene*
ANTONYM **uncomfortable**
2 feeling at ease: *I don't feel comfortable around him.*
at ease *He is not at ease in fancy restaurants.*
at home *We soon felt quite at home.*
contented *a contented life*
happy *I'm not very happy with that idea.*
relaxed *a relaxed attitude*
ANTONYM **uneasy**
See also **cosy, easy, leisurely, relaxed, wealthy**

comic *See* **funny**

comical *See* **funny, hysterical**

coming *See* **appearance, future, imminent**

command
▷ *VERB*

1 to order someone to do something: *I commanded the dog to lie down.*
bid FORMAL *The soldiers bade them to turn and go back.*
demand *They demanded that he leave.*
direct *His doctor has directed him to rest.*
order *The soldiers were ordered to cease fire.*
2 to be in charge of: *the general who commanded the UN troops*
control *She now controls the whole company.*
head *Who heads the firm?*

lead *William Lyon Mackenzie led Canada during World War II.*
manage *I manage a small team of workers.*
supervise *She supervised more than 400 volunteers.*
▷ NOUN
3 an order to do something: *The order was carried out at the emperor's command.*
bidding *They refused to leave at his bidding.*
decree *an official decree*
directive *a government directive*
injunction *A court injunction kept the protesters away from the building.*
instruction *They were just following instructions.*
order *I don't take orders from you.*
▷ NOUN
4 knowledge and ability: *a good command of English*
grasp *a good grasp of mathematics*
knowledge *He has no knowledge of law.*
mastery *a mastery of grammar*
See also **administer, control, direction, exact, instruct, lead, manage, order, tell**

commander See **leader, ruler**

commanding See **powerful**

commemorate
▷ VERB
to do something in memory of, or in honour of: *concerts to commemorate the anniversary of his birth*
celebrate *celebrating their wedding anniversary*
honour *celebrations to honour his memory*
See also **celebrate, honour**

commence See **begin, start**

commencement See **beginning, opening, start**

commend See **honour**

commendation See **credit, honour, praise**

comment
▷ VERB
1 to make a remark: *He refused to comment on the rumours.*
mention *I mentioned that I didn't like jazz.*
note *He noted that some issues remained to be settled.*
observe *"You're very pale," he observed.*
point out *I should point out that these figures are approximate.*
remark *Everyone had remarked on my new hairstyle.*
say *"Well done," she said.*

▷ NOUN
2 something you say: *sarcastic comments*
observation *a few general observations*
remark *snide remarks*
statement *That statement puzzled me.*
See also **observe, remark, word**

commentary See **review**

commerce See **business, finance, trade**

commercial See **advertisement, economic**

commission See **employ, hire**

commit
▷ VERB
to do something: *A crime has been committed.*
carry out *The work was carried out by a team of experts.*
do *They have done a lot of damage.*
perform *people who have performed acts of bravery*
perpetrate *A fraud has been perpetrated.*

committed See **fervent**

committee See **council**

commodity See **product**

common
▷ ADJECTIVE
1 of many people: *a common complaint*
general *the general opinion*
popular *a popular belief*
prevailing *The prevailing mood is not a happy one.*
prevalent *the kind of loyalty prevalent among old friends*
universal *The desire to feel well is universal.*
widespread *widespread support*
ANTONYM **rare**
2 not special: *the common cold*
average *the average teenager*
commonplace *a commonplace observation*
everyday *your everyday routine*
ordinary *an ordinary day*
plain *a plain doughnut*
standard *standard practice*
usual *My usual practice is to turn on the computer after dinner.*
3 having bad taste or manners: *a common, rude guest*
coarse *coarse humour*
rude *It's rude to stare.*
vulgar *vulgar remarks*
ANTONYM **refined**

C

See also **everyday, frequent, general, low, natural, popular, universal, usual, vulgar, widespread**

commonplace See **common**

common sense
▷ NOUN
the ability to make good judgments: *Use your common sense.*
good sense *He had the good sense to call me at once.*
judgment *I respect your judgment.*
level-headedness *He prides himself on his level-headedness.*
prudence *His lack of prudence led to financial problems.*
See also **head, sense**

commotion See **bustle, excitement, fuss, noise, racket**

communal See **public**

communicate
▷ VERB
1 to be in touch with someone: *We communicate mainly by e-mail.*
be in contact *I'll be in contact with him next week.*
be in touch *She hasn't been in touch with me yet.*
correspond *We correspond regularly.*
2 to pass on information: *The results will be communicated by mail.*
convey *They have conveyed their views to the government.*
impart *the ability to impart knowledge*
inform *Will you inform me of any changes?*
pass on *I'll pass on your good wishes.*
spread *She has spread the news to everyone.*
transmit *He transmitted the information over the Internet.*
See also **convey, express**

communicate with See **contact**

communication See **contact, message, note, word**

communicative See **talkative**

community See **colony, company, local, public**

companion
▷ NOUN
someone you travel with or spend time with: *They've been constant companions for the past six years.*
comrade *Unlike so many of his comrades, he survived the war.*

crony *He played pool with his cronies.*
friend *A group of friends spent a week at the cottage.*
pal INFORMAL *We've been pals for years.*
partner *a partner in crime*
See also **friend, partner**

companionship See **company, fellowship**

company
▷ NOUN
1 a business: *a publishing company*
business *a family business*
corporation *one of Canada's largest corporations*
establishment *a commercial establishment*
firm *a firm of engineers*
house *the world's top fashion houses*
2 a group of people: *the Canadian Opera Company*
assembly *an assembly of citizens*
band *a band of thieves*
circle *a large circle of friends*
community *the local business community*
crowd *That's not my type of crowd.*
ensemble *an ensemble of young musicians*
group *an environmental group*
party *a party of sightseers*
troupe *a troupe of actors*
3 the act of spending time with someone: *I could do with some company.*
companionship *He keeps a dog for companionship.*
presence *Your presence is not welcome here.*
See also **association, band, body, business, enterprise, firm, organization**

comparable See **similar**

compare
▷ VERB
to look at things for similarities or differences: *Compare these two illustrations.*
contrast *Contrast these very different works of art.*
juxtapose *a traditional style juxtaposed with a contemporary one*
weigh *She weighed her options.*

compartment
▷ NOUN
1 a section of a railway car: *We shared our compartment with a group of tourists.*
car *a crowded subway car*
2 one of the separate parts of an object: *the freezer compartment of the fridge*
bay *the cargo bays of an aircraft*
chamber *the chambers of the heart*

division *Each league was further split into several divisions.*

section *a toolbox with sections for various items*

compassion *See* **kindness, mercy, pity, sympathy**

compassionate
▷ *ADJECTIVE*

feeling or showing sympathy and pity for others: *My father is a deeply compassionate man.*

caring *a lovely child, very gentle and caring*

empathetic *She was empathetic and understood exactly how I felt.*

humane *She began to campaign for the humane treatment of animals.*

kind *Thank you for being so kind to me.*

kind-hearted *a warm, generous, and kind-hearted person*

merciful *a merciful judge*

sympathetic *She was very sympathetic to their problems.*

tender *Her voice was tender and reassuring.*

See also **benevolent, humane, kind, merciful, tender, understanding**

compassionately *See* **well**

compatible
▷ *ADJECTIVE*

going together: *Business partners should be compatible.*

congenial *congenial company*

consistent *injuries consistent with a car crash*

harmonious *a harmonious partnership*

in keeping *This behaviour was in keeping with his character.*

ANTONYM **incompatible**

compel *See* **drive, force, make, require**

compelling *See* **interesting, powerful, urgent**

compensate
▷ *VERB*

I to repay someone for loss or damage: *You will be properly compensated for your loss.*

atone *to atone for his wrongdoings*

refund *The company will refund the full cost.*

repay *The company repaid the money to all the unsatisfied customers.*

reward *Their patience was finally rewarded.*

2 to cancel out: *His lack of skill was compensated for by his enthusiasm.*

balance *The pros balance the cons.*

cancel out *The two influences cancel each other out.*

counteract *pills to counteract high blood pressure*

make up for *I'll make up for what I've done.*

offset *The loss is being offset by a new tax.*

See also **pay**

C

compensation
▷ *NOUN*

something that makes up for loss or damage: *compensation for his injuries*

amends *an attempt to make amends for the crime*

atonement *atonement for one's sins*

damages *damages for libel*

payment *The employees who lost their jobs each received a generous severance payment.*

compete
▷ *VERB*

to try to win: *companies competing for business*

contend *two teams contending for the cup*

contest *the candidates contesting the election*

fight *rivals fighting for first place*

vie *The contestants vied to finish first.*

See also **play**

competence *See* **ability, skill**

competent *See* **capable, efficient, proficient, skilful, skilled**

competently *See* **well**

competition
▷ *NOUN*

I an attempt to win: *There's a lot of competition for this year's Gemini Awards.*

contention *I'm in contention for the gold medal.*

contest *the trivia contest*

opposition *They are in direct opposition for the job.*

rivalry *the rivalry between the two leaders*

struggle *a power struggle*

2 a contest to find the winner in something: *a surfing competition*

championship *a swimming championship*

contest *a beauty contest*

event *major sporting events*

tournament *a judo tournament*

See also **competitor, contest, event, match**

competitive *See* **reasonable**

competitor
▷ *NOUN*

a person who competes for something: *one*

of the youngest competitors in the event
adversary *his political adversaries*
challenger *She's 20 seconds faster than the nearest challenger.*
competition *staying ahead of the competition*
contestant *contestants on the quiz show*
opponent *the best opponent I've played all season*
opposition *They can outplay the opposition.*
rival *a business rival*
See also **candidate**

complacent *See* **smug**

complain

▷ VERB

to express dissatisfaction: *They always complain about the noise.*
carp *Stop carping at me all the time.*
find fault *He's always finding fault with my work.*
grouse *You're always grousing about something.*
grumble *It's not in her nature to grumble.*
kick up a fuss INFORMAL *He kicks up a fuss when he doesn't get his own way.*
moan *moaning about the weather*
whine *whining children*
See also **grumble, moan, protest**

complaint

▷ NOUN

an instance of complaining about something: *There have been a number of complaints about the food.*
criticism *criticism that we don't get sufficient exercise*
grievance *They had a legitimate grievance against the company.*
grumble *Her main grumble is over the long hours she has to work.*
objection *I have no objections about the way I have been treated.*
protest *Despite our protests, they went ahead.*
See also **disorder, grumble, illness, protest**

complement *See* **augment, blend, foil, supplement**

complete

▷ ADJECTIVE

1 to the greatest degree possible: *a complete transformation*
absolute *absolute nonsense*
consummate *a consummate professional*
outright *an outright victory*
perfect *a perfect stranger*

thorough *a thorough snob*
total *a total failure*
utter *an utter shambles*
2 with nothing missing: *a complete set of tools*
entire *the entire plot*
full *a full report*
intact *the few buildings that have survived intact*
undivided *I want your undivided attention.*
whole *I told him the whole story.*
ANTONYM **incomplete**
▷ VERB
3 to finish: *He has just completed his first novel.*
conclude *The judge concluded her instructions to the jury.*
end *The crowd was in tears as she ended her speech.*
finish *I'll finish my report this week.*
See also **absolute, accomplish, achieve, finish, ideal, over, perfect, perform, pure, rank, sheer, thorough, total, utter, whole**

completely *See* **quite, well**

completion *See* **finish**

complex

▷ ADJECTIVE

1 having many different parts: *complex issues*
complicated *a very complicated voting system*
difficult *the difficult process of becoming a candidate*
intricate *intricate patterns*
involved *a long, involved explanation*
tangled *His personal life has become more tangled than ever.*
ANTONYM **simple**
▷ NOUN
2 an emotional problem: *I have never had a complex about my height.*
fixation *a fixation about cleanliness*
obsession *The majority of patients know their obsessions are irrational.*
phobia *The man had a phobia about flying.*
preoccupation *his total preoccupation with neatness*
problem *an emotional problem*
thing *He has a thing about eating outside.*
See also **complicated, elaborate, hard, obsession, sophisticated, tricky**

complicated

▷ ADJECTIVE

complex and difficult: *a complicated situation*
complex *a complex issue*
convoluted *a convoluted plot*

elaborate *an elaborate theory*
intricate *an intricate process*
involved *a long, involved explanation*
ANTONYM **simple**
See also **complex, confusing, elaborate, hard, sophisticated, tricky**

complication *See* **difficulty**

compliment *See* **flatter, tribute**

complimentary *See* **free**

comply *See* **follow, submit**

comply with *See* **obey**

component *See* **attachment, fitting, ingredient**

compose
▷ *VERB*
to create or write: *She has composed a symphony.*
create *She has created a new software program.*
devise *a play devised by the drama company*
invent *to invent a new art form*
produce *She has produced a book about the city.*
write *I've never been able to write poetry.*
See also **create, form, make up, write**

composed *See* **calm, cool, patient**

composition *See* **piece**

composure *See* **patience**

compound *See* **blend, mixture**

comprehend
▷ *VERB*
to understand or appreciate something: *I just cannot comprehend your attitude.*
appreciate *She has never really appreciated the enormity of the problem.*
fathom *I really couldn't fathom what he was talking about.*
grasp *The mayor has not yet grasped the seriousness of the crisis.*
see *I don't see why you're complaining.*
take in *I tried to explain, but I could tell they weren't taking it in.*
understand *They are too young to understand what's going on.*
work out *It took me some time to work out what was causing the problem.*
See also **know, read, realize, see, take in, understand**

comprehensible *See* **plain**

comprehension *See* **grasp, intelligence, understanding**

comprehensive *See* **broad, extensive, full, general, thorough**

compress *See* **press**

compressed *See* **firm**

comprise *See* **consist of, contain, make up**

compromise *See* **endanger**

compulsion *See* **force, urge**

compulsory
▷ *ADJECTIVE*
required by law: *School attendance is compulsory.*
mandatory *the mandatory retirement age*
obligatory *an obligatory final test*
required *the required reading for this course*
requisite *the requisite documents*
ANTONYM **voluntary**

comrade *See* **companion**

con
▷ *VERB*
1 to trick someone into doing or believing something: *He claimed that he'd been conned out of his life savings.*
cheat *a deliberate attempt to cheat employees out of their pensions*
deceive *She deceived herself into thinking that she was going to win.*
mislead *The reporter was not intentionally trying to mislead her readers.*
swindle *Investors were swindled out of millions of dollars.*
trick *They tricked him into parting with his life savings.*
▷ *NOUN*
2 a trick intended to mislead or disadvantage someone: *Snacks that offer miraculous weight loss are a con.*
bluff *The letter was a bluff.*
deception *You've been the victim of a rather cruel deception.*
fraud *victims of an online credit-card fraud*
scam *Seniors have been warned about the latest phone scam.*
swindle *a tax swindle*
trick *a cheap trick to encourage people to switch phone companies*
See also **cheat, deceive, dupe, fool, rob, take in, trick**

conceal *See* **cover, hide, obscure, suppress**

concealed *See* **invisible**

concede *See* **give in, grant**

conceit

▷ NOUN

excessive pride: *his insufferable conceit*
egotism *typical showbiz egotism*
pride *a blow to her pride*
self-importance *His air of self-importance is quite laughable.*
vanity *His preoccupation with his appearance is an act of pure vanity.*
See also **pride**

conceited

▷ ADJECTIVE

too proud: *She's smart and beautiful, but not conceited.*
bigheaded INFORMAL *a bigheaded baseball player who thinks the team revolves around him*
cocky *I was very cocky as a youngster.*
egotistical *an egotistical show-off*
self-important *self-important pop stars*
vain *a shallow, vain individual*
ANTONYM **modest**
See also **boastful, cocky, haughty, pretentious, smug, stuck-up, vain**

conceivable *See* **possible**

conceivably *See* **maybe, perhaps**

conceive *See* **imagine, invent**

conceive of *See* **picture**

concentrate

▷ VERB

1 to give something all your attention: *Concentrate on your studies.*
be engrossed in *He was engrossed in his work.*
focus your attention on *focusing her attention on the race*
give your attention to *I gave my attention to the question.*
put your mind to *You could do it if you put your mind to it.*
2 to be found in one place: *Condominiums are mostly concentrated in urban areas.*
accumulate *Cholesterol accumulates in the arteries.*
collect *dust collecting in the corners*
gather *Residents gathered at the neighbourhood meeting.*
See also **centre, essence, focus**

concentrated *See* **thick**

conception *See* **vision**

concern

▷ NOUN

1 a feeling of worry: *public concern about violence*
anxiety *anxiety about the economy*
apprehension *apprehension about the future*
disquiet *a growing sense of disquiet*
worry *She has no worries about his health.*
2 someone's duty or responsibility: *His private life is not my concern.*
affair *If you want to go, that's your affair.*
business *This is none of my business.*
responsibility *He's not my responsibility.*
▷ VERB

3 to make someone worried: *It concerns me that he doesn't want to go.*
bother *Nothing bothers me.*
distress *They are distressed by the accusations.*
disturb *disturbed by the news*
trouble *Is anything troubling you?*
worry *an issue that had worried him for some time*
▷ VERB

4 to affect or involve: *This concerns both of us.*
affect *the ways in which computers affect our lives*
apply to *This rule does not apply to us.*
be relevant to *These documents are relevant to the case.*
involve *meetings that involve most of the staff*
See also **anxiety, bother, care, consideration, enterprise, interest, issue, job, worry**

concerned *See* **anxious, worried**

concerning *See* **about**

concise

▷ ADJECTIVE

using no unnecessary words: *a concise guide*
brief *a brief description*
short *a short speech*
succinct *a succinct explanation*
terse *a terse statement*
ANTONYM **long**
See also **short**

conclude

▷ VERB

1 to decide something: *He concluded that she had been right.*
decide *I decided that it was time to leave.*
deduce *She deduced that I had written the letter.*
infer *His feelings were easily inferred from his reply.*
judge *The doctor judged that the athlete was*

not fit enough to play.

reckon INFORMAL *I reckon we should wait a while.*

suppose *There's no reason to suppose he'll be there.*

surmise *It is surmised that he must have known.*

2 to finish something: *He concluded the letter with a request.*

close *They closed the show with a song.*

end *Her speech ended on a happy note.*

finish *We finished the evening with a walk on the beach.*

round off *This butter tart rounded the meal off perfectly.*

wind up *She quickly wound up her conversation.*

ANTONYM **begin**

See also **complete, end, finish, gather, stop**

concluding See **final, last**

conclusion

▷ NOUN

1 a decision made after thinking carefully about something: *I've come to the conclusion that he was telling the truth.*

deduction *a shrewd deduction about what was going on*

inference *There were two inferences to be drawn from her letter.*

judgment *My judgment is that things are going to get worse.*

verdict *The doctor's verdict was that the patient was fine.*

2 the finish or ending of something: *the conclusion of the program*

close *bringing the talks to a close*

end *The speech is finally coming to an end.*

ending *a dramatic ending*

finish *the finish of the race*

termination *the termination of his employment*

ANTONYM **beginning**

See also **decision, finish, judgment, verdict**

conclusive See **convincing, final, positive**

concoct See **invent, make up**

concrete See **positive, real**

concur See **agree**

concur with See **accept**

concurrently See **together**

condemn

▷ VERB

1 to say that something is bad or

unacceptable: *He was condemned for his violent actions.*

blame *Some people blame television for the rise in violence.*

censure *a motion censuring the government*

criticize *She was criticized for her failure to act.*

damn *The report damns the government's handling of the crisis.*

denounce *denounced as a traitor*

2 to give a punishment: *condemned to life in prison*

doom *If you don't learn from your mistakes, you're doomed to repeat them.*

sentence *sentenced to ten years in prison*

See also **censure, criticize, disapprove**

condemnation See **censure, disapproval**

condemned See **doomed**

condense See **thicken**

condensed See **thick**

condescending See **superior**

condition

▷ NOUN

1 the state of something: *The house is in good condition.*

form *The comedian is in rare form tonight.*

shape *He's in great shape for his age.*

state *Look at the state of my car!*

2 something required for something else to be possible: *terms and conditions of the contract*

prerequisite *A science background is a prerequisite for the job.*

provision *a provision in his will forbidding the sale of the house*

proviso *The answer is yes, with one proviso.*

qualification *He agreed, but with some qualifications.*

requirement *The product meets all legal requirements.*

requisite *the main requisite for membership*

stipulation *The only dress stipulation was "no jeans."*

terms *the terms of the agreement*

See also **disorder, health, qualification, state**

conditions See **terms**

condone See **forgive**

conduct

▷ VERB

1 to carry out an activity or task: *to conduct*

a scientific experiment
carry out *carry out a survey*
direct *The new manager will direct day-to-day operations.*
do *I'm doing my homework right now.*
manage *his ability to manage the business*
organize *Her campaign was well organized.*
perform *Several skin grafts were performed during the operation.*
run *Each teacher will run a different workshop.*
▷ NOUN
2 the way someone behaves: *Other people judge you by your conduct.*
attitude *His attitude made me angry.*
behaviour *Make sure that good behaviour is rewarded.*
manners *He dressed well and had impeccable manners.*
ways *They urged him to alter his ways.*
See also **accompany, handle, lead, manner, take, way**

conduct yourself
▷ VERB
to behave in a particular way: *The way she conducts herself reflects on the school.*
act *He acted suspiciously before the surprise party.*
behave *He'd behaved badly.*

confectionery *See* **candy**

confederation *See* **association, body, organization, union**

confer with *See* **consult**

conference
▷ NOUN
a meeting for discussion: *a conference on education*
congress *the Canadian Labour Congress*
convention *The librarians' annual convention was held in Toronto.*
discussion *a round of formal discussions*
forum *a forum for trade negotiations*
meeting *a meeting of shareholders*
See also **convention, meeting**

confess
▷ VERB
to admit to something: *He confessed his love.*
acknowledge *He acknowledged that he was to blame.*
admit *I admit to feeling jealous.*
own up *The principal is waiting for someone to own up.*
ANTONYM **deny**

confession
▷ NOUN
the act of confessing: *a confession of her guilt*
acknowledgment *an acknowledgment of his mistakes*
admission *an admission of guilt*

confidant *See* **friend**

confidante *See* **friend**

confidence
▷ NOUN
1 a feeling of trust: *I have complete confidence in you.*
belief *his belief in his partner*
faith *He has great faith in her judgment.*
reliance *I don't put much reliance on that idea.*
trust *He destroyed my trust in people.*
ANTONYM **distrust**
2 sureness of yourself: *I've never had much confidence.*
aplomb *She handled the interview with aplomb.*
assurance *He led the orchestra with great assurance.*
self-assurance *his supreme self-assurance*
self-possession *an air of self-possession*
ANTONYM **shyness**
See also **belief, faith**

confident
▷ ADJECTIVE
1 sure about something: *confident of success*
certain *certain of getting a place on the team*
convinced *He is convinced it's your fault.*
positive *I'm positive it will happen.*
satisfied *We must be satisfied that the treatment is safe.*
secure *secure about his job prospects*
sure *I'm not sure I understand.*
ANTONYM **uncertain**
2 sure of yourself: *a confident attitude*
assured *His piano playing became more assured.*
self-assured *a self-assured young speaker*
self-possessed *a self-possessed young lawyer*
ANTONYM **shy**
See also **bold, certain, optimistic, positive, secure**

confidential *See* **private, secret**

confine
▷ VERB
1 to limit to something specified: *They confined themselves to talking about the weather.*
limit *I limit myself to three eggs a week.*

restrict *The patient was restricted to a salt-free diet.*
2 to prevent from leaving: *confined to bed for two days*
hem in *hemmed in by the surrounding crowd*
imprison *imprisoned in a tiny cell*
restrict *We were restricted to the building.*
shut up *He can't stand being shut up in the house.*
See also **imprison, limit, restrict**

confirm
▷ VERB
1 to say or show that something is true: *Police confirmed that they had received a call.*
bear out *The facts bear out his story.*
endorse *This theory has been endorsed by research.*
prove *The results prove his point.*
substantiate *no evidence to substantiate the claims*
validate *It is difficult to validate this belief.*
verify *I was asked to verify this statement.*
2 to make something definite: *Can we confirm the arrangements for tomorrow?*
fix *The date for the election was fixed.*
settle *I've settled on a time to see him.*
See also **determine, prove**

confirmation *See* proof

confiscate *See* seize

conflict
▷ NOUN
1 disagreement and argument: *conflict between workers and management*
antagonism *antagonism toward the other players*
disagreement *The meeting ended in disagreement.*
discord *public discord*
friction *friction between the rival players*
hostility *I sensed some hostility from the other students.*
opposition *a wave of opposition*
strife *a cause of strife in many marriages*
2 a war or battle: *the conflict in the Middle East*
battle *The enemies were engaged in a fierce battle.*
combat *We honour those who died in combat.*
fighting *Villagers have left their homes to avoid the fighting.*
strife *civil strife*
war *the war in Iraq*
▷ VERB
3 to differ or disagree: *conflicting ideas*
be at variance *His statements are at variance with the facts.*
be incompatible *These two principles are incompatible.*
clash *a decision that clashes with official policy*
differ *The two leaders differ on several issues.*
disagree *Governments disagree over the need for action.*
See also **clash, dispute, interfere, war**

conflicting *See* opposite

conform *See* agree, follow

conform to *See* suit

conformist *See* conventional

confrontation *See* clash

confuse
▷ VERB
1 to mix two things up: *confusing fact with fiction*
mistake *I mistook you for someone else.*
mix up *He sometimes mixes up his words.*
muddle up *I'm muddled up. Are you John or his twin brother?*
2 to puzzle or bewilder: *Politics confuse me.*
baffle *Police are baffled by the crime.*
bewilder *His silence bewildered her.*
mystify *I was mystified by his attitude.*
puzzle *One thing still puzzles me.*
See also **cloud, mix up, muddle, puzzle**

confuse with *See* mistake

confused
▷ ADJECTIVE
1 puzzled or bewildered: *confused about health risks*
baffled *He stared in baffled amazement.*
bewildered *bewildered tourists*
muddled *She was muddled about the date.*
perplexed *perplexed by recent events*
puzzled *a puzzled expression*
2 in an untidy mess: *The clothes lay in a confused heap.*
chaotic *the chaotic mess on his desk*
disordered *a disordered pile of papers*
disorganized *a disorganized lifestyle*
untidy *an untidy room*
ANTONYM **tidy**
See also **dazed, garbled, unclear**

confusing
▷ ADJECTIVE
puzzling or bewildering: *a confusing situation*
baffling *a baffling statement*

C

bewildering *a bewildering choice of products*
complicated *a complicated voting system*
puzzling *a puzzling problem*

confusion

▷ NOUN

an untidy mess: *My life is in confusion.*
chaos *economic chaos*
disarray *The house is in disarray.*
disorder *The emergency room was in disorder.*
disorganization *scenes of chaos and disorganization*
mess *He always leaves the bathroom in a mess.*
ANTONYM **order**
See also **disorder, fuss, muddle**

congeal *See* **thicken**

congealed *See* **firm**

congenial *See* **compatible**

congested *See* **crowded**

congratulate *See* **praise**

congratulation *See* **praise**

congregate *See* **assemble, crowd, gather, mass, meet**

congregation *See* **gathering**

congress *See* **conference, convention, meeting**

conjecture *See* **theory**

connect

▷ VERB

1 to join together: *Connect the pipe to the tap.*
affix *His name was affixed to his office door.*
attach *Attach the curtains to the rods with hooks.*
couple *The engine is coupled to a gearbox.*
fasten *Fasten the latch to the door.*
join *two springs joined together*
link *The Confederation Bridge links Prince Edward Island with New Brunswick.*
ANTONYM **separate**
2 to associate one thing with another: *evidence connecting them with the crime*
ally *We allied ourselves with the other political party.*
associate *symptoms associated with migraine headaches*
link *research that links smoking with cancer*
relate *Support from fans is related to the team's performance.*
See also **associate, attach, join, link**

connection

▷ NOUN

1 a link or relationship: *a connection between good health and lots of exercise*
affiliation *He has no affiliation with any political party.*
association *the association between the two companies*
bond *the bond between bears and their cubs*
correlation *the correlation between smoking and lung cancer*
correspondence *the correspondence between ancient practices and modern medicine*
link *a link between air pollution and breathing difficulties*
relation *This theory bears no relation to reality.*
relationship *the relationship between humans and their environment*
2 a point where things are joined: *The fault was just a loose connection.*
coupling *The coupling between the train cars nearly snapped.*
fastening *the fastening between the seat belt and its buckle*
junction *the junction between nerve and muscle*
link *The highway provides a link between the cities.*
See also **association, bond, contact, link, relation, relationship, tie**

conquer *See* **defeat, overcome, vanquish**

conqueror *See* **winner**

conquest *See* **defeat**

conscience

▷ NOUN

a sense of right and wrong: *He had a guilty conscience.*
principles *It's against my principles to eat meat.*
scruples *a man with no moral scruples*
sense of right and wrong *people with no sense of right and wrong*
See also **principle**

CONFUSABLES

Conscience means **knowing right from wrong**.
Conscious means **aware**.

---

conscientious *See* **industrious**

conscious *See* **deliberate**

conscious of *See* **aware of**

consciousness *See* **sense**

consecrate *See* **bless**

consecrated *See* **holy**

consent *See* **blessing, permission**

consent to *See* **accept, approve**

consequence *See* **effect, result**

consequently *See* **therefore**

conservative
▷ *ADJECTIVE*
unwilling to change: *People sometimes become more conservative as they grow older.*
conventional *conventional tastes*
traditional *a traditional school*
ANTONYM **radical**
See also **conventional, right-wing**

consider
▷ *VERB*
1 to think of someone or something as: *They do not consider him a suitable candidate.*
believe *I believe him to be innocent.*
deem *He was not deemed qualified for the position.*
judge *His work was judged unsatisfactory.*
rate *The movie was rated excellent.*
regard as *They regard the tax as unfair.*
think *Many people think him arrogant.*
2 to think carefully: *I will consider your offer.*
contemplate *He contemplated his fate.*
deliberate *The jury deliberated for three days.*
meditate *He meditated on the problem.*
muse *She sat there, musing on how unfair life was.*
ponder *pondering how to improve the team*
reflect *I reflected on the child's future.*
think about *I've been thinking about what you said.*
3 to take into account: *We should consider her feelings.*
bear in mind *There are a few points to bear in mind.*
make allowances for *Remember to make allowances for delays.*
respect *We will respect your wishes.*
take into account *another factor to be taken into account*
think about *more important things to think about*
See also **contemplate, feel, judge, ponder, rate, reckon, regard, think, view**

considerable *See* **extensive, handsome, respectable, significant**

considerably *See* **far**

considerate *See* **accommodating, kind, thoughtful, understanding**

considerately *See* **well**

consideration
▷ *NOUN*
1 careful thought about something: *a decision requiring careful consideration*
attention *I gave the question all my attention.*
contemplation *The problem deserves serious contemplation.*
deliberation *After much deliberation, he called the police.*
study *The proposals need careful study.*
thought *I've given the matter a great deal of thought.*
2 concern for someone: *Show some consideration for the other passengers.*
concern *concern for the homeless*
kindness *We have been treated with great kindness.*
respect *no respect for wildlife*
tact *She exhibited tact and diplomacy.*
3 something to be taken into account: *Safety is a major consideration.*
factor *an important factor in buying a house*
issue *Price is not the only issue.*
point *There is another point to remember.*
See also **aspect, factor, thought**

consignment *See* **load**

consistency *See* **texture**

consistent *See* **compatible, logical, regular, steady**

consist of
▷ *VERB*
to be made up of: *The brain consists of millions of nerve cells.*
be composed of *The committee is composed of ten people.*
be made up of *The bouquet was made up of roses and carnations.*
comprise *The art show comprises 50 paintings and sketches.*

consolation *See* **comfort**

console *See* **comfort**

consolidate *See* **strengthen**

conspicuous
▷ *ADJECTIVE*
easy to see or notice: *Her conspicuous lack of warmth confirmed her disapproval.*

apparent *It has been apparent that someone has been stealing.*
blatant *a blatant disregard for rules*
evident *He spoke with evident emotion about his ordeal.*
noticeable *the most noticeable effect of these changes*
obvious *an obvious injustice*
perceptible *a perceptible air of neglect*
See also **clear, manifest, noticeable, prominent, visible**

conspiracy See **plot**

conspire See **plot**

constant
▷ ADJECTIVE
1 going on all the time: *a government under constant attack from the media*
continual *continual interruptions*
continuous *continuous noise*
eternal *an eternal hum in the background*
nonstop *nonstop music*
perpetual *their perpetual complaints*
relentless *relentless pressure*
ANTONYM **periodic**
2 staying the same: *a constant temperature*
even *an even level of sound*
fixed *a fixed salary*
regular *a regular beat*
stable *a stable condition*
steady *travelling at a steady 60 km/h*
uniform *a uniform thickness*
ANTONYM **changeable**
See also **continual, continuous, devoted, even, loyal, permanent, regular, steadfast, steady**

constituent See **ingredient**

constitute See **form, make up**

constitution See **health, law**

constraint See **restriction**

constricted See **tight**

construct
▷ VERB
to build or make something: *to construct a model plane*
assemble *The computer was assembled at the factory.*
build *Our house was built 20 years ago.*
create *We created a makeshift platform for him to stand on.*
erect *The building was erected in 1900.*
make *The company now makes cars at two plants in Ontario.*

put together *We bought the desk in pieces and put it together at home.*
put up *She was putting up a new fence.*
See also **assemble, build, fashion, make, produce**

construction See **making, structure**

constructive See **helpful, positive, productive**

consult
▷ VERB
to go to for advice: *Consult your doctor before beginning an exercise program.*
ask for advice *I asked the coach for advice on diet and exercise.*
confer with *He is conferring with his lawyers.*
refer to *I had to refer to the manual.*
See also **refer**

consultant See **adviser**

consultation See **discussion**

consume See **drain, exhaust**

consumer See **customer**

consummate See **complete, ideal, perfect, utter**

contact
▷ NOUN
1 the state of being in touch with someone: *We keep in daily contact.*
communication *The leaders were in constant communication.*
touch *We stay in touch by e-mail.*
2 someone you know: *a contact in the music business*
acquaintance *We met through a mutual acquaintance.*
connection *She had a business connection in England.*
▷ VERB
3 to get in touch with: *We contacted the company to complain.*
approach *A journalist has approached me for a story.*
communicate with *We communicate mostly by e-mail.*
get hold of *I've been trying to get hold of you all week.*
get in touch with *I will get in touch with my lawyers.*
reach *Where can I reach you in an emergency?*

contagious See **infectious**

contain
▷ VERB
1 to include as a part of: *My diary contains*

personal information.
comprise *The band comprises two singers and two guitarists.*
include *The total price includes tax.*
2 to keep under control: *efforts to contain the disease*
control *He could hardly control his happiness.*
curb *measures to curb inflation*
repress *people who repress their emotions*
restrain *unable to restrain his anger*
stifle *stifling the urge to scream*
See also **curb, include, restrain, restrict, suppress**

container
▷ *NOUN*
something that holds things: *a plastic container for food*
holder *a pencil holder*
vessel *storage vessels*
See also **box, case**

contaminate *See* **infect, pollute**

contemplate
▷ *VERB*
I to think carefully about something: *She carefully contemplated her next move.*
consider *She paused to consider her options.*
examine *I have examined all the documents.*
muse on *He mused on the possible locations for his vacation.*
ponder *He didn't waste time pondering the question.*
reflect on *I reflected on the child's future.*
think about *Think about how you can improve the situation.*
2 to consider doing something: *He contemplated a career as a doctor.*
consider *Travellers should consider getting enough insurance.*
envisage *He had never envisaged spending so long at one job.*
plan *I had been planning a trip to the Atlantic provinces.*
think of *He was thinking of taking legal action against his employer.*
See also **consider, ponder, regard, study, think**

contemplation *See* **consideration, thought**

contemplative *See* **thoughtful**

contemporary *See* **current, modern**

contempt
▷ *NOUN*
complete lack of respect: *I shall treat that*

remark with the contempt it deserves.
derision *He was greeted with shouts of derision.*
disdain *to look at him with complete disdain*
disregard *total disregard for the safety of the public*
disrespect *complete disrespect for authority*
scorn *They greeted the proposal with scorn.*
ANTONYM **respect**
See also **scorn**

contemptible *See* **low, shabby**

contemptuous *See* **scornful**

contend *See* **compete**

contender *See* **candidate**

content *See* **satisfied**

contented *See* **comfortable, pleased, satisfied**

contention *See* **competition**

contest
▷ *NOUN*
I a competition or game: *first prize in the spelling contest*
competition *a debating competition*
game *the first game of the season*
match *They were watching a wrestling match.*
tournament *Here is a player capable of winning a world tournament.*
2 a struggle for power: *a bitter contest over the party's leadership*
battle *the eternal battle between good and evil*
fight *the fight for the class presidency*
struggle *locked in a power struggle with the prime minister*
▷ *VERB*
3 to object formally to a statement or decision: *Your former employer has 14 days to contest the case.*
challenge *The move was immediately challenged.*
dispute *She disputed the allegations.*
oppose *He opposed my promotion.*
question *It never occurs to them to question the doctor's decisions.*
ANTONYM **accept**
See also **compete, competition, dispute, event, game, match**

contestant *See* **competitor**

continual
▷ *ADJECTIVE*
happening again and again: *the continual*

ringing of his cellphone
frequent *prone to frequent colds*
recurrent *recurrent dreams*
regular *He is a regular visitor to our house.*
repeated *They did not return the money, despite repeated reminders.*
ANTONYM **occasional**
See also **constant, frequent**

CONFUSABLES

Continual means **often repeated.**
Continuous means **without interruption.**

---

continually *See* **always**

continue
▷ *VERB*
1 to keep doing something: *He continued to work for another year.*
carry on *The assistant carried on talking.*
go on *Unemployment is likely to go on rising.*
keep on *He kept on trying.*
persist *She persists in using his nickname.*
2 to go on existing: *The discussion continued after they'd left.*
carry on *My work will carry on after I'm gone.*
endure *Their friendship has endured for 30 years.*
last *Nothing lasts forever.*
persist *The problem persists.*
remain *The historic building remains to this day.*
survive *companies that survived after the recession*
3 to start doing again: *After a moment, she continued speaking.*
carry on *He took a deep breath, and then carried on.*
recommence *He recommenced work on his novel.*
resume *Police will resume the search today.*
See also **extend, last, proceed, remain, stretch**

continued *See* **continuous**

continuous
▷ *ADJECTIVE*
going on or happening all the time, without stopping: *continuous growth*
constant *under constant pressure*
continued *a continued improvement*
endless *endless demands for attention*
eternal *In the background was that eternal hum.*
extended *He took an extended leave of*

absence from the job.
nagging *a nagging pain between his shoulder blades*
perpetual *the perpetual thump of music*
prolonged *a prolonged drought*
uninterrupted *an uninterrupted view of the Rockies*
ANTONYM **periodic**
See also **constant, continual, gradual, steady**

continuously *See* **always**

contours *See* **form, outline, shape**

contract *See* **agreement, bond, develop, diminish, shrink**

contradict *See* **clash, deny, dispute**

contraption *See* **machine**

contrary *See* **opposite, reverse**

contrast *See* **compare, difference, foil**

contrasting *See* **different, opposite**

contravene *See* **break**

contribute *See* **provide**

contribute to *See* **lead to**

contribution *See* **gift**

control
▷ *NOUN*
1 power over something: *He was forced to give up control of the company.*
authority *You have no authority here.*
command *She has a good command of the language.*
direction *The team worked well under his direction.*
government *The entire country is under the government of one person.*
management *the day-to-day management of the business*
power *a position of great power*
rule *His rule of the kingdom ended after 20 years.*
supremacy *The political party has re-established its supremacy.*
▷ *VERB*
2 to be in charge of: *trying to control your mind*
administer *the authorities who administer the island*
be in charge of *She is in charge of the project.*
command *the general who commanded the troops*
direct *He will direct day-to-day operations.*
govern *her ability to govern the country*
have power over *The dictator has total*

power over the country.
manage *the government's ability to manage the economy*
rule *the dynasty that ruled China*
See also **administer, check, command, contain, curb, determine, direct, direction, grip, head, hold, influence, manage, management, possess, possession, power, restrain, restriction, run**

conundrum See **mystery, problem**

convalesce See **recover**

convene See **assemble, meet**

convenient
▷ ADJECTIVE
helpful or easy to use: *a convenient mode of transport*
handy *Credit cards can be handy.*
helpful *a helpful fact sheet*
useful *a useful search engine*
ANTONYM **inconvenient**
See also **handy, ready**

convention
▷ NOUN
1 an accepted way of behaving or doing something: *It's a social convention that men don't wear skirts.*
code *a code of conduct*
custom *The custom of lighting the Olympic flame goes back centuries.*
etiquette *the rules of etiquette*
practice *It's my usual practice to turn off the computer at the end of the day.*
tradition *cultural traditions different from ours*
2 a large meeting of an organization or group: *the annual convention of the Canadian Association of Journalists*
assembly *the general assembly of the Canadian Dental Association*
conference *a conference attended by 450 delegates*
congress *an international congress on conservation*
meeting *the weekly meeting of our club*
See also **conference, custom, habit, meeting, tradition**

conventional
▷ ADJECTIVE
1 having or relating to a very ordinary lifestyle: *His opinions are generally quite conventional.*
conformist *He may have become more conformist if he wants a promotion.*
conservative *a rather conservative style of dress*

C

unadventurous *He was a strong player, but rather unadventurous.*
2 familiar, or usually used: *the conventional treatment for diabetes*
customary *my customary semi-annual visit to the dentist*
ordinary *It has 25 percent less fat than ordinary ice cream.*
orthodox *Many of these ideas are being incorporated into orthodox medical treatment.*
regular *This is the regular brand of ketchup that I buy.*
standard *It was standard practice for paralegals to deal with simpler cases.*
traditional *traditional teaching methods*
See also **conservative, formal, normal, ordinary, popular, proper, traditional**

conversation See **chat, discussion, talk, word**

conversational See **colloquial**

converse See **opposite, reverse**

convert See **adapt, change, recruit, transform, turn**

convey
▷ VERB
to cause information or ideas to be known: *She conveyed her enthusiasm to her friends.*
communicate *They generously communicate their knowledge to others.*
express *I expressed my disapproval by frowning.*
get across *I wanted to get my message across.*
impart *the ability to impart knowledge*
See also **bear, bring, carry, communicate, take, transport**

convict See **prisoner**

convicted See **guilty**

conviction See **belief, idea, view, viewpoint**

convince
▷ VERB
to persuade that something is true: *I convinced him of my innocence.*
assure *The skater assured her fans that she would compete in the next Olympics.*
persuade *I had to persuade him of the advantages of saving money.*
satisfy *He had to satisfy the doctors that he was fit to play.*
See also **satisfy**

convinced See **certain, confident, positive, sure**

convincing
▷ ADJECTIVE
persuasive: *a convincing argument*
conclusive *conclusive proof*
effective *an effective speaker*
persuasive *persuasive reasons*
plausible *a plausible explanation*
powerful *a powerful speech*
telling *a telling criticism*
ANTONYM **unconvincing**
See also **powerful**

convoluted See **complicated**

cook
▷ VERB
to prepare food for eating by heating it in some way: *I enjoy cooking for friends.*
bake *a machine for baking bread*
barbecue *On the long weekend, we barbecued hamburgers.*
boil *Boil the potatoes in water until they are tender.*
fry *Fry the potatoes in hot oil.*
grill *Grill the fish for five minutes.*
microwave *Microwaved vegetables have a fresher flavour.*
poach *I had ordered poached eggs on toast for breakfast.*
roast *Roast the chicken in the oven until fully cooked.*
sauté *Sauté the onions in the oil.*
steam *salmon served with steamed vegetables*
stew *Stew the vegetables and meat for several hours.*
stir fry *Quickly stir fry the vegetables and diced chicken.*
toast *This raisin bread is delicious either plain or toasted.*

cool
▷ ADJECTIVE
1 having a low temperature: *a gust of cool air*
chilled *a chilled bottle of wine*
chilly *a chilly afternoon*
cold *Your dinner's getting cold.*
refreshing *a refreshing breeze*
ANTONYM **warm**
2 staying calm: *He kept cool through the whole thing.*
calm *Try to stay calm.*
collected *She was cool and collected throughout the interview.*
composed *I tried to look composed but I was furious inside.*

level-headed *She's level-headed and practical.*
relaxed *a relaxed manner*
serene *a serene smile*
ANTONYM **nervous**
▷ VERB
3 to make or become cool: *Put the cookies on a wire rack to cool.*
chill *a glass of chilled orange juice*
cool off *Dip the carrots in water to cool them off.*
freeze *Make double the quantity and freeze half for later.*
refrigerate *Refrigerate the dough overnight.*
ANTONYM **heat**
See also **apathetic, calm, patience, relaxed**

cool off See **cool**

cooperate
▷ VERB
to work together: *The family cooperated with the author of the book.*
collaborate *They collaborated on a CD.*
join forces *The two political parties are joining forces.*
pull together *Workers and management have pulled together.*
work together *industry and government working together*
See also **team**

cooperative See **helpful**

coordinate See **blend, oversee**

cope with See **deal, endure, manage, take care of**

copious See **abundant, plentiful**

copy
▷ NOUN
1 something made to look like something else: *He kept a copy of the letter.*
counterfeit *This credit card is a counterfeit.*
duplicate *I lost my key and had to get a duplicate made.*
fake *How do I know this painting isn't a fake?*
forgery *The letter was a forgery.*
imitation *Beware of cheap imitations!*
replica *a replica of the CN Tower*
reproduction *a reproduction of a famous painting*
▷ VERB
2 to do the same thing as someone else: *She tried to copy the author's writing style.*
ape *My little brother apes everything I do.*
emulate *The young player tried to emulate the star goalie.*

follow *Where a trendsetter goes, others will surely follow.*

imitate *Children sometimes imitate what they see on TV.*

mimic *He mimicked my singing voice.*

▷ VERB

3 to make a copy of: *documents copied by hand*

counterfeit *These bills are very easy to counterfeit.*

duplicate *DVDs are being illicitly duplicated all over the country.*

reproduce *a new method of reproducing oil paintings*

See also **fake, imitate, issue**

cordial See **friendly, warm**

core See **basis, centre, essence**

cork See **plug**

corner See **bend, trap**

corny

▷ ADJECTIVE

unoriginal or sentimental: *corny old love songs*

banal *banal dialogue*

hackneyed *a hackneyed plot*

maudlin *a maudlin film*

sentimental *a sentimental ballad*

stale *stale ideas*

stereotyped *a stereotyped image of Canada*

trite *a trite ending*

corporation See **business, company, firm**

corpse See **body**

correct

▷ ADJECTIVE

1 without mistakes: *a correct diagnosis*

accurate *an accurate weather forecast*

exact *an exact copy*

faultless *Her Spanish was faultless.*

flawless *a flawless performance*

precise *a precise total*

right *That clock never shows the right time.*

true *a true account*

ANTONYM **wrong**

2 socially acceptable: *correct behaviour*

acceptable *Online education is becoming more acceptable.*

appropriate *appropriate dress*

fitting *behaving in a manner not fitting for the occasion*

OK INFORMAL *Is it OK if I bring a friend with me?*

proper *In those days, it was not proper for children to talk at the dinner table.*

seemly *It is not seemly to joke about such things.*

ANTONYM **unacceptable**

▷ VERB

3 to make right: *trying to correct his faults*

amend *The government amended the movie-classification system.*

cure *a known cure for the virus*

improve *We must improve the situation.*

rectify *attempts to rectify the problem*

reform *the debate over Senate reform*

remedy *What is needed to remedy these deficiencies?*

right *I intend to right these wrongs.*

See also **accurate, appropriate, fitting, fix, formal, precise, proper, reform, revise, right, standard, true**

correction

▷ NOUN

the act of making something right: *The newspaper printed a correction of the story.*

adjustment *My car needs a brake adjustment.*

amendment *He has made lots of amendments to the script.*

righting *the righting of the country's domestic troubles*

See also **reform**

correlate See **correspond**

correlation See **connection, relation, relationship**

correspond

▷ VERB

to be similar or connected to something else: *The two maps correspond closely.*

agree *The Vancouver Canucks have agreed to extend the contract.*

be related *The problems are closely related.*

coincide *He was delighted to find that her feelings coincided with his own.*

correlate *The wearing of seat belts correlates with fewer injuries.*

fit *Must the punishment always fit the crime?*

match *Our value system does not match with theirs.*

tally *This description did not tally with what we saw.*

See also **communicate, fit, match, suit, write**

correspondence See **connection, resemblance**

corridor See **passage**

corrode See **eat away, erode, wear**

corrosion *See* **wear**

corrupt

▷ *ADJECTIVE*

1 acting dishonestly or illegally: *corrupt politicians*
crooked *a crooked cop*
dishonest *a dishonest worker*
fraudulent *The government is investigating fraudulent banking practices.*
shady INFORMAL *shady deals*
unscrupulous *unscrupulous dealings*
ANTONYM **honest**

▷ *VERB*

2 to make dishonest: *Power is said to corrupt some people.*
bribe *accused of bribing officials*
buy off *They say the manufacturer bought off the safety officials.*
fix INFORMAL *He tried to fix the match by bribing the boxers.*

▷ *VERB*

3 to make immoral: *Is TV really corrupting our children?*
deprave *music said to deprave anyone who listens to it*
pervert *attempts to pervert justice*
See also **criminal, crooked, dirty, dishonest**

corruption

▷ *NOUN*

dishonest and illegal behaviour: *charges of corruption*
bribery *on trial for bribery*
dishonesty *She accused the government of dishonesty and incompetence.*
fraud *jailed for fraud*
See also **dishonesty**

cosmopolitan *See* **sophisticated**

cosset *See* **spoil**

cost

▷ *NOUN*

1 the amount of money needed: *The cost of fuel has increased.*
charge *We can arrange this for a small charge.*
expense *household expenses*
outlay *Buying printer cartridges in bulk is well worth the outlay.*
payment *an initial payment of just $100*
price *The price of oil rose again.*
rate *the rate of exchange between the Canadian dollar and the euro*
2 loss or damage: *the total cost in human misery*

detriment *These changes are to the detriment of staff morale.*
expense *They cut down on practice drills at the expense of safety.*
penalty *paying the penalty for someone else's mistakes*

▷ *VERB*

3 to involve a cost of: *The air fares were going to cost a lot.*
come to *Lunch came to nearly $10.*
sell at *The books are selling at $20 per copy.*
set someone back INFORMAL *This wedding will set them back thousands of dollars.*
See also **charge, price, rate, value**

cost-effective *See* **economical**

costly *See* **dear, expensive, valuable**

costume *See* **clothes, dress**

cosy

▷ *ADJECTIVE*

1 warm and comfortable: *a cosy cottage by the lake*
comfortable *a comfortable fireside chair*
snug *a snug bed*
warm *warm blankets*
2 pleasant and friendly: *a cosy chat between friends*
friendly *a friendly little get-together*
informal *The house has an informal atmosphere.*
intimate *an intimate candlelit dinner for two*
relaxed *a relaxed evening at home*
See also **comfortable**

couch *See* **express**

council

▷ *NOUN*

a governing group of people: *the city council*
assembly *the National Assembly of Québec*
board *the Transportation Safety Board of Canada*
committee *the management committee*
panel *a panel of judges*

CONFUSABLES

Council is a noun that refers to a group of people.
Counsel means **advice** (n) or **advise** (v).

---

counsel *See* **advice, advise, guide, lawyer**

count

▷ *VERB*

1 to add up: *He counted the votes.*
add up *Add up the sales figures.*

calculate *First, calculate your monthly living expenses.*
tally *Computers now tally votes.*
2 to be important: *Our opinions don't count.*
carry weight *a politician whose words carry weight*
matter *Skills really matter when you're looking for a job.*
rate *This does not rate as one of my main concerns.*
signify *His absence does not signify much.*
weigh *This evidence did not weigh with the jury.*
▷ NOUN
3 a counting or number counted: *The count revealed that our party had the majority.*
calculation *I did a quick calculation in my head.*
reckoning *By my reckoning we were about 3 km from camp.*
sum *Can you work out the sum without a calculator?*
tally *They keep a tally of visitors to the museum.*
See also **calculate, matter, rate, reckon**

INFORMALLY SPEAKING

count for: be worth
count on: rely on

---

count on *See* **depend, trust**

count up *See* **add**

countenance *See* **expression, face**

counter *See* **foil, reply**

counteract
▷ VERB
to reduce the effect of something: *pills to counteract high blood pressure*
act against *The immune system acts against infection.*
offset *The slump was offset by a surge in sales.*
See also **compensate**

counterbalance *See* **reaction**

counterfeit *See* **copy, fake, mock, pretend**

countless
▷ ADJECTIVE
too many to count: *the star of countless movies*
infinite *an infinite number of atoms*
innumerable *innumerable problems*
myriad *music in all its myriad forms*
untold *untold wealth*
See also **many**

C

country
▷ NOUN
1 a political area: *the boundary between the two countries*
kingdom *the kingdom of Saudi Arabia*
land *Canada is a land of opportunity.*
state *a communist state*
2 land away from towns and cities: *He lives right out in the country.*
bush *During the summer, they worked in the bush.*
countryside *surrounded by beautiful countryside*
outdoors *We love the great outdoors.*
See also **land, state, territory**

countryside *See* **country**

couple *See* **associate, attach, connect, join, link**

coupling *See* **connection**

courage
▷ NOUN
lack of fear: *Her courage impressed everyone.*
bravery *an act of bravery*
daring *tales of daring and adventure*
grit *She demonstrated grit and determination.*
guts INFORMAL *He didn't have the guts to admit he was wrong.*
heroism *the young soldier's heroism*
nerve *I didn't have the nerve to complain, but I wanted to.*
pluck *You have to admire their pluck in refusing to be bullied.*
valour *They were decorated for valour in the war.*
ANTONYM **fear**
See also **bravery, daring**

courageous *See* **bold, brave**

courier *See* **messenger**

course
▷ NOUN
1 a series of lessons: *a course in information technology*
classes *I go to dance classes.*
curriculum *the history curriculum*
2 a policy of action: *The premier took the only course left open to her.*
plan *Your best plan is to see your doctor.*
policy *She decided the best policy was to wait.*
procedure *He did not follow the correct procedure.*

3 a way taken to get somewhere: *She sensed the plane had changed course.*
direction *He went off in the opposite direction.*
line *the birds' line of flight*
path *the path of an oncoming car*
route *the most direct route*
trajectory *the trajectory of the missile*
way *Do you know the fastest way to Lethbridge?*
See also **direction, line, passage, path, pour, route, sequence, way**

CONFUSABLES

Course has nothing to do with roughness. **Coarse** means **rough**.

course of action *See* **process**

court
▷ NOUN
I a place where legal matters are decided: *He ended up in court for theft.*
bench *He was brought before the bench.*
law court *The law courts are located downtown.*
tribunal *The international tribunal found the dictator guilty.*
▷ VERB
2 OLD-FASHIONED to intend to marry: *My grandparents courted for five years before they married.*
go steady *They've been going steady for six months now.*

courteous *See* **polite**

courteousness *See* **courtesy**

courtesy
▷ NOUN
polite and considerate behaviour: *a lack of courtesy to other drivers*
civility *Handle customers with tact and civility.*
courteousness *his courteousness and kindness*
gallantry *treated with old-fashioned gallantry*
good manners *the rules of good manners*
grace *He didn't even have the grace to apologize.*
graciousness *The team displayed graciousness in defeat.*
politeness *basic standards of politeness*
See also **favour, politeness**

cove *See* **bay**

cover
▷ VERB
I to protect or hide: *He covered his face.*
cloak *a land cloaked in mist*
conceal *The hat concealed her hair.*
cover up *I covered him up with a blanket.*
hide *His sunglasses hid his eyes.*
mask *A cloud masked the sun.*
obscure *One wall was obscured by a huge banner.*
screen *The road was screened by rows of trees.*
shade *shading his eyes from the glare*
ANTONYM **reveal**
2 to form a layer over: *Tears covered his face.*
coat *Coat the fish with flour.*
overlay *The floor was overlaid with rugs.*
▷ NOUN
3 something that protects or hides: *quilts, blankets, and other covers*
case *an eyeglass case*
coating *steel covered with a coating of zinc*
covering *a plastic covering*
jacket *the dust jacket of a book*
mask *a surgical mask*
screen *a solar screen to block the sun*
wrapper *Remove the wrapper from the chocolate.*
See also **defence, defend, include, protection, report, safeguard, shelter, spread, stretch**

cover up *See* **cover**

covering *See* **coating, cover, layer**

covert *See* **secret**

covet *See* **envy, long, want**

cow
▷ NOUN
a farm animal kept for its milk or meat: *a herd of dairy cows*
bovine *a field of bovines*
cattle *fields where cattle graze*

coward
▷ NOUN
someone who is easily scared: *too much of a coward to fight*
chicken SLANG *We called him a chicken.*
wimp INFORMAL *He doesn't seem like a wimp to me.*
wuss INFORMAL *Stop being such a wuss!*

cowardly
▷ ADJECTIVE
easily scared: *too cowardly to tell the truth*
chicken SLANG *I was too chicken to complain.*

faint-hearted *This is no time to be faint-hearted.*

gutless INFORMAL *a gutless coward*

ANTONYM **brave**

See also **timid**

cower

▷ VERB

to bend down with fear: *The hostages cowered in their seats.*

cringe *I cringed in horror.*

quail *She quailed at the sight.*

shrink *He shrank back in terror.*

co-worker *See* associate

crack

▷ VERB

1 to become damaged, with lines on the surface: *A gas main has cracked.*

break *I broke my leg skiing.*

fracture *You've fractured a rib.*

snap *The mast snapped like a dry twig.*

2 to find the answer to something: *We've managed to crack the problem.*

decipher *trying to decipher the code*

solve *attempts to solve the mystery*

work out *I've worked out the problem.*

▷ NOUN

3 a line or gap caused by damage: *a large crack in the wall*

break *a small break in the bone*

cleft *a cleft in the rocks*

crevice *They squeezed glue into the crevices.*

fracture *a hip fracture*

See also **attempt, bang, breach, burst, fissure, gap, leak, opening, solve, split**

INFORMALLY SPEAKING

crack up: respond with laughter; suffer a breakdown

crack down: impose stricter discipline

get cracking: hurry up

---

cracking *See* excellent, splendid

craft *See* work

craftsman *See* worker

crafty

▷ ADJECTIVE

clever and rather dishonest: *That crafty old devil has taken us for a ride!*

artful *an artful pickpocket*

cunning *a cunning plan to get us out of this mess*

devious *By devious means, she obtained the address.*

scheming *You're a scheming little rascal, aren't you?*

slippery *a slippery customer*

sly *a sly old character if ever there was one*

wily *the wily old fox*

See also **cunning, shrewd, sly, sneaky**

craggy *See* jagged, rough

cram

▷ VERB

to stuff something into a container or place: *She crammed the towel into her gym bag.*

jam *The place was jammed with people.*

pack *The drawers were packed with clothes.*

squeeze *The two of us were squeezed into one seat.*

stuff *wallets stuffed with bills*

See also **fill, jam, stuff**

cramped *See* tight, uncomfortable

crank *See* eccentric

crash

▷ NOUN

1 an accident involving a moving vehicle: *a plane crash*

accident *a serious car accident*

bump *a minor bump in which nobody was hurt*

collision *a head-on collision*

pile-up INFORMAL *a 14-car pile-up*

smash *a head-on car smash*

2 a loud noise: *There was a sudden crash outside.*

bang *The door slammed with a bang.*

clash *the clash of cymbals*

din *the din of battle*

smash *the smash of falling pots and pans*

3 the failure of a business: *a stock-market crash*

bankruptcy *Many firms are now facing bankruptcy.*

collapse *The economy is on the edge of collapse.*

depression *the Great Depression of the 1930s*

failure *a major cause of business failure*

ruin *Inflation has driven them to the brink of ruin.*

▷ VERB

4 to have an accident: *His car crashed into the rear of a minivan.*

bump *I've just bumped my car.*

collide *Two trains collided outside the city.*

drive into *He drove his car into a tree.*

have an accident *My brother's had an accident on his moped.*

hurtle into *The racing car hurtled into the spectator section.*

plough into *The plane had ploughed into the mountainside.*
wreck *He's wrecked his van.*
See also **dash**

crave *See* **desire, long, want**

craving *See* **desire, longing**

crawl
▷ VERB
to be full of: *The place is crawling with tourists.*
be alive with *The river was alive with frogs.*
be full of *The place was full of insects.*
be overrun SLANG *The area is overrun with visitors.*
swarm *The mall was swarming with shoppers.*
teem *ponds teeming with fish*

craze
▷ NOUN
a brief enthusiasm for something: *the latest fitness craze*
fad *a short-lived fad*
fashion *I can't keep track of the latest fashions.*
trend *the latest trend among movie stars*
vogue *a vogue for so-called health drinks*
See also **fashion, whim**

crazy
▷ ADJECTIVE
1 INFORMAL very strange or foolish: *People thought we were crazy when we told them our plans.*
foolish *It is foolish to risk skin cancer for the sake of a tan.*
insane *If you want my opinion, I think your idea is completely insane.*
mad *You'd be mad to work with him again.*
ridiculous *It was an absolutely ridiculous decision.*
wild *all sorts of wild ideas*
zany *zany humour*
ANTONYM **sensible**
2 INFORMAL very keen on something: *He's crazy about figure skating.*
fanatical *fanatical about computer games*
mad *She's not as mad about sports as I am.*
obsessed *He was obsessed with science-fiction movies.*
passionate *He is passionate about good food.*
smitten *They were totally smitten with each other.*
wild *I'm just wild about him!*
ANTONYM **uninterested**
See also **absurd, idiotic, irrational, mad**

crease *See* **crumple, fold**

create
▷ VERB
1 to make something happen: *The new factory created hundreds of jobs.*
bring about *helping to bring about peace*
cause *Wind and heavy rains caused traffic delays.*
lead to *The takeover led to widespread layoffs.*
occasion *the distress occasioned by his changing job situation*
2 to invent something: *creating a new style of painting*
coin *the man who coined the term "virtual reality"*
compose *Vivaldi composed many concertos.*
devise *We devised a plan to help him.*
formulate *They formulated their escape plan.*
invent *The paint roller was invented by Norman Breakey of Toronto.*
originate *About 90 percent of new toys originate from private inventors.*
See also **bring, bring about, cause, compose, construct, fashion, form, invent, make, produce, start**

creation *See* **making, piece**

creative
▷ ADJECTIVE
able to invent: *her creative talents*
fertile *a fertile imagination*
imaginative *an imaginative writer*
inspired *his inspired use of colour*
inventive *an inventive storyline*

creativity *See* **imagination**

creature *See* **animal**

credible *See* **believable**

credit
▷ NOUN
praise for something: *He took all the credit for my idea.*
commendation *Both teams deserve commendation.*
glory *basking in reflected glory*
praise *Praise is due to all concerned.*
recognition *She got no recognition for her work.*
thanks *He received no thanks for his efforts.*
See also **loan**

creed *See* **belief, faith**

creep *See* **ease, edge, slip, steal**

creepy

▷ ADJECTIVE

INFORMAL strange and frightening: *This place is really creepy at night.*
disturbing *There was something about her that we found disturbing.*
eerie *I walked down the eerie dark path.*
macabre *macabre stories*
scary INFORMAL *We watched scary movies.*
sinister *There was something sinister about him.*
spooky *The whole place has a slightly spooky atmosphere.*
unnatural *The altered landscape looks unnatural and weird.*
See also **scary, spooky**

crest See **peak, top**

crevice See **crack, fissure**

crew See **party, team**

crime

▷ NOUN

an act that breaks the law: *the problem of organized crime*
misdemeanour *a financial misdemeanour*
offence *a serious offence*
violation *a traffic violation*
wrong *I intend to right that wrong.*
See also **pity, sin, wrong**

criminal

▷ NOUN

1 someone who has committed a crime: *the country's most dangerous criminals*
crook INFORMAL *The man is a crook and a liar.*
culprit *the true culprit's identity*
offender *a first-time offender*
villain *an armed villain*

▷ ADJECTIVE

2 involving crime: *criminal activities*
corrupt *corrupt practices*
crooked *crooked business deals*
illegal *an illegal action*
illicit *illicit dealings with criminals*
unlawful *unlawful entry*
See also **crooked, guilty, illegal**

crimson See **blush**

cringe See **cower, flinch**

cripple

▷ VERB

1 to injure severely: *The dog was crippled in a car accident.*
disable *disabled by polio*
maim *land mines maiming and killing civilians*
paralyze *paralyzed in a riding accident*

2 to prevent from working: *The crisis may cripple the provincial economy.*
bring to a standstill *The strike brought France to a standstill.*
impair *Their actions will impair our national interests.*
put out of action *The port has been put out of action.*

crisis See **emergency**

crisscross See **cross**

criterion See **standard**

critical

▷ ADJECTIVE

1 very important: *a critical point in history*
crucial *Large voter turnout is crucial to their election.*
deciding *Price was a deciding factor.*
decisive *a decisive moment in my life*
momentous *a momentous decision*
pivotal *She played a pivotal role in winning the championship.*
vital *vital information*
ANTONYM **unimportant**
2 very serious: *a critical illness*
grave *grave danger*
precarious *a precarious financial situation*
serious *His condition is said to be serious.*
3 finding fault with something or someone: *critical remarks*
carping *carping comments*
derogatory *Derogatory expressions are hurtful.*
disapproving *a disapproving look*
disparaging *She spoke in disparaging tones.*
scathing *a scathing attack*
ANTONYM **complimentary**
See also **acute, crucial, grave, major, serious, severe, vital**

criticism

▷ NOUN

expression of disapproval: *The finance minister faced criticism over the budget.*
censure *They deserve praise rather than censure.*
disapproval *a chorus of disapproval*
disparagement *their disparagement of this book*
fault-finding *my boss's constant fault-finding*
flak INFORMAL *I got a lot of flak for that idea.*
ANTONYM **praise**
See also **censure, complaint, disapproval, review**

criticize

▷ VERB

to find fault: *The dictatorial regime has been harshly criticized.*
censure *a decision for which she was censured*
condemn *He refused to condemn their behaviour.*
find fault with *She keeps finding fault with my work.*
knock INFORMAL *Don't knock it till you've tried it.*
put down *The coach is always putting me down in front of the team.*
ANTONYM **praise**
See also **attack, censure, condemn, fault, put down**

croaky *See* **hoarse**

crony *See* **companion, friend**

crook

▷ NOUN

INFORMAL a criminal: *The man is a crook and a liar.*
cheat *a rotten cheat*
rogue *a lovable rogue*
scoundrel OLD-FASHIONED *He is a lying scoundrel!*
shark *Beware the sharks when you are deciding how to invest.*
swindler *Swindlers have cheated investors out of millions of dollars.*
thief *The thieves snatched the laptop.*
villain *Nobody expected her to be the villain of the story.*

crooked

▷ ADJECTIVE

1 bent or twisted: *a crooked tree*
bent *a bent back*
deformed *a deformed tree trunk*
distorted *a distorted image*
irregular *irregular lines*
out of shape *The wires were bent out of shape.*
twisted *bits of twisted metal*
warped *warped wooden shutters*
ANTONYM **straight**
2 dishonest or illegal: *crooked business practices*
corrupt *corrupt politicians*
criminal *criminal activities*
dishonest *dishonest salespeople*
fraudulent *a fraudulent claim*
illegal *illegal trading*
shady INFORMAL *shady deals*
ANTONYM **honest**

See also **corrupt, criminal, dirty, dishonest, dubious, wrong**

crop up *See* **appear**

cross

▷ VERB

1 to go across: *the bridge that crosses the river*
ford *trying to find a safe place to ford the stream*
go across *going across the road*
span *the bridge spanning the railway*
traverse *a valley traversed by streams*
2 to meet and go across: *the intersection where the roads cross*
crisscross *Phone wires crisscross the street.*
intersect *The circles intersect in two places.*
▷ NOUN
3 a mixture of two things: *a cross between a collie and a retriever*
blend *a blend of the old and the new*
combination *a combination of fear and anger*
mixture *a mixture of two emotions*
▷ ADJECTIVE
4 rather angry: *I'm really cross with you.*
angry *Are you angry with me?*
annoyed *I'm annoyed with myself for being so stupid.*
fractious *The children were getting fractious.*
fretful *a fretful expression on her face*
grumpy *It's a movie about grumpy old men.*
in a bad mood *He's in a bad mood about something.*
irritable *She had been restless and irritable all day.*
See also **angry**

cross out *See* **delete**

cross your mind *See* **occur**

crouch

▷ VERB

to squat down: *crouching behind the car*
bend down *I bent down and touched the grass.*
squat *He squatted on his heels to talk to the children.*
See also **bend**

crow *See* **boast, brag**

crowd

▷ NOUN

1 a large group of people: *a large crowd at the garage sale*
horde *hordes of tourists*
host FORMAL *a host of golden daffodils*

mass *a heaving mass of people*
mob *a mob of demonstrators*
multitude *surrounded by a noisy multitude*
swarm *swarms of visitors*
throng *An official pushed through the throng.*
▷ VERB
2 to gather close together: *Thousands of fans crowded into the stadium.*
congregate *A large crowd congregated outside the arena.*
gather *Dozens of people gathered to watch.*
swarm *Police swarmed into the area.*
throng *The crowds thronged into the mall on Boxing Day.*
See also **band, bunch, company, group, jam, lot, mass, number**

crowded
▷ ADJECTIVE
full of people: *a crowded room*
congested *congested cities*
full *The train was full.*
overflowing *buildings overflowing with students*
packed *By noon, the store was packed.*

crowing *See* boastful

crown *See* top

crucial
▷ ADJECTIVE
very important: *a crucial moment in her career*
central *central to the whole process*
critical *a critical point in the campaign*
decisive *ready to strike at the decisive moment*
momentous *a momentous event*
pivotal *He played a pivotal role in winning the World Series.*
vital *vital information*
See also **critical, essential, major, serious, vital**

crude
▷ ADJECTIVE
1 rough and simple: *a crude weapon*
primitive *They managed to make a primitive harness.*
rough *a rough sketch*
rudimentary *some form of rudimentary heating*
simple *a simple stringed instrument*
2 rude and offensive: *a crude sense of humour*
coarse *coarse speech*
dirty *a dirty joke*
indecent *indecent lyrics*
obscene *obscene language*

tasteless *a tasteless remark*
vulgar *a vulgar expression*
ANTONYM **refined**
See also **indecent, primitive, vulgar**

cruel
▷ ADJECTIVE
deliberately causing hurt: *I can't understand why people are cruel to animals.*
barbarous *a barbarous attack*
brutal *a brutal murder*
callous *callous treatment*
cold-blooded *a cold-blooded killer*
heartless *It was a heartless thing to do.*
inhumane *He was held under inhumane conditions.*
sadistic *mistreated by sadistic guards*
vicious *a vicious blow*
ANTONYM **kind**
See also **harsh, malicious, merciless, savage, spiteful, unkind, violent**

cruelty
▷ NOUN
cruel behaviour: *an act of unbelievable cruelty*
barbarity *the barbarity of war*
brutality *police brutality*
callousness *the callousness of his murder*
inhumanity *instances of inhumanity throughout history*
savagery *scenes of unimaginable savagery*
viciousness *the viciousness of the attacks*
ANTONYM **kindness**
See also **violence**

cruise *See* wander

crumb *See* bit

crumble *See* crush, disintegrate

crumple
▷ VERB
to squash and wrinkle: *She crumpled the paper in her hand.*
crease *Don't crease the material.*
crush *I crushed the empty can.*
wrinkle *trying not to wrinkle her silk skirt*
See also **crush, fold**

crunch *See* chew

crusade *See* campaign

crush
▷ VERB
1 to destroy the shape of by squeezing: *Their car was crushed, but nobody was seriously hurt.*
crumble *Crumble the cheese over the salad.*

C

crumple *She crumpled the note up and threw it away.*
mash *Mash the bananas with a fork.*
squash *She squashed the bug with her thumb.*
2 to defeat completely: *The Blue Jays crushed the Yankees.*
overcome *working to overcome the enemy forces*
put down *Soldiers moved in to put down the rebellion.*
quell *Troops eventually quelled the unrest.*
stamp out *steps to stamp out bullying in schools*
vanquish *his vanquished foe*
See also **crumple, dash, defeat, jam, press, subdue, suppress, vanquish**

cry
▷ *VERB*
1 to have tears coming from your eyes: *Stop crying and tell me what's wrong.*
See **WORD STUDY cry**
2 to call out loudly: *"See you soon!" they cried.*
call *She called to me across the room.*
exclaim *"You must be mad!" he exclaimed.*
shout *"Over here!" they shouted.*
yell *He yelled out of the window.*
▷ *NOUN*
3 a loud or high shout: *a cry of pain*
call *the call of a seagull*
exclamation *an exclamation of surprise*
shout *I heard a distant shout.*
yell *He let out a yell.*
See also **bay, call, scream, shout**

cryptic See **mysterious, obscure**

crystalline See **clear, transparent**

cuddle See **hug**

cue See **signal**

culminate See **peak**

culmination See **peak, top**

culprit See **criminal**

cultivate See **breed**

cultivated See **educated, sophisticated**

culture See **background, society**

cultured See **civilized, educated, polite, sophisticated**

cunning
▷ *ADJECTIVE*
1 clever and deceitful: *a cunning and ruthless plot*
artful *an artful crook*
crafty *a crafty plan*
devious *a devious mind*
sly *a sly trick*
wily *a wily politician*
ANTONYM **open**
▷ *NOUN*
2 cleverness and deceit: *the cunning of today's criminals*
deviousness *the deviousness of drug traffickers*
guile *She was without guile or pretence.*
See also **crafty, sly**

curb
▷ *VERB*
1 to keep something within limits: *He must learn to curb that temper of his.*
check *an attempt to check the spread of the disease*

WORD STUDY: CRY

There are a number of words that you can use instead of **cry**, if you want to say a little more about how someone cries.

- If you **weep**, you cry. This is quite a literary word.
The woman began to **weep** uncontrollably.

- If you **whimper**, you make a low. unhappy sound as if you are about to cry,
He huddled in a corner, **whimpering** with fear.

- If you **sob**, you cry in a noisy way, with short breaths.
My sister broke down and began to **sob** into her handkerchief.

- If you **blubber**, you cry noisily and in an unattractive way.
To our surprise, he began to **blubber** like a child.

- If you **howl** or **wail**, you cry with a long, loud noise.
The baby was **howling** in the next room.
The mother began to **wail** for her injured child.

- If you **bawl**, you cry very loudly.
One of the toddlers was **bawling**.

contain *A hundred firefighters are still trying to contain the fire.*
control *the need to control environmental pollution*
limit *He limited his speech to five minutes.*
restrain *efforts to restrain corruption*
suppress *to suppress freedom of expression*
▷ *NOUN*
2 an attempt to keep something within limits: *She called for stricter curbs on government spending.*
brake *Illness had put a brake on his progress.*
control *price controls*
limit *limits on government spending*
limitation *We need a limitation on the powers of the government.*
restraint *The government imposed new restraints on imports.*
See also **check, contain, halt, limit, moderate, restrain, restriction, suppress**

curdled *See* **sour**

cure
▷ *VERB*
1 to make well: *Doctors are still seeking a treatment that will cure the common cold.*
heal *plants used to heal wounds*
remedy *an operation to remedy a blood clot*
▷ *NOUN*
2 something that makes an illness better: *a cure for the disease*
medicine *herbal medicines*
remedy *a remedy for acne*
treatment *the most effective treatment for malaria*
See also **correct**

curiosity
▷ *NOUN*
1 the desire to know: *a curiosity about the past*
inquisitiveness *the inquisitiveness of children*
interest *an interest in current affairs*
2 something unusual: *a museum displaying relics and curiosities*
freak *The sudden storm was a freak of nature.*
marvel *a marvel of science*
novelty *in the days when a home computer was a novelty*
oddity *Tourists are still something of an oddity here.*
rarity *Mexican restaurants are a rarity here.*
See also **interest**

curious
▷ *ADJECTIVE*
1 wanting to know: *He was curious about*

my family.
inquiring *He gave me an inquiring look.*
inquisitive *Cats are very inquisitive.*
interested *A crowd of interested people gathered.*
nosy INFORMAL *nosy neighbours*
2 strange and unusual: *a curious mixture of the old and the new*
bizarre *his bizarre behaviour*
extraordinary *an extraordinary story*
odd *an odd coincidence*
peculiar *a peculiar smell*
singular *singular talent*
strange *a strange taste*
unusual *an unusual hobby*
ANTONYM **ordinary**
See also **bizarre, nosy, odd, peculiar, strange, unusual, weird**

curl *See* **coil, twist**

current
▷ *NOUN*
1 a strong continuous movement of water: *swept away by the strong current*
flow *the quiet flow of the blue-green water*
tide *We will sail with the tide.*
undertow *Dangerous undertows make swimming unsafe along the coastline.*
▷ *ADJECTIVE*
2 happening, being done, or being used now: *current trends*
contemporary *He has adopted a more contemporary style of dress.*
fashionable *the fashionable theory about this issue*
ongoing *an ongoing discussion on pollution control*
present *The house was skilfully renovated by the present owners.*
present-day *Even by present-day standards these are large aircraft.*
today's *In today's Canada, health care is a major issue.*
up-to-the-minute *up-to-the-minute reports on traffic conditions*
ANTONYM **past**
See also **fashionable, flow, modern, recent**

currently *See* **now**

curriculum *See* **course**

curriculum vitae *See* **record**

curse *See* **abuse**

cursed *See* **unlucky**

cursory *See* **casual, quick**

curt *See* **abrupt, impatient**

curtail *See* **reduce**

curve
▷ *NOUN*
1 a bending line: *a curve in the road*
arc *Our eyes followed the rainbow's arc.*
bend *a bend in the river*
trajectory *the trajectory of the football*
turn *every turn in the road*
▷ *VERB*
2 to move in a curve: *The road curved sharply to the left.*
arc *A rainbow arced over the town.*
arch *a domed ceiling arching overhead*
bend *The path bent to the right.*
swerve *The car swerved off the road.*
See also **bend**

custody *See* **possession**

custom
▷ *NOUN*
1 a traditional activity: *a family custom to have a birthday picnic*
convention *the conventions of Canadian football*
practice *a medical practice that's been around forever*
ritual *a ritual of the religion*
tradition *different cultural traditions*
2 something a person always does: *It was his custom to start work at 8:30.*
habit *his habit of making tactless remarks*
practice *her usual practice of arriving early*
routine *his daily routine*
wont FORMAL *He woke early, as was his wont.*
See also **convention, habit, practice, tradition, way**

customary *See* **conventional, regular, standard, usual**

customer
▷ *NOUN*
someone who buys something: *The store was filled with customers.*
buyer *The real estate agent showed the home to several potential buyers.*
client *a lawyer and her client*
consumer *the increasing demands of consumers*
patron *the restaurant's patrons*
purchaser *a prospective purchaser*
shopper *late-night shoppers on their way home*

cut
▷ *VERB*
1 to mark or injure with something sharp:

He accidentally cut his chin while he was shaving.
See WORD STUDY **cut** *on next page*
2 to reduce something: *The department's first priority is to cut costs.*
cut back *The government has decided to cut back on defence spending.*
decrease *calls to decrease income tax*
lower *The Bank of Canada has lowered interest rates.*
reduce *Gradually reduce the dosage of the medication.*
slash *Hotel prices have been slashed.*
ANTONYM **increase**
▷ *NOUN*
3 a mark or injury made by cutting: *a cut on his left eyebrow*
gash *There was a deep gash across his forehead.*
incision *a tiny incision in the skin*
slash *jeans with slashes*
slit *Make a slit in the middle of the piece of paper.*
▷ *NOUN*
4 a reduction in something: *another cut in interest rates*
cutback *cutbacks in funding*
decrease *a decrease in attendance at the games*
lowering *the lowering of taxes*
reduction *a reduction in the price of CD players*
saving *savings on second-hand DVDs*
ANTONYM **increase**
See also **carve, chop, lower, reduce, shorten**

INFORMALLY SPEAKING

cut down to size: humiliate
cut it fine: leave no room for error
cut it out: stop it
make the cut: be one of a limited number selected

---

cut back *See* **cut**

cut down *See* **decrease, reduce**

cut out *See* **eliminate, stop**

cut short *See* **halt**

cut up *See* **divide**

cutback *See* **cut, decrease**

cute
▷ *ADJECTIVE*
pretty or attractive: *You were such a cute baby!*
appealing *an appealing character*
attractive *I think you are very attractive.*

There are many useful synonyms for the word **cut**. Different words are appropriate substitutes, depending on what it is that is being cut, what is being used to do the cutting, or how deep or extensive the cutting is.

- If you **nick** something, you make a small cut on its surface.
He **nicked** his chin while he was shaving.

- If you **score** something, you cut a line or lines on its surface.
Lightly **score** the skin of the fish with a sharp knife.

- If you **pierce** something with a sharp object, or a sharp object **pierces** it, the object goes through it and makes a hole in it.
Pierce the skin of the potato with a fork.
The arrow had **pierced** the knight's armour, but he himself was not hurt.

- If something **penetrates** an object, it goes inside or it passes through it.
There sat the spider, with fangs big enough to **penetrate** skin.

- If you **slit** something, you make a long narrow cut in it.
He began to **slit** open each envelope.

- If you **gash** or **slash** something, you make a long, deep cut in it.
He **gashed** his leg on the barbed wire.
In the second act, the villain tried to **slash** the hero's throat.

- If you **trim** something, you cut off small amounts of it to make it look neater.
I have my hair **trimmed** every eight weeks.

- If you **mow** grass, you cut it with a lawnmower.
He **mowed** the lawn and did various other chores.

- If you **snip** something, you cut it with scissors or shears.
The hairdresser **snipped** off my split ends.

- If you **split** or **divide** something, you cut it into two or more parts.
Split the planks down the middle.
Divide the apple into four equal parts.

- If you **sever** something, you cut it off or cut right through it.
Dad **severed** the tendon of his thumb in an accident at work.

- If you **saw** something, you cut it with a saw.
She is **sawing** wood in the basement.

- If you **slice** something, you cut it into thin pieces.
I **sliced** the celery into thin strips.

- If you **chop** something, you cut it into pieces with strong downward movements.
You will need to **chop** the onions very finely.

- If you **carve** an object, you make it by cutting it out of a substance such as wood or stone.
He **carves** these figures from pine.

- If you **carve** meat, you cut slices from it.
Mother began to **carve** the chicken.

- If you **lop** something off, you cut it off with one quick stroke.
Somebody has **lopped** the heads off our tulips.

- If you **dock** an animal's tail, you cut it off.
I think it is cruel to **dock** the tail of any animal.

C

---

charming *a charming little cottage*
dear *Look at the puppies' dear little faces!*
good-looking *She's naturally good-looking.*
gorgeous *a gorgeous movie star*
pretty *a very pretty picture*
See also **pretty**

cycle See **sequence**

cylindrical See **round**

cynical

▷ ADJECTIVE

always thinking the worst of people: *a cynical attitude*
distrustful *distrustful of all politicians*
sceptical *a sceptical response*

Dd

dab *See* **blob**

daily *See* **everyday**

dainty *See* **fragile**

damage
▷ *VERB*
I to cause harm to something: *A fire had severely damaged the school.*
harm *a warning that the product may harm the environment*
hurt *He had hurt his back in a soccer game.*
injure *Fortunately, nobody was injured in the accident.*
▷ *NOUN*
2 harm that is done to something: *The flood caused extensive damage to the restaurant.*
harm *All dogs are capable of doing harm to humans.*
injury *He escaped without injury.*
See also **harm, injury, ruin, spoil**

damaged *See* **imperfect**

damages *See* **compensation**

damaging *See* **harmful**

damn *See* **condemn**

damp
▷ *ADJECTIVE*
slightly wet: *a damp towel*
clammy *clammy hands*
dank *The kitchen was dank and cheerless.*
humid *Visitors can expect hot and humid conditions.*
moist *The soil is reasonably moist after the September rain.*
sodden *Once inside, we changed our sodden clothes.*
soggy *soggy cheese sandwiches*
wet *My hair was still wet.*

dampen *See* **wet**

dampness
▷ *NOUN*
slight wetness: *There was dampness all over the walls.*
humidity *August's heat and humidity were intolerable.*
moisture *Compost helps the soil retain moisture.*
See also **wet**

danger
▷ *NOUN*
the possibility of harm: *Your life is in danger!*
hazard *a health hazard*
jeopardy *A series of setbacks have put the whole project in jeopardy.*
menace *a menace to the public*
peril *the perils of the sea*
risk *The inexperienced skier took a risk going down the difficult slope.*
threat *the threat of a tornado*
ANTONYM **safety**
See also **risk**

dangerous
▷ *ADJECTIVE*
likely to cause harm: *It's dangerous to ride a bike without a helmet.*
hazardous *It's hazardous to skate on thin ice.*
perilous *a perilous journey across the Arctic*
risky *Investing your money can be risky.*
treacherous *Freezing rain had made the roads treacherous.*
ANTONYM **safe**
See also **fierce, serious, treacherous**

dangle *See* **hang**

dank *See* **damp**

dare
▷ *VERB*
I to challenge someone to do something: *I dare you to ask him for a date.*
challenge *She challenged me to a game of tennis.*
defy *I defy you to eat just one chocolate.*
2 to have the courage to do something: *Nobody dared to complain.*
risk *The captain was not willing to risk sailing in the storm.*
venture *The hikers ventured further into the forest.*
See also **challenge, risk**

daring
▷ *ADJECTIVE*
I willing to take risks: *a daring escape by helicopter*
adventurous *an adventurous skier*
audacious *an audacious plan to win the election*
bold *bold economic reforms*
brave *She was brave enough to take on the top debater.*
fearless *They were young and strong and fearless.*
ANTONYM **cautious**
▷ *NOUN*
2 the courage to take risks: *His daring may have cost him his life.*
audacity *He had the audacity to criticize the world's leading expert on the subject.*
boldness *the boldness of the premier's economic program*

bravery *She received a medal for bravery.*
courage *He impressed everyone with his personal courage.*
guts INFORMAL *I haven't got the guts to tell him.*
nerve INFORMAL *She didn't have the nerve to meet me.*
ANTONYM **caution**
See also **bold, courage**

dark

▷ ADJECTIVE
1 lacking light: *It was too dark to see what was happening.*
cloudy *a cloudy sky*
dim *the dim outline of a small boat*
dingy *a dingy basement*
murky *the murky waters of the swamp*
overcast *a cold, windy, overcast afternoon*
shadowy *a shadowy corner*
ANTONYM **light**
2 dull in colour: *a dark suit*
black *a black leather coat*
swarthy *a swarthy complexion*
▷ NOUN
3 lack of light: *I've always been afraid of the dark.*
darkness *The room was plunged into darkness.*
dimness *I squinted to adjust my eyes to the dimness.*
dusk *She disappeared into the dusk.*
gloom *the gloom of a foggy November morning*
ANTONYM **light**
See also **dim, gloomy**

INFORMALLY SPEAKING

in the dark: not knowing or not understanding
keep dark: keep secret

---

darkness *See* **dark**

darling *See* **beloved, dear, favourite**

darn *See* **mend, repair**

dart *See* **fly, tear**

dash

▷ VERB
1 to rush somewhere: *Suddenly, the dog dashed into the street.*
bolt *I bolted for the exit.*
fly *She flew downstairs.*
race *The cyclists raced away out of sight.*
run *I ran after the man who had dropped his wallet.*
rush *Someone rushed out of the building.*
sprint *The officer sprinted to her car.*

tear *He tore off down the road.*
2 to throw or be thrown violently against something: *The waves dashed against the rocks.*
break *We watched the waves breaking against the shore.*
crash *Dishes and glasses crashed to the floor below.*
hurl *He hurled the box to the ground in rage.*
slam *She slammed her fist on the desk.*
smash *smashing the bottle against a wall*
3 to ruin or frustrate someone's hopes or ambitions: *They had their hopes raised and then dashed.*
crush *My dreams of becoming an actor have been crushed.*
destroy *The loss of the championship destroyed my confidence.*
disappoint *His Olympic hopes have been disappointed before.*
foil *Our plans to form a team were foiled by the lack of funds.*
frustrate *The government has deliberately frustrated his efforts.*
shatter *A failure would shatter all our hopes.*
thwart *The skater's gold medal dreams were thwarted when he missed the jump.*
▷ NOUN
4 a sudden movement or rush: *a dash to the hospital*
bolt *He made a bolt for the door.*
race *a race to the finish line*
run *One of the thieves made a run for it.*
rush *the mad rush not to be late for school*
sprint *a last-minute sprint to catch the bus*
stampede *There was a stampede for the exit.*
▷ NOUN
5 a small quantity of something: *a dash of vinegar*
drop *I'll have a drop of that milk in my tea.*
pinch *a pinch of salt*
splash *Add a splash of lemon juice.*
sprinkling *a light sprinkling of sugar*
See also **bolt, bustle, charge, fly, hurry, race, rush, tear, trace**

data *See* **information**

date *See* **appointment**

dated *See* **old-fashioned**

daunt *See* **discourage**

daunting *See* **formidable**

dawn *See* **start**

dawn on *See* **occur**

daydream

▷ *NOUN*

1 a series of pleasant thoughts: *He learned to escape into daydreams.*
dream *My dream is to have a house in the country.*
fantasy *fantasies of romance and love*

▷ *VERB*

2 to think about pleasant things: *She daydreams of being a famous journalist.*
dream *She used to dream of becoming an actress.*
fantasize *I fantasized about winning the Stanley Cup.*
See also **dream, vision**

days gone by *See* **the past**

day-to-day *See* **everyday**

dazed

▷ *ADJECTIVE*

unable to think clearly: *At the end of the interview, I was dazed and exhausted.*
bewildered *Some diners looked bewildered by the sheer variety of items on the menu.*
confused *Things were happening too quickly and I became confused.*
dizzy *Her head hurt and she felt dizzy.*
light-headed *If you miss breakfast, you may feel light-headed.*
numbed *I'm so numbed with shock that I can hardly think.*
stunned *a stunned silence*

dazzling *See* **bright, brilliant**

deluxe *See* **luxurious, superior**

dead

▷ *ADJECTIVE*

1 no longer alive: *Our cat's been dead a year now.*
deceased *his recently deceased grandfather*
departed *my dear departed aunt*
extinct *the bones of extinct animals*
late *her late husband*
ANTONYM **alive**
2 no longer functioning: *a dead language*
defunct *the now defunct Alliance Party*
not working *The DVD player is not working.*
See also **late, numb**

INFORMALLY SPEAKING

dead in the water: totally defeated
dead to the world: deeply asleep
over my dead body: I will resist to the end.
wouldn't be caught dead: be extremely unwilling to do

---

dead body *See* **body**

dead ringer *See* **look-alike**

deaden *See* **silence**

deadline *See* **limit**

deadly

▷ *ADJECTIVE*

causing death: *a deadly disease*
destructive *the destructive power of nuclear weapons*
fatal *a fatal heart attack*
lethal *a lethal dose of sleeping pills*
mortal *Our lives were in mortal danger.*
See also **fatal**

deadpan *See* **blank**

deafening *See* **loud, noisy**

deal

▷ *VERB*

to cope successfully with something: *He must learn to deal with stress.*
attend to *We have business to attend to first.*
cope with *They have had to cope with losing their business.*
handle *I have learned how to handle pressure.*
manage *As time passed, I learned to manage my temper.*
see to *My cousin saw to packing while I washed the car.*
take care of *They took care of all the arrangements.*
See also **administer, agreement, trade**

deal in *See* **sell, stock**

deal with *See* **handle, process, take care of, treat**

dealer *See* **trader**

dealings *See* **business**

dear

▷ *NOUN*

1 a person for whom you have affection: *What's the matter, dear?*
darling *Thank you, darling.*
sweetheart *Let me do that for you, sweetheart.*
treasure INFORMAL *That student over there? Oh, he's a treasure.*

▷ *ADJECTIVE*

2 much loved: *a dear friend of mine*
beloved *He lost his beloved wife last year.*
cherished *his most cherished possession*
darling *his darling son*
esteemed *my esteemed colleagues*
precious *Her family's support is very precious to her.*

prized *one of the gallery's most prized possessions*
treasured *one of my most treasured memories*
See also **cute**

dearest See **beloved, favourite**

dearth See **shortage**

debacle See **defeat**

debatable See **doubtful**

debate See **argue, deliberate, discuss, discussion**

debris See **garbage, remains**

debut See **appearance**

decay See **rot, ruin**

decayed See **rotten**

deceased See **dead, late**

deceit See **dishonesty, fraud, lie, lying**

deceitful See **dishonest, false, insincere, lying, sneaky, two-faced**

deceive
▷ VERB
to make someone believe something that is untrue: *I was really hurt that he had deceived me.*
con INFORMAL *We were conned into thinking we had won a free trip.*
double-cross *They were warned about being double-crossed.*
dupe *a plot to dupe collectors into buying fake stamps*
fool *They tried to fool you into thinking the party was for me.*
mislead *He was furious with his coach for having misled him.*
take in *I wasn't taken in for one moment.*
trick *I was tricked into giving away the secret.*
See also **cheat, con, dupe, fool, take in, trick**

decelerate See **slow (down)**

decency See **honour, politeness**

decent
▷ ADJECTIVE
1 of an acceptable standard: *to earn a decent salary*
adequate *an adequate diet*
passable *She speaks passable Spanish.*
reasonable *He couldn't make a reasonable living from his writing.*
respectable *a respectable interest rate*
satisfactory *I never got a satisfactory answer.*

tolerable *to make life more tolerable*
2 correct and respectable: *the decent thing to do*
proper *It is right and proper to do this.*
respectable *a perfectly respectable family*
ANTONYM **improper**
See also **respectable**

deception See **con, fraud, trick**

deceptive
▷ ADJECTIVE
likely to make people believe something that is untrue: *First impressions can be deceptive.*
false *"Thank you," she said with false enthusiasm.*
fraudulent *fraudulent claims about being a doctor*
illusory *Their moment of joy may be illusory.*
misleading *It would be misleading to say that we were friends.*
unreliable *His account of what happened is quite unreliable.*

decide
▷ VERB
to choose to do something: *She decided to write her autobiography.*
choose *They chose to close the school during the storm.*
come to a decision *Have you come to a decision about where you're going tonight?*
determine FORMAL *He determined to rescue the skiers.*
elect FORMAL *I have elected to stay.*
make up your mind *He can't make his mind up whether he should stay.*
reach a decision *She demanded to know all the facts before reaching any decision.*
resolve FORMAL *She resolved to report the matter to the authorities.*
See also **conclude, determine, resolve, settle**

decide on See **select, settle**

decide upon See **pick**

decided See **definite**

deciding See **critical**

decipher See **crack, read, solve**

decision
▷ NOUN
a judgment about something: *The umpire's decision is final.*
conclusion *I've come to the conclusion that she's a great musician.*

D

finding *It is the finding of this court that you are guilty.*
judgment *a landmark judgment by the Court of Appeal*
resolution *The committee passed a budget resolution.*
ruling *He tried to have the court ruling overturned.*
verdict *The judges will deliver their verdict in October.*
See also **verdict**

decisive *See* **critical, crucial**

deck *See* **decorate**

declaration
▷ *NOUN*
a forceful or official announcement: *a declaration of war*
affirmation *her first public affirmation as president*
protestation FORMAL *his protestations of innocence*
statement *He made a formal statement to the police.*
testimony *Their testimony was an important element in the case.*
See also **announcement, statement**

declare
▷ *VERB*
to state something forcefully or officially: *He declared that he was going to be famous.*
affirm *a speech in which she affirmed a commitment to lower taxes*
announce *They were planning to announce their engagement.*
assert *He asserted his innocence.*
certify *The mayor certified that the project would receive a grant of one million dollars.*
proclaim *He still proclaims his innocence.*
profess FORMAL *Why do organizations profess that they care?*
pronounce *The jury took time to pronounce its verdict.*
state *Please state your name.*
See also **state**

decline
▷ *VERB*
I to become smaller or weaker: *a declining birth rate*
decrease *The number of subway riders decreased last year.*
diminish *The threat of nuclear war has diminished.*
drop *His blood pressure had dropped.*
fall *The factory's output will fall by six percent.*

go down *Crime has gone down 70 percent.*
plummet *The candidate's popularity has plummeted to an all-time low.*
reduce *The number of contestants has been reduced from 12 to 10.*
ANTONYM **increase**
2 to refuse politely to accept or do something: *He declined their invitation.*
abstain *I will abstain from voting in the election.*
excuse yourself *I was invited, but I excused myself.*
refuse *He refused to comment after the trial.*
turn down *I thanked him for the offer, but turned it down.*
ANTONYM **accept**
▷ *NOUN*
3 a gradual weakening or decrease: *economic decline*
decrease *a decrease in the number of young people out of work*
downturn *a sharp downturn in sales*
drop *a drop in support for the political party*
fall *a sharp fall in the value of the Canadian dollar*
recession *The economy suffered a recession.*
shrinkage *a shrinkage in the factory's output*
slump *a slump in property prices*
ANTONYM **increase**
See also **decrease, drop, fail, fall, recession, refuse, reject, wither, worsen**

decompose *See* **rot**

decomposed *See* **rotten**

decorate
▷ *VERB*
to make more attractive: *He decorated his room with pictures.*
adorn *Several oil paintings adorn the walls.*
deck *The house was decked with flowers.*
do up INFORMAL *We did up the rec room for the party.*
renovate *The couple spent thousands renovating the house.*
See also **honour**

decorated *See* **fancy**

decoration *See* **ornament**

decorum *See* **ceremony**

decoy *See* **bait**

decrease
▷ *VERB*
I to become or make less: *Population growth is decreasing by 1.4 percent each year.*
cut down *He cut down his coffee intake.*

decline *The number of staff members has declined.*
diminish *The threat of nuclear war has diminished.*
drop *Temperatures can drop to freezing at night.*
dwindle *his dwindling authority*
lessen *changes to their diet that would lessen the risk of disease*
lower *The Bank of Canada has lowered interest rates.*
reduce *Consuming less fat reduces the risk of heart disease.*
shrink *The forests have shrunk to half their size due to fires.*
ANTONYM **increase**
▷ NOUN
2 a lessening in the amount of something: *a decrease in the number of unemployed*
cutback *cutbacks in military spending*
decline *the rate of decline in gas consumption*
drop *a drop in temperature*
lessening *a lessening of tension*
reduction *dramatic reductions in staff*
ANTONYM **increase**
See also **abate, cut, decline, diminish, drop, fall, lessen, lower, reduce**

decree *See* **command, law, order, rule**

dedicate *See* **bless**

dedicated *See* **devoted**

deduce *See* **conclude, reconstruct**

deduct *See* **subtract**

deduction *See* **conclusion**

deed *See* **achievement, act, action**

deem *See* **feel, think, view**

deep
▷ ADJECTIVE
1 being a long way to the bottom: *a deep hole*
bottomless *a bottomless pit*
yawning *a yawning chasm*
ANTONYM **shallow**
2 great or intense: *his deep love of his country*
extreme *extreme poverty*
grave *a grave crisis*
great *the great gulf between the two opinions*
intense *The pain was intense.*
profound *discoveries that had a profound effect on medicine*
serious *a serious problem*
3 low in sound: *a deep voice*
bass *a beautiful bass voice*

low *the dog's low growl*
ANTONYM **high**
See also **extreme, far, heavy, intense, serious, severe**

deeply *See* **very**

defeat
▷ VERB
1 to win a victory over someone or something: *to defeat the enemy*
beat *the team that beat us in the finals*
conquer *I conquered my fear of public speaking.*
crush *in a bid to crush the rebels*
rout *the battle at which the Norman army routed the English*
trounce *Canada trounced Sweden with four straight wins.*
vanquish FORMAL *The hero vanquished the dragon.*
▷ NOUN
2 a failure to win: *a 2-1 defeat by Russia*
conquest *the conquest of the Incas by Spain*
debacle FORMAL *It will be hard for them to recover from this debacle.*
rout *The retreat turned into a rout.*
trouncing *after a 6-2 trouncing on Sunday*
ANTONYM **victory**
See also **beat, failure, foil, subdue, vanquish**

defect
▷ NOUN
a fault or flaw: *A defect in the aircraft caused the crash.*
deficiency *a vitamin deficiency*
failing *Don't blame your failings on others.*
fault *a minor technical fault*
flaw *The flaw in his character is a short temper.*
imperfection *The vase is in excellent condition except for a slight imperfection.*
shortcoming *The book has its shortcomings.*
weakness *His weakness is his laziness.*
See also **fault, flaw, handicap, hole, weakness**

defective *See* **faulty, imperfect**

defence
▷ NOUN
1 action to protect something: *The high walls around the city made a good defence against attackers.*
cover *They could not provide adequate air cover for ground operations.*
protection *Such a diet is believed to offer*

protection against cancer.
resistance *Most people have a natural resistance to the disease.*
safeguard *legislation that offers safeguards against discrimination*
security *Airport security was tightened.*
2 an argument in support of something: *the mayor's defence of her position*
argument *There's a strong argument for lowering the price.*
excuse *There's no excuse for behaviour like that.*
explanation *The explanation for his behaviour was a little hard to believe.*
justification *There's no justification for the way they treat their animals.*
plea *a plea of insanity*
See also **safeguard**

defenceless   See **helpless**

defend

▷ VERB
I to protect from harm or damage: *The wolves defended their cubs.*
cover *travel insurance covering you against theft*
guard *security officers guarding the prince and princess*
protect *What can women do to protect themselves from heart disease?*
safeguard *action to safeguard the ozone layer*
shelter *a wooden house, sheltered by a low roof*
shield *He shielded his head from the sun with an old hat.*
2 to argue in support of: *I can't defend what he did.*
endorse *I can endorse their opinion wholeheartedly.*
justify *Can any argument justify a war?*
stick up for INFORMAL *Why do you always stick up for them?*
support *Would you support such a move?*
uphold *upholding the artist's right to creative freedom*
See also **champion, guard, justify, protect, safeguard, support**

defender

▷ NOUN
a person who argues in support of something: *a committed defender of human rights*
advocate *a strong advocate of free speech*
champion *a champion of environmental causes*

supporter *a major supporter of tax reform*
See also **champion**

defer   See **delay, postpone, put off**

deferential   See **meek**

deficiency

▷ NOUN
a lack of something: *signs of a vitamin deficiency*
deficit *a staffing deficit*
deprivation *sleep deprivation*
inadequacy *the inadequacies of the current system*
lack *a lack of people wanting to start new businesses*
ANTONYM **abundance**
See also **defect, failure, fault, lack, shortage, want**

deficient

▷ ADJECTIVE
lacking in something: *a diet deficient in vitamins*
inadequate *inadequate staffing*
lacking *Why was military intelligence so lacking?*
poor *soil that is poor in zinc*
short *The proposals were short on detail.*
wanting *He analyzed his game and found it wanting.*
See also **inadequate, incomplete, insufficient, weak**

deficit   See **deficiency**

define   See **describe, explain**

definite

▷ ADJECTIVE
I unlikely to be changed: *It's too soon to give a definite answer.*
assured *Victory was still not assured.*
certain *Very little in life is certain.*
decided *Is anything decided yet?*
fixed *The restaurant offers fixed prices for its dinners.*
guaranteed *Success is not guaranteed.*
settled *Nothing is settled yet.*
2 certainly true: *The police had nothing definite against them.*
clear *It was a clear case of nerves.*
positive *We have positive proof that he was a blackmailer.*
See also **certain, clear, final, sure**

definitely   See **certainly**

definitely not   See **no**

definition   See **explanation**

definitive   See **final**

deformed   See **distorted**

defraud *See* **cheat, rob**

defunct *See* **dead**

defy *See* **challenge, dare, disobey, rebel, resist**

degenerate *See* **worsen**

degree *See* **extent, measure**

dehydrate *See* **dry**

dejected *See* **disappointed, down, gloomy, miserable, sad**

dejection *See* **despair, disappointment, sadness**

delay

▷ VERB

1 to put something off until later: *the decision to delay the announcement until tomorrow*
defer *Customers often defer payment for as long as possible.*
postpone *The visit has been postponed indefinitely.*
procrastinate *Stop procrastinating and finish your homework.*
put off *They put off their visit until tomorrow.*
shelve *The project has now been shelved.*
suspend *The production was suspended until the problems were fixed.*
2 to slow or hinder something: *Various setbacks delayed production.*
check *a policy to check the growth in unemployment*
hinder *Further investigation was hindered by the loss of the e-mails.*
impede *Fallen rocks are impeding the progress of rescue workers.*
obstruct *The authorities are obstructing an investigation.*
set back *a strike that could set back production*
ANTONYM **hurry**
▷ NOUN
3 a time when something is delayed: *a seven-hour work stoppage that caused delays on most flights*
interruption *interruptions in the supply of food*
obstruction *Obstruction of justice is a criminal offence.*
setback *a setback for the peace process*
See also **hinder, impede, pause, postpone, put off, wait**

delayed *See* **late**

delectable *See* **delicious**

delegate *See* **representative**

delete

▷ VERB

to remove something written: *I accidentally deleted the e-mail.*
cross out *He crossed out the first sentence and wrote it again.*
erase *It was unfortunate that she had erased the message.*
rub out *She rubbed out the marks in the margin.*
See also **remove**

D

deliberate

▷ ADJECTIVE

1 done on purpose: *a deliberate act of sabotage*
calculated *a calculated attempt to cover up her crime*
conscious *I made a conscious decision not to hide.*
intentional *The kick was intentional.*
premeditated *a premeditated attack*
studied *"It's an interesting game," he said with studied understatement.*
ANTONYM **accidental**
2 careful and not hurried: *His movements were gentle and deliberate.*
careful *The trip needs careful planning.*
cautious *a cautious approach*
measured *walking at a measured pace*
methodical *Da Vinci was methodical in his research.*
ANTONYM **casual**
▷ VERB
3 to think carefully about something: *The jury deliberated for five days before reaching a verdict.*
debate *He was debating whether he should tell her.*
meditate *He meditated on the uncertainties of his future.*
mull over *The director had been mulling over an idea for a movie.*
ponder *He was pondering the problem when I drove up.*
reflect *I reflected on the child's future.*
See also **consider, think**

deliberately *See* **on purpose**

deliberation *See* **consideration, thought**

delicacy *See* **tact**

delicate *See* **fine, fragile, sheer, weak**

delicious

▷ ADJECTIVE

tasting very nice: *a wide selection of delicious foods*

appetizing *the appetizing smell of freshly baked bread*
delectable *delectable pie*
luscious *luscious fruit*
tasty *The food was very tasty.*
See also **tasty**

delight
▷ *NOUN*
1 great pleasure or joy: *To my great delight, it worked.*
glee *The victory was greeted with glee.*
happiness *Our happiness at being rescued knew no bounds.*
joy *the joys of being a grandparent*
pleasure *the pleasure of seeing your face*
rapture *gasps of rapture*
satisfaction *a feeling of satisfaction at the end of my speech*
▷ *VERB*
2 to give someone great pleasure: *The report has delighted environmentalists.*
amuse *a selection of toys to amuse the baby*
captivate *captivated the world with their extraordinary skating*
charm *She charmed her friends with her witty conversation.*
enchant *We were enchanted by the house.*
please *It pleased him to talk to her.*
thrill *The quadruple jumps thrilled the crowd.*
See also **charm, ecstasy, entertain, entrance, happiness, joy, please, pride, rejoice**

delight in *See* **enjoy**

delighted *See* **glad, joyful, pleased**

delightful *See* **agreeable, beautiful, lovely, pleasant**

delinquent *See* **criminal**

deliver *See* **give, issue, release, save**

delude *See* **dupe**

deluge *See* **flood, rain**

delusion *See* **illusion**

demand
▷ *VERB*
to need or require something: *This situation demands hard work.*
involve *Running a restaurant involves long hours.*
need *a problem that needs careful handling*
require *Then he'll know what's required of him.*
take *Walking across the room took all her strength.*

want *The windows wanted cleaning.*
See also **ask, command, expect, insist, need, require, requirement, take, want**

demanding *See* **difficult**

demean
▷ *VERB*
to humiliate someone: *I wasn't going to demean myself by becoming possessive.*
humiliate *How dare you humiliate me!*
See also **reduce**

demeanour *See* **manner**

demolish *See* **destroy**

demolished *See* **broken**

demolition *See* **destruction**

demonstrate *See* **agitate, prove, show**

demote *See* **reduce**

denote *See* **indicate, mean**

denounce *See* **accuse, censure, condemn, inform on**

dense *See* **slow, thick**

deny
▷ *VERB*
1 to say that something is untrue: *She denied both accusations.*
contradict *His version contradicted the official one.*
refute *He angrily refutes the charge.*
ANTONYM **admit**
2 to refuse to give something: *denied access to the property*
refuse *to refuse permission for the march*
reject *He rejected their claims.*
withhold *Financial aid to their country has been withheld.*
See also **dispute, reject**

deny oneself *See* **abstain**

depart *See* **leave**

departed *See* **dead, late**

department
▷ *NOUN*
a section of an organization: *the marketing department*
division *the restaurant chain's eastern division*
office *Contact your local tax office.*
section *a little-known section within the ministry*
unit *the health services research unit*
See also **division, field**

departure *See* **retreat, variation**

depend
▷ *VERB*
1 to rely on: *You can depend on me.*
bank on *The government is banking on the Olympics to bring in tourists.*
count on *I can always count on you to cheer me up.*
rely on *They can always be relied on to turn up.*
trust *I knew I could trust him to meet a tight deadline.*
2 to be affected by: *Success depends on the dedication of the team.*
be determined by *The weekend plans will be determined by the weather.*
hinge on *Victory or defeat hinged on the final serve.*

depend on *See* **require, trust**

dependable *See* **loyal, reliable, responsible, sure, trusty**

dependence *See* **habit**

dependency *See* **colony**

depict *See* **describe, represent**

deplete *See* **exhaust**

deplorable *See* **sorry**

deplore *See* **disapprove**

deport *See* **banish**

depose *See* **overthrow**

deposit
▷ *VERB*
to put down or leave somewhere: *The waiter deposited a hamburger in front of him.*
drop *He dropped me outside the hotel.*
lay *We laid the sandwiches on the picnic table.*
leave *Leave your key with a neighbour.*
place *I placed the book on the counter.*
put down *He put down the heavy shopping bag.*
See also **dump, keep, payment, place, put, set**

depot *See* **store**

deprave *See* **corrupt**

depraved *See* **evil, perverted, wicked**

depressed *See* **down, miserable, sad, unhappy**

depressing *See* **sad**

depression *See* **crash, misery, recession, sadness**

deprivation *See* **deficiency**

depth *See* **extreme**

depths *See* **bottom**

deputy *See* **helper, representative, substitute**

deranged *See* **mad**

D

derelict
▷ *ADJECTIVE*
abandoned and in poor condition: *a derelict warehouse*
abandoned *abandoned mines*
dilapidated *a dilapidated building*
neglected *a neglected garden*
ruined *a ruined castle*

deride *See* **belittle, make fun of, mock**

derision *See* **abuse, contempt, mockery, scorn**

derivation *See* **origin, source**

derive *See* **base, result**

derogatory *See* **critical**

descend
▷ *VERB*
to move downward: *as we descend to the basement*
dip *The sun dipped below the horizon.*
dive *The shark dived down and under the boat.*
fall *Heavy rain fell on the crops.*
go down *after the sun has gone down*
plummet *The team plummeted to the bottom of the NHL.*
sink *A fresh egg will sink, and a stale egg will float.*
ANTONYM **ascend**
See also **drop**

descendants *See* **family**

descent *See* **origin, stock**

describe
▷ *VERB*
to give an account of something: *Describe what you do in your spare time.*
define *Success can be defined in many ways.*
depict *a novel depicting a gloomy, futuristic country*
portray *a writer who accurately portrays city life*
See also **explain, report, represent**

description *See* **explanation, report**

desert *See* **abandon, barren, leave**

deserted *See* **empty, lonely**

deserve

▷ VERB

to have a right to something: *He deserves a rest.*

be entitled to *She is entitled to feel proud.*
be worthy of *The bank might think you're worthy of a loan.*
earn *You've earned this break.*
justify *The decision was fully justified by economic conditions.*
merit *Such ideas merit careful consideration.*
warrant *no evidence to warrant a murder investigation*
See also **merit**

design

▷ VERB

I to make a plan of something: *They wanted to design a new product that was both attractive and practical.*

draft *The legislation was drafted by the committee.*
draw up *to draw up a formal agreement*
outline *We outlined the proposal for review.*
plan *when we plan road construction*
▷ NOUN

2 a plan or drawing: *her design for a new office*

draft *We approved the draft.*
model *an architect's model of a new concert hall*
outline *She prepared an outline of her novel.*
plan *when you have drawn a plan of the garden*
▷ NOUN

3 the shape or style of something: *a new design of clock*

form *the form of the human body*
pattern *a pattern of coloured dots*
shape *a kidney shape*
style *Several styles of hat were available, including the toque and beret.*
See also **intend, layout, pattern, plan, structure**

designate *See* **class**

designation *See* **name, term**

designed *See* **calculated**

desirable *See* **right**

desire

▷ VERB

I to want something: *We can stay longer if you desire.*

crave *I crave chocolate cake.*
fancy *She fancied living in France.*
long for *He longed for the winter to be over.*
want *I want a sandwich.*

wish *We wished to return.*
yearn *He yearned to sleep.*
▷ NOUN

2 a feeling of wanting something: *a strong desire to help people*

appetite *She had lost her appetite for air travel.*
craving *a craving for sugar*
hankering *a hankering to be a singer*
longing *her longing to return home*
wish *Her wish is to be in movies.*
yearning *a yearning for a good night's sleep*
yen INFORMAL *a yen to go inline skating*
See also **longing, passion, urge, want, wish**

desist *See* **stop**

desist from *See* **cease**

desolate *See* **barren, lonely**

despair

▷ NOUN

I a loss of hope: *feelings of despair*
dejection *There was an air of dejection about them.*
despondency *There's a mood of despondency in the country.*
gloom *the deepening gloom over the team's record*
hopelessness *a feeling of hopelessness about the future*
▷ VERB

2 to lose hope: *Don't despair. I know things will be all right.*

feel dejected *We all have days when we feel dejected.*
feel despondent *The workers felt despondent when the factory closed.*
lose heart *He appealed to his supporters not to lose heart.*
lose hope *You mustn't lose hope.*
See also **misery**

despatch *See* **message**

desperate *See* **terrible**

despicable *See* **hateful, low, shabby**

despise *See* **hate, scorn**

despite

▷ PREPOSITION

in spite of: *Despite its condition, he bought the car anyway.*

in spite of *In spite of a recent injury, she won the race.*
notwithstanding FORMAL *Notwithstanding his age, he had an important job.*
regardless of *She wanted the computer, regardless of its cost.*
See also **in spite of**

despondency *See* **despair, disappointment, sadness**

despondent *See* **disappointed, pessimistic, unhappy**

destiny *See* **fate, luck**

destitute *See* **poor**

destitution *See* **hardship, poverty**

destroy

▷ *VERB*

to ruin something completely: *The building was completely destroyed.*

annihilate *The volcano's lava annihilated everything in its path.*

demolish *A storm moved over the island, demolishing buildings.*

devastate *A fire had devastated large parts of the building.*

obliterate *Whole villages were obliterated by fire.*

raze *The existing stadium will be razed.*

ruin *Don't ruin your health through worry.*

wreck *the injuries that nearly wrecked his hockey career*

See also **bomb, dash, eat away, erode, kill, put down, ruin, spoil**

destruction

▷ *NOUN*

the act of destroying something: *the destruction of the ozone layer*

annihilation *Leaders fear the annihilation of their people.*

demolition *the demolition of an old bridge*

devastation *A huge blast brought chaos and devastation.*

obliteration *the obliteration of three rainforests*

See also **ruin**

destructive *See* **deadly, harmful**

detach *See* **remove, separate**

detached *See* **alone, distant, impersonal, remote, separate**

detail

▷ *NOUN*

an individual feature of something: *We discussed every detail of the performance.*

aspect *Climate affects every aspect of our lives.*

element *one of the key elements of the peace plan*

particular *You will find all the particulars in the brochure.*

point *Many of the points in the report are correct.*

respect *At least in this respect we have something in common.*

detailed *See* **elaborate, full**

detain *See* **imprison, jail**

detect *See* **discern, find, notice, spot**

deter *See* **discourage**

deteriorate *See* **erode, worsen**

D

deterioration *See* **rot, wear**

determination

▷ *NOUN*

a firm decision to do something: *the government's determination to improve health care*

perseverance *Through perseverance, she managed to arrange an interview.*

persistence *She was determined to be a doctor, and her persistence paid off.*

resolution *She acted with resolution and courage.*

resolve FORMAL *a firm resolve to break the habit*

tenacity *Hard work and sheer tenacity are crucial to career success.*

See also **drive, resolve, will**

determine

▷ *VERB*

1 to cause or control a situation or result: *The size of the chicken pieces will determine the cooking time.*

control *Can anyone control the aging process?*

decide *The results will decide if she makes the team.*

dictate *A number of factors dictate how long the tree will survive.*

govern *the rules governing eligibility in the contest*

shape *the role of the government in shaping the future of Canada*

2 to decide or settle something firmly: *The final wording had not yet been determined.*

arrange *It was arranged that the guests would gather in the lobby.*

choose *Halifax was chosen as the site for the convention.*

decide *The matter was decided after a careful discussion.*

fix *The date of the election was fixed.*

resolve *She resolved to report the matter to the authorities.*

settle *That's settled then. We'll do it tomorrow.*

3 to find out the facts about something: *The investigation will determine what really happened.*

ascertain FORMAL *We need to ascertain the true facts.*
confirm *X-rays have confirmed that you have not broken any bones.*
discover *It was difficult for us to discover the reason for the decision.*
establish *to establish the cause of death*
find out *one family's campaign to find out the truth*
verify *Please verify that your e-mail address is correct.*
See also **calculate, decide, learn, resolve, see, settle**

determined
▷ ADJECTIVE
firmly decided: *She was determined not to repeat the error.*
bent on *They seem bent on inviting themselves to the party.*
dogged *dogged persistence*
intent on *She is intent on repeating her Olympic victory.*
persistent *He phoned again this morning. He's very persistent.*
purposeful *She had a purposeful air.*
resolute FORMAL *a decisive and resolute leader*
single-minded *a single-minded determination to win*
tenacious *a tenacious and persistent interviewer*
See also **firm, set on**

detest See **dislike, hate**

detested See **unpopular**

detonate See **explode, fire**

detonation See **bang**

detract from See **belittle**

detriment See **cost**

detrimental See **harmful**

devastate See **destroy, ruin**

devastation See **destruction, ruin**

develop
▷ VERB
I to grow or become more advanced: *to develop at different rates*
advance *tracing how medical technology has advanced to its present state*
evolve *Scientific knowledge evolves over the years.*
grow *The kittens grew into cats.*
mature *to mature physically and emotionally*
progress *Your piano playing has progressed noticeably.*

result *Ignore the warnings, and illness could result.*
spring *His anger seemed to spring from nowhere.*
2 to become affected by an illness or fault: *He developed a bad cold.*
catch *catch a cold*
come down with *Three members of the band came down with the flu.*
contract FORMAL *He contracted pneumonia.*
fall ill *to fall ill with measles*
pick up *They've picked up an infection from something they've eaten.*
succumb *I was determined not to succumb to the virus.*
See also **breed, build, elaborate, enlarge on, expand, expand on, extend, form, grow, progress, result, work out**

development See **advance, growth, improvement**

deviant See **perverted**

deviation See **variation**

device See **bomb, gadget, machine**

devious
▷ ADJECTIVE
getting what you want by sly methods: *devious ways of getting the starring role in the play*
calculating *a calculating politician*
scheming *He was branded a scheming liar.*
underhand *They used underhand tactics to win the election.*
wily *a wily old fox*
See also **crafty, cunning, sly, sneaky**

deviousness See **cunning**

devise See **compose, create, plan**

devoted
▷ ADJECTIVE
very loving and loyal: *a devoted parent*
constant *her constant companion*
dedicated *dedicated followers of classical music*
doting *doting grandparents*
faithful *a faithful old dog*
loving *a loving husband*
loyal *a loyal friend*
true *She is true to her friends.*
See also **ardent, enthusiastic, faithful, fond, loving**

devotee See **fan, fanatic**

devotion See **love, worship**

devotional See **religious**

devour See **gobble**

devout *See* **fervent, holy, religious**

dexterity *See* **skill**

diagnose *See* **identify**

diagram *See* **pattern, plan**

dialect *See* **language**

dialogue *See* **discussion**

dictate *See* **determine, impose, order**

dictatorial *See* **absolute, bossy**

die

▷ VERB

I to stop living: *to die in an accident*
expire FORMAL *before he finally expired*
pass away *He passed away last year.*
pass on *My grandfather passed on four years ago.*
perish FORMAL *the ferry disaster in which 193 passengers perished*
2 to fade away: *My love for you will never die.*
fade away *With time, they said, the pain will fade away.*
fade out *This type of store seems to be fading out.*
peter out *The six-month strike seemed to be petering out.*

INFORMALLY SPEAKING

die down: become calmer
die hard: resist to the end
to die for: excellent

---

die away *See* **cease, fade**

die out

▷ VERB

to cease to exist: *That custom has died out now.*
disappear *Huge areas of the countryside are disappearing.*
fade *Prospects for peace had already started to fade.*
vanish *those species that have vanished*
See also **disappear, vanish**

diet *See* **food**

differ *See* **clash, conflict, disagree**

difference

▷ NOUN

I a lack of similarity between things: *the vast difference in size*
contrast *the real contrast between the two poems*
discrepancy *discrepancies between their statements*
disparity *disparities between poor and wealthy nations*

distinction *a distinction between Canadian and American football*
divergence *a substantial divergence of opinion*
variation *a wide variation in the prices charged*
ANTONYM **similarity**
2 the amount by which two quantities differ: *The difference is 853.*
balance *They were due to pay the balance on delivery.*
remainder *They own a 75 percent stake. The remainder is owned by the bank.*
See also **change, disagreement, gap, variation**

difference of opinion *See* **division**

different

▷ ADJECTIVE

I unlike something else: *We have totally different views.*
contrasting *painted in contrasting colours*
disparate FORMAL *The countries are very disparate in size and wealth.*
dissimilar *His methods were not dissimilar to those used by his predecessor.*
divergent FORMAL *divergent opinions*
opposed *two opposed ideologies*
unlike *This restaurant serves unusual food, quite unlike what I'm used to.*
ANTONYM **similar**
2 unusual and out of the ordinary: *The result is interesting and different.*
special *a special variety of strawberry*
unique *Each person's signature is unique.*
3 distinct and separate: *to support a different charity each year*
another *My doctor referred me to a specialist.*
discrete FORMAL *two discrete sets of nerves*
distinct *A word may have two quite distinct meanings.*
individual *Each child needs individual attention.*
separate *The word "quarter" has two completely separate meanings.*
See also **various**

different from *See* **unlike**

differentiate *See* **distinguish**

difficult

▷ ADJECTIVE

I not easy to do or solve: *a difficult decision to make*
arduous *a long, arduous journey*
demanding *a demanding job*
hard *He found it hard to get work.*

intractable FORMAL *an intractable problem*
laborious *a laborious task*
uphill *an uphill battle*
ANTONYM **easy**
2 not easy to deal with: *I hope they're not going to be difficult.*
demanding *a demanding problem*
troublesome *a troublesome individual*
trying *The whole business has been very trying.*
See also **complex, formidable, hard, rough, serious, stiff, tough, tricky**

difficulty
▷ NOUN
I a problem: *The main difficulty is his inability to get along with others.*
complication *complications following surgery*
hassle INFORMAL *all the usual hassles at the airport*
hurdle *Preparing a résumé is the first hurdle in a job search.*
obstacle *To succeed, you must learn to overcome obstacles.*
pitfall *the pitfalls of a camping trip*
problem *He quit the team because of problems with the coach.*
snag *The only snag was that he had no means of transportation.*
trouble *What seems to be the trouble?*
2 the quality of being difficult: *a problem of great difficulty*
hardship *economic hardship*
strain *the stresses and strains of a busy career*
tribulation FORMAL *the trials and tribulations of everyday life*
See also **bother, distress, drawback, fix, hardship, obstacle, problem, snag, trouble**

diffident *See* **hesitant, timid**

diffuse *See* **distribute**

diffusion *See* **spread**

dig
▷ VERB
I to break up soil or sand: *to dig a hole in the ground*
burrow *Rabbits burrow into the ground.*
excavate *The archaeologists began by excavating the soil.*
gouge *quarries that have gouged great holes in the hills*
hollow out *The mice hollowed out their home from the cushions.*
quarry *The caves are quarried for limestone.*

till *freshly tilled fields*
tunnel *The prisoners tunnelled their way out of jail.*
2 to push something in: *He could feel the coins digging into his palm.*
jab *A needle was jabbed into the patient's arm.*
poke *She poked a fork into the baked potato.*
thrust *He thrust his hand into the sticky mess.*
▷ NOUN
3 a push or poke: *a dig in the ribs*
jab *a swift jab in the stomach*
poke *a playful poke in the arm*
prod *He gave the donkey a prod.*
thrust *knife thrusts*
See also **poke, stick**

INFORMALLY SPEAKING
dig in: begin to eat heartily
dig up: find by searching thoroughly

digest *See* **absorb, take in**

digit *See* **figure, number**

dignitary *See* **figure**

dilapidated *See* **derelict, shabby**

dilemma *See* **jam**

diligent *See* **industrious**

dilute *See* **thin**

diluted *See* **thin**

dim
▷ ADJECTIVE
I not bright or well lit: *a dim outline of a small boat*
dark *a dark corridor*
dull *The stamp was a dark, dull blue.*
grey *a grey, wet April Sunday*
murky *one murky November afternoon*
poorly lit *a poorly lit road*
shadowy *a shadowy corner*
2 vague or unclear: *a dim memory*
faint *a faint recollection*
hazy *Many details remain hazy.*
indistinct *the indistinct murmur of voices*
obscure *The origin of the custom is obscure.*
shadowy *the shadowy world of spies*
vague *I have a vague memory of the incident.*
ANTONYM **clear**
3 INFORMAL slow to understand: *He is rather dim.*
dense *Please repeat that. I'm feeling a bit dense today.*
obtuse *He's too obtuse to understand your point.*

slow *I'm a bit slow until I've had my morning shower.*
stupid *How could I have been so stupid?*
thick INFORMAL *I must have seemed incredibly thick.*
ANTONYM **bright**
See also **dark, fade, faint, slow, soft, stupid**

dimensions *See* **capacity, size**

diminish
▷ *VERB*
to reduce or become reduced: *The threat of war has diminished.*
contract *The factory's production fell last year and is expected to contract further.*
decrease *Gradually decrease your speed.*
lessen *New medications lessened the degree of allergic reactions.*
lower *This drug lowers cholesterol levels.*
reduce *It reduces the risk of heart disease.*
shrink *My interest in movies is starting to shrink.*
weaken *The prime minister's authority has been seriously weakened.*
See also **abate, decline, decrease, drop, fall, lessen, lower, reduce, shrink, weaken**

diminutive *See* **tiny**

dimness *See* **dark**

din *See* **crash, noise, racket, sound**

dine *See* **eat**

dingy *See* **dark, drab**

dinner *See* **function, meal**

dip *See* **descend**

diplomacy *See* **tact**

diplomatic *See* **tactful**

dire *See* **extreme, severe, terrible**

direct
▷ *ADJECTIVE*
1 in a straight line or with nothing in between: *the direct route*
first-hand *She has little first-hand experience in the theatre.*
immediate *She is my immediate superior at work.*
personal *I have no personal experience of this.*
straight *Keep the boat in a straight line.*
uninterrupted *an uninterrupted view*
ANTONYM **indirect**
2 open and honest: *He can sometimes be very direct.*
blunt *She is blunt to her customers.*
candid *I haven't been completely candid with you.*

forthright *forthright language*
frank *She is always very frank.*
straight *He never gives you a straight answer.*
straightforward *her straightforward manner*
ANTONYM **devious**
▷ *VERB*
3 to control and guide something: *She will direct day-to-day operations at work.*
control *He now controls the entire company.*
guide *He should have let his instinct guide him.*
lead *Mackenzie King led the country during World War II.*
manage *Within two years, she was managing the store.*
oversee *an architect to oversee the work*
run *Is this any way to run a country?*
supervise *I supervise the packing of all mail orders.*
See also **administer, command, conduct, control, express, focus, guide, head, immediate, influence, instruct, lead, manage, order, oversee, require, run, straightforward, supervise, tell**

direction
▷ *NOUN*
1 the line in which something is moving: *five kilometres in the opposite direction*
course *The pilot altered course.*
path *He nearly stepped into the path of an oncoming bus.*
route *We took the wrong route.*
way *Does anybody know the way to the washroom?*
2 control and guidance of something: *He was chopping vegetables under the chef's direction.*
charge *A few years ago she took charge of the company.*
command *Last year, she took command of the squadron.*
control *It was time to give up control of the company.*
guidance *the reports that were produced under his guidance*
leadership *The agency doubled in size under her leadership.*
management *The zoo needed better management.*
See also **control, course, management, path**

directive *See* **command, order**

directly *See* **immediately**

director *See* **boss, chief, head, leader, manager**

directors *See* **management**

directory *See* **list**

dirt

▷ NOUN

1 dust or mud: *I started to scrub off the dirt.*
dust *The furniture was covered in dust.*
filth *cleaning up the filth and sewage*
grime *I scrubbed the grime off my hands.*
muck *All this muck was interfering with the filter.*
mud *Their truck got stuck in the mud.*
2 earth or soil: *He drew a circle in the dirt with the stick.*
earth *a huge pile of earth*
soil *an area with very good soil*
See also **earth, gossip, ground, soil**

dirty

▷ ADJECTIVE

1 marked with dirt: *The kids' clothes are dirty.*
filthy *a pair of filthy jeans*
grimy *a grimy industrial city*
grubby *kids with grubby faces*
mucky *a mucky floor*
muddy *his muddy boots*
soiled *soiled white running shoes*
unclean *unclean water*
ANTONYM **clean**
2 unfair or dishonest: *a dirty fight*
corrupt *corrupt practices*
crooked *crooked business deals*
ANTONYM **honest**
3 sexually explicit: *a dirty joke*
blue *a blue movie*
filthy *a filthy book*
pornographic *pornographic writing*
rude *a rude joke*
See also **crude, indecent, obscene, shabby, soil, stain, vulgar**

disability *See* **handicap**

disable *See* **cripple**

disadvantage

▷ NOUN

an unfavourable circumstance: *the advantages and disadvantages of changing the law*
drawback *The apartment's only drawback was that it was too small.*
handicap *The star goalie's absence was undoubtedly a handicap to the team.*
minus *The plusses and minuses were about equal.*

weakness *the strengths and weaknesses of the argument*
ANTONYM **advantage**
See also **catch, handicap, snag**

disagree

▷ VERB

1 to have a different opinion: *They can communicate even when they disagree.*
differ *They differ on lots of issues.*
dispute *Nobody disputed that she was bright.*
dissent *dissenting views*
ANTONYM **agree**
2 to think that something is wrong: *I disagree with that policy in general.*
object *We objected strongly but were outvoted.*
oppose *protesters opposing nuclear tests*
take issue with *I take issue with much of what he said.*
See also **argue, clash, conflict, protest**

disagreeable

▷ ADJECTIVE

unpleasant in some way: *a disagreeable odour*
horrible *horrible behaviour*
horrid *What a horrid smell!*
nasty *What a nasty gossip you are!*
objectionable *an objectionable, stuck-up person*
obnoxious *One of the neighbours was a most obnoxious character.*
unfriendly *She spoke in a loud, rather unfriendly voice.*
unpleasant *The side effects can be unpleasant.*
ANTONYM **agreeable**
See also **horrible, nasty, sour, uncomfortable, unfriendly, unpleasant**

disagreement

▷ NOUN

1 a dispute about something: *My driving instructor and I had a brief disagreement.*
altercation FORMAL *an altercation with the referee*
argument *an argument about money*
difference *We have our differences, but we get along.*
dispute *a salary dispute*
quarrel *I had a terrible quarrel with my brother.*
row *a major diplomatic row*
squabble *minor squabbles about phone bills*
tiff *a lovers' tiff*
ANTONYM **agreement**
2 an objection to something: *Britain and France have expressed some disagreement with the proposal.*

dissent *voices of dissent*
objection *I have no objection to banks making money.*
opposition *their opposition to the project*
See also **conflict, dispute, quarrel, squabble**

disappear

▷ VERB

1 to go out of sight: *The aircraft disappeared off the radar.*
be lost to view *They observed the comet for 70 days before it was lost to view.*
drop out of sight *After his first movie, he dropped out of sight.*
fade *We watched the harbour fade into the mist.*
recede *The cyclist receded into the distance.*
vanish *Our dog vanished from outside our home the Wednesday before last.*
ANTONYM **appear**
2 to stop existing: *The pain has finally disappeared.*
cease FORMAL *At twelve noon, the rain ceased.*
die out *How did the dinosaurs die out?*
go away *All she wanted was for the pain to go away.*
melt away *His anger melted away.*
pass *He told her the fear would pass.*
vanish *species that have vanished*
See also **die out, melt, vanish**

disappoint *See* **dash**

disappointed

▷ ADJECTIVE

sad because something has not happened: *I was disappointed that my best friend was not there.*
dejected *Her refusal left him feeling dejected.*
despondent *After the interview, he became despondent.*
disenchanted *She has become very disenchanted with her boss.*
disillusioned *I've become very disillusioned with politics.*
downcast *After his defeat, the mayor looked downcast.*
saddened *He is saddened that they did not win anything.*
ANTONYM **satisfied**

disappointing *See* **unsatisfactory**

disappointment

▷ NOUN

1 a feeling of being disappointed: *Book early to avoid disappointment.*
dejection *There was an air of dejection about her.*

despondency *a mood of gloom and despondency*
regret *my one great regret in life*
2 something that disappoints you: *The reunion was a bitter disappointment.*
blow *It was a terrible blow when he was laid off.*
setback *a setback for the peace process*
See also **blow, failure**

D

disapproval

▷ NOUN

the belief that something is wrong: *their disapproval of his coaching style*
censure *He deserves support, not censure.*
condemnation *the ongoing condemnation of the war*
criticism *actions that have attracted fierce criticism*
ANTONYM **approval**
See also **censure, criticism, opposition**

disapprove

▷ VERB

to think that something is wrong: *Everyone disapproved of their marrying so young.*
condemn *Political leaders condemned the racist's speech.*
deplore FORMAL *He deplores violence.*
dislike *Her parents seemed to dislike her friends.*
find unacceptable *I find such behaviour totally unacceptable.*
take a dim view of *They took a dim view of such business practices.*
ANTONYM **approve**
See also **protest**

disapproving *See* **critical, severe**

disarray *See* **confusion, disorder, mess, muddle**

disaster

▷ NOUN

a very bad accident: *another air disaster*
calamity FORMAL *It could end only in calamity.*
catastrophe *War would be a catastrophe.*
misfortune *to enjoy the misfortunes of others*
tragedy *They have suffered an enormous personal tragedy.*

disastrous *See* **fatal**

discard

▷ VERB

to get rid of something: *Read the instructions before discarding the box.*

cast aside *Some societies seem to cast aside the elderly.*

dispose of *how he disposed of the murder weapon*

dump INFORMAL *The getaway car was dumped near the river.*

jettison *The crew jettisoned the disabled plane's excess fuel.*

shed *a snake that has shed its skin*

throw away *I never throw anything away.*

throw out *Why don't you throw out all those old magazines?*

See also **banish, dispose of**

discern

▷ VERB

FORMAL to notice or understand something clearly: *trying to discern a pattern in his behaviour*

detect *I could detect a certain sadness in the old man's face.*

make out *I could just make out a shadowy figure through the mist.*

notice *I noticed a bird sitting on the garage roof.*

observe *I observed a pattern in his behaviour.*

perceive *Get students to perceive the relationship between success and effort.*

see *I saw in her a future champion.*

spot *I've spotted an error in your calculations.*

See also **distinguish, notice, see, spot, tell**

discernment *See* **wisdom**

discharge

▷ VERB

1 to send something out: *The motorboat discharged fuel into the lake.*

emit *the amount of greenhouse gases emitted*

empty *companies that empty toxic by-products into rivers*

expel *Poisonous gas is expelled into the atmosphere.*

flush *Flush out all the sewage.*

give off *natural gas, which gives off less carbon dioxide than coal*

release *a weapon that releases toxic nerve gas*

2 to allow someone to leave the hospital or a prison: *He has a broken nose, but may be discharged today.*

free *The country will free more prisoners.*

let go *They held him for three hours and then let him go.*

liberate *They promised to liberate prisoners held in detention camps.*

release *She was released on bail.*

set free *More than 90 prisoners have been set free.*

3 to dismiss someone from a job: *discharged when caught stealing a computer*

dismiss *The commander has been dismissed.*

eject *ejected from his first job for persistent lateness*

fire *If he wasn't so good at his job, I'd fire him.*

sack INFORMAL *He was sacked after a week on the job.*

▷ NOUN

4 a sending away from a job or institution: *a dishonourable discharge from the army*

dismissal *shock over the manager's sudden dismissal*

ejection *These actions led to his ejection from office.*

expulsion *expulsion from the Liberal Party*

the sack INFORMAL *People who make dangerous mistakes can be given the sack.*

See also **drain, dump, fire, free, release, sack, the sack**

disciple *See* **follower**

discipline *See* **punish**

disclose *See* **reveal**

disclosure *See* **news**

discolour *See* **fade**

discomfort *See* **pain**

disconcert *See* **embarrass**

disconnect *See* **separate**

disconnected *See* **separate**

discontinue *See* **cease, interrupt, quit, stop**

discord *See* **conflict**

discount *See* **ignore**

discourage

▷ VERB

to make someone lose enthusiasm: *Don't let these problems discourage you.*

daunt *He was not the type of person to be daunted by adversity.*

deter *Would tougher prison sentences deter crime?*

dissuade *He considered moving, but his family managed to dissuade him.*

put off *I wouldn't let it put you off applying for the job.*

ANTONYM **encourage**

discourse *See* **discussion, lecture, speech, talk**

discover

▷ VERB

to find something or find out about something: *to discover a new planet*
come across *They came across the jawbone of a carnivorous dinosaur.*
find *The police found more evidence.*
find out *Watch the next episode to find out what happens.*
learn *The movie star, on learning who I was, wanted to meet me.*
realize *As soon as we realized something was wrong, we took action.*
stumble on or **stumble across** *They stumbled on a magnificent waterfall.*
unearth *Archaeologists have unearthed ancient fossils.*
See also **determine, find, hear, learn, observe, see**

discredit *See* **disgrace, disprove, shame**

discreet *See* **tactful**

discrepancy *See* **difference**

discrete *See* **different, individual, separate**

discretion *See* **freedom, tact**

discretionary *See* **flexible**

discriminate *See* **distinguish**

discriminating *See* **fussy**

discrimination *See* **injustice, prejudice**

discuss

▷ VERB

to talk about something: *I will be discussing the situation with students tomorrow.*
debate *The UN Security Council will debate the issue today.*
exchange views on *They exchanged views on a wide range of subjects.*
go into *We didn't go into that.*
talk about *What did you talk about?*

discussion

▷ NOUN

a talk about something: *informal discussions*
consultation *consultations between lawyers*
conversation *I struck up a conversation with him.*
debate *There has been a lot of debate among teachers about this.*
dialogue *a direct dialogue between the two nations*
discourse *a long tradition of political discourse*
talk *We had a long talk about it.*
See also **conference, word**

disdain *See* **contempt, scorn**

disdainful *See* **haughty, scornful, stuck-up, superior**

disease *See* **disorder, illness**

disenchanted *See* **disappointed**

disfigured *See* **distorted**

D

disgrace

▷ NOUN

1 lack of respect: *to bring disgrace upon the whole team*
scandal *Royal families often fear scandal.*
shame *to bring shame on the family name*
ANTONYM **credit**

▷ VERB

2 to bring shame upon: *to disgrace their family's name*
discredit *Certain practices have discredited the political party.*
shame *I wouldn't shame my family by doing that.*
See also **humble, humiliate, shame**

disgraceful

▷ ADJECTIVE

deserving of shame: *disgraceful behaviour*
scandalous *a scandalous waste of money*
shameful *the most shameful episode in the history of Canadian politics*
shocking *a shocking invasion of privacy*

disguised *See* **invisible**

disgust

▷ NOUN

1 a strong feeling of dislike: *his disgust at the incident*
nausea *I was overcome with a feeling of nausea.*
repulsion *a shudder of repulsion*
revulsion *They expressed their shock and revulsion at his senseless death.*

▷ VERB

2 to cause someone to feel disgust: *He disgusted many with his behaviour.*
repel *violent behaviour that frightened and repelled us*
revolt *The smell revolted me.*
sicken *What he saw there sickened him.*
See also **horrify, horror, repel, shock**

disgusting

▷ ADJECTIVE

very unpleasant or unacceptable: *one of the most disgusting sights I had ever seen*
foul *a foul stench*
gross *Don't be so gross!*

obnoxious *a most obnoxious character*
repellent *a very large, repellent toad*
revolting *The smell was revolting!*
sickening *a sickening attack on a defenceless person*
vile *a vile odour*
See also **nasty**

dishonest

▷ ADJECTIVE

not truthful: *It would be dishonest to mislead people.*
corrupt *corrupt police officers*
crooked *crooked business deals*
deceitful *She called the report deceitful and misleading.*
fraudulent *fraudulent insurance claims*
hypocritical *He's so hypocritical — saying one thing and doing the opposite.*
lying *a lying child*
ANTONYM **honest**
See also **corrupt, crooked, dubious, insincere, lying, sneaky, two-faced**

dishonesty

▷ NOUN

dishonest behaviour: *She accused the government of dishonesty.*
cheating *He was accused of cheating.*
corruption *The president faced 54 charges of corruption.*
deceit *the deceit and lies of the past*
trickery *They resorted to trickery in order to impress their clients.*
ANTONYM **honesty**
See also **corruption, lying**

dishonour See **shame**

disillusioned See **disappointed**

disinclined See **reluctant**

disintegrate

▷ VERB

to break into many pieces: *The sculpture fell off the table and disintegrated.*
break up *There was a danger of the ship breaking up completely.*
crumble *I crumbled some crackers into the soup.*
fall apart *Bit by bit, the building fell apart.*
fall to pieces *The coffee mug fell to pieces.*
fragment *The clouds fragmented, and out came the sun.*
See also **erode**

disinterested See **neutral**

dislike

▷ VERB

1 to consider something unpleasant: *We don't serve it often because many people dislike it.*
abhor FORMAL *a man who abhorred violence*
be averse to *He's not averse to a little publicity.*
detest *She detested being photographed.*
hate *to hate an evil person*
loathe *a play loathed by the critics*
not be able to abide *I can't abide liars.*
not be able to bear *I can't bear people who speak like that.*
not be able to stand *I can't stand the sound of that squeaky voice.*
ANTONYM **like**

▷ NOUN

2 a feeling of not liking something: *She looked at him with dislike.*
animosity *The animosity between the two men grew.*
antipathy *his antipathy to smoking*
aversion *I've always had an aversion to being part of a group.*
distaste *They looked at us with distaste.*
hatred *her hatred of racism*
hostility *hostility to his co-workers*
loathing *He made no secret of his loathing of the movie.*
ANTONYM **liking**
See also **animosity, disapprove, hate, hatred, resent**

disliked See **unpopular**

disloyal See **false, treacherous, two-faced**

dismal See **drab, gloomy, sad**

dismay See **horrify, panic**

dismiss See **banish, discharge, fire, sack**

dismissal See **discharge, the sack**

disobedient See **naughty**

disobey

▷ VERB

to refuse to follow instructions deliberately: *He was forever disobeying the rules.*
break *drivers breaking speed limits*
defy *the first time that I dared to defy my mother*
flout *illegal campers who persist in flouting the law*
infringe *He was adamant that he had infringed no rules.*
violate *They violated the ceasefire agreement.*
ANTONYM **obey**

disorder

▷ *NOUN*

1 a state of untidiness: *Inside, all was disorder.*
clutter *She prefers the counter to be free of clutter.*
disarray *Her closet was in disarray.*
muddle *a general muddle of pencils and boxes*
ANTONYM **order**
2 a lack of organization: *Regular fire drills prevent disorder in a real emergency.*
chaos *Their concerts often ended in chaos.*
confusion *There was confusion when someone shouted "Fire.".*
disarray *The nation is in disarray following the riots.*
turmoil *political turmoil*
3 a disease or illness: *a rare nerve disorder*
affliction *an affliction that is often hard to deal with*
ailment *an ailment that is difficult to treat*
complaint *a common skin complaint*
condition *a heart condition*
disease *heart disease*
illness *a serious illness*
See also **confusion, illness, mess, muddle, riot**

disordered *See* **confused**

disorganization *See* **confusion, muddle**

disorganized *See* **confused, inefficient**

disown *See* **renounce**

disparagement *See* **criticism**

disparaging *See* **abusive, critical**

disparate *See* **different, various**

disparity *See* **difference, gap**

dispassionate *See* **neutral**

dispatch *See* **message, news, send**

dispel *See* **banish**

dispense *See* **administer, distribute**

dispense with *See* **dispose of**

disperse *See* **distribute, melt**

dispirited *See* **down**

display *See* **flourish, show, sight**

displease *See* **annoy**

displeasure *See* **annoyance**

disposed *See* **prone**

dispose of

▷ *VERB*

to get rid of something: *Dispose of your*

garbage in the proper containers.
discard *Read the instructions before discarding the box.*
dispense with *The new evaluation system dispenses with final exams.*
dump *The government declared that it did not dump radioactive waste in the ocean.*
get rid of *The owner needs to get rid of the car for financial reasons.*
jettison *The crew jettisoned excess fuel and made an emergency landing.*
throw away *I never throw anything away.*
See also **discard, dump, get rid of, process, settle**

disprove

▷ *VERB*

to show that something is not true: *the statistics that will prove or disprove the statement*
discredit *There would be difficulties in discrediting the evidence.*
give the lie to *This survey gives the lie to the idea that the economy is recovering.*
invalidate *Some of the other criticisms were invalidated years ago.*
prove false *It is hard to prove such claims false.*
refute *the kind of rumour that is impossible to refute*
ANTONYM **prove**

dispute

▷ *NOUN*

1 an argument: *The dispute between them is settled.*
argument *a heated argument*
clash *the clash between union leaders and the government*
conflict *a lasting conflict between the two nations*
disagreement *disagreements among the member countries*
feud *a bitter feud between the two families*
row *a major diplomatic row with France*
wrangle *a legal wrangle*
▷ *VERB*
2 to question something's truth or wisdom: *He disputed the allegations.*
challenge *I challenge the wisdom of this decision.*
contest *Your former employer wants to contest the case.*
contradict *Her version contradicted that of the referee.*
deny *She denied both accusations.*
query *No one queried my decision.*
question *It never occurred to me to question*

the doctor's diagnosis.
ANTONYM **accept**
See also **argument, challenge, contest, disagree, disagreement, fight, quarrel, query, question, squabble**

disqualification *See* **ban**

disqualify *See* **ban**

disquiet *See* **concern**

disregard *See* **contempt, ignore, neglect, overlook**

disrepair *See* **ruin**

disreputable *See* **low, notorious**

disrespect *See* **contempt**

disrespectful
▷ *ADJECTIVE*
rude: *They were disrespectful to the older workers.*
impertinent *an impertinent question*
impudent *his rude and impudent behaviour*
insolent *a defiant, almost insolent look*
rude *Her rude language was offensive.*
See also **rude**

disrupt *See* **disturb, impede, interfere**

dissent *See* **disagree, disagreement**

dissimilar *See* **different**

dissimilar to *See* **unlike**

dissolve *See* **eat away, melt, vanish**

dissuade *See* **discourage**

distance *See* **length, space**

distant
▷ *ADJECTIVE*
1 far away in space or time: *a distant land*
far *Is it very far?*
outlying *outlying suburbs*
out-of-the-way *an out-of-the-way spot*
remote *a remote village*
ANTONYM **close**
2 cold and unfriendly: *He is polite, but distant.*
aloof *He seemed aloof and detached.*
detached *He observed me with a detached curiosity.*
reserved *She's quite a reserved person.*
withdrawn *to become withdrawn and moody*
ANTONYM **friendly**
See also **cold, far, foreign, remote**

distaste *See* **dislike**

distasteful *See* **unpleasant**

distilled *See* **refined**

distinct *See* **different, particular, plain**

distinct from *See* **unlike**

distinction *See* **difference, quality**

distinctive *See* **characteristic, individual, peculiar, special**

distinguish
▷ *VERB*
1 to see the difference between things: *Could he distinguish right from wrong?*
differentiate *At this age, your baby cannot differentiate one person from another.*
discriminate *He is unable to discriminate a good idea from a terrible one.*
tell *How do you tell one from another?*
tell apart *I can tell them apart only by the colour of their shoes.*
tell the difference *I can't tell the difference between the twins.*
2 to recognize something: *I heard shouting, but was unable to distinguish the words.*
discern *We could just discern a narrow ditch.*
make out *He couldn't make out what she was saying.*
pick out *Through my binoculars, I picked out a group of figures.*
recognize *He did not think they could recognize his car in the snow.*

distinguishable *See* **visible**

distinguished *See* **famous**

distinguishing *See* **characteristic, peculiar**

distort *See* **cloud, colour, misrepresent, twist**

distorted
▷ *ADJECTIVE*
abnormally shaped: *the distorted image caused by the projector*
deformed *a deformed right leg*
disfigured *the scarred, disfigured face*
See also **crooked, garbled**

distract
▷ *VERB*
to stop someone from concentrating: *Playing computer games distracts him from his homework.*
divert *They want to divert our attention from the real issues.*
draw away *to draw attention away from the crime*

distracted *See* **absent-minded**

distraction *See* **escape**

distress

▷ NOUN

1 great suffering: *Kindness eased their distress.*

heartache *the heartache of their loss*

pain *eyes that seemed filled with pain*

sorrow *a time of great sorrow*

suffering *an end to his suffering*

2 the state of needing help: *The ship might be in distress.*

difficulty *rumours about banks being in difficulty*

need *When you were in need, I loaned you money.*

straits *desperate financial straits*

trouble *a charity that helps those in trouble*

▷ VERB

3 to cause someone unhappiness: *Our fight greatly distressed me.*

bother *It bothered me that nobody ate dessert.*

disturb *dreams so vivid that they disturb me for days*

grieve *It grieved her to be separated from her family.*

pain *It pains me to think of you struggling all alone.*

sadden *The cruelty in the world saddens me deeply.*

trouble *He was troubled by the lack of business.*

upset *I'm sorry if I've upset you.*

worry *I didn't want to worry you.*

See also **agitate, alarm, concern, disturb, grief, grieve, hurt, pain, shake, shock, upset**

distress signal   See **alarm**

distressed   See **upset**

distressing   See **painful, tragic**

distribute

▷ VERB

1 to hand something out: *They publish and distribute flyers.*

circulate *He has circulated a draft of the proposal.*

hand out *One of my jobs was to hand out the prizes.*

pass around *Cookies were being passed around.*

2 to spread something through an area: *Distribute the berries evenly over the cake.*

diffuse *Interest in books is more widely diffused than ever.*

disperse *to disperse information over the Internet*

scatter *She scattered the petals over the floor.*

spread *A thick layer of wax was spread over the surface.*

3 to divide and share something: *Distribute chores equally among all family members.*

allocate *funds allocated for the school play*

allot *The tickets are allotted on a first-come, first-served basis.*

dispense *The government had already dispensed a million dollars in grants.*

divide *She divides her spare time between reading and sports.*

dole out *I opened my wallet and began to dole out the money.*

share *You could share the money a bit more evenly.*

See also **circulate**

district   See **area, local, region, territory**

distrust   See **question, suspect, suspicion**

distrustful   See **cynical, suspicious, wary**

disturb

▷ VERB

1 to intrude on someone's peace: *Don't disturb me while I'm studying.*

bother *I'm sorry to bother you.*

disrupt *Protesters disrupted the meeting.*

intrude on *I don't want to intrude on your privacy.*

2 to upset or worry someone: *Some scenes in the movie may disturb you.*

agitate *The thought agitated her.*

distress *The breakup had profoundly distressed me.*

shake *Well, it shook me quite a bit.*

trouble *He was troubled by their insensitive behaviour.*

unsettle *The presence of the two security guards unsettled me.*

upset *I'm sorry if I've upset you.*

worry *I didn't want to worry you.*

See also **agitate, bother, concern, distress, shake, trouble, upset**

disturbance   See **riot**

disturbing   See **creepy**

dither   See **hesitate**

dive

▷ VERB

to jump or fall into water: *She was standing by the pool, about to dive in.*

jump *He ran along the diving board and jumped in.*
leap *She leaped into the water.*
submerge *Hippos are unable to submerge in the few remaining water holes.*
See also **descend**

diverge *See* **split**

divergence *See* **difference, split**

divergent *See* **different**

divergent from *See* **unlike**

diverse *See* **various**

diversify *See* **vary**

diversion *See* **escape, hobby, pastime, variation**

divert *See* **distract**

divide

▷ VERB
1 to split something up: *Divide the pizza into six slices.*
cut up *Halve the tomatoes, and then cut them up.*
partition *a plan to partition the country*
segregate *to segregate the two groups*
separate *Fluff the rice with a fork to separate the grains.*
split *Split the chicken in half.*
split up *She split up the company.*
ANTONYM **join**
2 to form a barrier between things: *the border dividing Mexico from the United States*
bisect *The main street bisects the town.*
separate *the fence that separated the two yards*
3 to cause people to disagree: *the enormous differences that still divide them*
come between *It's difficult to imagine anything coming between them.*
set against one another *The incident has set neighbours against one another.*
split *Angry words from both sides have split the party.*
See also **distribute, separate, share, sort**

divine *See* **religious**

division

▷ NOUN
1 separation into parts: *equal division of the money*
partition *the partition of the room into smaller areas*
separation *the separation of the restaurant into casual and formal sections*
2 a disagreement: *There were divisions in the club over who should be in charge.*
breach *a serious breach in relations between the two countries*
difference of opinion *Was there a difference of opinion over what to do with the money?*
rupture *a rupture of the family unit*
split *They accused both sides of trying to provoke a split in the party.*
3 a section of something: *the research division of the toy company*
department *the company's information technology department*
section *The department is broken down into different sections*
sector *Canada's manufacturing sector*
See also **compartment, department, section, split**

divorce *See* **separate**

divorced *See* **separate**

divulge *See* **reveal**

dizzy

▷ ADJECTIVE
about to lose your balance: *He kept getting dizzy spells.*
giddy *She felt slightly giddy.*
lightheaded *If you skip breakfast, you may feel lightheaded.*
See also **dazed, faint**

do

▷ VERB
1 to carry out a task: *He just didn't want to do any work.*
carry out *Of course he didn't carry out his threat.*
execute FORMAL *The landing was skillfully executed.*
perform *people who have performed outstanding acts of bravery*
undertake *She undertook the task of monitoring the elections.*
2 to be sufficient: *Homemade soup is best, but canned soup will do.*
be adequate *Three small meals a day will be adequate for me.*
be sufficient *One teaspoon of sugar should be sufficient.*
suffice FORMAL *Often a far shorter letter will suffice.*
3 to perform well or badly: *She did well at school.*
fare *Some later expeditions fared better.*
get on *How did you get on when you lost your job?*
manage *How did you manage when the lights went out?*
See also **accomplish, achieve, commit,**

do away with *See* **abolish, eliminate**

do business *See* **trade**

do up *See* **decorate, renovate**

do well *See* **flourish, succeed, thrive**

do wrong *See* **sin**

do your best *See* **strive**

do your utmost *See* **strive**

docile *See* **meek, passive**

dock *See* **land**

doctrinal *See* **religious**

doctrine *See* **belief, principle**

document *See* **record**

dodge
> *VERB*

1 to move out of the way: *We dodged to the side as the joggers approached.*
duck *I ducked as the ball came whizzing in my direction.*
swerve *He swerved to avoid a truck.*
2 to avoid doing something: *dodging responsibilities by pretending to be ill*
avoid *They tried to avoid paying their fares.*
elude *She eluded the police for 13 years.*
evade *evading taxes*
get out of *He'll do almost anything to get out of paying his share.*
shirk *We can't shirk our responsibility.*
sidestep *Rarely, if ever, does she sidestep a question.*
See also **avoid, escape, manoeuvre**

dog
> *NOUN*

an animal often kept as a pet: *a children's book about dogs*
canine *a canine rescue program*
mongrel *a rescued mongrel called Prince*
mutt *a lovable mutt*
pooch *our pet pooch*

INFORMALLY SPEAKING

a dog's life: a miserable life
go to the dogs: be ruined
let sleeping dogs lie: avoid stirring up unnecessary trouble

---

dogged *See* **determined, obstinate, stubborn**

dogma *See* **belief**

dole out *See* **distribute**

domain *See* **field, territory**

domestic *See* **home**

dominance *See* **advantage, hold**

dominant *See* **powerful**

domineering *See* **bossy**

dominion *See* **colony, power, territory**

don *See* **wear**

donate *See* **give, present**

donation *See* **gift, present**

done *See* **over, right**

doom *See* **condemn**

doomed
> *ADJECTIVE*

certain to fail: *a doomed attempt to rescue the miners*
condemned *condemned to a life of hunger and poverty*
hopeless *I don't believe your situation is as hopeless as you think.*
ill-fated *an ill-fated attempt to break the world record*

door *See* **entrance, entry**

doorway *See* **entrance, entry**

dope *See* **fool**

doting *See* **devoted, fond, loving**

double
> *ADJECTIVE*

1 twice the usual size: *a double scoop*
twice *Income in that town is twice the national average.*
twofold *a twofold risk*
2 consisting of two parts: *a double check of her work*
dual *dual nationality*
twin *twin beds*
twofold *Their concern was twofold: personal and political.*
See also **lookalike**

double-cross *See* **betray, deceive**

doubt
> *NOUN*

1 a feeling of uncertainty: *This raises doubts about the point of advertising.*
misgiving *I had misgivings about his methods.*
qualm *I have no qualms about recommending this approach.*
scepticism *The report has been greeted with scepticism.*
uncertainty *the uncertainties regarding the*

expansion of the league
ANTONYM **certainty**
▷ VERB
2 to feel uncertain about something: *No one doubted his ability.*
be dubious *I was dubious about his claims.*
be sceptical *Other archaeologists are sceptical about her findings.*
query *No one queried my decision.*
question *It never occurs to them to question the doctor's decisions.*
ANTONYM **believe**
See also **question, suspect, suspicion**

doubtful
▷ ADJECTIVE
unlikely or uncertain: *It is doubtful whether she will compete in the next Olympics.*
debatable *He calls himself a singer, but that's debatable.*
dubious *This claim seems rather dubious to us.*
questionable *It is questionable whether the cost is justified.*
uncertain *It's uncertain whether they will accept the plan.*
ANTONYM **certain**
See also **dubious, hesitant, improbable, suspect, suspicious, uncertain, unpredictable**

doubtless See **probably**

dough See **money**

dovetail See **fit**

down
▷ ADVERB
1 toward the ground, or in a lower place: *We went down in the elevator.*
downward *She gazed downward.*
downstairs *The washroom is downstairs.*
ANTONYM **up**
▷ ADJECTIVE
2 depressed: *He sounded really down.*
dejected *We all have days when we feel dejected.*
depressed *They're very depressed about this situation.*
dispirited *I left feeling utterly dispirited.*
fed up INFORMAL *I'm just fed up and I don't know what to do.*
glum *No matter how we tried to cheer him up, he remained glum.*
melancholy *It is in the afternoon that I feel most melancholy.*
miserable *My work was making me really miserable.*

See also **below, gloomy, miserable, pile, sad, unhappy**

> **INFORMALLY SPEAKING**
>
> **come down with:** get sick with (a short-term illness)
> **down on:** disapprovingly critical

downcast See **disappointed, miserable, sad**

downfall
▷ NOUN
the failure of a person or thing: *Lack of support led to the team's downfall.*
collapse *Is the medical system facing collapse?*
fall *the fall of the military dictator*
ruin *Inflation has driven them to the brink of ruin.*
See also **collapse, failure, ruin**

downgrade See **belittle, reduce**

downpour See **flood, rain**

downright See **absolute, rank**

downstairs See **down**

down-to-earth See **realistic, sensible, sound**

downtrodden See **oppressed**

downturn See **decline, recession**

downward See **down**

doze See **sleep**

drab
▷ ADJECTIVE
dull and unattractive: *the same drab grey outfit*
dingy *his rather dingy office*
dismal *a dark, dismal day*
dreary *a dreary little town*
gloomy *the gloomy days of winter*
grey *a typically grey and cheerless November day*
sombre *the sombre colour of the afternoon sky*
ANTONYM **bright**
See also **dreary, dull**

draft See **design, plan, recruit**

drag
▷ VERB
to pull something along the ground: *He dragged his chair toward the table.*
draw *She drew her chair nearer the fire.*
haul *A crane was used to haul the car out of the stream.*
lug *Nobody wants to lug around huge suitcases.*

tow *They threatened to tow away my car.*

trail *She came down the stairs slowly, trailing the coat behind her.*

See also **annoyance, draw, pull, tug**

drag in: bring something irrelevant into a discussion
drag on: be boringly long
drag your feet: act slowly on purpose

drain
▷ VERB

1 to cause a liquid to flow somewhere: *We drained the pipes till the water ran clear.*
pump *to pump out water from the flooded garage*
2 to flow somewhere: *rivers that drain into lakes*
discharge *Blood was discharging from its nostrils.*
empty *The Red River empties into Lake Winnipeg.*
flow *Water flowed out of the washing machine and into the hallway.*
seep *Water seeped from the flood above us into our kitchen.*
3 to use something up: *The prolonged feud drained him of energy.*
consume *plans that will consume hours of time*
exhaust *People are exhausting natural resources.*
sap *The illness sapped his strength.*
tax *Stop taxing my patience!*
use up *They aren't the ones who use up the world's resources.*
See also **dry, empty, exhaust, tax, tire**

drained *See* tired, weary

drama *See* play

dramatic *See* exciting

drape *See* hang

drastic
▷ ADJECTIVE

severe and urgent: *It's time for drastic action.*
extreme *extreme safety measures following the earthquake*
harsh *harsh measures to fight poverty*
radical *radical economic reforms*
severe *a severe shortage of drinking water*
See also **extreme**

draw
▷ VERB

1 to make a picture: *to draw pictures of flowers*
paint *He is painting a portrait of his friend.*

sketch *She sketched a map on the back of a menu.*
trace *She learned to draw by tracing pictures from old books.*
2 to move somewhere: *as the car drew away*
move *She moved away from the window.*
pull *He pulled into the driveway.*
3 to pull something: *He drew his chair nearer the fire.*
drag *She dragged her chair toward the table.*
haul *A crane was used to haul the car out of the stream.*
pull *A tow truck easily pulled the car out of the ditch.*
See also **attract, drag, earn, extract, lure, pull, tie, tug**

beat to the draw: manage to do something before someone else
draw out: extend too much
draw the line: set a limit

draw away *See* distract

draw back *See* retreat

draw off *See* drain

draw up *See* design, form, halt

drawback
▷ NOUN

a problem that makes something less than perfect: *The only drawback was that the apartment was too small.*
difficulty *There is only one difficulty — I don't have the key.*
hitch *It's a great idea, but I can see a serious hitch.*
problem *The main problem with the house is its location.*
snag *It's a great play, but there's a snag. It's sold out for months.*
trouble *The trouble is that he might not agree with our plans.*
See also **catch, disadvantage, fault, handicap, snag**

drawing *See* picture

dread *See* fear, horror

dreadful
▷ ADJECTIVE

very bad or unpleasant: *He told us the dreadful news*
appalling *living under the most appalling conditions*

D

atrocious *The food here is atrocious!*
awful *Jeans look awful on me.*
frightful *The experience had been so frightful she couldn't talk about it.*
ghastly *The weather was ghastly.*
horrendous *the most horrendous experience of his life*
terrible *I'll never go back to that terrible restaurant.*
ANTONYM **wonderful**
See also **awful, horrible, terrible**

dream
▷ NOUN
I mental pictures while sleeping: *He had a dream about horses.*
hallucination *The medication induces hallucinations at high doses.*
trance *She seemed to be in a trance.*
vision *seeing his dead grandfather in a vision*
2 something that you want very much: *his dream of winning the race*
ambition *Her ambition is to sail around the world.*
aspiration *one of his greatest aspirations*
daydream *She learned to escape into daydreams of becoming a writer.*
fantasy *fantasies of adventure*
See also **daydream, hope, vision**

INFORMALLY SPEAKING

a dream come true: exactly what one would have wanted
dream up: have an idea, especially an unusual one
like a dream: perfectly

---

dreary
▷ ADJECTIVE
dull or boring: *the dreary winter months*
boring *a boring job*
drab *At times, the day's activities often seem drab.*
dull *There was scarcely a dull moment.*
humdrum *His daily routine seems rather humdrum.*
monotonous *It's monotonous work, like many factory jobs.*
tedious *Such lists are tedious to read.*
uneventful *a dull, uneventful life*
ANTONYM **exciting**
See also **drab, gloomy**

dregs See **remains**

drenched See **wet**

dress
▷ NOUN
I a piece of clothing: *a black dress*
garment *a shapeless garment*
gown *wedding gowns*
robe *a fur-lined robe*
2 clothing in general: *casual dress*
attire FORMAL *dressed in their finest attire*
clothes *comfortable clothes*
clothing *protective clothing*
costume *dressed in traditional costume*
garb FORMAL *his usual garb of a dark suit*
▷ VERB
3 to wear or put on clothes: *She often dressed in black.*
attire *attired in a smart blue suit*
clothe *He lay down on the bed fully clothed.*
garb FORMAL *garbed in her official uniform*
ANTONYM **undress**
See also **clothes**

dribble See **drip**

dried-up See **dry**

drift See **float, flow, meaning, wander**

drill See **pierce, practice, teach, train**

drink
▷ VERB
I to swallow liquid: *I drank some water.*
gulp *She quickly gulped her juice.*
guzzle *She guzzled the drink in a couple of gulps.*
sip *She sipped from her coffee mug.*
2 to drink alcohol: *He drinks little and eats carefully.*
booze INFORMAL *boozing until late in the night*
tipple *tippling from the sherry bottle*
See also **alcohol**

drip
▷ VERB
I to fall in small drops: *water dripping from the kitchen tap*
dribble *Perspiration dribbled down his face.*
splash *Rain splashed onto the surface of the lake.*
trickle *A tear trickled down his cheek.*
▷ NOUN
2 a small amount of a liquid: *drips of water*
bead *beads of sweat*
drop *a drop of blue ink*
droplet *water droplets*
See also **drop**

drive
▷ VERB
I to operate or power a machine or vehicle: *Don't drive a car after taking this medication.*

operate *He operated the Zamboni at the arena.*

pilot *She piloted her own plane to Charlottetown.*

power *The outboard motor powered the boat.*

propel *Attached is a tiny rocket designed to propel the spacecraft toward Mars.*

steer *What is it like to steer a ship this size?*

work *I learned how to work the forklift.*

2 to force or try to force someone to do something: *Her love of acting drove her into a life in the theatre.*

compel *He felt compelled to speak out against their actions.*

force *A back injury forced her to withdraw from the tournament.*

lead *His travels through the Arctic led him to write his first book.*

motivate *What motivates people to behave like this?*

prompt *The recession has prompted consumers to cut back on spending.*

push *Public pressure pushed the government into making reforms.*

spur *The adventure was spurred by a book he had read.*

3 to force something pointed into a surface: *I used the sledgehammer to drive in the pegs.*

hammer *Hammer the wooden peg into the hole.*

knock *She knocked a couple of nails into the wall.*

ram *He rammed the stake into the ground.*

sink *I sank my teeth into an apple.*

thrust *thrusting a knife into the watermelon*

▷ NOUN

4 a journey in a vehicle: *We might go for a drive on Sunday.*

excursion *an excursion to a local conservation area*

jaunt *a quick jaunt down to the beach*

journey *The journey from Ottawa to Montreal took several hours.*

ride *We took some friends for a ride in the family car.*

run *We went for a run in the new car.*

spin *I was thinking about going for a spin.*

trip *a bus trip through the Rockies*

▷ NOUN

5 energy and determination: *We remember her great drive and enthusiasm.*

ambition *When I was young, I never had any ambition.*

determination *her natural determination to succeed*

energy *You have enough energy for both of us!*

enterprise *the group's lack of enterprise*

initiative *We were disappointed by his lack of initiative.*

motivation *Their extraordinary motivation helped them win the finals.*

vigour *They played with great vigour.*

See also **blow, chase, energy, force, go, make, motivate, reduce, urge**

drive into *See* **crash**

drive off *See* **repel**

drive someone up the wall *See* **pester**

drivel *See* **garbage, nonsense, rubbish**

drizzle *See* **rain**

droop *See* **hang, wither**

drooping *See* **limp**

drop

▷ VERB

1 to fall downward: *She let her head drop.*

descend *as the aircraft descended*

fall *My keys fell out of my pocket.*

plummet *If his parachute hadn't opened, he would have plummeted to the ground.*

sink *He sank to his knees after winning the race.*

tumble *The coins tumbled out of my hand.*

2 to become less: *Temperatures can drop to freezing at night.*

decline *The number of workers has declined.*

decrease *Population in the village is decreasing each year.*

diminish *diminishing resources*

fall *Attendance fell toward the end of the season.*

plummet *The value of the dollar has plummeted.*

sink *Pay increases have sunk to about 7 percent.*

slump *Profits slumped by 41 percent.*

tumble *House prices have tumbled by almost 20 percent.*

ANTONYM **rise**

▷ NOUN

3 a small amount of a liquid: *a drop of blue ink*

bead *beads of sweat*

drip *drips of water*

droplet *water droplets*

See also **ball, blob, dash, decline,**

decrease, deposit, drip, dump, fall,
lose, lower, trace

INFORMALLY SPEAKING

a drop in the bucket: a comparatively
small amount
drop out: leave school without finishing
courses
drop the ball: make a mess of what one
is doing

drop out of sight *See* **disappear**

droplet *See* **blob, drip, drop**

drown *See* **flood**

drowsy *See* **sleepy, tired**

drug
▷ *NOUN*
1 a treatment for disease: *a new drug in the
fight against AIDS*
medication *She is not on any medication.*
medicine *herbal medicines*
2 an illegal substance: *She was sure her
cousin was taking drugs.*
narcotic *He was indicted for dealing in
narcotics.*
stimulant *the use of stimulants in sport*
See also **medicine**

drum *See* **advice, information**

drunk
▷ *ADJECTIVE*
1 having consumed too much alcohol: *He
got drunk.*
intoxicated *FORMAL He appeared
intoxicated.*
tipsy *I'm feeling a bit tipsy.*
ANTONYM **sober**
▷ *NOUN*
2 someone who consumes too much
alcohol: *A drunk lay in the alley.*
alcoholic *after admitting that he was an
alcoholic*
boozer *INFORMAL a bit of a boozer*

dry
▷ *ADJECTIVE*
1 without any liquid: *The path was dry after
the sunshine.*
arid *arid conditions*
dried-up *a dried-up riverbed*
parched *parched brown grass*
ANTONYM **wet**
▷ *VERB*
2 to remove liquid from something: *Wash
and dry the lettuce.*
dehydrate *Coffee can dehydrate the body.*

drain *People were mobilized to drain the
flooded land.*
ANTONYM **moisten**
See also **barren**

dual *See* **double**

dub *See* **name**

dubious
▷ *ADJECTIVE*
1 not entirely honest or reliable: *a rather
dubious claim*
crooked *expose their crooked business
deals*
dishonest *He had become rich by dishonest
means.*
questionable *allegations of questionable
business practices*
suspect *The whole affair is highly suspect.*
suspicious *two characters who looked
suspicious*
unreliable *a notoriously unreliable source of
information*
2 doubtful about something: *My parents
were a bit dubious about it all.*
doubtful *I was still very doubtful about our
chances for success.*
nervous *The team has become nervous
about its prospects of winning.*
sceptical *Other archaeologists are sceptical
about their findings.*
suspicious *I'm a little suspicious about his
motives.*
unconvinced *Most fans seem unconvinced
that the team will make a comeback.*
undecided *After university, she was still
undecided about a career.*
unsure *Fifty-two percent were unsure about
the idea.*
See also **doubtful, improbable, suspect,
suspicious, uncertain**

duck *See* **dodge, escape**

duck out of *See* **avoid**

due *See* **outstanding**

duel *See* **fight**

dull
▷ *ADJECTIVE*
1 not interesting: *I found the play rather
dull.*
boring *a boring job*
drab *The rest of the day's activities often
seem drab.*
humdrum *The new government seemed
rather humdrum.*
monotonous *It's monotonous work, like
most factory jobs.*
tedious *Such lists are tedious to read.*
uninteresting *That program has a*

reputation for being dull and uninteresting.
ANTONYM **interesting**
2 not bright or clear: *a dark, dull blue colour*
drab *the same drab grey outfit*
gloomy *Inside it's gloomy after all that sunshine.*
muted *He likes sombre, muted colours.*
sombre *an official in sombre black*
subdued *subdued lighting*
ANTONYM **bright**
3 covered with clouds: *It seems as if it's always dull and raining.*
cloudy *In the morning it was cloudy.*
leaden *a leaden sky*
murky *one murky November afternoon*
overcast *For three days it was overcast.*
See also **blank, blunt, boring, cloudy, dim, dreary, fade, flat, gloomy, numb, sleepy, stuffy**

dullness See **boredom**

dumb
▷ *ADJECTIVE*
unable to speak: *We were all struck dumb for a minute.*
mute *a mute look of appeal*
silent *Suddenly, they both fell silent.*
speechless *I was almost speechless with rage.*

dumbness See **silence**

dummy See **mock, model**

dump
▷ *VERB*
1 to get rid of something: *The thieves were arrested when they dumped the stolen car in the police station's parking lot.*
discharge *Pollutants were illegally discharged in the ocean.*
dispose of *how they disposed of the murder weapon*
get rid of *We finally got rid of the smelly garbage.*
jettison *The crew jettisoned their excess fuel.*
throw away *You should have thrown the letter away.*
throw out *You ought to throw out those empty bottles.*
2 to put something down: *We dumped our bags at the hotel and went for a walk.*
deposit *Imagine if you were suddenly deposited on a desert island.*
drop *The children had been dropped outside the stadium by their parents.*
See also **discard, dispose of, get rid of**

dunce See **fool**

D

dungeon See **prison**

dupe
▷ *VERB*
to trick someone: *I was duped into believing the autograph was authentic.*
cheat *They were arrested for cheating customers.*
con INFORMAL *The people have been conned by the advertiser.*
deceive *He has deceived us all.*
delude *We were deluded into thinking we'd win a prize.*
fool *The art dealer fooled a lot of people.*
play a trick on *She realized he had played a trick on her.*
trick *He'll be upset when he finds out you tricked him.*
See also **cheat, deceive, fool, take in, trap, trick**

duplicate See **copy**

durable See **sturdy, tough**

duration See **length**

duress See **force**

dusk See **dark**

dust See **clean, dirt**

duty
▷ *NOUN*
1 something that you ought to do: *Citizens have a duty to vote.*
obligation *He felt an obligation to help his old friend.*
responsibility *work and family responsibilities*
2 a task associated with a job: *He carried out his duties conscientiously.*
assignment *dangerous assignments*
job *One of my jobs was to answer the phone.*
responsibility *She handled her responsibilities as a counsellor very well.*
role *Both sides had important roles to play.*
3 tax paid to the government: *customs duties*
excise *excise tax on tobacco*
levy *The local government may order a one-time levy to pay for the new sports facility.*
tariff *The Auto Pact eliminated tariffs between Canada and the United States.*
tax *federal income tax*
See also **function, job, part, responsibility, task, tax, work**

dwell See **inhabit, live**

dwelling See **home, house**

dwindle *See* **decrease, fall, lessen, shrink**

dye *See* **colour**

dying, be dying for

▷ *VERB*

to want something very much: *I'm dying for a breath of fresh air!*

ache for *He ached for the time when he was young and carefree.*

hunger for *We hungered for adventure.*

long for *He longed for the winter to be over.*

pine for *I pine for the countryside.*

yearn for *They yearned for freedom.*

dynamic *See* **energetic, vital**

Ee

each *See* **all**

eager
▷ *ADJECTIVE*
wanting very much to do or have something:
She is eager to earn some extra money.
anxious *She was anxious to leave early.*
ardent *one of the government's most ardent supporters*
avid *He's always been an avid reader.*
enthusiastic *He usually seems very enthusiastic.*
keen *a keen swimmer*
raring to go *INFORMAL They're all ready and raring to go.*
See also **enthusiastic, impatient, keen, ready, willing**

eagerness *See* **enthusiasm**

earlier *See* **before, first, previous**

earliest *See* **first**

early
▷ *ADJECTIVE*
1 before the arranged or expected time:
You're not late — I'm early!
advance *an advance screening of the new movie*
premature *The injury put a premature end to his hockey career.*
untimely *an untimely death for the promising young singer*
ANTONYM **late**
2 near the beginning of a period of time: *the early 1990s*
primeval *These insects first appeared in the primeval forests of Europe.*
primitive *a fossil of a primitive birdlike creature*
▷ *ADVERB*
3 before the arranged or expected time: *We left early so we wouldn't have to line up.*
ahead of time *The bus always arrives ahead of time.*
beforehand *If you'd let me know beforehand, you could have come with us.*
in advance *You need to book in advance to get a good seat.*
in good time *We arrived at the airport in good time.*
prematurely *My dad went prematurely bald.*

earmark *See* **intend**

earn
▷ *VERB*
1 to get money in return for doing work: *He earns a lot more than I do.*
bring in *My job brings in just enough to pay the bills.*
get *How much do you get for mowing lawns?*
make *She makes a lot of money.*
obtain *the profits obtained from buying and selling baseball cards*
2 to receive something that you deserve: *She earned the respect of her team.*
acquire *She has acquired a reputation as a hard worker.*
attain *FORMAL He finally attained his pilot's licence.*
win *She won the admiration of all her co-workers.*
See also **deserve, gain, merit**

earnest *See* **intense, serious, solemn**

earnings *See* **income, pay, profit**

earth
▷ *NOUN*
1 the planet on which we live: *the tallest mountain on earth*
globe *from every corner of the globe*
planet *the effects of pollution on the atmosphere of our planet*
world *the first person to cycle around the world*
2 soil from the ground: *He filled a pot with earth and planted the seeds in it.*
clay *lumps of clay that stuck to his boots*
dirt *kneeling in the dirt*
ground *digging potatoes out of the ground*
soil *We planted some bulbs in the soil around the pond.*
See also **dirt, ground, soil**

ease
▷ *NOUN*
1 lack of difficulty or worry: *He passed his test with ease.*
leisure *living a life of leisure*
relaxation *The village has a feeling of relaxation and tranquillity about it.*
simplicity *The simplicity of the map has made it easy for tourists to get around the city.*
▷ *VERB*
2 to make or become less severe or intense: *The doctor gave him medication to ease the pain.*
abate *By morning, the storms had abated.*
calm *The government is taking steps to calm the situation.*
relax *He relaxed his grip on the axe.*
relieve *The pills will help relieve the pain.*
slacken *His grip on the rope slackened, and he fell back.*

E

▷ VERB

3 to move slowly or carefully: *He eased the door open and peered outside.*

creep *The car crept down the ramp.*

edge *She edged the van slowly back into the garage.*

guide *She guided the plane out onto the tarmac.*

inch *The ambulance inched its way through the crowds.*

lower *He lowered himself into the armchair.*

manoeuvre *We attempted to manoeuvre the canoe toward the shore.*

squeeze *I squeezed into the seat and put on my seatbelt.*

See also **comfort, moderate**

easily offended *See* **sensitive, touchy**

easily upset *See* **sensitive**

easy

▷ ADJECTIVE

1 able to be done without difficulty: *The software is very easy to install.*

light *a few light exercises to warm up*

painless *Finding somewhere to stay was pretty painless.*

simple *All you have to do is answer a few simple questions.*

smooth *a smooth transition to the new system*

straightforward *The route is fairly straightforward so you shouldn't need a map.*

ANTONYM **hard**

2 comfortable and without worries: *He has not had an easy life.*

carefree *a carefree summer spent at the cottage*

comfortable *I feel comfortable in her company.*

leisurely *a leisurely weekend spent with a few close friends*

quiet *a quiet weekend at the cottage*

relaxed *It's very relaxed here, so you can do what you like.*

See also **comfortable, fluent, informal, leisurely, relaxed, simple, straightforward**

INFORMALLY SPEAKING
easy come, easy go: easily obtained and easily lost
easy does it: act gently
take it easy: relax

easy to use *See* **handy**

eat

▷ VERB

1 to chew and swallow food: *For lunch he ate a cheese sandwich.*

See WORD STUDY **eat**

2 to have a meal: *We like to eat early.*

dine *We usually dine at about six.*

feed *Leopards feed only when they are hungry.*

have a meal *We could have a meal at the restaurant after the film.*

picnic *After our walk, we picnicked by the river.*

eat away

▷ VERB

to destroy something slowly: *The front of the car had been eaten away by rust.*

corrode *buildings corroded by acid rain*

destroy *Areas of the coast are being destroyed by erosion.*

dissolve *Chemicals in the water are dissolving the bridge.*

erode *the floods that erode the dry, loose soil*

rot *Too much candy will rot your teeth.*

wear away *The weather can wear away the paint on the buildings.*

See also **erode**

eavesdrop *See* **hear**

eavesdropping *See* **nosy**

ebb *See* **abate**

eccentric

▷ ADJECTIVE

1 regarded as odd or peculiar: *His math teacher was considered a bit eccentric.*

bizarre *He's quite a bizarre character.*

outlandish *His outlandish behaviour sometimes puts people off.*

outrageous *My aunt is conservative, but my uncle can be outrageous.*

quirky *a quirky, delightful TV series that is full of surprises*

strange *his strange views about UFOs*

weird *His taste in music is a bit weird.*

▷ NOUN

2 someone who is regarded as odd or peculiar: *He's always been regarded as a bit of an eccentric.*

character INFORMAL *a well-known character who lived in our town*

crank *People regarded vegetarians as cranks in those days.*

See also **bizarre**

echelon *See* **rank**

echo *See* **repeat**

eclipse *See* **blot out, top**

There are a number of more descriptive words which you can use instead of the basic **eat**, to say something about the way in which a person eats.

• If you **consume** something, you eat it. This is a formal word.
The family **consumed** nearly a kilo of cheese a day.

• When an animal **feeds**, or **feeds on** something, it eats.
After a few days, the caterpillars stopped **feeding**.
Slugs **feed on** decaying plant material.

• If you **swallow** something, you make it go from your mouth into your stomach.
Snakes **swallow** their prey whole.

• If you **snack**, you eat things between meals.
Instead of **snacking** on chips and chocolate, eat fruit.

• If you **chew** something, you break it up with your teeth so that it is easier to swallow.
I pulled out a filling while I was **chewing** a candy.

• If you **nibble** food, you eat it by biting very small pieces of it, perhaps because you are not very hungry.
She **nibbled** at a piece of toast.

• If you **munch** food, you eat it by chewing it slowly, and rather noisily.
He **munched** his sandwiches appreciatively.

• If you **stuff yourself**, you eat a lot of food.
They'd **stuffed themselves** with snacks before dinner.

• If you **gobble**, **guzzle**, or **wolf (down)** food, you eat it quickly and greedily. **Guzzle** and **wolf (down)** are informal words.
She **gobbled** all the pizza before anyone else arrived.
Some people **guzzle** chocolate whenever they are unhappy.
I was back in the changing room **wolfing** sandwiches.
She bought a hot dog from a stand and **wolfed it down**.

• If you **devour** something, you eat it quickly and eagerly.
She **devoured** half of the apple pie.

E

economic

▷ ADJECTIVE

concerning the way money is managed: *the need for economic reform*
budgetary *a summit meeting to discuss various budgetary matters*
commercial *a purely commercial decision*
financial *The financial pressures on the government are mounting.*
See also **economical, financial**

economical

▷ ADJECTIVE

I cheap to use and saving you money: *Our car may not be fast, but it's very economical.*
cheap *This isn't a very cheap way of mailing packages.*
cost-effective *the most cost-effective way of shopping for food*
economic *the most economic way to travel to Calgary*
inexpensive *There are several good, inexpensive restaurants in town.*

2 careful and sensible with money or materials: *He's never been very economical about shopping for clothes.*
careful *She's very careful with her money.*
frugal *his frugal lifestyle*
prudent *the prudent use of precious natural resources*
thrifty *My parents were very thrifty because they had so little spare cash.*
See also **cheap, thrifty**

economics See finance

economy

▷ NOUN

the careful use of things to save money: *improvements in the fuel economy of new cars*
frugality FORMAL *To survive, our grandparents needed to live with strict frugality.*
prudence *A lack of prudence could seriously affect his finances.*

restraint *We need to exercise some restraint in our spending.*
thrift *He was widely praised for his thrift and imagination.*

ecstasy
▷ *NOUN*
extreme happiness: *his feeling of ecstasy after winning the medal*
bliss *the newlyweds living together in bliss and harmony*
delight *He squealed with delight when we told him.*
elation *Her supporters reacted to the news with elation.*
euphoria *There was a sense of euphoria after our election victory.*
exaltation *the mood of exaltation that affected everyone*
joy *her joy at finding him after so long*
rapture *The speech was received with rapture by a huge crowd.*
See also **happiness, heaven, joy**

edge
▷ *NOUN*
1 the place where something ends or meets something else: *on the edge of the forest*
border *the border between Canada and the United States*
boundary *The area beyond the western boundary has not been cleared.*
brim *He kept climbing until he reached the brim of the crater.*
fringe *the areas on the fringes of the city*
lip *The lip of the jug was badly cracked.*
margin *standing on the margin of the land where it met the water*
rim *a large round mirror with a gold rim*
ANTONYM **centre**
▷ *VERB*
2 to move somewhere slowly: *He edged toward the phone, ready to grab it if it rang.*
creep *The car crept forward a few feet, then stopped.*
inch *The ambulance inched its way through the crowd.*
sidle *A man sidled up to him and tried to sell him a ticket.*
See also **bank, border, ease, outskirts, side**

INFORMALLY SPEAKING

on edge: nervous and tense
take the edge off: take away the sharpness of; blunt

edgy *See* **nervous, restless, tense**

edifice *See* **building, structure**

edit *See* **revise**

edition *See* **issue**

educate *See* **instruct, teach, train**

educated
▷ *ADJECTIVE*
having a high standard of learning: *an educated, tolerant, and reasonable person*
cultivated *an elegant, cultivated woman*
cultured *a cultured man with a wide circle of friends*
intellectual *He is the intellectual type.*
learned *She was a scholar, a very learned person.*

education
▷ *NOUN*
the process of learning or teaching: *the importance of a good education*
coaching *extra coaching to help him pass his exams*
instruction *All instruction is provided by qualified experts.*
schooling *He began to wish he'd paid more attention to his schooling.*
training *Her training as a chef proved very useful.*
See also **knowledge**

eerie *See* **creepy, scary, spooky**

effect
▷ *NOUN*
a direct result of something: *the effect that divorce has on children*
consequence *aware of the consequences of their actions*
end result *The end result of this process is still unclear.*
fruit *The new software is the fruit of three years' hard work.*
result *The result of all this practice is that we are prepared for the big game.*
upshot *The upshot is that we have a very unhappy team.*
See also **influence, result**

CONFUSABLES

Effect means **result**, and is usually a noun.
Affect means **influence**, and is a verb.

effective *See* **convincing, efficient, powerful, useful**

effectively *See* **well**

effectiveness *See* **value**

effects *See* **possessions, property, things**

efficient

▷ ADJECTIVE
able to work well without wasting time or energy: *The new hatchback has a much more efficient engine.*
businesslike *a highly businesslike approach that impressed everyone*
competent *an extremely competent piece of work*
economical *The new system is much more economical, and will save millions.*
effective *effective use of the time we have left*
organized *She seemed very organized, and completely in control of the situation.*
productive *farmers who are productive*
ANTONYM **inefficient**
See also **able, capable, proficient**

efficiently *See* **well**

effort

▷ NOUN
1 physical or mental energy: *It took a lot of effort, but we managed in the end.*
application *Her talent, application, and energy are a credit to the school.*
energy *He decided to devote his energy to writing another book.*
exertion *Is it really worth all the exertion?*
trouble *It's not worth the trouble.*
work *All the work I put in has now been wasted!*
2 an attempt or struggle: *an unsuccessful effort to ban Sunday shopping*
attempt *an attempt to obtain an interview with the rock star*
bid *a last-minute bid to stop the trial from going ahead*
stab INFORMAL *her latest stab at acting*
struggle *his struggle to clear his name*
See also **enterprise, hassle, labour, struggle, try**

effortless *See* **fluent**

egoistic *See* **selfish**

egoistical *See* **selfish**

egotism *See* **conceit, pride**

egotistic *See* **selfish**

egotistical *See* **boastful, conceited, selfish, vain**

eject *See* **banish, discharge, get rid of, remove**

ejection *See* **discharge**

elaborate

▷ ADJECTIVE
1 having many different parts: *an elaborate and costly research project*
complex *a complex explanation*
complicated *a complicated security system*
detailed *the detailed plans that have been drawn up*
intricate *an intricate system of levers and pulleys*
involved *a very involved heart operation, lasting many hours*
ANTONYM **simple**
2 highly decorated: *elaborate wooden carvings*
fancy *the fancy plasterwork on the ceiling*
fussy *a rather fussy design*
ornate *an ornate wrought-iron staircase*
▷ VERB
3 to add more information about something: *He promised to elaborate on what had been said last night.*
develop *Maybe we should develop this idea.*
enlarge *He was enlarging on proposals made earlier.*
expand *a view that I will expand on later*
See also **complicated, fancy, sophisticated**

elaborate on *See* **enlarge on, expand on**

elastic *See* **flexible**

elated *See* **joyful**

elation *See* **ecstasy, happiness, joy**

elbow *See* **poke**

elbow room *See* **room**

elect *See* **decide**

election *See* **appointment**

electrifying *See* **exciting**

elegance *See* **beauty, grace, polish, style**

elegant *See* **posh, smart**

element *See* **aspect, detail, factor, ingredient, substance**

elementary *See* **basic, simple, straightforward**

elevate *See* **lift, promote, raise**

elicit *See* **excite, extract**

eliminate

▷ VERB
1 to get rid of someone or something: *We've eliminated two of the four options so far.*
cut out *His guilty plea cut out the need for a long, costly trial.*

E

do away with *the attempt to do away with nuclear weapons altogether*

eradicate *Efforts to eradicate malaria seem to be failing.*

get rid of *Why don't we just get rid of this idea and start over?*

remove *You should try to remove these fatty foods from your diet.*

stamp out *We need to stamp out this disgusting practice.*

2 to beat someone in a competition: *Our team was eliminated in the first round.*

knock out *They were knocked out by the returning champions.*

put out *She finally put her fellow American out in the quarter final.*

See also **banish, exclude, remove**

elite *See* **pick, top**

elsewhere *See* **absent**

elude *See* **avoid, dodge, escape**

emaciated *See* **skinny**

emancipation *See* **freedom, release**

embargo *See* **ban, boycott, sanctions**

embark upon *See* **start**

embarrass
▷ *VERB*
to make someone feel ashamed or awkward: *You always embarrass me in front of my friends!*

disconcert *The way he was smirking disconcerted me.*

fluster *Nothing could fluster him.*

humiliate *How dare you humiliate me like that!*

shame *Their behaviour upset and shamed us.*

See also **humiliate, shame**

embarrassed
▷ *ADJECTIVE*
ashamed and awkward: *I was embarrassed about making a fool of myself in public.*

ashamed *I felt so ashamed, I wanted to hide.*

awkward *It was a very awkward situation.*

humiliated *He felt humiliated when such personal details appeared in the newspapers.*

red-faced *Red-faced executives had to explain this fact.*

self-conscious *I always feel self-conscious when I'm having my picture taken.*

sheepish *He looked very sheepish when he finally appeared.*

See also **ashamed, uncomfortable**

embarrassment
▷ *NOUN*
shame and awkwardness: *I laughed loudly to cover my embarrassment.*

awkwardness *the awkwardness of our first meeting*

bashfulness *Overcome with bashfulness, he lowered his voice.*

humiliation *the humiliation of having to ask for money*

self-consciousness *her painful self-consciousness*

shame *the shame he felt at having let her down*

See also **shame**

embittered *See* **bitter, resentful, sour**

emblem *See* **sign, symbol**

embrace *See* **clasp, grasp, hold, hug, include**

emerge *See* **appear**

emergence *See* **appearance**

emergency
▷ *NOUN*
an unexpected and difficult situation: *This is an emergency!*

crisis *the economic crisis affecting parts of Africa*

pinch *I don't mind working late in a pinch.*

emergent *See* **in the making**

eminence *See* **fame, success**

eminent *See* **important, leading, prominent**

emit
▷ *VERB*
to give out or release something: *She blinked and emitted a long sigh.*

exude *The sewage treatment plant exudes an extremely unpleasant smell.*

give off *The fumes it gives off are poisonous.*

give out *The alarm gave out a series of beeps, then stopped.*

release *The factory is still releasing toxic fumes.*

send out *The volcano has been sending out smoke for weeks.*

utter *He uttered a loud snort and continued eating.*

See also **discharge**

emotion *See* **feeling, passion**

emotional *See* **moving, passionate**

empathize with *See* **identify with**

empathy *See* **sympathy**

emphasis

▷ NOUN

special or extra importance: *too much emphasis on materialism*
accent *Under the new leader, the accent will be on co-operation.*
importance *There's not enough importance being given to environmental issues.*
prominence *Crime prevention has to be given more prominence.*
weight *This adds more weight to the government's case.*

emphasize

▷ VERB

to make something seem especially important or obvious: *He emphasized the need for everyone to remain calm.*
accent *a white dress accented by a brightly coloured scarf*
accentuate *His shaved head accentuates his round face.*
highlight *This situation has highlighted the difficulty faced by the club.*
play up *He played up his "Mr. Innocent" image.*
stress *I would like to stress that we are in complete agreement.*
underline *This underlines how important the new deal really is.*
See also **feature, stress**

employ

▷ VERB

1 to pay someone to work for you: *He was employed by the singer as a bodyguard.*
appoint *We need to appoint a successor to the treasurer.*
commission *She has been commissioned to design a new bridge.*
engage FORMAL *They have finally engaged a suitable choir director.*
hire *I was hired as a gardener.*
take on *the need to take on more workers for the summer*
2 to use something: *the tactics employed by the police*
bring to bear *We can bring two very different techniques to bear on this.*
make use of *He makes use of several highly effective terms to describe the situation.*
use *the methods used in the investigation*
utilize *Technicians will utilize a range of techniques to improve the program.*
See also **busy, hire, use**

employed *See* **busy**

employee

▷ NOUN

someone who is paid to work for someone

else: *the way they look after their employees*
hand *He's been working as a farmhand.*
worker *Workers at the plant have been laid off.*
See also **worker**

employees *See* **labour, staff**

employer

▷ NOUN

someone for whom other people work: *a meeting with her employer to discuss the issue*
boss *My boss has always been very fair.*
See also **boss**

E

employers *See* **management**

employment

▷ NOUN

the fact of employing people: *the employment of teenagers to work in restaurants*
engagement *the engagement of suitable staff*
enlistment *Enlistment in the Canadian Forces is falling.*
hiring *The hiring of new staff is our top priority.*
recruitment *new policies on recruitment and training*
taking on *Taking on extra staff would make life a lot easier.*
See also **job, use, work**

empty

▷ ADJECTIVE

1 having no people or things in it: *The roads were empty.*
bare *When he got there, the refrigerator was bare.*
blank *all the blank pages in his diary*
clear *The runway must be kept clear at all times.*
deserted *By nightfall, the square was deserted.*
unfurnished *The apartment was unfurnished when they moved in.*
uninhabited *The house has remained uninhabited since she moved out.*
vacant *two vacant lots in the subdivision*
ANTONYM **full**
2 boring or without value or meaning: *My life is empty without you.*
inane *a series of inane remarks*
meaningless *the feeling that his existence was meaningless*
worthless *a worthless movie, with nothing to say about anything*
▷ VERB
3 to remove people or things: *He emptied all*

the drawers before the guests arrived.
clear *The police cleared the building just in time.*
drain *She drained the bottles and washed them out.*
evacuate *Fortunately, the building had been evacuated.*
unload *It took only 20 minutes to unload the truck.*
ANTONYM **fill**
See also **bare, barren, blank, discharge, drain, fond**

emulate *See* **copy, imitate**

en masse *See* **together**

enable *See* **permit**

enchant *See* **delight**

enchanting *See* **lovable, magical**

encircle *See* **enclose, surround**

enclose
▷ *VERB*
to surround a thing or place completely: *The CDs arrived enclosed in a small brown box.*
border *The entire lawn was bordered with flowers.*
encircle *The area had been encircled by barbed wire.*
fence off *We decided to fence off the property.*
hem in *We were hemmed in by walls and hedges.*
surround *the low wall that surrounded the rose garden*
wrap *Wrap the chicken in foil and bake it in a medium oven.*
See also **surround**

encompass *See* **include, surround**

encounter *See* **experience, meet, meeting, receive**

encourage
▷ *VERB*
1 to give someone confidence: *We were very encouraged by the response.*
cheer *This news cheered us all and helped us keep going.*
hearten *I am heartened to hear that.*
reassure *He always reassures me when I'm feeling down.*
ANTONYM **discourage**
2 to support a person or activity: *the need to encourage people to be sensible*
aid *I tried to aid his creative efforts.*
boost *Efforts to boost the TV ratings seem to be succeeding.*

favour *conditions that favour growth in the economy*
help *policies aimed at helping small businesses*
incite *to incite a riot*
support *He will support me in this campaign.*
See also **back, push, reassure, strengthen, support**

encouragement *See* **incentive**

encroach *See* **intrude**

end
▷ *NOUN*
1 the last part of a period or event: *the end of the 20th century*
ANTONYM **beginning**
See WORD STUDY **end** *on next page*
2 the farthest point of something: *the room at the end of the hallway*
3 the purpose for which something is done: *The army is being used for political ends.*
▷ *VERB*
4 to come or bring to a finish: *talks being held to end the players' strike*
bring to an end *The treaty brought to an end 50 years of conflict.*
cease *By one o'clock, the storm had ceased.*
conclude *The evening concluded with the usual speeches.*
finish *waiting for the game to finish*
stop *When is it all going to stop?*
terminate *the decision to terminate their contract*
ANTONYM **begin**
See also **back, cease, complete, conclude, conclusion, extreme, finish, goal, halt, lift, stop, use**

INFORMALLY SPEAKING

at loose ends: not doing anything in particular
end up: do or be, eventually
jump (or go) off the deep end: act rashly
make both ends meet: spend no more than you have
no end: very much or very many

---

end result *See* **effect**

endanger
▷ *VERB*
to put someone or something in danger: *a dispute that could endanger the peace talks*
compromise *We will not allow safety to be compromised.*
jeopardize *a scandal that could jeopardize the government*

End is a commonly overused word. Depending on the context, you can use the following substitutes to add variety and interest to your writing.

• **of a period of time**
The company made $100 million by the **close** of the year.
It was the **ending** of a great era.
Tomorrow marks the **expiry** of my period of training.
The college basketball season is nearing its **finish**.

• **of an event**
The court was packed for the dramatic **climax** of the trial.
Yesterday was the **close** of the festival.
Stay tuned for the **conclusion** of this exciting episode.
Winning an award would be the remarkable **culmination** of a glittering career.
The film had a tragic **ending**.
Fireworks were planned as a grand **finale** to the week-long celebrations.
What a disappointing **finish** to our adventures.

• **the furthest part of something**
We walked along the **boundary** of the park.
The landscape beyond the **bounds** of the city is very flat.
He fell off the **edge** of the cliff.
The western **extremity** of the continent is very mountainous.

They live in an area outside the official city **limits**.
Agricultural regions start right at the forest **margin**.

• **the point of something long or sharp**
We walked to the southernmost **point** of the island.
The **tip** of the knife was broken off.

E

• **a leftover piece**
Don't throw away all those trimmings and **leftovers**.
The puppet is made from **remnants** of fabric.
She saves **scraps** of spare material.
The ticket **stub** was in my pocket.

• **the purpose of doing something**
The different groups were united by a common **aim**.
We're all working toward the same **goal**.
He concealed his real **intentions**.
What was the **object** of your mission?
The **objective** of all this effort was not clear to me.
He secretly told us the true **purpose** of his visit.
Is she here on holiday, or for business **reasons**?

---

put at risk *those who were put at risk by one person's stupidity*
risk *He is risking the lives of others.*
threaten *A breakdown in this system could threaten the whole project.*
See also **threaten**

endearing *See* **lovable**

endeavour *See* **attempt, enterprise, seek, strive, try, undertaking**

ending *See* **conclusion, finish**

endless *See* **continual**

endorse *See* **advocate, approve, back, confirm, defend, sanction**

endorsement *See* **approval**

endow *See* **equip**

endure
▷ *VERB*
I to experience something difficult: *He had*

to endure hours of discomfort.
cope with *We've had a lot to cope with in the last few weeks.*
experience *The team has experienced several injuries.*
go through *having to go through the public humiliation of a trial*
stand *I don't know how he stood it for so long.*
suffer *My grandfather has suffered years of pain from arthritis.*
2 to continue to exist: *Our friendship has endured through everything.*
last *a car that is built to last*
live on *Her name will live on as an inspiration to others.*
remain *When everything else is forgotten, this fact will remain.*
survive *the few traces of their civilization that have survived*
See also **bear, continue, go through,**

have, last, remain, suffer, survive, tolerate, undergo

enduring *See* **permanent**

enemy

▷ *NOUN*

someone who is against you: *She has many enemies in the government.*

adversary *face to face with his old adversary*

antagonist *He killed his antagonist in a duel.*

foe *He plays Dracula's foe, Dr. Van Helsing.*

opponent *Her opponents will be delighted at this news.*

ANTONYM **friend**

energetic

▷ *ADJECTIVE*

full of energy: *She is an able, energetic, and very determined politician.*

animated *an animated conversation about politics and sports*

dynamic *a dynamic and ambitious salesperson*

indefatigable *trying to keep up with their indefatigable boss*

spirited *a spirited defence of his new proposals*

tireless *a tireless campaigner for the homeless*

vigorous *a vigorous campaign*

See also **active, alive, lively, vital**

energy

▷ *NOUN*

the ability and strength to do things: *I'm saving my energy for tomorrow.*

drive *a person with immense drive and enthusiasm*

life *At 96, she's still as full of life as ever.*

spirit *Despite trailing 6-2, they played with a lot of spirit.*

strength *She put all her strength into finding a new job.*

vigour *They returned to their work with renewed vigour.*

vitality *someone with considerable charm and endless vitality*

See also **activity, drive, effort, spirit**

enforce *See* **impose**

engage *See* **book, busy, employ, hire**

engage in *See* **participate**

engaged *See* **active, busy**

engagement *See* **employment**

engineer *See* **stage**

engrave *See* **carve**

engrossed *See* **busy, preoccupied**

enhance *See* **benefit, flatter, improve**

enhancement *See* **improvement**

enigma *See* **mystery**

enigmatic *See* **mysterious**

enjoy

▷ *VERB*

to find pleasure in something: *I haven't enjoyed a movie as much as that in ages!*

appreciate *people who don't appreciate rock music*

delight in *He delights in playing practical jokes.*

like *I like shopping.*

love *She loves skiing.*

relish *She relished the opportunity to compete with me.*

revel in *The young player was revelling in all the attention.*

take pleasure from *He took no pleasure from the knowledge that he had won.*

take pleasure in *She seemed to take pleasure in my misery.*

See also **have, like, love, possess**

enjoyable *See* **agreeable, lovely, pleasant**

enjoyment *See* **entertainment, fun, pleasure**

enlarge

▷ *VERB*

to make something larger: *plans to enlarge the stadium*

add to *We've decided to add to this house rather than move again.*

expand *If we want to stay in business, we need to expand.*

extend *They extended the house by adding a new wing.*

increase *It's time to increase the memory in the computer.*

magnify *A more powerful lens will magnify the image.*

See also **elaborate, expand, extend, increase**

enlargement *See* **growth**

enlarge on

▷ *VERB*

to give more information about something: *I'd like you to enlarge on that last point.*

develop *Maybe I should develop this idea a little bit further.*

elaborate on *He refused to elaborate on what he had said earlier.*

expand on *an idea that I will expand on later*
See also **expand on**

enlighten *See* **inform**

enlightened *See* **civilized, rational**

enlist *See* **join, recruit**

enlistment *See* **employment**

enliven *See* **refresh**

enormous
▷ *ADJECTIVE*
very large in size or amount: *an enormous dust cloud*
colossal *a colossal waste of money*
gigantic *The road is bordered by gigantic rocks.*
huge *Several artists were working on a huge piece of canvas.*
immense *an immense cloud of smoke*
massive *The scale of the problem is massive.*
tremendous *I was under tremendous pressure at work.*
vast *vast stretches of land*
ANTONYM **tiny**
See also **colossal, excessive, huge, immense, large, vast**

enough *See* **adequate, ample, plenty, sufficient**

enrage *See* **anger, provoke**

enraged *See* **angry, furious, mad**

enrol *See* **join, recruit**

ensemble *See* **company**

ensue *See* **result**

ensuing *See* **next**

ensure
▷ *VERB*
to make sure about something: *We must ensure that this never happens again.*
guarantee *They guaranteed that we would have more ice time.*
make certain *to make certain that he'll get there*
make sure *I will personally make sure that the job gets done.*
See also **guarantee**

CONFUSABLES

ensure means **make sure**
assure means **instill confidence**
insure means **arrange for payment in case of accident or loss**

---

enter *See* **come, insert, invade, record**

enter into *See* **participate**

enterprise
▷ *NOUN*
1 a business or company: *a small enterprise that grew into a major corporation*
business *a medium-sized business*
company *a company that was doing very well*
concern *It's not a large concern, but it makes a profit.*
establishment *a modest establishment dedicated to skateboarding*
firm *a clothing firm*
operation *a one-person operation*
2 a project or task: *a creative enterprise such as painting or photography*
effort *her latest fundraising effort for cancer research*
endeavour *an endeavour that was bound to end in failure*
operation *He'd set up a small software operation.*
project *a project that will attract a lot of media attention*
undertaking *This undertaking will rely on the hard work of our volunteers.*
venture *a venture in which few were willing to invest*
See also **business, drive, firm, racket, undertaking**

entertain
▷ *VERB*
to keep people amused or interested: *things that might entertain children during the spring break*
amuse *He amused us all evening, singing and telling jokes.*
charm *He charmed us all with tales of life on the road.*
delight *a routine that will delight audiences*
enthral *She enthralled audiences throughout Canada.*
please *The comedian certainly knows how to please a crowd.*
See also **please, receive**

entertain oneself *See* **play**

entertaining *See* **interesting**

entertainment
▷ *NOUN*
enjoyable activities: *Their main form of entertainment is TV.*
amusement *looking for some amusement on a Saturday night*
enjoyment *We need a bit of enjoyment to cheer us up.*
fun *It's not really my idea of family fun.*

E

pleasure *lots of pleasure with just a deck of cards*
recreation *a healthy and enjoyable form of recreation*
See also **festival, fun**

enthral *See* **entertain, entrance, fascinate**

enthuse *See* **rave**

enthusiasm
▷ *NOUN*
eagerness and enjoyment in something: *We were disappointed by their lack of enthusiasm.*
eagerness *He could barely contain his eagerness.*
excitement *Her excitement got the better of her.*
interest *He doesn't show much interest in football.*
keenness *I don't doubt his keenness; it's his ability that worries me.*
warmth *She greeted us with her usual warmth and affection.*
See also **excitement, spirit**

enthusiastic
▷ *ADJECTIVE*
showing great excitement and eagerness for something: *He was very enthusiastic about the new plan.*
ardent *one of the government's most ardent supporters*
avid *an avid reader*
devoted *a devoted figure-skating fan*
eager *She is eager to learn more about photography.*
excited *We are very excited about getting a new dog.*
keen *a keen card player*
passionate *a passionate opponent of racism*
ANTONYM **apathetic**
See also **active, ardent, eager, excited, fervent, keen**

entice *See* **attract, lure, tempt**

entire *See* **complete, whole**

entirely *See* **quite**

entrails *See* **insides**

entrance
▷ *NOUN*
1 the way into a particular place: *I met my cousin in front of the arena entrance.*
door *She was waiting by the front door.*
doorway *the crowd of people blocking the doorway*
entry *the main entry to the theatre*

gate *the security guard at the main gate*
way in *Is this the way in?*
2 a person's arrival somewhere: *The actors made their entrance when the curtain went up.*
appearance *She made a brief appearance at the party.*
arrival *reporters awaiting the arrival of the team*
entry *He was welcomed on his entry into Canada.*
3 the right to enter somewhere: *His happy manner gained him entrance to the group.*
access *We were denied access to the stadium.*
admission *no admission without a ticket*
entry *I was unable to gain entry to the meeting.*
▷ *VERB*
4 to amaze and delight someone: *The audience was entranced by her voice.*
bewitch *My brother's smile bewitched everyone.*
captivate *I was captivated by her piercing blue eyes.*
charm *He charmed the crowd with his delightful stories.*
delight *a CD that will delight her many fans*
enthral *Audiences were enthralled by his spectacular stage act.*
fascinate *She never failed to fascinate him.*
See also **charm, entry**

entry
▷ *NOUN*
1 a person's arrival somewhere: *her dramatic entry*
appearance *She made her appearance to great applause.*
arrival *He apologized for his late arrival.*
entrance *My entrance was spoiled when I tripped over the carpet.*
2 the way into a particular place: *He was hanging around at the entry to the station.*
door *I'll meet you at the front door.*
doorway *A bicycle was blocking the doorway.*
entrance *The parcel had been left outside the entrance to the building.*
gate *Guards were posted at the main gate.*
way in *I can't find the way in.*
3 something that has been written down: *the final entry in his journal*
item *A number of interesting items appear in his diary.*
note *She made a note on the calendar before turning off the computer.*
record *There is no record of delivery.*
See also **entrance**

envelop *See* **surround**

envious *See* **jealous**

environment *See* **background, habitat, scene, surroundings**

environmental

▷ *ADJECTIVE*

concerned with environmental issues: *Children and adolescents are now aware of environmental issues.*

conservationist *protests from conservationist groups*

ecological *shared interest in ecological issues*

green *People are taking a greater interest in green issues.*

envisage *See* **contemplate, imagine**

envoy *See* **messenger**

envy

▷ *NOUN*

1 a feeling of resentment about what someone else has: *his feelings of envy toward his cousin*

jealousy *the jealousy people felt toward her because of her money*

resentment *All the anger, bitterness, and resentment suddenly melted away.*

▷ *VERB*

2 to want something that someone else has: *I don't envy you one bit.*

be envious *people who were envious of her good fortune*

begrudge *Surely you don't begrudge me one night out.*

be jealous *I couldn't help being jealous when I knew he had won.*

covet *She coveted his job.*

resent *Anyone with money was resented and ignored.*

ephemeral *See* **temporary**

epidemic *See* **rash**

episode *See* **event, experience, incident**

epithet *See* **name**

epitome *See* **ideal, model, ultimate**

equal

▷ *ADJECTIVE*

1 the same in size, amount, or value: *equal numbers of men and women*

equivalent *A kilogram is equivalent to about 2.2 pounds.*

identical *glasses containing identical amounts of water*

the same *different areas of research that have the same importance*

▷ *VERB*

2 to be as good as something else: *the runner's time equalled her previous record*

be equal to *The final score is equal to his personal best.*

match *able to match her previous time for the marathon*

See also **even, fair, rival, same**

equally *See* **alike**

equal to

▷ *ADJECTIVE*

having the necessary ability for something: *She was equal to any task they gave her.*

capable of *I'm no longer capable of this kind of work.*

up to *He said he wasn't up to a long walk.*

equilibrium *See* **balance**

equine *See* **horse**

equip

▷ *VERB*

to supply someone with something: *The boat was equipped with an outboard motor.*

arm *The children arrived armed with an assortment of games.*

endow *The male bird is endowed with a vicious-looking beak.*

fit out *fitted out with a new wardrobe*

provide *We provided them with sandwiches.*

supply *They supplied us with camping gear.*

See also **issue, provide, supply**

equipment

▷ *NOUN*

the things you need for a particular job: *a shed full of gardening equipment*

apparatus *All the firefighters were wearing breathing apparatus.*

gear *camping gear*

paraphernalia *backpacks, tents, and other hiking paraphernalia*

stuff *The builders had left all their stuff in the garden.*

tackle *They kept all their fishing tackle in the spare room.*

See also **stuff, supplies**

equitable *See* **fair**

equity *See* **balance, justice, right**

equivalence *See* **balance**

equivalent *See* **equal, same**

eradicate *See* **banish, eliminate**

erase *See* **delete, remove**

erect *See* **assemble, build, construct, straight**

erode

▷ VERB

to wear something away and destroy it:
*The cliffs were being eroded by the constant
pounding of the waves.*

corrode *buildings corroded by acid rain*
destroy *ancient monuments destroyed by
pollution*
deteriorate *The tapestry had deteriorated
badly where the roof was leaking.*
disintegrate *Once they were exposed to
light, the documents rapidly disintegrated.*
eat away *The chemicals in the water had
eaten away the cables.*
wear away *rocks worn away by the crashing
waves*
wear down *The dog's teeth were worn
down, but she could still chew on a bone.*
See also **eat away, wash, wear**

erosion See **wear**

erotic See **sexy**

err

▷ VERB

to make a mistake: *The builders had erred in
their original estimate.*
blunder *It was a costly blunder.*
go wrong *We must have gone wrong
somewhere in our calculations.*
make a mistake *Okay, I made a mistake;
I'm only human.*
miscalculate *They miscalculated, and now
they're in deep trouble.*

erratic See **changeable, irregular**

erroneous See **false, untrue**

error

▷ NOUN

a mistake: *a mathematical error*
blunder *She made a tactical blunder by
announcing the election.*
fault *Nobody's perfect; we all have faults.*
lapse *a serious lapse in judgment*
mistake *spelling mistakes*
slip *We must be careful — we can't afford
any slips.*
See also **hole, mistake, slip**

erudite See **learned**

erupt See **burst**

eruption See **outbreak, rash**

escalate See **jump**

escape

▷ VERB

I to manage to get away: *Three prisoners
who escaped have given themselves up.*
break free *He was handcuffed, but
managed to break free.*
break out *two prisoners who broke out of
the maximum security wing*
get away *She got away from her guards.*
make your escape *We made our escape
using knotted sheets.*
run away *I called him, but he just ran away.*
run off *The children ran off when they
spotted me.*
2 to manage to avoid something: *He was
lucky to escape injury.*
avoid *She has managed to avoid arrest so
far.*
dodge *He dodged his responsibilities by
pretending to be ill.*
duck *a pathetic attempt to duck their
responsibilities*
elude *He managed to elude the police for
13 years.*
evade *He has now been charged with
evading tax.*
▷ NOUN
3 something that distracts you from
something unpleasant: *Cycling gives her an
escape from the routine of work.*
distraction *a distraction from his troubles*
diversion *a pleasant diversion from my
studies*
relief *The piano provides me with relief from
all the stress.*
See also **bolt, flee, leak**

eschew See **avoid**

escort See **accompany, guide, lead,
take**

essence

▷ NOUN

the most basic and important part of
something: *The essence of good manners is
the ability to listen.*
core *the need to get to the core of the
problem*
heart *at the heart of the problem*
nature *the nature of what it is to be a nurse*
soul *a song that captures the soul of this
nation*
spirit *the spirit of modern technology*

essential

▷ ADJECTIVE

I extremely important: *Good ventilation is
essential in a greenhouse.*
crucial *Her speech was a crucial part of the
campaign.*
indispensable *She has become
indispensable to the department.*
vital *a vital aspect of the plans that everyone
has overlooked*

2 basic and important: *an essential part of any child's development*
basic *the basic laws of physics*
cardinal *He had broken one of the cardinal rules of business.*
fundamental *the fundamental principles of democracy*
key *She had a key role to play in the negotiations.*
main *an attempt to analyze the main points of his theory*
principal *the principal idea behind their argument*
See also **basic, necessary, requirement, vital**

essentials
▷ *PLURAL NOUN*
the things that are most important: *We had only enough food money for the essentials.*
basics *We need to get back to basics.*
fundamentals *the fundamentals of road safety*
necessities *Water, food, and shelter are the necessities of life.*
prerequisites *Self-confidence is one of the prerequisites for a happy life.*
rudiments *learning the rudiments of car maintenance*

establish See **determine, form, organize, prove, set up, start**

established See **certain, set, traditional**

establishment See **business, company, enterprise, introduction**

estate See **grounds, land, legacy, possessions, property**

esteem
▷ *NOUN*
admiration and respect for another person: *held in high esteem by her students*
admiration *I have always had the greatest admiration for him.*
estimation *He has gone down in my estimation.*
regard *I had a very high regard for him and his work.*
respect *I have tremendous respect for her.*
reverence *She is still spoken of with reverence by those who knew her.*
See also **admiration, approval, favour, prize, respect**

esteemed See **dear**

estimate
▷ *NOUN*
a guess at an amount, quantity, or outcome: *This figure is five times the original estimate.*

appraisal *an appraisal of their financial worth*
assessment *assessments of the property*
estimation *Their estimation of my height was surprisingly accurate.*
guess *an educated guess about the size of the room*
quote *We asked the painter for a quote before giving her the job.*
reckoning *By my reckoning, we were 12 km from the town.*
valuation *The valuations reflect prices at the end of the fiscal year.*
See also **guess, judge, price, reckon, tender, value**

estimated See **approximate, rough**

estimation See **esteem, estimate, opinion**

eternal
▷ *ADJECTIVE*
lasting forever: *the secret of eternal life*
everlasting *everlasting love*
immortal *immortal fame as an artist*
unchanging *the unchanging laws of the cosmos*
See also **constant, continual, infinite, permanent**

ethics See **standards**

ethnic group See **race**

etiquette See **ceremony, convention, politeness**

euphoria See **ecstasy**

evacuate See **empty**

evacuation See **retreat**

evade See **avoid, dodge, escape**

evaluate See **judge, value**

evaporate See **melt, vanish**

even
▷ *ADJECTIVE*
1 flat and level: *I need an even surface to write on.*
flat *a small cottage with a flat roof*
horizontal *He drew a series of horizontal lines on the paper.*
level *checking the floor to make sure it was level*
smooth *the smooth kitchen counter*
ANTONYM **uneven**
2 without changing or varying: *an even flow of liquid*
constant *The temperature in the room*

E

remained more or less constant.

regular *quiet, regular breathing*

smooth *He caught the ball and passed it in one smooth motion.*

steady *a steady stream of people*

uniform *The prices increases are not uniform across the country.*

3 the same: *At half-time, the scores were still even.*

equal *the fight for equal rights between women and men*

identical *At the end of the contest, our scores were identical.*

neck and neck *They're still neck and neck with two minutes to go.*

See also **constant, regular, steady, straight**

INFORMALLY SPEAKING

break even: have equal gains and losses
even out: become more level or balanced
get even: take revenge

---

even though *See* **in spite of**

event

▷ NOUN

1 something that happens: *still amazed at the events of last week*

affair *He preferred to forget the unpleasant affair.*

business *Do you remember that business with your cousin?*

circumstance *due to circumstances beyond our control*

episode *A rather embarrassing episode took place at the wedding.*

experience *an experience that changed his mind about going to university*

incident *the incident in the restaurant*

matter *She doesn't seem to be taking this matter seriously.*

2 a competition: *The next event is the long jump.*

bout *This is his fifth heavyweight fight in three months.*

competition *the first competition of the afternoon*

contest *She's out of the contest for good.*

See also **affair, competition, incident, occasion**

eventual *See* **final, ultimate**

eventually *See* **finally**

everlasting *See* **eternal, infinite**

every now and then *See* **sometimes**

every one *See* **all**

every so often *See* **sometimes**

every time *See* **always**

everyday

▷ ADJECTIVE

usual or ordinary: *the drudgery of everyday life*

common *a common occurrence*

daily *In our daily life we follow predictable patterns of behaviour.*

day-to-day *I use a lot of spices in my day-to-day cooking.*

mundane *the mundane realities of life*

ordinary *our ordinary dishes, not the fancy ones*

routine *routine maintenance of the machine*

See also **colloquial, common, frequent, natural, regular, routine**

everything *See* **all, whole**

evict *See* **banish**

evidence *See* **proof, sign, trace**

evident

▷ ADJECTIVE

easily noticed or understood: *He spoke with evident emotion about his ordeal.*

apparent *She spoke with apparent nonchalance about the experience.*

clear *It became clear that I hadn't convinced anyone.*

noticeable *a noticeable effect*

obvious *It's obvious that he doesn't like me.*

palpable *The tension between the two of them is palpable.*

plain *It was plain to me that they were having a dreadful time.*

visible *the most visible sign of his distress*

See also **clear, conspicuous, naked, noticeable, obvious, plain, visible**

evil

▷ NOUN

1 the force that causes bad things to happen: *the conflict between good and evil*

badness *behaving that way out of sheer badness*

immorality *the immorality that is typical of the drug trade*

sin *a place of sin and corruption*

vice *a business long associated with vice and immorality*

wickedness *the wickedness of his behaviour*

ANTONYM **good**

2 something unpleasant or harmful: *a lecture on the evils of alcohol*

affliction *Hay fever is an affliction that affects thousands.*

ill *Many of the economy's ills are his responsibility.*
misery *the misery of drug addiction*
sorrow *the joys and sorrows of family life*
▷ ADJECTIVE
3 morally wrong or bad: *an utterly evil person*
bad *He's not a bad man, he's just very unhappy.*
depraved *a thoroughly depraved story*
malevolent *a malevolent influence on the whole school*
sinful *a good person in a sinful world*
vile *vile acts of brutality*
wicked *a wicked attack on a helpless animal*
ANTONYM **good**
See also **sin, sinister, wicked, wrong**

evoke See **excite, provoke**

evolve See **develop**

exact
▷ ADJECTIVE
1 correct in every detail: *It's an exact reproduction of the first steam engine.*
accurate *an accurate description of the person*
authentic *The autograph is authentic.*
faithful *faithful copies of ancient stone tools*
faultless *Your Italian is faultless.*
precise *It's difficult to give a precise date for the painting.*
true *Is this a true picture of life in the Middle Ages?*
ANTONYM **approximate**
▷ VERB
2 FORMAL to demand and obtain something: *They are certain to exact a high price for their co-operation.*
command *an excellent surgeon who commanded the respect of all her colleagues*
extract *to extract the maximum advantage from this situation*
impose *to impose a fine for littering*
insist on *She insisted on conducting all the interviews herself.*
insist upon *He insists upon good service.*
wring *attempts to wring concessions from management*
See also **accurate, correct, faithful, particular, precise, right, strict**

exacting See **fussy, particular, stiff, tough**

exactly
▷ ADVERB
1 with complete accuracy and precision: *He arrived at exactly five o'clock.*
accurately *We cannot accurately predict where the missile will land.*

E

faithfully *I translated the play as faithfully as I could.*
just *There are no statistics about just how many people won't vote.*
on the dot *At nine o'clock on the dot, they have breakfast.*
precisely *Nobody knows precisely how many people attended the meeting.*
quite *That wasn't quite what I meant.*
ANTONYM **approximately**
▷ INTERJECTION
2 an expression implying total agreement: *"We'll never know the answer." "Exactly. So let's stop speculating."*
absolutely *"It's worrying, isn't it?" "Absolutely."*
indeed *"That's a topic that's getting a lot of media coverage." "Indeed."*
precisely *"So, you're suggesting we do away with these laws?" "Precisely."*
quite *"It's your choice, isn't it?" "Quite."*
See also **prompt**

exaggerate
▷ VERB
to make things seem more extreme than they are: *He thinks I'm exaggerating, but I'm not!*
overdo *I think he's overdoing it a bit when he complains like that.*
overestimate *I think we're overestimating their desire to co-operate.*
overstate *It's impossible to overstate the seriousness of this situation.*

exaggerated See **excessive**

exaltation See **ecstasy**

exam
▷ NOUN
a test to find out how much you know: *a final exam*
examination *a three-hour written examination*
test *I'm studying for my history test.*

examination
▷ NOUN
1 a careful inspection of something: *a careful examination of all the evidence*
analysis *an analysis of the author's writing style*
inspection *The police inspection of the crime scene found no fingerprints.*
study *A study of the wreckage revealed new information.*
2 a check carried out on someone by a doctor: *The doctor suggested an immediate examination of his ear.*

check *a quick check just to make sure everything's working properly*
checkup *my annual checkup at the clinic*
physical *It's time for my annual physical.*
See also **check, exam, research, review**

examine
▷ VERB
1 to look at something very carefully: *Police are examining the scene of the crash.*
analyze *We haven't had time to analyze all the samples yet.*
go over *I'll go over your report tomorrow.*
go through *We went through his belongings and found a notebook.*
inspect *Customs officials inspected the vehicle.*
look over *We'll look the items over and decide if we wish to buy them.*
study *Experts are studying the frozen remains of a mammoth.*
2 to give someone a medical examination: *I was examined by several specialists.*
check *The doctor checked my nose and throat.*
look at *She said she wanted to look at my chest again just to make sure.*
test *They tested my eyes, but my vision was fine.*
See also **check, contemplate, inspect, interrogate, investigate, question, research, scrutinize, study**

example
▷ NOUN
1 something that represents a group of things: *some examples of well-made horror movies*
illustration *Her Olympic performance is an illustration of her elegance as a skater.*
sample *This drawing is a sample of his early work.*
specimen *I had to submit a specimen of my handwriting for analysis.*
2 something that people can imitate: *His dedication is an example to us all.*
ideal *Everyone's ideal of beauty is different.*
model *His conduct at the meeting was a model of dignity.*
paragon *a paragon of neatness and efficiency*
prototype *the prototype of a well-mannered individual*
See also **case, ideal, model**

exasperate See **irritate**

excavate See **dig**

exceed See **pass, top**

exceeding See **above, over**

excellence See **merit**

excellent
▷ ADJECTIVE
extremely good: *It's an excellent book, one of my favourites.*
brilliant *What a brilliant performance!*
fine *There's a fine view from the bedroom window.*
first-class *a first-class effort*
great *She's a great player, and we'll be sorry to lose her.*
outstanding *an outstanding performance*
superb *a superb technician*
ANTONYM **terrible**
See also **exceptional, fine, first-rate, marvellous, outstanding, splendid, superb, wonderful**

except
▷ PREPOSITION
apart from: *I don't eat dessert, except for the occasional slice of pie.*
apart from *The room was empty apart from one man seated by the fire.*
but *I can't offer you anything but a glass of water.*
other than *She makes no reference to any research other than her own.*
save FORMAL *We had almost nothing to eat, save the few berries and nuts we could find.*
with the exception of *Yesterday was a day off for everybody, with the exception of my boss.*
See also **but**

CONFUSABLES
Except means **other than**, and is a preposition.
Accept means **receive**, and is a verb.

except for See **but**

exception See **qualification**

exceptional
▷ ADJECTIVE
1 unusually excellent, talented, or clever: *Her piano playing is exceptional.*
excellent *The recording quality is excellent.*
extraordinary *He is an extraordinary musician.*
outstanding *an outstanding athlete*
phenomenal *The performances have been absolutely phenomenal.*
remarkable *a remarkable achievement*
talented *She is a talented violinist.*
ANTONYM **mediocre**
2 unusual and likely to happen very rarely: *The traffic is exceptional for this time of day.*

isolated *They said the allegations related to an isolated case.*

out of the ordinary *I've noticed nothing out of the ordinary.*

rare *those rare occasions when he did eat alone*

special *In special cases, an exception to this rule may be made.*

unheard-of *buying these jeans at the unheard-of price of $20*

unusual *A smiling face is unusual for him.*

ANTONYM **common**

See also **extreme, first-rate, outstanding, particular, rare, singular, special, superior, uncommon, unusual**

excerpt See **extract, passage**

excess

▷ *NOUN*

1 behaviour that goes beyond what is acceptable: *a life of excess*

extravagance *Examples of their extravagance were everywhere.*

indulgence *a moment of sheer indulgence*

2 a larger amount than necessary: *An excess of houseplants made the room look like a jungle.*

glut *There's a glut of umbrellas on the market.*

overabundance *There seems to be an overabundance of peaches this year.*

surfeit *A surfeit of rich food did not help his digestive problems.*

surplus *a surplus of teachers in some countries*

ANTONYM **shortage**

▷ *ADJECTIVE*

3 more than is needed: *travelling with excess baggage*

extra *Pour any extra liquid into a bowl and set it aside.*

superfluous *all our superfluous belongings — things we don't need*

surplus *Farmers have to sell off their surplus livestock.*

See also **extra**

excessive

▷ *ADJECTIVE*

too great: *an excessive reliance on government funding*

enormous *They spent an enormous amount on clothes.*

exaggerated *the exaggerated claims made by their supporters*

needless *a movie that is full of needless violence*

undue *the need to avoid undue expenses*

unreasonable *unreasonable increases in the price of gasoline*

See also **extreme, steep**

excessively See **too**

exchange

▷ *VERB*

1 to give something in return for something else: *We exchanged phone numbers.*

barter *The farmers bartered apples for chickens.*

change *Can you change toonies for quarters?*

swap *I wouldn't swap places with them for anything!*

switch *They switched their tickets for another date.*

trade *to trade baseball cards*

▷ *NOUN*

2 the act of giving something for something else: *a ceasefire to allow the exchange of prisoners*

interchange *to encourage an interchange of ideas*

swap *The two teams agreed to a swap of the two players.*

switch *The switch went ahead as planned.*

trade *I am willing to make a trade with you.*

See also **change, substitute, swap**

exchange views on See **discuss**

excise See **duty, tax**

excite

▷ *VERB*

1 to make someone feel enthusiastic or nervous: *The idea of travelling across Canada really excited the kids.*

agitate *I've no idea what has agitated him.*

animate *There was plenty about the basketball game to animate the capacity crowd.*

thrill *The reception he got at the meeting thrilled him.*

titillate *a meal that will titillate the taste buds of every gourmet*

2 to cause a particular feeling or reaction: *The meeting failed to excite strong feelings in anyone.*

arouse *a move that has aroused deep public anger*

elicit *His proposal elicited a storm of protest.*

evoke *The movie has evoked a sense of nostalgia in many older people.*

incite *a failed attempt to incite a riot*

inspire *The appointment of the new manager certainly inspires confidence.*

provoke *The suggestion has provoked anger.*

stir up *He's just trying to stir up trouble.*

See also **thrill**

E

excited

▷ ADJECTIVE

happy and unable to relax: *We are very excited about getting a new dog.*
agitated *in an excited and agitated state*
enthusiastic *She generally seems very enthusiastic.*
feverish *a state of feverish anticipation*
thrilled *The children were thrilled when the snow finally arrived.*
ANTONYM **bored**
See also **enthusiastic**

excitement

▷ NOUN

interest and enthusiasm: *The release of her latest book has caused great excitement.*
activity *a scene of frenzied activity*
adventure *setting off in search of adventure*
agitation *He reacted to the news with considerable agitation.*
commotion *We decided to see what all the commotion was about.*
enthusiasm *They greeted our arrival with enthusiasm.*
thrill *the thrill of scuba diving*
See also **bustle, enthusiasm, heat, passion**

exciting

▷ ADJECTIVE

making you feel happy and enthusiastic: *the most exciting race I've ever seen*
dramatic *The arrival of the champions was dramatic and exciting.*
electrifying *It was an electrifying performance.*
exhilarating *an exhilarating walk along the coast*
rousing *a rousing speech*
stimulating *It's a stimulating book, full of ideas.*
thrilling *a thrilling opportunity to watch the lions as they feed*
ANTONYM **boring**
See also **impressive**

exclaim *See* **cry**

exclamation *See* **cry**

exclude

▷ VERB

1 to decide not to include something: *We cannot exclude this possibility altogether.*
eliminate *We can eliminate two more people from our list of suspects.*
ignore *We cannot afford to ignore this option.*
leave out *We can narrow down our choices*

by leaving out places that are too expensive.
omit *His name seems to have been omitted from the list.*
rule out *The police have ruled out foul play.*
ANTONYM **include**
2 to stop someone going somewhere or doing something: *Nobody is excluded from this club.*
ban *banned from driving for three years*
bar *barred from the restaurant*
forbid *They have forbidden us from attending future meetings.*
keep out *to keep out troublemakers*
See also **ban, boycott, forbid, omit**

exclusive

▷ ADJECTIVE

available only to a few rich people: *one of the city's most exclusive golf clubs*
chic *a chic nightclub in the trendy part of town*
classy *a very classy restaurant*
posh INFORMAL *They're staying at a posh hotel.*
select *a very lavish and very select party*
upscale *The area is much more upscale than it used to be.*
See also **posh, private, select**

excruciating *See* **painful**

excursion *See* **drive, journey, ramble, trip**

excuse

▷ NOUN

1 a reason or explanation: *Stop making excuses and get on with it!*
explanation *You'd better have a good explanation for your conduct.*
justification *What possible justification can there be for this?*
pretext *His pretext for leaving early was an upset stomach.*
reason *This gave me the perfect reason for visiting Victoria.*
▷ VERB
2 to forgive someone or someone's behaviour: *Please excuse my late arrival.*
forgive *Forgive me, I'm so sorry.*
overlook *the need to overlook each other's failings*
pardon *Pardon my ignorance, but who is in charge here?*
turn a blind eye to *We can't be expected to turn a blind eye to this behaviour.*
See also **defence, forgive, grounds, justify**

excuse yourself *See* **decline**

excused *See* **exempt**

execute *See* **administer, do, kill, perform**

executive *See* **manager, official**

exempt
▷ *ADJECTIVE*
excused from a duty or rule: *exempt from paying the tax*
excused *They are officially excused from attending the meeting.*
immune *The diplomat was immune from prosecution.*
not liable *They are not liable to pay for damages.*
See also **immune**

exemption *See* **freedom**

exercise
▷ *NOUN*
activity that keeps you fit: *I need to get more exercise.*
activity *a bit of physical activity to get the heart going*
exertion *I'm tired out by all this exertion.*
training *She needs to do a bit more training before the game.*
work *I'm doing a lot more work at the gym.*
See also **practice**

exertion *See* **effort, exercise, labour**

exhaust
▷ *VERB*
1 to make very tired: *Don't exhaust yourself by taking on too many projects.*
drain *My emotional turmoil had drained me.*
fatigue *He is easily fatigued.*
tire out *a great new job that tires me out*
wear out *Too much work and too much play wears you out.*
2 to use something up completely: *She has exhausted all my patience.*
consume *plans that will consume hours of time*
deplete *chemicals that deplete the earth's protective ozone shield*
run through *The project ran through its budget in a couple of months.*
use up *I've used up all my energy.*
See also **drain, tax, tire, wear out**

exhausted *See* **tired, weary, worn out**

exhausting *See* **hard**

exhaustive *See* **full, thorough**

exhibit *See* **bear**

exhibition *See* **fair, show**

exhilarating *See* **exciting**

exile *See* **banish**

exist *See* **live, occur**

existence *See* **life**

exotic *See* **foreign, strange, unfamiliar**

expand
▷ *VERB*
to make or become larger: *The rails expanded and buckled in the fierce heat.*
develop *We need to develop our minds as well as our muscles.*
enlarge *Plans to enlarge the stadium have been approved.*
extend *We're trying to extend our range of sportswear.*
fill out *The balloon had filled out and was already almost airborne.*
grow *Her popularity continues to grow.*
increase *to increase the computer's memory*
swell *The river had swollen rapidly.*
ANTONYM **decrease**
See also **bulge, elaborate, enlarge, extend, grow, increase, spread**

expand on
▷ *VERB*
to give more information about something: *an idea that I will expand on later*
develop *You should develop this theme a little bit further.*
elaborate on *He refused to elaborate on what he had said earlier.*
enlarge on *I'd like you to enlarge on that last point.*
See also **enlarge on**

expanse *See* **amount, area, stretch**

expansion *See* **growth, spread**

expansive *See* **broad, extensive, spacious**

expect
▷ *VERB*
1 to believe that something is going to happen: *The trial is expected to last several weeks.*
anticipate *We do not anticipate any problems.*
assume *He assumed that they would wait for him.*
believe *Experts believe the comet will pass close to the earth.*
imagine *The meal cost more than we had imagined.*
presume *I presume they'll be arriving shortly.*
reckon *We reckon it'll be a fairly brief visit.*
think *I thought the concert was cancelled.*

E

2 to believe that something is your right: *I was expecting to have a bit of time to myself.*
demand *a job that demands a lot of concentration*
rely on *I'm relying on you to help me.*
require *They require a lot of her — maybe too much.*
See also **figure, suppose**

expectation See **hope, prospect**

expected See **likely, supposed**

expedient See **measure**

expedition See **journey**

expel See **banish, discharge**

expense See **cost**

expensive
▷ ADJECTIVE
costing a lot of money: *a very expensive suit*
costly *a costly court case*
dear *The price of their coffee is rather dear.*
pricey *Medical insurance can be very pricey.*
ANTONYM **inexpensive**
See also **dear, precious, valuable**

experience
▷ NOUN
1 knowledge or skill in a particular activity: *They're looking for someone with experience.*
expertise *They lack the expertise to deal with such a complex case.*
know-how *Her technical know-how was invaluable.*
knowledge *We need someone with knowledge of programming.*
training *keyboard training*
understanding *someone with considerable understanding of the law*
2 something that happens to you: *a terrifying experience that they still talk about*
adventure *a series of hair-raising adventures*
affair *He seemed keen to forget the whole affair and never discussed it.*
encounter *his first encounter with poetry*
episode *The episode has proved deeply embarrassing for her.*
incident *an incident he would rather forget*
ordeal *a painful ordeal that is now over*
▷ VERB
3 to have something happen to you: *We are experiencing a few technical problems.*
encounter *The storms were the worst they had ever encountered.*
have *We're having a few difficulties with the computer.*

meet *The next time you meet a situation like this, be careful.*
undergo *to undergo an unpleasant experience*
See also **endure, event, feel, go through, have, suffer, undergo**

experienced
▷ ADJECTIVE
very skilful as a result of practice: *an experienced diver*
expert *an expert pilot*
knowledgeable *He's very knowledgeable in this field.*
practised *a practised and accomplished surgeon*
seasoned *a seasoned climber*
well versed *She is well versed in many styles of jazz.*
ANTONYM **inexperienced**
See also **expert, practical, skilled**

expert
▷ NOUN
1 a skilled or knowledgeable person: *A team of experts will be on hand to offer advice.*
ace INFORMAL *an ace race-car driver*
authority *an authority on ancient Egypt*
buff INFORMAL *She's a bit of a movie buff.*
guru *fashion gurus who predict the latest trends*
professional *She's widely respected in the theatre as a true professional.*
specialist *a specialist in tropical flowers*
wizard *a financial wizard who made millions*
ANTONYM **beginner**
▷ ADJECTIVE
2 skilled and knowledgeable: *Her expert approach impressed everyone.*
able *an able and dedicated surgeon*
adept *an adept guitar player*
experienced *He was an experienced traveller and knew the area well.*
knowledgeable *She's very knowledgeable about Canadian documentaries.*
proficient *proficient in several European languages*
skilful *the skilful use of light in the artist's early paintings*
skilled *a highly skilled photographer*
See also **able, experienced, perfect, skilful, skilled**

expertise See **ability, experience, skill**

expertly See **well**

explain
▷ VERB
to give extra information about something: *He explained to us how the system worked.*

define *Can you define what you mean by "excessive"?*

describe *an attempt to describe the whole process*

illustrate *Let me illustrate this point with an example.*

See also **justify**

explanation

▷ *NOUN*

a helpful or clear description: *her clear explanation of the parliamentary system*

clarification *Her clarification has done little to help matters.*

definition *a definition of what we mean by "coincidence"*

description *a fascinating description of how the pyramids were built*

exposition *It was a clear exposition of the poet's ideas.*

See also **defence, excuse, statement**

explicit See **clear**

explode

▷ *VERB*

1 to burst or cause to burst loudly: *the sound of fireworks exploding in the air*

blow up *Nobody was aboard when the boat blew up.*

burst *The child blew up the balloon until it burst.*

detonate *Troops managed to detonate the mine safely.*

go off *The bomb went off without any warning.*

set off *Nobody knows who planted the bomb, or how it was set off.*

2 to become angry suddenly: *I asked him if he'd finished, and he just exploded.*

blow up *When I finally told him, he blew up and walked out.*

go berserk *He'll go berserk if he ever finds out.*

go mad *He went mad when he read the letter.*

3 to increase suddenly and rapidly: *Sales of digital cameras have exploded in recent years.*

shoot up *Prices shot up, and the shelves were soon empty.*

skyrocket *Prices have skyrocketed in the last few months.*

soar *Demand for the new game has soared.*

See also **burst, fire**

exploit See **achievement, action, profit**

exploitation See **abuse**

exploration See **research**

explore See **investigate, research**

explosion

▷ *NOUN*

a violent burst of energy: *The explosion shattered windows all along the street.*

bang *A loud bang made me run for cover.*

blast *Three people were hurt in the blast.*

See also **bang, outbreak**

explosive See **bomb**

expose

▷ *VERB*

1 to make something visible: *The original floor was exposed as we began sanding.*

reveal *The purse was open, revealing a lot of cash.*

show *The stain still showed after she washed the blouse.*

uncover *Please remove your cap so that your head is uncovered.*

2 to tell the truth about someone or something: *He has been exposed as a liar and a cheat.*

bring to light *The truth will be brought to light eventually.*

reveal *an investigation that revealed widespread corruption*

show up *She was finally shown up as a hypocrite.*

uncover *We uncovered evidence of fraud.*

unearth *Investigators have unearthed new evidence.*

See also **betray, subject, uncover**

exposed See **bare, vulnerable**

exposition See **explanation**

express

▷ *VERB*

1 to say what you think: *She expressed interest in trying out for the part.*

communicate *People must learn to communicate their feelings.*

couch *Their demands, though extreme, are couched in moderate language.*

phrase *It sounds fine, but I would have phrased it differently.*

put *Absolutely — I couldn't have put it better.*

put across *the need to put across your message without offending anyone*

voice *Residents have voiced their concern over plans for a dump site in their township.*

▷ *ADJECTIVE*

2 very fast: *express delivery service*

direct *There's also a direct train.*

fast *a fast way of getting there*

high-speed *the high-speed train to Montréal*

E

non-stop *the new non-stop service to New York*
See also **convey, particular, state, swift**

express regret *See* **apologize**

expression
▷ *NOUN*
1 the look on your face that shows your feelings: *a pleasant expression*
countenance *the beaming countenance of the prime minister*
face *Why are you all wearing such long faces?*
2 a word or phrase used to communicate: *It's my grandmother's favourite expression.*
idiom *idioms such as "it's raining cats and dogs"*
phrase *What is the origin of the phrase?*
remark *She makes a friendly remark every time we meet.*
term *a slang term*
See also **look, term**

expulsion *See* **discharge**

exquisite *See* **superb**

extend
▷ *VERB*
1 to have a particular size or position: *The city will soon extend way beyond its present borders.*
continue *The sandy beach continues for several kilometres.*
hang *The branches hang down to the ground.*
reach *a long shirt that reached to her knees*
stretch *an area of forest stretching as far as the eye could see*
2 to stick out: *She extended her hand and shook mine.*
jut out *The tip of the island juts out like a finger into the sea.*
project *the ruins of a fort that projected from the mud*
protrude *a huge rock protruding from the surface of the lake*
stick out *pieces of rough metal that stuck out like spikes*
3 to make something larger: *We'd like to extend the house and build a sunroom.*
add to *I've been adding to my stamp collection.*
develop *She developed the British arm of the company.*
enlarge *plans to enlarge the club*
expand *The store expanded its range of footwear.*
widen *the need to widen the appeal of the group to a larger audience*
See also **build, enlarge, expand, increase, lengthen, range, spread, stretch**

extend to *See* **reach**

extended *See* **continuous**

extensive
▷ *ADJECTIVE*
1 covering a large area: *the mansion's extensive grounds*
broad *a broad expanse of green lawn*
expansive *an expansive play area*
large *a large country estate*
spacious *a spacious dining area*
sweeping *the sweeping curve of the bay*
vast *vast stretches of land*
wide *The desk is wide enough for the computer.*
2 very great in effect: *The blast caused extensive damage.*
comprehensive *comprehensive television coverage of last week's events*
considerable *She has considerable influence over the committee.*
far-reaching *a decision with far-reaching consequences*
great *great changes in Canadian politics*
pervasive *the pervasive influence of television in our lives*
untold *untold damage to one's health*
widespread *There is widespread support for the proposals.*
See also **broad, full, spacious, widespread**

extent
▷ *NOUN*
the length, area, or size of something: *The full extent of the damage was revealed yesterday.*
degree *To what degree were you in control of these events?*
level *the level of public concern over this issue*
measure *The full measure of the government's dilemma has become apparent.*
scale *Don't underestimate the scale of the problem.*
size *the size of the task*
See also **area, length, quantity, range, size, spread, stretch**

exterior *See* **face, front, outside**

exterminate *See* **kill**

external *See* **outside**

extinct *See* **dead**

extortionate *See* **steep**

extra

▷ *ADJECTIVE*

1 more than is usual or expected: *The company is taking on extra staff for the summer.*

added *The motel has the added advantage of being near the beach.*

additional *the need for additional funding*

excess *If there's any excess sauce, you can freeze it.*

further *the introduction of further restrictions*

more *We need three more forks.*

new *new rules in addition to all the other changes*

spare *There are spare blankets in the closet.*

▷ *NOUN*

2 something that is not included with other things: *the cost of the extras added to the price of the vacation.*

accessory *What accessories are you getting for the car?*

addition *the latest addition to the team*

bonus *The view from the hotel was an added bonus.*

See also **excess, luxury, more, spare, supplement**

extract

▷ *VERB*

1 to take or get something out of somewhere: *Citric acid can be extracted from orange juice.*

draw *They still have to draw their water from wells.*

mine *the finest gems, mined from all corners of the world*

obtain *Chocolate is obtained from cocoa beans.*

pull out *I can pull that information out of the database for you.*

remove *Three bullets were removed from the wall.*

take out *The dentist had to take the tooth out.*

2 to get information from someone: *She tried to extract further information from the witness.*

draw *They finally drew a confession from him.*

elicit FORMAL *the question of how far police should go to elicit a confession*

get *How did you get an admission like that out of her?*

glean *We're gleaning information from all sources.*

obtain *They have obtained statements from several witnesses.*

▷ *NOUN*

3 a small section of music or writing: *an extract from his latest novel*

excerpt *an excerpt from Tchaikovsky's Nutcracker*

passage *He read out a passage from the book.*

reading *The author treated us to a reading from her latest novel.*

section *Let's study a section of the text in more detail.*

snatch *We played them a snatch of a violin concerto.*

snippet *snippets of popular classical music*

▷ *NOUN*

4 a concentrated liquid: *vanilla extract*

concentrate *concentrate made from oranges*

See also **exact, passage, quote, remove, withdraw**

extraction *See* **origin, stock**

extraordinary

▷ *ADJECTIVE*

unusual or surprising: *He really is an extraordinary man.*

amazing *What an amazing coincidence!*

bizarre *It's such a bizarre thing to happen.*

odd *It's an odd combination of colours.*

singular *The child gave me a smile of singular sweetness.*

strange *It's a strange piece of music.*

surprising *A surprising number of people have seen that play.*

unusual *It's a most unusual way to spend your vacation.*

ANTONYM **ordinary**

See also **bizarre, curious, exceptional, incredible, singular, strange, uncommon, unusual, weird**

extravagance *See* **excess, luxury, waste**

extravagant *See* **extreme, fancy, ostentatious, wasteful**

extreme

▷ *ADJECTIVE*

1 very great in degree or intensity: *living in extreme poverty*

acute *a mistake that caused acute embarrassment for everyone concerned*

deep *a decision that caused deep resentment*

dire *He is in dire need of medical treatment.*

great *a change in the law that could cause many people great hardship*

intense *A number of people collapsed in the intense heat.*

profound *feelings of profound shock and anger*

E

severe *a business with severe financial problems*

2 unusual or unreasonable: *I think that's rather an extreme reaction.*

drastic *Let's not do anything too drastic.*

exceptional *I think this is an exceptional case.*

excessive *a newspaper feature about the government's excessive spending*

extravagant *All that money being spent on clothes seemed a bit extravagant.*

radical *a series of radical economic reforms*

unreasonable *I don't think she's being the least bit unreasonable.*

▷ *NOUN*

3 the highest or furthest degree or point: *We're just going from one extreme to the other.*

boundary *the boundaries of artistic freedom*

depth *the beauty of the countryside in the depths of winter*

end *both ends of the spectrum*

height *behaviour that was the height of bad manners*

limit *The ordeal tested the limits of their endurance.*

ultimate *the ultimate in luxury*

See also **acute, deep, drastic, intense, serious, severe, ultimate, uncommon**

extremely *See* **really, very**

extremist *See* **fanatic**

extricate *See* **release**

exude *See* **emit**

eye *See* **inspect, regard**

eye-catching *See* **prominent**

eyesight *See* **sight**

eyewitness *See* **spectator, witness**

Ff

fabric *See* **cloth, material, substance**

fabricate *See* **build, invent, make, make up, manufacture**

fabrication *See* **lie, lying, making, manufacture**

facade *See* **outside**

face

▷ *NOUN*

1 the front part of the head: *A strong wind was blowing in my face.*
countenance *The witness met each question with an impassive countenance.*
features *Her features were strongly defined.*
mug SLANG *He managed to get his funny mug on television.*
2 a surface or side of something: *the north face of Everest*
aspect *The house had a southwest aspect.*
exterior *The exterior of the building was made of brick.*
front *There was a large veranda at the front of the house.*
side *narrow valleys with steep sides*
surface *tiny waves on the surface of the water*
▷ *VERB*
3 to look toward something or someone: *a room that faces on to the street*
be opposite *I was opposite her at the breakfast table.*
look at *She turned to look at the person who was speaking.*
overlook *The pretty room overlooks a beautiful garden.*
See also **brave, expression, front, look, outside**

INFORMALLY SPEAKING

face someone down: confront someone and make that person lose confidence or feel embarrassed
face to face: in person
face up to: meet bravely and boldly
get in someone's face: be aggressive

---

face down *See* **prone**

facility *See* **capacity, skill**

fact

▷ *NOUN*

a piece of information that is true: *a statement of fact*
certainty *A general election became a certainty three weeks ago.*

reality *Fiction and reality became increasingly blurred.*
truth *In the town, very few know the whole truth.*
ANTONYM **lie**
See also **reality, truth**

faction *See* **movement, party, side**

factor

▷ *NOUN*

something that helps to cause a result: *Physical activity is an important factor in maintaining fitness.*
aspect *Test results illustrate only one aspect of a school's success.*
cause *Smoking is the biggest preventable cause of death and disease.*
consideration *Money was also a consideration.*
element *Fitness has now become an important element in our lives.*
influence *Tom Thomson was a major influence on the development of the Group of Seven.*
part *Respect is a very important part of any relationship.*
See also **aspect, consideration**

factory

▷ *NOUN*

a building where goods are made: *He owned furniture factories in several locations.*
mill *a textile mill*
plant *The plant produces most of the country's canned tomatoes.*
works *the steel works*

facts *See* **information**

factual *See* **real, right, true**

fad *See* **craze, fashion, whim**

fade

▷ *VERB*

to make or become less intense: *The fabric had faded in the bright sunlight.*
die away *The sound died away gradually.*
dim *The house lights dimmed.*
discolour *Exposure to bright light can cause wallpaper to discolour.*
dull *Repeated washing had dulled the bright finish.*
wash out *This dye won't wash out.*
See also **die out, disappear, vanish, wither**

fade away *See* **die, vanish**

fade out *See* **die**

faded *See* **faint, pale**

F

fail

▷ VERB

1 to be unsuccessful: *He failed in his attempt to fire the coach.*
be defeated *The vote to change the law was defeated.*
be in vain *It became clear that his efforts had been in vain.*
be unsuccessful *My job application was unsuccessful.*
come to grief *Many friendships have come to grief over money issues.*
fall through *Negotiations with the striking players fell through last night.*
flunk INFORMAL *He flunked his exam.*
ANTONYM **succeed**
2 to omit to do something: *They failed to e-mail her.*
neglect *They never neglect their duties.*
omit *He had omitted to tell her of the change in his plans.*
3 to become less effective: *His eyesight began to fail.*
cease *The secrecy about the plan had ceased to matter.*
decline *His strength declined as he grew older.*
give out *All machines give out eventually.*
sink *Her spirits sank lower and lower.*
stop working *The boat came to a halt when the engine stopped working.*
wane *her grandfather's waning strength*
See also **collapse, neglect, weaken**

fail to notice *See* miss

fail to remember *See* forget

failing *See* defect, fault

failure

▷ NOUN

1 a lack of success: *to end in failure*
breakdown *a breakdown of the talks between the parties*
defeat *It is important not to admit defeat.*
downfall *people wishing to see the downfall of the government*
fiasco *The evening was a total fiasco!*
miscarriage *a miscarriage of justice*
ANTONYM **success**
2 an unsuccessful person or thing: *The new business was a complete failure.*
disappointment *a disappointment to his family*
flop INFORMAL *The play turned out to be a flop.*
loser *Stop acting like a loser.*
3 a weakness in something: *a failure in the insurance system*
deficiency *a serious deficiency in their defence system*
shortcoming *The stage production has many shortcomings.*
See also **collapse, crash**

faint

▷ ADJECTIVE

1 lacking in intensity: *a faint smell of perfume*
dim *dim lighting*
faded *a faded sign on the side of the building*
indistinct *The lettering was worn and indistinct.*
low *He spoke in a low voice.*
muted *some muted cheers from the balcony*
vague *a vague memory*
ANTONYM **strong**
2 feeling dizzy and unsteady: *Feeling faint is one of the symptoms of lack of food.*
dizzy *suffering from dizzy spells*
giddy *He felt giddy after the ride.*
light-headed *She felt light-headed because she hadn't eaten.*
▷ VERB
3 to lose consciousness temporarily: *to faint from shock*
black out *The blood drained from his head and he blacked out.*
collapse *I collapsed when I heard the news.*
pass out *to pass out with pain*
See also **dim, slender, soft, weak**

faint-hearted *See* cowardly

fair

▷ ADJECTIVE

1 reasonable and just: *a fair trial*
equal *equal pay for work of equal value*
equitable *an equitable distribution of resources*
impartial *an impartial observer*
legitimate *a legitimate claim to the money*
proper *It's right and proper that he should be here.*
upright *an upright and trustworthy person*
ANTONYM **unfair**
2 having light-coloured hair or pale skin: *long, fair hair*
blond *a darker shade of blond*
light *a light complexion and blue eyes*
ANTONYM **dark**
▷ NOUN
3 an outdoor entertainment: *a country fair*
bazaar *a fundraising event*
carnival *the Winter Carnival in Québec*
exhibition *an international trade exhibition*
festival *a rock festival*
fete *The annual fete was a popular event.*
show *an agricultural show*

fairly See **pretty, quite, rather**

fairness See **justice, right**

faith

▷ *NOUN*

I trust in a thing or a person: *to have great faith in something*
confidence *They had no confidence in the captain.*
trust *complete trust in the team*
2 a person's or community's religion: *the faith of their family*
belief *united by belief*
creed *open to all, regardless of creed*
persuasion *people of all religious persuasions*
religion *the right to practise one's religion*
See also **belief, confidence**

faithful

▷ *ADJECTIVE*

I loyal to someone or something: *a faithful dog*
devoted *They are devoted to each other.*
loyal *a sign of true and loyal friendship*
staunch *a staunch member of the party*
true *a true believer*
ANTONYM **unfaithful**
2 accurate and truthful: *The play was faithful to the novel.*
accurate *an accurate description of the event*
exact *an exact copy of the original*
strict *We demand strict adherence to the rules.*
true *The movie was quite true to life.*
See also **accurate, devoted, exact, loyal, realistic, reliable, steadfast, trusty**

faithfully See **exactly**

faithless See **treacherous**

fake

▷ *NOUN*

I a deceitful imitation of a thing or person: *These paintings are fakes.*
copy *The sculpture was an excellent copy of the original.*
forgery *The signature was a forgery.*
fraud *The "doctor" turned out to be a fraud.*
imitation *The "antique" chair is in fact a clever imitation.*
reproduction *a reproduction of a famous painting*
sham *The election was denounced as a sham.*

▷ *ADJECTIVE*

2 imitation and not genuine: *fake fur*
artificial *an artificial sweetener.*
counterfeit *a large number of counterfeit documents*
false *a false passport*
imitation *bound in imitation leather*
phony INFORMAL *He used a phony accent.*
ANTONYM **real**

▷ *VERB*

3 to pretend to experience something: *He faked his own death.*
feign *to feign illness*
pretend *He pretended to be shocked.*
simulate *writhing around in simulated agony*
See also **copy, false, fraud, mock, phony, pretend**

fall

▷ *VERB*

I to descend toward the ground: *The tile fell from the roof.*
collapse *The bridge collapsed on to the road.*
drop *parachutes dropping from the sky*
plunge *A bus plunged into the river.*
topple *He toppled slowly backwards.*
trip *I tripped and broke my leg.*
ANTONYM **rise**
2 to become lower or less: *The value of the Canadian dollar fell last week.*
decline *a declining birth rate*
decrease *The number of tourists decreased last year.*
diminish *Resources are diminishing steadily.*
dwindle *his dwindling authority*
plummet *plummeting interest rates*
subside *The flood waters have subsided.*
ANTONYM **increase**

▷ *NOUN*

3 a reduction in amount: *a fall in the exchange rate*
decline *signs of economic decline*
decrease *an overall decrease of ten percent*
drop *the sharp drop in exports*
reduction *The bank announced a reduction in interest rates.*
slump *a slump in property prices*
ANTONYM **rise**
See also **decline, descend, downfall, drop, ruin, slope**

F

INFORMALLY SPEAKING

fall all over yourself: be extremely eager
fall for: be fooled by; fall in love with
fall off: decline
fall through: fail

fall apart *See* **disintegrate**

fall behind *See* **lag**

fall down *See* **collapse**

fall ill *See* **develop**

fall out *See* **argue, quarrel, squabble**

fall over *See* **trip**

fall to *See* **reach**

fall to pieces *See* **disintegrate**

fallacy *See* **illusion**

false
▷ *ADJECTIVE*
1 not true or correct: *He gave a false name and address.*
erroneous *to arrive at an erroneous conclusion*
fictitious *the source of the fictitious rumours*
incorrect *a decision based on incorrect information*
mistaken *I had a mistaken view of what had happened.*
untrue *The remarks were completely untrue.*
ANTONYM **true**
2 not genuine, but intended to seem so: *false eyelashes*
artificial *an artificial plant*
bogus *their bogus insurance claim*
fake *fake fur*
forged *They crossed the border using forged documents.*
simulated *a simulated display of affection*
ANTONYM **genuine**
3 unfaithful and deceitful: *They turned out to be false friends.*
deceitful *deceitful and misleading remarks*
disloyal *He was accused of being disloyal to the company.*
insincere *insincere flattery*
unfaithful *left alone by an unfaithful partner*
See also **deceptive, fake, insincere, lying, mock, phony, two-faced, untrue, wrong**

falsehood *See* **lie**

falsify *See* **misrepresent, pretend**

fame
▷ *NOUN*
the state of being very well known: *The movie brought her international fame.*
eminence *to achieve eminence as a politician*
glory *my moment of glory*
prominence *She came to prominence with her bestselling novel.*
renown *a singer of great renown*
reputation *the city's reputation as a place of romance*
See also **glory, success**

familiar
▷ *ADJECTIVE*
knowing something well: *Most children are familiar with fairy tales.*
acquainted with *I'm well acquainted with Margaret Atwood's works.*
aware of *aware of the dangers of smoking*
knowledgeable about *They were very knowledgeable about gardening.*
versed in *She was well versed in corporate law.*
ANTONYM **unfamiliar**
See also **accustomed, informal**

familiar with *See* **aware of**

family
▷ *NOUN*
1 a group of relatives: *My family is always supportive of me.*
descendants *The pioneers' descendants lived on the original farm for 150 years.*
relations *friends and relations*
relatives *cousins and other relatives*
2 a group of related species: *Tigers are members of the cat family.*
class *several classes of butterflies*
classification *The classification includes conifers.*
kind *different kinds of roses*
See also **kin, young**

famished *See* **hungry**

famous
▷ *ADJECTIVE*
very well known: *the most famous singer of her time*
celebrated *his most celebrated movie*
distinguished *a distinguished acting family*
illustrious *the most illustrious scientists of the century*
legendary *His skills are legendary.*
noted *She is noted for her generosity.*
renowned *The area is renowned for its scenery.*
ANTONYM **unknown**
See also **prominent**

famous name *See* **personality**

fan
▷ *NOUN*
an enthusiast about something or someone: *a fan of the new band*
adherent *The movement was gaining adherents everywhere.*
admirer *one of her many admirers*
devotee *a devotee of chamber music*
lover *an art lover*
supporter *supporters of the hometown team*
zealot *He was a supporter, but not a zealot.*
See also **follower, supporter**

fan out *See* **spread**

fanatic
▷ *NOUN*
someone who is extremely enthusiastic about something: *a soccer fanatic*
activist *political activists*
devotee *a devotee of yoga*
extremist *groups of religious extremists*
militant *The militants took over the organization.*
zealot *He was a supporter, but not a zealot.*

fanatical
▷ *ADJECTIVE*
showing extreme support for something: *a fanatical supporter of the baseball team*
fervent *a fervent admirer*
obsessive *obsessive about figure skating*
passionate *a passionate interest*
rabid *a rabid promoter of hate literature*
wild *I am wild about this band.*
See also **crazy**

fancy
▷ *VERB*
1 to want to have or do something: *He fancied an ice-cream cone.*
be attracted to *I am attracted to the idea of relocating.*
hanker after *to hanker after a bigger car*
have a yen for *a yen for some new clothes*
would like *I would really like some pizza.*
▷ *ADJECTIVE*
2 special and elaborate: *dressed up in fancy clothes*
decorated *She preferred decorated cakes to plain ones.*
elaborate *his elaborate costume ideas*
extravagant *the extravagant mosaics in the lobby*
intricate *covered with intricate patterns*
ornate *an ornate picture frame*
ANTONYM **plain**
See also **desire, elaborate, illusion, whim**

fantasize *See* **daydream, imagine**

fantastic *See* **splendid**

fantasy *See* **daydream, dream, vision**

far
▷ *ADVERB*
1 at a great distance from something: *The ocean was far below us.*
afar *seen from afar*
a great distance *They travelled a great distance.*
a long way *The guy's lonely and a long way from home.*
deep *deep into the bush*
2 to a great extent or degree: *far better than the others*
considerably *The dinners were considerably more relaxed than before.*
incomparably *Some countries are incomparably richer than others.*
much *I feel much better now.*
very much *The rain got very much worse in the afternoon.*
▷ *ADJECTIVE*
3 very distant: *in the far south of the country*
distant *the distant horizon*
long *a long distance from here*
outlying *The outlying areas are accessible only by air.*
remote *a cottage in a remote area of the province*
ANTONYM **near**
See also **distant**

far from *See* **unlike**

fare *See* **do, food**

far-fetched *See* **improbable, incredible**

far-off *See* **remote**

far-reaching *See* **extensive, serious**

fascinate
▷ *VERB*
to be of intense interest to someone: *He was fascinated by the new discovery.*
absorb *totally absorbed by her career*
bewitch *bewitched by her charm*
captivate *looks that captivated the whole world*
enthral *enthralled by the brilliant acting*
intrigue *Her story intrigued them.*
See also **appeal, entrance, interest**

fascination *See* **charm, interest**

fashion
▷ *NOUN*
1 a popular style of dress or behaviour: *changing fashions in clothing*
craze *the latest health craze*

F

fad *just a passing fad*
style *a revival of an old style*
trend *the current trend in sunglasses*
vogue *a vogue for fitness training*
2 a manner or way of doing something: *It works in a similar fashion.*
manner *in a friendly manner*
method *his usual method of fixing the plugged sink*
mode *a different mode of transportation*
way *in her usual resourceful way*
▷ *VERB*
3 to make and shape something: *fashioned from rough wood*
construct *an inner frame constructed from timber*
create *It was created from odds and ends.*
make *a quilt made from different fabrics*
mould *They moulded the cups from clay.*
shape *Shape the dough into a loaf.*
work *a machine for working the stone*
See also **craze, form, make, manner, model, shape**

fashionable

▷ *ADJECTIVE*
very popular: *a fashionable restaurant*
current *the current thinking on the subject*
in *INFORMAL Jogging was the in thing.*
latest *all the latest hairstyles*
popular *the most popular movie*
prevailing *contrary to prevailing attitudes*
ANTONYM **old-fashioned**
See also **current, popular, trendy**

fast

▷ *ADJECTIVE*
1 moving at great speed: *a fast train*
accelerated *at an accelerated pace*
hurried *He ate a hurried breakfast.*
quick *a quick learner*
rapid *a rapid rise through the company*
speedy *best wishes for a speedy recovery*
swift *as swift as an arrow*
ANTONYM **slow**
▷ *ADVERB*
2 quickly and without delay: *You'll have to move fast.*
hastily *hastily erected tents*
hurriedly *students hurriedly taking notes*
quickly *She worked quickly and methodically.*
rapidly *moving rapidly across the field*
swiftly *They had to act swiftly to save him.*
ANTONYM **slowly**
▷ *ADVERB*
3 firmly and strongly: *Hold fast to the rail.*
firmly *with windows firmly shut*

securely *The door was securely locked and bolted.*
tightly *held tightly in my arms*
See also **express, quick, quickly, swift**

fasten

▷ *VERB*
to close or attach something: *Fasten your seatbelts.*
attach *He attached a label to the folder.*
fix *It was fixed on the wall.*
join *joined together by wire*
lock *a locked door*
secure *The door was secured with a lock and chain.*
tie *Tie your shoelaces.*
See also **attach, bond, connect, fix, hang, join, link, secure, shut, tie**

fastened See **secure, shut**

fastener See **clasp**

fastening See **clasp, connection**

fastidious See **fine, fussy, particular**

fat

▷ *ADJECTIVE*
weighing too much: *a fat cat*
ANTONYM **thin**
See WORD STUDY **fat** on next page
See also **overweight, plump, thick**

fatal

▷ *ADJECTIVE*
1 causing death: *fatal injuries*
deadly *a deadly disease*
incurable *an incurable illness*
lethal *a lethal dose of sleeping pills*
mortal *They were in mortal danger.*
terminal *a terminal illness*
2 having an undesirable effect: *The mistake was fatal to my plans.*
calamitous *a calamitous air crash*
catastrophic *The water shortage is potentially catastrophic.*
disastrous *This could have disastrous consequences for the town.*
lethal *a lethal snake bite*
See also **deadly**

fate

▷ *NOUN*
a power believed to control events: *the fickleness of fate*
chance *a victim of chance*
destiny *Are we responsible for our own destiny?*
fortune *Some say that fortune favours the brave.*
providence *an act of providence*
See also **luck**

Some words used to describe a person who is overweight can be more hurtful or insulting than others. There are also words to describe varying degrees of being overweight.

- Someone who is **overweight** weighs more than is considered healthy. However, you can be just a little overweight as well as very overweight
Since having my baby, I feel slightly **overweight**.

- If you say someone is **pudgy**, you mean that he or she is slightly fat.
This is an informal word.
My dad is getting a little **pudgy** round the middle.

- If you describe someone as **fleshy**, you mean that he or she is slightly too fat.
He was well built, but too **fleshy** to be an imposing figure.

- A **chubby**, **tubby**, or **stout** person is rather fat.
I was greeted by a small, **chubby** child.
He had been a short, **tubby** man, but has recently lost weight.
My grandfather is a tall, **stout** man with grey hair.

- A **portly** person is rather fat.
This word is mostly used to describe men.
The salesperson was a **portly**, middle-aged man.

- You can use the word **plump** to describe someone who is rather fat or rounded, usually when you think this is a good quality.

The baby was a **plump** little thing, with a mass of dark curls.

- If you describe a woman's figure as **rounded**, you mean that it is attractive because it is well developed.
My aunt is a beautiful woman with blue eyes and a **rounded** figure.

- A **roly-poly** person is pleasantly fat and round.
This is an informal word.
The manager was a short, **roly-poly** woman, with laughing eyes.

- If you describe a woman as **buxom**, you mean that she looks healthy and attractive and has a rounded body and big breasts.
The tour guide was a tall, **buxom** blonde.

- If you describe someone as **obese**, you mean that he or she is extremely fat, to the point of being unhealthy.
Obese people tend to have higher blood pressure than lean people.

- If you describe someone as **gross**, you mean that he or she is extremely fat and unattractive.
This is a very insulting word to use.
He tried to raise his **gross** body from the sofa.

F

father *See* **parent**

fathom *See* **comprehend, understand**

fatigue *See* **exhaust, tire**

fatigued *See* **tired, weary, worn out**

fault

▷ *NOUN*

1 something for which someone is responsible: *It was all my fault!*
blame *They put the blame on me.*
liability *The company was forced to admit liability.*
responsibility *He accepted full responsibility for the error.*
2 a defective quality in something: *a minor technical fault*
blemish *a blemish on an otherwise*

outstanding career
defect *a manufacturing defect*
deficiency *serious deficiencies in the system*
drawback *The plan had one major drawback.*
failing *the team's many failings*
flaw *serious character flaws*
imperfection *small imperfections on the surface of the table*
weakness *his one weakness*
ANTONYM **strength**
▷ *VERB*
3 to find reasons to be critical of someone: *Her conduct cannot be faulted.*
blame *I don't blame him.*
censure *He was censured by the committee.*
criticize *The mayor criticized the committee.*

See also **blame, defect, error, fissure, flaw, hole, responsibility**

INFORMALLY SPEAKING

at fault: deserving the blame
find fault with: criticize in a negative way
to a fault: to a great degree

---

faultfinding *See* **criticism**

faultless *See* **correct, exact, perfect**

faulty
▷ *ADJECTIVE*
containing flaws or errors: *Faulty goods should be sent back.*
defective *a truck with defective brakes*
flawed *The test results were seriously flawed.*
imperfect *an imperfect plan*
invalid *That's an invalid argument.*
unsound *a building that is structurally unsound*
See also **imperfect, weak, wrong**

favour
▷ *NOUN*
1 a liking or approval of something: *The proposals met with favour.*
approval *to gain his boss's approval*
esteem *in high esteem*
grace *to fall from grace*
support *They gave us their full support.*
ANTONYM **disapproval**
2 a kind and helpful action: *Can you do me a favour?*
courtesy *the courtesy of replying to my e-mail*
good turn *to do someone a good turn*
kindness *She did me the kindness of calling.*
service *a service to your community*
ANTONYM **wrong**
▷ *VERB*
3 to prefer something or someone: *They favoured the cuter puppy.*
prefer *the preferred candidate*
single out *singled out for special treatment*
See also **advocate, approval, approve, back, encourage, goodwill, prefer**

favourable
▷ *ADJECTIVE*
1 of advantage and benefit to someone: *favourable conditions*
advantageous *the most advantageous plan of action*
beneficial *a beneficial effect on our health*
good *a very good deal*
opportune *an opportune moment to ask for a raise*

suitable *Conditions were not suitable for those plants.*
ANTONYM **unfavourable**
2 positive and expressing approval: *a positive response*
affirmative *to give an affirmative answer*
amicable *amicable discussions*
approving *a warm, approving glance*
friendly *The proposal was given a friendly reception.*
positive *have a positive effect on the situation*
sympathetic *a sympathetic judge*
welcoming *a welcoming atmosphere*
ANTONYM **unfavourable**

favourably *See* **well**

favoured *See* **favourite**

favourite
▷ *ADJECTIVE*
1 being someone's best-liked person or thing: *my favourite teacher*
best-loved *our best-loved music*
dearest *Her dearest wish was fulfilled.*
favoured *the favoured nephew of an elderly uncle*
preferred *his preferred method of exercise*
▷ *NOUN*
2 the thing or person someone likes best: *The collie was always her favourite.*
darling *the spoiled darling of the family*
idol *the idol of his fans*
pet *the teacher's pet*
pick *the pick of the litter*
See also **popular**

favouritism
▷ *NOUN*
unfair favour shown to a person or group: *There was never a hint of favouritism.*
bias *political bias in broadcasting*
one-sidedness *The judges must show no one-sidedness.*
ANTONYM **impartiality**
See also **bias**

fawn *See* **flatter**

fawning *See* **flattery**

fear
▷ *NOUN*
1 an unpleasant feeling of danger: *shivering with fear*
alarm *I looked at them with growing alarm.*
awe *in awe of their great powers*
dread *She thought with dread of the dangers of the coming storm.*
fright *He jumped with fright at the noise.*
panic *a moment of panic*
terror *to shake with terror*

▷ *VERB*

2 to feel frightened of something: *There is nothing to fear.*

be afraid *The dog was afraid of him.*
be frightened *I am frightened of thunder.*
be scared *Are you scared of snakes?*
dread *He dreaded the idea of performing.*
take fright *The horse took fright at the sudden noise.*
See also **anxiety, horror, panic, worry**

fearful *See* **afraid, anxious**

fearless *See* **bold, brave, daring**

feasible *See* **possible, probable**

feast *See* **meal**

feat *See* **achievement, act, action**

feature
▷ *NOUN*
I a particular characteristic of something: *an unusual feature of the room*
aspect *every aspect of our lives*
attribute *a normal attribute of human behaviour*
characteristic *their physical characteristics*
mark *distinguishing marks*
property *the magnetic properties of iron*
quality *skills and personal qualities*
2 a special article or program: *a news feature*
article *a travel article*
blog *Feel free to add comments to my blog.*
column *the advice column*
item *an item about acid rain*
piece *a specially written piece*
report *a special report on the scandal*
story *front-page news stories*
▷ *VERB*
3 to include and draw attention to something: *featuring an interview with the premier*
emphasize *to emphasize their differences*
give prominence to *The* Daily Star *is alone in giving prominence to the story.*
spotlight *a book spotlighting Canadian comedians*
star *starring a major Canadian actor*
See also **article, aspect, attribute, characteristic, item, point, property, quality**

features *See* **face**

fed up *See* **bored, down, sick of**

federation *See* **union**

fee *See* **charge, pay, price, rate**

feeble *See* **lame, pathetic, poor, puny, weak**

feed *See* **eat**

feedback *See* **reaction**

feel
▷ *VERB*
I to experience emotionally: *I felt enormous happiness.*
experience *They seem to experience more difficulties than anyone else.*
suffer *suffering from feelings of guilt*
undergo *to undergo a change of heart*
2 to believe that something is the case: *She feels she is in control of her life.*
believe *I believe they are right.*
consider *We consider them to be our friends.*
deem *I deemed it best to cancel the party.*
judge *They were judged to be capable of almost anything.*
think *I think I am very lucky.*
3 to touch something physically: *Feel this lovely material!*
finger *He was fingering the coins in his pocket.*
fondle *She fondled the dog's ears.*
stroke *I stroked the cat gently.*
touch *I touched the cactus very carefully.*
See also **handle, have, sense, suspect, texture, touch**

INFORMALLY SPEAKING

feel for: sympathize with
feel like: have a desire for
feel out: find out about, in a cautious way

feel dejected *See* **despair**

feel despondent *See* **despair**

feel for *See* **identify with, pity**

feel sorry for *See* **pity**

feel uneasy *See* **worry**

feeling
▷ *NOUN*
I the experiencing of an emotion: *feelings of envy*
emotion *trembling with emotion*
fervour *political fervour*
heat *He spoke with some heat about his experiences.*
passion *She argued with great passion.*
sentiment *I'm afraid I don't share your sentiments.*
2 a physical sensation: *a feeling of pain*
sensation *a very pleasant sensation*
sense *a slight sense of nausea*
3 an opinion on something: *strong feelings on politics*

F

inclination *neither the time nor the inclination*
opinion *a consensus of opinion*
perspective *Her perspective on the issue was quite interesting.*
point of view *an unusual point of view on the subject*
view *Make your views known.*
See also **guess, impression, instinct, sense, view, viewpoint**

feign *See* **fake, pretend**

feigned *See* **mock**

feline *See* **cat**

fell *See* **chop**

fellow *See* **boy**

fellow worker *See* **colleague**

fellowship
▷ *NOUN*
a feeling of friendliness within a group: *a sense of community and fellowship*
camaraderie *the camaraderie among the team members*
companionship *the companionship between old friends*

female
▷ *NOUN*
1 a person or animal that can have babies: *Hay fever affects males more than females.*
girl *a girls' school*
lady *a nice young lady*
woman *the number of women in the room*
▷ *ADJECTIVE*
2 relating to females: *the world's greatest female skater*
feminine *"La" is the feminine definite article in French.*
See also **woman**

feminine *See* **female**

fence *See* **barrier**

fence off *See* **enclose**

ferocious *See* **fierce, savage**

ferry *See* **take**

fertile
▷ *ADJECTIVE*
capable of producing plants or offspring: *fertile soil*
fruitful *The fruitful earth gave forth its treasures.*
productive *the most productive vineyards in British Columbia*
prolific *Chinchillas are prolific breeders.*

rich *This plant grows in moist, rich ground.*
ANTONYM **barren**
See also **creative, productive, rich**

fervent
▷ *ADJECTIVE*
showing sincere and enthusiastic feeling: *a fervent admirer of her work*
ardent *one of the most ardent supporters of the policy,*
committed *a committed volunteer*
devout *a devout follower of their philosophy*
enthusiastic *a huge and enthusiastic crowd*
impassioned *an impassioned appeal for peace*
passionate *I'm a passionate believer in freedom of the press.*
zealous *He was a recent convert, and very zealous.*
See also **ardent, fanatical, intense**

fervour *See* **feeling, heat, violence**

fester *See* **rot**

festival
▷ *NOUN*
1 an organized series of events: *the Toronto Film Festival*
carnival *The carnival lasted for three days.*
entertainment *theatrical entertainments*
fair *The book fair attracted many visitors.*
fete *an annual neighbourhood fete*
gala *the gala that followed the world premiere*
2 a day or period of religious celebration: *different religious festivals*
holiday *What does that holiday celebrate?*
See also **celebration, fair**

festivity *See* **celebration**

fetch *See* **get, take**

fetching *See* **attractive**

fete *See* **fair, festival**

feud *See* **argue, argument, dispute, quarrel, squabble**

feverish *See* **excited**

few
▷ *ADJECTIVE*
small in number: *a few moments ago*
infrequent *infrequent commercial breaks*
meagre *a society with meagre resources*
not many *Not many people attended the meeting.*
scarce *Resources are scarce.*
sparse *a bare landscape with sparse trees*
ANTONYM **many**
See also **rare, scarce, uncommon**

CONFUSABLES

fewer means **not so many**
less means **not so much**

fewest *See* **least**

fiasco *See* **failure**

fib *See* **lie**

fibbing *See* **lying**

fickle *See* **changeable**

fiction *See* **lie**

fictional *See* **imaginary**

fictitious *See* **false, imaginary, untrue**

fiddle *See* **fidget**

fidget

▷ *VERB*
to move and change position restlessly:
fidgeting in his seat
fiddle INFORMAL *She fiddled with her pencil.*
jiggle *He's jiggling his keys.*
squirm *He squirmed and wriggled with
impatience.*
twitch *Everybody twitched in their seats.*
See also **fuss**

fidgety *See* **restless**

field

▷ *NOUN*
I an area of farmland: *a field full of sheep*
meadow *a grassy meadow*
pasture *cows grazing in the pasture*
2 a particular subject or interest: *a
breakthrough in the field of physics*
area *a politically sensitive area*
department *Health care isn't my
department.*
domain *in the domain of art*
province *This is the province of a different
department.*
specialty *His specialty was mythology.*
territory *That's really not my territory.*
See also **range**

fierce

▷ *ADJECTIVE*
I wild and aggressive: *a fierce lion*
aggressive *the dog's aggressive behaviour*
dangerous *These snakes are dangerous.*
ferocious *two and a half days of ferocious
wind*
murderous *a murderous attack*
ANTONYM **gentle**
2 very intense: *fierce competition*
intense *We found ourselves standing in
intense heat.*
keen *a keen interest in cars*

relentless *The pressure was relentless.*
strong *a strong dislike*
See also **furious, intense, wild**

fight

▷ *VERB*
I to take part in a battle or contest: *He
fought the world boxing champion.*
battle *The gang battled with the police.*
brawl *brawling drunkenly in the street*
grapple *grappling with an alligator*
struggle *The tennis star was struggling with
her opponent.*
▷ *NOUN*
2 an aggressive physical struggle: *a fight
between gladiators*
action *wounded in action*
battle *a gun battle*
bout *a wrestling bout*
combat *the end of a long combat*
duel *killed in a duel*
skirmish *a minor border skirmish*
▷ *NOUN*
3 an angry disagreement: *a fight with my
best friend*
argument *an argument over something
stupid*
dispute *a dispute over a parking ticket*
row *My cousin and I had a terrible row.*
squabble *a family squabble over money*
See also **argue, argument, clash,
compete, contest, quarrel, resist,
squabble, war**

fight against *See* **oppose**

fight for *See* **champion**

fight shy of *See* **avoid**

fighter

▷ *NOUN*
someone who physically fights another
person: *a tough street fighter*
mercenary *an army of rebels and
mercenaries*
soldier *well-equipped soldiers*
warrior *a brave warrior*

fighting *See* **conflict, war**

figure

▷ *NOUN*
I a number, or an amount represented by a
number: *No one really knows the true figures.*
amount *to withdraw cash in amounts of
twenty dollars at a time*
digit *a five-digit code*
number *A lot of games ended in a tie, but
we don't know the exact number.*
numeral *the numeral six*

F

statistic *Statistics show salaries declining by 24 percent.*
total *Then he added everything together to arrive at the final total.*
2 a shape, or the shape of someone's body: *A figure appeared in the doorway.*
body *a sculpture of the model's body*
build *a tall person with an average build*
form *The shadowy form receded into the darkness.*
physique *the physique and energy of a man half his age*
silhouette *We saw the silhouette of a large man as we entered the dimly lit room.*
shape *tall, dark shapes moving in the mist*
3 a person: *international political figures*
character *What a funny character she is!*
dignitary *a visiting dignitary of great importance*
person *a person of some influence*
personality *The event was attended by many showbiz personalities.*
player *a key player in the negotiations*
▷ VERB
4 INFORMAL to guess or conclude something: *I figure I'll learn from experience*
expect *I expect you're just tired.*
guess *I guess he's right.*
reckon INFORMAL *She reckoned that it must be about three o'clock.*
suppose *What do you suppose he's up to?*
See also **body, build, number, outline, price, shape, symbol**

figure out *See* **reckon, work out**

file *See* **line, rank, record**

fill
▷ VERB
to make something full: *Fill the bottle with water.*
cram *Guests crammed into the small room.*
gorge *gorged with food*
pack *a truck packed with boxes*
stock *a pond stocked with trout*
stuff *Stuff everything into your backpack.*
ANTONYM **empty**
See also **load, plug, stuff**

INFORMALLY SPEAKING

fill someone in: bring someone up to date
fill the bill: be just what is needed

fill in *See* **brief**

fill out *See* **expand**

filled *See* **full**

film *See* **layer**

filtered *See* **refined**

filth *See* **dirt**

filthy *See* **dirty, obscene**

final
▷ ADJECTIVE
1 being the last one in a series: *the fifth and final day*
closing *in the closing stages of the race*
concluding *the concluding episode of the series*
eventual *the eventual aim of their policies*
last *his last chance*
ultimate *The ultimate outcome will be different.*
ANTONYM **first**
2 unable to be changed or questioned: *The judges' decision is final.*
absolute *absolute authority*
conclusive *conclusive proof*
definite *too soon to give a definite answer*
definitive *the definitive account of the War of 1812*
See also **last, ultimate**

finale *See* **finish**

finalize *See* **finish**

finally
▷ ADVERB
1 happening after a long time: *It finally arrived.*
at last *He showed up at last.*
at the last moment *They changed their minds at the last moment.*
eventually *The flight eventually left.*
in the end *It all turned out OK in the end.*
in the long run *a success in the long run*
2 in conclusion of something: *Finally, I'd like to talk about safety measures.*
in conclusion *In conclusion, we have to agree.*
in summary *It was, in summary, a delightful movie.*
lastly *Lastly, I would like to thank my parents.*

finance
▷ VERB
1 to provide the money for something: *financed by the government*
back *an event backed by local businesses*
fund *The project is funded by the banks.*
pay for *He paid for his trip out of his savings.*
support *She supported herself through university.*
▷ NOUN
2 the managing of money and investments: *the world of high finance*

banking *the international banking system*
budgeting *We must exercise caution in our budgeting this year.*
commerce *industry and commerce*
economics *the changing economics of the province*
investment *tax incentives to encourage investment*
See also **fund**

financial
▷ *ADJECTIVE*
relating to money: *financial difficulties*
economic *an economic crisis*
fiscal *the long-term fiscal policy of this country*
monetary *a monetary advantage*
See also **economic**

find
▷ *VERB*
1 to discover something: *I can't find that computer file.*
come across *He came across the book by chance.*
discover *They discovered hidden treasure in a cave.*
locate *locating the position of the constellation*
track down *to track down their old friends on the Internet*
turn up *The search failed to turn up any evidence.*
unearth *to unearth the missing copy*
ANTONYM **lose**
2 to realize or learn something: *We found that we had a lot in common.*
become aware *I became aware of his work last year.*
detect *I detected a note of envy in her voice.*
discover *It was discovered that the money was missing.*
learn *I learned of his award when I read the paper.*
realize *They realized too late that the map was wrong.*
See also **discover, locate**

find a solution to *See* **resolve**

find fault *See* **complain, put down**

find fault with *See* **criticize**

find out *See* **determine, discover, hear, learn, see**

find unacceptable *See* **disapprove**

finding *See* **decision, verdict**

fine
▷ *ADJECTIVE*
1 very good and admirable: *fine clothes*

admirable *with many admirable qualities*
beautiful *a beautiful view of the river*
excellent *big hotels with excellent restaurants*
magnificent *the museum's magnificent collection of jewels*
outstanding *an area of outstanding natural beauty*
splendid *a splendid assortment of comic books*
2 small in size or thickness: *powder with very fine particles*
delicate *delicate curtains to let in the light*
lightweight *certain lightweight fabrics*
powdery *soft, powdery dust*
sheer *fabric so sheer that you could see through it*
3 subtle and precise: *the fine details*
fastidious *fastidious attention to detail*
keen *a keen eye for a bargain*
precise *a gauge with precise adjustment*
refined *a person of refined tastes*
sensitive *The radio had very sensitive tuning.*
subtle *a very subtle distinction*
See also **beautiful, excellent, narrow, sheer, sound, splendid, thin**

finesse *See* **polish**

finger *See* **feel, handle, touch**

finish
▷ *VERB*
1 to complete something: *I have to finish a report.*
close *They have closed the deal.*
complete *She has completed her first novel.*
conclude *He concluded his speech.*
end *That ended our discussion.*
finalize *to finalize an agreement*
ANTONYM **start**
▷ *NOUN*
2 the last part of something: *to see it through to the finish*
close *to bring to a close*
completion *The project is nearing completion.*
conclusion *at the conclusion of the program*
end *the end of the race*
ending *The movie had an unexpected ending.*
finale *the grand finale of the evening*
ANTONYM **start**
▷ *NOUN*
3 the surface appearance of something: *a glossy finish*
grain *the smooth grain of the wood*

F

lustre *a lustre similar to silk*
polish *The chrome had a high polish.*
shine *It gives a beautiful shine to the hair.*
surface *a polished surface*
texture *fabric with a velvety texture*
See also **cease, complete, conclude, conclusion, end, stop**

finished *See* **over**

fire
▷ *NOUN*
1 the flames produced when something burns: *a ball of fire*
blaze *The firefighters were hurt in the blaze.*
combustion *Energy is released by combustion.*
flames *rescued from the flames*
inferno *The building was an inferno.*
▷ *VERB*
2 to shoot or detonate something: *to fire a starter's pistol*
detonate *to detonate an explosive device*
explode *to explode a bomb*
launch *They launched the missile from a boat.*
set off *the largest nuclear explosion ever set off*
shoot *shooting guns in all directions*
▷ *VERB*
3 INFORMAL to dismiss someone from a job: *She was fired yesterday.*
discharge *discharged from the army*
dismiss *He was dismissed by the bank.*
lay off *Many workers were laid off during the slow season.*
make redundant *jobs made redundant by new technology*
sack INFORMAL *He was sacked after a week on the job.*
See also **discharge, passion, sack, spirit**

INFORMALLY SPEAKING

fire away: go ahead and ask
light a fire under: encourage someone to act more quickly
play with fire: meddle with something dangerous

firm
▷ *ADJECTIVE*
1 solid and not soft: *Freeze the ice cream until it is firm.*
compressed *compressed wood pulp made into cardboard*
congealed *a bowl of congealed grease*
hard *The snow was hard and slippery.*

rigid *Pour the mixture into a rigid plastic container.*
set *The glue wasn't completely set.*
solid *a block of solid ice*
stiff *egg whites beaten until stiff*
ANTONYM **soft**
2 resolute and determined: *The debating team needs a firm coach.*
adamant *He was adamant that he would not resign.*
determined *She was determined to finish the game.*
inflexible *his inflexible routine*
resolute *a willingness to take resolute action*
staunch *many staunch supporters*
unshakable *an unshakable belief in democracy*
▷ *NOUN*
3 a commercial organization: *a firm of builders*
business *a gardening business*
company *his software development company*
corporation *one of the leading banking corporations*
enterprise *small business enterprises*
organization *a multinational corporation*
See also **business, company, enterprise, hard, positive, rigid, secure, set, solid, steadfast, steady, stiff, strict, tight, trusty**

firmly *See* **fast**

first
▷ *ADJECTIVE*
1 done or in existence before anything else: *the first moon landing*
earliest *The earliest bus leaves at seven.*
initial *our initial meeting*
opening *a standing ovation on opening night*
original *She was one of the original cast members.*
primeval *the primeval forests of British Columbia*
ANTONYM **last**
▷ *ADVERB*
2 done or occurring before anything else: *You must do that first.*
beforehand *She had prepared her speech beforehand.*
earlier *I did that one earlier.*
firstly *Firstly, I'd like to thank you all for being here.*
initially *not as bad as they initially predicted*
to begin with *To begin with, we must prepare the soil.*
3 more important than anything else: *our first responsibility*

chief *the chief pilot*
foremost *one of our foremost judges*
leading *the team's leading hitter*
prime *He was the prime suspect.*
principal *the principal reason*
See also **foremost, opening, original, principal**

first-class See **brilliant, excellent, first-rate, outstanding, select**

first-hand See **direct**

firstly See **first**

first-rate
▷ *ADJECTIVE*
excellent: *They were dealing with a first-rate professional.*
excellent *He does an excellent job as her personal assistant.*
exceptional *His piano playing is exceptional.*
first-class *The food was first-class.*
marvellous *He certainly is a marvellous actor.*
outstanding *an outstanding athlete*
splendid *We had a splendid meal.*
superb *a superb 18-hole golf course*
See also **able, marvellous, outstanding, prime, prize, select, superior**

fiscal See **financial**

fishy See **suspect, suspicious**

fissure
▷ *NOUN*
a deep crack in rock or the ground: *There was a rumbling, and a fissure opened up.*
cleft *a narrow cleft in the rocks*
crack *The building developed large cracks in walls and ceilings.*
crevice *a huge boulder with ferns growing in every crevice*
fault *The San Andreas Fault is responsible for many earthquakes.*
pothole *That highway has many dangerous potholes.*
rift *a deep rift in the marshy land*
split *The baseball bat has a split right down the middle.*
See also **abyss, leak, split**

fit
▷ *VERB*
1 to be the right shape or size: *made to fit a child*
belong *I just didn't belong there.*
correspond *The two angles didn't correspond exactly.*
dovetail *The club's interests dovetailed with her own.*
go *small enough to go in your pocket*

match *Match the pegs with the holes.*
2 to place something in position: *a fitted carpet*
adapt *shelves adapted to suit the smaller books*
arrange *Arrange the pieces to form a picture.*
place *Place the CDs in the holder.*
position *plants that are carefully positioned in the room*
▷ *ADJECTIVE*
3 in good physical condition: *a reasonably fit person*
healthy *a healthy mind in a healthy body*
in good condition *in good condition for their age*
robust *a strong, robust farmer*
trim *a trim figure*
well *You're looking well.*
ANTONYM **unfit**
See also **burst, correspond, healthy, match, right, sound, suitable, well**

fit out See **equip**

fitness See **health**

fitting
▷ *ADJECTIVE*
1 appropriate and suitable for something: *a fitting thank-you speech*
appropriate *an appropriate outfit for the occasion*
correct *the correct thing to say*
proper *It isn't proper that they should be here.*
right *He always says just the right thing.*
suitable *a photo suitable for framing*
▷ *NOUN*
2 a part attached to something else: *fixtures and fittings*
accessory *bicycle accessories*
attachment *a wide range of attachments*
component *special components*
part *Extra parts can be added later.*
unit *The unit plugs into most computers.*
See also **appropriate, attachment, correct, proper, right, suitable**

fix
▷ *VERB*
1 to attach or secure something: *fixed to the wall*
attach *The label was attached with glue.*
bind *sticks bound together with string*
fasten *Fasten the two parts securely.*
secure *firmly secured by strong nails*
stick *She stuck the pictures into the scrapbook.*

F

2 to repair something broken: *The bike is fixed now.*

correct *to correct our mistakes*

mend *They finally got around to mending the roof.*

patch up *Patch up those holes.*

repair *I had my shoes repaired.*

▷ NOUN

3 INFORMAL a difficult situation: *in a bit of a fix*

difficulty *financial difficulties*

mess *Their credit rating was in a mess.*

predicament *a tricky predicament*

quandary *in a quandary about what to do*

See also **confirm, corrupt, determine, fasten, focus, glue, hang, hole, jam, limit, mend, mess, predicament, repair, secure, settle, stick**

fix up See **arrange, restore**

fixation See **complex, obsession**

fixed See **constant, definite, rigid, secure, set**

fixture See **attachment**

fizz See **boil, foam**

flabby

▷ ADJECTIVE

soft and lacking firmness: *a flabby stomach*

floppy *the hound's floppy ears*

sagging *a sagging double chin*

slack *The skin around the eyelids is a little slack.*

ANTONYM **taut**

See also **limp**

flag See **label, weaken**

flagrant See **shameless**

flair See **gift, style, talent**

flak See **criticism**

flamboyant See **flashy, loud, ostentatious**

flame See **burn**

flames See **fire**

flap See **wave**

flare See **burn, flash**

flash

▷ NOUN

1 a sudden, short burst of light: *a flash of lightning*

burst *a burst of fire*

flare *the sudden flare of a match*

sparkle *sparkles from the sequinned costume*

▷ VERB

2 to shine briefly and often repeatedly: *They signalled by flashing a light.*

flare *fireworks flaring in the darkness*

glint *the low sun glinting off the windshield*

glitter *the glittering crown on his head*

sparkle *Diamonds sparkled on her wrist.*

twinkle *stars twinkling in the night sky*

See also **instant, minute, speed**

flashy

▷ ADJECTIVE

showy in a vulgar way: *flashy clothes*

flamboyant *a ridiculously flamboyant outfit*

garish *curtains in garish colours*

showy *an expensive and showy watch*

tacky INFORMAL *tacky jewellery*

ANTONYM **modest**

See also **bold, gaudy, loud, ostentatious, tasteless, vulgar**

flat

▷ ADJECTIVE

1 level and smooth: *a flat surface*

horizontal *horizontal with the ground*

level *a completely level base*

smooth *a smooth marble top*

unbroken *the unbroken surface of the lake*

ANTONYM **uneven**

2 without emotion or interest: *a dreadfully flat speech*

boring *a boring menu*

dull *He told some really dull stories.*

insipid *an insipid performance*

monotonous *an interesting story expressed in a monotonous voice*

weak *A weak ending spoiled the story.*

See also **boring, even, level, stale**

flatness See **boredom**

flatten See **level**

flatter

▷ VERB

1 to praise someone insincerely: *flattering remarks*

compliment *She was often complimented on her poetry.*

fawn *surrounded by fawning fans*

2 to make more attractive: *clothes that flatter your figure*

enhance *The moustache did not enhance his looks.*

set off *Blue sets off the colour of your eyes.*

suit *Those glasses really suit your face.*

See also **humour**

flattery

▷ NOUN

flattering words and behaviour: *susceptible to flattery*

adulation *received with adulation by the critics*
fawning *the constant fawning of his admirers*

flavour *See* taste

flaw

▷ *NOUN*
an imperfection in something: *a flaw in his argument*
blemish *A small blemish spoiled the surface of the desk.*
defect *a manufacturing defect*
fault *a fault in the engine*
imperfection *slight imperfections in the sweater*
See also **defect, fault, hole, weakness**

flawed *See* faulty, imperfect

flawless *See* correct, perfect

flee

▷ *VERB*
to run away from something: *to flee the country*
bolt *He bolted for the exit.*
escape *They escaped across the border.*
fly *to fly from danger*
leave *to leave the scene of the crime*
run away *to run away from the police*
take flight *Thousands of people took flight from the floods.*
See also **bolt**

fleece *See* cheat, coat

fleeting *See* brief, short, temporary

flexible

▷ *ADJECTIVE*
1 able to bend or be bent easily: *flexible wire*
elastic *an elastic band*
lithe *lithe and graceful movements*
pliable *baskets made from pliable wicker*
supple *exercises to keep you supple*
2 able to adapt or change: *flexible working hours*
adaptable *an adaptable attitude to work*
discretionary *the discretionary powers of the court*
open *an open mind*
See also **soft**

flick *See* flourish

flicker *See* burn

flight *See* retreat

flimsy *See* fragile, lame, light

flinch

▷ *VERB*
to move suddenly with fear or pain: *The sharp pain made me flinch.*

cringe *to cringe in terror*
shrink *to shrink in fear*
start *They started at the sudden noise.*
wince *I could see him wincing with pain.*

fling *See* affair, throw

flippant *See* frivolous

flit *See* fly

float

▷ *VERB*
1 to be supported by water: *leaves floating on the river*
be on the surface *The oil is on the surface of the ocean.*
bob *toys bobbing in the bathtub*
drift *to drift in on the tide*
lie on the surface *The boat lay on the surface of the lake.*
stay afloat *They could stay afloat without swimming.*
ANTONYM **sink**
2 to be carried on the air: *floating on the breeze*
drift *The music drifted in through the window.*
glide *eagles gliding above us*
hang *A haze of perfume hung in the room.*
hover *Butterflies hovered above the flowers.*

flock *See* gather

flood

▷ *NOUN*
1 a large amount of water coming suddenly: *Many people were drowned in the floods.*
deluge *houses destroyed by the deluge*
downpour *a downpour of torrential rain*
spate *The river was in spate.*
torrent *Torrents of water gushed into the reservoir.*
2 a sudden, large amount of something: *a flood of angry letters*
rush *a sudden rush of panic*
spate *a spate of horror movies*
stream *a stream of praise*
torrent *He replied with a torrent of anger.*
▷ *VERB*
3 to overflow with water: *The river flooded its banks.*
deluge *Heavy rain deluged the capital.*
overflow *an overflowing bathtub*
submerge *The overflowing river submerged the road.*
swamp *His small boat was swamped by the waves.*
See also **flow, rash, wave**

floor _See_ **bottom**

flop _See_ **failure**

floppy _See_ **flabby, limp**

flourish
▷ VERB
1 to develop or function successfully or healthily: _Business was flourishing._
bloom _He seemed to bloom when he changed schools._
boom _Sales are booming!_
do well _The new bookstore is doing well._
prosper _The restaurant chain continues to prosper._
succeed _the qualities needed to succeed in small businesses_
thrive _Today the company continues to thrive._
ANTONYM **fail**
2 to wave or display something: _She flourished her scarf for dramatic effect._
brandish LITERARY _He appeared onstage brandishing a sword._
display _She proudly displayed the letter and began to read it._
hold aloft _He held the cup aloft._
wave _Crowds were waving flags and applauding._
▷ NOUN
3 a bold sweeping or waving movement: _with a flourish of his hand_
flick _a flick of the wrist_
sweep _With one sweep of her hand, she introduced the guest speaker._
wave _She stopped him with a wave of the hand._
See also **grow, shake, succeed, thrive, wave**

flourishing _See_ **successful**

flout _See_ **disobey**

flow
▷ VERB
1 to move or happen in a continuous stream: _a river flowing gently down into the valley_
circulate _to circulate through the entire house_
glide _The skaters glided over the ice._
roll _rolling gently out to sea_
run _A stream ran beside the road._
slide _to slide down a banister_
▷ NOUN
2 a continuous movement of something: _traffic flow_
current _currents of air_
drift _the drift of people from the country to the cities and towns_
flood _a flood of complaints_
stream _a constant stream of visitors_
tide _to slow the tide of change_
See also **current, drain, gush, movement, pour**

flower _See_ **pick**

flowing _See_ **fluent**

fluctuate _See_ **vary**

fluctuating _See_ **uneven**

fluent
▷ ADJECTIVE
expressing yourself easily and without hesitation: _a fluent speaker of Italian_
articulate _an articulate young woman_
easy _the easy flow of her argument_
effortless _He spoke with effortless ease._
flowing _a smooth, flowing presentation_
ready _a ready answer_
ANTONYM **hesitant**

fluid _See_ **liquid**

flunk _See_ **fail**

flurry _See_ **bustle**

flush _See_ **blush, discharge**

fluster _See_ **embarrass**

flutter _See_ **blow, fly, wave**

fly
▷ VERB
1 to move through the air: _to fly to Paris_
flit _butterflies flitting among the flowers_
flutter _The birds fluttered on to the feeder._
sail _a kite sailing above the trees_
soar _eagles soaring in the sky_
2 to move very quickly: _She flew down the stairs._
dart _She darted to the window._
dash _We had to dash._
hurry _They hurried to catch the train._
race _I had to race around the mall._
rush _rushing off to work_
speed _The car sped off._
tear _He tore off down the road._
See also **bolt, dash, flee, go, hurry, race, rush, tear**

foam
▷ NOUN
1 a mass of tiny bubbles: _waves tipped with foam_
bubbles _The child liked to have bubbles in the bath._
froth _egg whites whipped to a froth_
head _the foamy head on beer_
lather _It took a lot of shampoo to get a good lather._

▷ VERB
2 to swell and form bubbles: *a foaming river*
bubble *The boiling liquid bubbled up.*
fizz *a drink fizzing in the glass*
froth *The boiling milk frothed up over the rim.*
See also **boil**

focal point See **focus**

focus
▷ VERB
1 to concentrate your vision on something: *His eyes began to focus.*
aim *Astronomers aimed telescopes in their direction.*
concentrate *concentrating his gaze on the goalie*
direct *He directed the light on to the roof.*
fix *eyes fixed on the tennis player*
▷ NOUN
2 the centre of attention: *the focus of the conversation*
centre *at the centre of an admiring crowd*
focal point *the focal point of the whole room*
hub *the hub of the financial world*
target *to aim the sales pitch at a particular target*
See also **centre**

focus your attention on See **concentrate**

foe See **enemy**

fog See **cloud**

WORDS FOR ... FOG	
air pollution	murk
haze	smog
mist	

foil
▷ VERB
1 to prevent something from happening: *The police foiled an armed robbery.*
check *to check the rise in his fever*
counter *countering the threat of a strike*
defeat *an important role in defeating the rebellion*
frustrate *a frustrated attempt*
thwart *to thwart someone's plans*
▷ NOUN
2 a contrast to something: *a perfect foil for his personality*
antithesis *the antithesis of his chatty brother*
background *a fitting background for the statue*
complement *The wallpaper was the perfect complement to the antique furniture.*

contrast *The black frame is in dramatic contrast to the colourful picture.*
See also **dash, frustrate, prevent**

fold
▷ VERB
1 to bend something: *He folded the paper carefully.*
bend *Bend the wire toward you.*
crease *Crease along the dotted line.*
crumple *He crumpled the note and put it in his pocket.*
tuck *Tuck in the bedsheets.*
turn under *The bottom was turned under.*
▷ NOUN
2 a crease in something: *hanging in folds*
bend *There was a bend in the photograph.*
crease *sharp creases in his shirt*
pleat *a skirt with pleats*
wrinkle *little wrinkles on the dog's face*
See also **collapse**

follow
▷ VERB
1 to pursue someone: *We were being followed.*
hound *constantly hounded by photographers*
pursue *pursued across several countries*
stalk *arrested for stalking the movie star*
track *They tracked him to his home.*
2 to come after someone or something: *Night follows day.*
come after *Summer comes after spring.*
succeed *The queen was succeeded by the prince.*
supersede *Horses were superseded by cars.*
ANTONYM **precede**
3 to act in accordance with something: *Follow the instructions carefully.*
comply *in order to comply with the club's rules*
conform *conforming to the new safety requirements*
obey *You must obey the law.*
observe *The army was observing a ceasefire.*
See also **copy, happen, heed, obey, practise, result, see, understand**

follower
▷ NOUN
a supporter of a person, group, or belief: *a loyal follower of the team*
believer *many devout believers in the faith*
disciple *one of the prophet's disciples*
fan *football fans*
supporter *a major supporter of the plan*
ANTONYM **leader**
See also **supporter**

F

following *See* **after, next**

folly *See* **stupidity**

fond

▷ *ADJECTIVE*

feeling or showing affection or liking: *a fond greeting*

adoring *an adoring fan*

affectionate *an affectionate smile*

devoted *a devoted couple*

doting *doting grandparents*

having a liking for *a great liking for chocolate*

loving *a loving child*

See also **affectionate, loving**

fond of *See* **keen**

fondle *See* **feel**

fondness *See* **affection, attachment, love, taste, weakness**

food

▷ *NOUN*

things eaten to provide nourishment: *our favourite food*

diet *a balanced diet*

fare *traditional regional fare*

foodstuffs *basic foodstuffs*

grub *INFORMAL* *Get yourself some grub.*

nourishment *unable to take nourishment*

provisions *The campers took enough provisions for two weeks.*

refreshment *Refreshments will be provided.*

foodstuffs *See* **food**

fool

▷ *NOUN*

1 an unintelligent or silly person: *I felt like such a fool!*

dunce *a complete dunce at chemistry*

idiot *acting like an idiot*

ignoramus *Don't be such an ignoramus.*

moron *They treated me like a moron.*

▷ *VERB*

2 to trick someone: *Don't let him fool you.*

con *INFORMAL* *conned out of all his money*

deceive *deceiving the audience*

dupe *in order to dupe the media*

mislead *a deliberately misleading statement*

trick *They tricked him into believing it.*

See also **deceive, dupe, idiot, take in, trick**

foolhardy *See* **mad, rash**

foolish

▷ *ADJECTIVE*

silly and unwise: *feeling foolish*

inane *an inane remark*

nonsensical *a nonsensical thing to say*

senseless *It would be senseless to stop them.*

silly *a silly thing to do*

unintelligent *What an unintelligent thing to say!*

unwise *He had made some unwise investments.*

ANTONYM **wise**

See also **crazy, fond, frivolous, idiotic, mad, silly, stupid, unwise**

foolishness *See* **stupidity**

foolproof *See* **sure**

foot *See* **base, bottom**

footpath *See* **path**

for that reason *See* **therefore**

forage *See* **look for, search**

foray *See* **raid**

forbid

▷ *VERB*

to order someone not to do something: *forbidden to go out*

ban *banned from driving*

exclude *Nobody was excluded from joining the club.*

outlaw *the outlawed freedom fighters*

prohibit *Fishing is prohibited.*

veto *Their decision was vetoed by the president.*

ANTONYM **allow**

See also **ban, exclude, prohibit, veto**

forbidding *See* **sinister**

force

▷ *VERB*

1 to compel someone to do something: *We were forced to turn right.*

compel *I felt compelled to say something.*

drive *The competition is driving the company into bankruptcy.*

make *They made me do it.*

oblige *We were obliged to abandon our goals.*

pressure *She tried to pressure us into voting for her.*

▷ *NOUN*

2 a pressure to do something: *They made him agree by force.*

compulsion *a compulsion to write*

duress *The work was carried out under duress.*

pressure *under pressure to resign*

▷ *NOUN*

3 the strength of something: *the force of the explosion*

impact *the impact of the blast*

might *the full might of the army*
power *the power of the spoken word*
pressure *the pressure of work*
strength *The storm was gaining strength.*
See also **bully, drive, jam, make, reduce, spirit, strength, stuff, violence**

forced *See* **stiff**

forceful
▷ *ADJECTIVE*
determined and having force: *She is notorious for her forceful nature.*
aggressive *a very aggressive business executive*
ambitious *You have to be ambitious to make it in this business.*
assertive *He has become more assertive over the last year.*
bossy *a rather bossy child*
obtrusive *"You are rude and obtrusive," he said to the reporter.*
pushy INFORMAL *a rather pushy customer*
See also **powerful, pushy**

ford *See* **cross**

forebear *See* **ancestor**

foreboding *See* **premonition**

forecast *See* **predict, prediction**

forefather *See* **ancestor**

foreign
▷ *ADJECTIVE*
relating to other countries: *foreign travel*
distant *in that distant land*
exotic *filmed in an exotic location*
overseas *a long overseas trip*
See also **strange, unfamiliar**

foremost
▷ *ADJECTIVE*
most important or best: *one of the world's foremost scholars*
best *the best player of the 20th century*
chief *my chief reason for leaving*
first *The first priority is to clean my room.*
greatest *one of Canada's greatest artists*
leading *the leading scientists in the country*
most important *the country's most important politicians*
prime *I regard this as my prime duty.*
principal *one of the city's principal department stores*
top *The queen met with her top advisers.*
See also **chief, first, important, main, principal, supreme, top**

forensic *See* **legal**

foresee *See* **predict**

foresight *See* **vision**

TYPES OF ... *FOREST*		
bush ✹	rainforest	woods
grove	thicket	
jungle	woodland	

foretell *See* **predict**

forever *See* **always**

forewarn *See* **alert, warn**

foreword *See* **introduction**

forfeit *See* **sacrifice**

forged *See* **false, phony**

forgery *See* **copy, fake, fraud**

forget
▷ *VERB*
to fail to remember something: *I forgot to lock the door.*
fail to remember *He failed to remember the appointment.*
omit *omitting to mention the details*
overlook *to overlook an important fact*
ANTONYM **remember**
See also **neglect, overlook**

forgetful *See* **absent-minded**

forgive
▷ *VERB*
to stop blaming someone for something: *Can you ever forgive me?*
absolve *The verdict absolved him from blame.*
condone *We cannot condone violence.*
excuse *Please excuse our bad behaviour.*
pardon *The prisoner was pardoned.*
ANTONYM **blame**
See also **excuse**

forgiveness
▷ *NOUN*
the act of forgiving: *I ask for your forgiveness.*
acquittal *The jury voted for acquittal.*
mercy *to beg for mercy*
pardon *granting a pardon to the prisoner*
See also **mercy**

forgiving *See* **merciful**

forgo *See* **abstain, sacrifice**

fork *See* **split**

forlorn *See* **futile, hopeless, lonely**

form
▷ *NOUN*
1 a type or kind: *a rare form of the illness*
class *a different class of car*
kind *a new kind of leadership*

F

sort *Try to do some sort of exercise every day.*

type *various types of cameras*

variant *The extinct quagga was a beautiful variant of the zebra.*

variety *an unusual variety of this common garden flower*

2 the shape or pattern of something: *Valleys often take the form of deep canyons.*

contours *the contours of the rolling hills*

layout *the layout of the page*

outline *I could just see the outline of a building in the mist.*

shape *cookies in the shape of stars*

structure *the chemical structure of this molecule*

▷ *VERB*

3 to be the elements that something consists of: *the ideas that formed the basis of the argument*

compose *The committee was composed of both teachers and students.*

constitute *Parkland constitutes about 15 percent of the city's total area.*

make up *Adults over 60 years old make up a growing proportion of the population.*

serve as *an arrangement of bricks and boards that served as a bookshelf*

▷ *VERB*

4 to organize, create, or come into existence: *The bowl was formed out of clay.*

assemble *a model assembled entirely from toothpicks*

create *These patterns were created by the action of water.*

develop *to develop closer ties with other countries*

draw up *We've drawn up a plan of action.*

establish *The museum was established in 1975.*

fashion *to fashion a necklace from seashells*

make *The organic waste decomposes to make compost.*

See also **body, build, condition, design, figure, make, make up, model, outline, shape**

formal

▷ *ADJECTIVE*

1 in accordance with convention or particular rules: *a formal dinner*

conventional *a conventional style of dress*

correct *polite and correct behaviour*

precise *They spoke very precise English.*

stiff *his stiff manner and lack of humour*

ANTONYM **informal**

2 official and publicly recognized: *No formal announcement has been made.*

approved *a legally approved document*

legal *They have a legal responsibility.*

official *according to the official source of information*

prescribed *There is a prescribed procedure for situations like this.*

regular *to proceed through the regular channels*

See also **impersonal, official, stiff, stuffy**

formality See **ceremony**

format See **layout**

former

▷ *ADJECTIVE*

existing in the past: *a former tennis champion*

ancient *the ancient civilizations*

bygone *memories of a bygone age*

old *our old school*

past *a long list of past winners*

See also **past, previous**

former times See **the past**

formerly See **before**

formidable

▷ *ADJECTIVE*

difficult to overcome: *They faced formidable obstacles.*

challenging *a more challenging job*

daunting *a daunting prospect*

difficult *A difficult task lay ahead.*

intimidating *She was an intimidating opponent.*

mammoth *a mammoth undertaking*

onerous *onerous responsibilities*

See also **stiff**

formulate See **create, invent, plan**

forsake See **leave**

forsaken See **lonely**

fort

▷ *NOUN*

a building for defence and shelter: *They had to abandon the fort.*

castle *a heavily guarded castle*

citadel *The citadel towered above the river.*

fortification *fortifications along the border*

fortress *an ancient fortress*

forthcoming See **future, imminent, near**

forthright See **blunt, direct, straight, straightforward**

fortification See **fort**

fortified See **secure**

fortify See **secure, strengthen**

fortitude See **bravery**

fortress *See* **fort**

fortuitous *See* **lucky**

fortunate *See* **lucky**

fortune *See* **chance, fate, luck, wealth**

forum *See* **conference**

forward *See* **bold, send**

foul *See* **disgusting, nasty, smelly, soil**

found *See* **base, start**

foundation *See* **base, fund, start, support**

founder *See* **collapse**

fraction *See* **part**

fractious *See* **cross**

fracture *See* **crack**

fractured *See* **broken**

fragile
▷ *ADJECTIVE*
easily broken or damaged: *fragile china dishes*
breakable *Anything breakable or sharp had to be removed.*
dainty *a dainty music box*
delicate *a delicate instrument*
flimsy *poorly packed in a flimsy box*
frail *a frail old handrail*
ANTONYM **tough**

fragility *See* **weakness**

fragment *See* **bit, disintegrate, part, piece**

fragmented *See* **broken**

fragrance
▷ *NOUN*
a pleasant smell: *the fragrance of the roses*
aroma *the aroma of fresh bread*
bouquet *a wine with a spicy bouquet*
perfume *enjoying the perfume of the lemon trees*
scent *flowers chosen for their scent*
smell *a sweet smell of pine*
See also **smell**

fragrant
▷ *ADJECTIVE*
having a pleasant smell: *fragrant oils*
aromatic *a plant with aromatic leaves*
perfumed *perfumed body cream*
sweet-smelling *sweet-smelling flowers*
ANTONYM **smelly**
See also **sweet**

frail *See* **fragile, puny, weak**

frailty *See* **weakness**

frame *See* **body, build**

frame of mind *See* **humour, mood**

frank
▷ *ADJECTIVE*
open and straightforward: *a frank discussion*
blunt *his blunt approach*
candid *She was completely candid with me.*
honest *my honest opinion*
open *an open, trusting nature*
plain *plain talking*
straightforward *spoken in a straightforward manner*
See also **blunt, candid, direct, natural, open, straight, straightforward**

frantic *See* **furious, hysterical, upset**

fraud
▷ *NOUN*
1 the act of deceiving someone: *The votes were recounted because of electoral fraud.*
deceit *deliberate deceit*
deception *obtaining money by deception*
guile *children's lack of guile*
hoax *The report of the discovery of a gold mine turned out to be a hoax.*
trickery *They had to resort to trickery.*
2 someone or something that deceives you: *Many psychics are frauds.*
charlatan *exposed as a charlatan*
cheater *Cheaters will be disqualified.*
fake *The painting was a fake.*
forgery *just a clever forgery*
imposter *an imposter with false documents*
quack *He tried all sorts of quacks before going to a doctor.*
See also **con, corruption, fake, racket**

fraudulent *See* **corrupt, crooked, deceptive, dishonest**

fray *See* **wear**

free
▷ *ADJECTIVE*
1 not being held prisoner: *a free person*
at large *Three prisoners are at large.*
at liberty *the last hijacker still at liberty*
liberated *newly liberated prisoners*
loose *He broke loose from his bonds.*
ANTONYM **captive**
2 available without payment: *a free brochure*
complimentary *complimentary tickets*
gratis *The meal was gratis.*
unpaid *unpaid voluntary work*
without charge *They fixed it without charge.*

F

▷ *VERB*

3 to release from captivity: *to free the caged animals*
discharge *discharged from prison*
liberate *liberated under the terms of the amnesty*
release *The hostages were soon released.*
set at liberty *She was set at liberty after ten years.*
set loose *The animals were set loose after treatment.*
ANTONYM **imprison**
See also **available, discharge, immune, independent, loose, release, spare, wild**

INFORMALLY SPEAKING

a free hand: freedom to behave as you see fit
free and easy: with little attention to rules and customs
make free (with): act as if you had complete rights to something

---

free time *See* **leisure**

freedom
▷ *NOUN*
I the ability to choose: *freedom of action*
discretion *Use your own discretion.*
latitude *There is more latitude for personal opinions.*
leeway *given greater leeway in her job*
licence *He thinks he has a licence to do just as he likes.*
scope *plenty of scope for improvement*
2 the state of being free or being set free: *gaining their freedom after months of captivity*
emancipation *the emancipation of the slaves*
liberty *three months' loss of liberty*
release *the immediate release of the prisoners*
ANTONYM **captivity**
3 the absence of something unpleasant: *freedom from pain*
exemption *granted exemption from all taxes*
immunity *information in exchange for immunity from prosecution*
See also **release**

freeze *See* **cool, harden, numb**

freezing *See* **cold**

freight *See* **load**

frenzied *See* **furious, hysterical**

frenzy
▷ *NOUN*
wild and uncontrolled behaviour: *The room was a frenzy of activity.*
agitation *in a state of intense agitation*
fury *She marched out in a fury.*
hysteria *mass hysteria*
madness *a moment of madness*
rage *He flew into a rage.*
See also **rage**

frequency *See* **rate**

frequent
▷ *ADJECTIVE*
I happening often: *his frequent visits*
common *a common occurrence*
continual *continual demands for money*
everyday *an everyday event*
habitual *a habitual daydreamer*
recurrent *a recurrent theme in her work*
repeated *His friends made repeated attempts to visit.*
ANTONYM **rare**
▷ *VERB*
2 to appear or go somewhere often: *a restaurant that we frequent*
attend *He often attends their hockey games.*
haunt *They haunt my dreams.*
patronize *to patronize a hotel*
visit *a place we often visit*
ANTONYM **avoid**
See also **continual**

frequently *See* **often**

fresh *See* **original, recent**

fret *See* **fuss, worry**

fretful *See* **cross, restless**

friction *See* **conflict**

friend
▷ *NOUN*
a person you know and like: *lifelong friends*
buddy *We've been best buddies for years.*
companion *my constant companion*
confidant or **confidante** *I shared my deepest thoughts with my trusted confidant.*
crony *surrounded by her cronies*
pal *We are great pals.*
ANTONYM **enemy**
See also **companion**

friendliness *See* **goodwill**

friendly
▷ *ADJECTIVE*
kind and pleasant: *a very friendly group of people*
affectionate *on affectionate terms*
amiable *He was very amiable company.*
close *The two were very close.*

cordial *a most cordial welcome*
genial *a genial host*
welcoming *a welcoming atmosphere*
ANTONYM **unfriendly**
See also **cosy, favourable, pleasant, sociable, warm**

friendship
▷ *NOUN*
a state of being friendly with someone: *I value our friendship.*
affection *to win their affection*
attachment *the deep attachment between them*
closeness *her closeness to her sister*
goodwill *as a gesture of goodwill*
ANTONYM **hostility**
See also **goodwill**

fright *See* **alarm, fear, horror, panic, scare**

frighten
▷ *VERB*
to make someone afraid: *trying to frighten us*
alarm *alarmed by the noise*
intimidate *He is intimidated by his boss.*
scare *You aren't scared of mice, are you?*
startle *I didn't mean to startle you.*
terrify *Heights terrified me.*
terrorize *The invaders terrorized the town.*
unnerve *an unnerving silence*
See also **alarm, scare**

frightened
▷ *ADJECTIVE*
having feelings of fear about something: *frightened of thunder*
afraid *Don't be afraid of the dog.*
alarmed *Don't be alarmed.*
petrified *petrified of snakes*
scared *scared of being alone in the house*
startled *a startled animal*
terrified *a terrified look*
See also **afraid**

frightening
▷ *ADJECTIVE*
causing someone to feel fear: *a frightening experience*
alarming *an alarming increase in the rate of unemployment*
hair-raising *at hair-raising speed*
intimidating *threatening and intimidating behaviour*
menacing *a menacing glance*
terrifying *a terrifying dream*
See also **scary, spooky**

frightful *See* **awful, dreadful, terrible**

frigid *See* **cold, frozen**

fringe *See* **border, edge**

fritter away *See* **waste**

frivolous
▷ *ADJECTIVE*
not serious or sensible: *a frivolous remark*
flippant *a flippant comment*
foolish *saying foolish and inappropriate things*
juvenile *juvenile behaviour*
puerile *your puerile humour*
silly *making silly jokes*
ANTONYM **serious**

F

frolic *See* **play**

from time to time *See* **sometimes**

front
▷ *NOUN*
1 the part that faces forward: *the front wall of the house*
face *the face of the building*
frontage *a cottage with a river frontage*
ANTONYM **back**
2 the outward appearance of something: *She put on a brave front.*
appearance *the appearance of fair treatment*
exterior *his tough exterior*
face *a happy face*
show *a convincing show of affection*

in front
▷ *PREPOSITION*
further forward: *too close to the car in front*
ahead *ahead of the rest of the players*
before *I'm before you.*
leading *the leading bicyclist*
See also **face, head**

frontage *See* **front**

frontier *See* **border**

froth *See* **boil, foam**

frown
▷ *VERB*
to draw the eyebrows together: *She frowned in displeasure.*
glare *The man glared angrily at me.*
glower *She glowered, but said nothing.*
scowl *He scowled at the server.*
See also **glare**

frozen
▷ *ADJECTIVE*
extremely cold: *I was frozen in the arena.*
arctic *arctic weather conditions*
chilled *chilled to the bone*
frigid *frigid temperatures*
icy *an icy wind*

numb *numb with cold*
See also **numb**

frugal See **economical, thrifty**

frugality See **economy**

fruit See **effect**

fruitful See **fertile, productive**

fruitless See **in vain, vain**

frustrate
▷ *VERB*
to prevent something from happening: *His efforts were frustrated.*
block *They are blocking the peace process.*
check *to check the spread of the virus*
foil *They foiled all my plans.*
thwart *thwarting the club's ambitions*
See also **dash, foil, hamper, hinder**

fry See **cook**

fulfill
▷ *VERB*
to carry out or achieve something: *He decided to fulfill his dream and become a photographer.*
accomplish *If they all work together, they can accomplish their goal.*
achieve *We will strive to achieve these goals.*
carry out *They have no intention of carrying out their promises.*
perform *Each component performs a different function.*
realize *The question is, will our hopes ever be realized?*
satisfy *These steps should satisfy the basic requirements.*
See also **accomplish, achieve, carry out, keep, meet, perform, satisfy**

full
▷ *ADJECTIVE*
1 filled with something: *full of books*
filled *filled up to the top*
loaded *The van was loaded with furniture.*
packed *The train was packed.*
saturated *completely saturated with liquid*
ANTONYM **empty**
2 missing nothing out: *I want a full account of what happened.*
comprehensive *a comprehensive guide to the area*
detailed *a detailed description*
exhaustive *exhaustive research*
extensive *extensive coverage of the earthquake*
maximum *taking maximum advantage of the free offer*

thorough *a thorough search*
3 loose-fitting: *a full skirt*
baggy *a baggy sweater*
loose *hidden under his loose shirt*
voluminous *voluminous sleeves*
See also **abundant, busy, complete, crowded, thorough, whole**

full of life See **alive**

full-grown See **mature**

fully See **quite, well**

fully-fledged See **mature**

fume See **rage**

fuming See **furious, mad**

fun
▷ *NOUN*
an enjoyable activity: *It was great fun.*
amusement *What do you do for amusement?*
enjoyment *It gave us much enjoyment.*
entertainment *little opportunity for entertainment*
pleasure *to mix business and pleasure*
recreation *time for recreation*

make fun of
▷ *VERB*
to tease someone: *Don't make fun of him.*
deride *This theory is widely derided.*
laugh at *They laughed at his hat.*
mock *He was often mocked by his classmates.*
ridicule *Don't allow them to ridicule you.*
taunt *It's cruel to taunt him like that.*
See also **entertainment**

function
▷ *NOUN*
1 the useful thing that something or someone does: *What is the function of this software?*
duty *lifeguard duty*
job *Their main job is to keep us healthy.*
purpose *The purpose of the sale was to raise money for charity.*
responsibility *He handled his responsibilities as a counsellor in an intelligent fashion.*
role *information about the drug's role in preventing infection*
2 a large formal dinner, reception, or party: *We were going to a function downtown.*
dinner *a series of official dinners*
gathering *I'm always shy at formal gatherings like that.*
party *They met at a party.*
reception *At the reception they served roast beef and salmon.*

▷ VERB

3 to operate or work: *The furnace was not functioning properly.*
go *My car won't go in this weather.*
operate *Ceiling and wall lights can operate independently.*
perform *How is your new boat performing?*
run *The system is now running smoothly.*
work *Is your cellphone working today?*
See also **act, behave, go, job, part, party, purpose**

functional See **practical**

fund

▷ NOUN

1 an amount of money: *the pension fund*
capital *difficulty in raising capital*
foundation *money from a research foundation*
pool *a reserve pool of cash*
reserve *a drain on the cash reserves*
supply *to curb money supply and inflation*
2 a large amount of something: *an extraordinary fund of energy*
hoard *his hoard of supplies*
mine *a mine of information*
reserve *oil reserves*
reservoir *the body's short-term reservoir of energy*
store *a store of fuel*

▷ VERB

3 to provide the money for something: *to raise money to fund scientific research*
finance *big projects financed by the banks*
pay for *His parents paid for his vacation.*
subsidize *heavily subsidized by the government*
support *She is supporting herself through university.*
See also **bank, finance, hoard, reserve, store, supply**

fundamental See **basic, basis, essential, principle**

fundamentals See **essentials**

funds See **money**

funny

▷ ADJECTIVE

1 being strange or odd: *They heard a funny noise.*
mysterious *in mysterious circumstances*
odd *There was something odd about their behaviour.*
peculiar *It tasted very peculiar.*
puzzling *a puzzling development*
strange *A strange thing happened.*
unusual *a most unusual person*
2 causing amusement: *a funny story*
amusing *a most amusing teacher*

comic *comic moments*
comical *the comical expression on his face*
hilarious *We thought it was hilarious.*
humorous *a humorous magazine*
witty *a very witty speech*
ANTONYM **serious**
See also **odd, peculiar, strange, suspicious, weird, witty**

funny feeling See **premonition**

fur See **coat, pile**

furious

F

▷ ADJECTIVE

1 extremely angry: *furious about the poor service they received*
enraged *I got more and more enraged about the situation.*
fuming *He was still fuming over the remark.*
infuriated *She knew how infuriated the conversation had made me.*
livid *She was absolutely livid about it.*
mad *I'm pretty mad about this, I can tell you.*
raging *I tried to hide my feelings, but inside I was raging.*
2 involving great energy, effort, or speed: *a furious battle*
breakneck *They drove at breakneck speed.*
fierce *Competition has been fierce between the rival groups.*
frantic *There was frantic activity behind the scenes.*
frenzied *the frenzied activity of the school election*
intense *Both sides are involved in intense activity.*
manic *Preparations continued at a manic pace.*
See also **angry, mad, violent**

furnish See **issue, provide, supply**

further See **benefit, extra, more**

furthermore See **also**

furtive See **mysterious, secret**

fury See **anger, frenzy, rage**

fuse See **bond, combine, stick**

fusion See **blend, mixture, union**

fuss

▷ NOUN

1 anxious or excited behaviour: *What's all the fuss about?*
agitation *in a state of intense agitation*
bother *I don't want any bother.*
commotion *a commotion in the ballpark*

confusion *In the confusion, I forgot my wallet.*

stir *The play caused a stir here.*

to-do *a big to-do*

▷ *VERB*

2 to behave in a nervous or restless way: *The servers fussed and hovered around our table.*

bustle *shoppers bustling about the store*

fidget *He was fidgeting with his tie.*

fret *Stop fretting about the details.*

See also **bustle**

fussy

▷ *ADJECTIVE*

difficult to please: *fussy about his food*

choosy *INFORMAL Cats can be choosy about what they eat.*

discriminating *hard to please because of her discriminating taste in food*

exacting *I failed to meet their exacting standards.*

fastidious *My mother is fastidious about cleanliness.*

particular *very particular about the colours he used*

See also **elaborate, particular**

futile

▷ *ADJECTIVE*

having no chance of success: *a futile effort to run away*

abortive *the rebels' abortive coup attempt*

forlorn *forlorn hopes of future improvement*

unsuccessful *an unsuccessful bid for the Olympics*

useless *It was useless even to try.*

vain *in the vain hope of success*

ANTONYM **successful**

See also **hopeless, useless, vain**

future

▷ *ADJECTIVE*

relating to a time after the present: *to predict future growth*

approaching *concerned about the approaching winter*

coming *in the coming months*

forthcoming *candidates for the forthcoming elections*

impending *their impending marriage*

later *We'll discuss it at a later date.*

prospective *my prospective employers*

ANTONYM **past**

See also **outlook**

Gg

gabble *See* **babble**

gadget
▷ *NOUN*
a small machine or tool: *kitchen gadgets such as blenders and can openers*
appliance *Switch off all electrical appliances when they're not in use.*
device *a device that warns you when the batteries need changing*
machine *a machine for slicing vegetables*
tool *a tool for cutting wood, metal, or plastic*

gaffe *See* **mistake**

gag *See* **joke, silence**

gaggle *See* **bunch**

gain
▷ *VERB*
1 to get something gradually: *Students can gain valuable experience by working.*
achieve *Achieving our goals makes us feel good.*
acquire *Companies should reward workers for acquiring more skills.*
earn *She has earned the respect of the world's top cyclists.*
obtain *You would need to obtain permission to copy the design.*
secure *He failed to secure enough votes for a victory.*
win *The long-term aim is to win her approval.*
2 to get an advantage: *Would any areas of the world gain from global warming?*
benefit *Both sides have benefited from the talks.*
profit *to profit from one's crimes*
▷ *NOUN*
3 an increase or improvement in something: *Our party has made substantial gains in local elections.*
advance *advances in digital photography*
growth *rapid population growth*
improvement *a major improvement in standards*
increase *an increase of seven percent in visitors to Prince Edward Island*
rise *a huge rise in the price of gasoline*
See also **acquire, advance, benefit, increase, secure, win**

gait *See* **walk**

gala *See* **celebration, festival**

gall *See* **impudence**

gallantry *See* **courtesy**

gallop *See* **run, speed**

gamble
▷ *VERB*
1 to bet money on something: *He gambled on the horses.*
bet *The poker player bet all his remaining chips.*
2 to take a risk: *Few networks seem willing to gamble on new TV series.*
chance *I wouldn't chance the rapids in a canoe.*
risk *He risked his popularity by supporting the other candidate.*
stake *He has staked his reputation on the outcome.*
▷ *NOUN*
3 a risk that someone takes: *We are taking a gamble on a young player.*
chance *You take a chance on the weather when you vacation in England.*
lottery *The odds of winning a lottery are very small.*
risk *How much risk are you prepared to take?*
wager *We made a small wager that he couldn't be silent for a whole hour.*
See also **risk**

game
▷ *NOUN*
an occasion or event at which people compete: *the Blue Jays' first game of the season*
clash *the clash between Australia and Canada*
contest *The rain spoiled a good contest.*
match *a football match*
See also **agreeable, contest, match, willing**

INFORMALLY SPEAKING

ahead of the game: winning rather than losing
game over: final defeat
off your game: not performing well
play the game: follow the rules

---

gamut *See* **range**

gang *See* **band, bunch, group, party, team**

gap
▷ *NOUN*
1 a space or a hole in something: *They squeezed through a gap in the fence.*
break *stars twinkling between the breaks in the clouds*

G

chink *All the walls have wide chinks in them.*

clearing *a clearing in the woods*

hole *a hole in the wall*

opening *an opening in the trees*

space *the space between their car and the one in front*

2 a period of time: *After a gap of nearly a decade, she returned to politics.*

hiatus FORMAL *The store is open again after a two-year hiatus.*

interlude *a happy interlude in my parents' life*

interval *There was a long interval of silence.*

lull *a lull in the conversation*

pause *Then, after a pause, he went on.*

3 a difference between people or things: *the gap between rich and poor*

difference *He denied there were any major differences between them.*

disparity FORMAL *disparities between poor and wealthy countries*

inconsistency *There were major inconsistencies in the witness's evidence.*

See also **breach, hole, interval, opening, space**

garb See **dress**

garbage

▷ NOUN

1 things that people throw away: *piles of garbage*

debris *screws, bolts, and other debris*

junk INFORMAL *What are you going to do with all that junk?*

litter *If you see litter in the corridor, pick it up.*

refuse *refuse collection and street cleaning*

trash *I forgot to take out the trash.*

waste *industrial waste*

2 INFORMAL ideas and opinions that are untrue or unimportant: *I personally think this is complete garbage.*

drivel *What absolute drivel!*

gibberish *a politician talking gibberish*

nonsense *all that poetic nonsense about love*

rubbish *He's talking rubbish.*

See also **nonsense, refuse, trash**

garbled

▷ ADJECTIVE

confused or incorrect: *a garbled voice-mail message*

confused *the latest twist in a confused story*

distorted *a distorted version of what was said*

incomprehensible *Her speech was incomprehensible.*

jumbled *his jumbled account of how his cousin had been hired*

unintelligible *He muttered something unintelligible.*

gardens See **grounds**

garish See **flashy, gaudy, loud, tasteless**

garments See **clothes**

gash See **cut**

gasp

▷ VERB

1 to breathe in quickly through your mouth: *She gasped for air.*

choke *People began to choke as smoke filled the air.*

gulp *She gulped air into her lungs.*

pant *The hikers panted as they climbed the steep hill.*

puff *I could see he was unfit because he was puffing.*

▷ NOUN

2 a short, quick breath of air: *An audible gasp went through the theatre.*

gulp *I took in a large gulp of air.*

puff *He blew out a little puff of air.*

gate See **entrance, entry**

gather

▷ VERB

1 to come together in a group: *We gathered around the fireplace.*

assemble *a place for students to assemble between classes*

congregate *Youngsters love to congregate here in the evenings.*

flock *The poor reviews will not stop people from flocking to the movie.*

mass *The general was massing his troops for a counterattack.*

round up *The police rounded up a number of suspects.*

ANTONYM **scatter**

2 to bring things together: *I suggest we gather enough firewood to last the night.*

accumulate *In five years the country has accumulated a huge debt.*

amass *She has amassed a personal fortune of \$38 million.*

collect *About 1.5 million signatures have been collected.*

hoard *They've begun to hoard food and gasoline.*

stockpile *People are stockpiling food for the coming blizzard.*

3 to learn or believe something: *"He speaks English." "I gathered that."*

assume *I assume the eggs are fresh.*
conclude *He concluded that surgery was the best option.*
hear *I heard that he was forced to resign.*
learn *She wasn't surprised to learn that he was involved.*
understand *I understand that his family will be moving.*
See also **assemble, collect, concentrate, crowd, hear, imagine, learn, mass, meet, pick, stockpile, understand**

gathering
▷ *NOUN*
a meeting with a purpose: *polite social gatherings*
assembly *an assembly of party members*
congregation *The congregation said prayers.*
get-together INFORMAL *family get-togethers*
meeting *Can we have a meeting to discuss that?*
rally *a pre-election rally*
See also **function, meeting, party**

gauche See **clumsy**

gaudy
▷ *ADJECTIVE*
colourful in a vulgar way: *gaudy fake jewellery*
bright *fake fur, dyed in bright colours*
flashy *dancers in flashy satin suits*
garish *They climbed the garish purple-carpeted stairs.*
loud *a loud checked shirt*
showy *He favoured large, showy flowers.*
See also **loud, tasteless, vulgar**

gauge See **measure**

gaze See **look, regard, stare**

gaze at See **watch**

gear See **clothes, equipment, stuff, things**

general
▷ *ADJECTIVE*
1 relating to the whole of something: *a general decline in employment*
broad *a broad outline of the organization's history*
comprehensive *a comprehensive guide to the Maritimes*
overall *The overall quality of students' work had shown a marked improvement.*
ANTONYM **specific**
2 widely true, suitable, or relevant: *The project should raise general awareness about animal rights.*
accepted *the accepted version of events*

broad *a book with broad appeal*
common *Such behaviour is common among young people.*
universal *Music and sports programs have a nearly universal appeal.*
widespread *The proposals have attracted widespread support.*
ANTONYM **special**
See also **broad, common, mass, popular, public, universal**

generally See **as a rule, mainly, on average**

generate See **bring about, cause**

generosity
▷ *NOUN*
willingness to give money, time, or help: *She is well known for her generosity.*
benevolence *Banks are not known for their benevolence.*
charity *private acts of charity*
kindness *We have been treated with such kindness by everybody.*
ANTONYM **meanness**

generous
▷ *ADJECTIVE*
1 willing to give money, time, or help: *Not all wealthy people are so generous.*
charitable *Individuals can be charitable and help their neighbours.*
hospitable *He was very hospitable to me when I came to New York.*
kind *She is warmhearted and kind to everyone.*
lavish *The princess received a number of lavish gifts from her hosts.*
liberal *Don't be too liberal with your spending.*
ANTONYM **mean**
2 very large: *a generous portion of spaghetti*
abundant *an abundant supply of hot food*
ample *There is ample space for a good-sized kitchen.*
plentiful *a plentiful supply of beverages*
ANTONYM **meagre**
See also **handsome, noble**

genial See **friendly, warm**

genius
▷ *NOUN*
1 an extremely smart or talented person: *a mathematical genius*
brain *the financial brain behind the company*
master *The award-winning sculptor is a master of his craft.*

G

mastermind *the mastermind of the plot to kidnap the prince*
virtuoso *a virtuoso of pop music*
2 extraordinary ability or talent: *a poet of genius*
brains *She has brains as well as beauty.*
brilliance *his brilliance as a director*
intellect *people of great intellect*
See also **talent**

genre *See* **class, kind**

genteel *See* **polite, refined**

gentle
▷ ADJECTIVE
not violent or rough: *a quiet and gentle man*
benign *a good-looking fellow with a benign expression*
kind *I fell in love with him because of his kind nature.*
kindly *a kindly old gentleman*
meek *a meek, mild-mannered person*
placid *a look of impatience on her normally placid face*
soft *He has a very soft heart.*
tender *Her voice was tender.*
ANTONYM **cruel**
See also **leisurely, mild, soft, tender**

gentleman *See* **man**

gentleness *See* **kindness**

genuine
▷ ADJECTIVE
not false: *They're convinced the picture is genuine.*
authentic *an authentic French recipe*
bona fide *We are happy to donate to bona fide charities.*
real *a real Emily Carr painting*
ANTONYM **fake**
See also **actual, authentic, natural, real, right, serious, sincere, true**

germ-free *See* **pure, sterile**

germinate *See* **grow**

gesticulate *See* **signal**

gesture *See* **signal**

get
▷ VERB
1 to fetch or receive something: *I'll get us all something to eat.*
acquire *I have recently acquired a new camera.*
fetch *He fetched a towel from the washroom.*
obtain *They were trying to obtain false passports.*

procure FORMAL *It remained very difficult to procure food.*
receive *I received your letter of November 7.*
secure FORMAL *He failed to secure enough votes for a victory.*
2 to change from one state to another: *People draw the curtains once it gets dark.*
become *The wind became stronger.*
grow *He grew to love his work.*
turn *The leaves have turned golden brown.*
See also **acquire, develop, earn, extract, grow, obtain, receive, secure, see, take in, understand, win**

get across *See* **convey**

get away *See* **escape**

get back *See* **recover**

get back at *See* **retaliate**

get better *See* **recover**

get even *See* **revenge**

get even with *See* **retaliate**

get going *See* **start**

get hold of *See* **contact, obtain**

get in the way *See* **impede**

get in touch with *See* **contact**

get off your chest *See* **reveal**

get on someone's nerves *See* **annoy, bother, pester**

get out of *See* **dodge**

get rid of *See* **dispose of, dump, eliminate, remove**

get through *See* **pass**

get to *See* **reach**

get together *See* **meet**

get well *See* **recover**

get your own back *See* **retaliate, revenge**

get on
▷ VERB
to enjoy someone's company: *I get on very well with his family.*
be compatible *My cousin and I are very compatible.*
hit it off INFORMAL *They hit it off right away.*
See also **do**

get-together *See* **gathering, meeting, party**

ghastly *See* **awful, dreadful**

ghost

▷ NOUN

the spirit of a dead person: *the ghost in the haunted house*

apparition *She felt as if she were seeing an apparition.*

phantom *The opera singer was relentlessly pursued by a phantom.*

spectre *The Tower of London is said to be haunted by the spectre of Anne Boleyn.*

spirit *the spirits of our dead ancestors*
See also **spirit**

ghostly See spooky

giant See huge, immense, large, vast

gibberish See garbage

giddy See dizzy, faint

gift

▷ NOUN

1 something you give someone: *He showered us with gifts.*

bequest FORMAL *They received a bequest of $310,000.*

contribution *companies that make charitable contributions*

donation *donations of food and clothing for victims of the hurricane*

legacy *What about the legacy from your uncle?*

present *This book would make a great birthday present.*

2 a natural skill or ability: *a gift for comedy*

ability *It's obvious he has an exceptional ability.*

aptitude *She realized she had an aptitude for writing.*

flair *He found he had a real flair for design.*

talent *Both her children have a talent for music.*
See also **blessing, capacity, present, talent**

gigantic See colossal, enormous, immense, large, vast

giggle See laugh

girl

▷ NOUN

a female child: *She was a strong girl, and quite tall.*

schoolgirl *a group of schoolgirls*
See also **female**

gist See meaning

give

▷ VERB

1 to provide someone with something: *I gave her a CD.*

award *The mayor awarded him a medal.*

deliver *They deliver for Meals on Wheels to shut-ins.*

donate *Others donated second-hand clothes.*

grant *Permission was granted a few weeks ago.*

hand *He handed me a glass of orange juice.*

present *The Governor General presented the awards.*

provide *to provide a comfortable bed*

supply *Who supplied the food for the trip?*
ANTONYM **take**

2 to collapse or break under pressure: *My knees gave out under me.*

buckle *His left wrist buckled under the strain.*

cave in *Half the ceiling caved in.*

collapse *The roof supports had collapsed.*

give way *He fell when a ledge gave way beneath him.*

yield *The handle yielded to her grasp.*
See also **grant, hand down, issue, present, spare, supply**

give a kick See thrill

give a talk See lecture

give back See return

give off See discharge, emit

give out See emit, fail, issue

give up See abstain, cease, quit, renounce, sacrifice, surrender

give way See collapse, give

give in

▷ VERB

to admit that you are defeated: *Who do you think will give in first?*

capitulate *They won't capitulate to the prisoners' demands.*

concede *The candidate is not ready to concede defeat.*

submit *He submitted to an operation on his right knee.*

succumb *The ambassador said her country would never succumb to pressure.*

surrender *He surrendered to the Roman troops.*

yield *an opponent who had shown no desire to yield*
See also **submit, surrender**

given See prone

glad

▷ ADJECTIVE

happy about something: *They'll be glad to get away from it all.*

delighted *She'll be delighted to see you.*

happy *I'm very happy that you are here.*

G

joyful *a joyful reunion with his family*
overjoyed *My old friend was overjoyed to see me.*
pleased *They're pleased to be going home.*
ANTONYM **sorry**
See also **pleased**

glance

▷ NOUN

1 a brief look at something: *The boys exchanged glances.*
glimpse *They caught a glimpse of the actor.*
look *I took a last look in the mirror.*
peek *Could I just have another quick peek at the bedroom?*
peep *Would you take a peep out of the window?*

▷ VERB

2 to look at something quickly: *He glanced at his watch.*
glimpse *I glimpsed a rabbit in the garden.*
look *I looked quickly at the elegant people around me.*
peek *She peeked through the hole in the fence.*
peep *Now and then the baby peeped at us.*
scan *She scanned the want ads of the newspaper.*

▷ VERB

3 to hit something quickly and bounce away: *The car glanced off the guardrail.*
bounce *The ball bounced off the opposite post.*
brush *She brushed her hand across her face.*
skim *pebbles skimming across the water*
See also **look, peek**

glance at *See* read

glare

▷ VERB

1 to look angrily at someone: *He glared at his brother.*
frown *She looked up to see me frowning at her.*
glower *He glowered at me but said nothing.*
scowl *She scowled and then slammed the door behind her.*

▷ NOUN

2 an angry look: *The server lowered his eyes to avoid my furious glare.*
frown *There was a deep frown on the boy's face.*
scowl *She met the remark with a scowl.*

▷ NOUN

3 very bright light: *the glare of the headlights*
blaze *There was a sudden blaze of light.*
brilliance *The brilliance of the sunset dazzled my eyes.*

flare *the sudden flare of a flashlight*
glow *the glow of the fire*
See also **frown, light**

glaring *See* manifest

glassy *See* clear, smooth

gleam *See* gloss, glow, shine, sparkle

gleaming *See* brilliant, shining

glean *See* extract

glee *See* delight

glide *See* float, flow

glimmer *See* glow

glimpse *See* glance, look, peek, see

glint *See* flash

glisten *See* sparkle

glitter *See* flash, sparkle

gloat *See* glory

globe *See* ball, earth

gloom *See* dark, despair

gloomy

▷ ADJECTIVE

1 feeling very sad: *They are gloomy about the team's chances of success.*
dejected *Everyone has days when they feel dejected.*
down *My uncle sounded really down.*
glum *What on earth are you looking so glum about?*
miserable *I feel miserable about what I said to him.*
sad *You must feel sad about what's happened.*
ANTONYM **cheerful**

2 dark and depressing: *a gloomy house on the edge of the park*
dark *The house looked dark and gloomy.*
dismal *damp and dismal weather*
dreary *a dreary room with not enough light*
dull *It's always dull and raining.*
ANTONYM **sunny**
See also **cloudy, drab, dull, miserable, pessimistic, sad**

glorify *See* honour, worship

glorious *See* splendid

glory

▷ NOUN

1 fame and admiration that someone gets: *It was her moment of glory.*
fame *The movie earned him international fame.*
honour *the honour of leading the parade*
immortality *Some people want to achieve*

immortality through their art.
praise *She deserves full praise for her efforts.*
prestige *I'm not in this job for the prestige.*
ANTONYM **disgrace**
2 something impressive or beautiful: *Spring arrived in all its glory.*
grandeur *the grandeur of the Rocky Mountains*
magnificence *the magnificence of the sunset*
majesty *the majesty of Niagara Falls*
splendour *the splendour of the palace of Versailles*
▷ VERB
3 to enjoy something very much: *The curling team was glorying in its unexpected win.*
gloat *Their rivals were gloating over their triumph.*
relish *He relished the idea of getting some cash.*
revel *Diners revelled in the restaurant's gourmet menu.*
See also **credit, fame, rejoice**

gloss
▷ NOUN
a bright shine on a surface: *paper with a high gloss finish*
brilliance *ceramic tiles of great brilliance*
gleam *the gleam of brass*
polish *His boots had a high polish.*
sheen *The carpet had a silvery sheen to it.*
shine *This gel gives a beautiful shine to the hair.*

glossy
▷ ADJECTIVE
bright and shiny: *glossy paint*
bright *eyes bright with excitement*
brilliant *a brilliant shine to the floors*
lustrous *The chrome had a lustrous sheen.*
polished *a highly polished floor*
shiny *a shiny new sports car*
sleek *sleek black hair*
See also **smooth**

glow
▷ NOUN
1 a dull steady light: *the glow of the fire*
gleam *the first gleam of dawn*
glimmer *In the east, there was the slightest glimmer of light.*
light *the light of the evening sun*
▷ VERB
2 to shine with a dull steady light: *A light glowed behind the curtains.*
gleam *Lights gleamed in the deepening mist.*
glimmer *A few stars still glimmered.*
shine *Scattered lights shone on the horizon.*
smoulder *A very small fire was smouldering in the grate.*

See also **blush, glare, light, shine**

glower *See* **frown, glare**

glowing *See* **bright, brilliant**

glue
▷ VERB
to stick things together: *Glue the two halves together.*
fix *Fix the label on the jar.*
paste *The children were busy pasting gold stars on a chart.*
seal *He sealed the envelope and put on a stamp.*
stick *I stuck the notice on the board.*
See also **bond, stick**

glum *See* **down, gloomy, pessimistic, sad**

glut *See* **excess**

gnaw *See* **bite, chew**

go
▷ VERB
1 to move or travel somewhere: *I went home on the weekend.*
advance *Rebel forces are advancing on the capital.*
drive *We drove to Lethbridge to see our grandparents.*
fly *He flew to St. John's.*
journey FORMAL *They intended to journey up the Amazon.*
leave *What time are you leaving?*
proceed FORMAL *The taxi proceeded along a lonely road.*
set off *He set off for the station.*
travel *Students often travel long distances to get here.*
2 to work properly: *stuck on the highway in a car that won't go*
function *All the instruments functioned properly.*
work *The pump doesn't work and we have no running water.*
▷ NOUN
3 an attempt to do something: *I always wanted to have a go at waterskiing.*
attempt *one of his rare attempts at humour*
shot INFORMAL *a shot at winning a brand-new car*
stab INFORMAL *Several sports stars have had a stab at acting and singing.*
try *After a few tries, she had given up.*
See also **attempt, fit, function, journey, leave, range, travel, try, turn, work out**

go across *See* **cross**

G

Like **bad**, the word **good** is used in so many ways to describe so many things that it has lost a great deal of its effectiveness. A wide range of synonyms is available, so try to vary your language and vocabulary by choosing one of these instead.

• in quality
He had reached an **acceptable** standard of education.
The film has some **awesome** special effects. (slang)
We had an **excellent** meal and **first-class** service.
They played a **first-rate** game and made some **great** saves.
I expect goods of a **satisfactory** quality.
We stayed in a **splendid** hotel with a **superb** view.

• of an experience
Her guests had an **agreeable** evening.
We spent a **delightful** few hours in the garden after a very **enjoyable** lunch.
I had a **lovely** time in Ottawa, which is a **pleasant** city.
The team has had a very **satisfactory** season.

• having a beneficial effect
These changes could be **advantageous** for our business.
Name the **beneficial** effects of exercise.
They were working under **favourable** conditions, and so produced **positive** results.

• morally virtuous
He showed **commendable** character in all his dealings with us.
No **decent** person would have said such a thing.
Here is an institution that prides itself on its **ethical** stance.
She's a hard-working, **honest** citizen.
An **honourable** person would have resigned.
I try to live a **virtuous** life.
We donate money to **worthy** causes.

• kind and thoughtful
He is a kindly and **benevolent** man.
She is too **charitable** to hurt his feelings.
He is a **humane** and caring person.
We gratefully accepted donations from **kind-hearted** colleagues.
She's an **obliging** person who is always glad to help.

It was very **thoughtful** of you to offer.

• skilled at something
My sister is a very **able** student, and an **accomplished** pianist.
Politicians are **adept** at manipulating the press.
She's a very **capable** and **efficient** manager.
This path is dangerous for inexperienced and **expert** cyclists alike.
He's a **proficient** painter and a **skilled** carpenter.
She's one of the country's most **talented** musicians.

• of behaviour
She's a comparatively meek and **docile** child.
We expect **orderly** behaviour from our pupils.
He's a **well-behaved** boy, who was brought up to be **well mannered**.

• of advice
Thank you for your **constructive** and **helpful** suggestions.
I need some **sound, practical** advice.
She gave some **useful** tips for beginners

• of an idea
We need a **sensible** way out of our difficulties.
That's a **wise** plan!

• of a price, sum of money, amount, or quantity
Is there an **ample** supply of food?
He has a **considerable** annual income.
She has been left a **substantial** amount of money.

• of a person's mood
His **buoyant** spirits showed an unfailingly **cheerful** nature.
I'm in a **genial** mood.
You have a naturally **happy** disposition.
Keep an **optimistic** frame of mind.
He was in an unusually **sunny** mood.

go against *See* **clash**

go as far as *See* **reach**

go away *See* **disappear, vanish**

go back *See* **return**

go beyond *See* **pass, top**

go down *See* **decline, descend**

go for *See* **like, prefer**

go into *See* **discuss**

go off *See* **explode**

go on *See* **continue, proceed, remain, stretch, take place**

go on at *See* **hassle**

go over *See* **examine**

go together with *See* **accompany**

go up *See* **rise**

go well *See* **blend**

go with *See* **accompany, match, suit**

go wrong *See* **err**

goad *See* **incite, provoke**

go-ahead *See* **permission**

goal
▷ *NOUN*
something that a person hopes to achieve: *The goal seems to be to make as much money as possible.*
aim *The aim of the concert is to raise awareness of world hunger.*
end *another plan designed to achieve the same end*
intention *She announced her intention to run for class president.*
object *The object of the auction is to raise money for charity.*
objective *Her objective was to play golf and win.*
purpose *Their purpose was to make a profit.*
target *She achieved her target of raising $200 for charity.*
See also **aim, intention, object, point**

gobble
▷ *VERB*
to eat food very quickly: *I gobbled all the beef stew.*
devour *I devoured the chocolate bar in three bites.*
wolf *I wolfed down a sandwich.*

godly *See* **religious**

gone *See* **absent, over**

good
▷ *ADJECTIVE*
1 pleasant, acceptable, or satisfactory: *We had a really good time.*
ANTONYM **bad**
2 skilful or successful: *I'm not very good at waterskiing.*
ANTONYM **incompetent**
3 kind, thoughtful, and loving: *You are so good to me.*
ANTONYM **unkind**
See WORD STUDY **good** *on previous page*
See also **benefit, favourable, kind, respectable, sound**

G

CONFUSABLES

Good is an adjective, and so always describes a noun.
Well is an adverb, and so always describes a verb.
Well can be used as an adjective, but only to mean **in good health**.

---

good afternoon *See* **hello**

good evening *See* **hello**

good-looking *See* **cute, handsome**

good morning *See* **hello**

goodness *See* **honour, virtue**

goods *See* **product, stock**

goodwill
▷ *NOUN*
kindness and helpfulness toward other people: *They invited us to dinner as a gesture of goodwill.*
benevolence *anonymous acts of benevolence*
favour *trying to gain the favour of those in power*
friendliness *Visitors remarked on the friendliness of the people.*
See also **friendship**

gorge *See* **abyss, fill**

gorgeous *See* **beautiful, cute, splendid**

gossip
▷ *NOUN*
informal conversation about other people: *Gossip doesn't interest me.*
dirt *the latest dirt on the other candidates*
hearsay *The evidence was hearsay that could not be verified.*
See also **chat, rumour**

go through

▷ VERB

to experience an unpleasant event: *I was going through a very difficult time.*
endure *He'd endured years of pain and sleepless nights.*
experience *He was experiencing nightmares.*
undergo *My grandmother underwent emergency surgery.*
See also **endure, examine, suffer, undergo**

gouge See **dig**

govern See **control, determine, guide, lead, rule**

government See **control**

governor See **chief, ruler**

gown See **dress**

grab

▷ VERB

to take hold of something roughly: *I grabbed him by the arm.*
clutch *He clutched the money tightly.*
grasp *He grasped both my hands.*
seize *The child seized the cards from my hand.*
snatch *The dog snatched the sandwich off the counter.*
See also **grasp, seize**

grace

▷ NOUN

an elegant way of moving: *the grace of a ballet dancer*
elegance *a person of style and elegance*
poise *Ballet classes are important for poise and grace.*
ANTONYM **clumsiness**
See also **courtesy, favour, polish**

graciousness See **courtesy**

grade

▷ VERB

to arrange things according to quality: *Eggs are graded according to quality.*
class *That brand of coffee was classed as superior.*
classify *Rocks can be classified according to their origin.*
group *The fact sheets are grouped into seven sections.*
rate *He was rated as one of the country's top young players.*
sort *In the game of bridge, the cards are sorted by suit.*
See also **class, classify, kind, level, quality, rank, sort**

gradient See **slope, tilt**

gradual

▷ ADJECTIVE

happening or changing slowly: *the gradual improvement in communications*
continuous *a policy of continuous improvement*
progressive *One symptom of the disease is the progressive loss of memory.*
slow *The distribution of prizes has been a slow process.*
steady *a steady rise in sales*
ANTONYM **sudden**
See also **slow**

gradually See **slowly**

graduate See **pass, qualify**

grain See **bit, finish**

grand

▷ ADJECTIVE

1 very impressive in size or appearance: *a grand building in the centre of town*
imposing *the imposing gates at the entrance to the museum*
impressive *The old boat presented an impressive sight.*
magnificent *magnificent views of the Okanagan Valley*
majestic *a stupendous vista of majestic peaks*
monumental *a monumental work of art*
splendid *a splendid vista of the autumn scenery*
2 INFORMAL pleasant or enjoyable: *It was a grand day.*
great INFORMAL *They had a great time at camp.*
marvellous *It was a marvellous day and we were all so happy.*
terrific *Everybody there was having a terrific time.*
wonderful *It was a wonderful experience.*
See also **impressive, splendid**

grandeur See **glory**

grandiose See **ostentatious, pompous**

grant

▷ NOUN

1 a money award given for a particular purpose: *My application for a grant has been accepted.*
allocation *The allocation of funds is under review.*
award *a graduate student research award*
bursary *The skater received a small bursary.*

subsidy *government subsidies for public transportation*
▷ VERB
2 to allow someone to have something: *France has agreed to grant him political asylum.*
allocate *The budget allocated another billion dollars for the program.*
allow *Children should be allowed the occasional treat.*
award *The court awarded them a million dollars in damages.*
give *We have been given permission to attend the meeting.*
permit *We were permitted entry to the movie set.*
ANTONYM **deny**
▷ VERB
3 to admit that something is true: *I grant that you had some justification for your actions.*
accept *I do not accept that there is a crisis in the medical system.*
acknowledge *He acknowledged that he had been partly to blame.*
admit *I admit that I do make mistakes.*
allow *I allow that your point of view makes sense.*
concede *I finally conceded that she was right.*
ANTONYM **deny**
See also **admit, allow, give, permit, present**

graphic *See* **colourful**

grapple *See* **fight**

grasp
▷ VERB
1 to hold something firmly: *He grasped both my hands.*
clutch *I staggered and had to clutch at a chair for support.*
grab *I grabbed him by the arm.*
grip *She gripped the rope.*
hold *He held the cup tightly in his hand.*
seize *He seized my arm to hold me back.*
snatch *I snatched at a hanging branch and pulled myself up.*
2 to understand an idea: *Has anybody grasped the seriousness of the problem?*
absorb *He absorbed only about half the information we gave him.*
appreciate *She doesn't really appreciate the seriousness of the situation.*
assimilate *My mind could assimilate only one concept at a time.*
realize *People don't realize how serious this drought has been.*
take in *He listens to the explanation, but*

you can see he's not taking it in.
understand *They are too young to understand what is going on.*
▷ NOUN
3 a firm hold: *She slipped her hand from my grasp.*
clasp *He gripped my hand in a strong clasp.*
embrace *a tight embrace*
grip *She relaxed her grip.*
hold *He released his hold on the camera.*
▷ NOUN
4 a person's understanding of something: *They have a good grasp of languages.*
awareness *The children demonstrated their awareness of environmental issues.*
comprehension *This was utterly beyond my comprehension.*
grip *He has lost his grip on reality.*
knowledge *She has a good knowledge of these processes.*
understanding *a basic understanding of the problem*
See also **command, comprehend, grab, grip, handle, hold, learn, master, realize, see, seize, take in, understand, understanding**

grate *See* **scrape**

grateful
▷ ADJECTIVE
pleased and wanting to thank someone: *I am grateful to you for your help.*
appreciative *We have been very appreciative of their support.*
indebted *I am deeply indebted to them for their help.*
thankful *I'm just thankful that I have a job.*
ANTONYM **ungrateful**

gratified *See* **proud**

gratify *See* **satisfy**

gratis *See* **free**

gratitude
▷ NOUN
the feeling of being grateful: *We wish to express our gratitude to the coach.*
appreciation *their appreciation of his efforts*
recognition *an honour given in recognition of their help to the school*
thanks *They accepted their certificates with words of thanks.*
ANTONYM **ingratitude**

grave
▷ NOUN
1 a place where a corpse is buried: *They visited the grave twice a year.*

G

mausoleum *the great mausoleum at the top of the hill*
pit *The bodies were buried in a shallow pit.*
tomb *the tomb of the Unknown Soldier*
▷ ADJECTIVE
2 FORMAL very serious: *The situation in his country is very grave.*
acute *The report has caused acute embarrassment to the government.*
critical *The company's finances are in a critical state.*
serious *serious difficulties*
sober *a room filled with sad, sober faces*
solemn *His solemn face broke into smiles.*
sombre *Her expression became increasingly sombre.*
See also **acute, critical, deep, grim, heavy, serious, severe, solemn, tomb**

graze
▷ VERB
1 to injure your skin slightly: *He fell and grazed his left arm.*
scrape *She stumbled and fell, scraping her palms and knees.*
scratch *The branches scratched my hands and face.*
skin *He fell and skinned both his knees.*
▷ NOUN
2 a slight injury to your skin: *He has just a slight graze on his elbow.*
abrasion FORMAL *severe abrasions to the right cheek*
scratch *scratches on my face*
See also **scrape, touch**

great
▷ ADJECTIVE
1 very large in size: *great columns of ice*
ANTONYM **small**
2 important or famous: *great teams of the NHL*
3 INFORMAL very good: *I thought it was a great idea.*
ANTONYM **terrible**
See WORD STUDY **great** on next page
See also **acute, brilliant, deep, excellent, extensive, extreme, grand, intense, large, outstanding, splendid, uncommon, vast, wonderful**

great deal See **plenty**

greatest See **foremost, supreme, ultimate**

greatly See **very**

greedy
▷ ADJECTIVE
wanting more than you need: *greedy people*

who take more than their fair share
materialistic *a very materialistic society*

SHADES OF ... *GREEN*	
avocado	olive
chartreuse	pea green
emerald	pistachio
jade	sage
khaki	sea green
lime	turquoise

greet
▷ VERB
to say hello to someone when they arrive: *The champions were greeted by their fans.*
meet *A nurse met me at the entrance.*
receive FORMAL *About 250 guests were received by the bride and groom.*
welcome *They were there to welcome us home.*
See also **receive**

gregarious See **sociable**

grey See also **dim, drab**

SHADES OF ... *GREY*	
ash	platinum
charcoal	silver
gunmetal	silvery
hoary	slate
leaden	stone
pewter	taupe

grief
▷ NOUN
a feeling of extreme sadness: *a huge outpouring of national grief*
distress *the intense distress they were causing my family*
heartache *She has suffered more heartache than anyone deserves.*
misery *All that money brought nothing but misery.*
sadness *It is with a mixture of sadness and joy that I say farewell.*
sorrow *a time of great sorrow*
unhappiness *There was a lot of unhappiness in their family.*
ANTONYM **happiness**
See also **misery, pain, regret, sorrow**

grief-stricken See **sad**

grievance See **complaint, wrong**

grieve
▷ VERB
1 to feel extremely sad: *He still grieves for his wife.*
lament *All who knew him will lament his death.*

There are a number of ways in which the word **great** can be used, depending on what you are referring to. Why not make your language more interesting and use one of the following instead?

• in size
He lives in a **big** house.
At the back of the building there was a **colossal** statue.
They erected a **huge** marquee in the park.
She stacked up a **large** pile of logs.
They entered an **enormous** hall.
The library has an **extensive** range of books.
They're building a **gigantic** theme park over there.
His office is in an **immense** building.
She'll need to spend a **stupendous** amount of money on that car.
It's a **tremendous** challenge.
The fire destroyed a **vast** area of forest.

• in degree
That job has a **high** degree of risk.
I don't believe these **extravagant** claims.
This film contains **extreme** violence.
The elephant had **tremendous** strength.

• in importance
This is one of our **chief** problems.
I have to ask you an **important** question.
Who's their **main** competitor?
That will be a **major** issue in the next election.
What a **momentous** occasion!
Make this your **principal** aim.
There's a **serious** deficiency in the system.
This is a **significant** step toward peace.

• in fame
JRR Tolkien is the **celebrated** author of *Lord of the Rings*.
My uncle is a **distinguished** architect.
The lab was run by two **eminent** scientists.
The **famed** actor was gracious to his fans.

Some of the world's most **illustrious** ballerinas have danced this role.
He is a good but not **notable** chess player.
Canada's most **prominent** and **renowned** heart surgeon will operate on her.

• in skill
I had an **excellent** math teacher.
These slopes are suitable for **expert** skiers only.
We watched an **outstanding** display of teamwork.
I'm not the most **skilful** hockey player in the world.
She's a **skilled** chef.
He proved himself a **superb** goalie.
She's a **superlative** thriller writer.
The company is run by a **talented** management team.

• in quality
He enjoys **good** food.
This is an **excellent** pasta sauce.
The room was full of **superb** works of art.
We saw a **fantastic** firework display. (informal)
They pride themselves on their **first-rate** service.
Over there is a **marvellous** restaurant. (informal)
The local art gallery displays some **outstanding** works of art.
Leading upstairs was a **superb** staircase made from oak.
It was a **terrific** party. (informal)
You've done a **tremendous** job. (informal)
I've had a **wonderful** time.

G

---

mourn *The whole nation mourns the death of their great leader.*
2 to make someone feel extremely sad: *It grieved us to be separated from our loved ones.*
distress *It distresses me that there is so much poverty in the world.*
pain *It pains me to think of you struggling all alone.*
sadden *The cruelty in the world saddens me.*

upset *The news upset me.*
ANTONYM **cheer**
See also **distress, lament, regret, upset**

grievous *See* **painful, serious**

grill *See* **cook, interrogate**

grim
▷ ADJECTIVE
looking very serious: *Her face was grim.*
grave *He was looking very grave, and he was expecting the worst.*

severe *He leaned toward me, a severe expression on his face.*

solemn *What a solemn-faced kid he had been.*

stern *She gave the dog a stern look.*

See also **horrible, serious, severe**

grime *See* dirt

grimy *See* dirty

grin *See* smile

grind *See* scrape

grip

▷ *NOUN*

1 a firm hold on something: *He tightened his grip on the wallet.*

clasp *They clasped hands and then said goodbye.*

grasp *The rock slipped from her grasp and fell to the ground.*

hold *He released his hold on the camera.*

2 someone's control over something: *The dictator maintains an iron grip on his country.*

clutches *to fall into the clutches of the wrong sort of person*

control *The port area is under the control of rebel forces.*

influence *He fell under the influence of a mysterious leader.*

power *The colonies were under the power of the king.*

▷ *VERB*

3 to hold something firmly: *I gripped the steering wheel and stared straight ahead.*

clutch *He clutched my arm.*

grasp *She grasped both my hands.*

hold *He was struggling to hold on to the rope.*

See also **clasp, grasp, handle, hold**

gripping *See* interesting

groan *See* grumble, moan

gross *See* disgusting

ground

▷ *NOUN*

the surface of the earth: *We slid down the roof and dropped to the ground.*

dirt *They sat on the dirt in the shade of a tree.*

earth *The road winds through parched earth.*

land *hundreds of hectares of agricultural land*

soil *fertile soil*

terrain *Farms give way to hilly terrain.*

See also **base, bottom, earth, soil**

INFORMALLY SPEAKING

break new ground: do something original

get off the ground: make a successful start

lose ground: give up what has been gained

stand your ground: refuse to give in or retreat

---

grounds

▷ *PLURAL NOUN*

1 the land surrounding a building: *the grounds of the university*

estate *the millionaire's estate overlooking the whole valley*

land *They built a cottage on the land they had purchased.*

2 the reason for doing or thinking something: *I'm against it on the grounds of expense.*

basis *Could you tell me on what basis the fee is calculated?*

cause *No one had cause to become angry or unpleasant.*

excuse *There's no excuse for behaviour like that.*

justification *There was no justification for what I was doing.*

reason *Who would have a reason to do that?*

See also **argument, cause, land, reason**

group

▷ *NOUN*

1 a number of people or things: *a group of football fans*

band *a band of rebels*

bunch *They're a nice bunch of people.*

collection *a collection of short stories by Canadian authors*

crowd *A small crowd of onlookers has gathered.*

gang *The old gang gets together every week.*

pack *a pack of journalists eager to question him*

party *a party of sightseers*

set *a set of dishes*

▷ *VERB*

2 to link people or things together: *Their responses are grouped into 11 categories.*

arrange *He started to arrange the books in piles.*

class *They are officially classed as an endangered species.*

classify *Rocks can be classified according to their origin.*

organize *I was organizing my DVDs.*

sort *My CDs are sorted by type of music.*

See also **arrange, association, band, bunch, category, class, club, collection, company, grade, lot, mass, movement, organization, society, sort, team, type**

grouping *See* **party**

grouse *See* **complain**

grow
▷ *VERB*
1 to increase in size or amount: *Bacteria grow more quickly once food is contaminated.*
develop *Fortunately, it did not develop into an epidemic.*
expand *Will the universe continue to expand forever?*
increase *Sales increased by 20 percent.*
multiply *Demands on the workers seemed to multiply.*
ANTONYM **shrink**
2 to be alive or exist: *Trees and bushes grew down to the water's edge.*
flourish *The plant flourishes in slightly milder climates.*
germinate *Heat will encourage seeds to germinate.*
sprout *It takes only a few days for beans to sprout.*
3 to change gradually: *The puppy grew more comfortable with us.*
become *The wind became stronger.*
get *The boys were getting bored.*
turn *In October it turned cold.*
See also **develop, expand, get, increase, rise, spread**

grow up *See* **mature**

grown *See* **mature**

grown-up *See* **adult, mature**

growth
▷ *NOUN*
the act of getting bigger: *the growth of the sport-fishing industry*
development *What are your plans for the development of your company?*
enlargement *the enlargement of the Canadian Forces*
expansion *a period of economic expansion*
increase *an increase in the number of homeless people*
See also **gain, increase, spread**

grub *See* **food**

grubby *See* **dirty**

grudge *See* **resentment**

grudging *See* **unwilling**

gruesome *See* **horrible**

gruff *See* **hoarse**

grumble
▷ *VERB*
1 to complain in a bad-tempered way: *"This is very inconvenient," he grumbled.*
carp *The actors had plenty to carp about.*
complain *They complained about the lack of sporting facilities.*
groan *parents groaning about the cost of tuition*
moan *moaning about the weather*
mutter *He muttered about the traffic as he tried to cross the street.*
whine *children who whine that they are bored*
▷ *NOUN*
2 a bad-tempered complaint: *I didn't hear any grumbles from anyone at the time.*
complaint *I get nothing but complaints about my cooking.*
murmur *She paid without a murmur.*
objection *If you have any objections, please raise them now.*
protest *Despite our protests, they went ahead with the plan.*
See also **complain, complaint, moan**

grumpy
▷ *ADJECTIVE*
bad-tempered and annoyed: *a grumpy old dog*
irritable *He had missed his dinner and grew irritable.*
sulky *His sulky expression can be annoying.*
sullen *Several unhappy workers have maintained a sullen silence.*
surly *They were surly, and sometimes downright rude to me.*
See also **cross**

grunt *See* **moan**

guarantee
▷ *NOUN*
1 something that makes another thing certain: *a guarantee of job security*
assurance *a written assurance that he would start work at once*
pledge *a pledge of support for our club*
promise *a promise that I would attend her party*
undertaking *She gave an undertaking not to repeat the allegations.*
word *He simply cannot be trusted to keep his word.*
▷ *VERB*
2 to make it certain that something will

G

happen: *Remarks of this kind are guaranteed to cause anxiety.*

ensure *We need to ensure that every student has basic literacy skills.*

pledge *Both sides pledged that a nuclear war would never be fought.*

promise *He promised that everyone would receive equal treatment.*

See also **ensure, promise**

guaranteed See **certain, definite**

guard

▷ VERB

1 to protect someone: *Police were guarding his home yesterday.*

defend *He and his friends defended themselves against the attackers.*

protect *What can people do to protect themselves from heart disease?*

safeguard *measures to safeguard our human rights*

shelter *A neighbour sheltered them for seven days.*

shield *Shield them from the truth.*

watch over *The faithful dog watched over him.*

2 to stop someone making trouble or escaping: *Soldiers were guarding the prisoners.*

patrol *Prison officers continued to patrol the grounds.*

police *It is difficult to police the border.*

supervise *Only two staff members were supervising 100 prisoners.*

▷ NOUN

3 someone who guards people or places: *The prisoners overpowered their guards and locked them in a cell.*

sentry *We can sneak past the sentries.*

warden *The warden worked to reform the prison system.*

See also **defend, protect, safeguard, watch**

guard against See **beware**

guarded See **cautious, wary**

guardian See **champion**

guess

▷ VERB

1 to form an idea or opinion about something: *I guessed that he was in the movie business.*

estimate *It's difficult to estimate how much money is involved.*

imagine *"Was he meeting someone?" "I imagine so."*

reckon *I reckon that it must be about three o'clock.*

speculate *The reader can speculate what will happen next.*

suppose *I suppose you'd like breakfast.*

suspect *I suspect they were right.*

think *I thought he was at least 17 years old.*

▷ NOUN

2 an attempt to give the right answer: *My guess is that the answer will be no.*

feeling *My feeling is that everything will turn out right for us.*

reckoning *By my reckoning, 50 percent of the team will be available.*

speculation *speculation about the future of the universe*

See also **assume, estimate, figure, idea, imagine, suppose, suspect**

guffaw See **laugh**

guidance See **advice, direction, help**

guide

▷ VERB

1 to lead someone somewhere: *He took the child by the arm and guided him to safety.*

accompany *We accompanied her to the studio downtown.*

direct *Officials directed him to the wrong airport.*

escort *I escorted him to the door.*

lead *The nurse led me to a large room.*

2 to influence someone: *He should have let his instinct guide him.*

counsel FORMAL *She was counselled not to talk to reporters.*

govern *Our thinking is as much governed by habit as by behaviour.*

influence *My teacher influenced me to become a social worker.*

See also **direct, ease, influence, lead, manoeuvre, take**

guideline See **rule, standard**

guild See **club, society**

guile See **cunning, fraud**

guileless See **innocent**

guilt See **blame, responsibility**

guilty

▷ ADJECTIVE

1 having done something wrong: *They were found guilty of the crime.*

convicted *a convicted fraud artist*

criminal *She had a criminal record for petty theft.*

ANTONYM **innocent**

2 unhappy because you have done something bad: *When she saw me, she looked guilty.*

ashamed *He said he was not ashamed of*

what he had done.
regretful *Surprisingly, she didn't feel regretful about her actions.*
remorseful FORMAL *He felt remorseful for what he had done.*
sorry *They were very sorry about all the trouble they'd caused.*
See also **ashamed, responsible**

gulf *See* **bay**

gullibility *See* **innocence**

gullible
▷ *ADJECTIVE*
easily tricked: *I'm so gullible I would have believed him.*
naive *It would be naive to believe their report.*
trusting *He has an open, trusting nature.*
ANTONYM **suspicious**
See also **impressionable**

gulp *See* **drink, gasp**

guru *See* **adviser, expert, teacher**

gush
▷ *VERB*
to flow in large quantities: *Water gushed out of the broken pipe.*
flow *Tears flowed down his cheeks.*
pour *Blood was pouring from the player's nose.*
spurt *a fountain that spurts water high into the air*
stream *water streaming over the rocks*
See also **pour, rave, rush**

gutless *See* **cowardly**

guts *See* **courage, daring, insides**

guy *See* **man**

guzzle *See* **drink**

G

Hh

habit

▷ NOUN

1 something that is done regularly: *his habit of smiling at everyone he sees*
convention *It's a social convention to make toasts at weddings.*
custom *an ancient Japanese custom*
practice *the practice of getting to school early*
routine *my daily routine*
tradition *a family tradition at birthdays*
2 an addiction to something: *a drug habit*
addiction *his addiction to gambling*
dependence *the effects of alcohol dependence*
See also **custom, practice**

habitat

▷ NOUN

the natural home of a plant or animal: *the habitat of the spotted owl*
environment *a safe environment for marine mammals*
home *A lion's natural home is the African plains.*
territory *a bird's territory*

habitual See **frequent, normal, regular, usual**

hack See **chop**

hackneyed

▷ ADJECTIVE

used too often to be meaningful: *hackneyed phrases like "tried and true"*
banal *banal lyrics*
clichéd *clichéd slogans*
stale *Their relationship has become stale.*
tired *a tired excuse*
trite *The movie is full of trite ideas.*
ANTONYM **original**
See also **corny, stock**

hail

▷ NOUN

1 a lot of things falling together: *a hail of bullets*
barrage *a barrage of angry questions*
bombardment *the sound of heavy aerial bombardment*
shower *a shower of rose petals*
storm *The announcement provoked a storm of protest.*
volley *A volley of shots rang out.*
▷ VERB

2 to attract someone's attention: *He hailed me from across the street.*
call *He called for the dog to come back.*

flag down *I ran onto the road and flagged down a taxi.*
signal to *The crossing guard signalled to me to stop.*

hair See **coat, pile**

hair-raising See **frightening, scary**

halfway See **middle**

halfway point See **middle**

hall See **passage**

hallmark See **property**

hallow See **bless**

hallowed See **holy**

hallucination See **dream, illusion, vision**

halt

▷ VERB

1 to come or bring to a stop: *She held her hand out to halt him.*
draw up *The car drew up outside the house.*
pull up *The cab pulled up, and the driver jumped out.*
stop *The event literally stopped the traffic.*
2 to bring something to an end: *Production was halted on the movie.*
cease *A small number of companies have ceased operating.*
check *We have managed to check the spread of the disease.*
curb *efforts to curb the spread of nuclear weapons*
cut short *They had to cut short their trip.*
end *They decided to end the meeting.*
terminate *His contract has been terminated.*
ANTONYM **begin**
▷ NOUN

3 an interruption or end to something: *He brought the car to a halt.*
close *Their meeting finally came to a close.*
end *The war came to an end.*
pause *There was a pause before he replied.*
standstill *The players' strike brought the season to a standstill.*
stop *He slowed the car almost to a stop.*
stoppage *Air and ground crews are staging a 24-hour work stoppage today.*
See also **block, check, pause, stop**

hammer See **bang, drive**

hamper

▷ VERB

to make movement or progress difficult: *I was hampered by a lack of information.*

frustrate *His attempt was frustrated by the weather.*
hinder *A thigh injury hindered her mobility.*
impede *Their work was being impeded by shortages of supplies.*
obstruct *charged with obstructing justice*
restrict *Her diet is restricted because of allergies.*
See also **handicap, hinder, impede, restrain, restrict**

hand *See* **employee, give**

hand down
▷ *VERB*
to pass from one generation to another: *stories handed down from parents to children*
bequeath *He bequeathed all his silver to his children.*
give *a watch given to me by my grandfather*
pass down *an heirloom passed down from generation to generation*
pass on *My parents passed on their love of classical music to me.*

handicap
▷ *NOUN*
1 something that makes progress difficult: *Being short was a slight handicap for the basketball player.*
barrier *Taxes are the most obvious barrier to free trade.*
disadvantage *the disadvantage of unemployment*
drawback *The apartment's only drawback was that it was too small.*
hindrance *She was a help rather than a hindrance to my work.*
impediment *an impediment to economic development*
obstacle *the main obstacle to the deal*
▷ *VERB*
2 to make something difficult for someone: *Greater levels of stress may handicap some students.*
burden *We decided not to burden him with the news.*
hamper *I was hampered by a lack of information.*
hinder *A thigh injury hindered her mobility.*
impede *Fallen rocks impeded the progress of the rescue workers.*
restrict *laws to restrict imports from Canada*
See also **barrier, disadvantage, restrict**

hand in *See* **submit, tender**

handle
▷ *NOUN*
1 the part of an object by which it is held: *a broom handle*

grip *He fitted a new grip on the golf club.*
hilt *the hilt of a sword*
knob *the knob on the door*
▷ *VERB*
2 to hold or move with the hands: *Wear protective gloves when handling chemicals.*
feel *The doctor felt his arm.*
finger *He fingered the few coins in his pocket.*
grasp *Grasp the end firmly.*
hold *Hold it by the edge.*
touch *She touched his hand reassuringly.*
▷ *VERB*
3 to control or deal with something: *She handled the travel arrangements.*
administer *The project is administered by the school committee.*
conduct *This is no way to conduct a business.*
deal with *The matter has been dealt with by the school.*
manage *Within two years, he was managing the store.*
supervise *I supervise the packing of all mail orders.*
take care of *He took care of the catering arrangements.*
See also **deal, process, take care of, touch**

hand out *See* **distribute, present**

handout *See* **grant**

hand-pick *See* **pick**

hand-picked *See* **select**

handsome
▷ *ADJECTIVE*
1 very attractive in appearance: *a handsome man*
attractive *an attractive young woman*
good-looking *good-looking actors*
ANTONYM **ugly**
2 large and generous: *a handsome profit*
ample *ample space for a good-sized kitchen*
considerable *his considerable wealth*
generous *a generous gift*
liberal *a liberal donation*
plentiful *a plentiful supply of vegetables*
sizable *They inherited a sizable fortune.*
ANTONYM **small**
See also **attractive**

handy
▷ *ADJECTIVE*
1 conveniently near: *Keep a pencil and paper handy.*
at hand *Having the right equipment at hand*

H

will be extremely useful.

at your fingertips *Thanks to the search engine, the answers are at my fingertips.*
close *a secluded area close to her home*
convenient *a convenient corner store*
nearby *He tossed the empty bag into a nearby garbage can.*
on hand *Experts are on hand to offer advice.*
2 easy to handle or use: *handy hints on looking after indoor plants*
convenient *a convenient way of paying*
easy to use *This DVD player is easy to use.*
helpful *helpful instructions*
neat *It had been such a neat, clever plan.*
practical *the most practical way of preventing crime*
useful *useful information*
See also **available, convenient, ready**

hang

▷ VERB

1 to be attached at the top with the lower part free: *His jacket hung from a hook behind the door.*
dangle *A gold bracelet dangled from his left wrist.*
droop *Wilting roses drooped from a vase.*
sag *The skin sagged on the old dog.*
2 to fasten something to another thing by its top: *to hang clothes on a line*
attach *He attached the picture to the wall with a nail.*
drape *The actor draped his cloak around his shoulders.*
fasten *stirrups fastened to the saddle*
fix *He fixed a pirate flag to the mast.*
suspend *The light fixture is suspended from the ceiling.*
See also **extend, float, stretch**

INFORMALLY SPEAKING

get the hang of: learn how to do or to operate
hang around: loiter aimlessly
hang back: be unwilling to go forward
hang in (there): be persistent
hang out: spend time with someone or in some place
hang together: be consistent

hang around *See* **stay**

hang out *See* **associate**

hanker after *See* **fancy**

hankering *See* **desire, longing, wish**

haphazard *See* **irregular, random**

haphazardly *See* **at random**

hapless *See* **unlucky**

happen

▷ VERB

to take place: *The accident happened on Wednesday.*
come about *It came about almost by accident.*
follow *A celebration followed the final performance.*
occur *The crash occurred on a sharp bend.*
result *Ignore the early warnings and illness could result.*
take place *The festival took place last June.*
See also **come, occur, result, take place, work out**

happening *See* **incident**

happiness

▷ NOUN

a feeling of great pleasure: *Money can't buy happiness.*
contentment *a feeling of contentment following the big dinner*
delight *To my delight, it worked perfectly.*
ecstasy *She was in ecstasy when she heard the great news.*
elation *His supporters reacted to the news with elation.*
joy *tears of joy*
pleasure *Everybody takes pleasure in eating.*
satisfaction *job satisfaction*
ANTONYM **sadness**
See also **delight, pleasure**

happy

▷ ADJECTIVE

1 feeling or causing joy: *a happy atmosphere*
ANTONYM **sad**
2 fortunate or lucky: *a happy coincidence*
ANTONYM **unlucky**
See WORD STUDY **happy**
See also **agreeable, bright, cheerful, cheery, comfortable, glad, pleased, ready, satisfied, willing**

harass *See* **hassle**

harbour *See* **bear, refuge, shelter**

hard

▷ ADJECTIVE

1 firm, solid, or rigid: *a hard piece of cheese*
firm *a firm mattress*
rigid *rigid plastic containers*
solid *solid rock*
stiff *stiff metal wires*
strong *It has a strong casing, which won't crack or chip.*
tough *an apple with a rather tough skin*
ANTONYM **soft**
2 requiring a lot of effort: *hard work*

WORD STUDY: HAPPY

Happy is an overused word. You can vary your language by choosing one of the alternatives shown here.

• **displaying a cheerful nature or mood**
I have a **cheerful** disposition
The character is portrayed as a **jolly**, fat person.
He broke into a **merry** laugh.
I love her for her unfailingly **sunny** nature.

• **feeling joy at something**
They seem **delighted** with their new home.
I was **ecstatic** to see my friends again.
She was **elated** that she had won the prize.
He is understandably **euphoric** over his success.
We're **glad** to be back.
He takes a **joyful** pride in his work.
She was **jubilant** over her election victory.
They were **overjoyed** to be reunited at last.
We're very **pleased** with the verdict.
I'm just **thrilled** to be playing again.

• **causing joy**
I had the **agreeable** task of telling him the good news.
They celebrated twenty years of **blissful** marriage.

It was a truly **festive** occasion.
We enjoyed a **gratifying** relationship.
A wedding is meant to be a **joyful** event.
We heard the **joyous** news that he had been found safe.
I don't have a single **pleasurable** memory of that place.

• **willing to do something**
She was **content** just to sit and watch.
I'm always **glad** to be of service.
I'll be **pleased** to take you there myself.
I'd be **prepared** to talk to him if you like.
He's **ready** to help anyone in trouble.
I'm **willing** to wait for you.

• **lucky**
It was not an **auspicious** start to his new job.
That is a **convenient** outcome for all concerned.
Will there be a **favourable** result?
We're in a very **fortunate** situation.
It was a **lucky** chance that you were here.
It was hardly an **opportune** moment to bring the subject up.
I appreciated his **timely** arrival.

---

arduous *a long, arduous journey*
exhausting *It's a pretty exhausting job.*
laborious *Weeding the garden can be a laborious task.*
rigorous *rigorous military training*
strenuous *Avoid strenuous exercise in the evening.*
tough *Change is often tough to deal with.*
ANTONYM **easy**
3 difficult to understand: *That's a very hard question.*
baffling *a baffling remark*
complex *a complex problem*
complicated *a complicated system of voting*
difficult *It was a very difficult decision to make.*
puzzling *The plot of this book is rather puzzling.*
ANTONYM **simple**
See also **difficult, firm, harsh, rigid, rough, severe, solid, stiff, tough, tricky**

hard up *See* poor

harden
▷ VERB
to make or become stiff or firm: *The cement finally hardened.*
bake *The soil had been baked solid by the heat wave.*
cake *The blood had begun to cake and turn brown.*
freeze *The lake freezes in winter.*
set *Lower the heat and allow the omelette to set.*
stiffen *paper that had been stiffened with paste*
ANTONYM **soften**
See also **strengthen**

hardened *See* tough

hardly
▷ ADVERB
not quite: *I could hardly believe what I was seeing.*
barely *His voice was barely audible.*
just *Her hand was just visible under her coat.*
only just *For many years, farmers there have only just managed to survive.*
scarcely *He could scarcely breathe.*
See also **barely**

hardship

▷ NOUN

difficult circumstances: *Many people are suffering economic hardship.*

adversity *They manage to enjoy life despite adversity.*

destitution *a life of poverty and destitution*

difficulty *Many social services are in serious financial difficulty.*

misfortune *She seemed to enjoy the misfortunes of others.*

want *They were fighting for freedom of speech and freedom from want.*

See also **difficulty, ordeal, poverty, sorrow**

hard-wearing *See* **tough**

hard-working *See* **active, industrious**

hardy *See* **sturdy, tough**

hark *See* **listen**

harm

▷ VERB

1 to injure someone or damage something: *The robbers seemed anxious not to harm anyone.*

abuse *Animals are still being exploited and abused.*

damage *He damaged his knee during training.*

hurt *He fell and hurt his back.*

ill-treat *We thought they had been ill-treating their cat.*

ruin *Don't ruin your health by worrying so much.*

wound *He was wounded in battle.*

▷ NOUN

2 injury or damage: *Even friendly bears are capable of doing harm to human beings.*

abuse *The abuse of animals is inexcusable.*

damage *The bomb caused extensive damage.*

hurt *His cruel words caused considerable hurt.*

injury *The two other passengers escaped serious injury.*

See also **abuse, damage, hurt, injure, injury, spoil**

harmful

▷ ADJECTIVE

having a bad effect on something: *Most stress is harmful, but some is beneficial.*

damaging *damaging rumours about his personal life*

destructive *the awesome destructive power of nuclear weapons*

detrimental *levels of radioactivity that are detrimental to public health*

hurtful *Her comments can only be hurtful to the family.*

ANTONYM **harmless**

See also **unhealthy**

harmless

▷ ADJECTIVE

safe to use or be near: *This experiment was harmless to the animals.*

innocuous *Both mushrooms look innocuous but are in fact deadly.*

nontoxic *a cheap and nontoxic method of cleaning up our water*

not dangerous *The tests are not dangerous to the environment.*

safe *The toy is safe for children.*

ANTONYM **harmful**

See also **safe**

harmonious *See* **compatible, sweet**

harmonize *See* **blend**

harmony *See* **order**

harrowing *See* **sad**

harsh

▷ ADJECTIVE

severe, difficult, and unpleasant: *harsh weather conditions*

austere *The explorers faced austere conditions.*

cruel *an unusually cruel winter*

hard *He had a hard life.*

ruthless *the ruthless treatment of traitors*

severe *My boss gave me a severe reprimand.*

stern *a stern warning*

ANTONYM **mild**

See also **drastic, severe**

harshness *See* **violence**

harvest *See* **pick**

hassle

▷ NOUN

1 INFORMAL something that is difficult or causes trouble: *It's not worth the hassle.*

bother *It's no bother if you join us for dinner.*

effort *This additional practice session is well worth the effort.*

inconvenience *the expense and inconvenience of installing a new hard drive*

trouble *You've caused us a lot of trouble.*

upheaval *Moving can cause a big upheaval in your life.*

▷ VERB

2 INFORMAL to annoy someone by nagging or making demands: *The picky customer hassled the server.*

badger *They kept badgering me to go back.*

bother *Go away and don't bother me.*
harass *The guard harassed some of the prisoners.*
nag *I know it's a bad habit, but stop nagging me about it.*
pester *I won't lend you my bike, so stop pestering me.*
See also **annoy, difficulty, nuisance, stress, trouble, worry**

haste *See* **speed**

hasten *See* **hurry, rush**

hastily *See* **fast, quickly**

hasty
▷ *ADJECTIVE*
done or happening suddenly and quickly: *The signs of their hasty departure could be seen everywhere.*
brisk *a brisk walk*
hurried *a hurried breakfast*
prompt *It is not too late, but prompt action is needed.*
rapid *a rapid retreat*
swift *my swift departure*
See also **quick, rash, sudden**

hatch *See* **plot**

hate
▷ *VERB*
1 to have a strong dislike for something or someone: *Most people hate him, but they don't care to say so.*
abhor *He abhorred violence.*
be sick of *We're sick of being ripped off.*
despise *I despise any kind of cruelty.*
detest *She detested being photographed.*
dislike *those who dislike change*
loathe *a play universally loathed by the critics*
ANTONYM **love**
▷ *NOUN*
2 a strong dislike: *a violent bully, destructive and full of hate*
animosity *The animosity between the two men grew.*
aversion *I've always had an aversion to being part of a group.*
dislike *Think about what your food likes and dislikes are.*
hatred *her hatred of authority*
hostility *He looked at them with open hostility.*
loathing *Critics are united in their loathing of the band.*
ANTONYM **love**
See also **dislike, hatred**

hateful
▷ *ADJECTIVE*
extremely unpleasant: *It was a hateful thing*

to say to me.
abhorrent *Discrimination is abhorrent to our entire staff.*
despicable *a despicable crime*
horrible *a horrible little child*
loathsome *the loathsome spectacle we were obliged to witness*
obnoxious *Your obnoxious behaviour gets on everyone's nerves.*
offensive *an offensive remark*

hatred
▷ *NOUN*
an extremely strong feeling of dislike: *He has been accused of inciting racial hatred.*
animosity *The animosity between the two men grew.*
antipathy *a surprising antipathy toward spiders*
aversion *my aversion to housework*
dislike *his dislike of modern buildings*
hate *These people are so full of hate.*
revulsion *They expressed their revulsion at his violent death.*
ANTONYM **love**
See also **animosity, dislike, hate, horror, hostility**

haughty
▷ *ADJECTIVE*
showing excessive pride: *He spoke in a haughty tone.*
arrogant *an air of arrogant indifference*
conceited *They had grown too conceited and pleased with themselves.*
disdainful *She cast a disdainful glance around her.*
proud *She was said to be proud and arrogant.*
snobbish *They had a snobbish dislike for some of the new students.*
stuck-up INFORMAL *She was a famous actress, but she wasn't a bit stuck-up.*
ANTONYM **humble**
See also **stuck-up, superior**

haul *See* **drag, draw, loot, pull, tug**

haunt *See* **frequent**

haunted *See* **spooky**

have
▷ *VERB*
1 to own something: *We have two tickets for the concert.*
hold *She holds a degree in engineering.*
keep *We keep chickens.*
own *His parents own a local diner.*
possess *He is said to possess a fortune.*

H

2 to experience something: *He had a marvellous time.*
endure *The company endured heavy losses.*
enjoy *Most workers at the factory enjoy a two-week vacation.*
experience *We experienced a few surprises during our trip.*
feel *I felt a sharp pain in my shoulder.*
sustain *He had sustained a cut above his left eyebrow.*
undergo *He recently underwent surgery.*
See also **bear, experience, own, possess**

have fun *See* **play**

have on *See* **wear**

haven *See* **refuge, retreat, shelter**

hawk *See* **sell**

hazard *See* **danger, threat**

hazardous *See* **dangerous, treacherous**

haze *See* **cloud**

hazy *See* **dim, vague**

head
▷ NOUN
1 a person's mind and mental abilities: *I don't have a head for business.*
aptitude *an aptitude for numbers*
brain *If you stop using your brain, you'll become boring.*
common sense *Use your common sense more often.*
intelligence *Try to use your intelligence to solve the puzzle. Don't just guess.*
mind *I'm trying to clear my mind of all this.*
wits *She has used her wits to get where she is today.*
2 the top, front, or start of something: *the head of the line*
beginning *the beginning of this chapter*
front *Stand at the front of the line.*
source *the source of this great river*
start *Go back to the start of this section.*
top *the top of the stairs*
ANTONYM **tail**
3 the person in charge of something: *heads of government*
boss *the boss of the new company*
chief *She's the new chief of security.*
director *the director of the intensive care unit*
leader *the leader of the Conservative Party*
manager *the manager of our division*
president *the president of the organization*
principal *the principal of the school*
▷ VERB

4 to be in charge of something: *She heads the department.*
be in charge of *She's in charge of the overseas division.*
control *He controls the largest fast-food empire in the world.*
direct *The new manager will direct day-to-day operations.*
lead *leading a campaign to save the rainforest*
manage *Within two years, he was managing the store.*
run *Each teacher will run a different workshop.*
See also **boss, chief, command, foam, lead, leader, mind, top**

INFORMALLY SPEAKING

come to a head: reach a climax
head off: successfully turn something back or aside
keep your head: remain calm
lose your head: lose control of yourself
put heads together: discuss

head of state *See* **ruler**

headquarters *See* **base**

headstrong *See* **obstinate**

headway *See* **progress**

heal *See* **cure**

healing *See* **recovery**

health
▷ NOUN
1 the condition of your body: *Smoking is bad for your health.*
condition *The patient remains in critical condition.*
constitution *She must have an extremely strong constitution.*
shape *He was still in better shape than many younger men.*
2 a state in which a person is feeling well: *In hospital they nursed me back to health.*
fitness *She has fitness problems.*
good condition *He is in good condition for a man of his age.*
well-being *Singing can create a sense of well-being.*
ANTONYM **illness**

healthy
▷ ADJECTIVE
1 having good health: *She was a very healthy child.*
active *an active lifestyle*
fit *She works hard at staying physically fit.*
in good shape *I keep in good shape by swimming.*

robust *a robust and vibrant young person*
strong *a strong constitution*
well *I'm not very well today.*
ANTONYM **ill**
2 INFORMAL producing good health: *a healthy diet*
beneficial *A balanced diet is beneficial to health.*
bracing *a bracing walk*
good for you *Regular, moderate exercise is good for you.*
nourishing *sensible, nourishing food*
nutritious *a hot, nutritious meal*
wholesome *fresh, wholesome ingredients*
ANTONYM **unhealthy**
See also **beneficial, fit, sound, well**

CONFUSABLES

The word **healthy** means **in good health**, and **healthful** means **good for the health**, but, in everyday speech, most people use **healthy** for both meanings.

---

heap
▷ NOUN
1 a pile of things: *a heap of garbage*
hoard *a hoard of silver and jewels*
mass *a mass of flowers*
mound *The bulldozers piled up huge mounds of dirt.*
pile *a pile of bills*
stack *stacks of books on the bedside table*
▷ VERB
2 to pile things up: *She heaped vegetables onto his plate.*
pile *He was piling clothes into the suitcase.*
stack *They stacked up pillows behind his back.*
See also **bunch, mass, pile**

hear
▷ VERB
1 to listen to something: *I heard the sound of a car backfiring.*
catch *I don't believe I caught your name.*
eavesdrop *I eavesdropped on their conversation in the elevator.*
heed *Few at the conference heeded his warning.*
listen in *Secret agents listened in on his phone calls.*
listen to *He spent his time listening to the radio.*
overhear *I overheard two doctors discussing my case.*
2 to learn about something: *I heard that he was forced to resign.*
ascertain *They had ascertained that he was not a spy.*
discover *She discovered that she had left the*

book in her locker.
find out *As soon as we found this out, we told the principal.*
gather *I gather the report is critical of the judge.*
learn *She wasn't surprised to learn that he was involved.*
understand *I understand that she's taken another job.*
See also **gather, learn, listen, understand**

hearsay See **gossip, rumour**

heart See **basis, centre, essence**

heartache See **distress, grief, sorrow**

heartbreaking See **pathetic, tragic**

hearten See **encourage**

heartfelt See **passionate, serious, sincere**

heartless See **callous, cruel, merciless**

heart-rending See **sad, tragic**

heat
▷ NOUN
1 the quality of being warm or hot: *the heat of the sun*
high temperature *The suffering caused by the high temperature has been great.*
warmth *the warmth of the sand under her feet*
ANTONYM **cold**
2 a state of strong emotion: *in the heat of the election campaign*
excitement *in a state of great excitement*
fervour *religious fervour*
intensity *the intensity of feeling about this issue*
passion *She spoke with great passion.*
vehemence *I was surprised by the vehemence of his criticism.*
▷ VERB
3 to raise the temperature of something: *Heat the oil in a frying pan.*
reheat *Reheat the soup to a gentle simmer.*
warm up *Before serving, warm up the pie.*
ANTONYM **cool**
See also **feeling, warm**

heat up See **warm**

heated See **hot, warm**

heave See **raise, tug, vomit**

heaven
▷ NOUN
INFORMAL a place or situation liked very

H

much: *I was in cinematic heaven.*
bliss *a scene of domestic bliss*
ecstasy *the ecstasy of being in love*
paradise *Whistler, British Columbia, is a skier's paradise.*
rapture *the sheer rapture of listening to Bach's music*

heavy

▷ ADJECTIVE
1 great in weight or force: *a heavy frying pan*
bulky *a bulky grey sweater*
massive *a massive blue whale*
ANTONYM **light**
2 serious or important: *a heavy speech*
deep *a period of deep personal crisis*
grave *the grave crisis facing the country*
profound *His remarks were profound.*
serious *The matter deserved serious consideration.*
solemn *a simple, solemn ceremony*
weighty *Surely such weighty matters merit a higher level of debate.*
ANTONYM **trivial**
See also **grave, stuffy**

heckle *See* **interrupt**

hectic *See* **busy**

heed

▷ VERB
1 to pay attention to someone's advice: *Few at the conference heeded his warning.*
follow *For once, he followed my advice.*
listen to *They won't listen to my advice.*
pay attention to *The food industry is now paying attention to young consumers.*
take notice of *We want the government to take notice of what we think.*
▷ NOUN
2 careful attention: *He paid little heed to her warning.*
attention *He never paid much attention to his audience.*
notice *So do they take any notice of public opinion?*
See also **hear**

hefty *See* **overweight**

height *See* **extreme, maximum, top, ultimate**

heirloom *See* **legacy**

heirlooms *See* **valuables**

hell

▷ NOUN
INFORMAL an unpleasant situation or place: *Bullies can make your life hell.*

agony *the agony of defeat*
anguish *the anguish of families unable to trace relatives who've disappeared*
misery *All that money brought nothing but sadness and misery.*
nightmare *The years in prison were a nightmare.*
ordeal *the painful ordeal of the last year*

INFORMALLY SPEAKING

from hell: of the worst possible kind
like hell: strenuously
raise hell: cause a lot of trouble

hello

▷ INTERJECTION
a greeting: *I dropped by to say hello.*
good afternoon *Good afternoon. Won't you sit down?*
good evening *Good evening, and welcome!*
good morning *Good morning, everyone.*
greetings *"Greetings, folks," she said with a smile.*
hi INFORMAL *She smiled and said, "Hi."*
how do you do? FORMAL *"How do you do?" he said, holding out his hand.*
ANTONYM **goodbye**

help

▷ VERB
1 to make something easier or better for someone: *He began to help with the chores.*
aid *a software system to aid managers*
assist *information to assist you*
lend a hand *I'd be glad to lend a hand.*
support *She thanked everyone who had supported her in the school election.*
▷ NOUN
2 assistance or support: *The books were not much help.*
advice *He has given me lots of good advice about public speaking.*
aid *millions of dollars of aid*
assistance *I would be grateful for any assistance.*
guidance *The yearbook was published under their guidance.*
helping hand *Most parents would be grateful for a helping hand.*
support *Only a few clubs pledged their support for the project.*
See also **benefit, blessing, comfort, encourage, support**

helper

▷ NOUN
a person who gives assistance: *There is an adult helper for every two children.*
aide *She is one of the prime minister's aides.*

assistant *a research assistant*

deputy *I can't make it, so I'll send my deputy.*

supporter *He is a strong supporter of the plan.*

See also **assistant**

helpful

▷ ADJECTIVE

1 giving assistance or advice: *The staff in the office are very helpful.*

accommodating *She was very accommodating and changed her plans so I could go too.*

co-operative *I made every effort to be co-operative.*

kind *I must thank you for being so kind to me.*

supportive *The coach was very supportive of my ideas.*

ANTONYM **unhelpful**

2 making a situation better: *Having the right equipment will be enormously helpful.*

advantageous *an advantageous arrangement*

beneficial *beneficial changes in the tax system*

constructive *constructive criticism*

profitable *a profitable exchange of ideas*

useful *useful information*

See also **accommodating, beneficial, convenient, handy, positive, useful, valuable**

helping   See **portion**

helping hand   See **help**

helpless

▷ ADJECTIVE

weak or unable to cope: *a helpless baby*

defenceless *a savage attack on a defenceless creature*

powerless *He was powerless to help.*

unprotected *They felt unprotected and defenceless.*

vulnerable *the most vulnerable members of society*

weak *still weak from a long illness*

See also **powerless**

hem   See **border**

hem in   See **confine, enclose, surround**

hence   See **therefore**

here   See **present**

heritage   See **inheritance**

hero   See **champion**

heroic   See **brave**

heroism   See **bravery, courage**

hesitant

▷ ADJECTIVE

uncertain about something: *At first he was hesitant to accept the role.*

diffident *My brother is as confident as I am diffident.*

doubtful *I was very doubtful about the chances for success.*

reluctant *She was reluctant to get involved.*

unsure *They made me feel awkward and unsure of myself.*

wavering *wavering voters*

See also **reluctant**

hesitate

▷ VERB

to pause or show uncertainty: *She hesitated before replying.*

dither *I'm still dithering over whether to take the job.*

pause *The crowd paused for a minute, wondering what to do next.*

waver *She never wavered in her determination.*

hi   See **hello**

hiatus   See **gap, interval**

hibernate   See **sleep**

hibernation   See **sleep**

hidden   See **invisible, secret**

hide

▷ VERB

1 to put something where it cannot be seen: *She hid her face in her hands.*

conceal *The hat concealed her hair.*

secrete *She secreted the cash in the kitchen cabinet.*

stash INFORMAL *He had stashed money away in a secret offshore account.*

▷ NOUN

2 the skin of a large animal: *the process of tanning hides*

pelt *beaver pelts*

skin *a coat of fake leopard skin*

See also **coat, cover, obscure, shelter**

high

▷ ADJECTIVE

1 tall or a long way above the ground: *a high tower*

ANTONYM **low**

2 great in degree, quantity, or intensity: *There is a high risk of heart disease.*

ANTONYM **low**

H

WORD STUDY: HIGH

High is another word that has a number of meanings. Depending on just what you are describing as **high**, you have a whole range of substitutes to choose from to give your writing some added variety and expressiveness.

• **of a building, ceiling, or mountain**
The apartment is in an **elevated** position overlooking the docks.
The churches all had **lofty** towers and **soaring** spires.
I hate climbing the **steep** hill up to her house.
The garden is sheltered by **tall** walls.
In the distance, I could see the **towering** red sandstone cliffs.

• **of an amount or degree**
I'm in a state of **acute** anxiety.
He was driving at **excessive** speed.
She drinks **extraordinary** quantities of water.
He seems to be acting under **extreme** emotional pressure.
The new software created a **great** level of interest.
There are **severe** penalties for smuggling.

• **of a cost or price**
Must we pay the **costly** premiums of private health insurance?
The membership fee is too **dear** for me.
I won't pay **expensive** charges for mediocre service.
The prices in that store are very **steep**. This is an informal word.

• **of a wind**
It was a morning of **blustery** breezes.
We were working in **extreme** wind and cold.
There will be thunder and **squally** winds.
Some **strong** gusts will reach 90 km/h.
Here's some video of the **violent** gales that have hit the Atlantic coast.

• **important**
He accepted the **chief** position in the company.
She's one of the country's most **eminent** scientists.
He moves in **exalted** circles.
She held an **important** post in the government.
He longed to have an **influential** place in the system.
She is a **leading** figure in her field.
He's one of the most **powerful** people in Britain.
She holds a **pre-eminent** position among jazz singers.
A host of **prominent** political figures attended the ceremony.
They treasure their **superior** status.

• **of a voice or sound**
A **high-pitched** cry split the air.
He gave a **penetrating** whistle, and the dog turned and ran back.
We all cringed as he hit another **piercing** note.
The child let out a **shrill** scream of pleasure.

• **of a person's spirits**
They remain in **buoyant** spirits.
They'd never seen him in such **cheerful** spirits.
I had that **elated** feeling you get when everything is going well.
She seemed to be in an **exhilarated** frame of mind.
He is in one of his **exuberant** moods.

See WORD STUDY **high**
See also **excited, steep, tall, thrill**

high point *See* **peak, top**

high temperature *See* **heat**

higher than *See* **above**

highest *See* **supreme, top**

highlight *See* **emphasize**

highly *See* **very, well**

high-ranking *See* **senior**

high-speed *See* **express**

hijack *See* **seize**

hike
▷ *NOUN*
1 a long walk in the countryside: *They went for a hike through the woods.*
excursion *an excursion into the hills*
ramble *a long ramble along the Bruce Trail*
stroll *The next day we took a stroll along the river's bank.*
walk *We often go for walks in the country.*
▷ *VERB*
2 to go for a long walk: *We hiked through the ravine.*

amble *ambling along a country lane*
stray *Several hikers strayed from the path.*
stroll *whistling as he strolled along the road*
walk *We finished the evening by walking along the beach.*
wander *He loved to wander in the woods.*
See also **walk**

hilarious *See* **funny, hysterical**

TYPES OF ... *HILL*	
bluff ✹	height of land ✹
butte ✹	knoll
dune	moraine
foothill	mound
height	prominence

hilt *See* **handle**

hinder
▷ *VERB*
to get in the way of someone or something: *A thigh injury hindered her mobility.*
block *The goalie blocked two shots.*
check *We have managed to check the spread of the disease.*
delay *Various problems have delayed production.*
frustrate *Rain frustrated our plans for a barbecue.*
hamper *I was hampered by a lack of information.*
impede *Fallen rocks are impeding the progress of rescue workers.*
See also **delay, hamper, handicap, impede, interfere, prevent, restrain**

hindrance *See* **barrier, handicap, obstacle**

hinge *See* **base**

hinge on *See* **depend**

hint
▷ *NOUN*
1 an indirect suggestion: *He gave a strong hint that I would make the team.*
clue *He hadn't a clue about who the mystery guest would be.*
indication *She gave no indication that she was ready to compromise.*
intimation *I did not have any intimation that he was going to resign.*
suggestion *We reject any suggestion that the team needs different uniforms.*
2 a helpful piece of advice: *I hope to get some fashion hints.*
advice *Don't be afraid to ask for advice.*
pointer *Here are a few pointers to help you make your choice.*

suggestion *May I give you a few suggestions?*
tip *tips for busy managers*
▷ *VERB*
3 to suggest something indirectly: *Criticism is merely hinted at.*
imply *The report implied that his death was inevitable.*
indicate *She has indicated that she may resign.*
insinuate *The newspaper article insinuated that he was lying.*
intimate *She intimated that she was contemplating a shakeup of the company.*
suggest *Are you suggesting that I need a makeover?*
See also **idea, indication, mention, note, sign, suggest, suggestion, trace**

hint at *See* **promise**

hire
▷ *VERB*
to employ the services of someone: *I was hired for a summer job.*
appoint *The prime minister has appointed a new justice minister.*
commission *You can commission her to paint something for you.*
employ *They employed me as a messenger.*
engage *We engaged the services of an engineer.*
sign up *He persuaded the company to sign her up.*
See also **employ**

hiring *See* **employment**

historic *See* **memorable**

history *See* **background**

histrionic *See* **melodramatic**

hit
▷ *VERB*
1 to strike someone or something forcefully: *He had been hit with a baseball bat.*
See WORD STUDY **hit** *on next page*
2 to collide with something: *The car had apparently hit a traffic sign.*
bang into *I fell after another skier banged into me.*
bump *The boat bumped against the dock.*
collide with *He almost collided with another skater.*
meet head-on *Their cars met head-on on a narrow road.*
run into *The bus nearly ran into the turning car.*
smash into *The car plunged down a cliff and smashed into a tree.*

H

The word **hit** is often overused. There are a number of more descriptive words that you can use to give additional information about the way in which something is hit, or how hard it is hit.

- If you **strike** someone or something, you hit them deliberately.
  This is a formal word.
  She stepped forward and **struck** him across the mouth.

- If you **tap** something, you hit it with a quick light blow or series of blows.
  Tap the egg gently with a teaspoon to crack the shell.

- If you **pat** something or someone, you tap them lightly, usually with your hand held flat.
  "Don't worry about it," he said, **patting** me on the knee.

- If you **rap** something, or **rap on** it, you hit it with a series of quick blows.
  She kept **rapping** the glass with the knuckles of her right hand.
  He **rapped on** the door with his cane.

- If you **slap** or **smack** something, you hit it with the palm of your hand.
  I **slapped** him on the back and said "Congratulations!"
  She **smacked** the mosquito, but it was too late to avoid being bitten.

- If you **swat** something such as an insect, you hit it with a quick, swinging movement using your hand or a flat object.
  Every time a fly came near, I **swatted** it with a newspaper.

- If you **knock** someone or something, you hit it roughly, especially so that it falls or moves.
  She accidentally **knocked** the can off the shelf.

- If you **knock** on something such as a door or window, you hit it, usually several times, to attract someone's attention.

She went to his apartment and **knocked** on the door.

- If you **beat** something, you hit it hard, usually several times or continuously for a period of time.
  While still **beating** drums, the students began to march in a circle.

- If you **hammer** on something, you hit it hard several times to make a noise.
  We had to **hammer** on the door and shout to attract their attention.

- If you **pound** something, you hit it with great force, usually loudly and repeatedly.
  He **pounded** the table with both fists.

- If you **batter** something, you hit it very hard, using your fists or a heavy object.
  I **battered** the door with my clenched fists, and that hurt.

- If you **bang** something, you hit it hard, making a loud noise.
  We **banged** on the window and shouted to be let out.

- If you **bang** a part of your body, you accidentally knock it against something and hurt it.
  She'd fallen and **banged** her head.

- If you **bash** something, you hit it hard. This is an informal word.
  One of the cars **bashed** into the other.

- If you **whack** something, you hit it hard. This is an informal word.
  By mistake, she missed the ball and **whacked** me with the baseball bat.

- If you **punch** something, you hit it hard with your fist.
  Punch down on the bread dough several times.

▷ *NOUN*
3 the action of hitting something: *Give the nail a good hard hit with the hammer.*
blow *a blow to the chin*
knock *a loud knock on the door*
rap *a rap on the knuckles*

slap *a slap on the wrist*
smack *a smack with a ruler*
See also **bang, beat, bump, success**

hit and miss *See* **unpredictable**

hit back *See* **retaliate, revenge**

hit it off *See* **get on**

hitch *See* **drawback**

hoard

▷ *VERB*

1 to store for future use: *People have begun to hoard food and gasoline.*
save *Save some money in case of an emergency.*
stockpile *People are stockpiling food for the coming blizzard.*
store *It's perfect for storing eggs or vegetables.*

▷ *NOUN*

2 a store of things: *a hoard of silver and jewels*
cache *a cache of weapons and explosives*
fund *a scholarship fund for engineering students*
reserve *the world's oil reserves*
stockpile *stockpiles of firewood for the winter*
store *I have a store of food and water here.*
supply *food supplies*
See also **bank, fund, gather, heap, pile, reserve, save, stockpile, store, supply**

CONFUSABLES

hoard means **store**
horde means **crowd**

hoarse

▷ *ADJECTIVE*

rough and deep in sound: *He became hoarse from shouting.*
croaky *He sounds a bit croaky after he wakes up.*
gruff *his gruff voice when he's in an unhappy mood*
husky *The actress's deep husky voice was her trademark.*
rasping *He sang in a deep rasping tone.*
ANTONYM **clear**

hoax *See* **fraud, trick**

hobbling *See* **lame**

hobby

▷ *NOUN*

an enjoyable activity pursued in your spare time: *My hobbies are music and photography.*
diversion *Playing cards is a pleasant diversion.*
leisure activity *Reading is my favourite leisure activity.*
leisure pursuit *Cycling is her main leisure pursuit.*
pastime *His favourite pastime is golf.*
See also **activity, interest, pastime**

hog *See* **pig**

hoist *See* **lift, raise**

hold

▷ *VERB*

1 to carry or support something: *Hold the baby while I load the car.*
carry *He was carrying a briefcase.*
clasp *She clasped the prize tightly.*
clutch *He was clutching a photograph.*
embrace *He embraced her when she stepped off the train.*
grasp *He grasped both my hands.*
grip *They gripped the rope tightly.*

▷ *NOUN*

2 power or control over someone or something: *The leader has a considerable hold over his people.*
control *She will have to give up her control of the company.*
dominance *the gang's dominance of the city's underworld*
sway *ideas that held sway for centuries*

▷ *NOUN*

3 the act or a way of holding something: *He grabbed the rope and got a hold on it.*
grasp *His hand was taken in a warm, firm grasp.*
grip *She relaxed her grip on the bag.*
See also **claim, clasp, grasp, grip, handle, have, influence, keep, possess, reserve, think**

INFORMALLY SPEAKING

get hold of: get in contact with
hold against: continue to resent
on hold: inactive

hold back *See* **restrain**

hold out *See* **offer**

hold up *See* **support**

holder *See* **container**

hole

▷ *NOUN*

1 an opening or hollow in something: *to punch holes in the paper*
gap *The wind was tearing through gaps in the windows.*
hollow *Water gathers in a hollow and forms a pond.*
opening *He squeezed through a narrow opening in the fence.*
pit *He lost his footing and began to slide into the pit.*
split *The seat has a few small splits around the corners.*
tear *I peeked through a tear in the curtains.*

H

2 a weakness in a theory or argument: *There are some holes in that theory.*

defect *A defect in the steering mechanism caused the crash.*

error *NASA discovered an error in its calculations.*

fault *There is a fault in the computer program.*

flaw *Almost all of these arguments have serious flaws.*

loophole *They found a loophole in the law.*

3 INFORMAL a difficult situation: *He admitted that the company was in a financial hole.*

fix INFORMAL *This will put homeowners in a fix.*

hot water INFORMAL *I'm in hot water because I missed the test.*

mess *the many reasons why the economy is in such a mess*

predicament *the once-great organization's current predicament*

tight spot *This was one tight spot she couldn't get out of.*

See also **breach, gap, jam, leak, opening, pit, tear**

INFORMALLY SPEAKING

hole up: go into hiding
in the hole: in debt
make a hole in: use up a large amount of
pick holes in: find fault with

---

holiday

▷ NOUN

1 time spent away from home for enjoyment: *I'm exhausted! I really need a holiday.*

break *They are currently taking a short break at their cottage.*

leave *Why don't you take a few days' leave?*

recess *Parliament returns today after its summer recess.*

time off *He took time off to go sailing with a friend.*

vacation *We went on vacation to Florida.*

See also **festival, leave, rest**

2 a festival or celebration: *The Thanksgiving holiday always falls on a Monday.*

celebration *The celebration was marked with fireworks.*

festival *a festival of lights*

hollow *See* **hole**

hollow out *See* **dig**

holy

▷ ADJECTIVE

1 relating to God or a particular religion: *We visited the city's holy places.*

consecrated *consecrated wine*

hallowed *hallowed ground*

sacred *sacred music*

sacrosanct *For him, the Sabbath was sacrosanct.*

venerated *Jerusalem is one of the world's most venerated places.*

2 religious and leading a good life: *There are holy people in all religions.*

devout *She is a devout Catholic.*

pious *He was brought up by pious relatives.*

religious *They are both very religious.*

saintly *his saintly aunt*

See also **religious**

homage *See* **honour, worship**

home

▷ NOUN

1 the building in which someone lives: *They stayed home and watched TV.*

abode *a luxurious abode*

dwelling *Various types of dwellings are planned for the area.*

house *our new house*

residence *the prime minister's official residence*

▷ ADJECTIVE

2 involving your own country or local area: *The home team is in town.*

domestic *over 100 domestic flights a day to 15 Canadian destinations*

internal *The government stepped up internal security.*

national *major national issues facing the country*

native *He was glad to be back on native soil.*

ANTONYM **foreign**

See also **house**

INFORMALLY SPEAKING

bring (or drive) home: make clear or convincing
hit home: make a forceful impression
home free: sure of success
home in on: narrow the attention to

---

homey

▷ ADJECTIVE

simple, ordinary, and comfortable: *The room was small and homey.*

comfortable *A home should be warm and comfortable.*

cosy *Guests can relax in the cosy sunroom.*

modest *the modest home of a family who lived off the land*

simple *a simple wedding, with just family members*

national

Jan 1: New Year's Day
Mar/Apr: Good Friday, Easter Sunday, Easter Monday
May: Victoria Day
Jul 1: Canada Day
Sep: Labour Day
Oct: Thanksgiving
Nov 11: Remembrance Day
Dec 25: Christmas Day
Dec 26: Boxing Day

provinces/territories

Alberta	*variable*
Feb: Family Day	Regatta Day
Aug: Heritage Day	**Nova Scotia**
British Columbia	Jul/Aug: Natal Day
Aug: B.C. Day	**Nothwest Territories**
Manitoba	Aug: Civic Holiday
Aug: Civic Holiday	**Ontario**
New Brunswick	Aug: Civic Holiday
Aug: New Brunswick Day	**Prince Edward Island**
Newfoundland & Labrador	Aug: Natal Day
Mar: St. Patrick's Day	**Québec**
Apr: St. George's Day	Jun 24: Fête nationale
Jun 24: Discovery Day	**Saskatchewan**
Jul 1: Memorial Day	Aug: Civic Holiday
Jul 12: Orangemen's Day	**Yukon**
	Aug: Discovery Day

H

welcoming *The restaurant is small and very welcoming.*
ANTONYM **grand**
See also **comfortable**

homicide *See* **murder**

hone *See* **perfect**

honest
▷ *ADJECTIVE*
truthful and trustworthy: *He is a very honest, decent man.*
law-abiding *law-abiding citizens*
reputable *a reputable car dealer*
trustworthy *a trustworthy and level-headed leader*
truthful *They could not give us a truthful answer.*
virtuous *a virtuous family man*
ANTONYM **dishonest**
See also **candid, frank, open, real, serious, straight, straightforward**

honesty *See* **honour**

honour
▷ *NOUN*
1 personal integrity: *I can no longer serve with honour in your government.*

decency *No one had the decency to tell me to my face.*
goodness *He retains a faith in human goodness.*
honesty *Her reputation for honesty helped to make her team captain.*
integrity *He was praised for his fairness and high integrity.*
ANTONYM **dishonour**
2 an award or mark of respect: *He was showered with honours — among them a Gemini award.*
accolade *the ultimate international accolade, the Nobel Peace Prize*
commendation *The officer received a commendation for brave conduct.*
homage *books that pay homage to great Canadians*
praise *He had won consistently high praise for his theatre work.*
recognition *At last, her writing has received recognition.*
tribute *He paid tribute to the organizers.*
▷ *VERB*
3 to give someone or something special praise: *She was honoured by the club with a gold medal.*

commemorate *The cenotaph commemorates those who died in the war.*
commend *I commended her for that action.*
decorate *He was decorated for bravery by being awarded the Distinguished Conduct Medal.*
glorify *The poet glorified her country.*
praise *He praised their excellent work.*
See also **character, commemorate, glory, keep, pay, prize, recognize, respect, right, tribute, worship**

honourable *See* **noble, respectable**

honoured *See* **proud**

hoodlum
▷ NOUN
a destructive and sometimes violent person: *The hoodlums hurled rocks at the building.*
hooligan *The hooligans were banned from the soccer match.*
lout *He was attacked by stone-throwing louts.*
tough *Residents may be too terrified of local toughs to protest.*
vandal *The windows were smashed by vandals.*
See also **thug**

hoop *See* ring

hope
▷ NOUN
a wish or feeling of desire and expectation: *There was little hope of recovery.*
ambition *Their ambition is to sail around the world.*
dream *her dream of becoming a pilot*
expectation *The hotel was being renovated in expectation of a tourist boom.*
See also **possibility, prospect**

hopeful *See* optimistic

hopeless
▷ ADJECTIVE
1 certain to fail or be unsuccessful: *Our situation is hopeless.*
forlorn *the forlorn hope of finding a better life*
futile *their futile attempts to avoid publicity*
impossible *It's impossible to have a conversation with him.*
pointless *a pointless exercise that would only waste more time*
useless *She knew it was useless to protest.*
vain *a vain attempt to catch the ball*
2 bad or inadequate: *I don't drive, and the buses are hopeless.*

inadequate *The problem lies with inadequate staffing.*
pathetic *the pathetic state of the railway system*
poor *The apartment was in a poor state of repair.*
useless INFORMAL *I'm pretty useless in the garden.*
See also **doomed, impossible, pessimistic**

hopelessness *See* despair

horde *See* crowd, number

horizontal *See* even, flat, level, straight

horrendous *See* awful, dreadful, terrible

horrible
▷ ADJECTIVE
1 disagreeable or unpleasant: *a horrible person to work with*
awful *I had an awful time.*
disagreeable *a disagreeable odour*
horrid *horrid behaviour*
mean *Why are you always so mean to me?*
nasty *This argument could turn nasty.*
unpleasant *He's a very unpleasant man.*
2 causing shock, fear, or disgust: *horrible crimes*
appalling *They have been living under the most appalling conditions.*
dreadful *She told me the dreadful news.*
grim *a grim discovery*
gruesome *gruesome murders*
terrifying *a terrifying experience*
See also **disagreeable, hateful, nasty, terrible**

horrid *See* disagreeable, horrible, terrible, unpleasant

horrify
▷ VERB
to cause to feel horror or shock: *a crime wave that horrified the city*
appal *I was appalled by her poor manners.*
disgust *He disgusted everyone with his boorish behaviour.*
dismay *We were deeply dismayed by the decision.*
outrage *I was outraged that my friend had cheated me.*
shock *Pictures of the victims shocked me.*
sicken *What he saw at the accident sickened him.*

horror
▷ NOUN
1 a strong feeling of alarm or disgust: *He gazed in horror at the knife.*

alarm *She sat up in alarm.*
dread *She thought with dread of the cold winter to come.*
fear *I stood there crying and shaking with fear.*
fright *He uttered a shriek and jumped with fright.*
panic *He felt a sudden rush of panic at the thought.*
terror *I shook with terror.*
2 a strong fear of something: *his horror of speaking in public*
abhorrence *their abhorrence of racism*
aversion *Many people have a natural aversion to insects.*
disgust *I threw the book aside in disgust.*
hatred *My hatred for him is intense.*
loathing *She looked at him with loathing.*
revulsion *They expressed their revulsion at his violent death.*

horse
▷ NOUN
an animal kept for riding: *a fall from a horse*
equine *the history and uses of equines*
nag INFORMAL *He unhitched his sorry-looking nag from a nearby post.*
pony *We took the kids on pony rides.*

hospitable *See* **accommodating, generous**

host *See* **crowd**

hostage *See* **prisoner**

hostel *See* **shelter**

hostile
▷ ADJECTIVE
unfriendly, aggressive, and unpleasant: *The umpire faced a hostile crowd.*
antagonistic *They were nearly all antagonistic to the idea.*
belligerent *belligerent language*
malevolent *a malevolent stare*
unkind *All last summer he'd been unkind to me.*
ANTONYM **friendly**
See also **aggressive, unfriendly**

hostile to *See* **against**

hostilities *See* **war**

hostility
▷ NOUN
aggressive or unfriendly behaviour toward someone or something: *hostility toward the rival team*
animosity *The animosity between the two men grew.*
antagonism *a history of antagonism between the two sides*

hatred *her lifelong hatred of authority*
ill will *He didn't bear anyone any ill will.*
malice *There was no malice in her voice.*
resentment *There is growing resentment against overpaid ballplayers.*
ANTONYM **friendship**
See also **animosity, conflict, dislike, hate, opposition**

hot
▷ ADJECTIVE
1 having a high temperature: *a hot climate*
boiling *It's boiling in here.*
heated *a heated swimming pool*
scalding *burned by scalding tea*
scorching *It was a scorching day.*
warm *a warm, dry summer*
ANTONYM **cold**
2 very spicy: *a hot, aromatic curry*
peppery *a rich, peppery stew*
spicy *a spicy sausage*
ANTONYM **bland**

INFORMALLY SPEAKING
hot and bothered: angry and upset
hot under the collar: angry
in the hot seat: in a potentially embarrassing position

hot air *See* **rubbish**

hot water *See* **hole, predicament**

hound *See* **chase, follow, persecute**

house
▷ NOUN
a building where a person or family lives: *They live in a large house with eight rooms.*
abode *a luxurious new abode*
building *Their apartment was on the first floor of the building.*
dwelling *various types of dwellings*
home *We stayed home and watched movies.*
residence *the prime minister's official residence*
See also **accommodate, accommodation, company, home**

INFORMALLY SPEAKING
bring down the house: be loudly applauded
like a house on fire: very well or very fast
on the house: free

H

household name *See* **personality**

housing *See* **accommodation**

hover *See* **float**

how do you do? *See* **hello**

howl *See* **bay, scream**

howling *See* **wild**

hub *See* **centre, focus**

hubbub *See* **noise, racket, sound**

huddle *See* **shelter**

hue *See* **colour**

huff *See* **resentment**

huffy *See* **resentful, sulky**

hug
▷ *VERB*
1 to hold someone close to you: *We hugged each other.*
clasp *He clasped the prize in his hand.*
cuddle *kissing and cuddling*
embrace *She embraced him as he stepped off the train.*
squeeze *He squeezed her hand gently.*
▷ *NOUN*
2 the act of holding someone close to you: *She gave him a hug.*
embrace *a couple locked in an embrace*
See also **clasp**

huge
▷ *ADJECTIVE*
extremely large in amount, size, or degree: *a huge crowd*
colossal *a colossal waste of money*
enormous *The bedroom is enormous.*
giant *a giant statue*
immense *He wielded immense power.*
massive *a massive surge in popularity*
vast *this vast area of northern Canada*
ANTONYM **tiny**
See also **colossal, enormous, immense, large, spacious, vast**

human *See* **person**

human being *See* **individual, person**

human beings *See* **people**

humane
▷ *ADJECTIVE*
showing kindness and sympathy toward others: *a more just and humane society*
benevolent *a most benevolent employer*
caring *a very caring boy*
charitable *charitable work*

compassionate *a deeply compassionate man*
kind *She is warmhearted and kind.*
merciful *a merciful ruler*
thoughtful *a very thoughtful gesture*
See also **benevolent, compassionate, kind, merciful**

CONFUSABLES

Humane refers to compassion towards others.
Human refers to qualities belonging specially to people rather than animals.

humanely *See* **well**

humanity *See* **kindness, man, people**

humankind
▷ *NOUN*
people in general: *the evolution of humankind*
humanity *She rendered a great service to humanity.*
human race *the future of the human race*
See also **people**

humans *See* **people**

humble
▷ *ADJECTIVE*
1 not vain or boastful: *He gave a great performance, but he was very humble.*
meek *He was meek and mild-mannered.*
modest *She's modest, as well as being a great player.*
unassuming *She has a gentle, unassuming manner.*
ANTONYM **haughty**
2 ordinary or unimportant: *Some fresh herbs will transform a humble stew.*
modest *her modest beginnings*
ordinary *It was just an ordinary weekend.*
simple *a simple dinner of rice and beans*
▷ *VERB*
3 to make someone feel humiliated: *the little car company that humbled the industry giants*
disgrace *I have disgraced the family's name.*
humiliate *The coach continually humiliated the players.*
See also **humiliate, modest, unknown**

humdrum *See* **boring, dreary, dull**

humid
▷ *ADJECTIVE*
damp and hot: *a hot, humid summer*
clammy *My shirt was clammy with perspiration.*
muggy *The weather was muggy and overcast.*
steamy *The air was hot and steamy.*

sticky *four hot, sticky days in the middle of August*
See also **damp, wet**

humidity See **damp**

humiliate
▷ VERB
to hurt someone's pride: *Why do you enjoy humiliating me?*
disgrace *I have disgraced my family.*
embarrass *It embarrassed him that he had no idea of what was going on.*
humble *The champion was humbled by the unseeded qualifier.*
put down *She has a habit of putting people down occasionally.*
shame *His life of crime had shamed them.*
See also **embarrass, humble, put down, shame**

humiliated See **ashamed, embarrassed**

humiliation See **embarrassment, shame**

humorous See **funny, witty**

humour
▷ NOUN
1 something that is thought to be funny: *The movie's humour contains a serious message.*
comedy *his career in comedy*
wit *She was known for her biting wit.*
2 the mood someone is in: *He hasn't been in a good humour lately.*
frame of mind *Clearly, she was not in the right frame of mind to continue.*
mood *The dog was in an aggressive mood.*
spirits *He was in very low spirits.*
temper *He stormed off the field in a furious temper.*
▷ VERB
3 to please someone so that they will not become upset: *I nodded, partly to humour him.*
flatter *I knew she was just flattering me.*
indulge *He did not agree with indulging children.*
mollify *The investigation was carried out primarily to mollify public concern.*
See also **mood**

humourless See **serious**

hump See **bulge, bump, lump**

hunch See **impression, suspicion**

hunger See **long, longing, wish**

hunger for See **be dying for**

hungry
▷ ADJECTIVE

wanting to eat: *I didn't have any lunch, so I'm really hungry.*
famished *Isn't dinner ready? I'm famished.*
peckish INFORMAL *Have a muffin if you're feeling peckish.*
ravenous *a pack of ravenous animals*
starving *He is hardly a starving student.*

hunk See **beauty, lump**

hunt See **chase, look for, search, seek**

hurdle See **barrier, difficulty, jump, obstacle**

hurl See **dash, throw**

hurried See **fast, hasty, quick, swift**

hurriedly See **fast, quickly**

H

hurry
▷ VERB
1 to move or do something as quickly as possible: *She hurried through the empty streets.*
dash *He dashed upstairs.*
fly *I must fly or I'll miss my train.*
get a move on INFORMAL *Get a move on! We're late for the play.*
rush *I've got to rush. I have a meeting in a few minutes.*
scurry *Reporters scurried to find their laptops.*
2 to make something happen more quickly: *an attempt to hurry the building process*
accelerate *The auto company is accelerating the development of their new car.*
hasten *This will hasten their decision.*
quicken *He quickened his pace a little.*
speed up *an effort to speed up the printer*
ANTONYM **slow down**
See also **accelerate, bustle, fly, race, rush, speed**

hurt
▷ VERB
1 to cause someone to feel pain: *I didn't mean to hurt anyone.*
harm *The hijackers seemed anxious not to harm anyone.*
injure *It was a miracle that nobody was seriously injured in the plane crash.*
wound *The explosion wounded five people.*
2 to upset someone or something: *What you said really hurt me.*
distress *I did not want to frighten or distress the horse.*
sadden *He is saddened that they did not win anything.*
upset *I'm sorry if I've upset you.*
wound *Her cruel words wounded me.*

▷ ADJECTIVE

3 upset or offended: *He felt hurt by all the lies.*

aggrieved *He is still aggrieved at the size of the fine.*

offended *She was offended at being left out.*

upset *I'm upset by your attitude.*

wounded *I think she feels desperately wounded.*

See also **abuse, damage, harm, injure, upset**

hurtful *See* **harmful**

hurtle into *See* **crash**

husband *See* **partner**

hush *See* **silence**

hushed *See* **quiet, silent**

husky *See* **hoarse**

hustle *See* **rush**

hygiene
▷ NOUN

the principles and practice of health and cleanliness: *Be extra careful about personal hygiene.*

cleanliness *Many of the beaches fail to meet minimum standards of cleanliness.*

sanitation *the hazards of contaminated water and poor sanitation*

hygienic *See* **clean**

hypnotize
▷ VERB

to put someone into a state in which they seem to be asleep but can respond to suggestions: *She said he would be hypnotized at the count of three.*

put in a trance *A stage hypnotist put her in a trance.*

put to sleep *First the hypnotist will put you to sleep.*

hypocritical *See* **two-faced**

hypothesis *See* **theory**

hypothetical *See* **imaginary**

hysteria *See* **frenzy, panic, scare**

hysterical
▷ ADJECTIVE

1 in a state of uncontrolled excitement or panic: *Calm down! Don't become hysterical.*

frantic *A bird had been locked in and was by now quite frantic.*

frenzied *her frenzied attempts to unlock the door quickly*

overwrought *One overwrought man had*

to be restrained by friends.

raving *He looked at me as if I was a raving lunatic.*

2 INFORMAL extremely funny: *His stand-up routine was hysterical.*

comical *Her expression is almost comical.*

hilarious *He has many hilarious jokes on the subject.*

Ii

icy *See* **cold, frozen**

idea

▷ *NOUN*

1 a plan or suggestion for something: *She said she'd had a brilliant idea.*
plan *I have a perfect plan.*
recommendation *a range of recommendations for change*
scheme *a scheme to develop the property*
solution *He came up with a solution to the problem.*
suggestion *Do you have a better suggestion?*
2 an opinion or belief about something: *old-fashioned ideas about health care*
belief *my personal beliefs*
conviction *It's my firm conviction that things have improved.*
impression *your first impressions of the new teacher*
notion *I have a notion of what he is like.*
opinion *a favourable opinion of our new neighbours*
view *Make your views known to local politicians.*
3 what you know about something: *They had no idea where they were.*
clue *I don't have a clue what you mean.*
guess *My guess is he went east.*
hint *She gave no hint about where she was.*
inkling *We had an inkling that something was happening.*
suspicion *I have a strong suspicion they are lying.*
See also **impression, intention, object, suspicion, thought**

INFORMALLY SPEAKING

don't get ideas: don't plan for things you shouldn't
have no idea: not know at all
The (very) idea!: Outrageous!

---

ideal

▷ *NOUN*

1 a principle or idea you try to achieve: *Live up to your ideals.*
principle *acts that go against your principles*
standard *a person with high moral standards*
value *the values of liberty and equality*
2 the best example of something: *That rose is the ideal of beauty.*
epitome *The hotel was the epitome of luxury.*

example *She was held up as an example of courage.*
model *a model of good manners*
paragon *a paragon of virtue*
standard *the standard by which we are compared*
▷ *ADJECTIVE*
3 being the best example of something: *the ideal person for the job*
classic *a classic example of hypocrisy*
complete *She is the complete athlete.*
consummate *a consummate politician*
model *a model student*
perfect *He is the perfect companion for me.*
supreme *a supreme example of kindness*
See also **cause, example, model, vision**

ideals *See* **standards**

identical *See* **alike, equal, even, like, same**

identification *See* **pass**

identify

▷ *VERB*

to recognize or name someone or something: *I tried to identify the perfume.*
diagnose *This illness is easily diagnosed.*
label *Poisonous substances should be labelled as such.*
name *The contest winners have been named.*
pinpoint *They could not pinpoint the cause of the problem.*
place *The man was familiar, but I couldn't place him.*
recognize *a woman I recognized as the former coach*

identify with

▷ *VERB*

to understand someone's feelings: *I can't identify with the characters in the play.*
associate with *I associate myself with the environmental movement.*
empathize with *I empathize with the people who live here.*
feel for *I felt for him after he lost his job.*
relate to *We have difficulty relating to each other.*
respond to *She responded to his unhappiness.*
See also **associate, recognize**

identity *See* **personality**

ideology *See* **belief**

idiom *See* **expression, language**

idiosyncratic *See* **individual**

idiot

▷ NOUN

a stupid person: *You're an idiot!*
fool *He'd been a fool to get involved.*
imbecile *I don't want to deal with these imbeciles!*
moron *I think that he's a complete moron.*
oaf *You clumsy oaf!*
twit INFORMAL *I feel like such a twit.*
See also **fool**

idiotic

▷ ADJECTIVE

extremely foolish or silly: *an idiotic thing to do*
crazy *You were crazy to leave before the ninth inning.*
foolish *It is foolish to risk injury.*
senseless *acts of senseless violence*
stupid *stupid ideas*
See also **silly, stupid, unwise**

idle

▷ ADJECTIVE

doing nothing: *idle, wealthy people*
jobless *Two in ten people in that town are jobless.*
unemployed *jobs for the unemployed*
ANTONYM **busy**
See also **laze, lazy, rest, unemployed**

idol *See* **favourite, star**

idolize *See* **worship**

ignite *See* **light**

ignominy *See* **shame**

ignoramus *See* **fool**

ignorant

▷ ADJECTIVE

1 not knowing about something: *He was completely ignorant of the rules.*
inexperienced *I am inexperienced at decorating.*
innocent *He is innocent about the harm he is doing.*
oblivious *He appeared oblivious to his surroundings.*
unaware *She was unaware that she was being filmed.*
unconscious *He was unconscious of his failure.*
2 not knowledgeable about things: *People are afraid to appear ignorant.*
green *The new worker is a little green, but she'll learn quickly.*
naive *a shy, naive man*
unaware *Young children are fairly unaware of danger.*
See also **unaware**

ignore

▷ VERB

to take no notice of someone or something: *Her cousin ignored her.*
discount *They simply discounted his feelings.*
disregard *He disregarded his father's advice.*
neglect *They never neglect their duties.*
overlook *a fact that we all tend to overlook*
See also **exclude, neglect, overlook**

ill

▷ ADJECTIVE

unhealthy or sick: *She was seriously ill with pneumonia.*
ailing *The mayor is said to be ailing.*
queasy *I feel queasy on boats.*
sick *He's very sick and he needs treatment.*
unhealthy *an unhealthy-looking man*
unwell *He felt unwell at the office.*
ANTONYM **healthy**
See also **queasy, sick, unhealthy, unwell**

ill at ease *See* **uncomfortable**

ill will *See* **animosity, hostility, spite**

illegal

▷ ADJECTIVE

forbidden by the law: *an illegal organization*
banned *banned substances*
criminal *a criminal offence*
illicit *illicit drugs*
outlawed *a place where hunting is outlawed*
prohibited *a country where alcohol is prohibited*
unlawful *unlawful acts*
ANTONYM **legal**
See also **criminal, crooked, wrong**

ill-fated *See* **doomed**

ill-fitting *See* **uncomfortable**

illicit *See* **criminal, illegal**

illness

▷ NOUN

a particular disease: *a mystery illness*
ailment *common ailments*
complaint *a skin complaint*
disease *He has been cured of the disease.*
disorder *a rare nervous disorder*
sickness *motion sickness*
See also **disorder**

illogical *See* **absurd, irrational**

ill-treat *See* **harm, mistreat, persecute**

ill-treatment *See* **abuse**

illuminate *See* **light**

illumination *See* **light**

illusion

▷ NOUN

1 a thing that you think you can see: *Artists create the illusion of space.*
hallucination *Perhaps the footprint you thought you saw was a hallucination.*
mirage *I began to see mirages.*
semblance *A semblance of normality has been restored.*
2 a false belief: *Their hopes proved to be an illusion.*
delusion *I was under the delusion that I could win.*
fallacy *It's a fallacy that the rich are always generous.*
fancy *childhood fancies*
misconception *There are many misconceptions about education.*
See also **vision**

CONFUSABLES

illusion means **misleading appearance**
allusion means **indirect reference**

---

illusory See **deceptive, imaginary**

illustrate See **explain**

illustration See **case, example, picture**

illustrative See **representative**

illustrious See **famous**

image See **appearance, vision**

imaginable See **believable, possible**

imaginary

▷ ADJECTIVE

existing in your mind but not in real life: *an imaginary friend*
fictional *a fictional character*
fictitious *a fictitious illness*
hypothetical *a hypothetical situation*
ideal *in an ideal world*
illusory *Some believe that freedom is illusory.*
invented *distorted or invented stories*
mythological *mythological creatures*
ANTONYM **real**

imagination

▷ NOUN

the ability to form new ideas: *a student who lacks imagination*
creativity *She paints with great creativity.*
ingenuity *the ingenuity of engineers*
inventiveness *the artistic inventiveness of Mozart*
originality *a composer of great originality*
vision *a leader with vision*
See also **mind, vision**

imaginative See **creative**

imagine

▷ VERB

1 to have an idea of something: *He could not imagine a more peaceful scene.*
conceive *I can't even conceive that much money.*
envisage *I envisage them getting back together.*
fantasize *I fantasized about playing in the major leagues.*
picture *I tried to picture the place.*
visualize *He could not visualize her as a young person.*
2 to believe that something is the case: *I imagine you're talking about my brother.*
assume *Don't assume we are similar.*
believe *I believe you have my pen.*
gather *I gather that his mother is a writer.*
guess INFORMAL *I guess he's right.*
suppose *He supposed I would be on the debating team this year.*
suspect *We suspected that things would get worse.*
See also **assume, expect, guess, picture, suppose, think**

imbecile See **idiot**

imitate

▷ VERB

to copy someone or something: *She imitated her parents.*
ape *He is aping his brother's behaviour.*
copy *I used to copy everything my older cousin did.*
emulate *The young skater tried to emulate the champion's style.*
impersonate *He could impersonate all the other students.*
mimic *The monkey mimicked everything we did.*
simulate *a machine that simulates animal sounds*
See also **copy**

imitation See **copy, fake, mock, parody**

immaculate See **clean**

immature See **childish, young**

immediate

▷ ADJECTIVE

1 happening or done without delay: *My immediate reaction was fear.*
instant *He took an instant dislike to them.*
instantaneous *The applause was instantaneous.*

2 most closely connected to you: *my immediate family*
close *I have a few close friends.*
direct *your direct descendants*
near *near relatives*
See also **direct, instant, prompt, urgent**

immediately
▷ *ADVERB*
I right away: *She answered my e-mail immediately.*
at once *You must come at once.*
directly *He will be there directly.*
instantly *Almost instantly she picked up the phone.*
now *Get out, now!*
promptly *The e-mail was answered promptly.*
right away *You'd better tell them right away.*
straightaway *I'd like to see you straightaway.*
2 very near in time or position: *immediately behind the house*
closely *He rushed out, closely followed by his dog.*
directly *I stopped directly under the window.*
right *He stood right behind me.*
See also **now**

immense
▷ *ADJECTIVE*
very large or huge: *an immense cloud of smoke*
colossal *a colossal waste of money*
enormous *The basement is enormous.*
giant *a giant oak table*
gigantic *a gigantic task*
huge *a huge new stadium*
massive *a massive cruise ship*
vast *a vast expanse of water*
ANTONYM **tiny**
See also **colossal, enormous, huge, large, vast**

immensity See **size**

immerse See **busy, steep**

immersed See **preoccupied**

imminent
▷ *ADJECTIVE*
going to happen very soon: *my sister's imminent arrival*
close *My birthday is quite close.*
coming *the coming dawn*
forthcoming *my forthcoming graduation*
impending *impending doom*
looming *My exams are looming.*

near *in the near future*
See also **near**

> ### CONFUSABLES
> **imminent** means **expected soon**
> **eminent** means **outstanding**

immoral See **perverted, wrong**

immorality See **evil**

immortal See **eternal**

immortality See **glory**

immovable See **steadfast**

immune
▷ *ADJECTIVE*
not subject to or affected by something: *She seems immune to pressure.*
exempt *She is exempt from blame.*
free *He was not completely free of guilt.*
protected *The diplomat is protected from the law.*
resistant *crops that are resistant to disease*
safe *I was safe from punishment.*
unaffected *She is unaffected by the sight of blood.*
See also **exempt**

immunity See **freedom, safety**

impact See **force**

impair See **cripple, ruin, spoil, undermine**

impart See **communicate, convey**

impartial See **fair, neutral**

impartiality See **justice**

impassioned See **fervent, intense, passionate**

impassive See **blank, calm, uninterested**

impatient
▷ *ADJECTIVE*
I easily annoyed: *You are too impatient with others.*
brusque *a brusque manner*
curt *He had spoken in a very curt tone of voice.*
irritable *He hadn't slept well and now felt irritable.*
ANTONYM **patient**
2 eager to do something: *He was impatient for the play to end.*
eager *Children are eager to learn.*
restless *The kids were bored and restless.*

impeccable See **clean**

impede

▷ *VERB*

to make someone's or something's progress difficult: *Fallen rocks are impeding the progress of rescue workers.*

block *The country has been trying to block these imports.*

delay *Various setbacks delayed production.*

disrupt *The drought has severely disrupted agricultural production.*

get in the way *She had a job that never got in the way of her hobbies.*

hamper *The bad weather hampered rescue operations.*

hinder *The investigation was hindered by the loss of vital information.*

obstruct *The lawyer's tactics were obstructing justice.*

See also **delay, hamper, handicap, hinder, interfere, prevent, restrict**

impediment *See* **barrier, handicap, obstacle**

impending *See* **future, imminent**

imperative *See* **necessary, urgent**

imperfect

▷ *ADJECTIVE*

having faults or problems: *We live in an imperfect world.*

broken *broken toys*

damaged *damaged goods*

defective *defective eyesight*

faulty *a car with faulty brakes*

flawed *a flawed character*

ANTONYM **perfect**

See also **faulty**

imperfection *See* **defect, fault, flaw, weakness**

imperial *See* **royal**

imperious *See* **bossy**

impersonal

▷ *ADJECTIVE*

not concerned with people and their feelings: *I found him strangely distant and impersonal.*

aloof *His manner was aloof.*

cold *My boss seemed very cold with me.*

detached *He felt emotionally detached from the victims.*

formal *Business relationships are usually formal.*

neutral *He told me the news in a neutral manner.*

remote *He was attractive, but remote.*

impersonate *See* **imitate, pose**

impertinence *See* **impudence**

impertinent *See* **cheeky, rude**

impetuous *See* **rash**

impinge on *See* **affect**

impish *See* **naughty, wicked**

implacable *See* **merciless**

implant *See* **insert**

implausible *See* **improbable, unbelievable, unlikely**

implement *See* **tool**

implore

▷ *VERB*

to beg someone to do something: *"Tell me what to do!" he implored us.*

beg *I begged him to come with me.*

beseech LITERARY *I beseech you to show him mercy.*

plead with *She pleaded with her coach to let her try the jump.*

See also **ask, beg, plead, press, urge**

imply *See* **hint, suggest**

importance *See* **emphasis, influence, value**

important

▷ *ADJECTIVE*

1 necessary or significant: *Their puppies are the most important thing to them.*

momentous *the momentous decision to drop out of school*

serious *a serious matter*

significant *a significant discovery*

weighty *We discussed weighty matters.*

ANTONYM **unimportant**

2 having great influence or power: *the most important person in the country*

eminent *an eminent scientist*

foremost *a foremost expert in Canadian history*

influential *one of the most influential books ever written*

leading *a leading expert in solar power*

notable *notable celebrities*

powerful *large, powerful countries*

See also **prominent, serious, significant, special, valuable, vital**

impose

▷ *VERB*

to force something on someone: *Fines were imposed on the culprits.*

dictate *The policy is dictated from the top.*

enforce *It is a difficult law to enforce.*

inflict *Inflicting punishment is cruel.*

levy *a tax levied on imported goods*

impose on

▷ VERB

to take advantage of someone: *I should stop imposing on your hospitality.*
abuse *They abused my hospitality by eating everything.*
take advantage of *He took advantage of her generosity.*
use *She's just using you.*
See also **administer, exact**

impose upon *See* **trouble**

imposing *See* **grand, splendid**

impossible

▷ ADJECTIVE

unable to happen or be believed: *You shouldn't promise impossible things.*
absurd *absurd claims to have met big movie stars*
hopeless *a hopeless task*
inconceivable *It's inconceivable that people can still be living in those conditions.*
ludicrous *his ludicrous plan to go swimming alone*
out of the question *Is a pay increase out of the question?*
unthinkable *The idea of splitting up is unthinkable.*
ANTONYM **possible**
See also **hopeless**

imposter *See* **fraud**

impotence *See* **inability**

impotent *See* **powerless**

impound *See* **seize**

impoverished *See* **poor**

impractical *See* **useless**

impregnable *See* **invincible, secure**

impression

▷ NOUN

the way someone or something seems to you: *your first impressions of high school*
feeling *the feeling that she was doing the right thing*
hunch *Was your hunch right or wrong?*
idea *I had my own ideas about what had happened.*
notion *I have a notion of what he is like.*
sense *She had the sense that she was in trouble.*

make an impression

▷ VERB

to have a strong effect on people: *He certainly made an impression on his teachers.*
cause a stir *News of her promotion caused a stir.*
influence *You can't do anything to influence him.*
make an impact *Events can make an impact on our lives.*
See also **idea, sense**

impressionable

▷ ADJECTIVE

easy to influence: *impressionable minds of children*
gullible *I'm so gullible, I actually believed his story.*
open *an open, trusting nature*
receptive *moulding their young, receptive minds*
sensitive *He was sensitive to criticism.*
susceptible *Children can be susceptible to advertisements.*
vulnerable *vulnerable older people*

impressive

▷ ADJECTIVE

tending to impress: *an impressive achievement*
awesome *awesome mountains, deserts, and lakes*
exciting *He tells the most exciting stories.*
grand *a grand old building*
powerful *a powerful image*
stirring *stirring music*
striking *her striking personality*
See also **grand, significant, splendid**

imprison

▷ VERB

to lock someone up: *imprisoned for murder*
confine *Keep your dog confined to the house.*
detain *They'll be detained and charged with theft.*
incarcerate *Prisoners were incarcerated in terrible conditions.*
jail *An innocent man was jailed.*
lock up *You people should be locked up!*
send to prison *The judge sent him to prison.*
ANTONYM **free**
See also **confine, jail**

improbable

▷ ADJECTIVE

unlikely or unbelievable: *improbable stories*
doubtful *It was doubtful if they would arrive on time.*
dubious *dubious evidence*
far-fetched *This all sounds a bit far-fetched.*
implausible *a movie with an implausible ending*
unbelievable *an unbelievable storyline*
unlikely *By now, they're unlikely to show up.*

improper *See* **inappropriate, indecent, unsuitable**

improve
▷ VERB
to get or make better: *They improved their house over the years.*
advance *Medical technology has advanced.*
better *They tried to better their working conditions.*
enhance *to enhance the quality of your life*
look up INFORMAL *Things are looking up for me now.*
progress *Her condition is progressing well.*
upgrade *You'll have to upgrade your computer.*
ANTONYM **worsen**
See also **correct, perfect, polish, progress, recover**

improve on *See* **top**

improvement
▷ NOUN
the fact or process of getting better: *dramatic improvements in conditions*
advance *ongoing advances in air safety*
development *his development as a comic actor*
enhancement *the enhancement of the digital image*
progress *The doctors are pleased with her progress.*
upturn *an upturn in the economy*
See also **gain, progress, recovery, reform, rise**

impudence
▷ NOUN
disrespectful talk or behaviour toward someone: *Have you ever heard such impudence?*
audacity *He had the audacity to challenge the guest speaker.*
boldness *I was amazed at his boldness toward the head of the company.*
chutzpah INFORMAL *He had the chutzpah to ask us to leave.*
gall *the most presumptuous question any interviewer has ever had the gall to ask*
impertinence *His words sounded like impertinence.*
insolence *I was punished for insolence.*
nerve *You've got a nerve showing up after what you've done.*

impudent *See* **bold, rude**

impulse *See* **instinct, urge, whim**

impulsive *See* **rash**

in *See* **fashionable, trendy**

in addition *See* **too**

in advance *See* **before, early**

in charge *See* **responsible**

in fact *See* **really**

in favour *See* **popular**

in keeping *See* **compatible**

in part *See* **partly**

in sight *See* **visible**

in spite of *See* **despite**

in the end *See* **finally**

in the long run *See* **finally**

in the middle of *See* **among**

inability
▷ NOUN
a lack of ability to do something: *an inability to concentrate*
impotence *a sense of impotence in the situation*
inadequacy *my inadequacy as a gardener*
incompetence *the incompetence of certain government officials*
ineptitude *mathematical ineptitude*
ANTONYM **ability**

inaccessible *See* **remote**

inaccurate *See* **untrue**

inadequacy *See* **deficiency, inability**

inadequate
▷ ADJECTIVE
1 not enough in quantity: *Supplies of medicine are inadequate.*
insufficient *insufficient food and water for the hiking trip*
lacking *Why are her communication skills so lacking?*
poor *poor wages*
scarce *the region's scarce energy reserves*
short *Deliveries are unreliable and food is short.*
2 not good enough: *We felt painfully inadequate in the crisis.*
deficient *He made me feel deficient as a friend.*
incapable *incapable as a server*
incompetent *He was fired for being incompetent at his job.*
inept *He was inept and lacked the skills to lead a team.*
pathetic *She made some pathetic excuse.*
useless *I'm useless around the house.*

ANTONYM **adequate**
See also **deficient, hopeless, insufficient, meagre, unsatisfactory, weak**

inadvertent See **accidental**

inane See **empty, foolish, silly, stupid**

inanity See **nonsense, stupidity**

inappropriate
▷ NOUN
not suitable for a purpose or occasion: *This behaviour is inappropriate.*
improper *the improper use of resources*
incongruous *an incongruous assortment of clothes*
unfit *unfit for the job*
unseemly *He thought crying was unseemly.*
unsuitable *food that is unsuitable for children*
untimely *their unjustified and untimely interference*
ANTONYM **appropriate**
See also **unsuitable**

inaudible See **quiet**

inaugural See **opening**

inaugurate See **begin, start**

inauguration See **introduction, start**

inborn See **natural**

incapable See **inadequate, incompetent, inefficient, powerless**

incarcerate See **imprison, jail**

incensed See **angry, mad**

incentive
▷ NOUN
something that encourages you to do something: *the incentive to work*
encouragement *She didn't get much encouragement to do anything.*
inducement *Are violent films an inducement to crime?*
motivation *Money is my motivation.*
stimulus *He needed all the stimulus he could get.*
See also **reason**

inception See **start**

incessant See **relentless**

inch See **ease, edge**

incident
▷ NOUN
an event: *Little incidents can shape our lives.*
circumstance *This is a fortunate circumstance.*

episode *I'm glad this episode is over.*
event *recent events in the Middle East*
happening *the latest happenings in the world*
occasion *I remember that occasion fondly.*
occurrence *I kept wondering about the strange occurrence.*
See also **event, experience**

incidental See **casual**

incinerate See **burn**

incision See **cut**

incite
▷ VERB
to excite someone into doing something: *Protestors tried to incite a riot.*
agitate for *Workers agitated for better conditions.*
goad *She tried to goad me into a response.*
instigate *The violence was instigated by a few people.*
provoke *I provoked him into doing something stupid.*
stir up *an attempt to stir up trouble*
See also **encourage, excite**

inclination See **feeling, tendency, will**

incline See **bend, slope, tilt**

incline toward See **prefer**

inclined See **prone**

include
▷ VERB
to have as a part: *Breakfast always includes pancakes with maple syrup.*
contain *This sheet contains a list of names.*
cover *The books cover many topics.*
embrace *a small county embracing one city and several towns*
encompass *classes that encompass a wide range of activities*
incorporate *The new cars incorporate many improvements.*
involve *a high-energy workout that involves nearly every muscle*
ANTONYM **exclude**
See also **contain**

income
▷ NOUN
the money someone or something earns: *a two-income family*
earnings *her earnings as an accountant*
pay *We complained about our pay.*
profits *The bank made profits of millions of dollars.*
salary *The lawyer was paid a good salary.*
wages *His wages have gone up.*
See also **pay**

incomparable

▷ ADJECTIVE

too good to be compared with anything else: *an area of incomparable beauty*
inimitable *his inimitable style*
peerless *He gave a peerless performance.*
superlative *The hotel has superlative views.*
supreme *the supreme piece of writing about Canada's history*
unparalleled *unparalleled happiness*
unrivalled *an unrivalled knowledge of music*

incomparably See **far**

incompetence See **inability**

incompetent

▷ ADJECTIVE

lacking the ability to do something properly: *You are incompetent, and you know it.*
bungling *a bungling amateur*
incapable *an incapable leader*
inept *an inept performance*
unable *He felt unable to handle the situation.*
useless *I felt useless.*
ANTONYM **competent**
See also **inadequate, inefficient**

incomplete

▷ ADJECTIVE

not finished or whole: *an incomplete book*
deficient *a deficient diet*
insufficient *insufficient information*
partial *The concert was a partial success.*
ANTONYM **complete**

incomprehensible See **garbled**

inconceivable See **impossible, unbelievable**

incongruous See **inappropriate**

inconsistency See **gap**

inconsistent See **uneven**

inconspicuous See **invisible**

inconvenience See **bother, hassle, nuisance, trouble**

incorporate See **include, involve**

incorrect See **false, untrue, wrong**

increase

▷ VERB

1 to make or become larger in amount: *The population continues to increase.*
enlarge *to enlarge the size of the picture*
expand *We will expand the size of the store.*
extend *She plans to extend her visit.*
grow *The sound grew in volume.*
multiply *viruses that can multiply rapidly in*

the human body
swell *His anger swelled within him.*
ANTONYM **decrease**

▷ NOUN

2 a rise in the amount of something: *a pay increase*
gain *a gain in speed*
growth *the growth of unemployment*
increment *My savings grew in tiny increments.*
rise *a rise in prices*
upsurge *an upsurge of interest in books*
ANTONYM **decrease**
See also **addition, augment, build, enlarge, expand, gain, grow, growth, jump, multiply, rise, spread**

incredible

▷ ADJECTIVE

1 totally amazing: *a champion with incredible skill*
amazing *an amazing success*
astonishing *an astonishing piece of good luck*
astounding *an astounding discovery*
extraordinary *extraordinary beauty*
marvellous *a marvellous thing to do*
sensational *a sensational performance*
2 impossible to believe: *the incredible stories of some children*
absurd *absurd ideas*
far-fetched *This all sounds very far-fetched to me.*
improbable *highly improbable claims*
unbelievable *The movie has an unbelievable plot.*
unimaginable *unimaginable wealth*
unthinkable *It's unthinkable that I forgot your birthday.*
See also **unbelievable, unlikely, wonderful**

CONFUSABLES

incredible means **hard to believe**
incredulous means **not willing to believe**

incredulity See **surprise**

increment See **increase**

incurable See **fatal**

indebted See **grateful**

indecent

▷ ADJECTIVE

shocking or rude: *indecent lyrics*
crude *crude pictures*
dirty *dirty jokes*

improper *improper behaviour*
lewd *lewd comments*
rude *a rude gesture*
vulgar *vulgar language*
See also **crude, obscene, vulgar**

indeed See **exactly**

indefatigable See **energetic**

indefinite See **uncertain, vague**

independent
▷ ADJECTIVE
1 separate from other people or things: *an independent politician*
autonomous *an autonomous country*
free *Do we have a free press?*
liberated *liberated countries*
separate *We live separate lives.*
unrelated *two unrelated incidents*
2 not needing or wanting other people's help: *a fiercely independent woman*
individualistic *individualistic behaviour*
liberated *a genuinely liberated young person*
self-sufficient *I am quite self-sufficient.*
unaided *For the first time since the operation, he walked unaided.*
See also **individual**

independently See **on your own**

indeterminate See **uncertain**

index See **list**

indicate
▷ VERB
to show that something is true: *a gesture that indicates his relief*
denote *A messy desk does not necessarily denote a messy mind.*
reveal *His diary revealed his feelings toward her.*
show *I would like to show my appreciation.*
signal *She signalled that everything was all right.*
signify *A white flag signifies surrender.*
See also **hint, mean, promise, show, specify, suggest**

indication
▷ NOUN
a sign of something: *She gave no indication that she had heard me.*
clue *Did she give any clue as to how she was feeling?*
hint *The mayor gave a strong hint that he intended to resign.*
sign *Your blood will be checked for any sign of iron deficiency.*

signal *They saw the visit as an important signal of support.*
suggestion *There is no suggestion that the two sides are any closer to agreeing.*
warning *a warning of impending doom*
See also **hint, lead, sign, suggestion, trace**

indifference See **neglect**

indifferent See **apathetic, callous, uninterested**

indignant See **resentful**

indignation See **resentment**

indirect
▷ ADJECTIVE
not done or going directly, but by another way: *an indirect route to school*
meandering *the meandering course of the river*
oblique *oblique threats*
rambling *In a rambling answer, he denied the charge.*
roundabout *a roundabout way of getting information*
tortuous *a tortuous path*
wandering *a wandering route through the woods*
ANTONYM **direct**

indiscriminate See **random**

indiscriminately See **at random**

indispensable See **essential, necessary, vital**

indistinct See **dim, faint, vague**

indistinguishable See **same**

individual
▷ ADJECTIVE
1 relating to separate people or things: *individual servings of pie*
discrete FORMAL *breaking down the job into discrete steps*
independent *two independent studies*
separate *Put the bananas and the apples in separate containers.*
single *every single house in the street*
2 different and unusual: *Develop your own individual writing style.*
characteristic *a characteristic feature of her skating*
distinctive *His voice was very distinctive.*
idiosyncratic *a highly idiosyncratic personality*
original *a chef with an original touch*
personal *his own personal style*
special *her own special way of doing things*
unique *Each person's signature is unique.*

▷ NOUN
3 a person, different from any other person: *the rights of the individual*
character *a remarkable character*
human being *another human being*
party *Who is the guilty party?*
person *There was only one person in the audience.*
soul *He's a jolly soul.*
See also **different, peculiar, person, personal, private, single, special**

individualistic *See* **independent**

individuality *See* **personality**

indomitable *See* **invincible**

induce *See* **occasion, persuade, prompt**

inducement *See* **bait, incentive**

indulge *See* **humour, satisfy, spoil**

indulgence *See* **excess, luxury**

industrious
▷ ADJECTIVE
tending to work hard: *industrious students*
busy *an exceptionally busy man*
conscientious *He was slow but conscientious.*
diligent *She was diligent about answering e-mails.*
hard-working *an exceptionally disciplined and hard-working student*
tireless *a tireless and willing worker*
ANTONYM **lazy**
See also **active**

industry *See* **business, labour**

inefficient
▷ ADJECTIVE
badly organized and slow: *an inefficient retrieval system*
disorganized *My boss is completely disorganized.*
incapable *If he fails, he will be considered incapable.*
incompetent *an incompetent officer*
inept *an inept use of power*
sloppy *sloppy management*
ANTONYM **efficient**

inept *See* **inadequate, incompetent, inefficient**

ineptitude *See* **inability**

inequality *See* **injustice**

inert *See* **still**

inevitable *See* **certain, necessary**

inexact *See* **approximate**

inexhaustible *See* **infinite**

inexorable *See* **necessary**

inexpensive *See* **cheap, economical, reasonable**

inexperience *See* **innocence**

inexperienced
▷ ADJECTIVE
lacking experience of a situation or activity: *inexperienced drivers*
green INFORMAL *He was new at the job and very green.*
new *a new player*
novice *a novice writer*
raw *raw talent*
unaccustomed *He's unaccustomed to being on TV.*
ANTONYM **experienced**
See also **ignorant**

infallible *See* **sure**

infamous *See* **notorious**

infant *See* **baby, child, young**

infantile *See* **childish**

infatuation *See* **love, passion**

infect
▷ VERB
to cause disease in something: *One mosquito can infect many people.*
affect *A few students have been affected by the virus.*
blight *trees blighted by pollution*
contaminate *These substances can contaminate fish.*
taint *blood that had been tainted*
See also **pollute**

infectious
▷ ADJECTIVE
spreading from one person to another: *infectious diseases*
catching *Yes, chicken pox is catching.*
contagious *a highly contagious disease*

infer *See* **conclude**

inference *See* **conclusion**

inferior
▷ ADJECTIVE
1 having a lower position than something or someone else: *Young people are considered to have inferior status.*
lesser *the work of lesser writers*
lower *lower animals*
minor *a minor celebrity*
secondary *He was relegated to a secondary position.*

second-class *treated as second-class citizens*
subordinate *Her subordinate officers followed her example.*
ANTONYM **superior**
2 of low quality: *inferior-quality DVDs*
mediocre *mediocre music*
poor *a poor standard of service*
second-class *a second-class education*
second-rate *second-rate restaurants*
shoddy *Customers no longer tolerate shoddy products.*
ANTONYM **superior**
▷ NOUN
3 a person in a lower position than another: *Don't treat me like an inferior.*
junior *the office junior*
subordinate *All her subordinates adored her.*
underling *Every underling feared him.*
ANTONYM **superior**
See also **cheap, junior, poor, rotten**

inferno *See* **fire, hell**

infertile *See* **barren**

infinite
▷ ADJECTIVE
without any limit or end: *an infinite number of possibilities*
boundless *boundless energy*
eternal *the secret of eternal youth*
everlasting *our everlasting friendship*
inexhaustible *an inexhaustible supply of ideas*
perpetual *a perpetual source of worry*
untold *untold wealth*
See also **countless, plentiful**

inflamed *See* **sore, tender**

inflexible *See* **firm, obstinate, rigid, stubborn**

inflict *See* **administer, bring, impose**

influence
▷ NOUN
1 power over other people: *They have quite a lot of influence.*
authority *You have no authority over me.*
control *Their coach has too much control over them.*
importance *a leader of great importance*
power *a position of power*
sway *My uncle holds sway in his home.*
2 an effect that someone or something has: *under the influence of alcohol*
effect *Your age has an effect on your views.*
hold *He is losing his hold on the public.*

magnetism *a speaker of great personal magnetism*
spell *under the spell of one of his friends*
weight *the weight of the law*
▷ VERB
3 to have an effect on someone or something: *His parents never try to influence him.*
affect *He will not let personal preference affect his choice.*
control *I can't control that dog.*
direct *I don't need you directing my life.*
guide *Let your instinct guide you.*
manipulate *I don't like the way he manipulates people.*
sway *efforts to sway voters*
See also **factor, grip, guide**

influential *See* **important, powerful**

inform
▷ VERB
to tell someone about something: *Please inform me of your progress.*
advise FORMAL *I can advise you of his whereabouts.*
enlighten *a history lesson that enlightens you*
notify *I was notified of my sister's illness.*
tell *Tell me what is going on.*
See also **advise, alert, brief, communicate, notify, tell**

informal
▷ ADJECTIVE
relaxed and casual: *His manner was informal and relaxed.*
casual *a casual attitude toward money*
colloquial *colloquial language*
easy *easy conversation*
familiar *His manner was too familiar, and seemed almost rude.*
natural *She was friendly and natural with us.*
relaxed *a relaxed atmosphere in class*
ANTONYM **formal**
See also **colloquial, cosy, relaxed**

information
▷ NOUN
the details you know about something: *I would never give any information about you.*
data *The survey provided valuable data.*
facts *Pass on all the facts to the police.*
material *highly secret material*
news *We have news of your brother.*
notice *advance notice of the event*
word *I received word that the guests had arrived.*
See also **news, word**

informed *See* **aware, wise**

inform of *See* **report**

inform on
▷ VERB
to tell the police about someone who has committed a crime: *Somebody must have informed on the thieves.*
betray *They betrayed their associates to the police.*
denounce *He was denounced as a dangerous rebel.*
tell on INFORMAL *It's all right; I won't tell on you.*
See also **betray**

infrequent *See* **few, uncommon**

infringe *See* **break, disobey, intrude**

infringed *See* **broken**

infringement *See* **breach**

infuriate *See* **anger**

infuriated *See* **furious, mad**

ingenious *See* **bright, smart**

ingenuity *See* **imagination**

ingredient
▷ NOUN
a thing that something is made from: *Place all the ingredients in a pan.*
component *the components of the computer*
constituent *the main constituent of fish oil*
element *the various elements in a picture*

inhabit
▷ VERB
to live in a place: *the people who inhabit these islands*
dwell *the people who dwell in the forest*
live *She has lived here for ten years.*
lodge *A number of students lodge in that house.*
occupy *Forty tenants occupy the building.*
populate *a swamp populated by huge birds*
reside FORMAL *They reside in the country.*
See also **live**

inhabitant
▷ NOUN
someone who lives in a place: *an inhabitant of Norway*
citizen *Canadian citizens*
inmate *prison inmates*
native *She lives in Canada, but she is a native of Italy.*
occupant *the previous occupant of the house*
resident *the residents of the retirement home*

inhabitants *See* **people**

inherent *See* **natural**

inheritance
▷ NOUN
something that is passed on: *This gold watch is my inheritance from my grandfather.*
bequest *Our aunt left a bequest for us in her will.*
heritage *This building is part of our city's heritage.*
legacy *His politeness was the legacy of his upbringing.*
See also **legacy**

inhibit *See* **check, interfere, restrain, restrict**

inhibited *See* **pent-up**

inhuman *See* **savage**

inhumane *See* **cruel**

inhumanity *See* **cruelty**

inimitable *See* **incomparable**

initial *See* **first, opening, original**

initially *See* **first**

initiate *See* **begin, start**

initiation *See* **introduction, start**

initiative *See* **drive**

injunction *See* **command**

injure
▷ VERB
to damage part of someone's body: *Five people were injured in the ferry accident.*
harm *The hijackers did not harm anyone.*
hurt *He hurt his back in an accident.*
maim *Land mines maim and kill civilians.*
wound *wounded by flying glass*
See also **damage, hurt**

injury
▷ NOUN
damage to part of the body: *He sustained serious injuries in the accident.*
damage *Fortunately, there was no brain damage.*
harm *Dogs can do harm to human beings.*
wound *a head wound*
See also **damage, harm**

injustice
▷ NOUN
unfairness and lack of justice: *the injustice of the system*

bias *He shows bias against women.*
discrimination *racial discrimination*
inequality *people concerned about social inequality*
prejudice *prejudice against workers over 55*
unfairness *the unfairness of the decision*
wrong *I intend to right past wrongs.*
ANTONYM **justice**
See also **wrong**

inkling *See* **idea**

inlet *See* **bay**

inmate *See* **inhabitant**

innards *See* **insides**

innate *See* **natural**

inner *See* **inside**

innermost *See* **inside**

innocence
▷ *NOUN*
inexperience of evil or unpleasant things: *the innocence of babies*
gullibility *I'm paying for my earlier gullibility.*
inexperience *their inexperience of the real world*
naivety *There was a youthful naivety to his honesty.*
simplicity *a childlike simplicity*

innocent
▷ *ADJECTIVE*
1 not guilty of a crime: *the arrest of innocent suspects*
blameless *a blameless life*
clear *He was cleared of blame for the accident.*
not guilty *Both men were found not guilty.*
spotless *a spotless record*
ANTONYM **guilty**
2 without experience of evil or unpleasant things: *They seem so young and innocent.*
childlike *childlike trust*
guileless *She is completely guileless, and thinks the best of everybody.*
naive *I was young and naive when I left home.*
pure *a pure life with little experience of the real world*
See also **ignorant**

innocuous *See* **harmless, safe**

innumerable *See* **countless, many**

inquire *See* **ask**

inquiring *See* **curious**

inquiry *See* **query**

inquisitive *See* **curious, nosy**

inquisitiveness *See* **curiosity**

inscribe *See* **carve, write**

insensitive *See* **callous, numb, thoughtless**

insert
▷ *VERB*
to put something into something else: *He inserted the key into the lock.*
enter *Enter your name in the box before mailing the application.*
implant *a device implanted in the arm*
introduce *to introduce a new subject into the conversation*
place *Cover the casserole tightly and place in the oven.*
put *She put a coin in the slot.*
set *diamonds set in gold*
See also **stick**

inside
▷ *ADJECTIVE*
surrounded by the main part and often hidden: *We booked an inside cabin.*
inner *the inner ear*
innermost *the innermost parts of the galaxy*
interior *a car with plenty of interior space*
internal *your internal organs*
ANTONYM **outside**

insides
▷ *PLURAL NOUN*
INFORMAL the parts inside your body: *My insides ached from eating too much.*
entrails *chicken entrails*
guts *fish guts*
innards *the innards of a human body*
internal organs *damage to internal organs*

insight *See* **vision, wisdom**

insignificant
▷ *ADJECTIVE*
small and unimportant: *a small, insignificant flaw in the sweater*
irrelevant *irrelevant details*
little *It seems such a little thing to get upset over.*
minor *Officials say the problem is minor.*
petty *Arguments can start over petty things.*
trifling *These difficulties may seem trifling to you.*
trivial *He tried to wave aside these issues as trivial matters.*
unimportant *The age difference seemed unimportant.*

ANTONYM **significant**
See also **petty, slight, trivial, unimportant**

insincere
▷ *ADJECTIVE*
saying things you do not mean: *insincere flattery*
deceitful *deceitful and misleading remarks*
dishonest *dishonest salespeople*
false *a false confession*
two-faced *the most two-faced liar in the world*
ANTONYM **sincere**
See also **false, two-faced**

insinuate *See* **hint, suggest**

insinuation *See* **suggestion**

insipid *See* **flat, mild, tasteless**

insist
▷ *VERB*
to demand something forcefully: *My family insisted I should not give in.*
demand *The teacher demanded an explanation.*
press *She is pressing for changes in the system.*
urge *We urge vigorous action be taken immediately.*
See also **claim**

insist on *See* **exact**

insist upon *See* **exact**

insolence *See* **impudence**

insolent *See* **rude**

insolvency *See* **poverty**

inspect
▷ *VERB*
to examine something carefully: *the right to inspect company files*
check *Check each item for obvious errors.*
examine *He examined the passport and stamped it.*
eye *We eyed each other thoughtfully.*
investigate *Police are investigating the scene of the crime.*
scan *The officer scanned the room.*
survey *They surveyed the ruins of the building.*
See also **check, examine, scrutinize**

inspection *See* **check, examination**

inspire *See* **excite, motivate, prompt**

inspired *See* **creative**

install *See* **set up**

instalment *See* **issue, payment, section**

instance *See* **case**

instant
▷ *NOUN*
1 a short period of time: *The pain disappeared in an instant.*
flash *It was all over in a flash.*
minute *I'll see you in a minute.*
moment *In a moment he was gone.*
second *Seconds later, the firefighters appeared.*
split second *Their eyes met for a split second.*
trice *She was back in a trice.*
▷ *ADJECTIVE*
2 immediate and without delay: *He had taken an instant dislike to me.*
immediate *We need an immediate reply.*
instantaneous *an instantaneous reaction to the e-mail*
prompt *Prompt action is needed.*
See also **immediate, minute, moment, prompt**

instantaneous *See* **immediate, instant, prompt**

instantly *See* **immediately**

instigate *See* **incite, start**

instinct
▷ *NOUN*
a natural tendency to do something: *My first instinct was to protect myself.*
feeling *You seem to have a feeling for drawing.*
impulse *The mother resisted an impulse to smile.*
intuition *You should trust your intuition.*
sixth sense *Some sixth sense told her to keep going.*
urge *He fought the urge to panic.*

instinctive *See* **automatic, natural**

institute *See* **set up, society, start**

institution *See* **association, introduction, organization**

instruct
▷ *VERB*
1 to tell someone to do something: *They have instructed their lawyers to sue.*
command *He commanded his troops to attack.*
direct *They have been directed to give attention to this problem.*
order *I ordered them to leave.*
tell *A passerby told me to move my bike.*
2 to teach someone about a subject or skill:

He instructs people in computer technology.
coach *He coached me in French.*
educate *We need to educate people about diet and exercise.*
school *She's been home-schooling her kids.*
teach *She taught us sign language.*
train *We're training them in restaurant management.*
tutor *He was tutoring me in math.*
See also **brief, order, require, show, teach, tell, train**

instruction *See* **command, education, order**

instructor *See* **teacher**

instrument *See* **machine, tool**

insufficient
▷ ADJECTIVE
not enough for a particular purpose: *insufficient information*
deficient *a deficient diet*
inadequate *The problem lies with inadequate staffing.*
lacking *My confidence is lacking.*
scant *He paid scant attention to what was going on.*
short *She was short of breath.*
ANTONYM **sufficient**
See also **inadequate, incomplete**

insular *See* **narrow-minded**

insult
▷ VERB
1 to offend someone by being rude to them: *I did not mean to insult you.*
abuse *obnoxious fans abusing referees*
affront *He pretended to be affronted by what I said.*
offend *I had no intention of offending the community.*
put down *They seemed to delight in putting me down.*
slight *They felt slighted by not being invited.*
snub *He snubbed me in public and made me feel foolish.*
ANTONYM **compliment**
▷ NOUN
2 a rude remark that offends someone: *The two men exchanged insults.*
abuse *The actor hurled verbal abuse at the director.*
affront *She took my words as a personal affront.*
offence *I meant no offence to you.*
slight *He is very sensitive to slights.*
snub *This was a deliberate snub to me.*
See also **abuse, offend, provoke**

insulting *See* **abusive, offensive**

insults *See* **abuse**

insurance *See* **precaution**

insurrection *See* **rebellion**

intact *See* **complete, sound**

integrate *See* **combine**

integrity *See* **character, honour, principle, right, virtue**

intellect *See* **genius, intelligence, mind, reason**

intellectual *See* **educated, learned**

intelligence
▷ NOUN
the ability to understand and learn things: *students of high intelligence*
cleverness *I can't get over the child's cleverness.*
comprehension *an idea beyond my comprehension*
intellect *Her intellect was obvious at a young age.*
perception *You have brilliant perception and insight.*
sense *They have the sense to seek help.*
understanding *a great understanding of human nature*
wit *He had the wit to see this was a good idea.*
See also **head, news, sense, word**

intelligent
▷ ADJECTIVE
able to understand and learn things: *Dolphins are intelligent animals.*
acute *His relaxed exterior hides a very acute mind.*
brainy INFORMAL *I don't consider myself brainy so I study extra hard.*
bright *an exceptionally bright child*
clever *a clever child*
quick *His quick mind soon grasped the situation.*
sharp *a very sharp intellect*
smart *He thinks he's as smart as I am.*
ANTONYM **stupid**
See also **bright, brilliant, clever, smart**

intend
▷ VERB
1 to decide or plan to do something: *She intended to move back to Saskatoon.*
aim *We aim to raise funds for charity.*
be determined *I'm determined to enjoy the day.*
mean *I didn't mean any harm.*
plan *He planned to leave Saint John on Monday.*

propose *Where do you propose building such a huge hotel?*

resolve *She resolved to report the matter.*

2 to mean for a certain use: *a book intended for serious students*

aim *children's games aimed at developing quick reflexes*

design *The house had been designed for a large family.*

earmark *That money was earmarked for repairs.*

mean *The cake was not meant for tonight's dinner.*

See also **aim, mean, resolve**

intended *See* **calculated**

intense

▷ *ADJECTIVE*

1 very great in strength or amount: *intense heat*

acute *an acute shortage of accommodation*

deep *He felt a deep sense of relief.*

extreme *Proceed with extreme caution.*

fierce *There was fierce competition for the job.*

great *a great sense of satisfaction*

powerful *I had a powerful urge to scream at him.*

profound *The book had a profound effect in Canada.*

severe *I had severe problems.*

2 tending to have strong feelings: *She was very intense before the important game.*

ardent *one of his most ardent supporters*

earnest *He is earnest about his beliefs.*

fervent *a fervent admirer of Beethoven's music*

fierce *fierce loyalty to his friends*

impassioned *She made an impassioned appeal for peace.*

passionate *He is very passionate about the project.*

vehement *a vehement critic of the plan*

See also **acute, ardent, colourful, deep, extreme, fierce, furious, passionate, serious, severe, uncommon, violent**

intensify *See* **build, rise**

intensity *See* **heat, passion, strength, violence**

intensive *See* **thorough**

intent *See* **set on**

intent on *See* **determined**

intention

▷ *NOUN*

a plan to do something: *He announced his intention of retiring.*

aim *The aim of this book is to inform you.*

goal *The goal is to raise a lot of money.*

idea *I bought books with the idea of reading them on my vacation.*

object *It was his object in life to find the island.*

objective *Her objective was to play on a professional hockey team.*

purpose *He did not know the purpose of their visit.*

See also **aim, goal, object, point, purpose**

intentional *See* **deliberate**

intentionally *See* **on purpose**

interchange *See* **change, exchange, substitute, swap**

interest

▷ *NOUN*

1 a feeling of wanting to know about something: *I have a great interest in that period of history.*

attention *The book attracted considerable attention.*

concern *How it happened is of little concern to me.*

curiosity *His reply satisfied our curiosity.*

fascination *a lifelong fascination with the sea*

2 a hobby: *He has a wide range of interests.*

activity *I enjoy outdoor activities like canoeing and rock climbing.*

hobby *My hobbies are skiing, photography, and tennis.*

pastime *His favourite pastime is golf.*

pursuit *favourite childhood pursuits*

▷ *VERB*

3 to attract someone's attention and curiosity: *This part of the book interests me most.*

appeal *The bright colours seem to appeal to children.*

captivate *this author's ability to captivate young minds*

fascinate *Politics fascinated my father.*

intrigue *The situation intrigued him.*

stimulate *She was stimulated by the challenge.*

ANTONYM **bore**

See also **activity, appeal, curiosity, enthusiasm**

interested *See* **curious**

CONFUSABLES

Interested has two antonyms:
uninterested means **not interested**
disinterested means **impartial**

---

interesting
▷ *ADJECTIVE*
making you want to know, learn, or hear
more: *an interesting hobby*
absorbing *an absorbing conversation*
compelling *compelling drama*
entertaining *an entertaining companion*
gripping *a gripping story*
intriguing *the most intriguing character in
the book*
stimulating *a stimulating trip to India*
ANTONYM **boring**
See also **colourful**

interfere
▷ *VERB*
1 to try to influence a situation: *Stop
interfering and leave me alone.*
butt in *I butted in where I didn't belong.*
intervene *You shouldn't have intervened in
their argument.*
intrude *I don't want to intrude on your
meeting.*
meddle *Do not meddle in my affairs.*
tamper *the price we pay for tampering with
the environment*
2 to have a damaging effect on a
situation: *His problems interfered with his
work.*
conflict *an evening that conflicted with my
work schedule*
disrupt *Strikes disrupted air traffic.*
hinder *An ankle injury hindered her
movement.*
impede *Fallen rocks impeded the progress of
the rescue workers.*
inhibit *factors that inhibit growth*
obstruct *Lack of funds obstructed our
progress.*
See also **pry**

interim *See* **temporary**

interior *See* **inside**

interlude *See* **break, gap, interval**

intermittent *See* **occasional**

internal *See* **home, inside**

internal organs *See* **insides**

interpret *See* **read**

interrogate
▷ *VERB*
to question someone thoroughly: *I
interrogated everyone even slightly involved.*
examine *Lawyers examined the witnesses.*
grill *He kept telling police who grilled him: "I
didn't do it."*
question *She was questioned by police.*
quiz *She quizzed me quite closely for a while.*
See also **ask, question**

interrupt
▷ *VERB*
1 to start talking when someone else is
talking: *He tried to speak, but she interrupted
him.*
butt in *He butted in without a greeting.*
heckle *It is easy to heckle from the safety of
the audience.*
2 to stop a process or activity for a time: *The
game was interrupted by rain.*
break *allowing passengers to break their trip
with a stay in Vancouver*
discontinue *Do not discontinue the
treatment without seeing your doctor.*
suspend *Work was suspended until the
electricity was restored.*
See also **intrude**

interruption *See* **delay, pause**

intersect *See* **cross**

interval
▷ *NOUN*
a period of time between two moments or
dates: *There was a long interval of silence.*
break *a short break from work*
gap *the gap between school terms*
hiatus *There was a momentary hiatus in the
sounds.*
interlude *It was a happy interlude in my
life.*
pause *a pause between two periods of
intense activity*
See also **break, gap, pause, period,
space, time, wait**

intervene
▷ *VERB*
to step in to prevent conflict: *I relied on them
to intervene if anything happened.*
arbitrate *A committee was set up to
arbitrate in the dispute.*
mediate *efforts to mediate between
management and labour*
See also **interfere**

interview *See* **appointment**

intimate *See* **cosy, hint, mention,
suggest**

intimation *See* **hint, notice, suggestion**

intimidate See **bully, frighten, scare**

intimidating See **formidable, frightening**

into See **keen**

into the bargain See **also, too**

intolerable See **unbearable**

intoxicated See **drunk**

intractable See **difficult, obstinate**

intrepid See **bold**

intricate See **complex, complicated, elaborate, fancy, sophisticated**

intrigue See **fascinate, interest, plot**

intriguing See **interesting**

introduce See **insert, raise, start**

introduction
▷ *NOUN*
1 the act of presenting someone or something new: *the introduction of the loonie in 1987*
establishment *the establishment of a democratic system*
inauguration *the inauguration of the president*
initiation *your initiation into adulthood*
institution *the institution of a new voting system*
launch *the launch of this popular author's new book*
2 a piece of writing at the beginning of a book: *The book contains a new introduction by the author.*
foreword *I am happy to write the foreword to this textbook.*
preface *I read through the preface quickly.*
prologue *I never read the prologue of a book.*
See also **appearance**

introductory See **opening**

intrude
▷ *VERB*
to disturb someone or something: *I don't want to intrude on your parents.*
butt in *I butted in where I didn't belong.*
encroach *Does your work encroach on your private life?*
infringe *She promised not to infringe on his space.*
interrupt *The ringing of the phone interrupted my thoughts.*
trespass *I don't like to trespass on your time.*
violate *to violate their privacy*
See also **interfere, pry**

intrude on See **disturb**

intuition See **instinct, vision**

intuitive See **natural**

invade
▷ *VERB*
to enter a country by force: *The allies invaded the mainland.*
attack *Planes attacked the town.*
enter *The troops entered from the west.*
occupy *Soldiers occupied the town within a few minutes.*
violate *An army helicopter violated neutral territory yesterday.*
See also **attack, raid**

invalid See **faulty, patient**

invalidate See **disprove, reverse**

invaluable See **precious**

invariably See **always**

invasion See **attack**

invective See **abuse**

invent
▷ *VERB*
1 to be the first person to think of a device: *He invented the first electric clock.*
coin *Jaron Lanier coined the term "virtual reality."*
come up with INFORMAL *She came up with a gadget to toss salads.*
conceive *He conceived the first portable computer.*
create *The company decided to create a new perfume.*
formulate *He formulated his plan for escape.*
originate *Jacques Plante was the hockey player who originated the goalie's mask.*
2 to make up a story or excuse: *I tried to invent a plausible excuse.*
concoct *A newspaper concocted an imaginary interview.*
fabricate *The evidence against them was fabricated.*
make up *He was known for making up stories about himself.*
manufacture *The children manufactured an elaborate tale.*
See also **compose, create, make up, produce**

invented See **imaginary**

inventive See **creative**

inventiveness See **imagination**

inventory See **list**

invest in See **buy**

investigate
▷ VERB
to find out all the facts about something:
Police are still investigating the incidents.
examine *I have examined all the evidence.*
explore *a book that explores the history of technology*
probe *He probed into my private life.*
research *I'm researching material about the Atlantic Provinces.*
sift *I sifted the evidence for conclusions.*
study *Experts are studying the security in the building.*
See also **inspect, research**

investigation See **research**

investment See **finance**

investments See **stock**

invincible
▷ ADJECTIVE
unable to be defeated: *When the skating pair is at their best, they're invincible.*
impregnable *an impregnable fortress*
indomitable *the indomitable spirit of the conquered people*
unbeatable *a performance record that is unbeatable*

invisible
▷ ADJECTIVE
unable to be seen: *His face was invisible beneath his hat.*
concealed *a concealed weapon*
disguised *a safe disguised as a panel in the wall*
hidden *a hidden camera*
inconspicuous *She tried to make herself inconspicuous.*
unseen *His work was guided by an unseen hand.*
ANTONYM **visible**

invite See **ask, challenge**

invoice See **bill**

involuntary See **automatic**

involve
▷ VERB
to have as a necessary part: *Running a kitchen involves a great deal of organization.*
incorporate *The program incorporates a range of activities.*
require *Caring for a baby requires special skills.*
take in *This study takes in a number of areas.*
See also **concern, demand, include**

involved See **active, complex, complicated, elaborate**

involvement See **part**

irate See **mad**

ironic See **sarcastic**

irrational
▷ ADJECTIVE
not based on logical reasons: *irrational fears*
absurd *It was an absurd overreaction.*
crazy *crazy ideas*
illogical *his completely illogical arguments*
nonsensical *Such an idea sounds downright nonsensical.*
unsound *The thinking is good-hearted, but muddled and unsound.*

irregular
▷ ADJECTIVE
1 not smooth or even: *an irregular surface*
asymmetrical *an asymmetrical design*
bumpy *bumpy roads*
jagged *jagged fragments of stained glass*
lopsided *his lopsided smile*
ragged *the ragged edges of a torn piece of paper*
uneven *uneven teeth*
ANTONYM **regular**
2 not forming a regular pattern: *She worked irregular hours.*
erratic *a planet with an erratic orbit*
haphazard *a haphazard system*
occasional *occasional rain showers*
patchy *Her career has been patchy.*
random *The stock market is random and unpredictable.*
variable *a variable rate of interest*
ANTONYM **regular**
See also **changeable, crooked, uneven**

irrelevant See **insignificant**

irresponsible
▷ ADJECTIVE
not concerned with the consequences of your actions: *an irresponsible attitude*
careless *a careless driver*
reckless *reckless spending*
thoughtless *a thoughtless remark*
wild *a wild idea*
ANTONYM **responsible**
See also **careless, unwise**

irrigate See **wet**

irritable
▷ ADJECTIVE
easily annoyed: *He's unusually tense and irritable.*
bad-tempered *You're very bad-tempered today.*

cantankerous *a cantankerous old man*
crabby *She's in a crabby mood today.*
petulant *He was like a petulant child.*
See also **grumpy, impatient, moody**

irritate

▷ *VERB*

to annoy someone: *Their attitude irritates me.*
anger *This article angered me.*
annoy *It just annoyed me to hear him criticize everyone.*
bother *Nothing bothers me.*
exasperate *We were exasperated by the delay.*
needle INFORMAL *If her remark needled him, he didn't show it.*
ruffle *He doesn't get ruffled by anything.*
See also **annoy, provoke**

irritation *See* **annoyance, bother, nuisance, pain**

isolated *See* **alone, exceptional, lonely, remote, separate**

isolation *See* **solitude**

issue

▷ *NOUN*

1 a subject that people are talking about: *important issues of the day*
concern *Political concerns continue to dominate the news.*
matter *He touched on many matters in his speech.*
problem *the energy problem*
question *The whole question of conservation is a tricky one.*
subject *the teacher's views on the subject*
topic *the main topic for discussion*
2 a particular edition of a newspaper or magazine: *the latest issue of* Maclean's *magazine*
copy *a copy of the* Free Press
edition *There's an article about the movie in next month's edition.*
instalment *a magazine published in monthly instalments*
▷ *VERB*
3 to make a formal statement: *They have issued a statement denying the allegations.*
deliver *She delivered a speech on the subject of pollution.*
give *He gave her his letter of resignation.*
make *He made an official statement.*
pronounce *The authorities took time to pronounce their verdicts.*
read out *She read out an announcement outside the court.*
release *The police are not releasing any more details.*

ANTONYM **withdraw**
▷ *VERB*
4 to give something officially: *Staff will be issued with badges.*
equip *plans to equip all reporters with laptops*
furnish *They will furnish you with the necessary items.*
give out *The prizes were given out by a local dignitary.*
provide *The players were provided with official uniforms.*
supply *an agreement not to supply nuclear reactors*
See also **affair, business, consideration, matter, question, release, subject**

INFORMALLY SPEAKING

a burning issue: a matter of great importance
make an issue (out) of: make into a point of argument
take issue: disagree

it could be *See* **maybe, perhaps**

item

▷ *NOUN*

1 one of a collection or list of things: *an item on the agenda*
article *articles of clothing*
matter *He dealt with a variety of matters.*
point *Many of the points in the report are correct.*
2 a newspaper or magazine article: *There was an item in the paper about them.*
article *a short article in the school paper*
feature *The magazine contained a special feature on our school science project.*
notice *notices in today's national newspapers*
piece *I enjoyed your recent piece about Canada's peacekeepers.*
report *an investigative report on the scandal*
See also **article, entry, feature**

itinerary *See* **route**

Jj

jab *See* **dig, poke, stick**

jack up *See* **organize**

jacket *See* **cover**

TYPES OF ... *JACKET*	
blazer	mackinaw
coat	parka
jerkin	windbreaker

jagged
▷ ADJECTIVE
sharp and spiky: *jagged cliffs*
barbed *barbed wire*
craggy *craggy mountains*
rough *the rough surface of the rock*
serrated *a serrated knife*
ANTONYM **smooth**
See also **irregular, sharp**

jail
▷ NOUN
1 a place where prisoners are held: *sentenced to six months in jail*
prison *his release from prison*
▷ VERB
2 to put in prison: *He was jailed for 20 years.*
detain *Police cannot detain a suspect indefinitely.*
imprison *imprisoned for 18 months on charges of theft*
incarcerate *They have been incarcerated as political prisoners.*
See also **imprison, prison**

jam
▷ NOUN
1 a crowded mass of people or things: *There was quite a traffic jam on the highway.*
crowd *elbowing his way through the crowd*
crush *We were separated in the crush.*
mass *a mass of excited fans*
mob *a growing mob of protesters*
multitude *surrounded by a noisy multitude*
throng *An official pushed through the throng.*
2 a difficult situation: *We're in a real jam now.*
dilemma *faced with a dilemma*
fix INFORMAL *a difficult economic fix*
hole SLANG *He admitted that the government was in a hole.*
plight *the plight of the earthquake victims*
predicament *We can find a way out of our predicament.*
quandary *We're in a quandary over our vacation plans.*

trouble *You are in serious trouble.*
▷ VERB
3 to push something somewhere roughly: *She jammed on the brakes.*
cram *He crammed the bills into his pocket.*
force *I forced the key into the ignition.*
ram *He lost control and rammed the bike into the wall.*
stuff *She stuffed the papers into the box.*
▷ VERB
4 to become stuck: *The paper has jammed in the photocopier again.*
stall *The engine stalled.*
stick *She tried to open the window, but it was stuck.*
See also **cram, mess, predicament, stick, stuff**

jar *See* **clash**

jargon *See* **language**

jaundiced *See* **sour**

jaunt *See* **drive, trip**

jaunty *See* **cheerful**

jazzy *See* **colourful**

jealous
▷ ADJECTIVE
wanting to have something that someone else has: *He was jealous of my success.*
envious *envious of the attention his brother was getting*
resentful *resentful of her friend's busy life*

jealousy *See* **envy**

jeering *See* **mockery**

jeopardize *See* **endanger, risk, threaten**

jeopardy *See* **danger**

jerk *See* **tug**

jest *See* **joke**

jettison *See* **discard, dispose of, dump, get rid of**

jiggle *See* **fidget**

jilt *See* **abandon**

jingle *See* **slogan**

jittery *See* **nervous, tense**

job
▷ NOUN
1 the work someone does to earn money: *I'm still looking for a job.*
employment *unable to find employment*
occupation *her occupation as a carpenter*

position *He's leaving to take a position at another firm.*
post *She has resigned her post as his assistant.*
profession *She chose law as her profession.*
trade *his trade as a welder*
2 a duty or responsibility: *It's your job to find out what's going on.*
concern *The technical aspects are the concern of the engineers.*
duty *I consider it my duty to write and thank you.*
function *an important function to fill*
responsibility *It's not my responsibility to look after your pets.*
role *Our role is to keep the peace.*
task *She had the task of breaking the bad news.*
See also **appointment, duty, function, task, undertaking, work**

jobless *See* **idle, unemployed**

jog *See* **run**

jog someone's memory *See* **remind**

join
▷ VERB
1 to become a member of something: *He joined the team last year.*
enlist *He enlisted in the Canadian Forces.*
enrol *She has enrolled in an acting class.*
sign up *I've signed up as a member.*
ANTONYM **resign**
2 to fasten two things together: *two sticks joined together by a chain*
attach *The gadget can be attached to any surface.*
connect *two rooms connected by a long hallway*
couple *two shafts coupled together*
fasten *a wooden bench fastened to the floor*
link *We linked arms and walked home together.*
tie *He tied the dog to a post.*
ANTONYM **separate**
See also **attach, connect, fasten, link, piece together, unite**

join forces *See* **co-operate, team, unite**

join in *See* **participate, take part in**

jointly *See* **together**

joke
▷ NOUN
1 something that makes people laugh: *I heard a great joke today.*
gag INFORMAL *He played a gag on us.*
jest *It was only intended as a jest.*
lark *They just did it for a lark.*
prank *The prank backfired on her.*

quip *a famous quip by my favourite comedian*
wisecrack *She was tempted to make a wisecrack.*
witticism *laughing at each other's witticisms*
▷ VERB
2 to say something funny: *She was always joking about her friends.*
banter *The comedian bantered with the audience.*
chaff *They chaffed us about our chances of winning.*
jest *jesting with his cronies*
kid INFORMAL *Don't worry, I'm only kidding.*
quip *"You'll be taller than me soon," he quipped.*
tease *"You must be famous," she teased.*

jolly *See* **bright, cheerful, cheery**

jolt *See* **bump, shake, surprise**

jotting *See* **note**

journal *See* **record**

journey
▷ NOUN
1 the act of travelling from one place to another: *the journey across the continent*
excursion *The trip includes an excursion to Niagara Falls.*
expedition *an expedition to the South Pole*
tour *a two-month tour of Europe*
trek *a trek through the Gobi Desert*
trip *a business trip*
voyage *the first space-shuttle voyage*
▷ VERB
2 to travel from one place to another: *Last year, she journeyed through South America.*
go *We went from one city to the next.*
proceed *proceeding along the road in the wrong direction*
tour *He toured China in 2004.*
travel *She travelled here by train.*
trek *trekking through the jungle*
voyage *They voyaged as far as Spain.*
See also **drive, go, travel, trip**

joy
▷ NOUN
great happiness: *Her face shone with joy.*
bliss *an expression of pure bliss*
delight *He let out a shout of delight.*
ecstasy *Her eyes closed in ecstasy at the good news.*
elation *He felt a surge of elation.*
rapture *Her speech was received with rapture.*
ANTONYM **misery**

See also **delight, ecstasy, happiness, pleasure**

joyful

▷ *ADJECTIVE*

extremely happy: *a joyful smile*
delighted *I'm delighted to be here.*
elated *the elated faces of the freed hostages*
jubilant *the jubilant crowd*
over the moon *INFORMAL I was over the moon to hear about your promotion.*
See also **glad**

jubilant *See* joyful

judge

▷ *NOUN*

1 the person in charge of a law court: *The judge sentenced her to three years in prison.*
justice *her appointment as a Justice of the Supreme Court*
2 someone who picks the winner or keeps control of a competition: *A panel of judges are selecting the finalists.*
referee *The referee ruled him out-of-bounds.*
umpire *The umpire's decision is final.*
▷ *VERB*
3 to form an opinion about someone or something: *Don't judge people by their looks.*
appraise *The technicians are appraised by a committee.*
assess *It is too early to assess the impact of the change.*
consider *We consider him to be dangerous.*
estimate *The cost of the damage is estimated at over a million dollars.*
evaluate *a test to evaluate an applicant's ability*
rate *The movie was rated a hit.*
▷ *VERB*
4 to pick the winner or keep control in a competition: *Entrants will be judged in two categories.*
referee *He has refereed in two World Cups.*
umpire *She umpired baseball games.*
See also **conclude, consider, feel, justice, reckon, regard, think, view**

judgment

▷ *NOUN*

an opinion or decision based on evidence: *It's hard to form a judgment without all the facts.*
appraisal *a calm appraisal of the situation*
assessment *my personal assessment of our position*
conclusion *I've come to the conclusion that she knows what she's talking about.*

opinion *Seek a medical opinion before you travel.*
ruling *a Supreme Court ruling*
verdict *The doctor's verdict was that he was completely healthy.*
view *In my view, things aren't going to get any better.*
See also **belief, common sense, conclusion, decision, opinion, reason, sense, verdict, wisdom**

judicial *See* legal

judiciary *See* legal

judicious *See* logical, sane, sensible, wise

jumble *See* muddle, tangle

jumbled *See* garbled, untidy

jump

▷ *VERB*

1 to leap up or over something: *I jumped over the fence.*
bound *He bounded up the steps.*
clear *The horse barely cleared the gate.*
hurdle *He crossed the lawn and hurdled the fence.*
leap *He had leaped from a window and escaped.*
spring *The lion roared once and sprang.*
vault *He vaulted over a fallen tree.*
2 to increase suddenly: *Sales jumped by 25 percent last year.*
escalate *Costs escalated dramatically.*
increase *The price of gas has dramatically increased this year.*
rise *Unemployment is rising rapidly.*
surge *We were worried when his temperature surged.*
▷ *NOUN*
3 a leap into the air: *the longest-ever jump by a human being*
bound *With one bound she was free.*
leap *He took the gold medal with a leap of 2.37 m.*
vault *She regained the record with a vault of 3.80 m.*
See also **bounce, dive, leap**

---

jumpy *See* nervous, restless, tense

junction *See* connection

junior

▷ *ADJECTIVE*

having a relatively low position compared to others: *a junior counsellor*
inferior *inferior status*
lesser *He resigned to take a lesser position and a cut in wages.*
lower *the lower ranks of committee members*
subordinate *a number of her subordinate officers*
ANTONYM **senior**
See also **inferior, young**

junk

▷ *NOUN*

old articles that people usually throw away: *What are you going to do with all that junk?*
clutter *They like to keep the kitchen counter free of clutter.*
odds and ends *The garage is full of useless odds and ends.*
refuse *a weekly collection of refuse*
rubbish *They disposed of the rubbish at the dump.*
scrap *a heap of scrap piled in the yard*
trash *cluttered with trash*
See also **garbage, refuse**

just *See* **barely, exactly, hardly, only**

just about *See* **nearly**

justice

▷ *NOUN*

1 fairness in the way that people are treated: *We want freedom, justice, and equality.*
equity *Income should be distributed with some sense of equity.*
fairness *concern about the fairness of the judging*
impartiality *a system lacking impartiality*
ANTONYM **injustice**
2 the person in charge of a law court: *his appointment as a justice of the Supreme Court*
judge *The judge asked the witness to speak louder.*
See also **judge, right**

justifiable *See* **reasonable**

justification *See* **cause, defence, excuse, grounds**

justify

▷ *VERB*

to show that something is reasonable or necessary: *How can you justify what you've done?*
defend *Her conduct is hard to defend.*
excuse *That still doesn't excuse his behaviour.*

explain *She left a note explaining her actions.*
vindicate *Ministers are confident their decision will be vindicated.*
warrant *These allegations warrant an investigation.*
See also **defend, deserve**

jut out *See* **extend**

jutting *See* **prominent**

juvenile *See* **child, childish, frivolous, young**

juxtapose *See* **compare**

J

Kk

keen

▷ ADJECTIVE

1 showing eagerness and enthusiasm for something: *a keen amateur photographer*
ardent *one of his most ardent supporters*
avid *an avid reader*
eager *We're eager to read the next book in the series.*
enthusiastic *He was very enthusiastic about the idea.*
fond of *Are you fond of cheesecake?*
into INFORMAL *I'm really into that game.*
2 quick to notice or understand things: *a keen intellect*
astute *an astute judge of character*
brilliant *She had a brilliant mind.*
perceptive *a perceptive gaze*
quick *His quick mind soon grasped the situation.*
shrewd *Her questions showed a shrewd perception.*
See also **acute, ardent, astute, eager, enthusiastic, fierce, fine, ready, sharp**

keenness *See* **enthusiasm**

keep

▷ VERB

1 to have and look after something: *I'd like to keep horses.*
care for *vintage cars lovingly cared for by their owners*
maintain *The house costs a fortune to maintain.*
preserve *the need to preserve the rainforests*
2 to store something: *He keeps his money under the mattress.*
deposit *Deposit your valuables in the hotel safe.*
hold *The money is held in a savings account.*
store *Store the cookies in an airtight container.*
3 to do what you said you would do: *I always keep my promises.*
carry out *He carried out his threat.*
fulfil *She fulfilled all her responsibilities.*
honour *They each honoured the agreement.*
See also **breed, have, own, reserve, save, store, upkeep**

INFORMALLY SPEAKING

for keeps: permanently
keep in with: keep friendship with
keep to yourself: not mix with others
keep up with: do as well as

keep an eye on *See* **mind, supervise**

keep on *See* **continue**

keep out *See* **exclude**

keep safe *See* **save**

keep your eyes open *See* **watch out**

keepsake *See* **souvenir**

key *See* **basic, chief, essential, leading**

kick *See* **thrill**

kick up a fuss *See* **complain**

kid *See* **child, joke**

kidnap

▷ VERB

to take someone away by force: *Four tourists have been kidnapped by rebels.*
abduct *people claiming to have been abducted by aliens*
capture *The guerrillas shot down one plane and captured the pilot.*
seize *hostages seized by terrorists*

kill

▷ VERB

to make someone or something die: *The earthquake killed 62 people.*
assassinate *the plot to assassinate the dictator*
butcher *That's the place where the pigs are butchered.*
destroy *The jockey was unhurt, but his horse had to be destroyed.*
execute *He was executed for treason.*
exterminate *an effort to exterminate all the rats*
massacre *More than 300 civilians have been massacred by the rebels.*
murder *the widow of the murdered leader*
slaughter *Whales are being slaughtered for commercial gain.*
slay *The fearless knight slew the dragon.*
See also **murder, put down**

killing *See* **murder**

kin

▷ NOUN

the people who are related to you: *"Next of kin" means the person most closely related to you.*
family *Everyone in our family has a great sense of humour.*
people *Her people are from the west coast.*
relations *I was staying with relations in Sackville.*
relatives *On Sundays, his relatives come to visit.*
See also **relation**

kind

▷ *NOUN*

1 a particular type of person or thing: *I don't like that kind of movie.*

brand *his favourite brand of chocolate*
breed *a rare breed of cattle*
category *What's your favourite category of music?*
class *a better class of restaurant*
classification *The three classifications are beginner, intermediate, and advanced.*
genre *Movie genres include thriller, romance, comedy, and adventure.*
grade *Which grade of gasoline is best for my new car?*
sort *different sorts of personalities*
species *a rare species of moth*
type *What type of chocolate was it?*
variety *a new variety of rose*

▷ *ADJECTIVE*

2 considerate toward other people: *Thank you for being so kind to me.*

benevolent *a very benevolent employer*
benign *a benign ruler*
charitable *a charitable nature*
compassionate *My father is a deeply compassionate man.*
considerate *a caring and considerate individual*
good *a good person driven to a desperate act*
humane *the humane treatment of animals*
kind-hearted *a kind-hearted and generous friend*
kindly *a kindly professor*
thoughtful *a thoughtful gesture*
unselfish *her generous and unselfish attitude toward others*
ANTONYM **cruel**
See also **accommodating, benevolent, breed, class, compassionate, family, form, generous, gentle, helpful, humane, merciful, sort, tender, thoughtful, type, variety**

INFORMALLY SPEAKING

all kinds of: plenty of
kind of: somewhat; rather
of a kind: of the same kind

---

kind of *See* **pretty**

kind-hearted *See* **compassionate, kind**

kindle *See* **light**

kindly *See* **gentle, kind, well**

kindness

▷ *NOUN*

the quality of being considerate toward other people: *They treated me with kindness.*

benevolence *an act of selfless benevolence*
charity *He is known for his many acts of charity.*
compassion *a nurse who shows great compassion*
gentleness *the gentleness with which she treated her grandparents*
humanity *Her speech showed great maturity and humanity.*
ANTONYM **cruelty**
See also **consideration, favour, generosity, mercy, pity**

kindred *See* **kin**

king

▷ *NOUN*

a man who is the head of a royal family: *the next king of England*

monarch *the coronation of the new monarch*
sovereign *Was the first British sovereign to visit the country a king or a queen?*

kingdom *See* **country, state**

kinsman *See* **relation**

kinswoman *See* **relation**

kitty *See* **cat**

knack *See* **skill, talent**

knick-knack *See* **ornament**

knit your brows *See* **frown**

knob *See* **bump**

knock *See* **bang, blow, bump, criticize, drive, hit**

knock down *See* **overturn**

knock out *See* **eliminate**

knock over *See* **overturn, upset**

knot *See* **tangle, tie**

know

▷ *VERB*

1 to understand or be aware of something: *I don't know a lot about cars.*

apprehend *It is impossible to apprehend the whole painting at once.*
be aware of *Are you aware of the risks involved?*
comprehend *They do not comprehend the nature of the problem.*
perceive *the world as we perceive it*
see *Don't you see what he's up to?*
understand *too young to understand what was happening*

K

2 to be familiar with a person or thing: *I believe you know my brother.*
be acquainted with *Are you acquainted with each other?*
be familiar with *I am familiar with her work.*
recognize *She recognized him at once.*
See also **recognize**

INFORMALLY SPEAKING

in the know: aware of information few people have
know the ropes: understand what to do
know what's what: be well informed

---

know-how *See* **experience**

knowingly *See* **on purpose**

knowledge
▷ *NOUN*
all you know about something: *She had no knowledge of world history.*
education *an extensive education*
learning *people of great learning*
scholarship *a lifetime of scholarship*
wisdom *a source of wisdom and knowledge*
See also **command, experience, grasp, understanding, wisdom**

knowledgeable *See* **aware, experienced, expert**

knowledgeable about *See* **familiar**

known *See* **certain**

LI

label
▷ NOUN
I a piece of paper or plastic attached to something for information: *He checked the label on the bottle.*
sticker *The sticker on the DVD showed the sale price.*
tag *a name tag*
ticket *a ticket for the movie*
▷ VERB
2 to put a label on something: *The shirt was labelled "Made in Canada."*
flag *Flag the pages that need corrections.*
sticker *products stickered at a special price*
tag *The pigeon was tagged with a numbered band.*
See also **identify**

laborious *See* **difficult, hard**

labour
▷ NOUN
I very hard work: *the labour involved in weeding and digging*
effort *The climb was worth the effort.*
exertion *My feet aren't used to such exertion.*
industry *Her contributions and industry were finally rewarded.*
toil *their day's toil in the fields*
work *All our work is starting to pay off.*
2 the workforce of a country or industry: *unskilled labour*
employees *How many employees are union members?*
workers *Thousands of workers have been laid off.*
workforce *a country where half the workforce is unemployed*
▷ VERB
3 to work very hard: *harvesters labouring in the fields*
slave *We've been slaving half the night to finish this.*
toil *workers toiling in poor conditions*
work *He works twelve hours a day.*
ANTONYM **relax**
See also **struggle, work**

labourer *See* **worker**

lack
▷ NOUN
I the shortage or absence of something that is needed: *a lack of funds*
absence *an absence of evidence*
deficiency *tests for vitamin deficiency*
scarcity *a scarcity of water*

shortage *a food shortage*
want FORMAL *becoming weak from want of rest*
ANTONYM **abundance**
▷ VERB
2 to be without something that is needed: *She lacks confidence.*
be deficient in *Your diet is deficient in vitamins.*
be short of *I'm short of cash.*
miss *Your jacket is missing a button.*
See also **deficiency, shortage, want**

lacking *See* **deficient, inadequate, insufficient**

lad *See* **boy**

lady *See* **female, woman**

ladylike *See* **refined**

lag
▷ VERB
I to make slower progress than other people or things: *He is now lagging a metre behind the champion.*
fall behind *The city is falling behind in attracting tourists.*
trail *The Liberal Party is trailing badly in the opinion polls.*

TYPES OF ... *LAKE*	
lagoon	slough
pond	tarn
reservoir	

lame
▷ ADJECTIVE
I unable to walk properly because of an injured leg: *lame in one leg*
limping *limping from a hamstring injury*
2 weak or unconvincing: *a lame excuse*
feeble *his feeble attempt at humour*
flimsy *The evidence was flimsy at best.*
pathetic *a pathetic attempt at humour*
poor *a poor effort*
unconvincing *an unconvincing argument*
weak *a weak performance*

lament
▷ VERB
I to express sorrow or regret over something: *She lamented the death of her friend.*
grieve *grieving over his loss*
mourn *We mourned the loss of our pet.*
wail *wailing uncontrollably after hearing the tragic news*
weep *weeping for her lost love*

L

▷ NOUN
2 something you say to express sorrow or regret: *a lament for his vanished youth*
moan *a moan of sorrow*
wail *wails of grief*
See also **grieve, regret**

lamentable See **pathetic**

lance See **pierce**

land
▷ NOUN
I an area of property: *a dispute over land*
estate *a party on the millionaire's estate*
grounds *the grounds of the prime minister's residence*
property *travellers who camped on his property*
2 a region or country: *the land of opportunity*
country *the boundary between the two countries*
nation *the nation's financial crisis*
province *British Columbia is Canada's westernmost province.*
region *the region of Tuscany*
territory *The dispute over the territory was reviewed by the United Nations.*
▷ VERB
3 to arrive on the ground after flying or sailing: *We landed in New York at noon.*
alight *The bird alighted on a nearby branch.*
dock *The ship docked in Halifax.*
touch down *The plane touched down in Florida.*
See also **country, ground, grounds, region, state, territory**

landscape See **scene, scenery, view**

lane See **way**

language
▷ NOUN
I the system of words people use to communicate: *She speaks four languages.*
dialect *the Cantonese dialect*
idiom *the Gaelic folk idiom*
jargon *scientific jargon*
lingo INFORMAL *I don't speak the lingo.*
tongue *The Germans feel passionately about their native tongue.*
vernacular *the vernacular of hockey*
vocabulary *a new word in the child's vocabulary*
2 the style in which you speak or write: *He explained the process in plain language.*
phrasing *The phrasing of this report is confusing.*
style *a simple writing style*

wording *The wording of the contract was unclear.*

lanky See **tall**

lap See **round, stage**

lapse See **error**

large
▷ ADJECTIVE
of a greater size or amount than usual: *a large room*
big *We've always had big dogs.*
colossal *a colossal task*
enormous *an enormous house*
giant *a giant bird*
gigantic *a gigantic spider*
great *the Great Wall of China*
huge *huge profits*
immense *an immense property*
massive *a massive ship*
vast *a vast desert*
ANTONYM **small**
See also **broad, extensive, spacious**

large numbers See **many**

largely See **mainly**

lark See **joke**

lash See **tie**

lass See **woman**

last
▷ ADJECTIVE
I the most recent: *last year*
latest *his latest thriller*
most recent *her most recent film*
preceding *a salary increase during the preceding year*
previous *his previous marriage*
ANTONYM **first**
2 happening or remaining after all the others of its kind: *the last three chapters of the book*
closing *the closing years of the century*
concluding *the concluding scene of the play*
final *This is your final chance.*
ultimate *the ultimate result of the move*
ANTONYM **first**
▷ VERB
3 to continue to exist or happen: *The movie lasted for two and a half hours.*
continue *The exhibition continues until November.*
endure *Somehow their friendship endures.*
persist *The problem persists.*
remain *The building remains to this day.*
survive *companies that survived after the recession*

See also **continue, endure, final, remain, remainder, stretch, survive, ultimate**

at last: after a long or seemingly long time
breathe your last: die
see the last of: not see ever again

lasting *See* **permanent**

lastly *See* **finally**

last-minute *See* **late**

latch *See* **catch, lock**

late
▷ *ADJECTIVE*
1 after the expected time: *The train was late.*
behind *I'm behind with my payments.*
behind schedule *Hurry up. We're behind schedule already.*
belated *a belated birthday card*
delayed *The plane's departure was delayed by four hours.*
last-minute *buying some last-minute birthday presents*
overdue *The book is two weeks overdue.*
ANTONYM **early**
2 dead, especially recently: *my late husband*
dead *She has been dead for a year now.*
deceased *his recently deceased mother*
departed *memories of departed friends*
See also **dead**

later *See* **after, future**

latest *See* **fashionable, last, modern, news, trendy**

lather *See* **foam**

latitude *See* **freedom**

laugh
▷ *VERB*
1 to make a noise that shows you are amused or happy: *You never laugh at my jokes.*
See WORD STUDY **laugh**
▷ *NOUN*
2 the noise you make when amused or happy: *She has a very infectious laugh.*
chortle *"That's what you think," he said with a chortle.*
chuckle *We had a quiet chuckle at his mistake.*
giggle *She gave a nervous giggle.*
guffaw *He let out a huge guffaw of amusement.*
snigger *barely able to stifle a snigger*
titter *A titter went around the room.*

laugh at: make fun of
laugh off: dismiss with a laugh

L

WORD STUDY: LAUGH

There are a number of more interesting or creative words you can use in place of the basic verb **laugh**. Try to say something about the way in which a person laughs.

• If you **chuckle**, you laugh quietly.
I **chuckled** to myself at the look on his face.

• If you **chortle**, you laugh in a pleased or amused way.
He sat there **chortling** at my predicament.

• If you **snigger**, you laugh in a quiet, sly way, perhaps at something rude or unkind.
Two boys were making silly faces and **sniggering**.

• If you **giggle**, you laugh in a high-pitched way, because you are amused, nervous, or embarrassed.
They followed me around, **giggling** every time I spoke.

• If you **titter**, you give a short, nervous laugh, often at something rude or because you are embarrassed.
The audience began to **titter** when the scenery started to shake.

• If you **cackle**, you laugh in a loud, harsh and unpleasant way, often at something bad which happens to someone else.
The woman **cackled** in glee at our embarrassment.

• If you **guffaw, howl,** or **roar**, you laugh very loudly because you think something is very funny.
They **guffawed** at me as I tripped over the garbage can.
The crowd **howled** at the antics of the clown.
He threw back his head and **roared** at the joke.

laugh at *See* **make fun of, mock**

laughable *See* **ridiculous**

launch *See* **fire, introduction, release, start**

launder *See* **wash**

laundered *See* **clean**

laurels *See* **victory**

lavish *See* **generous, luxurious**

law
▷ NOUN
1 a country's or other region's system of rules: *The sale of lottery tickets to minors is against the law.*
charter *the Canadian Charter of Rights and Freedoms*
code *a code of conduct*
constitution *proposed changes to the constitution*
2 one of the rules of a country or other region: *He was charged under the anti-stalking law.*
act *A new act has been passed by Parliament.*
bylaw *a municipal bylaw that enforces recycling*
code *a code designed to protect the rights of children*
decree *a decree lifting trade sanctions against certain countries*
regulation *regulations outlawing child labour*
rule *a rule that was imposed in 1962*
statute *a practice regulated by statute*
See also **principle, rule**

law court *See* **court**

law-abiding *See* **honest, obedient**

lawful *See* **legal**

lawsuit *See* **case**

lawyer
▷ NOUN
someone who advises people about the law: *I'm discussing the matter with my lawyer.*
advocate *A public advocate will be appointed to represent you.*
attorney *We phoned our attorney for advice.*
counsel *His counsel advised him to appeal against the verdict.*
solicitor *She took advice from a solicitor.*

lay
▷ VERB
1 to put something somewhere: *Lay a sheet of newspaper on the floor.*
place *He placed a mug of coffee in front of her.*
put *He put the photograph on the desk.*
set *She set her briefcase on the floor.*
set down *I set the glasses down on the table.*
spread *She spread a towel over the sand and lay down.*
2 to arrange or set something out: *to lay the carpet*
arrange *He started to arrange the books in piles.*
set out *The flower garden was set out with large beds of roses.*
See also **deposit, put, set**

INFORMALLY SPEAKING

lay away: put away for future use
lay in: put aside for an emergency
lay it on thick: flatter or exaggerate
lay off: give up something or stop doing something
lay on: supply with something
lay yourself out: make a big effort

lay out *See* **position**

layer
▷ NOUN
something that covers a surface or comes between two other things: *A fresh layer of snow covered the street.*
blanket *a blanket of fog*
coat *a coat of paint*
coating *a protective coating*
covering *a thin covering of dust*
film *a film of oil*
sheet *a sheet of ice*
stratum *the correct geological stratum*
See also **coating**

layout
▷ NOUN
the way in which something is arranged: *the layout of the pages*
arrangement *the arrangement of a room*
design *the design of the museum*
format *the format of the letter*
plan *a detailed plan of the house*
See also **form, plan**

laze
▷ VERB
to relax and do no work: *We spent a few days lazing around by the pool.*
idle *We spent hours idling in one of the cafés.*
loaf *loafing around the house all day*
lounge *They lounged in the shade.*
ANTONYM **work**
See also **relax, rest**

lazy

▷ ADJECTIVE

not willing to work: *a lazy and incompetent employee*

idle *an idle young man*

slack *Many workers have simply become too slack.*

ANTONYM **industrious**

lead

▷ VERB

1 to guide or take someone somewhere: *She led him into the house.*

conduct *He asked if he might conduct us to the concert.*

escort *They were escorted by police to their plane.*

guide *He took me by the arm and guided me out.*

steer *She steered them toward the door.*

usher *I ushered him into the office.*

2 to be in charge of: *Lester B. Pearson led the country between 1963 and 1968.*

command *the general who commanded the troops*

direct *He will direct day-to-day operations.*

govern *his ability to govern the country*

head *Who heads the firm?*

manage *I manage a small team of workers.*

supervise *He supervised more than 400 volunteers.*

▷ NOUN

3 a clue that may help solve a crime: *The police are following up several leads.*

clue *a vital clue to the killer's identity*

indication *All the indications suggest that he is the thief.*

trace *No traces of poison were found in his bloodstream.*

See also **bring, command, direct, drive, guide, head, motivate, rule, take, top**

INFORMALLY SPEAKING

lead nowhere: have no effect
lead off: begin or start
lead on: influence; deceive
lead up to: prepare the way for

leaden See **cloudy, dull**

leader

▷ NOUN

the person in charge of something: *the leader of the New Democratic Party*

boss INFORMAL *Who's the boss around here?*

captain *the captain of the team*

chief *the chief of police*

commander *a naval commander*

director *the director of the movie*

head *the head of the United Way campaign*

principal *the principal of the school*

ringleader *the ringleader of the gang*

ANTONYM **follower**

See also **boss, chief, head, ruler**

leadership See **direction**

leading

▷ ADJECTIVE

particularly important, respected, or advanced: *a leading industrial nation*

chief *one of her chief rivals*

eminent *an eminent surgeon*

key *the key witness at the trial*

major *Exercise has a major part to play in preventing disease.*

main *one of the main tourist areas of the city*

principal *one of the principal figures in politics today*

prominent *a prominent member of the Law Society*

top *a top model*

See also **first, foremost, important, in front, main, major, prime, supreme, top**

lead to

L

▷ VERB

to cause something to happen: *A proper diet can lead to better health.*

cause *A lack of calcium can cause weak bones.*

contribute to *injuries that contributed to his death*

produce *The drug produces side effects.*

See also **create, result in**

leaflet

▷ NOUN

a piece of paper or a pamphlet with information about a subject: *Protesters were handing out leaflets in the street.*

booklet *a booklet about the rules of the game*

brochure *a travel brochure*

circular *a circular sent out by the real estate firm*

flyer *The flyer featured the weekly specials at the supermarket.*

pamphlet *a pamphlet about preventing sports injuries*

league See **association, fellowship, society, union**

leak

▷ VERB

1 to escape from a container or other object: *The gas had leaked.*

escape *A vent was opened to let some air escape.*

ooze *Blood was oozing from the wound.*
seep *Radioactive water has seeped into underground reservoirs.*
spill *About 70 000 tonnes of oil spilled from the tanker.*
▷ NOUN
2 a hole or crack that lets gas or liquid escape: *Have you plugged the leaks?*
crack *The lava oozed through cracks in the rock.*
fissure *Water trickled out of fissures in the limestone.*
hole *The water was flowing in through the hole in the ship's hull.*
puncture *a small puncture in the tire of my bike*

lean *See* **bend, skinny, slender, tilt**

leaning *See* **tendency**

leap
▷ VERB
1 to jump a great distance or height: *The deer leaped into the air.*
bounce *She bounced up and down on the trampoline.*
bound *The dog came bounding up the stairs.*
jump *I jumped over the fence.*
spring *He sprang to his feet.*
vault *He could easily vault the wall.*
▷ NOUN
2 a jump of great distance or height: *a leap of 2.37 m*
jump *He placed second in the high jump.*
bound *With one bound, I was free.*
spring *The cheetah gave a great spring into the air.*
See also **dive, jump**

learn
▷ VERB
1 to gain knowledge by studying or training: *I am trying to learn Spanish.*
grasp *The basics of the language are easy to grasp.*
master *He's having trouble mastering the piano.*
pick up *You'll soon pick up enough Italian to get by.*
2 to find out about something: *On learning who she was, I asked to meet her.*
ascertain *They had ascertained that he was not a spy.*
determine *calculations to determine the rate of tax*
discover *She discovered that they'd escaped.*
find out *As soon as we found this out, we investigated the situation.*

gather *I gather the report is critical of the coach.*
hear *I heard he had moved away.*
understand *I understand that she's just taken early retirement.*
See also **discover, find, gather, hear, master, study, understand**

learned
▷ ADJECTIVE
having gained a lot of knowledge by studying: *a very learned person*
academic *I feel intimidated by academic people.*
erudite *a witty and erudite leader*
intellectual *an artistic and intellectual couple*
literate *a literate and educated readership*
scholarly *a scholarly researcher*
See also **educated**

learner *See* **beginner**

learning *See* **knowledge**

lease
▷ VERB
to let someone use your property for money: *She leases her house for the summer.*
rent *He rents rooms to students.*
See also **rent**

least
▷ ADJECTIVE
as small or few as possible: *Stick to foods with the least fat.*
fewest *Which product has the fewest calories?*
lowest *the lowest temperatures on record for this time of year*
minimum *the minimum height for a police officer*
slightest *He showed only the slightest hint of emotion.*
smallest *the smallest measurable unit of light*
ANTONYM **most**

least possible *See* **minimum**

leathery *See* **tough**

leave
▷ VERB
1 to go away from a person or place: *He is not allowed to leave the country.*
abandon *He claimed that they had abandoned the dog.*
depart *A number of staff members departed*

during his time as director.
desert *He deserted the army.*
forsake *He would never forsake his family.*
go *Let me know when you're ready to go.*
quit *He quit his job at the restaurant.*
withdraw *Troops withdrew from the country last month.*
▷ NOUN
2 a period of time off work: *Why don't you take a few days' leave?*
holiday *I still have several days' holiday to take.*
time off *They took time off to go sailing.*
vacation *We went on vacation to Mexico.*
See also **abandon, blessing, deposit, flee, go, holiday, quit, resign, will, withdraw**

leave behind *See* **abandon**

leave out *See* **exclude, omit**

lecherous *See* **lustful**

lecture
▷ NOUN
1 a formal talk about a particular subject: *In his lecture, he covered several topics.*
address *an address to the Canadian people*
discourse *a lengthy discourse on market strategy*
presentation *a business presentation*
sermon *his first sermon as a minister*
speech *She delivered her speech in French.*
talk *a brief talk on the history of the site*
2 a talk intended to scold or warn someone: *The police gave us a stern lecture on safety.*
reprimand *He has been given a severe reprimand.*
scolding *given a scolding for fighting with the other children*
warning *a severe warning from the referee*
▷ VERB
3 to teach by giving formal talks to audiences: *She has lectured all over the world.*
give a talk *He set about campaigning, giving talks, and raising money.*
speak *She's been invited to speak at the convention.*
talk *Today, I plan to talk about the issues of education and daycare.*
teach *She has taught at the university for 12 years.*
See also **lesson, scold, speech, talk**

lecturer *See* **teacher**

leeway *See* **freedom**

leftist *See* **left-wing**

leftover *See* **waste**

leftovers *See* **remains**

left-wing
▷ ADJECTIVE
believing in radical or liberal policies: *a left-wing demonstration*
leftist *three leftist guerrilla groups*
liberal *a politician with liberal views*
radical *a radical idea*
socialist *Europe's last socialist state*

legacy
▷ NOUN
property left when someone dies: *He left his children a generous legacy.*
bequest *She made a bequest to her favourite charity.*
estate *documents concerning the estate*
heirloom *This cabinet is a family heirloom.*
inheritance *a modest inheritance from her grandfather*
See also **gift, inheritance**

legal
▷ ADJECTIVE
1 relating to the law: *the Dutch legal system*
forensic *forensic medicine*
judicial *a judicial review*
judiciary *various levels of the judiciary system*
2 allowed by the law: *The strike was perfectly legal.*
authorized *an authorized procedure*
lawful *What I did was lawful and proper.*
legitimate *a legitimate business*
permissible *the current permissible levels of flavouring agents in food*
rightful *the rightful owner of the property*
valid *a valid passport*
ANTONYM **illegal**
See also **formal**

legality *See* **right**

legend *See* **story**

legendary *See* **famous**

legitimate *See* **fair, legal, real, reasonable**

leisure
▷ NOUN
time when you can relax: *There wasn't a lot of time for leisure.*
free time *He played piano in his free time.*
recreation *Saturday afternoons are for recreation.*
relaxation *Make time for a bit of relaxation.*
time off *I haven't had any time off all week.*
ANTONYM **work**
See also **ease, rest**

L

leisure activity *See* **hobby**

leisure pursuit *See* **hobby**

leisurely

▷ *ADJECTIVE*

unhurried or calm: *a leisurely walk along the beach*

comfortable *going at a comfortable speed*

easy *an easy pace*

gentle *His movements were gentle and deliberate.*

relaxed *a relaxed meal*

unhurried *an unhurried way of life*

See also **easy, slow**

lend *See* **loan**

lend a hand *See* **help**

length

▷ *NOUN*

1 the distance from one end of something to the other: *The length of the box is 45 cm.*

distance *Work out the distance between your house and mine.*

extent *the extent of the rainforest*

span *the span between a bird's wing tips*

2 the amount of time something lasts for: *The movie is over two hours in length.*

duration *The duration of the course is one year.*

period *for a limited period only*

space *A dramatic change takes place in the space of a few minutes.*

span *a span of four years between Olympics*

term *a 12-month term of service*

lengthen

▷ *VERB*

to make something longer: *The airport runway had to be lengthened.*

extend *They have extended the deadline.*

make longer *You can make your hair longer by using extensions.*

prolong *The adapter will prolong the life of your batteries.*

stretch *Be careful not to stretch the material.*

ANTONYM **shorten**

leniency *See* **mercy**

lenient *See* **merciful**

lessen

▷ *VERB*

to decrease in size or amount: *changes to their diet that would lessen the risk of disease*

abate *The storm gradually abated.*

decrease *Hunger decreases as you eat.*

diminish *The threat of war has diminished.*

dwindle *her dwindling authority*

lower *The Bank of Canada has lowered interest rates.*

minimize *Check your work to minimize the number of errors.*

reduce *Gradually reduce the dosage.*

shrink *The forests have shrunk to half their size.*

ANTONYM **increase**

See also **abate, decrease, diminish, lower, reduce, weaken**

CONFUSABLES

Less than means **not so much as**, and refers only to amount.

Fewer than means **not so many as**, and refers to countable things.

---

lessening *See* **decrease**

lesser *See* **inferior, junior, minor**

lesson

▷ *NOUN*

a period of time for being taught: *I'm taking piano lessons.*

class *I go to dance classes.*

coaching *He and I both need extra coaching in math.*

lecture *a series of lectures on art*

period *Our science periods are longer this year.*

tutoring *a growing demand for private tutoring*

lessons *See* **study**

let

▷ *VERB*

to allow someone to do something: *Don't let the cat out of the house.*

allow *I pleaded to be allowed to go.*

give permission *Who gave you permission to come here?*

permit *Permit me to express my opinion.*

sanction *The United Nations did not sanction the use of force.*

ANTONYM **forbid**

See also **allow**

INFORMALLY SPEAKING

let down: disappoint

let off: release or allow to go free

let off steam: give way to feelings

let someone in for: involve someone in something unpleasant

let up: stop or pause

---

let go *See* **discharge, release**

let in *See* **admit**

lethal *See* **deadly, fatal**

lethargic *See* **sleepy**

letter *See* **note**

level
▷ *ADJECTIVE*
1 completely flat: *a plateau of level ground*
flat *A pool table must be perfectly flat.*
horizontal *Every horizontal surface was covered with plants.*
ANTONYM **uneven**
▷ *VERB*
2 to make something flat: *We levelled the ground.*
flatten *Flatten the dough and cut it into four pieces.*
plane *She planed the surface of the wood until it was smooth.*
smooth *He smoothed his hair.*
▷ *NOUN*
3 a point on a scale that measures something: *Crime levels have started to decline.*
grade *the lowest grade of apples*
rank *She rose to the rank of captain.*
stage *an early stage of development*
standard *a decent standard of living*
status *This movie, I believe, deserves a higher status.*
See also **balance, even, extent, flat, rank, standard, straight**

level-headed *See* **cool, realistic, responsible, sane**

level-headedness *See* **common sense**

levelled *See* **flat**

levy *See* **charge, duty, impose, tax**

lewd *See* **indecent, lustful, naughty, obscene**

liability *See* **blame, fault, responsibility**

liable *See* **likely, prone**

liaison *See* **affair, relationship**

libel *See* **slander**

liberal *See* **generous, handsome, left-wing, tolerant**

liberate *See* **discharge, free, release**

liberated *See* **free, independent**

liberation *See* **release**

liberty *See* **freedom, release**

licence *See* **freedom, permission, permit, power**

licensed *See* **official**

lid *See* **top**

lie
▷ *VERB*
1 to rest somewhere horizontally: *I like to lie on my back when I sleep.*
loll *He was lolling on the beach.*
lounge *We lounged in the yard all day.*
recline *She reclined on the couch.*
sprawl *She sprawled in the hammock, snoozing.*
2 to say something that is not true: *He always lies about his age.*
fib *He fibbed when she asked him where he'd been.*
perjure oneself *All of the witnesses perjured themselves.*
tell a lie *He could never tell a lie or do anything devious.*
▷ *NOUN*
3 something you say that is not true: *His whole story was a lie.*
deceit *the deceits of political leaders*
fabrication *She described the magazine interview as "a complete fabrication."*
falsehood *He accused them of spreading falsehoods about him.*
fib *I caught her telling another fib.*
fiction *His account of events is a complete fiction.*

CONFUSABLES

Lie and **lay** both mean **rest on a surface.**
Lie does not take an object: **to lie on the floor.**
Lay always has an object: **to lay a new floor.**

life
▷ *NOUN*
the time during which you are alive: *a long and active life*
existence *a very miserable existence*
lifespan *This species of snake has a lifespan of up to 25 years.*
lifetime *a lifetime devoted to service to others*
See also **energy**

INFORMALLY SPEAKING

as large as life: in person
get a life: find something worthwhile to do
not on your life: under no circumstances
to save your life: even if your life depended on it

L

life force *See* **spirit**

lifespan *See* **life**

lifelike *See* **realistic**

lifetime *See* **life**

lift

▷ *VERB*

1 to move something to a higher position: *straining to lift heavy weights*

elevate *a mechanism to elevate the platform*

hoist *I hoisted my pack over my shoulder.*

pick up *He picked up the box from the floor.*

raise *She raised her hand to wave.*

ANTONYM **lower**

2 to remove something such as a ban or law: *the decision to lift sanctions against the country*

cancel *The government has cancelled the state of emergency.*

end *pressure to end the embargo*

relax *an attempt to persuade the company to relax the rules*

remove *She tried to remove one requirement from the contract.*

See also **raise**

light

▷ *NOUN*

1 brightness that enables you to see things: *Cracks of light filtered through the shutters.*

brightness *the brightness of the full moon*

brilliance *the brilliance of the sun*

glare *shading his eyes from the glare*

glow *the red glow of the dying fire*

illumination *The only illumination came from a small window.*

radiance *Indirect lighting casts a soft radiance on the walls.*

ANTONYM **dark**

▷ *ADJECTIVE*

2 pale in colour: *a light blue shirt*

bleached *bleached pine tables*

blonde or **blond** *blonde hair*

fair *to protect his fair skin*

pale *dressed in pale pink*

pastel *delicate pastel shades*

ANTONYM **dark**

▷ *ADJECTIVE*

3 not weighing much: *working out with light weights*

flimsy *a flimsy cardboard box*

lightweight *They will carry lightweight skis on their backs.*

portable *a portable TV*

slight *She is small and slight.*

ANTONYM **heavy**

▷ *VERB*

4 to make a place bright: *The room was lit by many candles.*

brighten *The late afternoon sun brightened the room.*

illuminate *No streetlights illuminated the road.*

light up *Fireworks lit up the sky.*

ANTONYM **darken**

▷ *VERB*

5 to make a fire start burning: *It's time to light the bonfire.*

ignite *A stray spark ignited the fireworks.*

kindle *I kindled a fire, and then we toasted marshmallows.*

ANTONYM **extinguish**

See also **easy, fair, glow, soft**

light up *See* **light**

light-headed *See* **dazed, dizzy, faint**

light-hearted *See* **bright, cheerful**

lightweight *See* **fine, light, sheer**

like

▷ *ADJECTIVE*

1 similar to another thing: *He looks just like his father.*

akin *She looked at me with something akin to disgust.*

alike *They are very alike in temperament.*

analogous *a process analogous to the growth of a plant from a seed*

identical *Nearly all the houses were identical.*

parallel *Our situation is parallel to yours.*

same *His jacket was exactly the same colour as the car.*

similar *a taste similar to that of celery*

ANTONYM **unlike**

▷ *VERB*

2 to find someone or something pleasant: *I really like this music.*

adore INFORMAL *All her employees adored her.*

appreciate *I know you appreciate good food.*

be fond of *I'm very fond of soup.*

be keen on *I'm not very keen on camping.*

be partial to *I'm partial to dark colours.*

enjoy *Most children enjoy cartoons.*

go for INFORMAL *He didn't go for the idea at all.*

have a soft spot for *I've always had a soft spot for spaniels.*

have a weakness for *I have a weakness for romantic movies.*

love *She loves reading.*

relish *He relished the idea of proving me wrong.*

revel in *He appears to revel in his misery.*
ANTONYM **dislike**
See also **enjoy, love, similar**

INFORMALLY SPEAKING

and the like: and similar things
like crazy (mad, etc.): with great speed, effort, etc.
nothing like: not nearly
something like: almost like
the likes of: someone or something like

like better *See* **prefer**

likeable *See* **pleasant**

likelihood *See* **chance, possibility, probability**

likely
▷ *ADJECTIVE*
having a good chance of happening: *It seems likely that he will come back.*
anticipated *the anticipated result*
expected *the expected response*
liable *He is liable to be a nuisance.*
possible *It's quite possible that I'm wrong.*
probable *the probable outcome*
ANTONYM **unlikely**
See also **believable, possible, potential, probable, probably**

likeness *See* **resemblance, similarity**

likewise *See* **too**

liking *See* **affection, attachment, love, taste, weakness**

limit
▷ *NOUN*
1 a point beyond which something cannot go: *the speed limit*
bounds *the bounds of good taste*
deadline *We finished the job ahead of the deadline.*
maximum *He was given two years in prison, the maximum allowed for the charges.*
ultimate *This hotel is the ultimate in luxury.*
utmost *His patience was tested to the utmost.*
▷ *VERB*
2 to prevent something from going any further: *Limit yourself to one evening out a week.*
confine *Damage was confined to a small portion of the building.*
curb *measures to curb inflation*
fix *The interest rate is fixed at five percent.*
ration *I'm rationing my portions till I lose some weight.*

restrict *The patient was restricted to a salt-free diet.*
See also **confine, curb, extreme, restrict**

limitation *See* **curb, restriction**

limited *See* **modest**

limits *See* **border, range**

limp
▷ *ADJECTIVE*
not stiff or firm: *a limp lettuce leaf*
drooping *the drooping branches of a birch tree*
flabby *a flabby stomach*
floppy *the dog's floppy ears*
soft *a soft clay*
ANTONYM **stiff**

limping *See* **lame**

line
▷ *NOUN*
1 a long thin mark on something: *Draw a line down the centre of the page.*
rule *He drew a rule under the last name.*
streak *dark streaks on the surface of the moon*
stripe *green jogging pants with white stripes down the sides*
2 a row of people or things: *a long line at the box office*
column *a column of numbers*
file *A file of mourners walked behind the coffin.*
queue *Files sent to a printer end up in a queue.*
rank *Soldiers lined up in ranks, side by side.*
row *a row of pretty little cottages*
3 the route along which something moves: *the line of flight*
course *the course of the river*
path *the flight path of the migrating birds*
route *the most direct route*
track *a railway track*
trajectory *the trajectory of the missile*
See also **border, course, rank, row, trade**

INFORMALLY SPEAKING

bring into line: cause to conform
cross the line: do something unacceptable
hold the line: stand firm against an attack or challenge
in line with: in agreement with
lay it on the line: state firmly and clearly
on the line: at risk
out of line: not suitable or proper

lineage *See* **origin, stock**

lines *See* **shape**

linger *See* **remain, stay, wait**

lingering *See* **slow**

lingo *See* **language**

link

▷ *NOUN*

1 a connection between two things: *the link between diet and health*
affiliation *He has no affiliation with any political party.*
association *the association between the two companies*
attachment *a close attachment between the brothers*
bond *The experience created a bond between us.*
connection *He has denied any connection to the hoax.*
relationship *the relationship between humans and their environment*
tie *She has ties with this town.*

▷ *VERB*

2 to connect two things: *He was linked to the crime.*
attach *Attach the curtains to the rods.*
connect *two rooms connected by French doors*
couple *Several shafts coupled together may be used.*
fasten *a wooden bench fastened to the floor*
join *the skin that joins the eye to the eyelid*
tie *He tied the cushion to the chair.*
ANTONYM **separate**
See also **associate, attach, bond, connect, connection, join, relation, relationship**

link up *See* **team, unite**

lip *See* **edge**

liquid

▷ *NOUN*

1 a substance that is not solid and can be poured: *a clear liquid*
fluid *Drink plenty of fluids during hot weather.*
solution *a solution of honey and vinegar*

▷ *ADJECTIVE*

2 in the form of a liquid: *wash in warm water with liquid detergent*
fluid *the substance's fluid properties*
molten *molten metal*
runny *The butter tart filling was sweet and runny.*

liquor *See* **alcohol**

list

▷ *NOUN*

1 a set of things written down one below the other: *There were six names on the list.*
catalogue *Check the library catalogue.*
directory *a telephone directory*
index *The book includes a comprehensive subject index.*
inventory *an inventory of goods*
listing *a listing of all the schools in the area*
record *Keep a record of everything you eat and drink.*
register *a register of births, deaths, and marriages*

▷ *VERB*

2 to set things down in a list: *All the ingredients are listed on the label.*
catalogue *I catalogued my CDs.*
index *The book has been carefully indexed.*
record *Nearly 400 species of fungi have been recorded.*
register *a registered charity*

listen

▷ *VERB*

to hear and pay attention to something: *I'll repeat that for those of you who weren't listening.*
hear *Will you hear me saying my lines?*
pay attention *Pay attention or you won't know what to do.*

listen in *See* **hear**

listen to *See* **hear, heed**

listing *See* **list**

literate *See* **learned**

lithe *See* **agile, flexible**

litter *See* **garbage, refuse, young**

little

▷ *ADJECTIVE*

1 small in size or amount: *a little kitten*
ANTONYM **large**
See WORD STUDY **little**

▷ *NOUN*

2 a small amount or degree: *Would you like a little juice?*
See also **insignificant, low, young**

little ones *See* **young**

live

▷ *VERB*

1 to have your home somewhere: *She has lived here for 20 years.*
dwell *the creatures who dwell in the forest*
inhabit *the fish that inhabit the coral reefs*
reside *He used to reside in England.*

Depending on what you are describing, you can choose from any of the following alternatives instead of the overused word **little**.

• of the physical size of objects
I ate several of the **dainty** sandwiches.
He grows **dwarf** tulips.
The machine resembled a **mini** laptop computer.
She owns a collection of **miniature** toy boats.
There must be a **minute** particle of dust in my eye.
We took my brother to a children's zoo that had **pygmy** goats.
She was dressed in a **skimpy** bikini.
They sat at a **small** table.
He tore the paper into **tiny** pieces.

• of the height of people
My **diminutive** stature has never stopped me from playing all kinds of sports.
Are these clothes specially designed for **petite** women?
I was too **short** to reach the top shelf.
In the dim light, I could just see a **squat** person at the door.
His mother is a **tiny** woman who only comes up to his shoulder.

• in duration
There was a **brief** pause.
We only got a **fleeting** glimpse of his face.
He took a **hasty** peek at the list.
It was just a **momentary** lapse of memory.
She gave me a **quick** smile.
I need a **short** break.

• in quantity
That's a **meagre** pay increase.
She served up a **measly** ration of food.

It's an interesting job, but the salary is **paltry**.
He paid **scant** attention to his colleagues.

• in age
This is my **baby** sister.
A mother with her **infant** son got on the bus.
She has two **small** kids to support.
He was only a **young** child when his parents died.

• in importance
Ignore it. It's an **insignificant** detail.
We had a **minor** squabble, but now we're friends again.
Their influence is **negligible**.
I won't listen to these **petty** complaints.
I don't want to bother you with such a **trifling** problem.
How much time have you wasted in discussing **trivial** matters?
He talked for ages about some **unimportant** event.

• a small amount
I wouldn't mind a **bit** of peace.
He spoke with a **dash** of bravado.
They only need a **fragment** of skin tissue to provide a DNA sample.
The chef made a delicate dish with just a **hint** of coriander.
I only carry a **small amount** of cash.
Just a **spot** of milk for me, thanks.
There was a **touch** of irritation in his voice.
The police found a **trace** of blood on the carpet.

L

---

2 to be alive: *She has lived a happy life.*
be alive *You are lucky to be alive.*
exist *the chances of finding life existing on Mars*
▷ *ADJECTIVE*
3 not dead or artificial: *a live spider*
alive *It is likely that he is still alive.*
animate *an animate object*
living *living tissue*
See also **inhabit, survive**

live it up: enjoy life to the full
live up to: act according to
live with: accept or tolerate

live on *See* **endure**

livelihood *See* **work**

liveliness *See* **activity**

lively
▷ *ADJECTIVE*
full of life and enthusiasm: *a lively personality*
active *an active youngster*
animated *an animated discussion*
energetic *She gave an energetic performance.*
perky *The puppy wasn't quite as perky as usual.*
sparkling *I was enjoying a sparkling conversation.*

sprightly *a sprightly fellow*
vivacious *She is vivacious and charming.*
ANTONYM **dull**
See also **active, alive, bright, busy, colourful, vital**

livid *See* **furious, mad**

living *See* **alive, live**

living soul *See* **person**

load
▷ NOUN
1 something being carried: *This truck can carry a large load.*
cargo *The boat was carrying its usual cargo of bananas.*
consignment *The first consignment of food has been sent.*
freight *Most of the freight was carried by rail.*
shipment *a shipment of new cars*
▷ VERB
2 to put a lot of things on or into: *The trucks were loaded with blankets and supplies.*
fill *The van was filled with crates.*
pack *helicopters packed with medical supplies*
pile *Her cart was piled with groceries.*
stack *shelves stacked with cans*
See also **bunch, burden, mass, stuff**

loaded *See* **full, rich**

loads
▷ PLURAL NOUN
INFORMAL plenty of something: *I've got loads of money.*
heaps *heaps of cash*
lots *lots of fun*
plenty *We've got plenty of time.*
stacks *stacks of magazines*
tons INFORMAL *I've got tons of work to do.*
See also **plenty**

loaf *See* **laze**

loan
▷ NOUN
1 a sum of money that you borrow: *a small business loan*
advance *She was paid a large advance on her next novel.*
credit *We bought the TV on credit.*
mortgage *They took out a second mortgage on the house.*
▷ VERB
2 to lend something to someone: *He loaned us the painting for our exhibition.*
advance *I advanced him some money till we got home.*

lend *Will you lend me your jacket?*

loath *See* **reluctant, unwilling**

loathe *See* **dislike, hate**

loathing *See* **dislike, hate, horror**

loathsome *See* **hateful**

lob *See* **throw**

lobby *See* **passage**

local
▷ ADJECTIVE
1 belonging to the area where you live: *We shop at our local stores.*
community *There's a real community spirit on our street.*
district *the district council*
neighbourhood *our neighbourhood library*
regional *the regional skating finals*
▷ NOUN
2 a person who lives in a particular area: *That's what the locals call the place.*
inhabitant *the inhabitants of our county*
resident *a petition signed by the local residents*

locality *See* **area, region**

locate
▷ VERB
to find out where someone or something is: *We have been unable to locate him.*
find *They can't find it on the map.*
pinpoint *They pinpointed the source of the fire.*
track down *She has spent years trying to track down her old roommate.*
See also **find, place, position, set, trace**

located
▷ ADJECTIVE
existing or standing in a particular place: *The restaurant is located near the park.*
placed *The hotel is wonderfully placed in the theatre district.*
situated *His hotel is situated in the heart of the city.*

location
▷ NOUN
a place or position: *a house in a beautiful location*
place *the place where the museum used to stand*
point *a popular meeting point for tourists*

position *The ship radioed its position to the coastguard.*

site *the site of the murder*

situation *The cabin is in a great situation by the lake.*

spot *Can you show me the spot where it happened?*

whereabouts *His exact whereabouts are still not known.*

See also **place, position, scene, spot, surroundings**

lock
▷ *VERB*

1 to close and fasten something with a key: *Are you sure you locked the door?*

latch *He latched the gate.*

padlock *The locker was padlocked.*

ANTONYM **unlock**

▷ *NOUN*

2 a device used to fasten something: *The lock had been forced open.*

latch *A key clicked in the latch of the front door.*

padlock *He put a padlock on the door of his apartment and snapped it shut.*

See also **fasten, secure**

lock up *See* imprison

locked *See* secure

lodge *See* inhabit, stick

lodgings *See* accommodation

lofty *See* superior, tall

log *See* record

logic *See* argument

logical
▷ *ADJECTIVE*

1 using logic to work something out: *a logical theory*

consistent *His arguments were consistent and well-presented.*

rational *a rational analysis*

reasoned *a reasoned discussion*

sound *His reasoning is sound.*

valid *Both sides put forward valid arguments.*

2 sensible in the circumstances: *a logical deduction*

judicious *a judicious application of sunscreen lotion*

obvious *I jumped to the obvious conclusion.*

plausible *a plausible explanation*

reasonable *a reasonable course of action*

sensible *the sensible thing to do*

wise *a wise decision*

ANTONYM **illogical**

See also **rational, reasonable**

logo *See* sign, symbol

loiter *See* stay

loll *See* lie

lone *See* single

loneliness *See* solitude

lonely
▷ *ADJECTIVE*

1 unhappy because of being alone: *He's lonely and just wants to talk.*

alone *scared of being alone in the house*

forlorn *He looked a forlorn figure as he left the ice.*

forsaken *a forsaken and bitter person*

lonesome *I'm lonesome without you.*

2 isolated and not visited by many people: *a lonely hillside*

deserted *a deserted farmhouse*

desolate *a desolate place*

isolated *Many of the villages are in isolated areas.*

remote *a remote outpost*

secluded *a secluded area close to her home*

uninhabited *an uninhabited island*

See also **remote**

lonesome *See* lonely

long
▷ *ADJECTIVE*

1 continuing for a great amount of time: *a long interval when nobody spoke*

ANTONYM **short**

2 great in length or distance: *a long line of people*

ANTONYM **short**

See WORD STUDY **long** *on next page*

▷ *VERB*

3 to want something very much: *He longed for peace and quiet.*

ache *He ached for the time when he was young and carefree.*

covet *He covets my job.*

crave *I crave chocolates.*

hunger *They hungered for adventure.*

lust *to lust for power*

pine *I pine for the countryside.*

yearn *He yearned for freedom.*

See also **far, wish**

long ago *See* past, the past

long for *See* be dying for, desire, miss

longing
▷ *NOUN*

a strong wish for something: *her longing to return home*

craving *a craving for sugar*

L

Try to vary your language by using one of these substitutes for **long**.

• in physical extent
The catfish has an **elongated** body.
The company stocks an **extensive** list of products.
There were **lengthy** queues for all of the movies.

• in duration
She suffered through an **extended** period of unemployment.
I had to listen to an **interminable** debate about GM foods.
There will be a **lengthy** delay between flights.
What will be the effects of a **long-drawn-out** war?
A **prolonged** labour is dangerous for both mother and child.
Negotiations over the pay raise were **protracted**.
Writing music is a **slow** process.
He had a **sustained** run of bad luck.

---

desire *her desire for privacy*
hankering *a hankering to be an actress*
hunger *a hunger for success*
thirst *a thirst for adventure*
yearning *a yearning to be part of their world*
See also **desire, urge, wish**

long-suffering *See* patient

long-winded *See* talkative

look

▷ VERB
1 to turn your eyes toward something and see it: *She looked at me with affection.*
See WORD STUDY **look** *on next page*
2 to appear or seem to be: *the desire to look older*
appear *He appeared confused.*
look like *You look like you need a good night's sleep.*
seem *She seemed tense.*
seem to be *They seem to be lacking in enthusiasm.*
▷ NOUN
3 the action of turning your eyes toward something: *He took a last look in the mirror.*
gaze *her concentrated gaze*
glance *a quick glance*
glimpse *a fleeting glimpse*
peek *Give me a peek at his letter.*
▷ NOUN
4 the way someone or something appears: *He had the look of a confident man.*
air *a nonchalant air*
appearance *She was fastidious about her appearance.*
bearing *a dignified bearing*
expression *I saw his puzzled expression.*
face *Why are you all wearing such long faces?*
semblance *a semblance of normality*
See also **appearance, glance, peek, regard, search, see, seem, stare**

look around: consider many possibilities
look bad: appear improper or unsuitable
look down on: despise
look into: investigate
look out for: take care of or protect
look over: examine or inspect
look up to: respect or admire

look after

▷ VERB
to take care of someone or something: *Will you look after my cats this weekend?*
care for *vintage cars lovingly cared for by their owners*
mind *She'll mind the store while I'm away.*
nurse *They nursed him back to good health.*
take care of *I'll take care of the house for you.*
tend *He tended his flower beds.*
watch *My father will watch the kids while we're out.*
See also **mind, run, safeguard, take care of, tend, watch**

look-alike

▷ NOUN
a person who looks like someone else: *an Elvis look-alike*
dead ringer INFORMAL *a dead ringer for his brother*
double *He's the exact double of his father at that age.*
spitting image INFORMAL *She is the spitting image of me.*

look at *See* examine, face, read, watch

look down on *See* scorn

look for

▷ VERB
to try to find a person or thing: *I'm looking for my winter boots.*
forage *foraging for food*

All of the following words mean **look**, but each one has an extra shade of meaning which makes it a more expressive substitute for the word **look** in particular situations or contexts.

- If you **glance**, **peek**, or **peep** at something, you look at it quickly, and often secretly.
He **glanced** at his watch as she spoke.
She **peeked** at him through the curtains.
He **peeped** at me to see if I was watching him.

- If you **scan** something written or printed, you look at it quickly.
She **scanned** the advertisement pages of the newspapers.

- If you **eye** or **regard** something, you look at it carefully.
The waiters **eyed** him with suspicion.
He **regarded** me curiously.

- If you **gaze** or **stare** at something, you look at it steadily for a long time, for example because you find it interesting or because you are thinking about something else. Staring is often thought to be rude, but gazing is not.
She sat **gazing** into the fire for a long time.
They **stared** silently into each other's eyes.

- If you **observe** or **watch** something, you look at it for a long period of time to see what is happening.
A woman was **observing** him from across the square.
I hate people **watching** me while I eat.

- If you **survey** or **view** something, you look at it carefully.
He stood up and **surveyed** the crowd.
The mourners filed past to **view** the body.

- If you **examine**, **scrutinize**, or **study** something, you look at it very carefully, often to find out information from it.
He **examined** all the evidence.
She **scrutinized** the passport before she stamped it.
We **studied** the menu for several minutes.

- If you **glare**, **glower**, or **scowl** at something, you stare at it angrily.
He **glared** resentfully at me.
She stood **glowering** at the TV screen.
He **scowled** at the two men as they came into the room.

- If you **peer** or **squint** at something, you try to see it more clearly by narrowing or screwing up your eyes as you look at it.
He was **peering** at me through the keyhole.
She **squinted** at the blackboard, trying to read what was on it.

- If you **gape** at something, you look at it in surprise, usually with your mouth open.
She was **gaping** at the wreckage, lost for words.

- If you **goggle** at something, you look at it with your eyes wide open, usually because you are surprised by it.
He **goggled** at me in disbelief.

L

---

hunt *Police are hunting for clues and asking for information.*
search *Rescue teams are searching for the missing crew members.*
seek *She's seeking work as a chef, but so far she has not had an interview.*
See also **seek**

look like *See* **look, resemble, seem**

look on *See* **regard**

look out *See* **beware, watch out**

look up *See* **improve, refer, visit**

looks *See* **appearance**

looming *See* **imminent, near**

loony *See* **mad**

loop *See* **bend, coil, ring**

loophole *See* **hole**

loose
▷ ADJECTIVE
1 not firmly held or fixed: *a loose tooth*
free *She broke her fall with her free hand.*
unsecured *unsecured objects*
wobbly *a wobbly bridge*
ANTONYM **secure**
2 not fitting closely: *Wear loose clothes for comfort.*

baggy *a baggy sweater*
slack *Those trousers are very slack on you.*
ANTONYM **tight**
See also **approximate, free, full, vague**

CONFUSABLES

loose means **not tight**
lose usually means **misplace** or **fail to keep**

---

loosen
▷ VERB
to make something looser: *He loosened his tie.*
slacken *We slackened the rope.*
undo *I undid the ribbon and opened the present.*
untie *He untied his shoes and slipped them off.*
ANTONYM **tighten**

loot
▷ VERB
1 to steal from a place, usually during a riot or battle: *Gangs began breaking windows and looting stores.*
pillage *The thieves pillaged the museum.*
plunder *They plundered and burned the town.*
raid *Cattle rustlers have raided some farms in the region.*
ransack *The invaders ransacked the house.*
▷ NOUN
2 stolen or illegal money or goods: *The loot was never recovered.*
booty *They divided the booty among themselves.*
haul *the biggest haul of diamonds ever seized*
plunder *pirates in search of easy plunder*
spoils *the spoils of war*
See also **rob**

lop *See* **chop**

lopsided *See* **irregular**

lord *See* **noble**

lose
▷ VERB
1 to be unable to find: *I've lost my keys.*
drop *She's dropped a contact lens.*
mislay *I seem to have mislaid my glasses.*
misplace *Somehow, my suitcase was misplaced.*
ANTONYM **find**

2 to be beaten: *We lost the game.*
be beaten *She was soundly beaten in the election.*
be defeated *They were defeated in the finals.*
ANTONYM **win**

lose hope *See* **despair**

lose your nerve *See* **panic**

lose your temper *See* **rage**

loser *See* **failure**

lost
▷ ADJECTIVE
1 not knowing where you are: *I think we're lost.*
adrift *adrift on a raft in the middle of the ocean*
astray *Our baggage went astray in transit.*
off course *After a while, I realized I was completely off course.*
2 unable to be found: *I wonder if my lost keys will ever turn up.*
mislaid *searching in his pockets for his mislaid keys*
misplaced *I've found your misplaced glasses.*
missing *a missing person*

lot, a lot, or lots
▷ NOUNS
1 a large amount of something: *Remember to drink lots of water.*
abundance *an abundance of food*
a great deal *I've spent a great deal of time on this project.*
masses INFORMAL *There were masses of flowers at her funeral.*
piles INFORMAL *He's got piles of money.*
plenty *We've got plenty of time.*
quantities *She drank quantities of hot, sweet tea.*
scores *There were scores of witnesses.*
▷ NOUN
2 an amount or number: *We've just sacked one lot of builders.*
batch *a batch of cookies*
bunch INFORMAL *My neighbours are a noisy bunch.*
crowd *They're a real crowd of villains.*
group *a small group of football supporters*
quantity *a small quantity of water*
set *a set of photographs*
See also **bunch, loads, many, numerous, plenty, whole**

lottery *See* **gamble**

loud

▷ *ADJECTIVE*

1 having a high level of sound: *a loud explosion*

blaring *a blaring television*
deafening *a deafening roar*
noisy *a noisy old car*
resounding *a resounding slap*
strident *his strident voice*
thunderous *thunderous applause from the crowd*
ANTONYM **quiet**

2 very brightly coloured: *a loud tie*
flamboyant *a flamboyant outfit*
flashy *flashy clothes*
garish *a garish outfit*
gaudy *a gaudy striped tuque*
lurid *She painted her toenails a lurid pink.*
ANTONYM **dull**
See also **bold, gaudy, noisy**

lounge *See* **laze, lie**

lousy *See* **rotten**

lout *See* **hoodlum, oaf**

lovable

▷ *ADJECTIVE*

easy to love: *His vulnerability makes him very lovable.*

adorable *an adorable black kitten*
charming *a charming young singer*
enchanting *an enchanting performance*
endearing *one of her most endearing qualities*
sweet *a sweet little child*
ANTONYM **hateful**

love

▷ *VERB*

1 to feel strong affection for someone: *They loved each other very much.*

adore *She adored her parents.*
cherish *We cherish our friendship.*
worship *to be worshipped from afar*
ANTONYM **hate**

2 to like something very much: *We both love fishing.*

appreciate *I know you appreciate good food.*
enjoy *Do you enjoy poetry?*
like *I've always liked horror films.*
relish *He relished the challenge of extreme sports.*
ANTONYM **hate**

▷ *NOUN*

3 a strong feeling of affection: *their love for their children*

adoration *The child star had been used to adoration all her life.*

affection *We thought of them with great affection.*
ardour *an attempt to rekindle their lost ardour*
devotion *After all these years, their devotion to each other remains strong.*
infatuation *consumed with infatuation for her*
passion *the object of his passion*
ANTONYM **hatred**

▷ *NOUN*

4 a strong liking for something: *her love of animals*

devotion *his devotion to his hobbies*
fondness *a fondness for good food*
liking *my liking for classical music*
weakness *He had a weakness for cats.*
ANTONYM **hatred**
See also **affection, attachment, enjoy, like, passion, worship**

loveliness *See* **beauty**

lovely

▷ *ADJECTIVE*

very attractive and pleasant: *You look lovely.*

attractive *an attractive harbour village*
beautiful *very beautiful scenery*
delightful *a delightful garden*
enjoyable *I've had a very enjoyable time.*
pleasant *a pleasant little apartment*
pretty *a pretty room overlooking a beautiful garden*
ANTONYM **horrible**
See also **agreeable, attractive, beautiful, pleasant, pretty**

lover *See* **fan**

loving

▷ *ADJECTIVE*

feeling or showing love: *their loving parents*

affectionate *openly affectionate with each other*
devoted *a devoted couple*
doting *a doting father*
fond *She gave him a fond smile.*
tender *Her voice was tender.*
warm *a warm and loving friendship*
ANTONYM **cold**
See also **affectionate, devoted, fond, romantic, tender, warm**

low

▷ *ADJECTIVE*

1 short or not far above the ground: *The sun was low in the sky.*

little *a little table*

L

short *a short flight of steps*
small *a small stool*
squat *squat log cabins*
stunted *stunted trees*
sunken *a sunken garden*
ANTONYM **high**
2 small in degree or quantity: *low prices*
minimal *Minimal experience is required.*
modest *a modest rate of unemployment*
poor *working for poor wages*
reduced *reduced customer demand*
scant *scant opportunity for promotion*
small *produced in small numbers*
ANTONYM **high**
See also **deep, faint, miserable, quiet, reasonable, sad, soft**

lower

▷ *VERB*
1 to move something downward: *They lowered the coffin into the grave.*
drop *He dropped his plate into the sink.*
let down *They let the barrier down.*
take down *The pilot took the helicopter down.*
ANTONYM **raise**
2 to make something less in amount: *a commitment to lower taxes*
cut *The first priority is to cut costs.*
decrease *The Bank of Canada plans to decrease interest rates.*
diminish *Over time, her grief diminished.*
lessen *a diet that would lessen the risk of disease*
minimize *attempts to minimize the risk of cancer*
reduce *Gradually reduce the dosage.*
slash *We're slashing our prices.*
ANTONYM **increase**
See also **below, cut, decrease, diminish, ease, inferior, junior, lessen, reduce**

lowering *See* **cut**

lowest *See* **bottom, least**

lowly

▷ *ADJECTIVE*
not considered respectable: *his lowly status*
contemptible *He associates with the most contemptible people in society.*
despicable *a despicable wretch*
disreputable *the company of disreputable types*
vulgar *She considers herself to be above the vulgar masses of society.*
See also **humble**

loyal

▷ *ADJECTIVE*
firm in your friendship or support: *a loyal friend*
constant *my best friend and constant companion*
dependable *a cheerful, dependable friend*
faithful *He remained a faithful companion.*
staunch *a staunch supporter*
true *a true friend*
trusty *a trusty ally*
ANTONYM **treacherous**
See also **devoted, faithful**

lucid *See* **sane**

luck

▷ *NOUN*
something that happens by chance: *It was just luck that we happened to meet.*
accident *It came about almost by accident.*
chance *We met by chance.*
destiny *Is it destiny that brings people together?*
fate *a simple twist of fate*
fortune *smiled on by fortune*
See also **chance**

luckless *See* **unlucky**

lucky

▷ *ADJECTIVE*
1 having a lot of good luck: *He had always been lucky at cards.*
blessed *being blessed with a cheerful disposition*
charmed *She seems to have a charmed life.*
fortunate *He was extremely fortunate to survive.*
ANTONYM **unlucky**
2 happening by chance with good consequences: *a lucky break*
fortuitous *a fortuitous combination of circumstances*
fortunate *His appearance at that moment was a fortunate accident.*
opportune *I had shown up at an opportune moment.*
timely *his timely arrival*
ANTONYM **unlucky**

lucrative *See* **successful**

ludicrous *See* **absurd, impossible, ridiculous**

lug *See* **carry, drag**

lukewarm *See* **cold, warm**

lull *See* **gap, silence**

lumbering *See* **clumsy**

luminary *See* **star**

luminous *See* **bright, brilliant, shining**

lump
▷ NOUN
1 a solid piece of something: *a big lump of clay*
ball *a ball of yarn*
cake *a cake of soap*
chunk *a chunk of bread*
hunk *a hunk of beef*
piece *a piece of cake*
wedge *a wedge of cheese*
2 a bump on the surface of something: *I've got a big lump on my head.*
bulge *My wallet made a bulge in my pocket.*
bump *a bump in the road*
hump *a hump on a camel's back*
swelling *a swelling over one eye*
See also **block, bulge, bump, mass**

lunch *See* **eat**

lure
▷ VERB
1 to attract someone somewhere or into doing something: *We are being lured into a trap.*
attract *Hot weather attracts blackflies.*
beckon *She beckoned me toward her table.*
draw *What drew him to the area was its proximity to the beach.*
entice *Retailers will do anything to entice shoppers through their doors.*
tempt *trying to tempt tourists to our province*
▷ NOUN
2 something that you find very attractive: *the lure of rural life*
attraction *the attraction of living on the waterfront*
bait *The company offered her a good salary, plus a car as added bait.*
magnet *The park is a magnet for cyclists.*
pull *to feel the pull of the past*
temptation *the many temptations to which they will be exposed*
See also **attract, bait, pull, tempt**

lurid *See* **loud**

lurk *See* **sneak**

luscious *See* **delicious, tasty**

lush *See* **thick**

lust *See* **long, passion**

lustful
▷ ADJECTIVE

feeling or showing strong sexual desire: *lustful thoughts*
carnal *carnal desires*
lecherous *a lecherous type*
lewd *arrested for lewd behaviour*

lustre *See* **finish**

luxuriant *See* **thick**

luxurious
▷ ADJECTIVE
expensive and full of luxury: *a luxurious lifestyle*
deluxe *deluxe surroundings*
lavish *a lavish party*
opulent *an opulent office*
plush INFORMAL *a plush hotel*
posh *posh surroundings*
sumptuous *a sumptuous feast*
ANTONYM **plain**

CONFUSABLES

luxurious usually means **full of luxury**
luxuriant means **growing thickly**

---

luxury

L

▷ NOUN
1 comfort in expensive surroundings: *a life of luxury*
affluence *the trappings of affluence*
opulence *the sheer opulence of their surroundings*
sumptuousness *The hotel lobby was sumptuousness itself.*
2 something enjoyable that you do not have often: *Telephones are still a luxury in some countries.*
extra *The car is a basic model with no extras.*
extravagance *Eating out is an extravagance.*
indulgence *This car is one of my few indulgences.*
treat *I eat cake only as a treat.*
See also **comfort**

lying
▷ NOUN
1 the action of telling lies: *I've had enough of your lying.*
deceit *the deceits of politicians*
dishonesty *deliberate dishonesty*
fabrication *His story is pure fabrication.*
fibbing *Her fibbing eventually got her into trouble.*
perjury *This witness has committed perjury.*
▷ ADJECTIVE
2 telling lies: *The man is just a lying cheat.*

deceitful *deceitful and misleading remarks*
dishonest *a dishonest account of events*
false *a false confession*
untruthful *She deliberately gave untruthful answers.*
ANTONYM **honest**
See also **dishonest**

Mm

macabre *See* **creepy**

mace *See* **stick**

machine

▷ NOUN

a piece of equipment: *a washing machine*
apparatus *an apparatus for use in fighting fires*
appliance *electrical appliances*
contraption *a contraption for stretching baseball caps*
device *a timer device for a bomb*
instrument *navigation instruments*
mechanism *a locking mechanism*
See also **gadget**

mad

▷ ADJECTIVE

I very foolish or unwise: *He'd be mad to refuse.*
crazy INFORMAL *People thought they were crazy to try it.*
foolhardy *Some described the act as foolhardy.*
foolish *It would be foolish to raise hopes unnecessarily.*
stupid *It would be stupid to pretend otherwise.*
2 angry about something: *They both got mad at me for interfering.*
angry *She was angry at her husband.*
crazy *This sitting around is driving me crazy.*
enraged *I became more and more enraged by the unfairness of it all.*
fuming *The neighbour was still fuming.*
furious *He is furious at the way his family has been treated.*
incensed *They were incensed at his lack of compassion.*
infuriated *He knew how infuriated this would make me.*
irate *The passenger was irate, shouting about the flight delay.*
livid *I am absolutely livid about it.*
See also **angry, crazy, furious**

madness *See* **frenzy**

magic

▷ NOUN

a special power: *They believe in magic.*
sorcery *the ancient use of sorcery to combat evil influences*
witchcraft *people who practise witchcraft*

magical

▷ ADJECTIVE

wonderful and exciting: *Paris is a magical city.*

bewitching *bewitching brown eyes*
enchanting *an enchanting child*

magnanimous *See* **noble**

magnet *See* **lure**

magnetism *See* **charm, influence, pull**

magnificence *See* **glory**

magnificent *See* **brilliant, fine, grand, marvellous, splendid, superb, wonderful**

magnify *See* **enlarge**

maim *See* **cripple, injure**

main

▷ ADJECTIVE

most important: *the main reason*
cardinal *one of the cardinal rules of movie reviewing*
chief *one of his chief rivals*
foremost *one of the foremost scholars on ancient languages*
leading *a leading industrial nation*
major *one of the major causes of cancer*
predominant *His predominant emotion was confusion.*
primary *the primary source of water in the region*
prime *the prime suspect*
principal *the principal source of salt in our diets*
See also **chief, essential, leading, prime, principal**

mainly

▷ ADVERB

true in most cases: *The staff members were mainly young.*
chiefly *He chiefly painted portraits.*
generally *It is generally true that the darker the fruit the higher its iron content.*
largely *Their early ideas were largely ignored.*
mostly *Cars are mostly metal.*
predominantly *Their business is conducted predominantly by phone.*
primarily *The body is made up primarily of bone, muscle, and fat.*
principally *This is principally because the stock market is weak.*
See also **as a rule**

maintain *See* **argue, claim, keep**

maintenance *See* **upkeep**

majestic *See* **grand**

majesty *See* **glory**

major

▷ ADJECTIVE

very important or serious: *a major problem*

critical *a critical factor*

crucial *The decision is important but not crucial.*

leading *a leading industrial nation*

outstanding *an outstanding contribution*

significant *a significant amount of damage*

ANTONYM **minor**

See also **leading, main, principal**

majority

▷ NOUN

more than half: *The majority of our cheeses are made with cow's milk.*

best part *for the best part of 24 hours*

better part *I spent the better part of this week's paycheque on clothes.*

bulk *She was responsible for the bulk of the work.*

most *Most of the book is true.*

make

▷ VERB

1 to construct something: *She makes all her own clothes.*

assemble *Workers were assembling planes.*

build *They built a new house at the site of the old one.*

construct *the campaign to construct a museum on the property*

create *It's great for a radio producer to create a show like this.*

fabricate *All the tools are fabricated from high-quality steel.*

fashion *necklaces fashioned from shells*

form *a sculpture formed from clay*

manufacture *They manufacture plastics.*

produce *We try to produce attractive and durable furniture.*

2 to force someone to do something: *He tried to make me lie for him.*

compel *legislation to compel cyclists to wear helmets*

drive *Jealousy drives people to do strange things.*

force *A back injury forced her to withdraw from the team.*

oblige *I was obliged to withdraw from the race.*

▷ NOUN

3 a particular type: *a certain make of wristwatch*

brand *a brand of coffee*

model *To keep the cost down, choose a basic model.*

See also **assemble, build, construct, earn, fashion, force, form, issue, manufacture, produce, reach, shape, sort, type**

INFORMALLY SPEAKING

make it: succeed

make like: imitate

make something of: start an argument

on the make: ambitiously trying for success

make a difference See **matter**

make a mistake See **err**

make an attempt See **try**

make an effort See **strive, try**

make certain See **ensure**

make fun of See **mock, tease**

make known See **advise, announce**

make out See **distinguish**

make sure See **ensure**

make up for See **compensate**

make up your mind See **decide, resolve**

make use of See **employ**

make up

▷ VERB

1 to form the parts of something: *Westerners make up the majority of the team.*

compose *The group was composed of students of all ages.*

comprise *The orchestra comprises various instruments.*

constitute *Young people constitute the majority of the contestants.*

form *Protein forms a large part of the diet.*

2 to invent a story: *It's very unkind of you to make up stories about him.*

concoct *The prisoner concocted the story to get a lighter sentence.*

fabricate *They fabricated evidence against him.*

invent *The author invented some fascinating characters.*

See also **form, invent**

makeup See **character, nature, personality, structure**

making

▷ NOUN

the act of creating something: *the making of this movie*

assembly *the assembly of a robot*
building *The building of the airport continues.*
construction *boat construction*
creation *the creation of large parks and forests*
fabrication *the design and fabrication of the space shuttle*
manufacture *the manufacture of car tires*
production *These proteins stimulate the production of blood cells.*

in the making
▷ *ADJECTIVE*
about to become something: *a captain in the making*
budding *a budding author*
emergent *an emergent nation*
potential *a potential champion*
up-and-coming *an up-and-coming golfer*
See also **manufacture**

male
▷ *NOUN*
1 a person or animal that can fertilize a female's eggs to produce young: *a pride of lions with three males, ten females, and six cubs*
boy *a boys' club*
gentleman *a perfect gentleman*
man *two men with beards*
▷ *ADJECTIVE*
2 relating to males: *the finest male actor in movies today*
masculine *masculine characteristics like facial hair*
See also **man**

malevolence *See* spite

malevolent *See* evil, hostile, malicious, spiteful

malice *See* animosity, hostility, spite

malicious
▷ *ADJECTIVE*
having the intention of being mean to someone: *She described the charges as malicious.*
cruel *Children can be so cruel.*
malevolent *FORMAL She gave me a malevolent stare.*
mean *Someone's played a mean trick on you.*
spiteful *spiteful telephone calls*
vicious *a vicious attack on an innocent man's character*
See also **spiteful, unkind**

malign *See* slander

mammoth *See* colossal, formidable

man
▷ *NOUN*
an adult male human being: *a young man*
gentleman *It seems this gentleman was waiting for the doctor.*
guy *INFORMAL There's some guy on the phone for you.*
male *The winners are equally divided between females and males.*

manage
▷ *VERB*
1 to succeed in doing something: *We managed to find somewhere to sit.*
cope with *How did my parents cope with so many children?*
succeed in *We have succeeded in persuading the library to buy the book.*
2 to be in charge of something: *Within two years, he was managing the store.*
be in charge of *Who's in charge here?*
command *Who would command the troops in the event of war?*
control *They now control the largest real estate company in the province.*
direct *She will direct day-to-day operations.*
run *Is this any way to run a country?*
See also **accomplish, administer, command, conduct, control, deal, direct, do, handle, head, lead, oversee, run, supervise, take care of**

management
▷ *NOUN*
1 the act of running an organization: *The zoo needed better management.*
control *The restructuring requires her to give up control of the company.*
direction *Organizations need clear direction.*
running *the day-to-day running of the clinic*
2 the people who run an organization: *The management is doing its best.*
administration *They would like the administration to exert more control over the university.*
board *a recommendation that he wants to put before the board*
bosses *INFORMAL a dispute between workers and bosses*
directors *the board of directors of a local hospital*
employers *Employers are said to be considering the demand.*
See also **control, direction**

manager
▷ *NOUN*
a person in charge of running an

M

organization: *the manager of the company's Atlantic division*
boss INFORMAL *He cannot stand his boss.*
director *the director of the finance department*
executive *an advertising executive*
See also **boss, chief, head, superior**

mandatory See **compulsory**

mangle See **twist**

mania See **obsession**

manic See **furious**

manifest
▷ ADJECTIVE
FORMAL obvious or easily seen: *the manifest failure of the policy*
blatant *a blatant attempt to spread the blame*
clear *a clear case of homicide*
conspicuous *They always dress in a conspicuous way.*
glaring *a glaring example of fraud*
obvious *an obvious injustice*
patent *This was patent nonsense.*
plain *She's made it plain that she wants to be involved.*
See also **betray, show, visible**

manipulate See **influence**

mankind See **humankind, people**

manly See **male**

manner
▷ NOUN
1 the way that something is done: *She smiled again in a friendly manner.*
fashion *a drug that works in a similar fashion*
mode *He switched automatically into his interview mode.*
style *an informal writing style*
way *He had a strange way of talking.*
2 the way that someone behaves: *her kind manner*
bearing *his military bearing*
behaviour *her antisocial behaviour*
conduct *principles of civilized conduct*
demeanour *a cheerful demeanour*
See also **fashion, style, way**

manners See **conduct**

manoeuvre
▷ VERB
1 to move someone or something skilfully: *It took expertise to manoeuvre the boat so close to the shore.*
guide *She guided them along the path.*

navigate *He attempted to navigate his way through the crowds.*
negotiate *I negotiated my way out of the airport.*
steer *I steered him toward the door.*
▷ NOUN
2 a clever action: *manoeuvres to block the changes on the team*
dodge *a tax dodge*
ploy *a marketing ploy*
ruse *This was a ruse to divide them.*
tactic *The tactic paid off.*
See also **ease, measure**

manslaughter See **murder**

manufacture
▷ VERB
1 to make goods by using machines, often in a factory: *Several models are being manufactured here.*
assemble *a factory where they assemble tractors*
fabricate *a plant that fabricates telephone components*
make *making cars at two plants in Ontario*
mass-produce *the invention of machinery to mass-produce footwear*
process *The material will be processed into plastic containers.*
produce *The company produced computer parts.*
▷ NOUN
2 the making of goods in a factory: *the manufacture of cardboard boxes*
assembly *the assembly of cars by robots*
fabrication *the design and fabrication of the Canadarm*
making *the steps that go into the making of a book*
mass production *the mass production of baby food*
production *We need to maintain the production of cars at last year's level.*
See also **invent, make, making, produce**

many
▷ ADJECTIVE
1 a large number: *Cooking is one of his many hobbies.*
countless *She brought joy to countless people.*
innumerable *He has invented innumerable excuses.*
myriad *the myriad other tasks we are trying to perform*
numerous *Her valuable contributions are too numerous to mention.*
umpteen INFORMAL *He has written umpteen books.*
ANTONYM **few**

▷ *NOUN*

2 a large number of people or things: *in many of these neighbourhoods*
a lot *A lot of people would agree with you.*
a mass *a mass of books and papers*
a multitude *for a multitude of reasons*
large numbers *Large numbers of people stayed away.*
lots INFORMAL *lots of food at the party*
plenty *plenty of vegetables*
scores *Scores of people were injured.*
ANTONYM **few**
See also **numerous**

mar *See* **botch, ruin, spoil**

march *See* **parade, walk**

margin *See* **border, edge**

marinate *See* **steep**

mark

▷ *NOUN*

1 a small stain: *I can't get this mark off the curtain.*
See WORD STUDY **mark** *on next page*

▷ *VERB*

2 to stain something: *to stop the shoes from marking the floor*
smudge *a face smudged with dirt*
stain *His clothing was stained with mud.*
streak *Rain had begun to streak the windows.*
See also **feature, quality, sign, spot, stain, symbol**

INFORMALLY SPEAKING

make your mark: succeed
miss the mark: fail to do what you tried to do
up to the mark: meeting a certain standard

---

marked *See* **particular, sharp, significant**

market

▷ *NOUN*

a place to buy or sell things: *the local market*
bazaar *an exotic bazaar*
fair *a fall fair*
See also **shop**

market price *See* **value**

marriage

▷ *NOUN*

1 the relationship between spouses: *six years of marriage*
matrimony FORMAL *the bonds of matrimony*
wedlock FORMAL *joined in wedlock*

TYPES OF ... MARSH

bayou	muskeg ❀
bog	quagmire
fen	quicksand
marshland	swamp
mire	swampland
morass	wetland
mud flat	

---

marvel *See* **curiosity, miracle, wonder**

marvellous

▷ *ADJECTIVE*

wonderful or excellent: *a marvellous actor*
brilliant *a brilliant performance*
excellent *He does an excellent job as my assistant.*
first-rate *The meal was absolutely first-rate.*
magnificent *She was magnificent as Anne of Green Gables.*
remarkable *a remarkable achievement*
splendid *splendid photographs*
superb *a superb novel*
wonderful *It's wonderful to see you.*
ANTONYM **terrible**
See also **brilliant, first-rate, grand, incredible, splendid, superb, wonderful**

M

masculine *See* **male**

mash *See* **crush, press**

mask *See* **cover, obscure**

masquerade as *See* **pose**

mass this

▷ *NOUN*

1 a large number or amount: *a mass of papers*
crowd *A huge crowd of people gathered.*
heap *a heap of bricks*
load *a load of kids*
lump *a lump of clay*
mob *a growing mob of demonstrators*
pile *a pile of sand*
throng *A shout went up from the throng of spectators.*

▷ *ADJECTIVE*

2 involving a large number of people: *mass unemployment*
general *We are trying to raise general awareness about this issue.*
popular *a popular decision*
universal *universal health care*
widespread *widespread support for the proposals*

▷ *VERB*

3 to gather together in a large group: *The crowd began to mass in the square.*

Mark is rather a vague word. Depending on what you are referring to, there are a number of more interesting synonyms that you can use in its place.

• a stain
There's an ink **blot** on your shirt.
A line of dirt ran across his face like a **scar**.
I tried to clean the oil **smudge** off my nose.
He noticed a grease **spot** on his pants.
The **stain** on the front of my jacket won't come out.
A **streak** of mud smudged her cheek.

• a damaged area
There are some slight **blemishes** on her skin.
He had big purple **blotches** all over his back.
Her hands were dotted with cuts and **bruises**.
There was a tiny **dent** on the hood.
The little **nicks** on his chin are from shaving.
The accident left a jagged **scar** on his forehead.
A long **scratch** ran across the tabletop.

• a written or printed symbol
She wore a jade pendant carved with Chinese **characters**.
The box was stamped with the royal **insignia**.

The company's **logo** is a red diamond.
Is that an x or a multiplication **sign**?
I can't read the date **stamp** on the envelope.
A dove is a **symbol** of peace.

• a characteristic of something
She shows all the essential **attributes** of a good leader.
The latest version has all the fundamental **features** that made the original so popular.
Thus began the compassion that was the **hallmark** of all her films.
It is a **measure** of how much things have changed.
The doctor could find no **symptoms** of depression.
Determination is a common **trait** of all great athletes.

• an indication of something
You should make a **gesture** of goodwill.
He bowed very low as an **indication** of his regard for the king.
Stand up as a **sign** of respect.
He wore black as a **symbol** of mourning.
The gifts were a **token** of our friendship.

---

assemble *Thousands of people assembled in the stadium.*
congregate *Youngsters congregate here in the evenings.*
gather *We gathered around the fireplace.*
group *The children grouped together under the trees.*
See also **assemble, crowd, gather, heap, jam, majority, tangle**

mass production *See* **manufacture**

massacre *See* **kill**

masses *See* **lot, public**

massive *See* **colossal, enormous, heavy, huge, immense, large, vast**

mass-produce *See* **manufacture**

master
▷ *VERB*
to learn how to do something: *She found it easy to master the latest technology.*

become proficient in *He quickly became proficient in the language.*
get the hang of *INFORMAL It's a bit tricky till you get the hang of it.*
grasp *It took her a while to grasp the basics of the process.*
learn *He enjoyed learning new skills.*
See also **expert, genius, learn, overcome, teacher**

masterly *See* **perfect, skilful, skilled**

mastermind *See* **genius**

mastery *See* **command**

mat *See* **tangle**

match
▷ *NOUN*
1 an organized game: *a tennis match*
competition *a surfing competition*
contest *one of the best contests in recent tennis history*
game *the Canucks' first game of the new season*

▷ VERB

2 to be similar to: *The shoes matched her dress.*
agree *Their statements do not agree.*
correspond *The two maps correspond closely.*
fit *Should the punishment fit the crime?*
go with *The curtains didn't go with the carpet.*
suit *the best insurance plan to suit your needs*
tally *The figures didn't seem to tally.*
See also **agree, blend, contest, correspond, equal, fit, game, rival, suit**

mate See **companion, friend, partner**

material
▷ NOUN

1 any type of cloth: *the thick material of her skirt*
cloth *a piece of cloth*
fabric *silk and other delicate fabrics*
2 a solid substance: *the materials needed to build the shed*
matter *waste matter from industries*
stuff *the stuff from which the universe is made*
substance *a crumbly black substance*
See also **cloth, information, matter, stuff, substance**

materialistic See **greedy**

materialize See **come**

matrimony See **marriage**

matter
▷ NOUN

1 something that you have to deal with: *business matters*
affair *The funeral was a sad affair.*
business *This whole business has upset me.*
issue *a major political issue*
question *the difficult question of unemployment*
situation *The situation is now under control.*
subject *a difficult subject on which to reach a compromise*
2 any substance: *The atom is the smallest divisible particle of matter.*
material *a conducting material such as metal*
stuff *curtains made from some flimsy stuff*
substance *a poisonous substance*
▷ VERB

3 to be important: *It doesn't matter what you wear to the party.*
be of consequence *Their choice is of no consequence to anyone but themselves.*
count *It's as if my opinions just don't count.*

make a difference *Exercise makes all the difference.*
See also **affair, business, count, event, issue, item, material, subject**

matter-of-fact See **realistic**

mature
▷ VERB

1 to become fully developed: *Some children mature earlier than others.*
come of age *The money was held in trust until he came of age.*
grow up *She grew up in Halifax.*
reach adulthood *He died before his children had reached adulthood.*
▷ ADJECTIVE

2 fully developed: *He's very mature for his age.*
adult *a pair of adult birds*
full-grown *a full-grown cat*
full-fledged *He has developed into a full-fledged adult.*
grown *a grown man*
grown-up *They have two grown-up children.*
See also **develop**

maudlin See **corny, sentimental**

maul See **savage**

mausoleum See **grave, tomb**

maxim See **saying**

maximum
▷ NOUN

1 the most that is possible: *The restaurant can seat a maximum of 30 people.*
ceiling *an agreement to put a ceiling on salaries*
height *when the population was at its height*
most *The most he'll get is a hundred dollars.*
upper limit *the need to put an upper limit on spending*
utmost *He did his utmost to make them agree.*
ANTONYM **minimum**
▷ ADJECTIVE

2 being the most that is possible: *the maximum recommended dosage*
top *a top speed of 100 km/h*
utmost *a question of the utmost importance*
ANTONYM **minimum**
See also **full, limit**

maybe
▷ ADVERB

it is possible that: *Maybe I should have done a bit more.*
conceivably *The project could conceivably*

M

be finished within a week.
it could be *That could be the reason why he refused.*
perhaps *Perhaps, in time, she'll understand.*
possibly *Carelessness is possibly to blame for this.*
See also **perhaps**

meadow See **field**

meagre
▷ ADJECTIVE
very small and inadequate: *a meagre pension*
inadequate *inadequate portions*
measly INFORMAL *Our bathroom measures a measly 3.5 m².*
paltry *a paltry fine of $20*
scant *He paid scant attention to my complaint.*
sparse *sparse vegetation*
See also **few**

meal
▷ NOUN
an occasion when people eat: *She sat next to me throughout the meal.*
banquet *a gala banquet at the prime minister's residence*
dinner *a series of official dinners*
feast *the wedding feast*

mean
▷ VERB
1 to convey a message: *The flashing signal means stop.*
denote *Red eyes denote strain and fatigue.*
indicate *Today's decision indicates a change in policy.*
signify *The music signified that the show was about to begin.*
2 to intend to do something: *I meant to phone you, but didn't have time.*
aim *I aim to arrive early.*
intend *She intended to move back to Manitoba.*
plan *They plan to marry in the summer.*
▷ ADJECTIVE
3 unkind: *Why are you being so mean to me?*
hurtful *a hurtful thing to say*
malicious *malicious thoughts*
nasty *a nasty trick to play on anyone*
spiteful *a spiteful thing to do*
▷ ADJECTIVE
4 unwilling to spend money: *Don't be mean with the tip.*
miserly *He is miserly with both his time and his money.*
tight INFORMAL *He was so tight that he wouldn't even buy new shoes.*
See also **horrible, intend, malicious,**

petty, represent, shabby, sneaky, unkind

meandering See **indirect**

meaning
▷ NOUN
the idea expressed by something: *the meaning of this dream*
drift *I was beginning to get his drift.*
gist *I could not get the gist of their conversation.*
message *The message of the movie escaped me.*
sense *The word has two main senses.*
significance *The message has more significance than you realise.*
See also **message**

meaningless See **empty, worthless**

means See **measure, process, way, wealth**

meant See **supposed**

measly See **meagre, petty**

measure
▷ VERB
1 to check the size of something: *We measured the size of the room.*
gauge *She gauged the wind at over 30 knots.*
survey *geological experts who surveyed the cliffs*
▷ NOUN
2 an amount of something: *There has been a measure of agreement.*
amount *a certain amount of disappointment*
degree *a degree of success*
portion *I have spent a considerable portion of my life here.*
proportion *A large proportion of my free time is spent reading.*
▷ NOUN
3 an action in order to achieve something: *Tough measures are needed to maintain safety.*
expedient *I reduced my spending by the simple expedient of destroying my credit card.*
manoeuvre *manoeuvres to advance the peace process*
means *The move is a means to fight crime.*
procedure *safety procedures*
step *steps to fight pollution*
See also **extent, quantity**

measured See **deliberate**

mechanical See **automatic**

mechanism See **machine**

meddle See **interfere**

meddler

▷ *NOUN*

a person who interferes in other people's business: *a meddler in everyone's personal affairs*
busybody *I wouldn't tell anything to that busybody.*
snooper *He's bossy, and he's a snooper.*

mediate *See* **intervene**

medical *See* **examination**

medication *See* **drug, medicine**

medicine

▷ *NOUN*

something you take to make you better: *Don't forget to take your medicine.*
drug *Three new drugs recently became available.*
medication *medication for her cough*
remedy *At the moment, we are trying a herbal remedy.*
See also **cure, drug**

mediocre *See* **inferior, poor, unsatisfactory**

meditate *See* **consider, deliberate, think**

meditation *See* **thought**

medium

▷ *ADJECTIVE*

1 average in size: *He was of medium height.*
average *a grey cat of average size*
medium-sized *a medium-sized pot*
middling *a person of middling intelligence*
▷ *NOUN*
2 a means of communication: *the medium of television*
channel *through diplomatic channels*
vehicle *The play seemed an ideal vehicle for his music.*
See also **moderate**

medium-sized *See* **medium**

medley *See* **mixture, variety**

meek

▷ *ADJECTIVE*

quiet and timid: *a meek, mild-mannered young man*
deferential *Wolves keep a deferential attitude to the pack leader.*
docile *a docile, obedient puppy*
submissive *submissive to authority*
timid *a timid child*
unassuming *very polite and unassuming*
ANTONYM **bold**
See also **gentle, humble, mild**

meet

▷ *VERB*

1 to be in the same place as someone: *I met him at the mall yesterday.*
bump into *INFORMAL I bumped into a friend of yours today.*
come upon *We turned the corner and came upon a group of hikers.*
encounter *the most gifted child we had ever encountered*
run across *We ran across some old friends.*
run into *Guess who I ran into the other day!*
2 to gather in a group: *We meet for lunch once a week.*
assemble *a convenient place for students to assemble between classes*
congregate *Youngsters congregate here in the evening.*
convene *The premiers convened in Fredericton.*
gather *We all gathered in the meeting room.*
get together *the last time we all got together*
3 to fulfill a need: *services intended to meet the needs of the elderly*
answer *Money alone can't answer my needs.*
fulfill *All the requirements were fulfilled.*
satisfy *Candidates must satisfy a number of requirements.*
See also **experience, greet, receive, satisfy, touch**

meet head-on *See* **hit**

meeting

▷ *NOUN*

1 an event at which people come together for a purpose: *a business meeting*
conference *a conference on education*
congress *a medical congress*
convention *the annual convention of the Canadian Library Association*
gathering *a social gathering*
get-together *INFORMAL a get-together I had at my home*
reunion *a family reunion*
2 an occasion when you meet someone: *a chance meeting*
encounter *an interesting encounter at the restaurant*
rendezvous *The couple arranged a six o'clock rendezvous.*
tryst *a lovers' tryst*
See also **appointment, conference, convention, gathering**

melancholy *See* **down, miserable, misery, sad, sadness, sorrow**

M

mellow *See* **soft, sweet**

melodious *See* **sweet**

melodramatic

▷ ADJECTIVE

behaving in an exaggerated way: *Don't you think you're being rather melodramatic?*
histrionic *She let out a histrionic groan.*
sensational *sensational newspaper reports in the tabloids*
theatrical *In a theatrical gesture, she raised her glass with a flourish.*

melody *See* **tune**

melt

▷ VERB

1 to become liquid: *The snow had melted.*
dissolve *Heat gently until the sugar dissolves.*
thaw *It's so cold the ice doesn't get a chance to thaw.*
2 to disappear: *My inhibitions melted.*
disappear *The immediate threat has disappeared.*
disperse *The crowd dispersed peacefully.*
dissolve *His new-found optimism dissolved.*
evaporate *My anger evaporated.*
vanish *All her fears suddenly vanished.*
See also **warm**

melt away *See* **disappear, vanish**

memento *See* **souvenir**

memo *See* **message, note**

memorable

▷ ADJECTIVE

likely to be remembered: *a memorable victory*
catchy *a catchy tune*
historic *a historic meeting*
notable *with a few notable exceptions*
striking *his most striking qualities*
unforgettable *an unforgettable experience*

memorandum *See* **message, note**

memory

▷ NOUN

the ability to remember: *Every detail is fresh in my memory.*
recall *She's blessed with total recall.*
remembrance FORMAL *My remembrance of the incident is somewhat hazy.*

menace *See* **danger, threat, threaten**

menacing *See* **frightening, sinister**

mend

▷ VERB

to repair something that is broken: *to mend a broken chain*
fix *If something is broken, we get it fixed right away.*
patch *They patched the barn roof.*
renovate *The couple spent thousands renovating the house.*
repair *to get her car repaired*
restore *experts who specialize in restoring old paintings*
See also **fix, piece together, repair, restore**

menial *See* **inferior**

mention

▷ VERB

1 to talk about something briefly: *I may not have mentioned it to her.*
allude to *She alluded to his absence in vague terms.*
bring up *Why are you bringing it up now?*
broach *I carefully broached the delicate subject.*
hint *The coach hinted that she might make some changes.*
intimate *He did intimate that he is seeking legal action.*
refer to *In his speech, he referred to a recent trip to Poland.*
touch on *The series touches on these issues, but only superficially.*
touch upon *I'd like to touch upon a more serious matter now.*

▷ NOUN

2 a brief comment about something: *There was no mention of elections.*
allusion *She made an allusion to the events in Los Angeles.*
reference *He made no reference to any agreement.*
See also **comment, note, observe, refer, remark**

mentor *See* **adviser**

merchandise *See* **product, stock**

merchant *See* **trader**

merciful

▷ ADJECTIVE

1 showing kindness: *merciful and sympathetic to others*
compassionate *a deeply compassionate person*
humane *the desire for a more humane society*
kind *She is good-hearted and kind to everyone.*
ANTONYM **merciless**
2 showing forgiveness: *We can only hope the court is merciful.*

forgiving *I don't think people are in a very forgiving mood.*

lenient *Are the courts too lenient to criminals?*

ANTONYM **merciless**

See also **compassionate, humane**

merciless

▷ ADJECTIVE

showing no kindness or forgiveness: *a merciless dictator*

callous *callous disregard for human life*

cruel *I don't understand how people can be cruel to animals.*

heartless *I couldn't believe they were so heartless.*

implacable *a powerful and implacable enemy*

ruthless *his ruthless treatment of employees*

ANTONYM **merciful**

mercy

▷ NOUN

1 the quality of kindness: *She showed no mercy.*

compassion *compassion for less fortunate people*

kindness *He was treated with kindness by strangers.*

pity *I saw no pity in their faces.*

2 the quality of forgiveness: *He threw himself upon the mercy of the court.*

forgiveness *He fell to his knees begging for forgiveness.*

leniency *The judge said she would show no leniency.*

See also **forgiveness, pity**

merely See only

merge See blend, combine, mix, unite

merit

▷ NOUN

1 worth or value: *Box-office success mattered more than artistic merit.*

excellence *the top award for excellence in journalism*

value *The value of this work experience should not be underestimated.*

virtue *There is little virtue in such an approach.*

worth *people who had already proved their worth to their companies*

2 a good quality that something has: *Despite its merits, the work would never be used.*

advantage *The great advantage of local produce is its flavour.*

asset *Her leadership qualities were her greatest asset.*

strength *The book's strength lay in its depiction of life in Upper Canada.*

strong point *Science was never my strong point at school.*

virtue *Its other great virtue is its durability.*

▷ VERB

3 to deserve something: *Such ideas merit careful consideration.*

be entitled to *She is entitled to feel proud.*

be worthy of *They didn't think she was worthy of a promotion.*

deserve *He deserves a rest.*

earn *Companies must earn a reputation for honesty.*

warrant *no evidence to warrant further investigation*

See also **deserve, quality, value, virtue**

merry See bright, cheerful

mess

▷ NOUN

1 a state of untidiness: *I'll clear up the mess later.*

chaos *Their concerts often ended in chaos.*

disarray *He found the room in disarray.*

disorder *Inside, all was disorder.*

2 a situation that is full of problems: *the reasons why the economy is in such a mess*

fix INFORMAL *The government has really got itself into a fix.*

jam INFORMAL *They were in a real jam.*

muddle *Our finances are in a muddle.*

turmoil *The league was in turmoil.*

▷ VERB

3 to spoil something: *He had messed up his career.*

botch up INFORMAL *They really botched up the repair job.*

bungle *Two prisoners bungled an escape bid.*

make a hash of INFORMAL *The so-called expert made a total hash of things.*

muck up SLANG *They have a way of mucking everything up.*

See also **confusion, fix, hole, muddle**

INFORMALLY SPEAKING

mess about (or around): be busy without seeming to accomplish anything
mess up: spoil; do wrong
mess with: defy; provoke

---

mess up See botch, ruin, spoil

message

▷ NOUN

1 a piece of information for someone: *He left a voice-mail message.*

bulletin *a news bulletin*

communication *The ambassador brought a communication from the prime minister.*

M

despatch *this despatch from our Ottawa correspondent*
memo *office memos*
memorandum *a memorandum from the head office*
note *I'll have to leave a note for my dad.*
word *There is no word from the hospital on his condition.*
2 the idea conveyed by something: *the story's anti-violence message*
meaning *We discussed the meaning of the play.*
moral *the moral of the story*
point *My point is that I'm not going to change.*
theme *The book's central theme is power.*
See also **meaning, note, word**

messenger
▷ NOUN
someone who carries a message: *A messenger will deliver the documents.*
courier *a bicycle courier*
envoy *an envoy to the king*

messy *See* **untidy**

method
▷ NOUN
a way of doing something: *her favourite method of making popcorn*
approach *different approaches to preparing for exams*
mode *a mode of transportation*
procedure *He did not follow the correct procedure.*
technique *the techniques of modern agriculture*
way *a way of making new friends*
See also **fashion, plan, practice, procedure, process, style, system, way**

methodical *See* **deliberate**

meticulous *See* **careful, particular, strict, thorough**

meticulously *See* **well**

metre *See* **beat**

metropolis *See* **city**

microscopic *See* **minute, tiny**

microwave *See* **cook**

middle
▷ NOUN
I the part farthest from the edges: *in the middle of the room*
centre *the centre of the table*
halfway point *in the lead at the halfway point of the race*

midst *a house in the midst of huge trees*
▷ ADJECTIVE
2 farthest from the edges: *the middle house*
central *the central part of town*
halfway *a point halfway between the two cities*
See also **centre**

middling *See* **medium, moderate, modest**

midst *See* **middle**

might *See* **force, power, strength**

mighty *See* **powerful**

migrate *See* **move**

mild
▷ ADJECTIVE
I not strong or powerful: *a mild shampoo*
insipid *It tasted bland and insipid.*
weak *weak tea*
ANTONYM **strong**
2 gentle and good-tempered: *a mild approach*
gentle *her gentle nature*
meek *a meek, mild-mannered person*
placid *a placid baby who rarely cried*
3 warmer than usual: *The area is famous for its mild winter climate.*
balmy *balmy summer evenings*
temperate *a temperate climate*
See also **calm, gentle, meek, quiet**

miles *See* **far**

militant *See* **fanatic**

mill *See* **factory**

mimic *See* **copy, imitate**

mind
▷ NOUN
I intelligence or the power that provides the ability to think: *You have a very suspicious mind.*
brain *She exercises her brain by doing crossword puzzles.*
head *I can't get that song out of my head.*
imagination *The magical world was alive in my imagination.*
intellect *good health and a lively intellect*
psyche *various elements of the human psyche*
▷ VERB
2 to be annoyed or concerned by something: *I don't mind what you do.*
be bothered *He's not bothered by mosquitoes.*
care *I don't care if it rains tomorrow.*
object *I don't object to his attitude.*
▷ VERB
3 to look after something: *My mother is*

keep an eye on *He asked me to keep an eye on the children.*

look after *I looked after the plants while they were away.*

take care of *There was no one else to take care of the children.*

watch *She bought the tickets while I watched her suitcase.*

See also **care, head, look after, take care of, watch, will**

INFORMALLY SPEAKING

have a mind to: intend to
keep in mind: remember
make up your mind: decide
never mind: pay no attention to
on your mind: much in your thoughts
take someone's mind off: distract someone from something unpleasant

---

mindful of *See* **aware of**

mine *See* **extract, fund**

mingle *See* **associate, blend, mix**

miniature *See* **tiny**

minimal *See* **low, minimum**

minimize *See* **lessen, lower**

minimum

▷ *ADJECTIVE*
being the least possible: *the minimum requirements for the job*
least possible *I try to cause the least amount of trouble possible.*
minimal *The aim is to incur minimal expense.*
ANTONYM **maximum**
See also **least**

minor

▷ *ADJECTIVE*
less important: *a minor injury*
lesser *They pleaded guilty to the lesser charges.*
petty *petty crime*
secondary *matters of secondary importance*
slight *We have a slight problem.*
trifling *Compared with what's happening in the world, our problems seem trifling.*
trivial *trivial details*
ANTONYM **major**
See also **child, inferior, insignificant, slight, trivial, unimportant**

minus *See* **disadvantage**

minute

▷ *NOUN*
1 a short period of time: *I'll be with you in*

---

just a minute.
flash *It was all over in a flash.*
instant *For an instant, I was tempted to leave the stage.*
moment *Stop for one moment and think about what you're doing!*
second *I'll be there in a second.*
▷ *ADJECTIVE*
2 extremely small: *Only a minute amount is needed.*
microscopic *microscopic fibres*
negligible *The differences between the two prices are negligible.*
slender *We won the vote by a slender margin.*
small *small particles of dust*
tiny *It may be a tiny cavity, but it's extremely painful.*
ANTONYM **vast**
See also **instant, moment, record, tiny**

miracle

▷ *NOUN*
a surprising and fortunate event: *It was a miracle that nobody was seriously hurt in the crash.*
marvel *a marvel of high technology*
wonder *the wonders of science*
See also **wonder**

mirage *See* **illusion, vision**

miscalculate *See* **err**

miscarriage *See* **failure**

miscellaneous *See* **various**

mischievous *See* **naughty, wicked**

misconception *See* **illusion**

misdemeanour *See* **crime**

miserable

▷ *ADJECTIVE*
1 very unhappy: *a job that made me miserable*
dejected *Everyone has days when they feel dejected.*
depressed *He seemed somewhat depressed.*
down *Try to support each other when one of you is feeling down.*
downcast *After the loss, the team's captain looked downcast.*
low *"I didn't ask for this job," he tells friends when he is low.*
melancholy *It was in these hours that she felt most melancholy.*
mournful *He looked mournful, even near to tears.*
sad *It left me feeling sad and empty.*

M

unhappy *She is desperately unhappy.*
wretched *I feel really confused and wretched.*
ANTONYM **cheerful**
2 causing unhappiness: *It's a miserable job, but someone has to do it.*
gloomy *The outlook for the team is gloomy.*
pathetic *a pathetic sight*
sorry *Competition has left our business in a sorry state.*
wretched *They didn't have to live in such wretched conditions.*
See also **down, gloomy, sorry, unhappy**

miserly *See* **mean**

misery
▷ *NOUN*
great unhappiness: *All that money brought nothing but misery.*
depression *He's been suffering from depression.*
despair *feelings of despair*
grief *her grief at her husband's death*
melancholy *with an air of melancholy*
sadness *with a mixture of sadness and joy*
sorrow *a time of great sorrow*
unhappiness *There was a lot of unhappiness in their lives.*
woe *a tale of woe*
ANTONYM **joy**
See also **evil, grief, hell, pain, sorrow**

misfortune
▷ *NOUN*
an unfortunate event: *I had the misfortune of seeing that movie.*
adversity *times of adversity*
bad luck *He has had his share of bad luck.*
See also **blow, disaster, hardship, sorrow**

misgiving *See* **anxiety, doubt, suspicion, worry**

misinterpret as *See* **mistake**

mislaid *See* **lost**

mislay *See* **lose**

mislead *See* **con, deceive, fool, take in**

misleading *See* **deceptive, untrue**

misplace *See* **lose**

misplaced *See* **lost**

misrepresent
▷ *VERB*
to give a false account of something: *The salesperson deliberately misrepresented the condition of the used printer.*

distort *The actor said his remarks had been distorted by the press.*
falsify *falsifying personal details on his website*
twist *You're twisting my words.*

miss
▷ *VERB*
1 to fail to notice: *It's on the second floor. You can't miss it.*
fail to notice *He failed to notice that the light had turned red.*
mistake *There's no mistaking her sincerity.*
overlook *a fact that we all tend to overlook*
2 to feel the loss of: *We missed our friends when we moved.*
long for *He longed for the good old days.*
pine for *Make sure your pet won't pine for you while you're away.*
yearn for *He yearned for his freedom.*
See also **lack, overlook**

miss out *See* **omit**

missile *See* **bomb**

missing *See* **absent, lost**

mission *See* **task**

mist *See* **cloud**

mistake
▷ *NOUN*
1 something that is wrong: *spelling mistakes*
blunder *It was a monumental blunder to give him that job.*
error *a mathematical error*
gaffe *a social gaffe*
oversight *By an unfortunate oversight, full instructions do not come with the product.*
slip-up *We don't want any slip-ups.*
▷ *VERB*
2 to think one thing is another thing: *I mistook her for the owner of the house.*
confuse with *I can't see how anyone could confuse you with your brother!*
misinterpret as *She misinterpreted his remarks as sarcasm.*
mix up with *People often mix me up with my sister.*
take for *She had taken her for a journalist.*
See also **confuse, error, miss, mix-up**

mistaken *See* **false, untrue, wrong**

mistreat
▷ *VERB*
to treat someone or something badly: *The dog had been mistreated by its former owner.*
abuse *He was arrested for abusing his pets.*
ill-treat *I thought he had been ill-treating his family.*

mistrust *See* **suspect, suspicion**

misty *See* **wet**

misunderstanding *See* **mix-up**

misuse *See* **waste**

mix
▷ VERB
to combine things: *Mix the ingredients together slowly.*
amalgamate *a need to amalgamate the two companies*
blend *Blend the butter with the sugar.*
combine *Combine the oil with 125 mL of lemon juice.*
merge *how to merge the graphics with text*
mingle *the mingled smell of coffee and bacon*
See also **associate, blend, combination, combine**

mixture
▷ NOUN
a combination of things: *a sticky mixture of flour and water*
alloy *an alloy of copper and tin*
amalgamation *an amalgamation of the two cities*
blend *a blend of lemonade and cranberry juice*
combination *a fantastic combination of colours*
compound *Salt is a compound of sodium and chlorine.*
fusion *fusions of jazz and pop music*
medley *We communicated in a medley of gestures and foreign words.*
See also **blend, combination, cross, union, variety**

mix up
▷ VERB
to confuse two things: *People often mix us up.*
confuse *Don't confuse the hot peppers with the sweet ones!*
muddle *Sports writers have begun to muddle the names of the two players.*
See also **confuse, muddle**

mix up with *See* **mistake**

mix-up
▷ NOUN
a mistake in something planned: *a mix-up in the hotel reservations*
mistake *There must be some mistake; my total doesn't agree with yours.*
misunderstanding *Ensure that there is no misunderstanding about the instructions.*
muddle *There's been a muddle about whose responsibility it is.*

moan
▷ VERB
1 to make a low sound: *He moaned in his sleep.*
groan *She began to groan with pain.*
grunt *The salesperson grunted when the customer changed his mind again.*
2 to complain about something: *He's always moaning about how much homework he has.*
complain *She's always complaining about the weather.*
groan *His parents were beginning to groan about the cost of tuition.*
grumble *A tourist grumbled about the condition of the roads.*
whine *They come to me to whine about their troubles.*
▷ NOUN
3 a low sound: *He let out a moan when he heard the sad news.*
groan *a groan of disappointment*
grunt *grunts of disapproval*
See also **complain, grumble, lament**

mob *See* **crowd, jam, mass**

mob violence *See* **riot**

mock
▷ VERB
1 to make fun of someone: *Don't mock me when I'm only trying to help.*
deride FORMAL *The country was derided for its hypocrisy.*
laugh at *They were laughing at me because my shirt was on backward.*
make fun of *Don't make fun of me.*
poke fun at *Don't poke fun at people's shortcomings.*
ridicule *He shouldn't have ridiculed my suggestions.*
scoff at *Some people may scoff at the idea that animals communicate.*
▷ ADJECTIVE
2 not genuine: *mock laughter*
artificial *artificial sweeteners*
bogus *their bogus insurance claim*
counterfeit *counterfeit money*
dummy *dummy weapons*
fake *a fake fur*
false *false teeth*
feigned *feigned surprise*
imitation *imitation leather*
phony INFORMAL *a phony excuse*
pretended *with pretended interest*
sham *a sham illness*
See also **make fun of, tease**

M

mockery

▷ NOUN

the act of mocking someone: *Was there a hint of mockery in his eyes?*

derision *shouts of derision*

jeering *There was a chorus of jeering, whistles, and laughter.*

ridicule *The mayor was subjected to public ridicule.*

See also **scorn**

mode See **fashion, manner, method, style**

model

▷ NOUN

1 a copy of something: *an architect's model of the new art gallery*

dummy *a crash-test dummy*

replica *a replica of the CN Tower*

representation *a representation of a human figure*

2 a perfect example of something: *The essay is a model of clarity.*

epitome *the epitome of good taste*

example *She is an example to the younger skaters.*

ideal *One person's ideal of beauty is different from another's.*

paragon *a paragon of virtue*

▷ VERB

3 to make something into a shape: *clay modelled into the shape of a bear*

carve *One of the prisoners had carved a wooden chess set.*

fashion *necklaces fashioned from seashells*

form *We formed a table out of twigs.*

mould *figures moulded from modelling clay*

sculpt *She sculpted a full-size replica of the bear.*

shape *Shape each half of the meat mixture into a loaf.*

See also **design, example, ideal, make, shape**

moderate

▷ ADJECTIVE

1 neither too much nor too little: *moderate exercise*

average *I was only average academically.*

fair *My cousin has a fair command of the language.*

medium *a medium size*

middling *After his number-one hit, he enjoyed only middling success.*

reasonable *reasonable prices*

▷ VERB

2 to become or make less extreme: *They are hoping he will moderate his views.*

abate *The storm had abated.*

curb *You must curb your extravagant tastes and start to save your money.*

ease *Tensions had eased.*

relax *Rules have been relaxed recently.*

soften *to soften the blow of steep price rises*

temper *He had to learn to temper his enthusiasm.*

tone down *She toned down her statements after the meeting.*

See also **change, modest, reasonable**

moderately See **quite**

modern

▷ ADJECTIVE

1 relating to the present time: *modern society*

contemporary *contemporary music*

current *the current situation*

present *the team's present difficulties*

present-day *Even by present-day standards, these were large aircraft.*

recent *in recent years*

2 new and involving the latest ideas: *modern technology*

latest *the latest fashions*

new *new methods of treating acne*

up-to-date *the most up-to-date computers*

up-to-the-minute *up-to-the-minute information*

ANTONYM **old-fashioned**

modernize See **renovate**

modest

▷ ADJECTIVE

1 small in size or amount: *a modest improvement*

limited *They may have only a limited amount of time.*

middling *After having only middling success for years, she recorded a number-one hit.*

moderate *moderate exercise*

small *a relatively small problem*

2 not boastful: *Although an award-winning writer, she is modest about her achievements.*

humble *He gave a great performance, but he was very humble.*

unassuming *She has a gentle, unassuming manner.*

ANTONYM **conceited**

See also **humble, low, reasonable**

modification See **change, qualification**

modify See **adapt, change, vary**

moist See **damp, wet**

moisten See **wet**

moisture See **damp**

mollify See **humour, pacify**

moment
▷ NOUN
1 a short period of time: *He paused for a moment.*
instant *The pain disappeared in an instant.*
minute *See you in a minute.*
second *Seconds later, firefighters reached the door.*
split second *Their eyes met for a split second.*
2 a point in time: *At that moment, the doorbell rang.*
instant *At that instant, the museum was plunged into darkness.*
point *At this point, my cousin arrived.*
time *It seemed like a good time to tell her.*
See also **instant, minute**

momentary *See* **brief, short, temporary**

momentous *See* **critical, crucial, important, serious**

momentum *See* **speed**

monarch *See* **king, ruler**

money
▷ NOUN
coins, bills, or cheques: *I needed to earn some money.*
capital *Companies are having difficulty in raising capital.*
cash *We were desperately short of cash.*
dough INFORMAL *He worked hard for his dough.*
funds *The concert will raise funds for AIDS research.*
See also **financial, wealth**

INFORMALLY SPEAKING

for my money: in my opinion
on the money: correct, or exact

mongrel *See* **dog**

monitor *See* **observe**

monotonous *See* **boring, dreary, dull, flat**

monotony *See* **boredom**

monster *See* **savage**

monumental *See* **grand**

mood
▷ NOUN
a state of mind: *She was in a really cheerful mood.*
frame of mind *He was not in the right frame of mind to continue.*

humour *Could that have been the source of her good humour?*
spirits *A bit of exercise will help lift your spirits.*
state of mind *I want you to get into a whole new state of mind.*
temper *I was in a bad temper last night.*
See also **humour**

moody
▷ ADJECTIVE
1 depressed or unhappy: *Despite his charm, he could sulk and be moody.*
irritable *He had missed his dinner, and grew irritable.*
morose *He was morose for a long time following their breakup.*
sulky *a sulky adolescent*
sullen *a sullen and resentful workforce*
2 liable to change your mood: *What a moody person — cheerful one moment and miserable the next.*
temperamental *He is very temperamental.*
volatile *He has a volatile temper.*
See also **sulky**

moor *See* **secure**

moot *See* **raise**

moral *See* **message**

morality *See* **right, virtue**

morals *See* **principle, standards**

more
▷ ADJECTIVE
greater than something else, or additional: *I have more fries than you.*
added *For added flavour, include onions in the mixture.*
additional *The hotel hires additional staff during the summer months.*
extra *There are some extra features on the DVD.*
further *There are likely to be further delays.*
ANTONYM **less**
See also **extra**

more than *See* **over**

moreover *See* **also, too**

moron *See* **fool, idiot**

morose *See* **moody**

mortal *See* **deadly, fatal**

mortgage *See* **loan**

most *See* **majority, maximum**

most important *See* **foremost**

M

most recent *See* **last**

mostly *See* **mainly**

mother *See* **parent**

motif *See* **pattern**

motion *See* **movement, question, signal**

motionless *See* **still**

motivate

▷ VERB

to cause a particular behaviour: *What motivates athletes to excel?*

drive *Jealousy drives people to do all sorts of things.*

inspire *What inspired you to become a director?*

lead *His Arctic travels led him to write the book.*

move *What moved you in the direction of this kind of music?*

prompt *What prompted you to write fiction?*

provoke *The vandalism has provoked much anger.*

See also **drive, prompt**

motivation *See* **cause, drive, incentive**

motive *See* **cause, reason**

motto *See* **slogan**

mould *See* **fashion, model, rot, shape**

mouldy *See* **rotten**

mound *See* **heap, pile**

mount *See* **climb, rise, stage**

mourn *See* **grieve, lament, regret**

mournful *See* **miserable, sad**

mourning *See* **sorrow**

mouthful *See* **taste**

move

▷ VERB

1 to change position: *The train began to move.*

See WORD STUDY **move** *on next page*

2 to change residence: *She had often considered moving to the Maritimes.*

migrate *The birds have migrated south.*

relocate *The company has relocated from Ontario to Alberta.*

3 to cause a deep emotion: *The story moved us to tears.*

affect *Her death still clearly affects us.*

touch *Their enthusiasm touched me.*

See also **draw, motivate, touch**

move to *See* **settle**

move up *See* **rise**

moved *See* **sorry**

movement

▷ NOUN

1 a change of position: *They monitor the movement of the fish swimming upstream.*

flow *the frantic flow of cars and buses along the street*

motion *the wind from the car's motion*

2 a group of people with similar aims: *the peace movement*

campaign *the campaign against public smoking*

faction *the leaders of the warring factions*

group *members of an environmental group*

organization *Canada's national Inuit organization*

See also **campaign, cause, wave**

moving

▷ ADJECTIVE

causing deep emotion: *It was a moving moment.*

affecting *one of the most affecting scenes in the movie*

emotional *an emotional reunion*

poignant *a poignant love story*

stirring *a stirring speech*

touching *the touching tale of how one family overcame many hardships*

See also **sad, touching**

much *See* **far**

muck *See* **dirt**

muck up *See* **mess**

mucky *See* **dirty**

mud *See* **dirt**

muddle

▷ NOUN

1 a state of disorder: *Our finances are in a muddle.*

chaos *Their games often ended in chaos.*

confusion *There was confusion when the lights went out in the building.*

disarray *He found the room in disarray.*

disorder *Inside, all was disorder.*

disorganization *a state of complete disorganization*

Move is not a very expressive word. If you can use a more descriptive substitute to say something about the way in which a person or thing moves, it will give your writing variety and interest.

• When a person **crawls**, they move forward on their hands and knees.
He tried to **crawl** away, but had no strength left.

• When an insect **crawls** somewhere, it moves there quite slowly.
I watched the moth **crawl** up the outside of the lampshade.

• If a person or animal **creeps** somewhere, they move quietly and slowly.
I tried to **creep** upstairs without being heard.

• To **inch** somewhere means to move there very carefully and slowly.
He began to **inch** across the face of the cliff.

• If you **edge** somewhere, you move very slowly in that direction.
He **edged** closer to the door.

• If a person or animal **slithers** somewhere, they move by sliding along the ground in an uneven way.
She lost her footing and **slithered** down the bank.
The snake **slithered** into the water.

• If you **wriggle** somewhere, for example through a small space, you move there by twisting and turning your body.
I **wriggled** through a gap in the fence.

• When people or small animals **scamper** or **scuttle** somewhere, they move there quickly with small, light steps.
The children got off the bus and **scampered** into the playground.
The crabs **scuttled** along the muddy bank.

• When people or small animals **scurry** somewhere, they move there quickly and hurriedly, often because they are frightened.
The thunder rolled, sending the spectators **scurrying** for cover.

• If you **hurry**, **race**, or **rush** somewhere, you go there as quickly as you can.
She **hurried** along the path.
He **raced** across town to the hospital.
The girl **rushed** into her room and slammed the door.

• If you **hasten** somewhere, you hurry there.
This is a formal word
He **hastened** along the corridor toward the back door.

• If you **dash**, **dart**, or **shoot** somewhere, you run or go there quickly and suddenly.
He jumped up and **dashed** out of the room.
The girl turned and **darted** away through the trees.
They had almost reached the boat when a figure **shot** past them.

• If you say that someone or something **flies** in a particular direction, you are emphasizing that they move there with a lot of speed and force.
I **flew** downstairs to answer the doorbell.

• If you **tear** somewhere, you move there very quickly, often in an uncontrolled or dangerous way.
Without looking to left or right, he **tore** off up the street.

• When you **run**, you move quickly because you are in a hurry to get somewhere.
I excused myself and **ran** back to the house.

• If you **jog**, you run slowly.
She **jogged** off in the direction he had indicated.

• If you **sprint**, you run as fast as you can over a short distance.
The firefighter **sprinted** to the burning car.

• If you **gallop**, you run somewhere very quickly.
They were **galloping** round the garden, yelling and waving their arms.

• If a person or animal **bolts**, they suddenly start to run very fast, often because something has frightened them.
I made some excuse and **bolted** toward the exit.

• If a group of animals or people **stampede**, they run in a wild, uncontrolled way.
The crowd **stampeded** out of the hall.

M

jumble *a meaningless jumble of words*
mess *the reasons why the economy is in such a mess*
tangle *a tangle of wires*
▷ VERB
2 to mix things up: *Their names are so similar, they often get muddled.*
confuse *Take care to avoid confusing the two bottles.*
jumble *The paper clips and staples were all jumbled together.*
mix up *People often mix us up.*
See also **cloud, disorder, mess, mix up, mix-up, tangle**

muddle up *See* **confuse**

muddled *See* **confused**

muddy *See* **cloudy, dirty**

muffle *See* **silence**

mug *See* **face**

mugger *See* **thief**

muggy *See* **humid, stuffy**

mull over *See* **deliberate, ponder, think**

multiply
▷ VERB
to increase in number: *The problems with my old computer just seem to multiply.*
increase *The population continues to increase.*
proliferate *Doughnut shops are proliferating fast.*
spread *Cholera is not spreading as quickly as it did in the past.*
See also **breed, grow, increase**

multitude *See* **bunch, crowd, jam, number**

mumble
▷ VERB
to speak quietly: *He mumbled a few words.*
murmur *He murmured something to the teacher.*
mutter *He sat there muttering to himself.*

munch *See* **chew**

mundane *See* **everyday**

murder
▷ NOUN
1 the act of killing someone: *after being found guilty of murder*
assassination *the assassination of John F. Kennedy*
homicide *the scene of the homicide*

killing *a brutal killing*
manslaughter *She was found guilty of manslaughter.*
slaughter *the slaughter of innocent civilians*
slaying LITERARY *a trail of motiveless slayings*
▷ VERB
2 to kill someone: *a book about two men who murder a third*
assassinate *Robert Kennedy was assassinated in 1968.*
kill *He was nearly killed during the break-in.*
slaughter *Families were slaughtered by the invaders.*
slay LITERARY *the field where the dragon was slain*
take the life of *He confessed to taking the lives of others.*
See also **kill**

murderous *See* **fierce, violent**

murky *See* **cloudy, dark, dim, dull**

murmur *See* **grumble, mumble**

muscle *See* **strength**

muse *See* **consider, think**

muse on *See* **contemplate**

mushy *See* **sentimental**

musical *See* **sweet**

muster *See* **recruit**

mutate *See* **turn**

mute *See* **dumb, silent**

muted *See* **dull, faint, soft**

muteness *See* **silence**

mutiny *See* **rebel, rebellion**

mutt *See* **dog**

mutter *See* **grumble, mumble**

myriad *See* **countless, many**

mysterious
▷ ADJECTIVE
1 strange and not well understood: *He died in mysterious circumstances.*
arcane FORMAL *the arcane world of high finance*
baffling *a baffling array of wires*
cryptic *cryptic jottings in the diary*
enigmatic *one of the most enigmatic films of the decade*
mystifying *I find your attitude rather mystifying.*
2 secretive about something: *Stop being so mysterious.*
furtive *with a quick, furtive glance over her shoulder*

mystery

▷ *NOUN*

something that is not understood: *the mystery surrounding her fortune*

conundrum *this philosophical conundrum*
enigma *Whatever motivated him to do such a thing will remain an enigma.*
puzzle *"You are a puzzle," he said to his son.*
riddle *the answer to the riddle of why it was never finished*

mystify *See* **confuse, puzzle**

mystifying *See* **mysterious**

mythological *See* **imaginary**

M

Nn

nag *See* **hassle, horse**

nagging *See* **continual**

naive *See* **gullible, ignorant, innocent**

naivety *See* **innocence**

naked

▷ ADJECTIVE

1 not wearing any clothes: *a naked body*
bare *her bare feet*
nude *nude bathing*
unclothed *an unclothed mannequin in a store window*
ANTONYM **clothed**
2 openly displayed or shown: *naked aggression*
blatant *evidence of blatant discrimination*
evident *We loved his evident enthusiasm.*
manifest *her manifest dislike of me*
open *open opposition to the government*
unmistakable *with unmistakable amusement in his eyes*
ANTONYM **secret**
See also **bare**

name

▷ NOUN

1 a word that identifies a person or thing:
My name is Joe.
designation *The code is a designation reserved for serious incidents.*
epithet *"Grit" is an epithet for a member of Canada's Liberal Party.*
nickname *He's heard your nickname is Cuddles.*
term *I don't know the medical term for it.*
title *Your title will be business manager.*
2 the opinion people have about someone:
to protect his good name
character *a series of personal attacks on my character*
reputation *I know he has a bad reputation.*
▷ VERB

3 to give a name to someone or something:
a little girl named Anna
call *in a town called Come-by-Chance*
dub *They dubbed him "the Memory Wizard."*
term *He was termed a temporary employee.*
See also **celebrity, identify, nominate, reputation, specify, term**

INFORMALLY SPEAKING

call names: insult by swearing at
name after: give someone the same name as
name of the game: the main objective

---

naming *See* **appointment**

nap *See* **pile, sleep**

narcotic *See* **drug**

narrative *See* **plot, story**

narrow

▷ ADJECTIVE

having a small distance from side to side: *a narrow stream*
fine *the fine hairs on my arms*
slender *long, slender legs*
slim *a slim volume of Irving Layton's poems*
thin *a thin layer of clay*
ANTONYM **wide**
See also **shrink, thin**

narrow-minded

▷ ADJECTIVE

unwilling to consider new ideas or other people's opinions: *their own narrow-minded view of the world*
biased *a biased view*
bigoted *bigoted opinions*
insular *insular travellers who don't even try the local foods*
opinionated *the most opinionated rubbish I have read*
prejudiced *prejudiced ideas about minorities*
ANTONYM **tolerant**

nasty

▷ ADJECTIVE

very unpleasant: *a nasty taste*
disagreeable *a disagreeable experience*
disgusting *the most disgusting behaviour*
foul *the foul smell of rotten eggs*
horrible *I've got a horrible feeling about this one.*
repellent *the most repellent human being I have ever met*
unpleasant *some unpleasant surprises*
vile *All the food is vile.*
ANTONYM **pleasant**
See also **disagreeable, horrible, spiteful, unkind, unpleasant**

nation *See* **land, public, race, state**

national *See* **home**

native *See* **home, inhabitant, local**

natter *See* **chat**

natural

▷ ADJECTIVE

1 normal and to be expected: *the natural reaction to such sad news*
common *It is a common response.*

everyday *the everyday drudgery of work*
normal *Biting is normal for puppies when they are teething.*
ordinary *The cottage looks quite ordinary from the road.*
typical *typical symptoms of stress*
usual *It was not usual for the meeting to be so brief.*
ANTONYM **unnatural**

2 not trying to pretend: *He was so natural with the children.*
candid *rather candid about her marriage*
frank *an unusually frank interview*
genuine *He always seems so genuine.*
real *She came across as a real person.*
unaffected *She sang with unaffected simplicity.*
ANTONYM **false**

3 existing from birth and not learned: *He's a natural comedian.*
inborn *an inborn sense of optimism*
inherent *the inherent goodness of people*
innate *the child's innate kindness*
instinctive *an instinctive distrust of authority*
intuitive *an intuitive understanding of econonics*
See also **automatic, informal, wild**

nature
▷ NOUN
someone's character: *It's not in my nature to sit still.*
character *the funny side of her character*
makeup *Compromise was never part of his makeup.*
personality *a dominating personality*
See also **character, essence, personality**

naughty
▷ ADJECTIVE
1 tending to behave badly: *a naughty child*
bad *the bad manners of some tourists*
disobedient *a disobedient puppy*
impish *an impish sense of humour*
mischievous *a mischievous child*
wayward *He tried to control his wayward nephew.*
ANTONYM **well-behaved**

2 rude or indecent: *naughty song lyrics*
bawdy *a series of bawdy jokes*
lewd *arrested for lewd behaviour*
obscene *making obscene gestures to the crowd*
vulgar *He used a vulgar expression.*
See also **wicked**

nausea *See* disgust

nauseous *See* queasy, sick

navigate *See* manoeuvre

near
▷ ADJECTIVE
1 not far away in distance: *The Rockies are near.*
adjacent *an adjacent room*
adjoining *A phone rang in an adjoining office.*
close *a close neighbour*
nearby *the nearby village*
ANTONYM **far**

2 not far away in time: *The time of birth is near.*
approaching *an approaching deadline*
forthcoming *the forthcoming football season*
imminent *The day of our departure was imminent.*
looming *Exams are looming and the students are panicking.*
upcoming *the upcoming elections*
▷ PREPOSITION
3 not far from: *He drew his chair near the fire.*
adjacent to *a garden adjacent to the castle*
alongside *the huts set up alongside the river*
close to *We parked close to the pavement.*
next to *I realized someone was standing next to me.*
not far from *a parking lot not far from the entrance*
See also **beside, immediate, imminent**

nearby *See* handy, near

nearest *See* next

nearly
▷ ADVERB
not completely, but almost: *The beach was nearly empty.*
almost *Over the past decade their wages have almost doubled.*
as good as *The hockey season is as good as over.*
just about *We are just about finished with this section.*
practically *The house was practically a wreck.*
virtually *Their country is virtually bankrupt.*
See also **about, almost**

neat
▷ ADJECTIVE
having everything arranged in a tidy way: *The house was clean and neat.*
orderly *an orderly room*
smart *a smart navy blue suit*
tidy *He always kept his bedroom tidy.*

N

trim *a street of trim little bungalows*
ANTONYM **untidy**
See also **handy, orderly, smart, tidy**

necessary

▷ ADJECTIVE
1 needed so that something can happen:
Make the necessary arrangements.
essential *It is essential that you visit a
dentist.*
imperative *It is imperative that we end up
with a win.*
indispensable *an indispensable part of the
peace process*
required *That book is required reading.*
vital *Bone marrow is vital for producing
blood cells.*
ANTONYM **unnecessary**
2 certain to happen or exist: *a necessary
consequence of overindulgence*
certain *one certain outcome of the
conference*
inevitable *It appears that defeat is
inevitable.*
inexorable *The growth in travel has been
inexorable.*
unavoidable *Job losses are unavoidable.*
See also **basic, vital**

necessities *See* essentials

necessity *See* requirement

neck and neck *See* even

need

▷ VERB
to believe you must have or do something:
You need some fresh air.
demand *The children demand our
attention.*
require *If you require further information,
please check our website.*
want *I want a drink.*
See also **demand, distress, require,
requirement, want**

needle *See* irritate, tease

needless *See* excessive, unnecessary

neglect

▷ VERB
1 to fail to look after someone or something:
unhappy and neglected children
ignore *They see the government ignoring
poor people.*
overlook *Pensioners feel they are being
overlooked.*
turn your back on *Do not turn your back
on the unemployed.*
2 to fail to do something: *He had neglected
to give her his address.*
fail *I failed to tell her the most important
part of the story.*
forget *She forgot to lock her door.*
omit *He omitted to mention his position on
the team.*
▷ NOUN
3 lack of care: *Most of her plants died from
neglect.*
disregard *a callous disregard for the
homeless*
indifference *Indifference to patients is rare
at our hospital.*
unconcern *the corporation's unconcern for
the environment*
See also **fail, ignore, overlook**

neglected *See* derelict

neglectful *See* careless

negligible *See* minute, slight, tiny,
trivial

negotiate *See* manoeuvre

neighbourhood *See* area, local,
surroundings

neighbouring *See* next

nerve

▷ NOUN
speech or behaviour that is rude or
disrespectful: *I'm amazed they had the nerve
to ask in the first place.*
audacity *He had the audacity to ask me for
a loan.*
gall *She had the gall to invite herself to the
party.*
impudence *My sister had the impudence to
go out with my ex-boyfriend.*
insolence *I could not believe his insolence in
front of the principal.*
rudeness *They were upset by her rudeness.*
See also **courage, daring, impudence**

nerve-racking *See* tense

nervous

▷ ADJECTIVE
worried about something: *She had been
nervous before the finals.*
anxious *I was very anxious about their safety.*
apprehensive *Their families are
apprehensive about the trip.*
edgy *I was edgy and tired.*
jittery *She still feels jittery when she visits
her sister.*
jumpy *More people are getting jumpy about
security.*
tense *too tense to sleep*
uptight *My parents aren't as uptight as they
seem.*

worried *You had me worried for a moment.*
ANTONYM **calm**
See also **afraid, anxious, dubious, tense, timid, uneasy, worried**

nervousness *See* **alarm, anxiety**

net *See* **trap**

neutral
▷ ADJECTIVE
not supporting either side: *We stayed neutral during their dispute.*
disinterested *a disinterested observer*
dispassionate *a full and dispassionate account*
impartial *How can he give impartial advice?*
nonaligned *nonaligned members of the UN*
ANTONYM **biased**
See also **impersonal**

never
▷ ADVERB
at no time at all: *I never said I was leaving.*
at no time *At no time did he see the helicopter.*
not ever *The problem won't ever go away.*

new
▷ ADJECTIVE
I recently created or discovered: *a new fast-food restaurant*
ANTONYM **old**
See WORD STUDY **new**
See also **extra, inexperienced, modern, original, recent, strange, unfamiliar**

news
▷ NOUN
information about things that have happened: *news about the trial*
bulletin *a late bulletin about the fire*
disclosure *disclosures about his private life*
dispatch *the latest dispatches from the war zone*
information *up-to-date information on the blizzard*
intelligence *military intelligence from behind enemy lines*
latest INFORMAL *the latest on the hostage situation*
tidings FORMAL *the bearer of bad tidings*
word *There is no word about casualties.*
See also **information, word**

next
▷ ADJECTIVE
I coming immediately after something else: *Their next car will be a convertible.*
ensuing *the ensuing floods*
following *The following day I went to work as usual.*
subsequent *As subsequent events showed, he was wrong.*
succeeding *succeeding generations of students*
▷ ADVERB
2 coming immediately after something else: *My brother arrived next.*
afterwards *I felt dizzy afterwards and had to sit down.*

N

WORD STUDY: NEW

Depending on the sense of **new** that you mean, there are a number of alternatives which you can use to vary your writing and make it more interesting.

• recently discovered or created
These are the trial results of the company's **newest** drug.
He reads all the **current** gossip on the stars.
We followed the **fresh** footprints in the snow.
She then made a **groundbreaking** discovery.
We review all the **latest** movies.
Modern technology has improved much of our daily life.
Is that his most **recent** novel?
That's an **ultramodern** shopping mall.
The computer's loaded with the most **up-to-date** software.
We bring you **up-to-the-minute** information.

• not used or owned before
I can't afford a **brand-new** car.
He turned to a **fresh** page in his notebook.
There are two stores that sell **unused** wedding dresses.

• unfamiliar
We need a completely **different** idea to attract the tourist market.
That's a **novel** way to exercise!
He's never had an **original** idea.
I was alone in a **strange** country.
She loved the **unaccustomed** experience of having money to spend.
I like visiting **unfamiliar** places.
This terrain is completely **unknown** to me.

subsequently *He was subsequently signed to the Flames.*

3 in a position nearest to something: *in the next room*

adjacent *I pulled into the adjacent driveway.*

adjoining *in adjoining streets*

closest *Canada's closest neighbours*

nearest *the nearest Italian restaurant*

neighbouring *The refugees fled to neighbouring countries.*

next to *See* **beside, near**

next world *See* **heaven**

nib *See* **point**

nibble *See* **bite**

nice

▷ ADJECTIVE

attractive or enjoyable: *We had a nice vacation.*
See WORD STUDY **nice**
See also **agreeable, pleasant**

niceties *See* **ceremony**

nick *See* **arrest, steal**

nickname *See* **name**

nigh *See* **near**

nightmare *See* **hell, ordeal**

nil *See* **zero**

nimble *See* **agile**

nip *See* **bite**

no

▷ INTERJECTION

not at all: *"Any problems?" "No, everything's fine."*

absolutely not *"Did they consult you?" "Absolutely not."*

certainly not *"Perhaps it would be better if I withdrew." "Certainly not!"*

definitely not *"Are you going to the party?" "Definitely not."*

not at all *"You're not upset, are you?" "Not at all."*

of course not *"Do you mind if I use your computer?" "Of course not!"*

ANTONYM **yes**

noble

▷ ADJECTIVE

1 deserving admiration because of honesty, bravery, and unselfishness: *a good and noble thing to do*

generous *It reflects her generous nature.*

honourable *His colleagues were honourable people.*

magnanimous *a magnanimous gift*

upright *a very upright, trustworthy man*

virtuous *a virtuous life*

worthy *less worthy members of our profession*

ANTONYM **ignoble**

▷ NOUN

2 someone from the highest social rank: *He claims to come from a family of British nobles.*

aristocrat *She married a European aristocrat.*

nobleman *a Spanish nobleman*

nobleman *See* **noble**

nod *See* **signal**

noise

▷ NOUN

a loud or unpleasant sound: *He is making an awful noise.*

commotion *There was a commotion in the corridor.*

din *The spectators made quite a din.*

hubbub *What's all the hubbub about?*

pandemonium *There was pandemonium in the classroom.*

racket *There was a terrible racket going on.*

uproar *The courtroom was in an uproar.*

ANTONYM **silence**
See also **racket, sound**

noisy

▷ ADJECTIVE

making a lot of noise: *a noisy audience of schoolchildren*

deafening *a deafening roar*

loud *The music was a little too loud.*

piercing *a piercing laugh*

strident *His strident voice is annoying.*

tumultuous *She took the field to tumultuous applause.*

vociferous *vociferous support from the fans*

ANTONYM **quiet**
See also **loud, rowdy**

nominate

▷ VERB

to suggest someone for a position: *The party refused to nominate him as its candidate.*

name *She'll be naming a new captain.*

propose *Her name was proposed for the coaching position.*

recommend *He recommended me as his successor at the firm.*

select *no prospect of being selected for the team*

submit *We submitted a list of 200 names.*

suggest *Some commentators have suggested the former mayor for the job.*

nomination *See* **appointment**

nonaligned *See* **neutral**

WORD STUDY: NICE

When you are writing or talking and you are going to use the word **nice**, try to think of a more descriptive and interesting word instead. Here are some ideas for words and phrases that you might use to describe different aspects of people and things.

• of someone's appearance
She's grown into an **attractive** young woman.
You're looking very **beautiful** today.
She's going out with a really **cute** guy.
Her son is **good-looking**, but very shy.
I think he's really **gorgeous**.
That's a very **handsome** young man.
He married a **lovely** woman.
You look very **pretty** in that outfit.

• of an object, place, or view
We found a **beautiful** little restaurant.
They live in a **charming** fishing village.
What a **delightful** place for a holiday!
She showed us some **lovely** pictures.
There's a **pretty** room overlooking the pool.

• of clothing
I admired his **chic** designer jacket.
That's a very **elegant** pair of shoes you're wearing.
What a **fetching** outfit!
I was wearing **smart** black pants.
She always has such **stylish** clothes.

• of an event or occasion
It's not a very **agreeable** way to spend your day off.
We had a **delightful** time.
The trip was much more **enjoyable** than I had expected.

Thanks for giving me such a **fantastic** party.
Have a **lovely** holiday!
It was not a **pleasant** experience.
There's nothing like the **pleasurable** sensation of getting into a warm bath.

• of someone's personality
I've always found him a very **amiable** man.
He's very **considerate** toward his sisters.
They aren't very **friendly** to strangers.
She is unfailingly **good-natured**.
I try to be **kind** to everyone.
Grandfather was a **kindly** man.
She was an immensely **likeable** person.
That was a very **thoughtful** gesture.

• of food and drink
An **appetizing** smell was coming from the kitchen.
We bought some **delectable** raspberries.
The food here is **delicious**.
These are **luscious** peaches.
I stared longingly at the **mouthwatering** dessert.
This café serves **tasty** meals.

• of the weather
It was a **beautiful** morning.
I'll cut the grass if the weather is **fine**.
It's a **glorious** day!

N

---

nonchalant *See* **careless, casual, uninterested**

nonsense
▷ *NOUN*
foolish words or behaviour: *I say the accusation is complete nonsense.*
drivel *mindless drivel aimed at the masses*
garbage INFORMAL *One source claimed the rumours were complete garbage.*
inanity *the inanities of the tabloids*
rubbish *complete and utter rubbish*
See also **garbage, rubbish**

nonsensical *See* **absurd, foolish, irrational**

non-specific *See* **broad**

non-stop *See* **constant, express, relentless, steady**

norm *See* **standard**

normal
▷ *ADJECTIVE*
usual and ordinary: *my normal routine*
average *What's your average day like?*
conventional *conventional tastes*
habitual *their country of habitual residence*
ordinary *It was just an ordinary weekend.*
regular *It looks like a regular onion, but it's very sweet.*
routine *a routine medical check*
standard *standard practice*
typical *A typical day begins at 8:30.*
usual *Pick me up at the usual time.*
ANTONYM **unusual**
See also **average, natural, ordinary, regular, routine, sane, standard, typical, usual**

normally *See* **as a rule, on average**

nostalgic *See* **sentimental**

nosy

▷ *ADJECTIVE*

trying to find out about other people's business: *nosy neighbours watching us through the curtains*

curious *surrounded by a group of curious visitors*

eavesdropping *We don't want to be overheard by eavesdropping diners.*

inquisitive *Bears are naturally inquisitive creatures.*

prying *I hid it away, safe from prying eyes.* *See also* **curious**

not at all *See* **no**

not be able to abide *See* **dislike**

not be able to bear *See* **dislike**

not be able to stand *See* **dislike**

not dangerous *See* **harmless**

not ever *See* **never**

not far from *See* **near**

not guilty *See* **innocent**

not level *See* **uneven**

not liable *See* **exempt**

not many *See* **few**

not quite *See* **almost**

not smooth *See* **uneven**

not well *See* **unhealthy**

notable *See* **important, memorable, particular, prominent, significant**

note

▷ *NOUN*

1 a short letter: *I wrote him a note asking him to visit.*

communication FORMAL *a communication from the Governor General*

e-mail *He didn't reply to my e-mail.*

letter *I have received a letter from a friend.*

memo *a leaked memo to managers*

memorandum *A memorandum has been sent to the members of the committee.*

message *He sent his son over with a message for me.*

reminder *We keep getting reminders from the garage to pay our repair bill.*

2 a written record that helps you remember something: *I made a note of his address.*

account *Keep an account of all your expenses.*

jotting *Carry a notebook with you for your jottings.*

record *Keep a record of all payments.*

3 an atmosphere, feeling, or quality: *I detected a note of bitterness in his voice.*

hint *Was there a hint of irony in that remark?*

tone *She laughed again, this time with a cold, sharp tone.*

touch *There is an unmistakable touch of pathos in his last film.*

trace *I could detect a trace of sarcasm in her tone.*

▷ *VERB*

4 to become aware of or mention a fact: *I noted that the rain had stopped.*

mention *I mentioned that I liked her essay.*

notice *Contact the police if you notice anything suspicious.*

observe *She observed a change in his attitude.*

perceive *He perceived a certain tension between them.*

register *The sound was so familiar that she didn't register it.*

remark *Everyone remarks about his bright, blue eyes.*

see *A lot of people saw what was happening.* *See also* **comment, entry, message, notice, observe, record**

noted *See* **famous, prominent**

nothing *See* **zero**

notice

▷ *VERB*

1 to become aware of something: *Then I noticed he wasn't laughing.*

detect *I detect a change in your mood.*

discern *I did not discern any change in attitudes.*

note *I noted that the rain had stopped.*

observe *I've observed how hard you work.*

perceive *gradually perceiving the possibilities*

see *I saw that the lobby was swarming with reporters.*

spot *I spotted him on the other side of the dance floor.*

▷ *NOUN*

2 a written announcement: *a handwritten notice posted on the wall*

advertisement *one advertisement in a local paper*

bill *students posting bills near the campus*

poster *a poster advertising a charity concert*

sign *a large cardboard sign*

▷ NOUN

3 warning that something is going to happen: *She was transferred without notice.*
advance warning *advance warning of the attack*
intimation *He has given no intimation of an intention to resign.*
notification *Official notification is expected to arrive today.*
warning *I was fired without warning.*
See also **advertisement, discern, heed, information, item, note, observe, review, see, sign, warning**

noticeable

▷ ADJECTIVE

obvious and easy to see: *a noticeable improvement*
conspicuous *a conspicuous lack of sympathy*
evident *He ate with evident enjoyment.*
obvious *There are obvious dangers.*
perceptible *The team is showing a perceptible improvement.*
unmistakable *a growing but unmistakable impatience*
See also **conspicuous, evident, prominent, visible**

notification See **notice**

notify

▷ VERB

to inform someone of something officially: *The skipper notified the coastguard of the difficulty.*
advise FORMAL *I think it best that I advise you of my decision first.*
inform *They informed us of their progress.*
tell *She told me I was due for a promotion.*
warn *They warned him of the dangers.*
See also **advise, alert, inform, report, tell, warn**

notion See **idea, impression, thought**

notorious

▷ ADJECTIVE

well-known for something bad: *The district was notorious for violent crime.*
disreputable *a low and disreputable character*
infamous *an industry infamous for late payment of debts*
scandalous *his scandalous behaviour*

notwithstanding See **despite, in spite of**

nourishing See **healthy**

nourishment See **food**

novel See **original, strange, unfamiliar**

novelty See **curiosity**

novice See **beginner, recruit**

now

▷ ADVERB

at the present time or moment: *I need to talk to him now.*
at once *I really must go at once.*
currently *The vaccines are currently being tested.*
immediately *Please phone me immediately.*
nowadays *I don't see much of my cousin nowadays.*
right now *Stop that noise right now!*
straightaway *I think you should see a doctor straightaway.*
without delay *We'll visit our sick friend without delay.*
See also **immediately**

now and again See **sometimes**

now and then See **sometimes**

nowadays See **now**

noxious See **poisonous, unhealthy**

nude See **bare, naked**

nudge See **poke**

nuisance

▷ NOUN

someone or something that is annoying: *Sorry to be a nuisance.*
annoyance *Snoring can be an annoyance.*
bother *Most men hate the bother of shaving.*
hassle *Cleaning my room is a hassle.*
inconvenience *the inconvenience of a transit strike*
irritation *He describes the tourists as "an irritation."*
pain INFORMAL *I found dressing up for the occasion a real pain.*
pest *The neighbour is becoming a pest.*
See also **annoyance, pest**

numb

▷ ADJECTIVE

1 unable to feel anything: *Your right arm goes numb.*
frozen *A frozen shoulder can be very painful.*
insensitive *The brain itself is insensitive to pain.*
paralyzed *a paralyzed arm*
▷ VERB

2 to make you unable to feel anything: *The cold numbed my fingers.*
dull *morphine to dull the pain*

N

freeze *The dentist said she would freeze my mouth.*

paralyze *people paralyzed by illness or injury*

stun *a dart used to stun an animal*

See also **frozen, shock**

numbed *See* **dazed**

number

▷ *NOUN*

1 a word or symbol used for counting: *Pick a number between one and ten.*

digit *a six-digit password*

figure *a figure between a hundred and a thousand*

numeral *Roman numerals*

2 a quantity of things or people: *She has introduced me to a large number of people.*

collection *a huge collection of books about Canadian history*

crowd *a huge crowd of supporters*

horde *hordes of mosquitoes*

multitude *Bands often play to a multitude of fans.*

See also **figure, quantity**

INFORMALLY SPEAKING

do a number on someone: treat someone unfairly or harshly

have someone's number: know someone's character

someone's number is up: someone is doomed

---

numeral *See* **figure, number**

numerous

▷ *ADJECTIVE*

existing or happening in large numbers: *on numerous occasions*

lots *I've got lots of photos of the kids.*

many *I have seen many plays.*

several *He is fluent in several languages.*

See also **many**

nurse *See* **look after, take care of, tend, treat**

nurture *See* **breed, raise**

nutritious *See* **healthy**

Oo

oaf

▷ NOUN

a clumsy or aggressive person: *You stupid oaf!*

brute *Stop behaving like such a brute.*
lout *a bad-mannered lout*
See also **idiot**

oath

▷ NOUN

a formal promise: *an oath of loyalty to the government*

pledge *The meeting ended with a pledge to work harder.*
promise *If you make a promise, you should keep it.*
vow *I made a silent vow to be more careful.*
See also **word**

obedient

▷ ADJECTIVE

tending to do what you are told: *He was always very obedient to his parents.*

law-abiding *law-abiding citizens*
submissive *a very submissive dog*
subservient *He was finally acting in a more independent and less subservient manner.*
ANTONYM **disobedient**

obese See **overweight**

obey

▷ VERB

to do what you are told: *Most people obey the law.*

abide by *They have got to abide by the rules.*
adhere to *All members adhere to a strict code of practice.*
comply with *The army will comply with the ceasefire.*
follow *Be sure to follow the instructions carefully.*
observe *to observe the speed limit*
ANTONYM **disobey**
See also **follow**

object

▷ NOUN

1 anything solid and non-living: *everyday objects such as wooden spoons*
article *household articles*
thing *What's that thing in the middle of the fountain?*
2 an aim or purpose: *The object of the exercise is to raise money for the charity.*
aim *The aim of the program is to provide a better picture of the ozone layer.*
goal *The goal is to raise as much money as possible by the end of the year.*
idea *The idea is to give children the freedom to explore.*
intention *It is my intention to remain in my position.*
objective *His objective was to win.*
purpose *What is the purpose of your visit?*
▷ VERB
3 to express disapproval: *A lot of people will object to the book.*
oppose *She opposed our suggested changes to the format of the yearbook.*
protest *residents protesting against the closing of the playground*
ANTONYM **approve**
See also **article, disagree, goal, intention, mind, point, protest, purpose, subject, thing, use**

object to See **query, resent**

objection

▷ NOUN

disapproval of something: *despite objections by the committee*
opposition *Opposition to this plan has come from an unexpected source.*
protest *protests against the government*
ANTONYM **support**
See also **complaint, disagreement, grumble, protest**

objectionable See **disagreeable, offensive, unpleasant**

objective See **aim, goal, intention, object**

obligation See **bond, duty, responsibility**

obligatory See **compulsory**

oblige See **force, make, require**

obliged See **supposed**

obliging See **accommodating**

oblique See **indirect**

obliterate See **blot out, destroy**

obliteration See **destruction**

oblivious See **ignorant, preoccupied, unaware, unconscious**

obnoxious See **disagreeable, disgusting, hateful, unpleasant**

obscene

▷ ADJECTIVE

indecent and likely to upset people: *obscene pictures*
bawdy *a bawdy song*

blue *a blue movie*
dirty *a dirty book*
filthy *a filthy joke*
indecent *an indecent suggestion*
lewd *lewd comments*
pornographic *a pornographic magazine*
See also **crude, naughty**

obscure

▷ *ADJECTIVE*

1 known by only a few people: *an obscure Canadian law*
little-known *a little-known Canadian composer*
unknown *an unknown writer*
ANTONYM **famous**

2 difficult to understand: *The news was shrouded in obscure language.*
arcane *the arcane world of contemporary classical music*
cryptic *cryptic comments*
opaque *the opaque language of the official reports*
ANTONYM **simple**

▷ *VERB*

3 to make something difficult to see: *His view was obscured by trees.*
cloak *a land permanently cloaked in mist*
cloud *Perhaps anger had clouded his judgment.*
conceal *The hat concealed her hair.*
hide *The cottage was hidden by trees and shrubs.*
mask *A thick grey cloud masked the sun.*
screen *Most of the road was screened by a row of trees.*
shroud *Mist shrouded the outline of Parliament Hill.*
ANTONYM **expose**
See also **blot out, cover, dim, unknown**

observable *See* **visible**

observance *See* **ceremony**

observant

▷ *ADJECTIVE*

good at noticing things: *Painting makes you really observant of things.*
attentive *the attentive audience*
perceptive *a perceptive remark*
vigilant *He warned the public to be vigilant at all times.*
watchful *Keep a watchful eye on the campfire, please.*
See also **alert, sharp**

observation *See* **comment, remark, watch**

observe

▷ *VERB*

1 to watch something carefully: *He has spent years observing the habits of frogs.*
monitor *I have been monitoring their progress carefully.*
scrutinize *She scrutinized his features to see if he was telling the truth.*
study *She studied her friend's face for a moment.*
survey *She surveys trends in television programming.*
view *the best time to view the eclipse*
watch *A man was watching him from across the square.*

2 to notice something: *I observed a number of strange phenomena.*
discover *They discovered that they were being watched.*
note *People noted how much care she took with her work.*
notice *Contact the police if you notice anything unusual.*
see *I saw a man coming toward me.*
spot *Moments later, smoke was spotted coming out of the kitchen.*
witness *Anyone who witnessed the accident should call the police.*

3 to make a comment about something: *"You've had your hair cut," he observed.*
comment *She commented that this was true.*
mention *I mentioned that I didn't like contemporary music.*
remark *"Some people have more money than sense," he remarked.*
say *She said that I looked tired.*
state *He stated that this was, indeed, the case.*
See also **comment, discern, follow, note, notice, obey, practise, remark, see, spot, watch, witness**

observer *See* **spectator, witness**

obsessed *See* **crazy**

obsession

▷ *NOUN*

a compulsion to think about something: *Chess is an obsession of mine.*
complex *I have never had a complex about my height.*
fixation *the country's fixation on the war*
preoccupation *a preoccupation with neatness*
thing INFORMAL *He's got this thing about eating outside.*
See also **complex**

obsessive *See* **fanatical**

obsolete *See* **old-fashioned, out of date**

obstacle

▷ NOUN

something that makes it difficult to go forward: *a large obstacle to improving the team's standing*

barrier *Taxes are the most obvious barrier to free trade.*

difficulty *the difficulties ahead*

hindrance *The higher rates have been a hindrance to economic recovery.*

hurdle *The swimming team overcame many hurdles before winning the semifinals.*

impediment *a serious impediment to economic growth*

obstruction *an obstruction in the road*

See also **barrier, difficulty, handicap**

obstinate

▷ ADJECTIVE

unwilling to change your mind: *He is obstinate and will not give up.*

dogged *her dogged insistence on her rights*

headstrong *He's young and headstrong.*

inflexible *His opponents viewed him as dogmatic and inflexible.*

intractable *I protested, but she was intractable.*

stubborn *a stubborn character who is used to getting her own way*

wilful *a wilful child*

ANTONYM **flexible**

See also **stubborn**

obstruct

▷ VERB

to block a road or path: *Trucks obstructed the road.*

bar *He stood there, barring our way.*

block *Some protesters blocked the highway.*

choke *The roads are choked with cars.*

clog *Traffic clogged the bridge.*

See also **bar, block, close, delay, hamper, impede, interfere**

obstruction *See* **barrier, blockage, delay, obstacle**

obtain

▷ VERB

to get something: *to obtain a false passport*

acquire *I recently acquired a new laptop.*

get *trying to get enough food to live*

get hold of *It's hard to get hold of him on the phone.*

get your hands on INFORMAL *reading everything she could get her hands on*

procure FORMAL *It became hard to procure fuel.*

secure FORMAL *continuing their efforts to secure a photograph of their great aunt*

See also **acquire, buy, earn, extract, gain, get, secure**

obtrusive *See* **pushy**

obtuse *See* **dim, slow, stupid**

obvious

▷ ADJECTIVE

easy to see or understand: *an obvious injustice*

apparent *It was apparent that he had lost interest.*

blatant *a blatant lie*

clear *a clear breach of the rules*

evident *His love of nature is evident in his paintings.*

overt *a display of overt affection*

palpable *The tension between them is palpable.*

plain *It was plain to him that I was not enjoying myself.*

self-evident *The implications for this country are self-evident.*

See also **clear, conspicuous, evident, logical, manifest, noticeable, plain, prominent, visible**

occasion

▷ NOUN

1 an important event: *The launch of a ship was a big occasion.*

affair *The visit was to be a purely private affair.*

event *A new book in the series is always an event.*

2 an opportunity to do something: *an important occasion for celebrating our friendship*

chance *the chance to practise medicine in Canadian hospitals*

opportunity *I had an opportunity to go to New York.*

time *This was no time to make a speech.*

▷ VERB

3 FORMAL to cause something: *damage occasioned by fire*

bring about *the only way to bring about peace*

give rise to *The judge's decision gave rise to practical problems.*

induce *an economic crisis induced by high oil prices*

produce *The drug is known to produce side-effects in some people.*

prompt *The demonstration prompted fears of more violence.*

provoke *The incident has provoked outrage in the capital.*

See also **case, chance, create, incident**

occasional

▷ ADJECTIVE

happening sometimes: *an occasional fumble of the ball*
intermittent *after three hours of intermittent rain*
odd *at odd moments*
periodic *periodic bouts of illness*
sporadic *a year of sporadic fighting*
ANTONYM **frequent**
See also **irregular**

occasionally See **sometimes**

occupant See **inhabitant**

occupation See **job, profession, trade, work**

occupied See **active, busy**

occupy See **busy, inhabit, invade, possess**

occur

▷ VERB

1 to happen or exist: *The changes occurred over a long period.*
appear *a test to reveal infection before symptoms appear*
arise *A problem may arise later.*
be present *This vitamin is present in milk.*
exist *A conflict of interest may exist in such situations.*
happen *The accident happened close to the provincial park.*
take place *Elections will take place on October 2.*
2 to come into your mind: *It didn't occur to me to check.*
cross your mind *The possibility of failure did cross my mind.*
dawn on *It dawned on me that I shouldn't give up without a fight.*
strike *A thought struck her.*
See also **come, happen, take place**

occurrence See **case, incident**

odd

▷ ADJECTIVE

strange or unusual: *an odd coincidence*
bizarre *his bizarre behaviour*
curious *a curious mixture of the ancient and modern*
funny *There's something funny about him.*
peculiar *Don't you think the sandwich tastes peculiar?*
singular FORMAL *Such maturity is singular in so young a person.*
strange *Then a strange thing happened.*
weird *That first day was weird.*

ANTONYM **frequent**
See also **bizarre, curious, extraordinary, funny, occasional, peculiar, strange, weird**

oddity See **curiosity**

odds See **chance, possibility, probability**

odds and ends See **junk**

odour See **smell**

of course not See **no**

off See **sour**

offence See **breach, crime, insult, sin**

offend

▷ VERB

to upset or embarrass someone: *He says he had no intention of offending the community.*
affront *He pretended to be affronted, but inwardly he was pleased.*
insult *The defendant says he was insulted by the judge's remarks.*
outrage *Many people have been outraged by what was said.*
ANTONYM **please**
See also **insult, repel, shock**

offended See **hurt, resentful**

offender See **criminal**

offensive

▷ ADJECTIVE

rude and upsetting: *offensive behaviour*
abusive *abusive language*
insulting *an insulting remark*
objectionable *I find your tone highly objectionable.*
See also **abusive, attack, hateful**

offer

▷ VERB

1 to ask if someone wants something: *I offered him an apple.*
hold out *I held out my ticket for him to check.*
tender *She has tendered her resignation.*
▷ NOUN
2 something that someone offers you: *She had refused several excellent job offers.*
proposition *I made them a proposition.*
tender *a tender for a government contract*
See also **tender**

offering See **present**

offhand See **careless, casual**

office See **department, room**

officer See **official**

official

▷ ADJECTIVE

1 approved by someone in authority: *the*

official figures
authorized *the authorized biography*
certified *a certified accountant*
formal *No formal announcement has been made.*
licensed *a licensed mechanic*
ANTONYM **unofficial**
▷ NOUN
2 someone in authority: *a senior UN official*
executive *a senior bank executive*
officer *an Officer of the Order of Canada*
representative *trade union representatives*
See also **formal**

CONFUSABLES
official means **authorized**
officious means **self-important**

officialdom *See* **bureaucracy**

offset *See* **compensate, counteract**

offspring *See* **child, young**

often
▷ ADVERB
happening many times: *They often spent their summers at the lake.*
frequently *He was frequently late.*
repeatedly *They have repeatedly ignored the warnings.*

ogle *See* **stare**

OK
▷ ADJECTIVE
acceptable or satisfactory: *Is it OK if I show up early?*
acceptable *It is becoming more acceptable to dress casually at work.*
all right *if it's all right with you*
See **all right, correct, right, safe, tolerable, yes**

old
▷ ADJECTIVE
1 having lived for a long time: *an old turtle*
ANTONYM **young**
2 in the past: *my old art teacher*
ANTONYM **new**
See WORD STUDY **old** *on next page*
See also **former, stale**

olden *See* **past**

old-fashioned
▷ ADJECTIVE
no longer fashionable: *old-fashioned shoes*
antiquated *an antiquated system*
archaic *archaic practices such as these*
dated *Some of the language sounds quite dated.*
obsolete *So much equipment becomes obsolete almost as soon as it's made.*

outdated *outdated attitudes*
outmoded *outmoded working conditions*
out of date *My computer is already out of date.*
passé *That music is already passé.*
ANTONYM **fashionable**
See also **out of date, stuffy**

omen
▷ NOUN
a sign of what will happen: *Her showing up at this moment is an omen of disaster.*
sign *people who look to the skies for signs*
warning *a warning of trouble to come*
See also **premonition**

ominous
▷ ADJECTIVE
suggesting that something bad will happen: *an ominous silence*
sinister *a sinister message*
threatening *a threatening sky*
See also **sinister**

omit
▷ VERB
to not include something: *Omit the salt in this recipe.*
exclude *She was excluded from the meeting for several reasons.*
leave out *Several good players had to be left out of the team.*
skip *It is all too easy to skip meals.*
See also **exclude, fail, forget, neglect**

on *See* **about**

on account of *See* **by virtue of**

on edge *See* **restless**

on guard *See* **alert**

on hand *See* **handy**

on the dot *See* **exactly, prompt**

on the whole *See* **as a rule**

on time *See* **punctual**

once in a while *See* **sometimes**

once more *See* **again**

one *See* **only, single**

onerous *See* **formidable**

one-sided *See* **biased**

one-sidedness *See* **favouritism**

one-time *See* **previous**

ongoing *See* **current**

onlooker *See* **spectator, witness**

Depending on the sense of **old** that you mean, there are a number of alternatives which you can use to vary your writing and make it more interesting.

• **having lived for a long time**
He was very attentive to his **ancient** great-grandparents.
My grandmother is a beautiful, **elderly** woman.

• **out of date**
Antiquated ideas have no place in today's world.
Fortunately, **archaic** practices such as these are on the way out.
These buildings are very much **behind the times** in terms of design.
Some of the language sounds quite **dated** now.
Computers are **obsolete** almost as soon as they're hooked up.
The **old-fashioned** style of writing seems to suit the book's theme.
She condemned the **outdated** attitudes of the members of the club.
Working with **outmoded** equipment is quite a challenge.

That car model is now **out of date**.
Who says that kind of music is **passé**?

• **in the past**
We gazed in awe at these relics of **ancient** cultures.
I am fascinated by the rituals of **bygone** civilizations.
He had two children from an **earlier** marriage.
Who are your favourites from the **early** days of rock music?
His **ex**-wife recently remarried.
I saw my **former** boyfriend yesterday.
Life was much harder in **olden** times.
He talked and talked about **past** grievances.
The **previous** tenants obviously liked the colour purple.
They discovered his **prior** criminal convictions.
Retired ball players love harking back to their **remote** days of glory.

only

▷ *ADVERB*
1 involving one person or thing: *Only the singer herself knows whether she will make a comeback.*
just *It's not just a financial matter.*
merely *She was far from being merely an entertainer.*
purely *a racing machine, designed purely for speed*
simply *Most of the damage was simply because of fallen trees.*
solely *decisions based solely upon what we see in magazines*
▷ *ADJECTIVE*
2 having no other examples: *their only hit single*
one *My one aim is to look after the horses well.*
sole *Our sole intention is to reunite the band.*
See also **single**

only just *See* **hardly**

onset *See* **start**

onslaught *See* **attack**

onus *See* **responsibility**

ooze *See* **leak**

opaque *See* **cloudy, obscure**

open

▷ *VERB*
1 to cause something not to be closed: *She opened the door.*
uncover *She uncovered the container and discovered some cold spaghetti.*
undo *I carefully undid the knot.*
unlock *She unlocked the door.*
ANTONYM **shut**
▷ *ADJECTIVE*
2 not closed: *an open box of chocolates*
ajar *He left the door ajar.*
uncovered *The uncovered bucket in the corner stank.*
undone *Your shirt's undone.*
unlocked *an unlocked room*
ANTONYM **shut**
▷ *ADJECTIVE*
3 not trying to deceive someone: *He had always been open with her.*
candid *I haven't been completely candid with him.*
frank *My client has been less than frank with me.*
honest *May I be perfectly honest with you?*
See also **bare, candid, flexible, frank, impressionable, spread, start, straightforward, uncover**

INFORMALLY SPEAKING

be open with: speak candidly
into the open: not concealed
open up: fully reveal

opening

▷ *ADJECTIVE*
1 coming first: *the opening day of the fishing season*
first *the first night of the play*
inaugural *his inaugural address*
initial *the aim of this initial meeting*
introductory *an introductory offer*
ANTONYM **closing**
▷ *NOUN*
2 the first part of something: *The opening was the best part of the movie.*
beginning *the beginning of the book*
commencement FORMAL *at the commencement of the course*
start *four years after the start of the space program*
ANTONYM **conclusion**
▷ *NOUN*
3 a hole or gap: *a narrow opening in the fence*
chink *a chink in the wall*
cleft *a narrow cleft in the rocks*
crack *I saw him through a crack in the curtains.*
gap *the wind tearing through gaps between skyscrapers*
hole *a hole in the wall*
slot *a slot in which to insert a coin*
space *a tiny space between the curtains*
vent *Steam escaped from the vent at the front of the machine.*
See also **beginning, breach, chance, first, gap, hole, start**

open-minded See **tolerant**

operate See **act, behave, drive, function, use**

operation See **action, campaign, enterprise, undertaking, use**

opinion

▷ *NOUN*
a belief or view: *I wasn't asking for your opinion.*
assessment *What is your assessment of the situation?*
belief *their religious beliefs*
estimation *He has gone down considerably in my estimation.*
judgment *In your judgment, how has the situation changed?*
point of view *Thanks for your point of view on the subject.*
view *Make your views known to your Member of Parliament.*
viewpoint *to include as many viewpoints as possible*
See also **advice, belief, feeling, idea, judgment, thought, verdict, view, viewpoint**

opinionated See **narrow-minded**

opponent See **competitor, enemy, rival**

opportune See **favourable, lucky**

opportunity See **chance, occasion, turn**

oppose

▷ *VERB*
to disagree with something: *students opposing the new rules*
fight against *a lifetime fighting against racism*
resist *They resisted our attempts to change the menu.*
speak out against *He spoke out strongly against some of the proposed changes.*
ANTONYM **support**
See also **contest, disagree, object, protest, resist**

opposed See **different, opposite**

opposite

▷ *ADJECTIVE*
1 completely different to something: *I take a completely opposite view.*
conflicting *three powers with conflicting interests*
contrary *She has a contrary opinion about everything.*
contrasting *two men with completely contrasting viewpoints*
opposed *Her ideas are often directly opposed to mine.*
reverse *The wrong attitude will have exactly the reverse effect.*
▷ *NOUN*
2 a completely different person or thing: *He was the complete opposite of his cousin.*
antithesis *His choice in music is the antithesis of mine.*
contrary *Quite the contrary; I'm in favour of your ideas.*
converse *Don't you think that the converse might also be possible?*
reverse *This didn't upset him at all; in fact, quite the reverse.*
See also **reverse**

O

opposition

▷ *NOUN*

disagreement about something: *Much of the opposition to this plan has come from the media.*

disapproval *The decision had been greeted with almost universal disapproval.*

hostility *There is hostility to this plan among many of the old-timers.*

resistance *Initially, I met resistance from my own family.*

ANTONYM **support**

See also **competition, competitor, conflict, disagreement, objection**

oppress See **bully, persecute**

oppressed

▷ *ADJECTIVE*

treated cruelly or unfairly: *a member of an oppressed minority*

abused *those who work with abused children*

downtrodden *They work to help the downtrodden of society.*

oppression

▷ *NOUN*

cruel or unfair treatment: *the oppression of slaves*

persecution *the persecution of minorities*

tyranny *The 1930s was a decade of tyranny in Europe.*

See also **abuse**

oppressive See **stuffy, unbearable**

oppressor See **bully**

opt See **vote**

opt for See **choose, pick, select**

optimistic

▷ *ADJECTIVE*

hopeful about the future: *He is in an optimistic mood.*

buoyant *She was in a buoyant mood.*

confident *I am confident that everything will turn out right in time.*

hopeful *I am hopeful this misunderstanding will be rectified.*

positive *a positive frame of mind*

sanguine *They have begun to take a more sanguine view.*

ANTONYM **pessimistic**

option See **choice**

opulence See **luxury**

opulent See **luxurious, rich, wealthy**

oral

▷ *ADJECTIVE*

spoken rather than written: *oral history*

spoken *the spoken word*

verbal *a verbal agreement*

See also **exam**

SHADES OF ... ORANGE

amber	peach
apricot	tangerine
carrot	

orchestra See **band**

orchestrate See **stage**

ordain See **impose, order**

ordeal

▷ *NOUN*

a difficult and unpleasant experience: *the ordeal of being arrested*

hardship *One of the worst hardships is having so little time.*

nightmare *Taking their grandson to a restaurant was a nightmare.*

torture *Waiting for the result was torture.*

trial *the trials of adolescence*

tribulation *the trials and tribulations of everyday life*

See also **experience, hell**

order

▷ *NOUN*

1 a command by someone in authority: *I don't take orders from them any more.*

command *The tanker failed to respond to a command to stop.*

decree *He issued a decree ordering all armed groups to disband.*

dictate *to ensure that the dictates of government are followed*

directive *a new directive from the head of the company*

instruction *We received our instructions on what to bring to the picnic.*

2 a well-organized situation: *the wish to impose order upon confusion*

harmony *the harmony of the universe*

regularity *the regularity of a field of corn*

symmetry *the beauty and symmetry of a snowflake*

ANTONYM **disorder**

▷ *VERB*

3 to tell someone to do something: *The troops were ordered to withdraw.*

command *commanded to attack*

decree *the rule that decreed no fishing without a licence*

direct *a court order directing the strikers to return to work*

instruct *The family has instructed their lawyers to sue the company.*
ordain *These policies were ordained by the legislature.*
ANTONYM **forbid**
See also **arrange, command, instruct, require, routine, rule, sequence, tell**

INFORMALLY SPEAKING

in short order: quickly
order about (or around): constantly command
out of order: not arranged properly or not working properly

---

orderly

▷ *ADJECTIVE*
well-organized or well-arranged: *Their bicycles were parked in orderly rows.*
neat *She put her wet clothes in a neat pile in the corner.*
regular *regular rows of tomato plants*
tidy *a tidy desk*
ANTONYM **disorderly**
See also **neat, tidy**

ordinary

▷ *ADJECTIVE*
not special or different: *an ordinary day*
conventional *a person with conventional opinions*
normal *He lives a normal life.*
regular *my regular day off*
routine *a routine procedure*
standard *It was standard practice.*
usual *all the usual problems*
ANTONYM **special**
See also **common, conventional, everyday, humble, natural, normal, regular, routine**

organization

▷ *NOUN*
1 a group or business: *charitable organizations*
association *research associations*
body *the head of the student body*
company *the Ford Motor Company of Canada*
confederation *Confederation Day is July 1.*
group *an environmental group*
institution *financial institutions*
outfit *We are a professional outfit.*
2 the planning and arranging of something: *We were involved in the organization of the picnic.*
organizing *His duties involved the organizing of transport.*
planning *The trip needs careful planning.*
structuring *improvements in the*

structuring of courses
See also **body, business, firm, movement, society, structure**

organize

▷ *VERB*
to plan and arrange something: *Organizing a wedding takes time.*
arrange *The bank can arrange a loan for students.*
establish *How do you establish a workable timetable?*
plan *A team meeting was planned for last night.*
set up *The committee was set up by a group of teachers and students.*
See also **arrange, book, conduct, group, set up, stage**

organized *See* **efficient, ready**

organizing *See* **organization**

origin

▷ *NOUN*
1 the beginning or cause of something: *the origins of the custom*
derivation *The derivation of the word is interesting.*
root *Rock'n'roll has its roots in other forms of music.*
source *the source of the problem*
2 someone's family background: *She was of Swedish origin.*
ancestry *I can trace my ancestry back to India.*
descent *After World War II, many people of Dutch descent settled in Canada.*
extraction *a Canadian citizen of Ukrainian extraction*
lineage *I'm trying to trace my grandparents' lineage.*
stock *He claims to be of United Empire Loyalist stock.*
See also **beginning, cause, source, stock**

original

▷ *ADJECTIVE*
1 being the first example of something: *the original owner of the cottage*
first *Her first reaction was disgust.*
initial *His initial response was to trust her.*
2 imaginative and clever: *a stunningly original idea*
fresh *These designers are full of fresh ideas.*
new *These proposals aren't new.*
novel *a novel way of making pizza*
ANTONYM **unoriginal**
See also **first, individual**

O

originality *See* **imagination**

originate *See* **begin, create, invent, start**

originator *See* **source**

ornament
▷ *NOUN*
an object that you display: *a shelf containing ornaments*
adornment *a building without any adornments*
bauble *glass beads and other baubles*
decoration *balloons and other party decorations*
knick-knack *Their apartment is crammed with knick-knacks.*
trinket *She sold trinkets to tourists.*
See also **decorate**

ornate *See* **elaborate, fancy**

orthodox *See* **conventional, proper, standard**

ostentatious
▷ *ADJECTIVE*
intended to impress people with appearances: *an ostentatious lifestyle*
extravagant *They make extravagant shows of generosity.*
flamboyant *flamboyant clothes*
flashy *a flashy sports car*
grandiose *the grandiose building that housed the mayor's offices*
pretentious *This restaurant was smaller and less pretentious.*
showy *large, showy flowers*
See also **pompous, pretentious, vain**

others *See* **remainder, rest**

oust *See* **overthrow**

out loud *See* **aloud**

out of danger *See* **safe**

out of shape *See* **crooked**

out of the ordinary *See* **exceptional, uncommon**

out of the question *See* **impossible**

out-and-out *See* **total, utter**

outback *See* **country**

outbreak
▷ *NOUN*
a sudden occurrence of something: *the outbreak of war*
eruption *this sudden eruption of violence*
explosion *the global explosion of interest in*
the Internet
See also **burst, rash**

outcome *See* **result**

outcry *See* **protest**

outdated *See* **old-fashioned, out of date**

outdo
▷ *VERB*
to do something better than another person: *She would love to outdo the previous champion.*
go one better than *You always have to go one better than anyone else.*
outshine *My cousin has begun to outshine me in tennis.*
surpass *determined to surpass the achievements of last year's debating team*
top *How are you going to top that?*
See also **beat, pass, top**

outdoor *See* **outside**

outdoors *See* **country**

outer *See* **outside**

outfit *See* **clothes, organization, provide, set**

outgoing *See* **sociable**

outing *See* **trip**

outlandish *See* **bizarre, eccentric**

outlaw *See* **ban, forbid, prohibit**

outlawed *See* **illegal**

outlay *See* **cost**

outline
▷ *VERB*
1 to describe something in a general way: *The mayor outlined his plan to clean up the town.*
sketch *He sketched his vision of the society under new leadership.*
summarize *The article can be summarized in three sentences.*
▷ *NOUN*
2 a general description of something: *an outline of the archaeologist's findings*
rundown *Here's a rundown of the events.*
summary *a summary of the report*
synopsis *a brief synopsis of the book*
▷ *NOUN*
3 the shape of something: *the hazy outline of the buildings*
contours *the contours of the body*
figure *I saw the dim figure of my grandmother in the chair.*
form *She'd never been so glad to see his bulky form.*

shape *dark shapes silhouetted against the moon*
silhouette *the dark silhouette of the castle*
See also **form, shape, summary**

outlive See **survive**

outlook
▷ NOUN
I your general attitude toward life: *I adopted a positive outlook on life.*
attitude *Poor working conditions produce negative attitudes.*
perspective *It gave him a new perspective on life.*
view *an optimistic view of the future*
2 the future prospects of something: *The economic outlook is one of rising unemployment.*
future *a meeting to discuss the program's future*
prospects *a detailed review of the company's prospects*
See also **attitude, prospect**

outlying See **distant, far, remote**

outmoded See **old-fashioned, out of date**

out of date
▷ ADJECTIVE
no longer useful: *The information is already out of date.*
antiquated *an antiquated plumbing system*
archaic *archaic practices such as these*
obsolete *So much equipment becomes obsolete almost as soon as it's made.*
old-fashioned *old-fashioned shoes*
outdated *outdated attitudes*
outmoded *outmoded working conditions*
ANTONYM **modern**
See also **old-fashioned**

out-of-the-way See **distant**

outpost See **colony**

outrage See **anger, horrify, offend, shock**

outright See **complete, pure, straight, total, utter**

outset See **beginning, start**

outshine See **outdo**

outside
▷ NOUN
I the outer part of something: *The moth was on the outside of the glass.*
exterior *the exterior of the building*
facade *the refurbishing of the city hall's facade*
face *the face of the watch*

surface *the surface of the road*
ANTONYM **inside**
▷ ADJECTIVE
2 not inside: *an outside water tap*
exterior *cleaning the car's exterior surfaces*
external *the external walls*
outdoor *outdoor activities*
outer *the outer suburbs of the city*
outward *with no outward sign of injury*
surface *Its total surface area was 650 m².*
ANTONYM **inside**

INFORMALLY SPEAKING

at the outside: at the most
outside of: with the exception of

outskirts
▷ PLURAL NOUN
the edges of an area: *the outskirts of Toronto*
edge *We were on a hill, right on the edge of town.*
perimeter *the perimeter of the airport*
periphery *suburbs on the periphery of large cities*

outspoken See **blunt**

outstanding
▷ ADJECTIVE
I extremely good: *an outstanding tennis player*
brilliant *a brilliant performance*
excellent *The recording quality is excellent.*
exceptional *children with exceptional ability*
first-class *first-class service*
first-rate *The show was first-rate.*
great *great scholastic achievements*
superb *superb skateboarding facilities*
2 still owed: *The total debt outstanding is $2 billion.*
due *They sent me $50 and advised me that no further payment was due.*
overdue *overdue salaries*
owing *There is still some money owing for the rent.*
payable *The amount payable is $10.*
unpaid *The bills remained unpaid.*
See also **brilliant, excellent, exceptional, fine, first-rate, major, prize, superb**

outstrip See **beat, pass, top**

outward See **outside**

over
▷ PREPOSITION
I more than a particular amount: *It cost over a million dollars.*
above *speeds above 80 km/h*

exceeding *a city budget exceeding $700 million a year*
in excess of *a fortune in excess of $10 million*
more than *The airport had been closed for more than a year.*
▷ ADJECTIVE
2 completely finished: *I am glad it's all over.*
at an end *The matter is now at an end.*
complete *The work on my project is finally complete.*
done *Are the dishes done yet?*
finished *once the season's finished*
gone *Any chance of winning was now gone.*
past *The time for regret is past.*
up *when the six weeks were up*
See also **above, past**

INFORMALLY SPEAKING

over again: once more
over and over: again and again
over with or **over and done with:** finished

---

over- *See* **too**

over the moon *See* **joyful**

overall *See* **general**

overbearing *See* **bossy**

overcast *See* **cloudy, dark, dull**

overcome
▷ VERB
to manage to deal with something: *I had overcome my fear of flying.*
conquer *He is trying to conquer his smoking habit.*
get the better of *Don't allow your emotions to get the better of you.*
master *Thanks to her determination, she has mastered the latest crisis.*
surmount *I realized I had to surmount the language barrier.*
triumph over *a symbol of good triumphing over evil*
vanquish FORMAL *the man who helped vanquish Napoleon*
See also **beat, crush, resolve, subdue, vanquish**

overconfident *See* **cocky**

overdo *See* **exaggerate**

overdose *See* **excess**

overdue *See* **late, outstanding**

overestimate *See* **exaggerate**

overflow *See* **flood**

overflowing *See* **crowded**

overheads *See* **upkeep**

overhear *See* **hear**

overjoyed *See* **glad**

overlay *See* **cover, spread**

overlook
▷ VERB
to ignore or fail to notice something: *We tend to overlook warning signals about our health.*
disregard *Some players will always disregard the rules.*
forget *She never forgets his birthday.*
ignore *For years her talents were ignored by the film industry.*
miss *His searching eye never missed a detail.*
neglect *She never neglects her duties.*
turn a blind eye to *They turned a blind eye to the environmental problems.*
See also **excuse, face, forget, ignore, miss, neglect**

overly *See* **too**

overpower *See* **subdue**

overrule
▷ VERB
to reject a decision officially: *The Court of Appeal overruled this decision.*
overturn *The new boss has overturned some of the office rules.*
reverse *They will not reverse the decision to increase prices.*
See also **overturn, reverse**

overseas *See* **foreign**

oversee
▷ VERB
to make sure a job is done properly: *Get a supervisor to oversee the work.*
be in charge of *She is in charge of day-to-day operations.*
coordinate *Government officials have been sent to coordinate the relief effort.*
direct *She directed the entire rescue mission.*
manage *Within two years, she was managing the project.*
preside *Who will be presiding over the day's meeting?*
supervise *He supervises the new department.*
See also **direct, supervise**

oversight *See* **mistake**

overstate *See* **exaggerate**

overt *See* **obvious**

overtake *See* **pass**

overthrow

▷ *VERB*

to remove someone from power by force:
The government was overthrown in a military coup.

bring down *They brought down the government by withdrawing their support.*

depose *He fled to the capital after being deposed as president.*

oust *Her opponents tried to oust her with a vote of no confidence.*

topple *the revolution that toppled the regime*

overturn

▷ *VERB*

1 to knock something over: *to overturn a can of paint*

capsize *I didn't count on his capsizing the raft.*

knock over *The child knocked over the box of cornflakes.*

tip over *He tipped the table over in front of him.*

topple *Winds and rain toppled trees and electricity lines.*

upset *Don't upset the stack of CDs.*

2 to reject a decision officially: *The referee's decision was overturned.*

overrule *The Court of Appeal overruled this decision.*

reverse *They will not reverse the decision to increase prices.*

See also **abolish, overrule, reverse, upset**

overused *See* **stock**

overweight

▷ *ADJECTIVE*

weighing too much, and therefore unhealthy: *Being overweight increases your risk of heart problems.*

fat *I could eat what I liked without getting fat.*

hefty *quite a hefty build*

obese *Obese people tend to have higher blood pressure than lean people.*

stout *a stout man with grey hair*

overwhelm *See* **beat**

overwork *See* **strain**

overwrought *See* **hysterical**

owing *See* **outstanding**

own

▷ *ADJECTIVE*

1 belonging to a particular person or thing: *I have my own website.*

personal *That's my personal opinion.*

private *Each guest room has a private bathroom.*

▷ *VERB*

2 to have something that belongs to you: *His parents own a hardware store.*

have *They have a new cat.*

possess *I would give them everything I possess.*

on your own

▷ *ADVERB*

without other people: *I work best on my own.*

alone *She lives alone.*

by oneself *I didn't know if I could run a business by myself.*

independently *several people working independently*

unaided *She brought us up completely unaided.*

See also **have, personal**

own up *See* **confess**

owner

▷ *NOUN*

the person to whom something belongs: *the owner of the store*

possessor *the proud possessor of a truly incredible voice*

proprietor *the proprietor of a local restaurant*

ownership *See* **possession**

Pp

pace *See* **rate, speed, walk**

pacify

▷ VERB

to calm down someone who is angry: *They tried to pacify the upset fans.*

appease *The offer has not appeased the protesters.*

calm *Milk calms my nerves.*

mollify *The investigation was undertaken to mollify pressure groups.*

placate *She went aboard to placate the angry passengers.*

soothe *She took the puppy in her arms and soothed him.*

pack *See* **cram, fill, group, load, stuff**

package *See* **tender**

packed *See* **crowded, full**

pact *See* **agreement, understanding**

padlock *See* **lock**

pageant *See* **parade**

pain

▷ NOUN

1 an unpleasant feeling of physical hurt: *I felt a sharp pain in my lower back.*

ache *Poor posture can cause neck aches.*

discomfort *I have some discomfort, but no real pain.*

irritation *The cream may cause irritation to sensitive skin.*

soreness *The soreness in my wrist lasted for about six weeks.*

trouble *back trouble*

twinge *He felt a slight twinge in his hamstring.*

2 a feeling of deep unhappiness: *the pain of rejection*

agony *the agony of war*

anguish *The family was in anguish over the tragedy.*

distress *Jealousy causes distress and painful emotions.*

grief *The grief soon gave way to anger.*

misery *All that money brought nothing but sadness and misery.*

See also **annoyance, distress, grieve, nuisance, pest, sorrow**

pain in the neck *See* **annoyance, pest**

painful

▷ ADJECTIVE

1 causing emotional pain: *painful memories*

distressing *one of the most distressing episodes in his life*

grievous *a grievous blow to the community*

saddening *a saddening experience*

unpleasant *an unpleasant truth*

2 causing physical pain: *a painful cramp in the stomach*

aching *his aching joints*

excruciating *an excruciating headache*

sore *a sore throat*

tender *My leg is very tender and sore.*

See also **sore, tender, uncomfortable**

painless *See* **easy**

pains *See* **care**

painstaking *See* **careful, thorough**

paint *See* **colour, draw**

painting *See* **picture**

pair up *See* **team**

pal *See* **companion, friend**

palatable *See* **tasty**

pale

▷ ADJECTIVE

rather white or without much colour: *Migrating birds filled the pale sky.*

ashen *He fell back, shocked, his face ashen.*

colourless *a colourless liquid*

faded *faded jeans*

sallow *His face was sallow and shiny with perspiration.*

wan *He looked wan and tired.*

See also **light, soft**

palpable *See* **evident, obvious**

paltry *See* **meagre, trivial, unimportant, worthless**

pamper *See* **spoil**

pamphlet *See* **leaflet**

pan *See* **criticize**

pandemonium *See* **noise**

pander to *See* **humour**

panel *See* **council**

pang of conscience *See* **regret**

panic

▷ NOUN

1 a very strong feeling of fear or anxiety: *The earthquake caused panic among the population.*

alarm *She sat up in alarm.*

dismay *To my dismay, I learned that the trip was cancelled.*

fear *my fear of the dark*

fright *To hide my fright, I asked a question.*

hysteria *mass hysteria*
terror *I shook with terror.*
▷ VERB
2 to become afraid or anxious: *I panicked when the elevator came to a sudden stop between floors and didn't move.*
become hysterical *One hostage remained calm but the other became hysterical.*
go to pieces *He went to pieces when he heard about the accident.*
lose your nerve *They lost their nerve and pulled out of the deal.*
See also **alarm, fear, horror, scare**

panorama *See* **scene, scenery, view**

pant *See* **gasp**

pantomime *See* **play**

parade
▷ NOUN
a line of people moving as a display: *the Grey Cup parade*
march *Organizers expect 300 000 protesters to join the march.*
motorcade *a motorcade of limousines and police motorcycles*
pageant *a traditional holiday pageant*
procession *religious processions*

paradise *See* **heaven**

paragon *See* **example, ideal, model**

PARTS OF … A PARAGRAPH	
clause	sentence
phrase	word

parallel *See* **like, relationship, resemblance, resemble**

paralyzed *See* **numb**

paramount *See* **supreme, ultimate**

paraphernalia *See* **equipment**

parched *See* **dry**

pardon *See* **excuse, forgive, forgiveness, spare**

parent *See* **father, mother**

parentage *See* **stock**

parity *See* **balance**

parody
▷ NOUN
an amusing imitation of someone else's style: *a parody of the newscast*
imitation *I can do a pretty good imitation of a barking dog.*
satire *a biting satire on the Canadian political process*
spoof INFORMAL *a spoof on Hollywood life*

takeoff INFORMAL *She did a brilliant takeoff of the TV star.*

part
▷ NOUN
1 a piece or section of something: *I like that part of Hamilton.*
bit *a bit of paper*
fraction *a fraction of a second*
fragment *fragments of glass*
piece *a piece of cheese*
portion *Damage was confined to a small portion of the building.*
section *a large orchestra, with a vast percussion section*
2 a person's involvement in something: *He tried to conceal his part in the accident.*
capacity *He has served the club in many capacities.*
duty *My duty is to look after the animals.*
function *Their main function is to publicize our games.*
involvement *You have no proof of my involvement.*
role *the drug's role in preventing infection*
See also **aspect, attachment, bit, factor, fitting, piece, portion, quantity, section, separate, split**

INFORMALLY SPEAKING
for my part: as far as I am concerned **for the most part:** mostly **in part:** to some extent **part and parcel:** a necessary or essential part **part with:** give up or let go **play a part:** be a contributing factor

P

take part in
▷ VERB
to do an activity with other people: *Thousands took part in the celebrations.*
be instrumental in *He was instrumental in tracking down the criminals.*
be involved in *My grandparents are involved in a volunteer group.*
have a hand in *She had a hand in three of the goals.*
join in *I hope that everyone will be able to join in the fun.*
participate in *They expected him to participate in the ceremony.*
play a part in *He continued to play a part in our education.*

partial *See* **biased, incomplete**

partially *See* **partly**

participate

▷ VERB

to take part in an activity: *More than half the class participated in the event.*
be involved in *Almost everyone was involved in the production.*
engage in *Students and faculty members are engaged in discussion.*
enter into *We entered into discussions with them weeks ago.*
join in *Their rivals refused to join in any price war.*
take part *The oldest car taking part was built in 1950.*
See also **play**

participate in See take part in

particular

▷ ADJECTIVE

1 relating to only one thing or person: *That particular place is dangerous.*
discrete *the discrete components of the machine*
distinct *The book is divided into two distinct parts.*
exact *Do you think I could get the exact thing I want?*
express *I bought the camera for the express purpose of taking railway photographs.*
peculiar *This is not a problem peculiar to our neighbourhood.*
precise *the precise location of the ship*
specific *There are several specific problems to be dealt with.*
2 especially great or intense: *Pay particular attention to the instructions.*
exceptional *children with exceptional ability*
marked *a marked increase in crime in the area*
notable *Two other notable events took place last week.*
singular *a flower of singular beauty*
special *a special occasion*
uncommon *Both are blessed with an uncommon ability to fix things.*
3 not easily satisfied: *He was very particular about the colours he used.*
choosy INFORMAL *Travellers should be choosy about the insurance policy they buy.*
exacting *exacting standards of craftsmanship*
fastidious *He was fastidious about his appearance.*
fussy *She is very fussy about her food.*
meticulous *meticulous attention to detail*

See also **detail, fussy, personal, precise, special, strict**

partition See divide, division

partly

▷ ADVERB

to some extent but not completely: *This is partly my fault.*
in part *The levels of blood glucose depend in part on what you eat.*
partially *You are each partially right.*
to some degree *These statements are, to some degree, correct.*
to some extent *Her concern is, to some extent, understandable.*

partner

▷ NOUN

1 either member of a couple in a relationship: *My partner moved in with me last year.*
husband or **wife** *Are husbands and wives included in the invitation?*
mate *She has found her ideal mate.*
spouse *The company's health-plan benefits are for both employee and spouse.*
2 the person someone is doing something with: *my tennis partner*
companion *her travelling companion*
teammate *They were teammates before he was traded to the Oilers.*
See also **colleague, companion**

PARTS OF ... *SPEECH*

adjective	noun
adverb	preposition
conjunction	pronoun
interjection	verb

---

party

▷ NOUN

1 a social event where people enjoy themselves: *Most teenagers like to go to parties.*
celebration *a New Year's Eve celebration*
function *a charity function at the hotel*
gathering *a gathering of friends and relatives*
get-together *a family get-together*
reception *a wedding reception*
2 an organization for people with the same political beliefs: *his resignation as mayor*
alliance *The two parties have agreed to form an alliance.*
coalition *a coalition between the two minority parties*
faction *the party's free-trade faction*
3 a group of people doing something together: *a search party looking for the lost child*

band *a small but dedicated band of supporters*
crew *a ship's crew*
gang *a gang of criminals*
squad *the demolition squad*
team *She led a team of doctors.*
unit *the health services research unit*
See also **band, celebrate, celebration, company, function, group, individual, side**

pass
▷ *VERB*
1 to exceed or go past something: *She gave a triumphant wave as she passed the finish line.*
exceed *The demand for these products exceeds the supply.*
go beyond *Did your relationship go beyond mere friendship?*
outdo *You've outdone yourself with this meal.*
outstrip *Demand continues to outstrip supply.*
overtake *It overtook* Lucky *as the week's highest-grossing movie.*
surpass *He was determined to surpass me as the company's top salesperson.*
2 to be successful in a test: *I just passed my driving test.*
get through *I barely got through my finals.*
graduate *He graduated in engineering.*
succeed *the skills and qualities needed to succeed*
ANTONYM **fail**
▷ *NOUN*
3 a document that allows you to go somewhere: *a free pass to the movies*
identification *You need a driver's licence plus one other piece of identification.*
passport *We showed our passports at the border.*
ticket *We're not going to renew our season tickets.*
See also **disappear, permit, vanish**

INFORMALLY SPEAKING
pass out: lose consciousness
pass over: fail to notice
pass up: give up or renounce

pass around *See* **distribute**

pass away *See* **die**

pass down *See* **hand down**

pass on *See* **communicate, die, hand down, will**

pass out *See* **faint**

pass round *See* **distribute**

passable *See* **acceptable, decent, satisfactory, tolerable**

passage
▷ *NOUN*
1 a space that connects two places: *He cleared a passage through the crowd.*
channel *A channel connects the two lakes.*
course *the river's twisting course*
path *A group of reporters blocked the path.*
road *the road between the two villages*
route *the most direct route to our cabin*
way *This is the way in.*
2 a narrow space that connects one place with another: *up some stairs and along a narrow passage toward a door*
aisle *the frozen-food aisle of the supermarket*
corridor *They sat crowded together in the hospital corridor.*
hall *The lights were on in the hall and in the bedroom.*
3 a section of a book or piece of music: *a passage from Shakespeare*
excerpt *an excerpt from her speech*
extract *an extract from his new book*
quotation *a favourite quotation from Stephen Leacock*
section *a section from the first movement of Beethoven's* Eroica *symphony*
See also **extract, journey, path**

passé *See* **old-fashioned**

passing *See* **temporary**

passion
▷ *NOUN*
any strong emotion: *She spoke with great passion.*
emotion *Her voice trembled with emotion.*
excitement *I was in a state of great excitement.*
fire *His speeches were full of fire.*
intensity *His intensity alarmed me.*
warmth *He greeted us with both warmth and affection.*
zeal *his zeal for teaching*
See also **feeling, heat, love, weakness**

passionate
▷ *ADJECTIVE*
expressing very strong feelings about something: *I'm a passionate believer in equal rights.*
ardent *ardent supporters of a peace treaty*
emotional *an emotional farewell*
heartfelt *My heartfelt sympathy goes out to all the relatives.*
impassioned *He made an impassioned appeal for peace.*

P

intense *intense opposition to the war*
strong *Many viewers have strong opinions about violence on TV.*
See also **ardent, crazy, enthusiastic, fanatical, fervent, intense, romantic**

passive

▷ *ADJECTIVE*
submissive or not playing an active part: *His passive attitude made things easier for me.*
docile *docile cows*
receptive *The voters had seemed receptive to his ideas.*
resigned *She was already resigned to losing her job.*
submissive *We wondered if the submissive dog had been abused.*
See also **apathetic, uninterested**

passport *See* **pass, permit**

past, the past

▷ *NOUN*
the period of time before the present: *We would like to put the past behind us.*
antiquity *famous monuments of classical antiquity*
days gone by *This brings back memories of days gone by.*
former times *In former times, he would have been punished for his actions.*
long ago *The old folks told stories of long ago.*

past

▷ *ADJECTIVE*
1 happening or existing before the present: *details of his past activities*
ancient *ancient history*
bygone *a bygone era*
former *Remember him as he was in his former years.*
olden *We were talking about the olden days on their farm.*
previous *a teenage daughter from a previous marriage*
ANTONYM **future**
▷ *PREPOSITION*
2 situated on the other side of somewhere: *It's just past the station.*
beyond *Beyond the garden was a small orchard.*
by *She was sitting in a chair by the window.*
over *He lived in a house over the hill.*
See also **former, over, previous**

paste *See* **bond, glue, stick**

pastel *See* **light, soft**

pasteurized *See* **pure**

pastime

▷ *NOUN*
a hobby or something done for pleasure: *Her favourite pastime is curling.*
activity *activities that range from canoeing to birdwatching*
diversion *Fingerpainting is very messy but an excellent diversion.*
hobby *My hobbies are collecting stamps and building model planes.*
recreation *Saturday afternoon is for family recreation.*
See also **activity, hobby, interest**

pasture *See* **field**

patch *See* **mend, repair**

patch together *See* **piece together**

patch up *See* **fix, repair**

patchy *See* **irregular, uneven**

patent *See* **manifest**

path

▷ *NOUN*
1 a strip of ground for people to walk on: *We followed the paths alongside the river.*
footpath *The waterfall is accessible only by footpath.*
pathway *a pathway leading toward the nearby river*
track *We set off over a rough mountain track.*
trail *He was following a broad trail through the trees.*
2 the space ahead of someone as he or she moves along: *A group of reporters stood in his path.*
course *obstacles blocking our course*
direction *Moncton was 10 km in the opposite direction.*
passage *We elbowed a passage through the shoppers.*
route *All escape routes were blocked by police.*
way *Get out of my way!*
See also **course, direction, line, passage, route, way**

pathetic

▷ *ADJECTIVE*
1 causing someone to feel pity: *small, shrunken, and looking pathetic*
heartbreaking *a heartbreaking series of tragedies*
sad *He seemed a rather sad figure.*
2 very poor or unsuccessful: *pathetic excuses*
feeble *This is a particularly feeble argument.*
lamentable *a lamentable effort by the former champions*
pitiful *They are paid pitiful wages.*

poor *The apartment was in a poor state of repair.*
sorry *Their manufacturing industry is in a sorry state.*
See also **hopeless, inadequate, lame, miserable, sad, sorry**

pathway *See* **path**

patience
▷ NOUN
the ability to stay calm in a difficult situation: *It was exacting work and required all her patience.*
calmness *calmness under pressure*
composure *He regained his composure and went on to win the game.*
cool INFORMAL *Despite the pressure, she never lost her cool.*
restraint *They behaved with more restraint than I'd expected.*
tolerance *a low tolerance for pain*

patient
▷ ADJECTIVE
1 staying calm in a difficult situation: *Please be patient — your cheque will arrive.*
calm *She remains calm under pressure.*
composed *a composed and charming manner*
long-suffering *long-suffering train commuters*
philosophical *He is philosophical about the defeat.*
serene *looking dreamily into the distance — serene, calm, and happy*
ANTONYM **impatient**
▷ NOUN
2 a person receiving medical treatment: *patients who wish to change their doctor*
case *He is a suitable case for treatment.*
invalid *elderly invalids*
sick person *an emergency room full of very sick people*
sufferer *asthma sufferers*

patriarch *See* **parent**

patrol *See* **guard**

patron *See* **customer**

patronize *See* **frequent**

patronizing *See* **superior**

pattern
▷ NOUN
1 a decorative design of repeated shapes: *red and purple thread stitched into a pattern of flames*
design *plates decorated with a floral design*
motif *a rose motif*
2 a diagram or shape used as a guide for

making something: *sewing patterns*
blueprint *the architect's blueprint for the new condominium*
design *They drew up the design for the brick patio.*
diagram *Follow the diagram on page 20.*
plan *a plan of the garden*
stencil *flower stencils*
template *Make a paper template of the seat of the chair.*
See also **design, routine, sequence**

paunch *See* **stomach**

pause
▷ VERB
1 to stop doing something for a short time: *On leaving, she paused for a moment at the door.*
break *They broke for lunch.*
delay *Various problems delayed the launch.*
halt *Striking workers halted production at the plant.*
rest *He rested briefly before pressing on.*
take a break *He needs to take a break from work.*
wait *I waited to see how she responded.*
▷ NOUN
2 a short period when activity stops: *There was a pause between the first and second acts.*
break *Do you want to have a little break?*
halt *Production was brought to a temporary halt.*
intermission *I had a drink during the intermission.*
interruption *The sudden interruption made me forget what I was saying.*
interval *After a brief interval, the train began moving again.*
rest *I think he's due for a rest now.*
stoppage *Miners have voted for a work stoppage.*
See also **break, gap, halt, hesitate, interval, wait**

pay
▷ VERB
1 to give money to someone to settle a debt: *You can pay by credit card.*
compensate *Farmers could be compensated for their loss of crops.*
honour *The bank refused to honour the cheque.*
settle *I settled the bill for our dinner.*
2 to give someone a benefit: *It pays to be honest.*
be advantageous *It would be advantageous to do extra research.*

P

be worthwhile *She believed the effort had been worthwhile.*

▷ NOUN

3 money paid to someone for work done: *their complaints about pay and conditions*

earnings *his earnings as an accountant*
fee *the lawyer's fee*
income *a modest income*
payment *payment for work done*
salary *He took a cut in salary.*
wages *Her wages have gone up.*
See also **income**

INFORMALLY SPEAKING

pay back: give the same treatment as you receive
pay off: give all the money that is owed
pay up: pay in full

---

pay attention *See* **listen, watch**

pay attention to *See* **heed**

pay back *See* **repay, return**

pay for *See* **buy, finance, fund**

pay someone back *See* **retaliate, revenge**

pay tribute to *See* **praise**

payable *See* **outstanding**

payment
▷ NOUN
an amount of money that is paid to someone: *mortgage payments*
advance *The author received a $50 000 advance for her next two novels.*
deposit *A $50 deposit is required when ordering.*
instalment *We paid for the stove in three monthly instalments.*
premium *higher insurance premiums*
remittance *Please make your remittance payable in US funds.*
See also **charge, compensation, cost, pay, reward**

peace
▷ NOUN
1 a state of undisturbed calm and quiet: *They left me in peace to recover from my exhaustion.*
calm *the calm of the lake after the storm*
quiet *She wants some peace and quiet before the big game.*
silence *They stood in silence.*
stillness *An explosion shattered the stillness of the night air.*

tranquility *The hotel is a haven of tranquility.*
2 freedom from war: *The people do not believe that the leaders want peace.*
armistice *the armistice between North Korea and the United Nations*
cessation of hostilities *a resolution calling for an immediate cessation of hostilities*
truce *an uneasy truce between the two sides*
ANTONYM **war**
See also **calm, quiet, silence**

peaceful
▷ ADJECTIVE
quiet and calm: *a peaceful house in the heart of the countryside*
calm *a calm spot amid the bustle of the city*
placid *the placid waters of Lake Erie*
quiet *The street was unnaturally quiet.*
serene *a beautiful, serene park*
still *In the garden, it was very still.*
tranquil *the tranquil paradise of the tropical island*
See also **quiet, relaxed**

peacefulness *See* **calm**

peak
▷ NOUN
1 the point at which something is at its greatest or best: *the peak of the morning rush hour*
climax *The tournament is building up to a dramatic climax.*
culmination *The marriage was the culmination of an eight-month romance.*
high point *The high point of this trip was camping at the provincial park.*
zenith *His career is now at its zenith.*
2 the pointed top of a mountain: *snow-covered peaks*
brow *He overtook a car as he approached the brow of a hill.*
crest *the crest of the hill*
pinnacle *He plunged 25 m from a rocky pinnacle.*
summit *the first person to reach the summit of Mount Everest*
top *the top of Mount Logan*
▷ VERB
3 to reach the highest point or greatest level: *Her career peaked when she was in her 40s.*
be at its height *when the Canadian art scene was at its height*
climax *a tour that climaxed with a three-night stint at the Air Canada Centre*
come to a head *Hostilities came to a head after the attack.*
culminate *The celebration of the centenary will culminate with a banquet.*

reach its highest point *The stock market reached its highest point in ten years.*
See also **top, ultimate**

peal See **ring, sound**

peculiar
▷ ADJECTIVE
1 strange and sometimes unpleasant: *a very peculiar sense of humour*
bizarre *bizarre behaviour*
curious *a curious mixture of the ancient and modern*
funny *Children get some funny ideas sometimes.*
odd *Something odd began to happen.*
strange *There was something strange about the flickering blue light.*
weird *It must be weird to be so rich.*
2 associated with one particular person or thing: *He has his own peculiar way of doing things.*
distinctive *She has a very distinctive laugh.*
distinguishing *Does he have any distinguishing features?*
individual *all part of her very individual personality*
personal *cultivating their own personal style*
special *Everyone has his or her own special problems and fears.*
unique *a feature unique to humans*
See also **bizarre, curious, funny, odd, particular, personal, special, strange, weird**

peddle See **sell**

pedestal See **base**

peek
▷ VERB
1 to have a quick look at something: *She peeked at him through a crack in the wall.*
catch a glimpse *Spectators lined the street to catch a glimpse of the singer.*
glance *He glanced at his watch.*
peep *Children came to peep at us round the doorway.*
sneak a look *We sneaked a look at his diary.*
▷ NOUN
2 a quick look at something: *He took his first peek at the new stadium.*
glance *We exchanged glances.*
glimpse *Some people had waited all day to catch a glimpse of her.*
look *She took a last look in the mirror.*
peep *He took a peep at his watch.*
See also **glance, look**

peep See **glance, peek**

peer See **noble**

peerless See **incomparable**

pellet See **ball**

pelt See **coat, hide**

penal institution See **prison**

penalize See **punish**

penalties See **sanctions**

penalty See **cost, punishment**

penchant See **taste, weakness**

penetrate See **pierce**

penetrating See **perceptive, shrill**

penitence See **regret**

penitent See **sorry**

penniless See **poor**

pensive See **serious, thoughtful**

pent-up
▷ ADJECTIVE
held back for a long time without release: *a lot of pent-up anger to release*
inhibited *an inhibited response*
repressed *repressed hostility*
suppressed *Deep sleep allowed suppressed anxieties to surface.*

people
▷ PLURAL NOUN
1 men, women, and children: *Hundreds of people lost their homes in the earthquake.*
human beings *The disease can be transmitted to human beings.*
humanity *crimes against humanity*
humankind *the evolution of humankind*
humans *before humans appeared on earth*
2 all the men, women, and children of a particular place: *It's a triumph for the Canadian people.*
citizens *the citizens of New York City*
inhabitants *the inhabitants of Hong Kong*
population *the continent's rapidly rising population*
public *the Canadian public*
See also **kin, public, race, settle**

peppery See **hot**

perceive See **appreciate, discern, know, note, notice, see**

percentage See **proportion**

perceptible See **conspicuous, noticeable, visible**

perception See **intelligence, understanding**

P

perceptive

▷ ADJECTIVE

good at noticing or realizing things: *a perceptive account of the poet's life*
acute *Her relaxed exterior hides an extremely acute mind.*
astute *He made a series of astute business decisions.*
aware *They are politically very aware.*
penetrating *He never stopped asking penetrating questions.*
sharp *She has a sharp eye and an excellent memory.*
See also **acute, astute, brilliant, keen, observant, sharp, shrewd, wise**

perfect

▷ ADJECTIVE

I of the highest standard and without fault: *His English was perfect.*
expert *There is a great deal to learn from her expert approach.*
faultless *faultless technique*
flawless *her flawless complexion*
masterly *a masterly performance*
polished *a polished production of the play*
skilled *a skilled repair job*
ANTONYM **imperfect**
2 complete or absolute: *They have a perfect right to say so.*
absolute *absolute nonsense*
complete *The resignation came as a complete surprise.*
consummate *He acted the part with consummate skill.*
sheer *an act of sheer desperation*
unmitigated *Last year's crop was an unmitigated disaster.*
utter *utter nonsense*
▷ VERB
3 to make something as good as it can be: *The technique was perfected last year.*
hone *a chance to hone their skills*
improve *Their Italian has improved enormously.*
polish *He spent time polishing the script.*
refine *Surgical techniques are constantly being refined.*
See also **complete, ideal, polish, utter**

perfectly See **quite**

perform

▷ VERB

I to carry out a task or action: *people who have performed acts of bravery*
carry out *The attacks were carried out at night.*
complete *He completed the test quickly.*
do *He crashed trying to do a tricky manoeuvre.*
execute *The landing was skilfully executed.*
fulfill *She fulfilled her various obligations.*
2 to act, dance, or play music in public: *students performing Shakespeare's Macbeth*
act *acting in an adventure movie*
do *I've always wanted to do a play at Stratford.*
play *His ambition is to play the part of Dracula.*
present *The company is presenting a new production of Hamlet.*
put on *The band is hoping to put on a new show.*
stage *The group staged their first play ten years ago.*
See also **achieve, act, administer, appear, carry out, commit, conduct, do, fulfill, function**

perfume See **fragrance, smell**

perfumed See **fragrant, sweet**

perfunctory See **quick**

perhaps

▷ ADVERB

maybe: *Perhaps you're right.*
conceivably *The mission could conceivably be accomplished in a week.*
it could be *It could be that he's upset at what you said.*
maybe *Maybe she is in love.*
possibly *Do you think that he could possibly be right?*
See also **maybe**

peril See **danger, risk**

perilous See **dangerous, treacherous**

perimeter See **outskirts**

period

▷ NOUN

a particular length of time: *a period of a few months*
interval *a long interval when nobody spoke*
spell *a long spell of dry weather*
stretch *an 18-month stretch in the army*
term *a 5-year prison term*
time *At 17, he left home for a short time.*
while *I haven't seen him for a long while.*
See also **length, lesson, round, space, stage, stretch, term, time**

periodic See **occasional, regular**

periphery See **outskirts**

perish See **die**

perjure oneself See **lie**

perjury *See* **lying**

perky *See* **lively**

permanent
▷ *ADJECTIVE*
lasting forever or present all the time: *a permanent end to the hostilities*
abiding *one of his abiding interests*
constant *Inflation is a constant threat.*
enduring *an enduring friendship*
eternal *the quest for eternal youth*
lasting *We are well on our way to a lasting peace.*
perpetual *a perpetual source of worry*
ANTONYM **temporary**

permeate *See* **soak**

permissible *See* **legal**

permission
▷ *NOUN*
authorization to do something: *He asked permission to leave the room.*
approval *The plan will require official approval.*
assent *He requires the assent of Parliament.*
authorization *his request for authorization to spend the funds*
consent *parental consent for the child's surgery*
go-ahead *After several delays, the project was given the go-ahead.*
licence *He has given me licence to do the job as I see fit.*
ANTONYM **ban**
See also **approval, blessing, permit, sanction**

permit
▷ *VERB*
1 to allow something or make it possible: *We aren't permitted to bring our own food to the movies.*
allow *Smoking will not be allowed.*
authorize *They are expected to authorize the use of military force.*
enable *The test should enable doctors to detect the disease early.*
give the green light to *She has been given the green light to begin writing the screenplay.*
grant *Permission was granted a few weeks ago.*
sanction *Our manager will not sanction the proposed new policy.*
ANTONYM **ban**
▷ *NOUN*
2 an official document allowing someone to do something: *a work permit*
authorization *We didn't have authorization to go.*
licence *a driver's licence*

pass *a train pass*
passport *My passport expires next year.*
permission *Permission for the march has not been granted.*
warrant *Police issued a warrant for her arrest.*
See also **allow, approve, grant, let, sanction**

pernicious *See* **harmful**

perpendicular *See* **sheer, straight**

perpetrate *See* **commit**

perpetual *See* **constant, continual, infinite, permanent**

perpetually *See* **always**

perplexed *See* **confused**

persecute
▷ *VERB*
to treat someone with continual cruelty and unfairness: *persecuted for religious beliefs*
hound *He has been hounded by the press.*
ill-treat *They thought he had been ill-treating his dog.*
oppress *Minorities in that country have been oppressed for generations.*
pick on *She was repeatedly picked on by the manager.*
torment *They were tormented by other students.*
torture *He tortured me with his endless putdowns.*
See also **bully**

CONFUSABLES

persecute means **harass**
prosecute means **take legal action against**

---

persecution *See* **oppression**

persecutor *See* **bully**

perseverance *See* **determination**

persist *See* **continue, last**

persistence *See* **determination**

persistent *See* **determined, relentless**

person
▷ *NOUN*
a man, woman, or child: *The amount of sleep we need varies from person to person.*
human *Anxiety is a human condition.*
human being *This protein occurs naturally in human beings.*
individual *the rights of the individual*

P

living soul *The nearest living soul was 20 km away.*
soul *a tiny village of only a hundred souls*
See also **figure, individual**

personal

▷ ADJECTIVE
belonging to a particular person or thing: *personal belongings*
individual *three individual portions*
own *I decided to design my own website.*
particular *his particular style of teaching*
peculiar *her peculiar talents*
private *my private life*
special *Every person has his or her own special problems.*
unique *a unique way of laughing*
See also **direct, individual, own, peculiar, private**

personality

▷ NOUN
I a person's character and nature: *She has such a kind, friendly personality.*
character *a negative side to his character*
identity *our own sense of cultural identity*
individuality *People should be free to express their individuality.*
makeup *There was some fundamental flaw in his makeup.*
nature *She trusted people. That was her nature.*
psyche *disturbing elements of the human psyche*
2 a famous person in entertainment or sport: *television personalities*
big name *the big names in Canadian cinema*
celebrity *Hollywood celebrities*
famous name *a famous name from the past*
household name *the TV series that made him a household name*
star *movie stars*
See also **celebrity, character, figure, nature**

personnel See **staff**

perspective See **attitude, outlook, view**

persuade

▷ VERB
to make someone do something by reason or charm: *He persuaded the company to sign her up.*
bring around INFORMAL *We will do what we can to bring them around to our point of view.*

coax *She coaxed him into talking about himself.*
induce *I would do anything to induce them to stay.*
sway *Don't ever be swayed by fashion.*
talk into *He talked me into travelling with him.*
win over *By the end of the day, she had won over the crowd.*
See also **coax, convince, push, reason, satisfy**

persuasion See **faith**

persuasive See **convincing, powerful**

pertinent See **relevant**

perturbed See **uneasy**

pervasive See **extensive, widespread**

pervert See **corrupt**

perverted

▷ ADJECTIVE
practising abnormal and unacceptable behaviour: *perverted phone calls and letters*
depraved *the work of depraved and evil criminals*
deviant *deviant practices*
immoral *those who think that his books are immoral*
unhealthy *His interest developed into an unhealthy obsession.*

pessimistic

▷ ADJECTIVE
believing that bad things will happen: *a pessimistic view of life*
despondent *despondent about their economic future*
gloomy *a gloomy view of the future*
glum *They are not entirely glum about the car industry's prospects.*
hopeless *He left the doctor's office feeling hopeless.*
ANTONYM **optimistic**

pest

▷ NOUN
I an insect or animal that damages crops or livestock: *Aphids and other pests destroyed much of the crop.*
bane *The groundhog is the bane of many farmers.*
blight *potato blight*
scourge *The Colorado beetle is a scourge for potato farmers.*
2 an annoying person: *I didn't want to be a cry baby or a pest.*
bane *Student journalists were the bane of her life.*
bore *I don't enjoy his company. He's a bore and a fool.*

nuisance *He can be a real nuisance when he wants something.*
pain INFORMAL *She's been a real pain recently.*
pain in the neck INFORMAL *You've been a pain in the neck sending all those e-mails.*
See also **annoyance, nuisance**

pester
▷ VERB
to bother someone continually: *He gets fed up with people pestering him for money.*
annoy *She kept on annoying me.*
badger *She badgered her doctor time and again.*
bother *Stop bothering me with your phone calls.*
bug INFORMAL *Stop bugging me!*
drive someone up the wall INFORMAL *I teased my sister and drove her up the wall.*
get on someone's nerves INFORMAL *I was beginning to get on her nerves.*
See also **hassle, worry**

pet *See* **favourite**

peter out *See* **die**

petition *See* **appeal, beg, press**

petrified *See* **frightened**

petty
▷ ADJECTIVE
1 small and unimportant: *endless rules and petty regulations*
insignificant *an insignificant amount of money*
measly INFORMAL *The pay is measly.*
trifling *The amount involved is trifling.*
trivial *trivial details*
unimportant *an unimportant argument*
2 selfish and small-minded: *I think that attitude is a bit petty.*
cheap *politicians making cheap political points*
mean *I'd feel mean saying no.*
small-minded *their small-minded preoccupation with gossip*
See also **insignificant, minor, trivial**

petulant *See* **irritable, sulky**

phantom *See* **ghost, spirit, vision**

phase *See* **stage**

phenomenal *See* **exceptional**

phenomenon *See* **wonder**

philosophical *See* **patient**

phobia *See* **complex**

phony
▷ ADJECTIVE

1 false and intended to deceive: *a phony accent*
bogus *a bogus insurance claim*
counterfeit *counterfeit currency*
fake *fake certificates*
false *a false name and address*
forged *forged documents*
sham *a sham contest*
ANTONYM **genuine**
See also **fake, mock**

photograph *See* **picture**

phrase *See* **express, expression, put**

phrasing *See* **language**

physique *See* **body, build, figure**

pick
▷ VERB
1 to choose something: *She picked ten people to interview for six sales jobs.*
choose *There are several options to choose from.*
decide upon *He decided upon a career in publishing.*
hand-pick *He was hand-picked for his job by the manager.*
opt for *I think we should opt for a more cautious approach.*
select *the committee's policy of selecting candidates*
settle on *I finally settled on a model of bike.*
2 to remove a flower or fruit with your fingers: *I picked the most beautiful rose.*
gather *We spent the afternoon gathering berries.*
harvest *We'll start harvesting the corn next week.*
pluck *I plucked a lemon from the tree.*
▷ NOUN
3 the best: *the pick of the country's young athletes*
elite *the elite of women's tennis*
pride *the Avro Arrow, the pride of Canadian aeronautical engineering*
See also **choose, favourite, select**

P

INFORMALLY SPEAKING

pick and choose: be very fussy
pick apart: find many flaws in
pick up on: notice and understand

pick on
▷ VERB
to criticize someone unfairly or treat him or her unkindly: *Bullies pick on younger or weaker children.*
bait *He delighted in baiting his younger brother.*

tease *He teased me mercilessly.*
torment *They were tormented by other students.*
See also **bully, persecute**

pick out *See* **distinguish**

pick up *See* **acquire, develop, learn, lift, receive**

pickpocket *See* **thief**

picnic *See* **eat**

picture
▷ NOUN
1 a drawing, painting, or photograph: *I have a picture of you as my screen saver.*
drawing *She did a drawing of me.*
illustration *Tolkien's illustrations for* The Hobbit
painting *his collection of Group of Seven paintings*
photograph *He wants to take some photographs of the house.*
portrait *a self-portrait by Emily Carr*
sketch *pencil sketches*
▷ VERB
2 to imagine something clearly: *He pictured her with long black hair.*
conceive of *I can't conceive of doing work that doesn't interest me.*
imagine *It's difficult to imagine anything coming between them.*
see *A good idea, but can you see my brother trying it?*
visualize *He could visualize himself as a famous rock star.*
See also **imagine, represent**

INFORMALLY SPEAKING

get the picture: understand without further explanation
out of the picture: not part of a certain situation

piece
▷ NOUN
1 a portion or part of something: *a piece of cheese*
bit *a bit of paper*
chunk *a can of pineapple chunks*
fragment *There were fragments of cork in the bottle.*
part *The engine has only three moving parts.*
portion *Damage was confined to a small portion of the castle.*
slice *a slice of bread*
2 something that has been written, created, or composed: *I read his piece on hockey parents.*

article *a newspaper article*
composition *Schubert's piano compositions*
creation *the fashion designer's latest creations*
study *the artist's studies of horses*
work *In my opinion, this is Shakespeare's greatest work.*
See also **article, bit, block, feature, item, lump, part, portion, section**

INFORMALLY SPEAKING

go to pieces: break down or collapse
piece of cake: a very easy task
piece of my mind: a scolding
piece of work: a difficult person to deal with
speak your piece: express your opinion

piece together
▷ VERB
to assemble things or parts to make something complete: *Doctors painstakingly pieced together the broken bones.*
assemble *She is assembling evidence concerning a murder.*
join *Join all the sections together.*
mend *I should have had it mended, but never got around to it.*
patch together *A hasty deal was patched together.*
repair *the cost of repairing earthquake damage*
restore *The heritage society is playing a leading part in restoring old buildings.*
See also **reconstruct**

pierce
▷ VERB
to make a hole in something with a sharp instrument: *Pierce the potato with a fork.*
bore *Bore a hole through the board and attach to the wall with a bolt.*
drill *I drilled five holes at equal distance.*
lance *It's a painful experience having the boil lanced.*
penetrate *The earth's atmosphere was penetrated by a meteor.*
puncture *The bullet nearly punctured his lung.*

piercing *See* **noisy, shrill**

pig
▷ NOUN
a farm animal kept for meat: *the number of pigs at the trough*
hog *a hog farm*
piggy INFORMAL *These two piggies are going to market!*
swine *herds of oxen, sheep, and swine*

pigment *See* **colour**

pigmentation *See* **colour**

pile

▷ NOUN

1 a quantity of things lying one on top of another: *a pile of books*
heap *a compost heap*
hoard *a hoard of jewels*
mound *The bulldozers piled up huge mounds of dirt.*
mountain *I have mountains of papers to read.*
stack *a stack of magazines on the table*
2 the raised fibres of a soft surface: *the carpet's thick pile*
down *The baby duck is covered with fine down.*
fur *This creature's fur is short and dense.*
hair *He has black hair.*
nap *The cotton is lightly brushed to heighten the nap.*

▷ VERB

3 to put things one on top of another: *A few newspapers were piled on the table.*
heap *She heaped more carrots onto the plate.*
hoard *They've begun to hoard gas and food.*
stack *They are stacked neatly in piles of three.*
See also **bunch, heap, load, mass**

piles *See* **lot**

pile-up *See* **crash**

pilfer *See* **steal**

pillage *See* **loot**

pillar *See* **support**

pilot *See* **drive**

pinch *See* **dash, emergency, steal**

pine *See* **long**

pine for *See* **be dying for, miss**

SHADES OF ... *PINK*	
coral	salmon
flesh	shell pink
fuchsia	shocking pink
rose	

pinnacle *See* **peak, top**

pinpoint *See* **identify, locate**

pioneer *See* **start**

pious *See* **holy, religious**

pirouette *See* **spin**

pit

▷ NOUN

a large hole in something: *He lost his footing and began to slide into the pit.*
chasm *The bike plunged down into the chasm.*
hole *The builders had cut holes into the soft stone.*
pothole *I try to avoid roads with deep potholes.*
See also **abyss, grave, hole**

pitch *See* **throw**

pitfall *See* **difficulty, risk**

pitiful *See* **pathetic, sorry**

pity

▷ VERB

1 to feel sorry for someone: *I don't know whether to hate or pity him.*
feel for *She had a terrible day and I really felt for her.*
feel sorry for *I felt sorry for the families whose homes were flooded.*
sympathize with *I sympathize with you for your loss.*

▷ NOUN

2 sympathy for other people's suffering: *She saw no pity in their faces.*
charity *They showed a lack of charity and understanding to us.*
compassion *his compassion for a helpless old dog*
kindness *He was treated with kindness by numerous officials.*
mercy *Neither side showed any mercy.*
sympathy *We expressed our sympathy for their loss.*
understanding *We would like to thank them for their patience and understanding.*

▷ NOUN

3 a regrettable fact: *It's a pity they can't all have the same opportunities.*
crime *It would be a crime to travel to Australia and not stop in Sydney.*
crying shame *It would be a crying shame to split up a winning partnership.*
shame *It's a shame the play had to close.*
See also **mercy, sympathy**

pivotal *See* **critical, crucial, vital**

placard *See* **sign**

placate *See* **pacify**

place

▷ NOUN

any point or area: *The pain is always in the same place.*

P

area *a picnic area*
location *What's the location of the restaurant?*
point *The pain originated from a point in his right thigh.*
position *the ship's position*
site *a bat sanctuary with special nesting sites*
spot *the island's top tourist spots*

take place

▷ VERB

to happen: *The meeting took place on Thursday.*
come about *That came about when we went to Winnipeg last year.*
go on *This has been going on for about a year.*
happen *We cannot say for sure what will happen.*
occur *When did the crash occur?*

place

▷ VERB

to put something somewhere: *Chairs were placed in rows for the parents.*
deposit *Imagine if you were suddenly deposited on a desert island.*
locate *the best city in which to locate a business*
plant *So far no one has admitted to planting the bomb.*
position *flowers that are carefully positioned in the room*
put *She put the photograph on her desk.*
situate *The hotel is situated next to the railway station.*
See also **appointment, deposit, fit, identify, insert, lay, location, position, put, recognize, scene, set, spot**

INFORMALLY SPEAKING

all over the place: everywhere; disorderly
go places: achieve success
put someone in his or her place: tell or show that someone is conceited

placed *See* **located**

placid *See* **gentle, mild, peaceful**

plague *See* **annoy, rash, worry**

plain

▷ ADJECTIVE

1 very simple in style with no decoration: *It was a plain, grey stone house.*
austere *The room was austere and simple.*
bare *bare wooden floors*

spartan *her spartan home in a tiny village*
stark *a stark white fireplace*
ANTONYM **fancy**

2 obvious and easy to recognize or understand: *It was plain to him that I was bored.*
clear *The book is clear and readable.*
comprehensible *a comprehensible manual*
distinct *a distinct smell of burning leaves*
evident *His footprints were clearly evident in the heavy dust.*
obvious *an obvious injustice*
unmistakable *Her voice was unmistakable.*
See also **blank, clear, common, evident, frank, manifest, obvious, simple, straight, straightforward, ugly, visible**

TYPES OF ... *PLAIN*

flat	plateau
flatland	prairie
grassland	savannah
llano	steppe
lowland	tableland
mesa	

plan

▷ NOUN

1 a way thought out to do something: *a plan to merge the two teams*
method *He did it by his usual method.*
proposal *The proposals need careful study.*
scheme *The scheme was a total failure.*
strategy *What should our marketing strategy achieve?*
system *the advantages of the new system over the old one*

2 a detailed diagram of something that is to be made: *a detailed plan of the science project*
blueprint *a blueprint for a new arena*
diagram *a diagram of the room*
layout *the layout of the page*
scale drawing *scale drawings of the new mall*

▷ VERB

3 to decide in detail what is to be done: *when we plan road construction*
arrange *We arranged a family reunion once a year.*
design *He approached me to design the restaurant.*
devise *We devised a plan.*
draft *The legislation was drafted by the committee.*
formulate *She formulated a plan for escape.*
See also **aim, arrange, contemplate, course, design, idea, intend, layout,**

mean, organize, pattern, plot,
suggestion

plane *See* **level**

planet *See* **earth**

planned *See* **calculated**

planning *See* **organization**

plant *See* **factory, place**

plaster *See* **spread**

plausible *See* **believable, convincing,
logical, probable**

play
▷ *VERB*
1 to take part in games or use toys: *The child
was playing with her teddy bear.*
amuse oneself *He amused himself by
playing solitaire.*
entertain oneself *I used to entertain
myself by building model planes.*
frolic *Tourists sunbathe and frolic in the
ocean.*
have fun *having fun with your friends*
2 to take part in a sport or game: *I was
playing cards with my friends.*
compete *Eight people competed for the
prize.*
participate *Sixteen teams participated in
the tournament.*
take on *They took on the top team and
won.*
take part *The teams taking part are
hockey's finest.*
vie with *The Blue Jays vied with the Phillies
for the World Series.*
▷ *NOUN*
3 a piece of drama performed on stage,
radio, or television: *Shakespeare's most
popular play*
comedy *a romantic comedy*
drama *He also wrote radio dramas.*
show *a one-woman show*
tragedy *Shakespeare's tragedies*
See also **act, appear, perform**

INFORMALLY SPEAKING
play for time: delay in order to gain an
advantage
play it safe (or smart, or cool, etc.):
act in a safe (or smart, etc.) way to achieve
a certain result
play on: take advantage of
play up to: try to get some benefit
through flattery

play a part *See* **appear**

play a part in *See* **take part in**

play a trick on *See* **dupe**

play the part of *See* **act**

play up *See* **emphasize**

player *See* **figure**

plea *See* **appeal, defence, request**

plead
▷ *VERB*
to beg someone for something: *I pleaded
with them to come home.*
appeal *The United Nations appealed for aid
from the international community.*
ask *I've asked you time and again not to do
that.*
beg *We are not going to beg for help ever
again.*
beseech FORMAL *He beseeched them to
show mercy.*
implore *Residents implored the authorities
to install traffic lights at the intersection.*
See also **appeal, ask, beg, press, urge**

plead with *See* **implore**

pleasant
▷ *ADJECTIVE*
1 enjoyable or attractive: *a pleasant little
apartment*
agreeable *workers in more agreeable and
better-paid occupations*
delightful *It was the most delightful garden
I'd ever seen.*
enjoyable *an enjoyable meal*
lovely *He had a lovely voice.*
nice *It's nice to be here together again.*
pleasurable *He found sailing more
pleasurable than skiing.*
ANTONYM **unpleasant**
2 friendly or charming: *an extremely
pleasant and obliging person*
affable *an affable and approachable
woman*
amiable *She was surprised at how amiable
and polite he seemed.*
charming *He can be charming to his
friends.*
friendly *She has a friendly manner.*
likable *She's an immensely likable person.*
nice *He's a nice fellow, very quiet and
courteous.*
ANTONYM **unpleasant**
See also **agreeable, lovely, warm**

please
▷ *VERB*
to give pleasure to: *I was tidying my bedroom
to please my parents.*

P

amuse *The thought seemed to amuse them.*
charm *He charmed all of us.*
delight *music that has delighted audiences all over the world*
entertain *Children's TV not only entertains but also teaches.*
See also **appeal, delight, entertain, satisfy, suit**

pleased

▷ ADJECTIVE

happy or satisfied: *I'm pleased with the way things have been going.*
contented *She had a contented smile on her face.*
delighted *I know he will be delighted to see you.*
glad *I'm glad he eventually changed his mind.*
happy *a confident and happy child*
satisfied *satisfied customers*
See also **glad, proud, satisfied**

pleasing *See* **beautiful**

pleasurable *See* **agreeable, pleasant**

pleasure

▷ NOUN

a feeling of happiness and satisfaction: *Almost everybody takes pleasure in eating.*
amusement *Her impersonations provided great amusement.*
enjoyment *her enjoyment of the countryside*
happiness *My current happiness has helped to erase the bad memories.*
joy *tears of joy*
satisfaction *job satisfaction*
See also **delight, entertainment, fun, happiness, pride**

pleat *See* **fold**

plebiscite *See* **vote**

pledge *See* **bond, guarantee, oath, promise, word**

plentiful

▷ ADJECTIVE

existing in large amounts: *a plentiful supply*
abundant *Birds are abundant in the woods.*
ample *The design created ample space for a large kitchen.*
bountiful *a bountiful harvest*
copious *He attended the lecture and took copious notes.*
infinite *an infinite variety of landscapes*
ANTONYM **scarce**
See also **abundant, generous, handsome, rich**

plenty

▷ NOUN

a lot of something: *There's plenty to go around.*
enough *Have you had enough?*
great deal *I've spent a great deal of time on this project.*
heaps INFORMAL *You have heaps of time.*
lots *She has made lots of changes to the script.*
plethora *a plethora of new products*
See also **a lot** or **lots, abundance, many, wealth**

plenty of *See* **ample**

plethora *See* **plenty**

pliable *See* **flexible, soft**

plight *See* **jam, situation, state**

plot

▷ NOUN

1 a secret plan made by a group of people: *the plot to assassinate the dictator*
conspiracy *a conspiracy to steal the secret formula*
intrigue *political intrigue*
plan *a secret government plan to build a nuclear waste dump*
scheme *an elaborate scheme to dupe the police*
2 the story of a novel, short story, play, or movie: *This book has a ludicrously complicated plot.*
narrative *a fast-moving narrative*
scenario *The scenario is far-fetched.*
story *lots of special effects, but a weak story*
storyline *It sounds like a typical storyline from a soap opera.*
▷ VERB

3 to plan something secretly with others: *Prosecutors allege that the defendants plotted to overthrow the government.*
conspire *The countries had conspired to acquire nuclear weapons.*
hatch *He hatched a plot to murder his rival.*
plan *I suspect they are secretly planning to raise taxes.*
scheme *He claimed that they were scheming against him.*

plough into *See* **crash**

ploy *See* **manoeuvre, trick**

pluck *See* **bravery, courage, pick, tug**

plucky *See* **brave**

plug

▷ NOUN

1 a small, round object for blocking a hole: *She put the plug in the sink.*

cork *the sound of popping champagne corks*
stopper *a bottle sealed with a cork stopper*
▷ VERB
2 to block a hole with something: *working to plug a major oil leak*
block *If the beavers build a dam, it will block the stream.*
fill *Fill the small holes with earth.*
seal *She filled the jars with jam and sealed them with wax.*
See also **advertise, advertisement, block, promote, publicity, publicize**

plummet *See* **decline, descend, drop, fall**

plump
▷ ADJECTIVE
rather fat: *a plump chicken*
beefy *beefy bodyguards*
burly *burly shipyard workers*
chubby *I was quite chubby as a child.*
fat *I could eat what I liked without getting fat.*
stout *He was a tall, stout man of 60.*

plunder *See* **loot, raid**

plunge *See* **fall**

plus *See* **virtue**

plush *See* **luxurious**

poach *See* **cook**

poignant *See* **moving, sad, touching**

point
▷ NOUN
1 the purpose or meaning something has: *Cutting costs is not the point of the exercise.*
aim *The aim of this book is to inform you.*
goal *The goal is to raise a lot of money.*
intention *It was never my intention to injure anyone.*
object *It was his object in life to find the island.*
purpose *He did not know the purpose of their visit.*
2 a quality or feature: *Tact was never her strong point.*
attribute *Cruelty is a regrettable attribute of human behaviour.*
characteristic *their physical characteristics*
feature *It's one of my best features.*
quality *mature people with leadership qualities*
side *the dark side of his character*
trait *Creativity is a human trait.*
3 the thin, sharp end of something: *the point of a needle*

nib *the nib of my pen*
prong *the prongs of a fork*
tip *the tip of the tongue*
See also **aspect, consideration, detail, item, location, message, moment, place, position, purpose, question, spot, stage, subject, use**

point of view *See* **attitude, feeling, opinion, view, viewpoint**

point out *See* **comment**

point-blank *See* **straight**

pointed *See* **sharp**

pointer *See* **hint**

pointless *See* **hopeless, unnecessary**

poise *See* **grace**

poison
▷ NOUN
a substance that can kill people or animals: *Mercury is a known poison.*
toxin *the liver's ability to break down toxins*
venom *the cobra's deadly venom*
See also **pollute**

poisonous
▷ ADJECTIVE
containing something that causes death or illness: *a large cloud of poisonous gas*
noxious *Many household products give off noxious fumes.*
toxic *the cost of cleaning up toxic waste*
venomous *a venomous snake*

poke
▷ VERB
1 to jab or prod someone or something: *She poked a fork into the turkey skin.*
dig *Stop digging your fingernails into my arm!*
elbow *He elbowed me out of the way.*
jab *Somebody jabbed an umbrella into his leg.*
nudge *She nudged me awake after I dozed off.*
prod *She prodded me till I stopped snoring.*
stab *He stabbed at me with his forefinger.*
▷ NOUN
2 a jab or prod: *She gave him a playful poke.*
dig *a sharp dig in the small of the back*
jab *a quick jab with my elbow*
nudge *She slipped her arm under his and gave him a nudge.*
prod *He gave me a gentle prod when I dozed off in the theatre.*
See also **dig, stick**

P

poke fun at *See* **mock**

poke your nose in *See* **pry**

pole *See* **bar, stick**

police *See* **guard**

policy *See* **course, procedure**

polish
▷ VERB
1 to make smooth and shiny by rubbing: *polishing the furniture*
buff *buffing the metal surface*
shine *shining his shoes*
wax *a Sunday morning spent washing and waxing the car*
2 to improve a skill or technique: *Polish your writing skills.*
brush up *She spent the summer brushing up on her driving skills.*
improve *I want to improve my golf game.*
perfect *We perfected our wallpapering technique.*
refine *Surgical techniques are constantly being refined.*
▷ NOUN
3 elegance or refinement: *The early stories lacked the polish of his later work.*
class INFORMAL *For sheer class, she is the top tennis player around.*
elegance *The furniture combined practicality with elegance.*
finesse *He's a good, strong player, but his game lacks finesse.*
grace *Ballet classes are important for learning poise and grace.*
refinement *She possesses both dignity and refinement.*
style *Paris, you have to admit, has style.*
See also **finish, gloss, perfect, practise**

polished *See* **glossy, perfect, smooth**

polite
▷ ADJECTIVE
1 having good manners: *It's not polite to point at people.*
civil *I have to force myself to be civil to him.*
courteous *Her reply was courteous but firm.*
respectful *Their children are always respectful to their elders.*
well-behaved *a well-behaved child*
well-mannered *a well-mannered student*
ANTONYM **rude**
2 cultivated or refined: *Certain words are not acceptable in polite society.*
cultured *He is immensely cultured and well-read.*

genteel *He's genteel in an old-fashioned way.*
refined *Her speech and manner are very refined.*
sophisticated *Recently her tastes have become more sophisticated.*
urbane *She describes him as charming and urbane.*
See also **refined**

politeness
▷ NOUN
the quality of being civil to someone: *She listened to him, but only out of politeness.*
civility *Handle customers with tact and civility.*
courtesy *He did not even have the courtesy to reply to my e-mail.*
decency *He should have had the decency to inform me.*
etiquette *the rules of diplomatic etiquette*
See also **courtesy**

polls *See* **vote**

pollute
▷ VERB
to contaminate with something harmful: *Heavy industry pollutes our rivers with noxious chemicals.*
contaminate *Have any fish been contaminated in the Arctic Ocean?*
infect *a virus that is spread mainly by infected blood*
poison *Drilling operations have poisoned the Nile delta.*
taint *blood tainted with the hepatitis viruses*
See also **soil**

pomp *See* **ceremony**

pompous
▷ ADJECTIVE
behaving in a way that is too serious and self-important: *a pompous man with a high opinion of his own capabilities*
arrogant *an air of arrogant indifference*
grandiose *grandiose plans that never got off the ground*
ostentatious *an ostentatious wedding reception*
pretentious *His response was full of pretentious nonsense.*
puffed up *She is puffed up with her own importance.*
See also **pretentious**

ponder
▷ VERB
to think about something deeply: *I'm continually pondering how to improve the team.*

brood *I guess everyone broods over things once in a while.*

consider *You have to consider the feelings of those around you.*

contemplate *He lay in bed contemplating his future.*

mull over *I'll leave you alone so you can mull it over.*

reflect *I reflected on the child's future.*

think *I have often thought about this problem.*

See also **consider, contemplate, deliberate, think, wonder**

ponderous *See* **slow**

pony *See* **horse**

pooch *See* **dog**

pool *See* **fund**

poor
▷ ADJECTIVE
1 having little money: *a poor family*
broke INFORMAL *They were broke when they got married.*
destitute *destitute people living on the streets*
hard up INFORMAL *He's not as hard up as he pretends to be.*
impoverished *one of the most impoverished suburbs of Rio de Janeiro*
penniless *a penniless refugee*
poverty-stricken *the story of a poverty-stricken child*
ANTONYM **rich**
2 of a low quality or standard: *He was a poor actor.*
feeble *a feeble attempt to score a goal*
inferior *The CDs were of inferior quality.*
mediocre *His school record was mediocre.*
second-rate *Passengers are fed up using a second-rate service.*
shoddy *shoddy goods*
unsatisfactory *questions to which she received unsatisfactory answers*
See also **deficient, hopeless, inadequate, inferior, lame, low, pathetic, remote, rotten, sorry, unsatisfactory, worthless**

poorly *See* **ill, sick, unhealthy, unwell**

populace *See* **public**

popular
▷ ADJECTIVE
1 liked or approved of by a lot of people: *These delicious pastries will be very popular.*
fashionable *fashionable restaurants*
favourite *Canada's favourite radio host*
in demand *She was much in demand as a lecturer.*

in favour *He is now back in favour with the manager.*
sought-after *one of the most sought-after new names in Hollywood*
well-liked *She was very sociable and well-liked by the other students.*
ANTONYM **unpopular**
2 involving or intended for ordinary people: *the popular press*
common *Shakespeare wrote his plays for the common people.*
conventional *conventional opinions*
general *general awareness of the problems*
prevalent *an increasingly prevalent trend*
universal *universal health care*
See also **common, fashionable, mass, public**

populate *See* **inhabit, settle**

population *See* **people**

pore over *See* **read, scrutinize, study**

pornographic *See* **dirty, obscene**

portable *See* **light**

portion
▷ NOUN
a part or amount of something: *I have spent a considerable portion of my life here.*
bit *I missed the first bit of the meeting.*
chunk *Cut the melon into chunks.*
helping *extra helpings of ice cream*
part *A large part of his salary was spent on rent.*
piece *Do you want another piece?*
segment *the middle segment of her journey*
serving *Each serving contains 240 calories.*
See also **measure, part, piece, section, share**

portrait *See* **picture**

portray *See* **act, describe, represent**

pose
▷ VERB
1 to ask a question: *When I finally posed the question "Why?" he merely shrugged.*
ask *I wasn't the only one asking questions.*
put *He put the question to me at an unexpected moment.*
submit *The audience is invited to submit questions.*
2 to pretend to be someone else: *The police officers posed as gamblers.*
impersonate *He was once arrested for impersonating a police officer.*

P

masquerade as *She masqueraded as a doctor and fooled everyone.*
pass oneself off as *He frequently passed himself off as a lawyer.*
pretend to be *We spent the afternoon pretending to be foreign tourists.*
See also **show**

poser *See* **puzzle**

posh
▷ ADJECTIVE
INFORMAL smart, fashionable, and expensive: *a posh hotel*
classy INFORMAL *expensive cars with classy upholstery*
elegant *an elegant society ball*
exclusive *a member of the country's most exclusive club*
fashionable *fashionable restaurants*
smart *smart dinner parties*
stylish *stylish décor*
upscale *an upscale food market aimed at young professionals*

position
▷ NOUN
I the place where someone or something is: *The ship's name and position were reported to the coastguard.*
location *She knew the exact location of their headquarters.*
place *The pain is always in the same place.*
point *The pain originated from a point above his right eye.*
whereabouts *Finding her whereabouts proved surprisingly easy.*
▷ VERB
2 to put something somewhere: *Position the plants near the edge of the garden.*
arrange *Arrange the books in neat piles.*
lay out *He laid out the cards and began playing solitaire.*
locate *the best city in which to locate a business*
place *Chairs were placed in rows for the parents.*
put *She put the photograph on her desk.*
See also **appointment, attitude, fit, job, location, place, put, set, spot, state, status**

positive
▷ ADJECTIVE
I completely sure about something: *I was positive he'd known about that money.*
certain *It wasn't a balloon — I'm certain about that.*
confident *The publisher is confident of success.*

convinced *He was convinced that I was part of the problem.*
sure *It is impossible to be sure about the value of the land.*
2 providing definite proof of the truth or identity of something: *positive evidence*
clear *a clear case of mistaken identity*
clear-cut *The issue is not so clear-cut.*
conclusive *Research on the matter is far from conclusive.*
concrete *He had no concrete evidence.*
firm *There is no firm evidence to prove this.*
3 tending to emphasize what is good: *I anticipate a positive response.*
constructive *We welcome constructive criticism.*
helpful *Thanks for your helpful comments.*
See also **certain, confident, definite, favourable, optimistic, sure**

possess
▷ VERB
I to have something as a quality: *He possesses both stamina and creativity.*
be blessed with *She was blessed with a photographic memory.*
be born with *Mozart was born with perfect pitch.*
enjoy *I have always enjoyed good health.*
have *They have talent in abundance.*
2 to own something: *He was said to possess a huge fortune.*
acquire *I have acquired a new DVD player.*
control *She now controls the entire company.*
hold *to hold a university degree*
occupy *Foreign forces now occupy part of the country.*
seize *Troops have seized the airport and railway terminals.*
take over *They plan to take over another airline.*
See also **have, own**

possession
▷ NOUN
ownership of something: *How did this picture come into your possession?*
control *The restructuring involves his giving up control of the firm.*
custody *He will have custody of their two children.*
ownership *the growth of home ownership*
tenure *the professor's long tenure at the University of Prince Edward Island*

possessions
▷ PLURAL NOUN
the things owned by someone: *People had lost all their possessions.*

assets *The group had assets worth over $10 million.*

belongings *personal belongings*

effects *His children were collecting his effects.*

estate *She left her entire estate to a charity.*

property *the rightful owner of the property*

things *She told him to take all his things and not to return.*

See also **property, things**

possessor *See* **owner**

possibility

▷ NOUN

something that might be true or might happen: *the possibility of a strike*

chance *There's no chance of that happening.*

hope *We had absolutely no hope of raising the money.*

likelihood *the likelihood of infection*

odds *What are the odds of that happening?*

prospect *There is little prospect of peace.*

risk *It reduces the risk of heart disease.*

See also **chance**

possible

▷ ADJECTIVE

1 likely to happen or able to be done: *I am grateful to my teachers for making this project possible.*

attainable *I always thought promotion was attainable.*

feasible *Whether such co-operation is feasible is a matter of doubt.*

practicable *It was not practicable for the writer to attend the official opening of his play.*

viable *commercially viable products*

workable *This isn't a workable solution in most cases.*

2 likely or capable of being true or correct: *It's possible there's an explanation for all this.*

conceivable *It is conceivable that a survivor might be found.*

imaginable *a place of no imaginable strategic value*

likely *Experts say a "yes" vote is still the likely outcome.*

potential *the network's potential audience*

See also **believable, likely, potential**

possibly *See* **maybe, perhaps**

post *See* **appointment, base, job, support**

poster *See* **notice**

posterior *See* **bottom**

postpone

▷ VERB

to put off to a later time: *The visit has been postponed until tomorrow.*

adjourn *The proceedings have been adjourned until next week.*

defer *Customers often defer payments for as long as possible.*

delay *I wanted to delay my departure until June.*

put back *The news conference has been put back a couple of hours.*

put off *The club has put off the event until October.*

shelve *Sadly, the project has now been shelved.*

See also **delay, put off**

potency *See* **strength**

potential

▷ ADJECTIVE

1 possible but not yet actual: *potential sources of funding*

likely *A tied game is the likely outcome.*

possible *Her family is discussing a possible move out West.*

probable *Faulty wiring was the most probable cause of the fire.*

▷ NOUN

2 ability to achieve future success: *recognizing the potential of solar energy*

ability *You have the ability to become a good pianist.*

aptitude *a natural aptitude for drawing*

capability *the country's nuclear capability*

capacity *people's creative capacities*

power *the power of speech*

wherewithal *They didn't have the financial wherewithal to do it.*

See also **capacity, in the making, possible**

pothole *See* **pit**

pound *See* **bang, beat**

pour

▷ VERB

to flow quickly and in large quantities: *Blood was pouring from his broken nose.*

course *The tears coursed down my cheeks.*

flow *The river flowed rapidly toward the falls.*

gush *Hot water gushed out of the tap.*

run *Water was running down the walls.*

spout *a fountain that spouts water high into the air*

stream *She came in, rain streaming from her clothes and hair.*

See also **gush, rain**

poverty

▷ NOUN

the state of being very poor: *The artist died in loneliness and poverty.*

destitution *refugees living in destitution*

hardship *Many people are suffering economic hardship.*

insolvency *Several companies are on the brink of insolvency.*

want *We are fighting for freedom from want.*

poverty-stricken See poor

powdery See fine

power

▷ NOUN

1 control over people and activities: *a position of great power and influence*

ascendancy *The extremists in the political party are gaining ascendancy.*

control *She has been forced to give up control over the company.*

dominion *They truly believe they have dominion over us.*

sovereignty *the resumption of Chinese sovereignty over Hong Kong in 1997*

supremacy *The track team has re-established its supremacy.*

2 authority to do something: *the power to change the rules*

authority *The judge had no authority to order a second trial.*

authorization *I don't have the authorization to make such a decision.*

licence *He has given me licence to do the job as I see fit.*

privilege *Senior students have more privileges.*

right *the right to vote*

3 physical strength: *Power and speed are vital to success in hockey.*

brawn *He's got plenty of brains as well as brawn.*

might *They worked with all their might.*

strength *She threw it forward with all her strength.*

vigour *He shovelled the snow with lots of vigour.*

See also **capacity, control, drive, force, grip, influence, potential, strength**

powerful

▷ ADJECTIVE

1 able to control people and events: *a large, powerful country*

commanding *We're in a commanding position.*

dominant *a dominant figure in the Italian film industry*

influential *She had been influential in shaping the fashion industry.*

2 physically strong: *It's such a powerful dog.*

mighty *a mighty river*

strapping *He was a bricklayer — a big, strapping fellow.*

strong *I'm not strong enough to carry you.*

sturdy *The camera was mounted on a sturdy tripod.*

vigorous *He was a vigorous, handsome young man.*

ANTONYM **weak**

3 having a strong effect: *a powerful argument*

compelling *a compelling reason to leave*

convincing *convincing evidence*

effective *Antibiotics are effective against this organism.*

forceful *forceful action to stop the suffering*

persuasive *The debater made a persuasive case for her side.*

telling *He spoke reasonably, carefully, and with telling effect.*

See also **convincing, important, impressive, intense, violent**

powerless

▷ ADJECTIVE

unable to control or influence events: *I was powerless to do anything.*

helpless *Many people felt helpless against the violence.*

impotent *Voters rejected their impotent leader, choosing someone who could act effectively.*

incapable *He is incapable as a manager.*

See also **helpless, weak**

practicable See possible

CONFUSABLES
practicable means **doable**   **practical** means **effective**

practical

▷ ADJECTIVE

1 involving experience rather than theory: *practical suggestions for a nutritious diet*

applied *plans to put more money into applied research*

pragmatic *a pragmatic approach to the problems of the league*

2 likely to be effective: *The clothes are lightweight and practical for camping.*

functional *The design is functional but stylish.*

sensible *sensible shoes*

ANTONYM **impractical**

See also **handy, realistic, sensible, useful**

practice
▷ NOUN

1 something that people do regularly: *My usual practice is to wake up early.*
custom *I have tried to adapt to local customs.*
habit *a survey on eating habits*
method *her usual method of getting through the traffic*
routine *We had to change our daily routine.*
way *a return to the old ways of doing things*
2 regular training or exercise: *I need more practice in this area.*
drill *The teacher ran them through the drill again.*
exercise *Lack of exercise can lead to feelings of exhaustion.*
preparation *Behind any successful event lie months of preparation.*
rehearsal *rehearsals for a concert tour*
training *her busy training schedule*
See also **convention, custom, habit, procedure, routine, way**

practise
▷ VERB

1 to do something repeatedly so as to gain skill: *She practises the piano every day.*
polish *They just need to polish their technique.*
rehearse *She was in her room rehearsing her lines.*
train *He was training for the new season.*
2 to take part in the activities of a religion, craft, or custom: *Acupuncture has been practised in China for thousands of years.*
observe *We observed the holiday quietly.*

practised See **experienced**

pragmatic See **practical**

praise
▷ VERB

1 to express strong approval of someone: *Many others praised her for taking a strong stand.*
admire *All those who knew him will admire him for his work.*
applaud *They should be applauded for their courage.*
approve *Not everyone approves of her methods.*
congratulate *I must congratulate the organizers for a well-run event.*
pay tribute to *He paid tribute to his teachers.*
ANTONYM **criticize**
▷ NOUN
2 something said, written, or done to show

approval: *She is full of praise for her co-workers.*
accolade *the ultimate international accolade, the Nobel Peace Prize*
approval *an obsessive drive to gain his employer's approval*
commendation *They received a commendation from the art society.*
congratulation *I offered her my congratulations.*
tribute *The speech was a moving tribute to the coach.*
ANTONYM **criticism**
See also **approval, approve, credit, glory, honour, tribute, worship**

prank See **joke**

prattle See **babble**

pray to See **worship**

precarious See **critical, serious, unsteady**

precaution
▷ NOUN

an action intended to prevent something from happening: *taking precautions against accidents*
insurance *Farmers grew a mixture of crops as insurance against crop failure.*
preventive measure *a preventive measure against heart disease*
protection *protection against damage to buildings*
provision *People need to make provisions for their old age.*
safeguard *legislation that offers safeguards against discrimination*

preceding See **last, previous**

precious
▷ ADJECTIVE

of great value and importance: *precious jewels*
expensive *an expensive new coat*
invaluable *I gained invaluable experience that year.*
priceless *his priceless collection of antiques*
prized *These CDs are my prized possessions.*
valuable *valuable books*
ANTONYM **worthless**
See also **beloved, dear, valuable**

TYPES OF ... *PRECIPITATION*	
drizzle	shower
freezing rain	sleet
hail	snow
rain	

precise

▷ *ADJECTIVE*

exact and accurate: *We may never know the precise details.*

accurate *an accurate description of the events*

actual *The actual number of voters is higher than initially believed.*

correct *This information was correct at press time.*

exact *The exact number of winners has not been revealed.*

particular *a very particular account of events*

specific *I asked him to be more specific.*

very *Those were his very words.*

ANTONYM **vague**

See also **accurate, careful, correct, exact, fine, formal, particular, right, strict**

precisely See **exactly, prompt**

preconception See **prejudice**

predetermined See **set**

predicament

▷ *NOUN*

a difficult situation: *He found himself in a peculiar predicament.*

fix INFORMAL *I'm in quite a fix, and I don't know what to do next.*

hot water INFORMAL *His antics keep landing him in hot water.*

jam INFORMAL *We are in a real jam now.*

scrape *He's had a few scrapes with the law.*

tight spot *This was one tight spot she couldn't get out of.*

See also **fix, hole, jam, problem, state**

predict

▷ *VERB*

to say that something will happen in the future: *The opinion polls are predicting a very close vote.*

forecast *He forecasts that attendance will rise by five percent this year.*

foresee *She did not foresee any problems.*

foretell *prophets who have foretold the end of the world*

prophesy *She prophesied a bad ending for the expedition.*

prediction

▷ *NOUN*

something that is forecast in advance: *He was unwilling to make a prediction for the coming year.*

forecast *a forecast of heavy weather to come*

prophecy *a prophecy about the end of the world*

predominant See **main**

predominantly See **mainly**

pre-eminent See **supreme, top**

preface See **introduction**

prefer

▷ *VERB*

to like one thing more than another thing: *Does she prefer a particular type of music?*

be partial to *I'm quite partial to onion rings.*

favour *Both sides favour a diplomatic solution.*

go for *They went for a more contemporary approach.*

incline toward *The majority of voters are inclined toward a change in leadership.*

like better *I like the flat shoes better.*

See also **favour**

preferred See **favourite**

PREFIXES		
ante-	intra-	pseudo-
anti-	mega-	re-
auto-	micro-	self-
bi-	mid-	semi-
centi-	milli-	step-
co-	mini-	sub-
contra-	mono-	super-
de-	multi-	tele-
demi-	neo-	trans-
dis-	non-	tri-
ex-	over-	ultra-
extra-	poly-	un-
hyper-	post-	under-
in-	pre-	vice-
inter-	pro-	

prejudice

▷ *NOUN*

1 an unreasonable or unfair dislike or preference: *prejudice against workers over 55*

bias *Bias against women continues in certain industries.*

preconception *preconceptions about the sort of people who take cruises*

2 intolerance toward certain people or groups: *racial prejudice*

bigotry *religious bigotry*

chauvinism *male chauvinism*
discrimination *discrimination against certain groups of people*
racism *the fight to rid sport of racism*
sexism *sexism in the workplace*
See also **bias, colour, injustice**

prejudiced See **biased, narrow-minded**

premature See **early**

prematurely See **early**

premeditated See **deliberate**

premier See **top**

premise See **basis**

premium See **payment**

premonition

▷ NOUN
a feeling that something unpleasant is going to happen: *He had a premonition that he would die.*
foreboding *Her triumph was overshadowed by an uneasy sense of foreboding.*
funny feeling INFORMAL *I have a funny feeling something unpleasant is about to happen.*
omen *The excellent weather is a good omen for our snowmobile trip.*
See also **warning**

preoccupation See **complex, obsession**

preoccupied

▷ ADJECTIVE
totally involved with something, or deep in thought: *I am preoccupied with my tennis career.*
absorbed *She was completely absorbed in her book.*
engrossed *He didn't notice because he was too engrossed in his work.*
immersed *immersed in her studies*
oblivious *totally oblivious to everybody else*
wrapped up *She's wrapped up in her new hobby.*

preparation See **practice**

prepare See **brief**

prepared See **agreeable, ready, willing**

preposterous See **ridiculous, unbelievable**

prerequisite See **condition**

prerequisites See **essentials**

prescribed See **formal**

presence See **company**

present

▷ ADJECTIVE
1 being at a place or event: *He had been present at the meeting.*
at hand *Having the right equipment at hand is important.*
here *He was here a minute ago.*
in attendance *In attendance were several celebrities.*
there *The group of old buildings is still there today.*
ANTONYM **absent**
▷ NOUN
2 something given to someone: *a birthday present*
donation *Employees make regular donations to charity.*
gift *a birthday gift*
offering *Flowers given as a peace offering.*
▷ VERB
3 to give something to someone: *The mayor presented the prizes.*
award *For his dedication, he was awarded a medal of merit.*
bestow *The title "Student of the Year" was bestowed on her.*
donate *He frequently donates large amounts to charity.*
give *She gave me a pen for my birthday.*
grant *France has agreed to grant him political asylum.*
hand out *My job is to hand out the prizes.*
See also **current, gift, give, modern, perform, submit**

presentation See **lecture, show**

present-day See **current, modern, recent**

presently See **soon**

preservation See **upkeep**

preserve See **keep, safeguard, save**

preside See **oversee**

president See **head**

press

▷ VERB
1 to apply force or weight to something: *Press the blue button.*
compress *Poor posture compresses the body's organs.*
crush *Peel and crush the garlic.*
mash *Mash the bananas with a fork.*
push *She pushed the door open.*
squeeze *He squeezed my arm reassuringly.*
2 to try hard to persuade someone to do

P

something: *The journalist was pressed to reveal her sources.*

beg *I begged him to come back with me.*

implore *"Tell me what to do!" he implored us.*

petition *The Olympics committee petitioned the government for additional funding.*

plead *I pleaded to be allowed to go.*

pressure *He thought she was trying to pressure him.*

urge *He had urged her to come to Victoria.*

See also **clasp, insist, push, rush, urge**

press on See **advance**

pressing See **serious, urgent**

pressure See **bully, force, press, rush, strain, stress**

prestige See **glory, status**

presumably See **probably**

presume See **believe, expect, suppose**

presumed See **supposed**

pretence See **show**

pretend

▷ VERB

to claim or give the appearance of something untrue: *Sometimes the boy pretended to be asleep.*

counterfeit *the $20 bills he is alleged to have counterfeited*

fake *He faked his own death last year.*

falsify *She was charged with falsifying business records.*

feign *accused of feigning injury*

pass oneself off as *She tried to pass herself off as an actress.*

See also **fake**

pretend to be See **pose**

pretended See **mock**

pretentious

▷ ADJECTIVE

making unjustified claims to importance: *Many critics thought his work and ideas pretentious and empty.*

affected *Her affected airs didn't fool anyone.*

conceited *I thought him conceited and arrogant.*

ostentatious *an ostentatious wedding reception*

pompous *He's pompous and has a high opinion of his own capabilities.*

snobbish *a snobbish type who thinks he's better than we are*

See also **ostentatious, pompous**

pretext See **excuse**

pretty

▷ ADJECTIVE

1 attractive in a delicate way: *a very charming and very pretty girl*

attractive *an attractive face*

beautiful *a beautiful child*

cute *a cute little baby*

lovely *his lovely children*

▷ ADVERB

2 quite or rather: *He's a pretty good card player.*

fairly *Both ships are fairly new.*

kind of INFORMAL *I was kind of embarrassed about it.*

quite *It was quite hard.*

rather *She's rather vain.*

See also **attractive, cute, lovely, rather**

prevail See **triumph, win**

prevailing See **chief, common, fashionable**

prevalent See **common, popular, widespread**

prevent

▷ VERB

to stop something from happening: *the most practical way of preventing crime*

avert *A fresh tragedy was narrowly averted yesterday.*

foil *The plot was foiled by police officers.*

hinder *Research is hindered by a lack of cash.*

impede *Fallen rocks are impeding the progress of the rescue workers.*

stop *a new initiative to try to stop the strike*

thwart *Her ambition to become an artist was thwarted by failing eyesight.*

See also **bar, prohibit, stop**

preventive measure See **precaution**

previous

▷ ADJECTIVE

happening or existing before something else: *the previous year*

earlier *Her earlier works include impressive still lifes.*

former *a former president of Mexico*

one-time *the country's one-time rulers*

past *a return to the turbulence of past centuries*

preceding *This is examined in detail in the preceding chapter.*

prior *I can't make it. I have a prior engagement.*

See also **last, past**

previously See **before**

price

▷ NOUN

1 the amount of money paid for something: *a sharp increase in the price of gasoline*
amount *I was asked to pay the full amount.*
charge *a delivery charge of $25*
cost *the cost of a loaf of bread*
fee *the annual membership fee*
figure *A figure of $200 was mentioned.*
value *The value of the company rose to $5.5 billion.*

▷ VERB

2 to fix the price or value of something: *I just can't imagine why it has been priced at this level.*
appraise *They had their antique toy collection appraised.*
cost *We hope it won't cost too much.*
estimate *Their personal riches were estimated at $368 million.*
put a price on *The auctioneer has refused to put a price on the value of the painting.*
value *I had my jewellery valued for insurance purposes.*
See also **charge, cost, rate, value**

priceless *See* **precious**

pricey *See* **dear, expensive**

pride

▷ NOUN

1 a feeling of satisfaction about your achievements: *We take pride in offering you the highest standards in the industry.*
delight *She took obvious delight in proving her critics wrong.*
pleasure *Our first win gave me great pleasure.*
satisfaction *His success was a great source of satisfaction to him.*
2 an excessively high opinion of yourself: *His pride may still be his downfall.*
arrogance *She has a swaggering arrogance.*
conceit *She knew, without conceit, that she was considered a genius.*
egotism *typical showbiz egotism*
smugness *a trace of smugness in his voice*
snobbery *intellectual snobbery*
vanity *her vanity about her long hair*
ANTONYM **humility**
See also **conceit, pick**

prim

▷ ADJECTIVE

behaving very correctly and easily shocked by anything rude: *We tend to assume our great-grandparents were very prim and proper.*
proper *He was very pompous and proper.*
prudish *I'm not prudish, but I think those*

photos are disgusting.
puritanical *a puritanical attitude*
straitlaced *He was very straitlaced and narrow-minded.*

primarily *See* **mainly**

primary *See* **chief, main, principal**

prime

▷ ADJECTIVE

1 main or most important: *a prime cause of traffic accidents*
chief *The job went to one of her chief rivals.*
leading *a leading industrial nation*
main *the city's main tourist area*
principal *our principal source of income*
2 of the best quality: *prime beef*
best *He'll have the best care.*
choice *our choicest chocolates*
first-rate *a first-rate sailor*
select *With that historic win, he now joins a select group of golfers.*
superior *superior coffee beans*
See also **brief, chief, first, foremost, main, principal, select, top**

primed *See* **ready**

primeval *See* **early, first**

primitive

▷ ADJECTIVE

very simple or basic: *a primitive shack*
crude *crude stone carvings*
rough *a rough wooden table*
rude *He constructed a rude cabin for himself.*
rudimentary *a rudimentary shelter*
simple *a simple cottage*
See also **crude, early**

principal

▷ ADJECTIVE

main or most important: *His principal concern is that of winning the school election.*
chief *her chief reason for withdrawing*
first *The first duty of this government is to tackle poverty.*
foremost *one of the world's foremost chess players*
main *What are the main differences between them?*
major *the major factor in her decision*
primary *the primary cause of his problems*
prime *Police will see me as the prime suspect!*
See also **chief, essential, first, foremost, head, leader, leading, main, prime, supreme, top**

principally *See* **mainly**

P

principle

▷ *NOUN*

1 a set of moral rules guiding personal conduct: *a person of principle*
conscience *It's simply a matter of conscience.*
integrity *He has always been a man of integrity.*
morals *public morals*
scruples *no moral scruples*
sense of duty *She did it out of a sense of duty to her company.*
2 a general rule or scientific law: *the basic principles of capitalism*
axiom *the long-held axiom that education leads to higher income*
canon *the canons of political economy*
doctrine *religious doctrine*
fundamental *the fundamentals of astronomy*
law *the laws of motion*
See also **basis, belief, ideal**

principles *See* **conscience, standards**

print *See* **publish**

prior *See* **previous**

prison

▷ *NOUN*

a building where criminals are kept in captivity: *a high-security prison*
dungeon *The castle's dungeons haven't been used for centuries.*
jail *Three prisoners escaped from the jail.*
penal institution *Thirty years in a penal institution is indeed a harsh penalty.*
penitentiary *Ontario's Kingston Penitentiary*
See also **jail**

prisoner

▷ *NOUN*

someone kept in prison or captivity: *top-security prisoners*
captive *the difficulties of spending four months as a captive*
convict *convicts serving life sentences*
hostage *negotiations to release the hostages*

privacy *See* **solitude**

private

▷ *ADJECTIVE*

1 for few people rather than people in general: *a private bathroom*
exclusive *Many of these clothes are exclusive to our stores.*
individual *Divide the vegetables among four individual dishes.*

personal *It's for my own personal use.*
special *her own special diet*
2 taking place among a small number of people: *a private wedding*
clandestine *a clandestine meeting with the spy*
confidential *confidential information about my private life*
secret *a secret friendship*
ANTONYM **public**
See also **own, personal**

privilege *See* **power**

prize

▷ *NOUN*

1 a reward given to the winner of something: *first prize at the piano competition*
accolade *the ultimate international accolade, the Nobel Peace Prize*
award *a Governor General's award for children's literature*
honour *He was showered with honours — among them an Oscar.*
trophy *They haven't won a trophy since 1991.*
▷ *ADJECTIVE*
2 of the highest quality or standard: *a prize bull*
award-winning *an award-winning restaurant*
first-rate *a first-rate thriller writer*
outstanding *an outstanding horse*
top *Canada's top curler*
▷ *VERB*
3 to value highly: *These ornaments are prized by collectors.*
cherish *We cherish our independence.*
esteem *one of the country's most esteemed awards*
treasure *She treasures her memories of those joyous days.*
value *I value the work he gives me.*
See also **appreciate, reward, treasure, value**

prized *See* **dear, precious, valuable**

probability

▷ *NOUN*

the likelihood of something happening: *the probability of a serious earthquake*
chances *The chances of success for the team are good.*
likelihood *the likelihood of infection*
odds *The odds are that you are going to win.*
prospect *the prospect for peace in the Middle East*
See also **chance**

probable

▷ ADJECTIVE

likely to be true or to happen: *a misunderstanding about the probable cost*
apparent *There is no apparent reason for the crime.*
feasible *Whether this is feasible is a matter of doubt.*
in the cards *A promotion is in the cards.*
likely *Further delays are likely.*
plausible *a plausible explanation*
ANTONYM **improbable**
See also **believable, likely, potential**

probably

▷ ADVERB

in all likelihood: *The wedding is probably going to be in late August.*
doubtless *He will doubtless try to change my mind.*
in all probability *Today's victory will, in all probability, earn Canada the title.*
likely *The entire surplus will most likely be handed over.*
presumably *The knife is presumably the weapon.*

probe *See* **investigate, question**

problem

▷ NOUN

1 an unsatisfactory situation causing difficulties: *the economic problems of the city*
difficulty *This company is facing great difficulties.*
predicament *the once-great club's current predicament*
quandary *We're in a quandary over our vacation plans.*
trouble *I had trouble getting out of bed this morning.*
2 a puzzle that needs to be solved: *a mathematical problem*
conundrum *The conundrum was who had left the parcel at our door.*
puzzle *The findings have presented astronomers with a puzzle.*
riddle *the riddle of the birth of the universe*
See also **business, complex, difficulty, drawback, issue, puzzle, snag, trouble**

problematic *See* **tricky**

procedure

▷ NOUN

the correct or usual way of doing something: *He did not follow the correct procedure in applying for a permit.*
method *new teaching methods*
policy *It is our policy to prosecute shoplifters.*
practice *a public inquiry into bank practices*
process *the production process*

strategy *a strategy for controlling malaria*
system *an efficient filing system*
See also **course, measure, method, process, routine, system, way**

proceed

▷ VERB

1 to start doing or continue to do something: *I had no idea how to proceed.*
begin *He stood up and began to move about the room.*
carry on *"May I start with a couple of questions?" — "Carry on."*
continue *I need some advice before I can continue with this task.*
get under way *Rehearsals got under way last week.*
go on *Go on with your work.*
start *I started to follow him up the stairs.*
ANTONYM **cease**
2 to move in a particular direction: *She proceeded along the hallway.*
advance *I advanced slowly, one step at a time.*
continue *She continued rapidly up the path.*
go on *They went on through the forest.*
make your way *He made his way to the plaza.*
progress *She progressed slowly along the coast in an easterly direction.*
travel *You can travel to Moncton tomorrow.*
See also **advance, go, journey, start**

CONFUSABLES

proceed means **move forward**
precede means **go before**

P

proceedings *See* **case**

proceeds *See* **profit**

process

▷ NOUN

1 a method of doing or producing something: *The building process was spread over three years.*
course of action *It is important that we take the right course of action.*
means *This is a means to fight crime.*
method *new teaching methods*
procedure *the correct procedure for applying for a permit*
system *an efficient filing system*
▷ VERB
2 to deal with or treat something: *Your application is being processed.*
deal with *the way that stores deal with complaints*

dispose of *They disposed of the problem quickly.*
handle *She didn't know how to handle the problem.*
take care of *They left it to me to try and take care of the problem.*
See also **action, manufacture, procedure**

processed See **refined**

procession See **parade**

proclaim See **announce, declare**

proclamation See **statement**

procure See **acquire, buy, get, obtain, secure**

prod See **dig, poke**

produce
▷ VERB
1 to make something: *clothing produced from the finest materials*
construct *an inner frame constructed from timber*
create *The doll was created from odds and ends.*
invent *Canadian Gideon Sundback invented the zipper.*
make *One of my jobs was to make the coffee.*
manufacture *They manufacture plastic products.*
2 to bring out something so it can be seen or discussed: *To rent a car, you must produce a driver's licence.*
advance *Many new theories have been advanced recently.*
bring forward *We will bring forward new proposals.*
bring to light *new evidence brought to light by the police*
put forward *She has put forward new peace proposals.*
See also **breed, bring, bring about, cause, compose, lead to, make, manufacture, occasion, product, provoke**

product
▷ NOUN
something that is made to be sold: *Many household products give off noxious fumes.*
commodity *basic commodities such as bread and milk*
goods *imported goods*
merchandise *The club sells a wide range of merchandise.*
produce *locally grown produce*
See also **result**

production See **making, manufacture**

productive
▷ ADJECTIVE
1 producing a large number of things: *Training makes workers highly productive.*
fertile *a product of his fertile imagination*
fruitful *Everyone agreed that the meeting had been fruitful.*
prolific *She is a prolific writer of novels and short stories.*
ANTONYM **unproductive**
2 bringing favourable results: *I'm hopeful the talks will be productive.*
constructive *constructive criticism*
useful *We made some progress during a useful exchange of ideas.*
valuable *The experience was highly valuable.*
worthwhile *It had been a worthwhile discussion.*
ANTONYM **unproductive**
See also **economic, efficient, fertile**

profess See **claim, declare**

profession
▷ NOUN
a job that requires advanced education or training: *a teacher by profession*
business *May I ask you what business you're in?*
career *a career in journalism*
occupation *her new occupation as a journalist*
See also **job, trade, work**

professional See **expert, skilled**

professionally See **well**

professor See **teacher**

proficiency See **skill**

proficient
▷ ADJECTIVE
able to do something well: *They tend to be proficient in foreign languages.*
able *an able young rider*
accomplished *an accomplished photographer*
adept *an adept guitar player*
capable *a very capable speaker*
competent *a competent public servant*
efficient *a team of efficient workers*
skilful *In that job, you have to be skilful at managing people.*
skilled *a highly skilled machinist*
ANTONYM **incompetent**
See also **capable, expert, practical, skilful, skilled**

profit

▷ *NOUN*

I money gained in business or trade: *The bank made pre-tax profits of $3.5 million.*
earnings *his earnings as an accountant*
proceeds *The proceeds from the concert will go to charity.*
revenue *tax revenue*
surplus *Japan's trade surplus*
takings *the restaurant's weekly takings*
ANTONYM **loss**

▷ *VERB*

2 to benefit from something: *He profited shamefully at the expense of my family.*
capitalize on *Don't capitalize on someone else's misfortune.*
exploit *to exploit child labour*
make the most of *Happiness is the ability to make the most of what you have.*
take advantage of *Take advantage of your time off to catch up on your reading.*
See also **benefit, gain**

profitable

▷ *ADJECTIVE*

making a profit: *Our new venture has proved highly profitable.*
economical *goods that are economical to produce*
moneymaking *moneymaking enterprises*
productive *the need to make these industries more productive*
viable *businesses that are no longer viable*
See also **helpful, successful**

profits See **income**

profound See **deep, extreme, heavy, intense, serious**

program

▷ *NOUN*

I a planned series of events: *We attended several training programs.*
agenda *This is sure to be an item on the agenda again next week.*
schedule *We both have such hectic schedules.*
timetable *We've finally managed to agree on a timetable for discussions.*
2 a broadcast on radio or television: *local news programs*
broadcast *a broadcast by the prime minister*
show *my favourite TV show*
See also **routine**

progress

▷ *NOUN*

I improvement or development: *progress in the fight against cancer*
advance *dramatic advances in road safety*
breakthrough *a breakthrough in their research*
headway *The police are making little headway in the investigation.*
improvement *considerable room for improvement*

▷ *VERB*

2 to become more advanced or skilful: *His piano playing is progressing well.*
advance *She has advanced to another level.*
blossom *In just a few years, skateboarding has blossomed into an international event.*
develop *workshops designed to develop acting skills*
improve *Their Spanish has improved enormously.*
See also **advance, develop, improve, improvement, proceed**

progression See **sequence, spread**

progressive See **gradual**

prohibit

▷ *VERB*

to forbid something or make it illegal: *a law that prohibits parking during certain hours*
ban *to ban smoking in all offices*
forbid *The country's constitution forbids the military use of nuclear energy.*
outlaw *The country outlawed child labour.*
prevent *She was prevented from participating in the race.*
ANTONYM **allow**
See also **ban, forbid, veto**

prohibited See **illegal**

prohibition See **ban, veto**

project See **enterprise, extend, undertaking**

proliferate See **multiply, spread**

proliferation See **spread**

prolific See **fertile, productive**

prologue See **introduction**

prolong See **lengthen**

prolonged See **continuous**

prominence See **emphasis, fame**

prominent

▷ *ADJECTIVE*

I important: *a prominent journalist*
eminent *an eminent scientist*
famous *Canada's most famous modern artist*
important *an important figure in the media*
notable *a list of notable astronomers*

P

noted *a noted Canadian author*
renowned *Frederick Banting, the renowned research scientist*
well-known *He liked to surround himself with well-known people.*
2 very noticeable, or sticking out a long way: *a prominent feature of the landscape*
conspicuous *a conspicuous landmark*
eye-catching *She wore an eye-catching gown to the awards ceremony.*
jutting *a jutting chin*
noticeable *That pimple is hardly noticeable.*
obvious *His cultural roots are most obvious in his poetry.*
pronounced *The exhibition has a pronounced Western theme.*
striking *a striking aspect of these statistics*
See also **leading**

promise

▷ VERB
1 to say that you will definitely do or not do something: *I promise not to be back too late.*
assure *She assured me that she would deal with the problem.*
give your word *He had given us his word he would go on the hike with us.*
guarantee *Most countries guarantee the right to free education.*
pledge *They have pledged to support the team.*
vow *I vowed that someday I would finish writing the book.*
2 to show signs of: *This promised to be a very long night.*
hint at *The child's talent hints at a bright future.*
indicate *His early work indicates an interest in abstract art.*
show signs of *Already, she shows signs of musical talent.*
▷ NOUN
3 an undertaking to do or not do something: *If you make a promise, you should keep it.*
assurance *He gave written assurance that he would start work at once.*
guarantee *They can give no guarantee that they will fulfill their obligations.*
pledge *a pledge to step up co-operation between the two countries*
undertaking *an undertaking that requires constant effort*
vow *marriage vows*
See also **bond, guarantee, oath, prospect, word**

promote

▷ VERB
1 to encourage the progress or success of something: *All attempts to promote interest in putting on a school musical have failed.*
back *She backed the new initiative enthusiastically.*
support *He thanked everyone who had supported him.*
2 to encourage the sale of a product by advertising: *She's in Europe promoting her new movie.*
advertise *She is contracted to advertise their beauty products.*
plug INFORMAL *He appeared on the radio program to plug his latest book.*
publicize *to publicize a book*
3 to raise someone to a higher rank or position: *He has been promoted twice in two years.*
elevate *She was elevated to the position of assistant coach.*
upgrade *He was upgraded to supervisor.*
See also **advertise, advocate, back, champion, publicize, support**

promotion *See* **publicity**

prompt

▷ VERB
1 to make someone decide to do something: *The uncertain economy has prompted consumers to stop buying new cars.*
cause *What caused you to leave?*
induce *Many teachers were induced to take early retirement.*
inspire *These herbs will inspire you to try all sorts of recipes.*
motivate *How do you motivate people to work hard?*
spur *What spurs these people to risk their lives?*
2 to encourage someone to say something: *"What was that you were saying about a guided tour?" he prompted her.*
coax *"Tell us what happened next," he coaxed me.*
remind *"You stopped in the middle of your story," I reminded him.*
▷ ADJECTIVE
3 done without any delay: *a serious condition that needs prompt treatment*
immediate *These incidents had an immediate effect.*
instant *He took an instant dislike to the customer.*
instantaneous *This would result in his instantaneous dismissal.*
quick *hoping for a quick end to the dispute*
rapid *their rapid response to the situation*

swift *Make a swift decision.*
See also **drive, hasty, instant, motivate, occasion, provoke, punctual, quick, swift**

promptly
▷ *ADVERB*
exactly at the time mentioned: *He showed up for the interview promptly at ten.*
exactly *He arrived at exactly five o'clock.*
on the dot *At nine o'clock on the dot, they have breakfast.*
precisely *The meeting began at precisely 4:00 p.m.*
sharp *She planned to get up at 8:00 sharp.*
See also **immediately**

prone
▷ *ADJECTIVE*
1 having a tendency to be affected by or do something: *He is prone to depression.*
disposed *I might have been disposed to like him in other circumstances.*
given *I am not very given to emotional displays.*
inclined *Nobody felt inclined to argue with her.*
liable *equipment that is liable to break*
susceptible *She's very susceptible to colds.*
2 lying flat and face downward: *We were lying prone on the grass.*
face down *He was lying face down on his bed.*
prostrate *The injured jockey lay prostrate on the ground.*

prong *See* **point**

pronounce *See* **declare, issue**

pronounced *See* **prominent, significant**

proof
▷ *NOUN*
evidence that confirms that something is true or exists: *We were asked for proof of our age.*
confirmation *further confirmation that this will be her last season*
evidence *To date there is no evidence to support this theory.*
testimony *His testimony was an important element in the prosecution's case.*
verification *verification of her story*

prop *See* **support**

prop up *See* **support**

propagate *See* **breed, circulate**

propel *See* **drive**

propensity *See* **tendency**

proper
▷ *ADJECTIVE*
1 correct or most suitable: *the proper course of action*
appropriate *a smart outfit appropriate to the job*
apt *an apt title for the book*
correct *the correct way to do things*
fitting *His speech was a fitting end to a bitter campaign.*
right *the right person for the job*
suitable *She had no other dress suitable for the occasion.*
ANTONYM **improper**
2 accepted or conventional: *It seemed the proper thing to do.*
accepted *the accepted way of doing things*
conventional *conventional surgical methods*
orthodox *orthodox police methods*
See also **appropriate, correct, decent, fair, fitting, prim, respectable, right, suitable**

property
▷ *NOUN*
1 the things that belong to someone: *her personal property*
assets *The company has assets of $3.5 billion.*
belongings *I collected my belongings and left.*
effects *A week following the funeral, he sorted his father's personal effects.*
estate *His estate was valued at $150 000.*
possessions *People had lost their homes and all their possessions.*
2 a characteristic or quality: *Mint is said to have powerful healing properties.*
attribute *a normal attribute of human behaviour*
characteristic *their physical characteristics*
feature *a feature of the local culture*
hallmark *The robbery had the hallmarks of a professional crime.*
quality *mature people with leadership qualities*
trait *Creativity is a human trait.*
See also **attribute, characteristic, feature, land, possessions, quality**

prophecy *See* **prediction**

prophesy *See* **predict**

proportion
▷ *NOUN*
part of an amount or group: *a tiny proportion of the population*

P

percentage *It has a high percentage of protein.*

quota *Spain's fishing quota has been cut.*

segment *a fast-growing segment of the economy*

share *I pay a share of the cable bill.*

See also **measure**

proportions *See* **size**

proposal *See* **plan, suggestion**

propose *See* **aim, intend, nominate, submit, suggest, vote**

proposition *See* **offer, suggestion**

proprietor *See* **owner**

prospect

▷ *NOUN*

expectation or something anticipated: *There was no prospect of going home.*

expectation *The hotel was being renovated in expectation of a tourist boom.*

hope *There is little hope of improvement now.*

outlook *Officials say the outlook for next year is gloomy.*

promise *New Year's Day brought the promise of better things to come.*

See also **chance, possibility, probability**

prospective *See* **future**

prospects *See* **outlook**

prosper *See* **flourish, succeed, thrive**

prosperity *See* **success, wealth**

prosperous *See* **rich, wealthy**

prostrate *See* **prone**

protect

▷ *VERB*

to prevent someone or something from being harmed: *Bank tellers are protected by security barrier shields.*

defend *I had to defend myself against the attack.*

guard *Soldiers guarded the border crossing.*

safeguard *action to safeguard the ozone layer*

shelter *The beach is sheltered by the harbour.*

shield *Tall trees shielded us from the wind.*

See also **defend, guard, safeguard, save, shelter, take care of**

protected *See* **immune, safe, secure**

protection

▷ *NOUN*

something that protects: *a diet believed to*

offer protection against some diseases

barrier *a flood barrier*

buffer *Keep savings as a buffer against unexpected expenses.*

cover *The cave provided cover during the storm.*

safeguard *a safeguard against weeds*

shelter *We waited in the bus shelter.*

See also **defence, precaution, safeguard, safety, shelter**

protector *See* **champion**

protest

▷ *VERB*

1 to disagree with someone or object to something: *She protested that the new hours of work were unfair.*

complain *People always complain that the big banks are unhelpful.*

disagree *I disagree with the school board's policy on that issue.*

disapprove *Her parents disapproved of the way she dressed.*

object *We objected strongly but were outvoted.*

oppose *They opposed the war on humanitarian grounds.*

▷ *NOUN*

2 a strong objection: *The council has ignored their protests by granting a building permit.*

complaint *the way that banks deal with complaints*

objection *I questioned the logic of his objections.*

outcry *The incident caused an international outcry.*

See also **agitate, complaint, grumble, object, objection**

protestation *See* **declaration**

protocol *See* **ceremony**

prototype *See* **example, ideal**

protrude *See* **bulge, extend**

protrusion *See* **bulge**

proud

▷ *ADJECTIVE*

feeling pleasure or satisfaction: *I was proud of our players today.*

gratified *He was gratified by the audience's response.*

honoured *I am honoured to work with her.*

pleased *I was pleased to call him my friend.*

See also **haughty, stuck-up, vain**

prove

▷ *VERB*

to provide evidence that something is

definitely true: *History will prove him to have been right all along.*

ascertain *They had ascertained that she was not a spy.*
confirm *X-rays confirmed that he had not broken any bones.*
demonstrate *You have to demonstrate that you are reliable.*
establish *The autopsy established the cause of death.*
verify *I can verify that it takes about 30 seconds.*
ANTONYM **disprove**
See also **confirm, show**

prove false *See* **disprove**

proverb *See* **saying**

provide
▷ VERB
to make something available to someone: *I'll be glad to provide a copy of this.*
contribute *Canada agreed to contribute peacekeepers to the area.*
equip *The climbers were equipped with a supply of oxygen.*
furnish *They'll be able to furnish you with the rest of the details.*
outfit *They outfitted us with camping gear.*
supply *the blood vessels supplying oxygen to the brain*
See also **equip, give, issue, supply**

providence *See* **fate**

province *See* **field, land, range, territory**

provision *See* **condition, precaution**

provisional *See* **temporary**

provisions *See* **food, supplies, terms**

proviso *See* **condition, terms**

provoke
▷ VERB
1 to try to make someone angry: *I didn't want to do anything to provoke him.*
anger *It's important not to anger her.*
annoy *You're just trying to annoy me.*
enrage *He enraged the group by going back on the agreement.*
goad *My little brother was always goading me.*
insult *I didn't mean to insult you.*
irritate *If you go on irritating that dog, it'll bite you.*
tease *I'm sorry, I shouldn't tease you like that.*
2 to cause an unpleasant reaction: *His comments have provoked an unexpected response.*

cause *These policies are likely to cause problems.*
evoke *The program has evoked a storm of protest.*
produce *The decision produced a furious reaction among fans.*
prompt *The allegations prompted an indignant response from the accused.*
rouse *This roused a feeling of rebellion in him.*
set off *Aftershocks from the earthquake set off new fears.*
spark *a political crisis sparked by a minor incident*
See also **bring about, cause, excite, incite, motivate, occasion**

proxy *See* **replacement, representative, substitute**

prudence *See* **caution, common sense, economy**

prudent *See* **careful, economical, sensible, thrifty**

prudish *See* **prim**

pry
▷ VERB
to try to find out about someone else's private business: *We do not want people prying into our business.*
interfere *I wish everyone would stop interfering and just leave me alone.*
intrude *The press was intruding into my personal life.*
poke your nose in INFORMAL *Who asked you to poke your nose in?*
snoop INFORMAL *He was snooping around the hotel room.*

prying *See* **nosy**

psyche *See* **mind, personality**

public
▷ NOUN
1 people in general: *the public's confidence in health care*
masses *bringing the Internet to the masses*
nation *The prime minister spoke to the nation.*
people *the will of the people*
populace *a large proportion of the populace*
society *a menace to society*
▷ ADJECTIVE
2 relating to people in general: *public support for the idea*
civic *a sense of civic pride*
general *The project should raise general awareness about the issue.*

P

popular *popular support for the idea*
universal *the universal outrage at the crime*
▷ ADJECTIVE
3 provided for everyone to use or open to anyone: *public transit*
communal *a communal dining room*
community *a local community centre*
open to the public *Part of the historic jail is now open to the public.*
universal *universal health care*
ANTONYM **private**
See also **people**

publication *See* **book**

publicity
▷ NOUN
information or advertisements about an item or event: *The book's publicity campaign included television and newspaper interviews.*
advertising *Those articles are little more than free advertising for the movie.*
plug INFORMAL *The interview was an unashamed plug for her new CD.*
promotion *They've spent a lot of money on advertising and promotion.*

publicize
▷ VERB
to advertise something or make it widely known: *The author appeared on TV to publicize her book.*
advertise *The launch of the DVD has been advertised on TV.*
plug INFORMAL *another celebrity plugging his latest book*
promote *a tour to promote her second solo album*
See also **advertise, promote**

publish
▷ VERB
to make a piece of writing available for reading: *We publish a range of titles.*
bring out *The newspapers all brought out special editions.*
print *a letter printed in the* Free Press *yesterday*
See also **release**

puerile *See* **childish, frivolous**

puff *See* **gasp**

puffed up *See* **pompous**

pull
▷ VERB
1 to draw an object toward you: *a wooden plough pulled by oxen*
drag *She dragged her chair toward the table.*
draw *He drew his chair closer to the fire.*

haul *A crane was used to haul the car out of the stream.*
tow *They threatened to tow away my car.*
tug *She tugged his thick hair.*
yank *She yanked open the drawer.*
ANTONYM **push**
▷ NOUN
2 the attraction or influence of something: *The pull of Mexico was too strong to resist.*
attraction *The attraction of Hollywood began to pall.*
lure *The lure of rural life is as strong as ever.*
magnetism *the sheer magnetism of his presence*
See also **attract, draw, lure, tug**

INFORMALLY SPEAKING

pull down: receive as a salary
pull for: give help to
pull off: successfully complete

---

pull back *See* **retreat**

pull out *See* **extract, withdraw**

pull through *See* **survive**

pull together *See* **co-operate, unite**

pull up *See* **halt**

pulse *See* **rhythm**

pump *See* **drain**

punctual
▷ ADJECTIVE
1 arriving or leaving at the correct time: *The most punctual airline last year was Swissair.*
in good time *It is now 8 a.m., and we are leaving in good time.*
on time *I'm generally early or on time for an appointment.*
prompt *We expect you to be prompt for all your classes.*

TYPES OF ... *PUNCTUATION*

apostrophe	exclamation mark
asterisk	hyphen
bracket	period
colon	question mark
comma	semicolon
dash	quotation marks

---

puncture *See* **burst, leak, pierce**

pungent *See* **sour**

punish
▷ VERB
to make someone suffer a penalty for some misbehaviour: *The child was punished for teasing the puppy.*
discipline *He was disciplined by his*

company, but not dismissed.

grounded *Her parents grounded her for two weeks.*

penalize *The player was penalized for fighting on the ice.*

rap someone's knuckles *The company got its knuckles rapped for this advertisement.*

sentence *He was found guilty and will be sentenced later.*

throw the book at *The Olympic committee seems certain to throw the book at him.*

punishment
▷ *NOUN*

a penalty for a crime or offence: *a punishment that fits the crime*

penalty *Canada abolished the death penalty completely in 1998.*

retribution *He didn't want any further involvement for fear of retribution.*

puny
▷ *ADJECTIVE*

very small and weak: *It's hard to believe he was a puny child.*

feeble *feeling old and feeble*

frail *She lay in bed looking frail.*

sickly *He has been a sickly child.*

skinny *a skinny little kid*

weak *His arms and legs were weak.*

See also **weak**

pupil *See* **student**

purchase *See* **buy**

purchaser *See* **customer**

pure
▷ *ADJECTIVE*

1 clean and free from harmful substances: *The water is pure enough to drink.*

clean *Tiled kitchen floors are easy to keep clean.*

germ-free *a germ-free environment*

pasteurized *The milk is pasteurized to kill bacteria.*

spotless *They kept the kitchen spotless.*

sterilized *sterilized surgical equipment*

ANTONYM **impure**

2 complete and total: *a matter of pure luck*

absolute *You're talking absolute nonsense.*

complete *complete and utter rubbish*

outright *an outright rejection of the deal*

sheer *acts of sheer desperation*

unmitigated *Last year's crop was an unmitigated disaster.*

utter *This, of course, is utter nonsense.*

See also **absolute, innocent, neat, refined, sheer, utter**

purely *See* **only**

purified *See* **clean, refined**

puritanical *See* **prim**

SHADES OF ... *PURPLE*	
amethyst	lilac
aubergine	magenta
gentian	mauve
heather	mulberry
heliotrope	plum
indigo	puce
lavender	violet

purpose
▷ *NOUN*

the reason for something: *What is the purpose of this meeting?*

aim *the aim of the policy*

function *Their main function is to provide guidance.*

intention *The intention of the plan is to encourage faster sales.*

object *the object of the exercise*

point *I don't see the point of it.*

reason *What is the real reason for the delay?*

on purpose
▷ *ADVERB*

deliberately: *Did you do that on purpose?*

by design *The pair met often — at first by chance, but later by design.*

deliberately *It looks as if the fire was started deliberately.*

intentionally *He intentionally revealed the secret.*

knowingly *I've never knowingly hurt anyone.*

purposely *They are purposely withholding information.*

See also **function, goal, intention, object, point, reason, use, will**

purposeful *See* **determined**

purposely *See* **on purpose**

pursue *See* **chase, follow**

pursuit *See* **activity, interest**

push
▷ *VERB*

1 to apply force to something in order to move it: *She pushed the door open.*

press *He pressed his back against the door.*

ram *He rammed the key into the lock.*

shove *He shoved her out of the path of the oncoming car.*

thrust *She thrust me aside and left the room.*

ANTONYM **pull**

P

2 to persuade someone to do something: *They tried to push me into playing street hockey.*

encourage *She encouraged me to stick to the diet.*

persuade *They persuaded him to moderate his views.*

press *They pressed him to make a decision.*

urge *He had urged her to come to Regina.*

See also **advertise, agitate, campaign, drive, press, rush, stick, stuff**

INFORMALLY SPEAKING

push around: treat roughly or with contempt
pushed for: limited by some lack
push for: promote strongly

---

pushy
▷ *ADJECTIVE*
INFORMAL unpleasantly forceful and determined: *a pushy salesperson*

aggressive *a very aggressive business executive*

ambitious *You have to be ambitious to make it in this business.*

assertive *I used to be shy, but I'm becoming more assertive.*

bossy *She remembers being a rather bossy little child.*

forceful *He has a forceful personality.*

forward *He's extremely forward, asking rather personal questions.*

obtrusive *Her personality is strong, though not obtrusive.*

puss See **cat**

pussy See **cat**

pussycat See **cat**

put
▷ *VERB*
1 to place something somewhere: *She put the photograph on the desk.*

deposit *On his way out, he deposited a glass in front of me.*

lay *Lay a sheet of newspaper on the floor.*

place *He placed it in the inside pocket of his jacket.*

position *Plants were carefully positioned in the lobby.*

rest *She rested her arms on the back of the chair.*

2 to express something: *I think you put that very well.*

phrase *I would have phrased it quite differently.*

word *You misinterpreted his letter, or else he worded it poorly.*

See also **express, insert, lay, place, pose, position, set, stick**

put across See **express**

put back See **postpone, put off**

put by See **reserve, save**

put down
▷ *VERB*
1 to criticize someone and make them appear foolish: *Racist jokes come from wanting to put down other people.*

belittle *The coach has a habit of belittling the players in public.*

criticize *She rarely criticized any of her children.*

find fault *I wish you wouldn't find fault with me so often.*

humiliate *His brother humiliated him in front of his friends.*

2 to kill an animal that is ill or dangerous: *The judge ordered the dog to be put down immediately.*

destroy *The horse had to be destroyed.*

kill *Animals should be killed humanely.*

put out of its misery *The bird was so badly injured I decided to put it out of its misery.*

put to sleep *Take the dog to the vet's and have her put to sleep.*

See also **attack, criticize, crush, deposit, humiliate, insult**

put forward See **produce, submit**

put off
▷ *VERB*
to delay something: *The House of Commons has put off the vote until next month.*

defer *Customers often defer payment for as long as possible.*

delay *She wants to delay the wedding.*

postpone *The visit has been postponed indefinitely.*

put back *The news conference has been put back a couple of hours.*

put on ice *The decision has been put on ice until October.*

reschedule *Since I'll be away, I'd like to reschedule the meeting.*

See also **delay, discourage, postpone**

put on See **perform, wear**

put out See **eliminate, publish, release, trouble**

put through See **subject**

put to sleep See **hypnotize, put down**

put together See **assemble, construct**

put up with

▷ *VERB*

to tolerate something disagreeable: *They won't put up with a return to the bad old days.*

abide *I can't abide arrogant people.*

bear *He can't bear to talk about it.*

stand *She cannot stand being late.*

stand for *We won't stand for it any more.*

stomach *He could not stomach violence.*

tolerate *She can no longer tolerate the position she is in.*

See also **tolerate**

puzzle

▷ *VERB*

1 to perplex and confuse: *There was something about her that puzzled me.*

baffle *An apple tree producing square fruit is baffling experts.*

bewilder *His silence bewildered her.*

confuse *Her sudden appearance surprised and confused him.*

mystify *The audience was mystified by the plot.*

stump *I was stumped by an unexpected question.*

▷ *NOUN*

2 a game or question that requires a lot of thought to solve: *a crossword puzzle*

brainteaser *It took me ages to solve that brainteaser.*

problem *a mathematical problem*

riddle *See if you can answer this riddle.*

See also **confuse, mystery, problem, wonder**

puzzled *See* **confused**

puzzling *See* **confusing, funny, hard, tricky**

P

Qq

quack See **fraud**

quail See **cower**

quake See **shake**

qualification

▷ NOUN

1 a skill or achievement: *Her qualifications are impressive.*
ability *a man of considerable abilities*
accomplishment *I was proud of my sister's accomplishments.*
achievement *the highest academic achievement*
capability *Her capabilities were not fully appreciated.*
quality *his leadership qualities*
skill *a skill you can use*
2 something added to make a statement less strong: *The argument is not true without qualification.*
condition *There were several conditions to her offer.*
exception *a major exception to this general argument*
modification *to consider modifications to his proposal*
reservation *people whose work I admire without reservation*
See also **condition**

qualify

▷ VERB

to pass the tests necessary for an activity: *She qualified as a doctor 20 years ago.*
be certified *They wanted to be certified as divers.*
become licensed *You can become licensed only by completing an accredited course.*
graduate *She graduated as a physiotherapist.*
See also **pass**

quality

▷ NOUN

1 the measure of how good something is: *The quality of food is very poor.*
calibre *a man of your calibre*
distinction *a chef of great distinction*
grade *top-grade meat and poultry*
merit *a work of real merit*
value *He set a high value upon their friendship.*
worth *a person's true worth*
2 a characteristic of something: *These qualities are essential for success.*
aspect *every aspect of our lives*
characteristic *their physical characteristics*

feature *the most striking feature of his work*
mark *the mark of a great composer*
property *the magnetic properties of iron*
trait *personality traits*
See also **attribute, characteristic, feature, point, property, qualification, standard**

qualm See **doubt**

quandary See **fix, jam, problem**

quantities See **lot**

quantity

▷ NOUN

1 an amount you can measure or count: *a large quantity of candy*
amount *a small amount of mayonnaise*
number *There are a limited number of seats available.*
part *the greater part of his wealth*
sum *a large sum of money*
2 the amount of something that there is: *emphasis on quality rather than quantity*
extent *the extent of the damage*
measure *The team has had a fair measure of success.*
size *He gauged the size of the audience.*
volume *the sheer volume of traffic*
See also **amount, lot**

quarrel

▷ NOUN

1 an angry argument: *I had a terrible quarrel with my brother.*
argument *an argument about money*
disagreement *My instructor and I had a brief disagreement.*
dispute *a dispute between the owners*
feud *a two-year feud between neighbours*
fight *It was a silly fight about where to go on the weekend.*
row *a noisy row*
squabble *minor squabbles about phone bills*
▷ VERB
2 to have an angry argument: *My brother quarrelled with my cousin.*
argue *They were still arguing later.*
bicker *They bickered endlessly over silly things.*
clash *She had clashed with him in the past.*
fight *The couple often fought in public.*
squabble *The children were squabbling over the remote control.*
See also **argue, clash, disagreement, row, squabble**

quarrelsome See **aggressive**

quarry See **dig**

quarter *See* **region**

quarters *See* **accommodation**

quash *See* **cancel, suppress**

queasy
▷ ADJECTIVE
feeling slightly sick: *He already felt queasy.*
ill *I was feeling ill.*
nauseous *The medication may make you feel nauseous.*
sick *The very thought of food made her feel sick.*
unwell *He felt unwell this afternoon.*
See also **ill, sick, unwell**

queer *See* **bizarre, odd, peculiar, strange, weird**

quell *See* **crush, subdue, suppress**

query *See* **question**

quest *See* **search**

question
▷ NOUN
1 a remark that requires a reply: *If you have any questions, please contact us.*
inquiry *I'll be happy to answer all your inquiries, if I can.*
query *The premier refused to answer further queries on the subject.*
ANTONYM **response**
2 a problem that needs to be discussed: *Can we get back to the question of the car?*
issue *What is your view on this issue?*
motion *The committee is now debating the motion.*
point *There is another point to consider.*
subject *He raised the subject of money.*
topic *the topic of where to go on vacation*
▷ VERB
3 to ask about something because it seems wrong: *No one questioned my decision.*
challenge *The move was challenged by her opponent.*
dispute *He disputed the allegations.*
object to *A lot of people objected to the plan.*
query *It never occurred to me to query him about it.*
▷ VERB
4 to ask someone questions: *A man is being questioned by police.*
examine *Lawyers examined the witnesses.*
interrogate *I interrogated everyone even slightly involved.*
probe *journalists probing us for details*
quiz *She quizzed me quite closely.*
ANTONYM **answer**
▷ VERB
5 to express doubts about something: *He*

never stopped questioning his decision.
challenge *She convincingly challenged the story.*
dispute *Nobody disputed that she was smart.*
distrust *I distrusted my ability to keep quiet.*
doubt *Nobody doubted his sincerity.*
query *No one queried my decision.*
suspect *Do we suspect the motives of our friends?*
See also **affair, ask, business, challenge, contest, dispute, doubt, interrogate, issue, matter, subject**

questionable *See* **doubtful, dubious, suspect, suspicious**

queue *See* **line, row**

quick
▷ ADJECTIVE
1 moving with great speed: *You'll have to be quick to catch the flight.*
brisk *a brisk walk*
fast *a very fast driver*
hasty *He spoke in a hasty, nervous way.*
rapid *a rapid rise through the company*
speedy *a speedy recovery*
swift *She is as swift as an arrow.*
ANTONYM **slow**
2 lasting only a short time: *a quick chat*
brief *a brief meeting*
cursory *a cursory glance inside the van*
fast *a fast meal of bread and soup*
hurried *He ate a hurried breakfast.*
perfunctory *With a perfunctory smile, she walked past me.*
ANTONYM **long**
3 happening without any delay: *a quick response*
hasty *This is no hasty decision.*
prompt *Prompt action is needed.*
sudden *this week's sudden cold snap*
See also **acute, astute, brief, fast, intelligent, keen, prompt, sharp, sudden, swift**

quicken *See* **accelerate, hurry**

quickly
▷ ADVERB
with great speed: *Stop me if I'm speaking too quickly.*
fast *How fast were you driving?*
hastily *taking shelter in hastily erected tents*
hurriedly *students hurriedly taking notes*
rapidly *moving rapidly across the field*
speedily *She recovered speedily.*
swiftly *They had to act swiftly.*
ANTONYM **slowly**
See also **fast**

Q

quick-witted See sharp

quiet

▷ ADJECTIVE

1 making very little noise: *The children were quiet for a change.*
hushed *Stories were exchanged in hushed tones.*
inaudible *a tiny, almost inaudible squeak*
low *I spoke in a low voice to her.*
silent *The audience was silent.*
soft *There was some soft music playing.*
ANTONYM **noisy**

2 peaceful and calm: *a quiet evening at home*
calm *The city seems relatively calm today.*
mild *The night was mild.*
peaceful *a peaceful old house*
restful *a restful scene*
serene *the beautiful, serene park*
tranquil *a tranquil lake*
▷ NOUN

3 silence or lack of noise: *The teacher called for quiet.*
calmness *the calmness of this area*
peace *I enjoy peace and quiet.*
serenity *the peace and serenity of a tropical sunset*
silence *There was a silence around the table.*
stillness *the stillness of the summer night*
tranquility *the tranquility of village life*
ANTONYM **noise**
See also **calm, easy, peace, peaceful, silence, silent, sleepy, soft**

quieten See calm, silence

quip See joke

quirky See eccentric

quit

▷ VERB

to leave a place or stop doing something: *He quit his job at the pizza place.*
discontinue *Do not discontinue the treatment without seeing your doctor.*
give up *She gave up smoking last year.*
leave *He left university after the first year.*
resign *I resigned from the firm.*
retire *She retired from her job when she reached 60.*
stop *I stopped working last year and returned to school.*
See also **leave, resign, stop**

quite

▷ ADVERB

1 fairly but not very: *He is quite old.*
fairly *Both ships are fairly new.*
moderately *a moderately attractive man*
rather *I made some rather bad mistakes.*
reasonably *I can dance reasonably well.*
somewhat *He's somewhat puzzled about what he should do.*

2 completely and totally: *The dog lay quite still.*
absolutely *I absolutely refuse to do that.*
completely *something completely different*
entirely *an entirely new approach*
fully *He has still not fully recovered.*
perfectly *The pies are perfectly safe to eat.*
totally *The fire totally destroyed the house.*
See also **exactly, pretty, rather**

quiver See shake

quiz See ask, interrogate, question

quota See proportion, share

quotation See passage

quote

▷ VERB

to repeat the exact words someone has said: *She quoted a great line from Shakespeare.*
cite *She cited a favourite poem.*
extract *This material has been extracted from the handbook.*
recite *They recited poetry to one another.*
repeat *Could you repeat the whole interview word for word?*
See also **estimate**

Rr

rabid *See* **fanatical**

race

▷ *NOUN*

1 a group of human beings with similar inherited physical characteristics: *Discrimination on the grounds of race is illegal.*

ethnic group *Ethnic group and nationality are often different.*

nation *a nation tolerant of all people*

people *an address to the Canadian people*

▷ *VERB*

2 to move very quickly: *Her heart raced uncontrollably.*

dash *He dashed upstairs.*

fly *I must fly or I'll miss my train.*

hurry *They hurried down the street.*

run *I ran to catch the plane.*

speed *speeding along as fast as I could*

tear *The door flew open and she tore into the room.*

See also **dash, fly, rush, speed, tear**

racism *See* **prejudice**

racket

▷ *NOUN*

1 a lot of noise: *The racket went on past midnight.*

clamour *She could hear a clamour in the road.*

commotion *He heard a commotion outside.*

din *make themselves heard over the din of the crowd*

hubbub *His voice was drowned out by the hubbub of the fans.*

noise *There was too much noise in the room.*

rumpus *There was such a rumpus, she had to shout to make herself heard.*

2 an illegal way of making money: *an investment racket*

con *INFORMAL It's a con, so don't fall for it.*

enterprise *a money-laundering enterprise*

fraud *tax fraud*

scam *a scam designed to swindle parents of young children*

scheme *a quick moneymaking scheme*

See also **noise, sound**

radiance *See* **light**

radiant *See* **bright, brilliant, shining**

radiate *See* **shine**

radical *See* **drastic, extreme, left-wing**

rage

▷ *NOUN*

1 a feeling of very strong anger: *trembling with rage*

anger *She felt deep anger at what he had said.*

frenzy *Their behaviour drove him into a frenzy.*

fury *a face distorted with fury and pain*

wrath *He incurred the wrath of the referee.*

▷ *VERB*

2 to be angry or speak angrily about something: *He was raging at their lack of response.*

be furious *He is furious at the way his complaint has been treated.*

fume *I was still fuming over her remark.*

lose your temper *They had never seen me lose my temper before.*

rave *There's no need to rant and rave like that.*

storm *"It's a disaster," he stormed.*

▷ *VERB*

3 to continue with great force: *The fire raged out of control.*

be at its height *when the storm was at its height*

rampage *a mob rampaging through the town*

storm *armies storming across the continent*

surge *The flood surged through the village.*

See also **anger, frenzy, rampage, rave**

ragged *See* **irregular, scruffy, shabby**

raging *See* **furious, violent, wild**

raid

▷ *VERB*

1 to attack something by force: *Soldiers raided the capital.*

assault *Their stronghold was assaulted by pirates.*

attack *We are being attacked!*

break into *No one saw them break into the warehouse.*

invade *The invading army took all their food supplies.*

plunder *plundering the homes of the inhabitants*

▷ *NOUN*

2 an attack on something: *Our raid on the kitchen provided enough food for the hike.*

attack *a surprise attack on the house*

break-in *The break-in occurred last night.*

foray *Guerrillas made forays into enemy territory.*

See also **attack, loot**

R

rail *See* **bar**

rain

▷ *NOUN*

1 water falling from the clouds: *A few drops of rain fell on her hand.*

deluge *homes damaged in the deluge*

downpour *A two-day downpour swelled water levels.*

drizzle *The drizzle had stopped, and the sun was shining.*

rainfall *four years of below-average rainfall*

showers *bright spells followed by scattered showers*

▷ *VERB*

2 to fall from the sky in drops: *It rained the whole weekend.*

drizzle *It was starting to drizzle when I left.*

pour *We drove all the way in pouring rain.*

teem *It teemed the entire day.*

rainfall *See* **rain**

rainy *See* **wet**

raise

▷ *VERB*

1 to make something higher: *a drive to raise standards of literacy*

elevate *Emotional stress can elevate blood pressure.*

heave *He heaved his injured leg into an easier position.*

hoist *He climbed on the roof to hoist the flag.*

lift *She lifted the last of her drink to her lips.*

ANTONYM **lower**

2 to look after children until they are grown up: *the house where she was raised*

bring up *They brought up a large family.*

nurture *the best way to nurture a child to adulthood*

rear *He reared his sister's family as well as his own.*

3 to mention or suggest something: *He had raised no objections at the time.*

advance *Some important ideas were advanced at the conference.*

bring up *I hesitate to bring up this matter with you, but I have no choice.*

broach *Eventually I broached the subject of her early life.*

introduce *always willing to introduce a new topic*

suggest *one possibility that might be suggested*

See also **breed, collect, lift**

CONFUSABLES

raise means **lift up**

rise means **get up** or **go up**

---

rally *See* **gathering, revive**

ram *See* **drive, jam, push, stick, stuff**

ramble *See* **hike, walk, wander**

rambling *See* **indirect**

ramp *See* **slope**

rampage

▷ *VERB*

to rush about angrily or violently: *children rampaging around the garden*

go berserk *The crowd went berserk at the sight of the movie star.*

rage *a raging mob*

run amok *The bull ran amok through the streets.*

run riot *The prisoners ran riot after the announcement.*

on the rampage

▷ *ADJECTIVE*

rushing about in a wild and violent way: *a wild animal on the rampage*

amok *He was arrested after running amok with a knife.*

berserk *The fans went berserk and mobbed the stage.*

wild *They just went wild after he left.*

See also **rage, riot**

rancid *See* **sour**

rancorous *See* **bitter**

rancour *See* **resentment**

random

▷ *ADJECTIVE*

not based on a definite plan: *random acts of kindness*

aimless *after hours of aimless wandering*

arbitrary *Arbitrary arrests were common.*

haphazard *He had never seen such a haphazard approach to writing.*

indiscriminate *the indiscriminate use of pesticides*

spot *picked up in a spot check*

at random

▷ *ADVERB*

without any definite plan: *chosen at random*

aimlessly *wandering around aimlessly*

arbitrarily *The questions were chosen quite arbitrarily.*

haphazardly *The books were stacked haphazardly on the shelves.*

indiscriminately *This disease strikes indiscriminately.*
randomly *a randomly selected sample*
See also **absent-minded, accidental, irregular**

randomly *See at* **random**

range
▷ NOUN
I the maximum limits of something: *What is the range of your cellphone?*
bounds *the bounds of good taste*
extent *the full extent of my knowledge*
field *The subject covers a very wide field.*
limits *outside the city limits*
province *This doesn't fall within our province.*
scope *He promised to widen the scope of their responsibilities.*
2 a number of different things of the same kind: *a wide range of colours*
assortment *There was a good assortment to choose from.*
class *Printers in this class are more expensive.*
gamut *I experienced the whole gamut of emotions.*
selection *a wide selection of delicious meals*
series *I have every book in this series.*
variety *a variety of fruit and vegetables*
▷ VERB
3 to vary between two extremes: *items ranging between the everyday and the exotic*
extend *The reclaimed land extends from here to the river.*
go *Their sizes go from very small to enormous.*
run *Accommodation runs from log cabins to luxury hotels.*
stretch *with interests that stretched from reading to extreme sports*
vary *Temperatures in Canada have varied from -63°C to +45°C.*
See also **area, choice, variety, wander**

rank
▷ NOUN
I someone's level in a group: *She rose to the rank of captain.*
class *He acts like he's a member of the moneyed classes.*
echelon *the upper echelons of society*
grade *She prefers to teach children in the primary grades.*
level *various levels of the legal system*
standing *a woman of wealth and social standing*
station *a humble station in life*
status *promoted to the status of foreperson*
2 a row of people or things: *ranks of police*

column *a column of numbers*
file *They walked in single file.*
line *He waited in a line of slow-moving vehicles.*
row *We sat in the eighth row of the theatre.*
▷ ADJECTIVE
3 complete and absolute: *It was rank stupidity to go there alone.*
absolute *not intended for absolute beginners*
complete *complete silence*
downright *That was just downright rudeness.*
sheer *his sheer stupidity*
unmitigated *The play was an unmitigated disaster.*
utter *his utter disregard for other people*
See also **class, classify, level, line, rate, row, status**

ransack *See* **loot**

rant *See* **rave**

rap *See* **blame, hit**

rap someone's knuckles *See* **punish**

rapid *See* **fast, hasty, prompt, quick, swift**

rapidity *See* **speed**

rapidly *See* **fast, quickly**

rapport *See* **relationship**

rapture *See* **delight, ecstasy, heaven, joy**

rare
▷ ADJECTIVE
not common or frequent: *a rare species of bird*
exceptional *in exceptional circumstances*
few *Genuine friends are few.*
scarce *Jobs are becoming increasingly scarce.*
sparse *Information about the tryouts is sparse.*
sporadic *occurring at only sporadic moments*
uncommon *The disease is uncommon in younger people.*
unusual *an unusual type of question*
ANTONYM **common**
See also **exceptional, scarce, singular, uncommon, unusual**

raring to go *See* **eager**

rarity *See* **curiosity**

rash
▷ ADJECTIVE
I acting in a hasty and foolish way: *It would*

R

be rash to act on such flimsy evidence.
foolhardy *Some described his behaviour as foolhardy.*
hasty *This is no hasty decision.*
impetuous *As usual, he reacted in a heated and impetuous way.*
impulsive *She is too impulsive to take on this responsibility.*
reckless *reckless driving*
▷ *NOUN*
2 an irritated area on your skin: *I noticed a rash on my leg.*
eruption *an unpleasant skin eruption*
outbreak *an outbreak of blisters around the mouth*
▷ *NOUN*
3 a large number of events happening together: *a rash of computer viruses*
epidemic *an epidemic of silly new love songs*
flood *a flood of complaints about the program*
plague *a plague of dreadful new movies*
spate *a spate of new TV shows about doctors*
wave *the current wave of violent attacks*
See also **unwise**

rasp See **scrape**

rasping See **hoarse**

rate
▷ *NOUN*
1 the speed or frequency of something: *appearing at the rate of one a week*
frequency *She phoned with increasing frequency.*
pace *at an accelerated pace*
speed *moving at the speed of light*
tempo *They wanted to speed up the tempo of change.*
velocity *changes in wind velocity*
2 the cost or charge for something: *cheap telephone rates*
charge *An annual charge will be made for this service.*
cost *the cost of clothes*
fee *They did a good job and charged a reasonable fee.*
price *the price of a new pair of jeans*
tariff *U.S. tariffs on imports of Canadian lumber*
▷ *VERB*
3 to give an opinion of someone's qualities: *He was rated as one of the best.*
appraise *She gave me an appraising glance.*
class *classed as one of the top ten athletes*
consider *I considered myself to be*

reasonably good at math.
count *That would be counted as wrong.*
rank *The hotel was ranked as one of the world's best.*
regard *a highly regarded member of the committee*
See also **class, consider, cost, count, grade, judge**

rate highly See **appreciate, value**

rather
▷ *ADVERB*
to a certain extent: *We got along rather well.*
fairly *Both ships are fairly new.*
pretty *I'm pretty tired now.*
quite *The cottage looks quite ordinary from the road.*
relatively *I think I'm relatively easy to get along with.*
slightly *slightly startled by his sudden appearance*
somewhat *He said, somewhat reluctantly, that he would pay.*
See also **pretty, quite**

ration See **limit, share**

rational
▷ *ADJECTIVE*
using reason rather than emotion: *to arrive at a rational conclusion*
enlightened *enlightened companies that take a practical approach*
logical *There must be a logical explanation for it.*
reasonable *a perfectly reasonable decision*
sensible *The sensible thing is to leave them alone.*
See also **logical, reasonable, sane, sensible, wise**

rationality See **reason**

rations See **supplies**

rattle See **shake**

rave
▷ *VERB*
1 to talk in an uncontrolled way: *He started raving about being treated badly.*
babble *They babbled on and on about their plans.*
rage *He was raging at their lack of response.*
rant *She started ranting about her boss's attitude.*
2 *INFORMAL* to be enthusiastic about

something: *She raved about the facilities there.*

be wild about INFORMAL *He was just wild about the play.*

enthuse *She enthused about the local architecture.*

gush *"It was brilliant," he gushed.*

See also **rage**

ravenous See **hungry**

raving See **hysterical**

raw See **cold, inexperienced, sore, tender**

raze See **destroy**

razor-sharp See **sharp**

reach

▷ VERB

1 to arrive somewhere: *He did not stop until he reached the door.*

arrive at *to arrive at an erroneous conclusion*

attain *She worked hard to attain a state of calm.*

get as far as *If we get as far as Nova Scotia, we will be quite satisfied.*

get to *I finally got to the end of the book.*

make it to *They didn't think they would make it to the summit.*

2 to extend as far as something: *Her coat nearly reached to the ground.*

extend to *The boundaries extend to the edge of the lake.*

touch *I could touch both walls with my arms extended.*

3 to arrive at a certain stage or level: *Unemployment has reached record levels.*

arrive at *They planted a flag when they arrived at the top.*

attain *He was close to attaining his personal best.*

climb to *Attendance climbed to a record level this year.*

fall to *Profits are expected to fall to their lowest level.*

rise to *She rose rapidly to the top of her profession.*

See also **contact, extend, stretch**

reaction

▷ NOUN

1 a person's response to something: *Reaction to the visit was mixed.*

acknowledgment *She made no acknowledgment of my question.*

answer *In answer to the question, the mayor said she would not be running for re-election.*

feedback *Continue to ask for feedback on your work.*

response *in response to a request from the members*

2 a response to something unpopular: *a reaction against rising prices*

backlash *the student backlash against cutbacks*

counterbalance *a committee set up as a counterbalance to the official one*

reactionary See **right-wing**

read

▷ VERB

1 to look at something written: *I love to read in bed.*

glance at *He just glanced briefly at the article.*

look at *She was looking at the evening paper.*

peruse *I perused the report before going to the meeting.*

pore over *poring over a dictionary*

scan *There's only time to scan through it quickly.*

study *I'll study the text more closely later.*

2 to understand what someone means: *as if he could read my thoughts*

comprehend *Her expression was difficult to comprehend.*

decipher *She was still no closer to deciphering the code.*

interpret *You have to interpret their gestures, too.*

INFORMALLY SPEAKING

read between the lines: find a meaning not actually expressed
read into: interpret in a certain way
read up on: research by reading

R

read out See **issue**

read up See **study**

reading See **extract**

ready

▷ ADJECTIVE

1 prepared for action or use: *The plums are ready to eat now.*

organized *Everything is organized for the party tomorrow.*

prepared *He was prepared for a tough fight.*

primed *The other side is primed for battle.*

ripe *Are those bananas ripe yet?*

set *We'll be set to go in five minutes.*

2 willing to do something: *She was always ready to give interviews.*

agreeable *We can go ahead if you are agreeable.*

eager *Children are eager to learn.*
happy *always happy to help*
keen *He wasn't keen about becoming involved.*
willing *questions that they were not willing to answer*
3 easily produced or obtained: *ready cash*
accessible *The system should be accessible to everyone.*
available *Food is available around the clock.*
convenient *a convenient excuse*
handy *Keep a pencil and paper handy.*
See also **agreeable, fluent, willing**

real

▷ ADJECTIVE

1 actually existing and not imagined: *You're dealing with real life now.*
actual *She was the actual basis for the leading character.*
authentic *containing authentic details of what happened*
concrete *I don't have any concrete evidence.*
factual *a factual account*
genuine *His worries about the future were genuine.*
legitimate *These are legitimate concerns.*
tangible *I cannot see any tangible benefits in these changes.*
true *the true story of his life*
ANTONYM **imaginary**
2 genuine and not imitation: *Is that a real diamond?*
authentic *an authentic French recipe*
bona fide *We are happy to donate to bona fide charities.*
genuine *It's a genuine Emily Carr painting, all right.*
honest *It was an honest attempt to set things right.*
sincere *His remorse was completely sincere, not just an act.*
rightful *the rightful heir to the throne*
true *He is a true believer in human rights.*
unaffected *She had genuine and unaffected sympathy for the victims.*
ANTONYM **fake**
See also **authentic, genuine, natural, sincere, true**

realism *See* reality

realistic

▷ ADJECTIVE

1 accepting the true situation: *It's only realistic to admit that things will go wrong.*
down-to-earth *We welcomed her down-to-earth approach.*

level-headed *a sensible, level-headed approach*
matter-of-fact *He sounded matter-of-fact and unemotional.*
practical *a highly practical attitude to life*
sensible *I'm trying to persuade you to be more sensible.*
sober *a more sober assessment of the situation*
2 true to real life: *His novels are more realistic than his short stories.*
authentic *The costumes have to look authentic.*
faithful *faithful copies of the original prints*
lifelike *almost as lifelike as a photograph*
true *It gave a true picture of how things were.*
See also **actual**

reality

▷ NOUN

something that is true and not imagined: *Fiction and reality were increasingly blurred.*
authenticity *The movie's authenticity impressed the critics.*
fact *No one knew how much of what he said was fact.*
realism *the realism of her stories*
truth *I must tell you the truth about this situation.*
See also **fact, truth**

realize

▷ VERB

to become aware of something: *People don't realize how serious it is.*
appreciate *He appreciates the difficulties we face.*
comprehend *They do not comprehend the nature of the problem.*
grasp *She still couldn't grasp what had really happened.*
recognize *Of course, I recognize the weaknesses of the team.*
understand *I didn't understand what he meant until later.*
See also **appreciate, discover, find, fulfill, grasp, see, sense, understand**

really

▷ ADVERB

1 very or certainly: *I've had a really good time.*
absolutely *feeling absolutely exhausted*
certainly *I am certainly getting tired of hearing about it.*
extremely *My laptop is extremely useful.*
remarkably *They have been remarkably successful.*
terribly *I'm terribly sorry to bother you.*
truly *a truly wonderful party*

very *learning very quickly*
2 in actual fact: *He didn't really understand the question.*
actually *I pretended I was interested, but I was actually half asleep.*
in fact *It sounds simple, but in fact, it's very difficult.*
in reality *He came across as streetwise, but in reality, he was not.*
truly *I truly never minded caring for your dogs.*
See also **very**

reappear *See* **return**

rear *See* **back, bottom, breed, raise**

reason
▷ NOUN
1 the cause of something that happens: *for a multitude of reasons*
cause *The true cause of the accident may never be known.*
grounds *some grounds for optimism*
incentive *There is no incentive to practise any harder.*
motive *Police have ruled out robbery as a motive.*
purpose *the purpose of their visit*
2 the ability to think: *a conflict between emotion and reason*
intellect *good health and a lively intellect*
judgment *His judgment was impaired.*
rationality *We live in a time of rationality.*
reasoning *a lack of sound reasoning and logic*
sense *He should have had more sense.*
▷ VERB
3 to try to persuade someone of something: *It's better to reason with them than to use force.*
bring around *We'll try to bring you around to our point of view.*
persuade *I had to persuade him of the advantages.*
win over *They still hoped to win her over to their way of thinking.*
See also **argue, cause, excuse, grounds, purpose, sense, wisdom**

reasonable
▷ ADJECTIVE
1 fair and sensible: *a reasonable sort of person*
fair *You can be sure she will be fair with you.*
moderate *an easygoing man of very moderate views*
rational *Please try to be rational about this.*
sane *No sane person wishes to have a war.*
sensible *She was a sensible person and did not panic.*
sober *We are now more sober and realistic.*

wise *You're a wise man: tell me what to do.*
2 based on good reasoning: *It seems reasonable to expect rapid urban growth.*
justifiable *Her annoyance was justifiable, given the poor service.*
legitimate *That's a perfectly legitimate fear.*
logical *There was a logical explanation.*
sensible *a sensible solution*
sound *sound advice*
understandable *Her unhappiness was understandable.*
3 not too expensive: *His fees were quite reasonable.*
cheap *These jeans are definitely not cheap.*
competitive *homes offered for sale at competitive prices*
fair *It's a fair price for a bike like that.*
inexpensive *an inexpensive computer*
low *The low prices and friendly service made for a pleasant shopping trip.*
modest *a modest charge*
See also **cheap, decent, logical, moderate, rational, respectable, sane, sound, tolerable**

reasonably *See* **quite**

reasoned *See* **logical**

reasoning *See* **argument, reason**

reassure
▷ VERB
to make someone feel less worried: *She reassured me that everything was fine.*
bolster *measures intended to bolster morale*
cheer up *I wrote it just to cheer myself up.*
comfort *He tried to comfort me as much as he could.*
encourage *Fans were encouraged by the news.*
See also **comfort, encourage, satisfy**

reassured *See* **secure**

rebel
▷ VERB
to fight against authority and accepted values: *I rebelled against everything when I was younger.*
defy *It was the first time she had defied her parents.*
mutiny *Sailors mutinied against their officers.*
resist *protesters who resisted arrest*
revolt *The islanders revolted against the unfair tax.*

rebellion
▷ NOUN
an organized opposition to authority: *the*

R

ruthless suppression of the rebellion
insurrection *They were plotting to stage an armed insurrection.*
mutiny *convicted of mutiny and high treason*
revolt *The revolt ended in failure.*
revolution *the French Revolution*
uprising *Isolated attacks turned into a full-scale uprising.*

rebuff *See* **reject**

rebuild *See* **reconstruct, restore**

rebuke *See* **scold**

recall *See* **memory, remember**

recapitulate *See* **sum up**

recapture *See* **recover, recovery**

recede *See* **disappear, vanish**

receive
▷ VERB
I to accept something from someone: *Did they receive my letter?*
accept *They accepted the package gratefully.*
be given *We were all given presents.*
get *She got some lovely things.*
pick up *She picked up an award for her performance.*
take *Will you take this package for your neighbour?*
2 to experience something: *We received a very warm welcome.*
encounter *He encountered some unexpected opposition.*
suffer *He suffered some scrapes and bruises.*
sustain *She had sustained a cut on her arm.*
undergo *You may have to undergo some minor surgery.*
3 to welcome visitors: *She was officially received by the prime minister.*
entertain *She loved to entertain friends at home.*
greet *They greeted the visitors at the door.*
meet *I'll come down to meet you.*
take in *The country took in many refugees.*
welcome *Several people dropped in to welcome me.*
See also **admit, get, greet**

recent
▷ ADJECTIVE
happening a short time ago: *his most recent acquisition*
current *a sound knowledge of current affairs*
fresh *fresh footprints in the snow*
new *the subject of a new movie*

present-day *Even by present-day standards these were large aircraft.*
up-to-date *the most up-to-date digital cameras*
See also **modern**

reception *See* **function, party**

receptive *See* **impressionable, passive**

recess *See* **break, holiday**

recession
▷ NOUN
a decline in economic conditions: *companies that survived the recession*
decline *signs of economic decline*
depression *the Great Depression of the 1930s*
downturn *due to a sharp downturn in the industry*
slump *Many jobs were lost during the slump.*
See also **decline**

recite *See* **quote**

reckless *See* **irresponsible, rash**

recklessness *See* **abandon**

reckon
▷ VERB
I INFORMAL to think or believe something is the case: *I reckon they're still fond of each other.*
assume *If mistakes occurred, they were assumed to be my fault.*
believe *"You've never heard of him?" "I don't believe so."*
consider *I consider your behaviour to be immature.*
judge *I would judge that my salary is considerably lower than yours.*
suppose *I suppose I'd better do some homework.*
think *I think there should be a ban on phones in cars.*
2 to calculate an amount: *The figure is now reckoned to be 20 percent.*
calculate *We calculate that the average size farm in the county is 1.5 ha.*
count *These three months counted as part of the prison sentence.*
estimate *We estimate the population to be 1.3 million.*
figure out *I roughly figured out the total.*
work out *It is proving hard to work out the value of their assets.*
See also **calculate, conclude, expect, figure, guess, think**

reckoning *See* **count, estimate, guess**

reclamation *See* **recovery**

recline *See* **lie**

recognition See **credit, gratitude, honour**

recognize

▷ VERB

I to know who or what someone or something is: *I recognized him at once.*
identify *She tried to identify the perfume.*
know *You'd know him if you saw him again.*
place *He couldn't place my voice immediately.*
spot *I spotted the house quite easily.*
2 to accept or acknowledge something: *She was recognized as an outstanding pilot.*
acknowledge *Her great bravery was acknowledged.*
appreciate *In time, you'll appreciate his good points.*
honour *achievements honoured with a Nobel Prize*
salute *We salute your great courage.*
See also **appreciate, distinguish, identify, know, realize, remember**

recommence See **continue, renew**

recommend See **advise, advocate, nominate, suggest, vote**

recommendation See **idea, suggestion**

reconcile See **settle**

reconcile oneself See **resign oneself**

recondition See **renovate**

reconstruct

▷ VERB

I to rebuild something that has been damaged: *The old bridge has been completely reconstructed.*
rebuild *The task of rebuilding would be very expensive.*
recreate *They try to recreate the atmosphere of former times.*
regenerate *the ability to regenerate damaged tissues*
renovate *The hotel was being renovated.*
restore *experts who specialize in restoring old furniture*
2 to put together from small details: *The police reconstructed the scene of the crime.*
deduce *The date can be deduced from other documents.*
piece together *It was easy to piece together the shattered fragments.*
See also **restore**

record

▷ NOUN

I a stored account of something: *medical records*
account *The company keeps detailed accounts.*

archives *Earlier issues of the magazine are stored in the archives.*
file *the right to inspect electronic files*
journal *He kept a journal while he was travelling.*
minutes *Did you read the minutes of the last meeting?*
register *a register of births, deaths, and marriages*
2 what someone has done in the past: *You will be rejected if you have a criminal record.*
background *His background was in engineering.*
career *Her career spoke for itself.*
curriculum vitae *I must update my curriculum vitae.*
résumé *He attached the résumé to the e-mail.*
track record INFORMAL *Her track record as a teacher was impeccable.*
▷ VERB
3 to note and store information: *Her diary records her daily life in detail.*
document *All these facts have been well documented.*
enter *All the names are entered in this book.*
log *They log everyone who comes in or out.*
make a note of *I must make a note of your birthday.*
register *We registered his birth with the government.*
write down *If I don't write it down, I'll forget it.*
See also **entry, list, note, trace, write**

recoup See **recover**

recover

▷ VERB

I to get better again: *He has still not fully recovered.*
convalesce *those convalescing from illness or surgery*
get better *He never really got better again.*
get well *Get well soon!*
improve *Your mobility will soon improve.*
recuperate *recuperating from a serious injury*
revive *Business revived once she returned.*
2 to get something back again: *They took legal action to recover the money.*
get back *We got everything back after the burglary.*
recapture *trying to recapture the atmosphere of our holiday*
recoup *trying to recoup their losses*
regain *It took him a while to regain his composure.*
retrieve *I retrieved my bag from the back seat.*

R

recovery

▷ NOUN

1 the act of getting better again: *He made a remarkable recovery after his illness.*
healing *She claims that humour is an integral part of healing.*
improvement *a noticeable improvement in the team's performance*
recuperation *great powers of recuperation*
revival *little chance of a revival of interest*
2 the act of getting something back: *a reward for the recovery of the painting*
recapture *the recapture of the championship*
reclamation *the reclamation of dry land from the marshes*
restoration *She owed the restoration of her sight to a remarkable new technique.*
retrieval *electronic storage and retrieval systems*

recreate *See* **reconstruct**

recreation *See* **entertainment, fun, leisure, pastime**

recruit

▷ VERB

1 to persuade people to join a group: *He helped to recruit volunteers.*
draft *drafted into the armed forces*
enlist *I had to enlist the help of six people to move it.*
enrol *She enrolled me in the evening course.*
muster *trying to muster support for the group*
▷ NOUN
2 someone who has recently joined a group: *the latest batch of recruits*
beginner *a course suitable for beginners.*
convert *a recent convert to the religion*
novice *I'm a novice at these things.*
trainee *My first job was as a bank trainee.*

recruitment *See* **employment**

rectify *See* **correct, reform**

recuperate *See* **recover**

recuperation *See* **recovery**

recurrent *See* **continual, frequent**

SHADES OF ... RED	
burgundy	magenta
cardinal	maroon
carmine	poppy
cerise	raspberry
cherry	ruby
claret	scarlet
crimson	strawberry
flame	vermilion

red tape *See* **bureaucracy**

redeem *See* **save**

red-faced *See* **embarrassed**

reduce

▷ VERB

1 to make something smaller in size or amount: *Gradually reduce the dosage.*
curtail *His powers will be severely curtailed.*
cut *The first priority is to cut costs.*
cut down *Try to cut down your coffee consumption.*
decrease *The government plans to decrease interest rates.*
diminish *The strength of the storm began to diminish.*
lessen *a diet that would lessen the risk of disease*
lower *a commitment to lower taxes*
shorten *taking steps to shorten waiting times*
ANTONYM **increase**
2 to bring to a weaker or inferior state: *The village was reduced to rubble.*
degrade *I wouldn't degrade myself by borrowing money.*
demote *He was demoted to the position of assistant coach.*
downgrade *The hurricane was downgraded to a tropical storm.*
drive *What drove him to such a pathetic state?*
force *He was forced to beg for his old job back.*
See also **cut, decline, decrease, diminish, lessen, lower, weaken**

reduced *See* **low**

reduction *See* **cut, decrease, fall**

redundant *See* **idle, unemployed**

reek *See* **smell, stink**

reeking *See* **smelly**

re-establish *See* **renew, restore**

refer

▷ VERB

1 to mention something: *In his speech, he referred to a recent trip to the Maritimes.*
allude *She alluded to his absence in vague terms.*
bring up *Why are you bringing that up now?*
cite *She cites a favourite story by Alice Munro.*
mention *She did not mention her mother's illness.*
2 to look at to find something out: *I had to refer to the manual.*

refer to *See* **consult, mention**

referee *See* **judge**

reference *See* **mention**

referendum *See* **vote**

refine *See* **perfect, polish**

refined

▷ *ADJECTIVE*

1 polite and well-mannered: *His speech and manner are very refined.*
civilized *the demands of civilized behaviour*
genteel *her genteel manner and soft voice*
polite *polite and correct behaviour*
ANTONYM **common**
2 processed to remove impurities: *refined oil*
distilled *distilled water*
filtered *a litre of spring or filtered water*
pure *The air was crisp and pure.*
purified *purified drinking water*
See also **fine, polite, sophisticated**

refinement *See* **polish**

reflect *See* **consider, deliberate, ponder, think**

reflect on *See* **contemplate**

reflection *See* **thought**

reflective *See* **thoughtful**

reflex *See* **automatic**

reform

▷ *NOUN*

1 a major change or improvement: *radical economic reforms*
amendment *an amendment to the Canadian Charter of Rights and Freedoms*
correction *a correction of an injustice*
improvement *She is pressing for improvements to the cafeteria food.*
rehabilitation *the rehabilitation of young offenders*
▷ *VERB*
2 to make major changes or improvements to something: *their plans to reform the economy*
amend *They want to amend the current system.*
better *taking action to better their working conditions*
correct *eager to correct injustices*
rectify *attempts to rectify the financial situation*
rehabilitate *efforts to rehabilitate repeat offenders*
See also **change, correct, transform**

refrain *See* **abstain**

refrain from *See* **avoid**

refresh

▷ *VERB*

to make you feel more energetic: *A glass of juice will refresh you.*
brace *a bracing walk*
enliven *Music can enliven the spirit.*
rejuvenate *He was told that the climate would rejuvenate him.*
revive *The cold water revived me a bit.*
stimulate *a lotion to stimulate the skin*

refreshing *See* **cool**

refreshment *See* **food**

refrigerate *See* **cool**

refuge

▷ *NOUN*

a place where you go for safety: *During the storm, we took refuge in the abandoned cabin.*
asylum *political asylum*
harbour *providing a harbour to refugees*
haven *The island is a haven for international criminals.*
sanctuary *a sanctuary from the outside world*
shelter *an animal shelter*
See also **retreat, shelter**

refund *See* **compensate, repay, return**

refurbish *See* **renovate, restore**

refuse

▷ *VERB*

1 to say you will not do something: *He refused to divulge the contents of the letter.*
abstain *people who abstain from eating meat*
decline *He declined to comment on the story.*
withhold *Financial support has been withheld.*
2 to say you will not allow or accept something: *He offered me a sandwich, which I refused.*
decline *He declined their invitation.*
reject *They rejected all my suggestions.*
spurn *We spurned her last offer.*
turn down *He has turned down the job.*
ANTONYM **accept**
▷ *NOUN*
3 garbage or waste: *a weekly collection of refuse*
garbage *rotting piles of garbage*
junk INFORMAL *What are you going to do with all that junk?*

R

litter *If you see litter in the corridor, pick it up.*
rubbish *They had piled most of their rubbish into boxes.*
trash *I forgot to take out the trash.*
waste *a law that regulates the disposal of waste*
See also **decline, deny, garbage, junk, reject, resist, rubbish, trash**

refute See **deny, disprove**

regain See **recover**

regal See **royal**

regard
▷ VERB
1 to have particular views about someone or something: *I regard creativity as a gift.*
consider *I consider such activities a waste of time.*
judge *This may or may not be judged as reasonable.*
look on *A lot of people looked on him as a healer.*
see *I don't see it as my duty to take sides.*
think of *We all thought of him as a friend.*
view *They view Canada as a land of opportunity.*
2 to look at someone in a particular way: *She regarded him curiously for a moment.*
contemplate *He contemplated her in silence.*
eye *We eyed each other thoughtfully.*
gaze *gazing at himself in the mirror*
look *She looked at him earnestly.*
scrutinize *She scrutinized his features to see if he was to be trusted.*
watch *I watched him sipping his drink.*
See also **admiration, esteem, rate, respect, view**

regard as See **consider**

regarding See **about**

regardless of See **despite, in spite of**

regenerate See **reconstruct**

region
▷ NOUN
a large area of land: *a remote mountainous region*
area *The area is renowned for its cuisine.*
district *I walked around the business district.*
land *a land rich in history*
locality *It's a popular restaurant among people living in the locality.*
quarter *We wandered through the poorest quarter of the city.*
sector *the northeast sector of Bosnia*
territory *unexplored territory*
tract *They cleared large tracts of forest.*
zone *a different time zone*
See also **area, land**

regional See **local**

register See **list, note, record**

regret
▷ VERB
1 to be sorry something has happened: *I gave in to him, and I have regretted it ever since.*
be sorry *I'm sorry you feel that way about it.*
grieve *grieving over the death of his wife*
lament *We lament the loss of a fine novelist.*
mourn *to mourn the loss of a loved one*
repent *to repent past sins*
▷ NOUN
2 the feeling of being sorry about something: *He expressed regret that he had caused any offence.*
grief *grief over the failed relationship*
pang of conscience *You need not feel any pangs of conscience over your decision.*
penitence *a true display of penitence*
remorse *She expressed remorse over her own foolishness.*
repentance *an apparent lack of genuine repentance*
sorrow *I feel real sorrow about the incident.*
See also **disappointment, sorrow**

regretful See **guilty, sorry**

CONFUSABLES

regrettable means **unfortunate** or **unwelcome**
regretful means **sorry**

---

regular
▷ ADJECTIVE
1 even or equally spaced: *soft music with a regular beat*
consistent *a consistent heartbeat*
constant *a constant temperature*
even *an even level of sound*
periodic *Periodic checks are carried out.*
rhythmic *the rhythmic beating of the drum*
steady *a steady pace*
uniform *The earth rotates on its axis at a uniform rate.*
ANTONYM **irregular**
2 usual or normal: *I was filling in for the regular server.*
customary *her customary place at the table*
everyday *part of everyday life*

habitual *habitual practices*
normal *a normal day*
ordinary *It was just an ordinary weekend.*
routine *a routine knee operation*
typical *My typical day begins at 8:30.*
usual *In a usual week, I watch about 15 hours of television.*
See also **average, constant, continual, conventional, even, formal, normal, orderly, ordinary, routine, standard, steady, typical, usual**

regularity *See* **order**

regulation *See* **law, restriction, rule**

regulations *See* **bureaucracy**

regurgitate *See* **vomit**

rehabilitate *See* **reform**

rehabilitation *See* **reform**

rehearsal *See* **practice**

rehearse *See* **practise**

reheat *See* **heat**

reign *See* **rule**

reinforce *See* **augment, strengthen, supplement, support**

reinstate *See* **restore**

reintroduce *See* **restore**

reiterate *See* **repeat**

reject
▷ VERB
to refuse to accept or agree to something: *All my suggestions were rejected.*
decline *They declined our offer of assistance.*
deny *He denied our request for help.*
rebuff *She rebuffed his offer.*
refuse *He offered me a sandwich, which I refused.*
renounce *She renounced her former ways.*
say no to *Just say no to the offer.*
spurn *He spurned the advice of experts.*
turn down *She turned down the offer of a job.*
ANTONYM **accept**
See also **boycott, deny, refuse, renounce**

rejoice
▷ VERB
to be very happy about something: *Today we can rejoice in our success.*
be overjoyed *I was overjoyed to see them.*
celebrate *We should celebrate our victory.*
delight *He delighted in her success.*
glory *glorying in the achievement*
See also **celebrate**

rejuvenate *See* **refresh**

relate *See* **connect**

relate to *See* **identify with**

relating to *See* **about**

relation
▷ NOUN
1 a connection between two things: *This theory bears no relation to reality.*
bearing *Diet has an important bearing on your general health.*
bond *the bond between bears and their cubs*
connection *the connection between good health and exercise*
correlation *the correlation between unemployment and crime*
link *the link between air pollution and breathing difficulties*
relationship *the relationship between success and effort*
2 a member of your family: *I was staying with relations in Edmonton.*
kin *I gave your name as my next of kin.*
relative *A relative looked after the children.*
See also **bond, connection**

relations *See* **family, kin**

relationship
▷ NOUN
1 the way people act toward each other: *He has a friendly relationship with his customers.*
affinity *the natural affinity among the players*
association *the association between the two countries*
bond *The experience created a bond between us.*
connection *She felt a personal connection with us.*
rapport *He has a terrific rapport with kids.*
2 the connection between two things: *the relationship between humans and their environment*
connection *the connection between good work habits and success*
correlation *the correlation between air pollution and breathing difficulties*
link *the link between smoking and lung cancer*
parallel *the parallel between painting and music*
See also **association, connection, link, relation, tie**

relative *See* **relation**

relatively *See* **rather**

R

relatives *See* **family, kin**

relax

▷ *VERB*

to be calm and become less worried: *I never have any time to relax.*

laze *I'm just going to laze around and do nothing.*

rest *Try to rest as much as you can.*

take it easy *the chance just to take it easy for a week or two*

unwind *It helps them to unwind after a busy day at work.*

veg out SLANG *I need to veg out this weekend.*

See also **calm, ease, lift, moderate, rest**

relaxation *See* **ease, leisure, rest**

relaxed

▷ *ADJECTIVE*

1 calm and not worried or tense: *As soon as I made the decision, I felt more relaxed.*

at ease *It is important to feel at ease with your doctor.*

calm *The witness felt calm and unafraid as she entered the courtroom.*

comfortable *He liked me and I felt comfortable with him.*

cool *She was marvellously cool, smiling as if nothing had happened.*

easy *By then, I was feeling a little easier about the situation.*

serene *that serene smile of his*

unflustered *He has a calm, unflustered temperament.*

ANTONYM **tense**

2 calm and peaceful: *The atmosphere at lunch was relaxed.*

calm *The city appears relatively calm today.*

casual *We have a very casual relationship.*

comfortable *a comfortable silence*

informal *an informal occasion*

peaceful *Sundays are usually quiet and peaceful in our house.*

ANTONYM **tense**

See also **calm, casual, comfortable, cool, cosy, easy, informal, leisurely, secure**

relaxing *See* **comfortable**

release

▷ *VERB*

1 to set someone or something free: *negotiations to release the hostages*

deliver *They were ordered to deliver the captives.*

discharge *He may be discharged from hospital today.*

extricate *They managed to extricate the survivors from the wreckage.*

free *Several political prisoners were freed.*

let go *They held him for three hours and then let him go.*

liberate *liberated under the terms of the amnesty*

set free *birds set free into the wild*

2 to make something available: *The DVD will be released next week.*

issue *She has issued a statement to the press.*

launch *The company has just launched a new range of products.*

publish *His latest book will be published in May.*

put out *They're putting out a series of novels by Governor General Award winners.*

▷ *NOUN*

3 the setting free of someone or something: *his release from prison*

discharge *a discharge from the army*

emancipation *the emancipation of slaves in the 19th century*

freedom *The prisoner campaigned for his freedom.*

liberation *their liberation from a Nazi concentration camp*

liberty *her television appearances pleading for his liberty*

See also **discharge, emit, free, freedom, issue**

relentless

▷ *ADJECTIVE*

never stopping or becoming less intense: *The pressure was relentless.*

incessant *incessant rain*

non-stop *non-stop background music*

persistent *in the face of persistent criticism*

sustained *a sustained attack*

unrelenting *unrelenting protests*

unremitting *the unremitting demands of the job*

See also **constant, fierce**

relevant

▷ *ADJECTIVE*

connected with what is being discussed: *We have passed along all relevant information.*

applicable *Several questions on the form were not applicable to me.*

appropriate *The name seemed very appropriate.*

apt *an apt comment*

pertinent *She had asked some pertinent questions.*

ANTONYM **irrelevant**

reliable

▷ *ADJECTIVE*

able to be trusted: *You have to demonstrate*

that you are reliable.
dependable *dependable information*
faithful *a faithful friend*
safe *It's all right, you're in safe hands.*
sound *sound advice*
staunch *a staunch supporter*
sure *a sure sign of rain*
true *a true account*
trustworthy *a trustworthy and level-headed leader*
ANTONYM **unreliable**
See also **responsible, sound, sure, trusty**

reliance *See* **confidence**

relic *See* **souvenir**

relics *See* **remains**

relief *See* **comfort, escape**

relieve *See* **ease**

relieve from *See* **spare**

TYPES OF ... *RELIGION*	
animism	Judaism
Baha'ism	Rastafarianism
Buddhism	shamanism
Christianity	Shinto
Confucianism	Sikhism
Hinduism	Taoism
Islam	Zen
Jainism	Zoroastrianism

religious
▷ *ADJECTIVE*
1 connected with religion: *religious worship*
devotional *an altar covered with devotional pictures*
doctrinal *their doctrinal differences*
holy *To Tibetans, this is a holy place.*
sacred *Bach's sacred music*
spiritual *no spiritual values*
theological *theological studies*
2 having a strong belief in a god or gods: *They are both very religious.*
devout *She is very devout.*
godly *godly ways*
pious *He was brought up by pious relatives.*
righteous *struggling to be righteous*
See also **holy**

relinquish *See* **renounce, surrender**

relish *See* **enjoy, glory, like, love**

relocate *See* **move**

reluctant
▷ *ADJECTIVE*
unwilling to do something: *He was reluctant to ask for help.*
averse to *I'm not averse to going along with the idea.*

disinclined *He was disinclined to talk about himself.*
hesitant *Her coach is hesitant to let her do the extra jump.*
loath *The finance minister is loath to cut income tax.*
slow *The world community has been slow to respond to the crisis.*
unwilling *For months, I had been unwilling to go through with the training program.*
ANTONYM **eager**
See also **hesitant, unwilling**

rely on *See* **depend, expect**

rely upon *See* **trust**

remain
▷ *VERB*
1 to stay somewhere: *You'll have to remain in hospital for the time being.*
be left *He was left in the car.*
linger *I lingered over my lunch at the mall.*
stay behind *I was told to stay behind after the class.*
wait *Wait here until I come back.*
2 to stay the same: *The men remained silent.*
continue *This state of affairs cannot continue.*
endure *Somehow their friendship endures.*
go on *The debate goes on.*
last *Nothing lasts forever.*
stay *They could stay afloat without swimming.*
survive *teams that survived after the restructuring*
See also **continue, endure, last, stay, wait**

remainder
▷ *NOUN*
the part that is left of something: *He gulped down the remainder of his milk.*
balance *Pay the balance on delivery.*
last *She finished off the last of the juice.*
others *She took one and put the others back.*
remnants *Just crumbs were the remnants of the cookie jar.*
remains *tidying up the remains of their picnic*
rest *I'm going to throw a party, and then invest the rest of the money.*
See also **difference, rest**

remains
▷ *PLURAL NOUN*
the parts of something left over: *the remains of an ancient dwelling*
debris *screws, bolts, and other debris from a scrapyard*

R

dregs *He drained the dregs from his cup.*
leftovers *Refrigerate any leftovers.*
relics *a museum of war relics*
remnants *Beneath the present building were remnants of Roman flooring.*
residue *Discard the milky residue left behind.*
scraps *the scraps from the dinner table*
vestiges *an attempt to destroy the last vestiges of evidence*
See also **body, remainder, ruin**

remark

▷ *VERB*

1 to mention or comment on something: *She had remarked on the boy's improvement.*
comment *So far, he has not commented on these reports.*
mention *I mentioned that I didn't like jazz.*
observe *"You're very pale," he observed.*
say *"Well done," she said.*
state *We stated that he had resigned.*

▷ *NOUN*

2 something you say: *a funny remark*
comment *her witty comments*
observation *a few general observations*
statement *That statement puzzled me.*
utterance *admirers who hung on to her every utterance*
word *No one had an unkind word to say about him.*
See also **comment, expression, note, observe, word**

remarkable *See* **exceptional, marvellous, singular, uncommon, wonderful**

remarkably *See* **really**

remedy *See* **correct, cure, medicine**

remember

▷ *VERB*

to bring to mind something from the past: *I do not remember the exact words.*
call to mind *That story calls to mind another one.*
recall *He tried to recall the layout of the farmhouse.*
recognize *I don't recognize that name.*
retain *information that can be retained in the memory*
ANTONYM **forget**

remembrance *See* **memory**

remind

▷ *VERB*

to make someone remember something: *He reminds me of myself at that age.*

bring back to *Talking about my summer job brought it all back to me.*
jog someone's memory *See if this picture helps jog your memory.*
make someone remember *Your article made me remember my first summer job.*
put in mind *His eagerness to please put her in mind of a puppy.*
refresh someone's memory *I read through the list to refresh my memory.*
See also **prompt**

reminder *See* **note, souvenir**

remission *See* **forgiveness**

remit *See* **function, send**

remittance *See* **payment**

remnant *See* **trace**

remnants *See* **remainder, remains**

remorse *See* **regret**

remorseful *See* **guilty, sorry**

remote

▷ *ADJECTIVE*

1 far off in distance or in the past: *a remote cabin in the mountains*
distant *in that distant land*
far-off *She has entirely forgotten those far-off days.*
inaccessible *people living in inaccessible parts of the country*
isolated *an isolated fishing village*
lonely *It felt like the loneliest place in the world.*
outlying *Tourists can arrange to visit outlying areas.*
2 not wanting to be friendly: *She appeared remote and not interested in meeting anyone.*
aloof *He seemed aloof, standing and watching the others.*
cold *What a cold, unfeeling person you are.*
detached *He tries to remain emotionally detached from the others in the group.*
distant *He is courteous but distant.*
reserved *She's quite a reserved person.*
withdrawn *He had become withdrawn and moody.*
3 not very great: *The chances of his making the team are pretty remote.*
poor *The odds of it happening again are very poor.*
slender *There is a slender possibility that the plan would work.*
slight *Is there even a slight hope that she will change her mind?*
slim *There's still a slim chance that she will run for office.*

small *There was still a small possibility that he would phone.*
See also **distant, far, impersonal, lonely, slender**

remove
▷ *VERB*
to take something off or away: *I removed the splinter from my finger.*
delete *He deleted several files before logging off.*
detach *Detach and keep the bottom part of the form.*
eject *He was ejected from the restaurant.*
eliminate *Eliminate dairy products from your diet.*
erase *She had erased the message.*
extract *She is having a tooth extracted today.*
get rid of *You can't get rid of the problem by avoiding it.*
take away *She took away the tray.*
take off *I won't take my coat off, since I'm not staying.*
take out *Take that dog out of here.*
withdraw *She withdrew her support for the candidate.*
See also **banish, eliminate, extract, get rid of, lift, withdraw**

rendezvous See **appointment, meeting**

renew
▷ *VERB*
to begin something again: *The two countries renewed diplomatic relations.*
begin again *The audience began applauding again.*
recommence *He recommenced work on his novel.*
re-establish *Three years later, they re-established their friendship.*
reopen *Please don't reopen that old argument.*
resume *The two countries have resumed peace talks.*

renounce
▷ *VERB*
FORMAL to reject something or give it up: *She renounced her claim to the inheritance.*
disown *They disowned any part in the ridiculous plan.*
give up *He did not want to give up his coaching job.*
reject *children who reject their parents' political beliefs*
relinquish *He does not intend to relinquish power.*
See also **deny, reject, surrender**

renovate
▷ *VERB*
to repair an old building or machine: *They spent thousands renovating the house.*
make over *He felt it was time to make over his bedroom.*
modernize *plans to modernize the refinery*
recondition *The company specializes in reconditioning photocopiers.*
refurbish *This hotel has been completely refurbished.*
repair *She has repaired the roof to make the house more windproof.*
restore *The old town square has been beautifully restored.*
revamp *plans to revamp the airport*
See also **decorate, mend, reconstruct, repair, restore**

renown See **fame, reputation**

renowned See **famous, prominent**

rent
▷ *VERB*
to pay money to use something: *They rented an apartment downtown.*
charter *They chartered a jet to fly her home.*
hire *They hired a limousine to take them to the prom.*
lease *He leased a car instead of buying one.*

renunciation See **sacrifice**

reopen See **renew**

repair
▷ *NOUN*
1 a mending of something that is damaged: *She did the house repairs herself.*
mend *a sewing technique that makes the mend invisible*
patch *jackets with patches on the elbows*
restoration *the restoration of a damaged building*
▷ *VERB*
2 to mend something that is damaged: *The money will be used to repair faulty equipment.*
fix *If something is broken, get it fixed.*
mend *They mended it without charge.*
patch *They patched the barn roof.*
patch up *Patch up those holes.*
renovate *They spent thousands renovating the house.*
restore *experts who specialize in restoring old paintings*
See also **fix, mend, piece together, renovate, restore**

R

repay

▷ VERB

to give back money that is owed: *It will take me years to repay the loan.*

pay back *I'll pay you back that money tomorrow.*

refund *Any extra money that you have paid will be refunded.*

settle up *If we owe you anything, we can settle up when you visit.*

See also **compensate, return**

repeal   See **cancel**

repeat

▷ VERB

to say or write something again: *Since you didn't listen, I'll repeat that.*

echo *"Are you frightened?" "Frightened?" he echoed. "Of what?"*

reiterate *The lawyer could only reiterate what he had said before.*

say again *"I'm sorry," she said again.*

See also **quote, stress**

repeated   See **continual, frequent**

repeatedly   See **often**

repel

▷ VERB

1 to horrify and disgust: *The thought of spiders repels me.*

disgust *He disgusted everyone with his obnoxious behaviour.*

offend *viewers who are easily offended*

revolt *The smell revolted me.*

sicken *What he saw there sickened him.*

ANTONYM **attract**

2 to fight and drive back enemy forces: *troops along the border ready to repel an enemy attack*

drive off *They drove the guerrillas off with air strikes.*

repulse *Tanks were sent to repulse the enemy forces.*

resist *They rose up and resisted the invaders.*

See also **disgust**

repellent   See **disgusting, nasty**

repent   See **regret**

repentance   See **regret**

repentant   See **sorry**

replace

▷ VERB

to take the place of something else: *She replaced the singer at the last minute.*

succeed *The king was succeeded by his daughter.*

supersede *Horses were superseded by cars.*

supplant *Anger supplanted all other feelings.*

take over from *She took over from me when I left the job.*

take the place of *Debit cards are taking the place of cash and cheques.*

See also **change, substitute, succeed**

replacement

▷ NOUN

a person or thing that takes the place of another: *He has nominated his assistant as his replacement.*

proxy *They must nominate a proxy to vote on their behalf.*

stand-in *She was a stand-in for my regular doctor.*

substitute *a synthetic substitute for silk*

successor *He recommended me as his successor.*

surrogate *They had expected me to be a surrogate for my sister.*

See also **substitute**

replica   See **copy, model**

reply

▷ VERB

1 to give someone an answer: *He did not even have the courtesy to reply to my e-mail.*

answer *He avoided answering the question.*

counter *"It's not that simple," she countered in a firm voice.*

respond *"It's my decision, not yours," I responded.*

retort *"Nobody asked you," he retorted.*

return *"I can manage," she returned coldly.*

▷ NOUN

2 an answer given to someone: *There was a trace of irony in his reply.*

answer *She could not give him a truthful answer.*

response *Her response was brusque.*

retort *His sharp retort clearly made an impact.*

See also **answer**

report

▷ VERB

1 to tell about or give an official account of something: *He reported the theft to the police.*

cover *The news media will cover the trial closely.*

describe *His condition was described as "improving."*

inform of *Inform the police of any suspicious activity.*

notify *The skipper notified the coastguard of the accident.*

state *The ad stated that all jeans would be on sale.*

▷ NOUN

2 an account of an event or situation: *reports of a tornado touching down*
account *a dishonest account of events*
description *a detailed description*
statement *a deliberately misleading statement*
See also **announcement, feature, item, review, statement**

represent
▷ VERB

1 to stand for something else: *Locate the icon on the desktop that represents your connection.*
mean *That sound means the elevator door is about to open.*
stand for *The maple leaf stands for Canada.*
symbolize *The olive branch symbolizes peace.*
2 to describe something in a particular way: *The media tends to represent him as a hero.*
depict *Children's books usually depict farm animals as lovable.*
describe *She was always described as an intellectual.*
picture *In the press, she was pictured as a eccentric.*
portray *He was portrayed as a heartless person.*
show *She was shown as an intelligent and courageous woman.*

representation *See* **model, symbol**

representative
▷ NOUN

1 a person who acts on behalf of another or others: *Employees from each department elect a representative.*
agent *The singer recently hired a new agent.*
delegate *a student delegate*
deputy *I can't make it, so I'll send my deputy.*
proxy *They must nominate a proxy to vote on their behalf.*
spokesperson *A spokesperson for the team made the announcement.*
▷ ADJECTIVE

2 typical of the group to which it belongs: *fairly representative groups of adults*
characteristic *a characteristic feature*
illustrative *an illustrative example*
typical *a typical Italian menu*
See also **official, substitute, typical**

repress *See* **contain, suppress**

repressed *See* **pent-up**

reprimand *See* **caution, lecture, scold**

reprisal *See* **revenge**

reproach *See* **censure**

reproduce *See* **breed, copy**

reproduction *See* **copy, fake**

republic *See* **state**

repulse *See* **repel**

repulsion *See* **disgust**

repulsive *See* **unpleasant**

reputable *See* **honest, respectable**

reputation
▷ NOUN

the opinion that people have of a person or thing: *The college has a good reputation.*
character *a person of good character*
name *She has a good name in the tennis world.*
renown *a singer of great renown*
repute *a writer and scholar of some repute*
standing *This has done nothing to improve his standing.*
stature *her stature as the world's greatest cellist*
See also **fame, name**

repute *See* **reputation**

reputed *See* **supposed**

request
▷ VERB

1 to ask for something politely or formally: *She requested that the door be left open.*
ask *The government is being asked to consider the plan.*
beg *May I beg a favour of you?*
seek *You should seek a medical opinion.*
▷ NOUN

2 the action of asking for something politely or formally: *The principal agreed to our request.*
appeal *an appeal for witnesses to come forward*
application *Their application was vetoed.*
call *calls to decrease income tax*
plea *his plea for help in solving the crime*
See also **appeal**

require
▷ VERB

1 to need something: *A baby requires warmth and security.*
be in need of *The house was in need of a makeover.*
demand *The task would demand patience and hard work.*
depend on *I depend on this money to survive.*

R

need *He desperately needed a job.*
want *The windows wanted cleaning.*
2 to say that someone must do something: *The rules require employers to provide safety training.*
compel *legislation that would compel cyclists to wear helmets*
demand *This letter demands an immediate reply.*
direct *a court order directing the group to leave the area*
instruct *They have instructed their lawyer to sue for compensation.*
oblige *The law obliges us to wear seatbelts.*
order *The court ordered him to pay the amount in full.*
See also **demand, expect, involve, need, take, want**

required See **compulsory, necessary, supposed**

requirement
  ▷ *NOUN*
something that you must have or do: *The products met all safety requirements.*
demand *the demands and challenges of his new job*
essential *the basic essentials for the camping trip*
necessity *food and other daily necessities*
need *special nutritional needs*
specification *These companies will have to meet strict new specifications.*
See also **condition, standard**

requisite See **compulsory, condition**

reschedule See **put off**

rescue See **save**

research
  ▷ *NOUN*
I the act of studying and finding out about something: *funds for AIDS research*
analysis *They collected blood samples for laboratory analysis.*
examination *A close examination of the painting revealed that it was a forgery.*
exploration *an exploration of classical myths*
investigation *Further investigation was hindered by the loss of the computer files.*
study *a study on the effects of acid rain*
  ▷ *VERB*
2 to study and find out about something: *I'm researching the history of the fisheries.*
analyze *We haven't had time to analyze those samples yet.*
examine *The spacecraft will examine how*

solar wind affects the earth's magnetic field.
explore *I would probably be wise to explore the matter further.*
investigate *Officials are investigating the cause of the explosion.*
study *She's been studying chimpanzees for 30 years.*
See also **investigate, study**

resemblance
  ▷ *NOUN*
a similarity between two things: *I can see a resemblance between you.*
analogy *the analogy between skiing and driving*
correspondence *There's little correspondence between your lifestyle and mine.*
likeness *These myths have a startling likeness to one another.*
parallel *There were parallels between the two cases.*
similarity *similarities between the brothers*
See also **similarity**

resemble
  ▷ *VERB*
to be similar to something else: *He resembles his grandfather when he was a young man.*
bear a resemblance to *She bears a resemblance to her cousin.*
be like *The ground is like concrete.*
be similar to *Your recipe is similar to mine.*
look like *He looks like his father.*
parallel *His fate paralleled that of his predecessor.*
take after *You take after your grandmother.*

resent
  ▷ *VERB*
to feel bitter and angry about something: *I resent the slur on my character.*
be angry about *I was angry at the way he spoke to me.*
be offended by *She was offended by my comments.*
dislike *I dislike his patronizing attitude.*
object to *I object to being treated like an idiot.*
take offence at *She took offence at the implied criticism.*
See also **envy**

resentful
  ▷ *ADJECTIVE*
bitter about something that has happened: *an unhappy and resentful team*
aggrieved *He is still aggrieved at the size of the fine.*
angry *I was angry that I wasn't consulted.*
bitter *a forsaken and bitter man*

embittered *She had grown into an embittered, hardened adult.*

huffy *He's so huffy if he doesn't get his own way.*

indignant *They were indignant that they had not been consulted.*

offended *He was offended at being left out.*
See also **bitter, jealous, sulky**

resentment
▷ *NOUN*
a feeling of anger and bitterness: *There is growing resentment against the new owners.*

anger *We could not understand the reason for his anger.*

animosity *The animosity between the two countries grew.*

bitterness *I feel bitterness toward the person who fired me.*

grudge *It was an accident and I bear no grudges.*

huff *She went off in a huff.*

indignation *He could hardly contain his indignation.*

rancour *There was no trace of envy or rancour in her face.*
See also **animosity, envy, hostility**

reservation *See* **qualification**

reserve
▷ *VERB*
1 to keep for a particular person or purpose: *Hotel rooms have been reserved for us.*

hoard *They've begun to hoard food and fuel.*

hold *The information is held in a database.*

keep *Grate the lemon zest and keep it for later.*

put away *She had enough put away for emergencies.*

save *Save me a seat.*

set aside *money set aside for education*

stockpile *People are stockpiling food for the coming blizzard.*

store *potatoes stored for the winter*
▷ *NOUN*
2 a supply kept for future use: *a drain on the cash reserves*

cache *a cache of peanuts hidden by the squirrel*

fund *a pension fund*

hoard *a hoard of food and fuel*

stock *Our stock of paper is getting low.*

stockpile *stockpiles of bottled water*

store *a secret store of chocolates*

supply *food supplies*
See also **bank, book, fund, hoard, save, stock, stockpile, store, supply**

reserved *See* **cold, distant, remote, secretive**

reservoir *See* **fund, stock, store**

reside *See* **inhabit, live**

residence *See* **home, house**

resident *See* **inhabitant, local**

residue *See* **remains**

resign
▷ *VERB*
to leave a job: *I resigned from the company.*

abdicate *The king abdicated to marry a commoner.*

hand in your notice *I handed in my notice on Friday.*

leave *I am leaving to become a teacher.*

quit *He quit his job at the restaurant.*

step down *In 2003, Jean Chrétien officially stepped down as prime minister.*

resign oneself
▷ *VERB*
to accept an unpleasant situation: *She had resigned herself to losing her job.*

accept *You've got to accept the fact that he's moved away.*

bow *He bowed to the inevitable and got on with his life.*

reconcile oneself *She had reconciled herself to never seeing him again.*
See also **quit**

resigned *See* **passive**

resilient *See* **tough**

resist
▷ *VERB*
to refuse to accept something and try to prevent it: *They resisted our attempts to change the yearbook's format.*

defy *arrested for defying the law*

fight *He vigorously fought the proposal.*

oppose *Many students opposed the changes.*

refuse *The patient has the right to refuse treatment.*

struggle against *small companies struggling against takeovers by large corporations*
ANTONYM **accept**
See also **oppose, rebel, repel**

resistance *See* **defence, opposition**

resistant *See* **immune**

resolute *See* **determined, firm, serious, steadfast**

resolution *See* **decision, determination, resolve, will**

R

resolve

▷ VERB

1 to decide firmly to do something: *She resolved to report the matter.*

decide *She decided to quit smoking.*

determine *They determined to rescue the whale.*

intend *I intended to teach him a lesson.*

make up your mind *Once she made up her mind to do it, there was no stopping her.*

2 to find a solution to a problem: *We must find a way to resolve these problems.*

clear up *The confusion was soon cleared up.*

find a solution to *the ability to find an effective solution to the crisis*

overcome *Find a way to overcome your difficulties.*

solve *These reforms did not solve the problem of unemployment.*

sort out *The two friends have sorted out their differences.*

work out *It seems like a nightmare, but I'm sure we can work it out.*

▷ NOUN

3 absolute determination: *He didn't weaken in his resolve.*

determination *the expression of fierce determination on her face*

resolution *"I'm going on a diet," he said, with sudden resolution.*

tenacity *Hard work and sheer tenacity are crucial to career success.*

See also **decide, determination, determine, intend, settle, solve, will, work out**

resolved *See* **serious**

resonate *See* **ring**

resounding *See* **loud**

respect

▷ VERB

1 to have a good opinion of someone: *I want her to respect me as a dedicated student.*

admire *I admire him for his honesty.*

have a good opinion of *Nobody seems to have a good opinion of him.*

have a high opinion of *They had a very high opinion of the young journalist.*

honour *They honoured us with their respect.*

look up to *He looks up to his dad.*

think highly of *I think highly of her.*

venerate *The musician venerated the great composer.*

ANTONYM **disrespect**

▷ NOUN

2 a good opinion of someone: *We have no respect for him at all.*

admiration *I have always had the greatest admiration for them.*

esteem *We have to win the trust and esteem of our clients.*

regard *I hold them in high regard.*

reverence *What makes a great hockey book is reverence for the game.*

ANTONYM **disrespect**

See also **admiration, admire, appreciate, approval, approve, consider, consideration, detail, esteem, value**

respectable

▷ ADJECTIVE

1 considered to be acceptable and correct: *respectable families*

decent *Sending a note of apology was the decent thing to do.*

good *a good family*

honourable *His colleagues were honourable people.*

proper *It was right and proper to return the lost wallet.*

reputable *a reputable firm*

upright *an upright and trustworthy individual*

worthy *worthy citizens*

2 adequate or reasonable: *a respectable rate of economic growth*

appreciable *making appreciable progress*

considerable *a considerable amount*

decent *a decent standard of living*

fair *She had a fair command of the language.*

reasonable *He couldn't make a reasonable living from his writing.*

See also **decent**

respectful *See* **polite**

respite *See* **break, rest**

respond *See* **answer, reply**

respond to *See* **identify with**

response *See* **answer, reaction, reply**

responsibility

▷ NOUN

1 the duty to deal with or take care of something: *The garden is your responsibility.*

duty *My duty is to look after the animals.*

obligation *You have an obligation to help him.*

onus *The onus was on me to prove my innocence.*

2 the blame for something that has happened: *We must all accept responsibility for our mistakes.*

blame *I'm not going to take the blame for this.*

fault *This is all your fault.*
guilt *She was not completely free of guilt.*
liability *He admitted liability for the damage.*
See also **blame, concern, duty, fault, function, job**

responsible
▷ ADJECTIVE
1 being the person in charge of something: *The music teacher is responsible for the band.*
in charge *I wish someone else was in charge of the project.*
in control *Who is in control of the operation?*
2 being to blame for something: *I hold you responsible for this mess.*
at fault *The driver making the left turn was found to be at fault.*
guilty *I still maintain that I am not guilty.*
to blame *Television is possibly to blame for this.*
3 sensible and dependable: *He had to show that he would be a responsible pet owner.*
dependable *a dependable, trustworthy teacher*
level-headed *a sensible, level-headed approach*
reliable *You have to demonstrate that you are reliable.*
sensible *He's sensible, if a bit headstrong.*
sound *sound advice*
trustworthy *She is a trustworthy leader.*
ANTONYM **irresponsible**

rest
▷ NOUN
1 the remaining parts of something: *Take what you want and leave the rest.*
balance *You pay half now and the balance on delivery.*
others *She took one and put the others back.*
remainder *He gulped down the remainder of his coffee.*
surplus *Coat the chicken with flour, shaking off the surplus.*
2 a period when you relax and do nothing: *I'll start again after a rest.*
break *He needs to take a break from work.*
holiday *I could really do with a holiday.*
leisure *What do you do in your leisure time?*
relaxation *Make time for a bit of relaxation.*
respite *a respite from the rush of everyday life*
▷ VERB
3 to relax and do nothing for a while: *She rested briefly before going on.*
have a break *He felt he had to have a break.*
idle *He sat idling in his room.*

laze *lazing on the beach*
put your feet up *Nobody's home, so I can put my feet up for a while.*
relax *They relaxed in the student lounge.*
sit down *I'll have to sit down for a minute.*
take it easy *the chance to just take it easy for a couple of weeks*
See also **break, pause, put, relax, remainder, set**

restful See **comfortable, quiet**

restless
▷ ADJECTIVE
unable to sit still or relax: *She had been restless and irritable all day.*
edgy *He was nervous and edgy as he sat in traffic.*
fidgety *bored, fidgety youngsters*
fretful *The family was fretful as they waited for news.*
jumpy *If she can't go outside, she gets jumpy and irritable.*
on edge *He's been on edge for weeks.*
unsettled *The workers were unsettled and demoralized.*
See also **active, busy, impatient**

restoration See **recovery, repair**

restore
▷ VERB
1 to cause something to return to its previous state: *He was anxious to restore his reputation.*
re-establish *an attempt to re-establish diplomatic relations*
reinstate *the failure to reinstate proper guidelines*
reintroduce *the plan to reintroduce that model of car*
return *attempts to return the team to its old glory*
2 to clean and repair something: *experts who specialize in restoring old paintings*
fix up *It took us months to fix this house up.*
mend *They finally got around to mending the roof.*
rebuild *plans to rebuild the arena*
reconstruct *reconstructing the old bridge*
refurbish *refurbishing the city hall's facade*
renovate *The hotel was being renovated.*
repair *The money will be used to repair faulty equipment.*
See also **mend, piece together, reconstruct, renovate, repair**

restrain
▷ VERB
to hold someone or something back: *He had*

R

to be restrained by his friends.
contain *He could hardly contain his rage.*
control *She tried to control her excitement.*
curb *She couldn't curb her enthusiasm.*
hamper *I was hampered by a lack of information.*
hinder *Expansion of the league is hindered by lack of cash.*
hold back *He could no longer hold back his laughter.*
inhibit *factors that inhibit growth*
See also **check, contain, curb, restrict, suppress**

restraint *See* **curb, economy, patience, restriction**

restrict

▷ *VERB*
to limit the movement or actions of someone or something: *laws to restrict foreign imports*
confine *They kept the dog confined to the house.*
contain *The fire had been contained.*
hamper *I was hampered by a lack of information.*
handicap *handicapped by the terms of the contract*
impede *Their work was being impeded by shortages of supplies.*
inhibit *factors that inhibit growth*
limit *Her practice sessions were limited to three a week.*
restrain *the need to restrain price increases*
See also **confine, hamper, handicap, limit**

restriction

▷ *NOUN*
a rule or situation that limits what you can do: *travel restrictions*
constraint *financial constraints*
control *a call for stricter gun control*
curb *a curb on lumber imports*
limit *a speed limit*
limitation *A slipped disc causes severe limitation of movement.*
regulation *regulations outlawing child labour*
restraint *a restraint placed on an injured animal*
stipulation *The only dress stipulation was "no jeans."*

result

▷ *NOUN*
1 the situation that is caused by something: *the result of many rehearsals*
consequence *This could have disastrous consequences for us.*

effect *the intended effect of the new requirements*
outcome *The ultimate outcome will be different.*
product *the product of five years' work*
upshot *The upshot is that our employees are all unhappy.*
▷ *VERB*
2 to be caused by something: *The crash resulted from a defect in the aircraft.*
arise *the publicity that arises from incidents of this kind*
derive *Much of my sense of humour derived from childhood experiences.*
develop *a determination which has developed from his new-found confidence*
ensue *If the system collapses, chaos will ensue.*
follow *the consequences that followed his release from prison*
happen *What will happen if you can't get online?*
stem *His dislike of broccoli stems from eating so much of it as a child.*
See also **develop, effect, happen**

result in

▷ *VERB*
to cause something to happen: *Fifty percent of road accidents result in head injuries.*
bring about *A shortage of gasoline will bring about an increase in price.*
cause *The play caused a stir here.*
lead to *brain damage which leads to paralysis*
See also **bring**

resume *See* **continue, renew**

resuscitate *See* **revive**

retain *See* **remember**

retaliate

▷ *VERB*
to do something to someone in return for what he or she did: *The army will retaliate against any attacks.*
get back at *a desire to get back at the person who did this*
get even with *He wanted to get even with the practical joker.*
get your own back *the opportunity to get your own back on your old adversary*
hit back *In this article, she hits back at her critics.*
pay someone back *I'll pay him back for what he's done.*
take revenge *taking revenge for his friend's death*
See also **revenge**

retaliation *See* **revenge**

reticence *See* **silence**

reticent *See* **secretive**

retire *See* **quit, withdraw**

retiring *See* **shy**

retort *See* **answer, reply**

retract *See* **reverse**

retreat

▷ *VERB*

1 to move away from someone or something: *The rebels retreated from the town.*

back away *She put up her hands in protest and began to back away.*

back off *I stood up for myself and they backed off.*

draw back *They drew back in fear.*

pull back *Their forces have pulled back in all areas.*

withdraw *Troops withdrew from the country last month.*

ANTONYM **advance**

▷ *NOUN*

2 the action of moving away from someone or something: *the long retreat from the capital*

departure *Her departure from the company was a mistake.*

evacuation *the evacuation of residents from the neighbourhood*

flight *their flight from danger*

withdrawal *the withdrawal of enemy troops*

ANTONYM **advance**

▷ *NOUN*

3 a quiet place you can go to: *He spent the day hidden away in his country retreat.*

haven *The hotel is a haven of tranquillity.*

refuge *My cabin in the woods is a refuge from the harsh realities of the world.*

sanctuary *a sanctuary located on an island*

See also **withdraw**

retribution *See* **punishment, revenge**

retrieval *See* **recovery**

retrieve *See* **recover**

return

▷ *VERB*

1 to go back to a place: *The plane failed to return at the scheduled time.*

come back *She said she'd come back later.*

go back *I love going back home.*

reappear *He reappeared two nights later.*

turn back *We've come too far now to turn back.*

2 to give something back: *You can return the coat if it doesn't fit.*

give back *He is refusing to give the dog back.*

pay back *Of course you have to pay back the loan.*

refund *The company will refund the full cost.*

repay *I can afford to repay the loan.*

See also **reply, restore, vote**

reunion *See* **meeting**

revamp *See* **renovate, revise**

reveal

▷ *VERB*

1 to tell people about something: *They were not ready to reveal any of the details.*

announce *They were planning to announce their engagement.*

disclose *She will not disclose the name of her patient.*

divulge *I do not want to divulge the source of my information.*

get off your chest INFORMAL *I feel it's done me good to get it off my chest.*

2 to uncover something that is hidden: *The carpet was removed to reveal the original pine floor.*

bring to light *The truth is unlikely to be brought to light.*

lay bare *His real motives were laid bare.*

uncover *They uncovered evidence of fraud.*

unearth *Archaeologists have unearthed ancient coins.*

unveil *The statue will be unveiled next week.*

See also **announce, betray, expose, indicate, show, uncover**

revel *See* **glory**

revel in *See* **enjoy, like**

revelation *See* **surprise**

revenge

▷ *NOUN*

1 vengeance for wrongs or injury received: *acts of revenge*

reprisal *witnesses unwilling to testify for fear of reprisal*

retaliation *The attack was in retaliation for the murder.*

retribution *They did not want their names used for fear of retribution.*

vengeance *He swore vengeance on everyone involved in the murder.*

▷ *VERB*

2 to take vengeance on someone: *He vowed to revenge himself on his enemies.*

avenge *He said he was trying to avenge the death of his friend.*

get even *I'm going to get even with you for this.*

R

get your own back *I simply want to get my own back on him.*
hit back *She hit back at those who criticized her.*
pay someone back *Some day I'll pay you back for this.*
retaliate *I was sorely tempted to retaliate.*

revenue See **profit**

reverence See **esteem, respect**

reverse
▷ VERB
1 to change into something different or contrary: *They won't reverse the decision to increase prices.*
change *They should change the rules to make this practice illegal.*
invalidate *A contract signed now might be invalidated at a future date.*
overrule *The umpire's decision was later overruled.*
overturn *The Court of Appeal overturned the original decision.*
retract *He was asked to retract his comments but refused.*
▷ NOUN
2 the opposite of what has just been said or done: *The reverse seldom applies.*
contrary *I'm not a fan of hers. Quite the contrary.*
converse *In fact, the converse is true.*
opposite *When I told him to do something, he always did the opposite.*
See also **back, opposite, overrule, overturn**

review
▷ NOUN
1 a critical assessment of a book or performance: *The school play received excellent reviews.*
commentary *He'll be writing a weekly commentary on popular culture.*
criticism *literary criticism*
notice *The singer's solo work received good notices.*
2 a general survey or report: *a review of safety procedures*
analysis *an analysis of Canadian trade policy*
examination *an examination of the top 250 companies*
report *the committee's annual report*
study *a recent study of treatments for back pain*
survey *a survey of 250 students*
See also **summary**

revise
▷ VERB
to alter or correct something: *The second edition was completely revised.*
amend *They voted unanimously to amend the constitution.*
correct *time spent correcting his students' work*
edit *We have the right to edit this book once it's finished.*
revamp *It is time to revamp the system.*
update *She was back in the office, updating the work schedule.*

revival See **recovery**

revive
▷ VERB
to make or become lively or active again: *an attempt to revive the stagnant economy*
rally *The stock market began to rally.*
resuscitate *a bid to resuscitate the weekly magazine*
See also **recover, refresh**

revoke See **cancel**

revolt See **disgust, rebel, rebellion, repel**

revolting See **disgusting**

revolution See **rebellion**

revolutionize See **transform**

revolve See **centre, spin**

revulsion See **disgust, hatred, horror**

reward
▷ NOUN
something given in return for a service: *As a reward for good behaviour, praise your child.*
bonus *a year-end bonus at work*
bounty *a bounty on wolves*
payment *Players now expect payment for interviews.*
prize *He won first prize.*
See also **compensate**

rewarding See **successful**

rhythm
▷ NOUN
a regular movement or beat: *His body twists and sways to the rhythm.*
beat *the thumping beat of rock music*
pulse *the repetitive pulse of the drumbeat*
tempo *The composer supplied her works with precise indications of tempo.*
time *The waltz is in three-quarter time.*
See also **beat**

rhythmic See **regular**

rich

▷ ADJECTIVE

I having a lot of money and possessions: *You're going to be a very rich person.*

affluent *an affluent neighbourhood*

loaded SLANG *Of course he can afford it. He's loaded.*

opulent *her opulent lifestyle*

prosperous *the youngest child of a relatively prosperous family*

wealthy *a wealthy industrialist*

well off *My grandparents were quite well off.*

ANTONYM **poor**

2 abundant in something: *Bananas are rich in vitamin A.*

abundant *the earth's most abundant natural resources*

fertile *a fertile imagination*

plentiful *a plentiful supply of vegetables*

See also **colourful, fertile, wealthy**

riches See **wealth**

rickety See **shaky, unsteady**

ricochet See **bounce**

rid or **get rid of**

▷ VERB

to remove or destroy something: *a coach who wanted to get rid of me*

dispose of *He disposed of the murder weapon.*

dump *We dumped our bags at the hotel.*

eject *Officials used guard dogs to eject the protestors.*

jettison *The crew jettisoned the excess fuel.*

remove *Most of their fears had been removed.*

weed out *We must weed these problems out as soon as possible.*

riddle See **mystery, problem, puzzle**

ride See **drive**

ridge See **top**

ridicule See **make fun of, mock, mockery**

ridiculous

▷ ADJECTIVE

very foolish: *It is ridiculous to suggest we are having secret meetings.*

absurd *absurd claims to have met big stars*

laughable *He claims the allegations are "laughable."*

ludicrous *It's a completely ludicrous idea.*

preposterous *their preposterous claim that they had unearthed a plot*

See also **absurd, crazy, silly**

rife See **widespread**

rift See **breach, fissure, split**

right

▷ ADJECTIVE

I in accordance with the facts: *That clock never tells the right time.*

accurate *an accurate record of events*

correct *The correct answers can be found at the bottom of the page.*

exact *I need to know the exact time.*

factual *His version of events is not strictly factual.*

genuine *a genuine eyewitness account*

precise *Officials did not give precise figures.*

strict *She has never been a star in the strict sense of the word.*

true *The true cost is higher than the estimated cost.*

valid *Your point is a valid one.*

ANTONYM **wrong**

2 most suitable: *The time is right for our escape.*

acceptable *This was beyond the bounds of acceptable behaviour.*

appropriate *an appropriate outfit for the occasion*

desirable *This goal is neither achievable nor desirable.*

done *Behaving that way just isn't done.*

fit *a subject that is not fit for discussion*

fitting *a fitting end to an exciting game*

OK INFORMAL *Is it OK if I bring a friend with me?*

proper *It's proper to send them a thank-you note.*

seemly *the rules of civility and seemly conduct*

suitable *the most suitable person for the job*

▷ NOUN

3 what is just and fair: *At least he knew right from wrong.*

fairness *a decision based not on fairness but on expediency*

equity *pay equity for men and women*

honour *Her whole life was dominated by a sense of honour.*

integrity *They always strove to maintain a high level of integrity.*

justice *He has no sense of justice or fair play.*

legality *They are expected to observe the principles of legality.*

morality *standards of morality and justice in society*

virtue *the special qualities of virtue*

R

See also **accurate, correct, fitting, immediately, power, proper, suitable**

INFORMALLY SPEAKING

in the right: morally correct
right now (or off): immediately

---

right away See **immediately**

right now See **now**

righteous See **religious**

rightful See **legal, real**

right-hand man See **assistant, helper**

righting See **correction**

right-wing
▷ ADJECTIVE
believing in conservative policies: *some right-wing groups*
conservative *conservative thinking*
reactionary *the most reactionary leader of that century*

rigid
▷ ADJECTIVE
I unchangeable and often considered severe: *Hospital routines for nurses are sometimes very rigid.*
fixed *fixed laws*
inflexible *Workers said the system was too inflexible.*
set *They have very set ideas about how to achieve this goal.*
strict *a strict diet*
stringent *stringent rules*
2 not easy to bend: *rigid plastic containers*
firm *Pack the dishes in a firm, strong box.*
hard *Something hard pressed into his back.*
solid *The concrete will stay as solid as a rock.*
stiff *Her fingers were stiff with cold.*
ANTONYM **flexible**
See also **firm, hard, stiff, strict, tense, tight**

rigorous See **hard, stiff, strict**

rigorously See **well**

rim See **border, edge**

ring
▷ VERB
I to make a loud clear sound: *He heard the school bell ring.*
chime *The clock chimed three o'clock.*
clang *The clock tower's bell clanged.*
peal *Bells pealed at the stroke of midnight.*
resonate *The chimes of the grandfather clock resonated through the house.*

toll *The tourists tolled the bell.*
▷ NOUN
2 an object or group of things in the shape of a circle: *a ring of blue smoke*
band *a wedding band*
circle *Cut out four circles of cardboard.*
hoop *a steel hoop*
loop *a loop of garden hose*
round *Slice a round of bread in half.*
▷ NOUN
3 a group of people involved in an illegal activity: *a drug-trafficking ring*
band *a small band of petty thieves*
cell *a cell of terrorists*
syndicate *a major crime syndicate*
See also **sound**

ringleader See **leader**

rinse See **wash**

riot
▷ NOUN
I a disturbance made by an unruly mob: *a prison riot*
anarchy *a decade of civil war and anarchy*
disorder *mass public disorder*
disturbance *Three fans were injured in a disturbance outside the stadium.*
mob violence *mob violence in a climate of war*
strife *the cause of neighbourhood strife*
▷ VERB
2 to take part in a riot: *They rioted in protest against the government.*
go on the rampage *Rock fans went on the rampage after a concert.*
rampage *A curfew was imposed as gangs rampaged through the streets.*
run riot *hoodlums running riot in the streets*
take to the streets *Workers and students took to the streets in protest.*

rip See **split, tear**

rip off See **cheat**

ripe See **ready**

ripple See **wave**

rise
▷ VERB
I to move upward: *smoke rising from the volcano*
ascend *She held my hand as we ascended the steps.*
climb *We climbed onto the bridge.*
go up *He went up the ladder quickly.*
move up *They moved up to second place after their win.*
2 to increase: *House prices are expected to rise this year.*

go up *Life expectancy has gone up from 60 to 79.*

grow *The economy continues to grow.*

increase *the decision to increase prices*

intensify *The conflict is bound to intensify.*

mount *For several hours the tension mounted.*

ANTONYM **fall**

▷ NOUN

3 an increase in something: *a rise in prices*

improvement *a major improvement in standards*

increase *a substantial increase in my workload*

upsurge *an upsurge of interest in books*

ANTONYM **fall**

See also **gain, increase, jump, slope**

CONFUSABLES

rise means **get up** or **go up**
raise means **lift up**

---

rise to *See* **reach**

risk

▷ NOUN

I a chance that something unpleasant might happen: *That's a risk I'm happy to take.*

danger *the dangers of smoking*

gamble *Booking a last-minute vacation can be a gamble.*

peril *the perils of starring in a TV commercial*

pitfall *the pitfalls of working at home*

▷ VERB

2 to do something knowing that something unpleasant might happen: *If he doesn't play, he risks losing his place in the team.*

chance *He wondered if he should chance singing in public.*

dare *Few people dared to go anywhere on foot.*

gamble *gambling their life savings on the stock market*

jeopardize *The talks may still be jeopardized by disputes.*

put in jeopardy *A series of setbacks have put the whole project in jeopardy.*

See also **danger, dare, endanger, gamble, possibility, threat**

risky *See* **dangerous**

rite *See* **ceremony**

ritual *See* **ceremony, custom**

rival

▷ NOUN

I the person someone is competing with: *She is well ahead of her nearest rival.*

adversary *political adversaries*

antagonist *In* Hamlet, *the king is the prince's antagonist.*

challenger *his only challenger for the position*

opponent *He's a tough opponent, but I'm too good for him.*

▷ VERB

2 to be the equal or near equal of: *For beauty, few beaches rival those of Prince Edward Island.*

be a match for *On the day of the game, we were a match for any team.*

equal *The victory equalled her personal best.*

match *I think we matched them in every department.*

See also **competitor**

rivalry *See* **competition**

TYPES OF ... *RIVER*

brook	stream
creek	tributary
estuary	watercourse
rivulet	waterway

---

road

▷ NOUN

a route used by travellers and vehicles: *There was very little traffic on the mining road.*

highway *The Trans-Canada Highway was officially completed in 1962.*

route *the most direct route to the downtown area*

street *He walked briskly down the street.*

track *a rough mountain track*

See also **route, way**

roam *See* **wander**

roar *See* **shout**

roast *See* **cook**

rob

▷ VERB

to take something from a person illegally: *He was robbed of all his money.*

burglarize *Their home had been burglarized during the night.*

con INFORMAL *Several people had been conned out of their life savings.*

defraud *charges of conspiracy to defraud the government*

loot *thugs who have looted stores*

steal from *trying to steal from my locker*

swindle *two executives who swindled their employer*

robber *See* **thief**

robbery *See* **theft**

R

robe *See* **dress**

robot *See* **automatic**

robust *See* **fit, healthy, sound, sturdy, tough, well**

rocket *See* **bomb, explode**

rocky *See* **rough**

rod *See* **bar, stick**

rogue *See* **crook**

role *See* **duty, function, job, part**

roll *See* **flow**

romantic
▷ ADJECTIVE
connected with sexual love: *a romantic relationship*
amorous *Who is the object of your amorous intentions?*
loving *a loving husband*
passionate *a passionate love affair*
tender *They embraced and kissed. It was a tender moment.*

room
▷ NOUN
1 a separate section in a building: *You can stay in my room.*
chamber *the judge's chambers*
office *I'm in the office at the end of the hallway.*
2 unoccupied space: *There wasn't enough room in the car.*
capacity *a seating capacity of 17 000*
elbow room *There wasn't too much elbow room in the cockpit.*
space *the high cost of office space*
See also **capacity, space**

rooms *See* **apartment**

root *See* **cause, origin**

rope *See* **tie**

rot
▷ VERB
1 to become rotten: *The grain started rotting in the silos.*
decay *The tooth was beginning to decay.*
decompose *The food scraps slowly decomposed into compost.*
fester *The wound is festering.*
spoil *Fats spoil by becoming rancid.*
▷ NOUN
2 the condition that affects things when they rot: *The wood was not protected against rot.*
decay *tooth decay*

deterioration *deterioration of the musty, damp suitcase*
mould *He scraped the mould off the cheese.*
See also **eat away, rubbish**

rotate *See* **spin, turn**

rotten
▷ ADJECTIVE
1 decayed and no longer of use: *The old wooden window frame is rotten.*
bad *That milk in the fridge is bad.*
decayed *teeth so decayed they need to be pulled*
decomposed *The body was too badly decomposed to be identified.*
mouldy *mouldy bread*
sour *sour milk*
2 INFORMAL of very poor quality: *It's a rotten idea.*
inferior *overpriced and inferior products*
lousy SLANG *The menu is limited and the food is lousy.*
poor *The food here is very poor.*
unsatisfactory *unsatisfactory goods or services*
See also **shabby, terrible**

rough
▷ ADJECTIVE
1 uneven and not smooth: *My bicycle bumped along the rough ground.*
bumpy *bumpy cobbled streets*
craggy *craggy mountains*
rocky *a bleak and rocky shore*
rugged *a remote and rugged hiking trail*
uneven *an uneven surface*
ANTONYM **smooth**
2 difficult or unpleasant: *He's been through a rough time.*
difficult *It's been a difficult month for us.*
hard *I've had a hard life.*
tough *She had a pretty tough childhood.*
unpleasant *The last few weeks here have been very unpleasant.*
3 only approximately correct: *I can give you a rough idea of the time.*
approximate *All times are approximate.*
estimated *There are an estimated 90 000 gangsters in the country.*
sketchy *a sketchy account of the incident*
vague *She could give only a vague description of the intruder.*
See also **approximate, broad, crude, jagged, primitive, uneven, violent, wild**

INFORMALLY SPEAKING

rough in (or out): shape or sketch roughly
rough it: do without conveniences

round

▷ *ADJECTIVE*

1 shaped like a ball or a circle: *a round pizza in a square box*

circular *a circular hole 4 m wide*
cylindrical *a cylindrical container*
rounded *a low, rounded hill*
spherical *a spherical fish bowl*

▷ *NOUN*

2 one of a series of events: *After round three, two contestants shared the lead.*

lap *the last lap of the race*
period *the second overtime period*
session *our first practice session*
stage *the second stage of the Tour de France*
See also **ring**

round off *See* **conclude**

round up *See* **gather**

roundabout *See* **indirect**

rounded *See* **blunt, round**

rouse *See* **provoke, wake**

rousing *See* **exciting**

rout *See* **defeat, vanquish**

route

▷ *NOUN*

a way from one place to another: *the direct route to the downtown area*

channel *a safe shipping channel, avoiding the reefs*
course *The ship was on a course that followed the coastline.*
itinerary *The next place on our itinerary was Mount Robson.*
path *We followed the hiking path.*
road *The coastal road is longer, but more scenic.*
way *I'm afraid I can't remember the way.*
See also **course, direction, line, passage, path, road, way**

routine

▷ *ADJECTIVE*

1 ordinary, and done regularly: *a series of routine medical tests*

everyday *an everyday occurrence*
normal *The hospital claimed it was following its normal procedure.*
ordinary *It was just an ordinary weekend for us.*
regular *one of the regular checks we carry out*
standard *It was standard practice for untrained clerks to do this work.*
typical *This was a fairly typical morning scene in our house.*

usual *The usual methods were not effective.*

▷ *NOUN*

2 the usual way or order someone does things: *The players had to change their daily routine.*

order *Babies respond well to order in their daily lives.*
pattern *All three attacks followed the same pattern.*
practice *a public inquiry into bank practices*
procedure *The Prime Minister's Office said there would be no change in procedure.*
program *It is best to follow some sort of structured program.*
schedule *He has been forced to adjust his schedule.*
system *an efficient filing system*
See also **custom, everyday, habit, normal, ordinary, practice, regular, stock, straightforward, system**

row

▷ *NOUN*

1 several things arranged in a line: *She was greeted by a row of glum faces.*

bank *a bank of elevators*
column *a column of numbers*
line *a sparse line of spectators*
queue *a queue of printing jobs*
rank *a long rank of taxis*

2 a serious disagreement: *This could provoke a major diplomatic row with neighbouring countries.*

altercation *He had an altercation with the umpire.*
argument *an argument about money*
quarrel *I had a terrible quarrel with my brother.*
squabble *There have been minor squabbles about who gets to use the computer.*
See also **argue, argument, disagreement, dispute, fight, line, noise, quarrel, racket, rank, squabble**

rowdy

▷ *ADJECTIVE*

rough and noisy: *He complained to the police about rowdy neighbours.*

boisterous *Most of the children were noisy and boisterous.*
noisy *My neighbours are a noisy bunch.*
unruly *They took the unruly child out of the restaurant.*
wild *fast cars and wild parties*
See also **wild**

royal

▷ *ADJECTIVE*

concerning a king or a queen or his or her

R

family: *the royal yacht*
imperial *the Imperial Palace in Tokyo*
regal *Never has she looked more regal.*
sovereign *the queen's sovereign authority*

rub *See* **wear**

rub out *See* **delete**

rubbish

▷ *NOUN*

1 unwanted things or waste material: *tons of rubbish waiting to be dumped*
garbage *Please take out the garbage and the recycling box.*
litter *fines for dropping litter*
refuse *We took the refuse to the dump.*
trash *The yards are overgrown and covered with trash.*
waste *the safe disposal of toxic waste*
2 foolish words or speech: *Don't talk rubbish!*
drivel *mindless drivel*
garbage *I personally think this is complete garbage.*
hot air INFORMAL *His excuse was just hot air.*
nonsense *all that poetic nonsense about love*
rot *What a load of rot!*
See also **garbage, junk, nonsense, refuse, trash**

rude

▷ *ADJECTIVE*

1 not polite: *He is rude to her friends.*
disrespectful *They shouldn't treat their parents in this disrespectful way.*
impertinent *I don't like being asked impertinent questions.*
impudent *his rude and impudent behaviour*
insolent *a defiant, almost insolent look*
ANTONYM **polite**
2 unexpected and unpleasant: *a rude awakening*
abrupt *The incident brought an abrupt end to his happiness.*
unpleasant *an unpleasant surprise*
violent *violent mood swings*
See also **abrupt, abusive, common, dirty, indecent, primitive, unpleasant, vulgar**

rudimentary *See* **crude, primitive**

rudiments *See* **essentials**

ruffle *See* **irritate, upset**

rugged *See* **rough, tough**

ruin

▷ *VERB*

1 to destroy or spoil something: *The crops have been ruined.*
break *He's broken all his toys.*
damage *This could damage our chances of winning.*
destroy *a recipe for destroying the economy*
devastate *Fires had devastated a large part of the forest.*
impair *The flavour is impaired by overcooking.*
mar *The celebrations were marred by violence.*
mess up INFORMAL *She's messed up her chances.*
spoil *Don't let a stupid mistake spoil your life.*
undo *He intends to undo everything I have fought for.*
wreck *The storm wrecked the garden.*
▷ *NOUN*
2 the state of being destroyed or spoiled: *The old factory was in a state of ruin.*
decay *The house fell into a state of decay.*
destruction *the destruction caused by the rioters*
devastation *devastation where the tornado came down*
disrepair *Many of the buildings had fallen into disrepair.*
downfall *A lack of experience led to his downfall.*
fall *the fall of the Roman Empire*
▷ *NOUN*
3 the remaining parts of a severely damaged thing: *the burned-out ruins of the building*
remains *the remains of an old fort*
shell *the shells of burned buildings*
wreck *We thought of buying the house as a wreck and fixing it up.*
See also **crash, destroy, downfall, harm, spoil**

ruined *See* **derelict**

rule

▷ *NOUN*

a statement of what is allowed: *This was against the rules.*
decree *a decree lifting sanctions against the country*
guideline *strict guidelines for recycling*
law *traffic laws*
order *He was suspended for disobeying orders.*
regulation *new safety regulations*

as a rule

▷ *ADVERB*

usually or generally: *As a rule, I eat my meals*

in front of the TV.
generally *It is generally true that the darker the fruit, the higher its iron content.*
mainly *Mainly, I work alone.*
normally *Normally, the transit system carries 50 000 passengers a day.*
on the whole *Their clothing line is, on the whole, of a very high standard.*
usually *I'm usually a calm and diplomatic person.*

rule
▷ VERB
to govern people: *He rules the country with a strong hand.*
administer *calls for the UN to administer the country until the election*
be in power *They were in power for 18 years.*
govern *The citizens are thankful they are not governed by a dictator.*
lead *Brian Mulroney led the country between 1984 and 1993.*
reign *King Henry II reigned from 1154 to 1189.*
See also **control, law, line**

rule out *See* **exclude**

ruler
▷ NOUN
a person who rules or commands: *He was a weak-willed and indecisive ruler.*
commander *The Governor General is commander of Canada's armed forces.*
head of state *the heads of state of all the countries in the western hemisphere*
leader *the leader of the New Democratic Party*
monarch *the coronation of the new monarch*
premier *the provincial premiers*
prime minister *the prime minister of Canada*
sovereign *the first British sovereign to set foot on Spanish soil*

rules *See* **standards**

ruling *See* **decision, judgment**

rumour
▷ NOUN
a story that may or may not be true: *persistent rumours of problems within the team*
gossip *We spent the first hour exchanging gossip.*
hearsay *Much of what was reported to them was hearsay.*
whisper *I've heard a whisper that she intends to quit.*
word *What's the latest word from Ottawa?*

rumoured *See* **supposed**

rumpus *See* **racket**

run
▷ VERB
1 to move on foot at a rapid pace: *I excused myself and ran back to the telephone.*
bolt *The students bolted out the door.*
gallop *The horses galloped away.*
jog *I could scarcely jog around the block that first day.*
sprint *She sprinted to the car.*
2 to manage: *He ran a small hotel.*
administer *the authorities who administer the island*
be in charge of *She is in charge of public safety.*
control *They now control a large property management empire.*
direct *She will direct day-to-day operations.*
look after *I look after the family's finances.*
manage *Within two years, she was managing the store.*
See also **administer, conduct, dash, direct, drive, flow, function, head, manage, pour, race, range, rush, series, stretch, supervise**

INFORMALLY SPEAKING

run across (or into): meet by chance
run out on: desert someone
run up against: face a problem or difficulty
run with: go ahead creatively with a plan

run across *See* **meet**

run amok *See* **rampage**

run around *See* **associate**

run away *See* **bolt, escape, flee**

run into *See* **hit, meet**

run off *See* **bolt, escape**

run riot *See* **rampage, riot**

run through *See* **exhaust**

rundown *See* **outline, summary**

runner *See* **messenger**

running *See* **management, upkeep**

runny *See* **liquid, thin**

rupture *See* **burst, division, tear**

ruse *See* **manoeuvre, trick**

R

rush

▷ *VERB*

1 to move fast or do something quickly: *Someone rushed out of the building.*

dash *She dashed in from the garden.*

fly *I must fly or I'll miss my train.*

gush *Piping-hot water gushed out.*

hasten *One of them hastened toward me.*

hurry *He had to hurry home to look after his son.*

hustle *Please hustle! I'm ready.*

race *He raced across town to her house.*

run *I excused myself and ran to the door.*

scurry *Reporters scurried to get to their laptops.*

shoot *The car shot into the intersection and nearly smashed into them.*

2 to force into immediate action without sufficient preparation: *Ministers won't be rushed into a response.*

hurry *I don't want to hurry you.*

press *attempting to press me into making a statement*

pressure *Do not be pressured into making your decision immediately*

push *Don't be pushed into signing anything.*

▷ *NOUN*

3 a state of hurrying: *the rush not to be late for school*

bustle *the bustle of modern life*

dash *a 100 km dash to the hospital*

hurry *We left the house in a hurry.*

race *a race to get the work finished before the deadline*

scramble *the scramble to get good seats for the movie*

stampede *There was a stampede for the exit.*

See also **bolt, burst, bustle, charge, dash, flood, fly, hurry, speed, wave**

ruthless See **harsh, merciless**

Ss

sack
▷ VERB
INFORMAL to dismiss from a job: *sacked for missing work so often*
discharge *discharged from the army*
dismiss *the power to dismiss employees*
fire *She was fired for insulting customers.*

the sack
▷ NOUN
INFORMAL dismissal from a job: *He got the sack after three months.*
discharge *He plans to appeal his discharge.*
dismissal *the case for his dismissal*
termination of employment *wrongful termination of employment*
See also **discharge, fire**

sacred See **holy, religious**

sacrifice
▷ VERB
1 to give something up: *He sacrificed his personal life for his career.*
forfeit *The company is forfeiting safety for the sake of profit.*
forgo *If we forgo our summer vacation, we can afford a car.*
give up *I gave up my job to be with you.*
surrender *They surrendered their independence for economic gain.*
▷ NOUN
2 the action of giving something up: *He was willing to make any sacrifice for peace.*
renunciation *renunciation of the crown for the sake of love*
self-denial *an unprecedented act of self-denial*

sacrosanct See **holy**

sad
▷ ADJECTIVE
1 feeling unhappy about something: *The loss of our friendship makes me sad.*
blue *I don't know why I'm feeling so blue today.*
dejected *Everyone has days when they feel dejected.*
depressed *She's depressed about this whole situation.*
dismal *What are you all looking so dismal about?*
down *My uncle sounded really down.*
downcast *a downcast expression*
glum *a row of glum faces*
gloomy *Don't look so gloomy! Things will get better.*
grief-stricken *grief-stricken relatives*

low *He comforted me when I was feeling low.*
melancholy *melancholy thoughts*
mournful *the mournful expression on his face*
unhappy *I hate to see you so unhappy.*
wistful *I found myself feeling wistful at the memory of him.*
ANTONYM **happy**
2 making you feel unhappy: *a sad song*
depressing *a depressing movie*
dismal *a dark, dismal day*
gloomy *a gloomy tale of a poor orphan*
harrowing *a harrowing documentary about the homeless*
heart-rending *heart-rending pictures of the victims*
melancholy *the melancholy music used throughout the movie*
mournful *a mournful ballad*
moving *a deeply moving account of her life*
pathetic *the pathetic sight of oil-covered seabirds*
poignant *a poignant love story*
tragic *his tragic death*
upsetting *I'm afraid I have some upsetting news for you.*
See also **gloomy, miserable, pathetic, sorry, unhappy**

sadden See **distress, grieve, hurt**

saddened See **disappointed**

saddening See **painful**

sadistic See **cruel**

sadness
▷ NOUN
the feeling of being unhappy: *I said goodbye with a mixture of sadness and joy.*
dejection *a feeling of dejection and despair*
depression *plunged into the deepest depression*
despondency *Deep despondency set in again.*
melancholy *He seems to have shaken off his melancholy.*
unhappiness *His unhappiness shows in his face.*
ANTONYM **happiness**
See also **grief, misery, sorrow**

safe
▷ ADJECTIVE
1 not causing harm or danger: *This is not a safe place after dark.*
harmless *harmless substances*
innocuous *Both mushrooms look innocuous but are in fact deadly.*

S

wholesome *fresh, wholesome ingredients*
ANTONYM **dangerous**
2 not in any danger: *I feel warm and safe with you.*
all right *I'll be all right on my own.*
in safe hands *It's all right; you're in safe hands.*
OK INFORMAL *Could you check that the baby's OK?*
out of danger *We were not out of danger yet.*
out of harm's way *I'm keeping him well out of harm's way.*
protected *Keep the plants protected from frost.*
safe and sound *I'm sure he will come home safe and sound.*
secure *I would like to feel financially secure.*
See also **harmless, immune, reliable, secure**

safe and sound See **safe**

safeguard
▷ VERB
1 to protect something: *international action to safeguard the ozone layer*
defend *his courage in defending religious and civil rights*
guard *He closely guarded her identity.*
look after *People tend to look after their own property.*
preserve *We need to preserve the forest.*
protect *What can we do to protect ourselves against heart disease?*
save *A knowledge of CPR could help you save someone from choking.*
shield *They moved to shield their children from adverse publicity.*
▷ NOUN
2 something that protects people or things: *adequate safeguards for civil liberties*
barrier *a barrier against the outside world*
cover *Airlines are required to provide insurance cover against such incidents.*
defence *The immune system is our main defence against disease.*
protection *Innocence is no protection from the evils in our society.*
See also **defence, defend, guard, precaution, protect, protection, save**

safety
▷ NOUN
the state of being safe from harm or danger: *I was very anxious about their safety.*
immunity *natural immunity to the disease*
protection *protection from the sun's harmful rays*

security *a false sense of security*
ANTONYM **danger**
See also **shelter**

sagging See **flabby**

sail See **fly**

saintly See **holy**

salary See **income, pay**

sallow See **pale**

salted See **salty**

salty
▷ ADJECTIVE
tasting of or containing salt: *salty bacon*
brackish *the brackish shallow water near the dam wall*
briny *the flow of the briny water*
salted *salted butter*

salute See **recognize**

salvage See **save**

same
▷ ADJECTIVE
exactly like one another: *The two words sound the same but have different spellings.*
alike *No two families are alike.*
equal *Mix equal quantities of soy sauce and vinegar.*
equivalent *a litre is roughly equivalent to a quart.*
identical *Nearly all the houses were identical.*
indistinguishable *symptoms indistinguishable from those of flu*
ANTONYM **different**
See also **like**

sameness See **similarity**

sample See **example, try**

sanction
▷ VERB
1 to officially approve of or allow something: *He is ready to sanction the use of force.*
allow *I will not allow violence on school premises.*
approve *Parliament has approved a program of economic reforms.*
authorize *Are you authorized to sign the cheque?*
back *persuading the principal to back our plan*
endorse *policies endorsed by the voting public*
permit *The government refused to permit the deportation.*
support *The city is under pressure to support the parade.*

ANTONYM **veto**

▷ *NOUN*

2 official approval of something: *The treaty required the sanction of Parliament.*
approval *The manager has given her approval.*
authorization *You will need the authorization of a parent or guardian.*
backing *Our fundraising project has the backing of the entire school.*
blessing *With the blessing of the mayor, we will hold the parade next week.*
permission *Finally she gave permission for him to travel alone.*
support *The prime minister gave his support to the reforms.*
See also **approval, approve, let, permit**

sanctions

▷ *NOUN*

penalties for countries that break the law: *Canada is considering imposing sanctions against the regime.*
ban *After four years, he lifted the ban.*
boycott *the lifting of the economic boycott against the country*
embargo *They called on the government to lift its embargo on trade with the country.*
penalties *legally binding penalties against treaty violators*

sanctuary *See* **refuge, retreat, shelter**

sands *See* **beach**

sane

▷ *ADJECTIVE*

I having a normal healthy mind: *This was not the act of a sane person.*
lucid *She was lucid right up until her death.*
normal *the question of what constitutes normal behaviour*
rational *She seemed perfectly rational to me.*
ANTONYM **mad**
2 showing good sense: *a sane and practical policy*
judicious *the judicious use of authority*
level-headed *a sensible, level-headed approach*
rational *a rational analysis*
reasonable *a reasonable course of action*
sensible *the sensible thing to do*
sound *sound advice*
See also **reasonable**

sanguine *See* **optimistic**

sanitation *See* **hygiene**

sap *See* **drain, tax, undermine, weaken**

sarcastic

▷ *ADJECTIVE*

saying the opposite of what you mean in

order to make fun of someone: *A sarcastic remark was on the tip of her tongue.*
caustic *His caustic comments hurt.*
ironic *an ironic remark*
sardonic *a sardonic sense of humour*
satirical *a satirical TV show*

sarcophagus *See* **tomb**

sardonic *See* **sarcastic**

satire *See* **parody**

satirical *See* **sarcastic**

satisfaction *See* **comfort, delight, happiness, pleasure, pride**

satisfactorily *See* **well**

satisfactory

▷ *ADJECTIVE*

acceptable or adequate: *a satisfactory explanation*
acceptable *The air pollution exceeds acceptable levels.*
adequate *Their income was barely adequate for a family of four.*
all right *The meal was all right, but nothing special.*
good enough *He's not good enough for you.*
passable *She speaks passable Italian.*
sufficient *One spoonful of sugar should be sufficient.*
ANTONYM **unsatisfactory**
See also **acceptable, adequate, decent, suitable**

satisfied

▷ *ADJECTIVE*

happy because you have got what you want: *We are not satisfied with these results.*
content *I'm perfectly content where I am.*
contented *She led a quiet, contented life.*
happy *I'm not happy with the situation.*
pleased *He seemed pleased with the arrangement.*
ANTONYM **disappointed**
See also **certain, confident, pleased, sure**

satisfy

▷ *VERB*

I to give someone as much of something as they want: *a solution that I hope will satisfy everyone*
gratify *He was gratified by the audience's response.*
indulge *I don't believe in indulging children.*
please *Our prime objective is to please our customers.*
2 to convince someone of something: *He*

S

had to satisfy the doctors that he was fit to play.
convince *trying to convince the public that its product is safe*
persuade *I had to persuade her of the advantages.*
put someone's mind at rest *He has done his best to put my mind at rest.*
reassure *I tried to reassure them, but they knew I was worried, too.*
3 to fulfill a requirement: *Applicants must satisfy the conditions for admission.*
fulfill *All the requirements were fulfilled.*
meet *The current arrangements are inadequate to meet their needs.*
See also **convince, fulfill, meet, suit**

saturated *See* **full, wet**

savage
▷ ADJECTIVE
1 cruel and violent: *a savage attack*
barbarous *Such a barbarous act should never be repeated.*
barbaric *a particularly barbaric act of violence*
brutal *a very brutal murder*
cruel *the cruel practice of bullfighting*
ferocious *the most ferocious violence ever seen in our city*
inhuman *the inhuman slaughter of these beautiful creatures*
vicious *a vicious blow to the head*
violent *violent crimes*
▷ NOUN
2 a violent and uncivilized person: *They really are a bunch of savages.*
barbarian *Our last coach was a complete barbarian.*
beast *You beast! Let the poor squirrrel go!*
brute *He was a brute and he deserved his fate.*
lout *a loud-mouthed lout*
monster *They were total monsters.*
▷ VERB
3 to attack and bite someone: *savaged to death by the animal*
attack *A lion attacked him when he was a child.*
bite *Every year, thousands of children are bitten by dogs.*
maul *The dog went berserk and mauled one of the children.*
See also **violent**

savagery *See* **cruelty, violence**

save
▷ VERB
1 to rescue someone or something: *He saved my life.*

come to someone's rescue *His uncle came to his rescue.*
deliver *delivered from the pain*
redeem *This is what it means to be redeemed from sickness and poverty.*
rescue *rescued from the flames*
salvage *salvaging some equipment from the wreckage*
2 to keep someone or something safe: *a new surgical technique which could save lives*
keep safe *to keep our home safe from germs*
preserve *preserving old buildings*
protect *What can we do to protect ourselves from heart disease?*
safeguard *measures to safeguard the ozone layer*
3 to keep something for later use: *I'm saving for a new computer.*
hoard *They've begun to hoard food and gas.*
keep *Grate the lemon zest and keep it for later.*
reserve *Drain the fruit and reserve the juice.*
set aside *The funds would be set aside for repairs to schools.*
ANTONYM **waste**
See also **but, except, hoard, reserve, safeguard, stockpile, store**

save from *See* **spare**

saving *See* **cut**

say
▷ VERB
1 to speak words: *She said they were very impressed.*
See WORD STUDY **say** *on the next two pages*
▷ NOUN
2 a chance to express your opinion: *voters who want a say in the matter*
voice *Parents are given a voice in decision making.*
vote *All the workers felt they had a vote in the company's future.*
See also **choice, comment, observe, remark, state**

say again *See* **repeat**

say no to *See* **reject**

say sorry *See* **apologize**

saying
▷ NOUN
a well-known sentence or phrase: *the saying "charity begins at home"*
adage *the old adage "the show must go on"*
axiom *the long-held axiom that education leads to higher income*
maxim *I believe in the maxim "If it ain't broke, don't fix it."*

WORD STUDY: SAY

There are a number of more interesting or creative words you can use in place of the basic verbs **say**, **speak**, and **talk**, if you want to describe the way in which a person says something. See this page and the next.

- If someone **utters** sounds or words, they say them.
This is a literary word.
They left without **uttering** a single word.

- If you **comment** on something, you say something about it.
He has refused to **comment** on these reports.

- If you **remark** that something is the case, you say that it is the case.
"I don't see you complaining," she **remarked**.

- If you **state** something, you say it in a formal or definite way.
Could you please **state** your name for the record?

- If you **mention** something, you say something about it, usually briefly.
He never **mentioned** that he was an only child.

- If you **note** something, you mention it in order to bring people's attention to it.
"It's already getting dark," she **noted**.

- If you **observe** that something is the case, you make a comment about it, especially when it is something you have noticed or thought about a lot.
"She's a very loyal friend," he **observed**.

- If you **point out** a fact or mistake, you tell someone about it or draw attention to it.
"You've not done so badly out of the deal," she **pointed out**.

- If you **announce** something, you tell people about it publicly or officially.
"I passed the test!" he **announced**.

- If you **affirm**, **assert**, or **declare** something, you state it firmly.
"I'm staying right here," she **affirmed**.
"The facts are clear," the prime minister **asserted**.
"I'm absolutely thrilled with the result," he **declared**.

- If you **add** something when you are speaking, you say something more.
"Anyway, it serves you right," she **added**.

- If you **interrupt**, you say something while someone else is speaking.
"I don't think you quite understand," he **interrupted**.

- When people **chat**, they talk to each other in a friendly and informal way.
We were just standing **chatting** in the corridor.

- If you **converse** with someone, you talk to them.
This is a formal word.
They were **conversing** in French.

- If you **gossip** with someone, you talk informally, especially about other people or events.
We sat and **gossiped** well into the evening.

- If you **explain** something, you give details about it so that it can be understood.
"We were only joking," she **explained**.

- If you **ask** something, you say it in the form of a question because you want to know the answer.
"How are you?" he **asked**.

- If you **inquire** about something, you ask for information about it.
This is a formal word.
"Is something wrong?" he **inquired**.

- To **query** or **question** means to ask a question.
"Can I help you?" the salesperson **queried**.
"What if something goes wrong?" he **questioned** anxiously.

- When you **answer**, **reply**, or **respond** to someone who has just spoken, you say something back to them.
"When are you leaving?" she asked.
"Tomorrow," he **answered**.
"That's a nice outfit," he commented.
"Thanks," she **replied**.
"Are you well enough to carry on?" "Of course," she **responded** scornfully.

S

WORD STUDY: SAY

- If you **riposte**, you make a quick, clever response to something that someone has just said. This is a formal word.
"It's tough at the top," I said. – "It's even tougher at the bottom," he **riposted**.

- To **retort** means to reply angrily to someone. This is a formal word.
"I don't agree," I said. – "Who cares what you think?" she **retorted**.

- If you **chatter**, you talk quickly and excitedly about things which are not important.
Everyone was **chattering** away in different languages.

- If you **gabble**, you say things so quickly that it is difficult for people to understand you.
She rushed into the room, **gabbling** excitedly.

- If you **prattle**, you talk a great deal about something unimportant.
She was **prattling** on about some guy she had met the day before.

- If someone **rambles**, they talk but do not make much sense because they keep going off the subject.
I was feeling sleepy, and **rambled** about the movie we had just seen.

- If someone **breathes** something, they say it very quietly. This is a literary word.
"Oh, I'm so glad you're here," he **breathed**.

- When you **whisper**, you say something very quietly, using your breath rather than your throat.
"Keep your voice down," I **whispered**.

- If you **hiss** something, you say it forcefully in a whisper.
"Stay here and don't make a sound," he **hissed**.

- If you **mumble**, you speak very quietly and not at all clearly, so that your words are hard to make out.
"I didn't know I was supposed to do it," she **mumbled**.

- If you **murmur** something, you speak very quietly, so that not many people can hear you.

"How convenient," I **murmured**.

- If you **mutter**, you speak very quietly, often because you are complaining about something.
"Oh great," he **muttered**, "that's all I need."

- If you **croak** something, you say it in a low, rough voice.
"Water!" he **croaked**.

- If you **grunt** something, you say it in a low voice, often because you are annoyed or not interested.
"Nonsense," I **grunted**, "you just didn't try hard enough."

- If you **rasp** something, you say it in a harsh, unpleasant voice.
"Get into the car," he **rasped**.

- If you **wheeze** something, you say it with a whistling sound, for example, because you cannot get your breath.
"I'm really out of condition," I **wheezed**.

- If you **gasp** something, you say it in a short, breathless way, especially because you are surprised, shocked, or in pain.
"What do you mean?" she **gasped**.

- If you **pant** something, you say it while breathing loudly and quickly with your mouth open because you have been doing something energetic.
"Let me get my breath back," he **panted**. "I'm not as fit as I used to be."

- If you **groan** or **moan** something, you say it in a low voice, usually because you are unhappy or in pain.
"My leg — I think it's broken," he **groaned**. "I can't stand it any longer," she **moaned**.

- When someone **growls** something, they say it in a low, rough, and angry voice.
"It's all your fault," he **growled**.

- If you **snarl** something, you say it in a fierce, angry way.
"Get out of here," she **snarled**.

- If you **snap** at someone, you speak to them in a sharp, unfriendly way.
"Of course you can't have it," he **snapped**.

proverb *"Things are not always what they seem" is an old proverb.*

scalding *See* **hot**

scale *See* **climb, extent**

scale drawing *See* **plan**

scan *See* **glance, inspect, read, scrutinize**

scandal *See* **disgrace, shame, slander**

scandalous *See* **disgraceful, notorious**

scant *See* **insufficient, low, meagre**

scanty *See* **few**

scarce
▷ ADJECTIVE
rare or uncommon: *Jobs are becoming increasingly scarce.*
few *Our options are few.*
rare *The northern spotted owl is now rare in Canada.*
uncommon *an extreme but by no means uncommon case*
unusual *To be appreciated as a parent is quite unusual.*
ANTONYM **common**
See also **few, inadequate, rare, uncommon**

scarcely *See* **barely, hardly**

scarcity *See* **lack, shortage, want**

scare
▷ VERB
1 to frighten someone: *You're scaring me!*
alarm *We could not see what had alarmed him.*
frighten *He knew that his sister was trying to frighten him.*
give someone a fright *The snake moved and gave everyone a fright.*
intimidate *She had set out to intimidate her new assistant.*
startle *Sorry, I didn't mean to startle you.*
terrify *Flying terrifies him.*
terrorize *terrorized by bullies*
unnerve *We were unnerved by the total silence.*
▷ NOUN
2 a short period of feeling very frightened: *We had a bit of a scare.*
fright *Go to see Dracula if you want a real fright.*
shock *It gave me quite a shock to see his face on the screen.*
start *The sudden noise gave me quite a start.*
3 a situation where people worry about something: *Despite the health scare, there are no plans to withdraw the drug.*
alert *a security alert*
hysteria *Everyone was getting carried away by the hysteria.*
panic *the panic over the contaminated meat scare*
See also **alarm, frighten**

scared *See* **afraid, frightened**

scary
▷ ADJECTIVE
INFORMAL frightening: *Camping can be scary at night.*
alarming *an alarming report on the rise of street crime*
chilling *a chilling account of the accident*
creepy INFORMAL *places that are really creepy at night*
eerie *the eerie, dark path*
frightening *a very frightening experience*
hair-raising *a hair-raising encounter with a bull on the loose*
spooky *The empty house has a slightly spooky atmosphere.*
terrifying *I find it terrifying to be surrounded by a crowd of people.*
unnerving *It was unnerving having to walk along the busy highway.*
See also **creepy, spooky**

scathing *See* **abusive, critical, scornful**

scatter
▷ VERB
to throw or drop things all over an area: *She scattered the rose petals.*
shower *meteors showering the night sky*
sow *Sow the seeds in a warm place.*
sprinkle *Sprinkle a spoonful of sugar over the fruit.*
throw about *They started throwing food about.*
ANTONYM **gather**
See also **distribute**

scenario *See* **plot, situation**

scene
▷ NOUN
1 a picture or view of something: *a village scene*
landscape *Saskatchewan's prairie landscape*
panorama *a panorama of fertile valleys*
view *a view of the lake*
2 the place where something happens: *the scene of the crime*
location *filmed in an exotic location*
place *Can you show me the place where you lost your wallet?*

S

setting *Rome is the perfect setting for romance.*
site *the site of the battle*
spot *the ideal spot for a picnic*
3 an area of activity: *the music scene*
arena *the political arena*
business *the potential to revolutionize the publishing business*
environment *the Canadian business environment*
world *the fashion world*
See also **sight, spot, view**

scenery
▷ *NOUN*
the things you see in the countryside: *Drive slowly and enjoy the scenery.*
landscape *Ontario's hilly landscape*
panorama *admiring the distant mountain panorama*
surroundings *a vacation home in beautiful surroundings*
terrain *The terrain changed from arable land to desert.*
view *The view from our window was spectacular.*

scent *See* **fragrance, smell**

sceptical *See* **cynical, dubious, suspicious**

scepticism *See* **doubt, suspicion**

schedule *See* **arrange, book, program, routine, time**

scheduled *See* **set**

scheme *See* **idea, plan, plot, racket**

scheming *See* **crafty, devious, sly**

schism *See* **split**

scholar *See* **pupil**

scholarly *See* **learned**

scholarship *See* **knowledge**

school *See* **instruct, teach, train**

schooling *See* **education**

scoff at *See* **mock**

scold
▷ *VERB*
to find fault with someone; to tell someone off: *She scolded the child for being naughty.*
chide *He chided himself for worrying.*
lecture *My parents lectured me about not eating properly.*
rebuke *I turned to him and sharply rebuked him.*

reprimand *reprimanded for talking during the exam*
tell off *INFORMAL The teacher really told me off.*
See also **abuse**

scolding *See* **lecture**

scope *See* **freedom, range**

scorch *See* **burn**

scorching *See* **hot**

score *See* **line**

scores *See* **lot, many**

scorn
▷ *NOUN*
1 great contempt felt for something: *The proposal was greeted with scorn.*
contempt *I treated the nasty remark with the contempt it deserved.*
derision *shouts of derision*
disdain *She looked at him with disdain.*
mockery *their mockery of our school spirit*
▷ *VERB*
2 to treat with great contempt: *He scorns the work of others.*
despise *She secretly despises him.*
disdain *He disdained the suggestion that he was a coward.*
look down on *I wasn't successful, so they looked down on me.*
slight *He felt slighted by this treatment.*
See also **belittle, contempt**

scornful
▷ *ADJECTIVE*
showing contempt for something: *He is deeply scornful of his rivals.*
contemptuous *a contemptuous little laugh*
disdainful *disdainful of crooked politicians*
scathing *He made some scathing comments about the design.*
sneering *a sneering tone*
supercilious *His manner is supercilious and arrogant.*
withering *I gave her a withering look.*

scoundrel *See* **crook**

scour *See* **clean, scrape, search**

scourge *See* **pest**

scowl *See* **frown, glare**

scramble *See* **rush**

scrap *See* **bit, junk**

scrape
▷ *VERB*
1 to rub a rough or sharp object against something: *We had to scrape the frost from the windshield.*

graze *He had grazed his knees a little.*
scour *Scour the pans.*
scratch *The branches scratched my face and hands.*
scuff *scuffed shoes*
skin *I found that I had skinned my knuckles.*
2 to make a harsh noise by rubbing: *her shoes scraping across the ground*
grate *His chair grated as he stood up.*
grind *Blocks of ice ground against each other.*
rasp *The wind rasped through the trees.*
scratch *The dog is scratching at the door.*
See also **graze, predicament**

scraps *See* **remains**

scratch *See* **graze, scrape, tear**

scrawny *See* **skinny**

scream
▷ *VERB*
1 to shout or cry in a high-pitched voice: *lots of people screaming on a roller coaster*
cry *a crying baby*
howl *He howled like a wounded animal.*
screech *"Get me some water!" I screeched.*
shout *I shouted at him to call the police.*
shriek *shrieks of laughter*
squeal *They squealed with delight.*
yell *Stop yelling at me!*
▷ *NOUN*
2 a loud, high-pitched cry: *The child let out a scream.*
cry *a cry of horror*
howl *a howl of rage*
screech *a screech that sent chills up my spine*
shriek *a shriek of joy*
squeal *the squeal of piglets*
yell *Scared, I let out a yell.*
See also **shout**

screech *See* **scream**

screen *See* **cover, obscure**

scriptural *See* **religious**

scrounge
▷ *VERB*
to get something by asking rather than working for it: *He's always scrounging for money.*
beg *They managed to beg a ride from a passing neighbour.*
sponge *INFORMAL I got tired of them sponging off me.*

scrub *See* **clean, wash**

scruffy
▷ *ADJECTIVE*
dirty and untidy: *four scruffy boys*

ragged *ragged clothes*
seedy *He looked pretty seedy after the camping trip.*
shabby *a shabby suitcase*
tatty *a tatty old sweater*
unkempt *His hair was unkempt and filthy.*
ANTONYM **smart**
See also **shabby**

scruples *See* **conscience, principle, standards**

scrupulous *See* **thorough**

scrutinize
▷ *VERB*
to examine something very carefully: *She scrutinized his features.*
examine *He examined her passport.*
inspect *He inspected the lettuce for bugs.*
pore over *We spent hours poring over the files.*
scan *She kept scanning the crowd for her cousin.*
search *Her eyes searched his face.*
study *I studied the document for a moment.*
See also **observe, regard**

scuff *See* **scrape**

sculpt *See* **carve, model**

scurry *See* **bustle, hurry, rush**

scuttle *See* **bustle**

seal *See* **close, glue, plug**

sealed *See* **shut**

search
▷ *VERB*
1 to look for something: *The RCMP is searching for the missing men.*
comb *Police combed the woods for the murder weapon.*
forage *foraging for food*
hunt *hunting for a job*
look *He's looking for a way out of this situation.*
scour *They had scoured the field for signs of animals.*
seek *the man he had been seeking for weeks*
sift *sifting through the wreckage for clues*
▷ *NOUN*
2 the action of looking for something: *Police will resume the search today.*
hunt *the hunt for my lost key*
quest *his quest to find his long-lost relatives*

search for *See* **seek**

S

seashore *See* **beach**

seaside *See* **beach, coast**

seasoned *See* **experienced, practical**

secluded *See* **lonely**

seclusion *See* **solitude**

second *See* **instant, minute, moment, support**

secondary *See* **inferior, minor**

second-class *See* **inferior**

second-rate *See* **cheap, inferior, poor**

secret
> *ADJECTIVE*

known about by only a few people: *a secret location*
closet *INFORMAL a closet drinker*
confidential *a confidential report*
covert *She gave him a covert glance.*
furtive *furtive meetings*
hidden *a hidden camera*
undercover *undercover agents*
underground *the underground political movement*
See also **private**

secrete *See* **hide**

secretive
> *ADJECTIVE*

hiding your feelings and intentions: *He was very secretive about his family affairs.*
cagey *INFORMAL He is cagey about how much his card collection is worth.*
reserved *She was unemotional and reserved.*
reticent *She is very reticent about her achievements.*
See also **mysterious**

section
> *NOUN*

one of the parts into which something is divided: *this section of the Trans-Canada Highway*
division *the company's sales division*
instalment *Payment can be made in instalments.*
part *the upper part of the body*
piece *The equipment was taken apart in pieces.*
portion *I ate a large portion of macaroni and cheese.*
segment *the third segment of the trip*
See also **compartment, department, division, extract, part, passage**

sector *See* **division, region**

secure
> *VERB*

1 *FORMAL* to manage to get something: *His achievements helped him to secure the job.*
acquire *The company acquired a 50 percent stake in the supermarket chain.*
gain *He gained a promotion at the firm.*
get *I got a job at the sawmill.*
obtain *She tried to obtain a false passport.*
procure *trying to procure the release of the hostages*
2 to make something safe: *We need to secure the building against attack.*
fortify *Soldiers are working to fortify the base.*
make impregnable *Their intention was to make the fort impregnable.*
make safe *Here are some ways to make your home safe.*
strengthen *to strengthen the walled city against enemy attack*
3 to fasten or attach something firmly: *to secure the picture to the wall*
attach *The gadget can be attached to any vertical surface.*
bind *Bind the twigs together with twine.*
fasten *Her long hair was fastened by an elastic band.*
fix *The fence post was firmly fixed in place.*
lock *Are you sure you locked the front door?*
moor *She moored the boat on the river bank.*
tie up *They dismounted and tied up their horses.*
ANTONYM **release**
> *ADJECTIVE*

4 tightly locked or well protected: *Make sure your home is as secure as possible.*
fortified *The door is fortified against flooding.*
impregnable *The old castle was impregnable against raids.*
protected *protected from sexual harassment*
safe *We didn't feel safe in that motel.*
shielded *The company is shielded from takeover attempts.*
5 firmly fixed in place: *Those bookshelves don't look very secure.*
fastened *Make sure the safety belt is fastened.*
firm *Is the ladder firm enough?*
fixed *Check that the microwave oven is fixed in its place on the wall.*
locked *Leave doors and windows locked.*
solid *I pulled on the bracket to see if it was solid.*
stable *The structure must be stable.*

tight *She kept a tight hold on the dog's leash.*
6 feeling safe and happy: *They felt secure when they were with each other.*
confident *In time he became more confident.*
protected *It's good to have a place in which you feel protected and loved.*
reassured *I felt reassured following my annual health check.*
relaxed *There are very few people with whom he feels relaxed.*
safe *The entire family felt safe and secure.*
ANTONYM **insecure**
See also **acquire, close, confident, fasten, fix, gain, get, obtain, safe, steady, tie, tight, win**

securely *See* **fast**

security *See* **defence, safety**

seduce *See* **tempt**

seductive *See* **sexy**

see
▷ VERB
1 to look at or notice something: *Did you see what happened?*
behold *It was as if he beheld a vision.*
discern *We could barely discern the outline of the island.*
glimpse *She glimpsed his face briefly.*
look *She turned to look at him.*
notice *He noticed a bird sitting on the roof.*
observe *She observed a reddish spot on the planet's surface.*
perceive *Infants start to perceive objects at a very early age.*
sight *A fleet of Spanish ships was sighted.*
spot *I think he spotted me but didn't want to be seen.*
2 to realize or understand something: *I see what you mean.*
appreciate *He appreciates the difficulties.*
comprehend *They do not comprehend the nature of the problem.*
follow *Do you follow what I'm saying?*
get *You don't seem to get the point.*
grasp *They have not grasped the seriousness of the crisis.*
realize *They realized too late that they were wrong.*
understand *I'm not sure I understand.*
3 to find something out: *I'll see what's happening outside.*
ascertain *Ascertain what services your bank provides.*
determine *The investigation will determine what really happened.*
discover *Try to discover what you are good at.*

find out *Watch the next episode to find out what happens.*
See also **comprehend, discern, know, note, notice, observe, picture, regard, sight, spot, tell, understand, watch, witness**

see eye to eye *See* **agree**

see to *See* **deal, take care of**

seedy *See* **scruffy, shabby**

seek
▷ VERB
1 to try to find something: *The police were still seeking information.*
be after *At last I found what I was after.*
hunt *Police are hunting for clues.*
look for *I'm looking for a lost wallet.*
search for *searching for answers*
2 to try to do something: *She is seeking re-election as class president.*
aim *We aim to raise funds for charity.*
aspire to *He aspired to work in the field of journalism.*
attempt *She was forever attempting to arrange deals.*
endeavour *They are endeavouring to protect the environment.*
strive *The school strives to treat students as individuals.*
try *We are trying to bring about a better world.*
See also **ask, attempt, look for, request, search, strive, try**

seem
▷ VERB
to appear to be: *He seemed such a quiet man.*
appear *She appeared intoxicated.*
give the impression *He gave the impression of being the perfect employee.*
look *The cottage looks quite ordinary from the road.*
look like *You look like a nice guy.*
See also **look**

seem to be *See* **look**

seemly *See* **correct, right**

seep *See* **drain, leak**

segment *See* **portion, proportion, section**

segregate *See* **divide**

seize
▷ VERB
1 to grab something firmly: *He seized the phone.*

S

grab *I grabbed him by the tail of his shirt.*
grasp *He grasped both my hands.*
snatch *He snatched the cards from my hand.*
2 to take control of something: *Rebels have seized the airport.*
annex *the plan to invade and annex the tiny country*
appropriate *The land was appropriated illegally.*
confiscate *The police confiscated weapons and ammunition.*
hijack *Almost 250 trucks were hijacked.*
impound *The ship was impounded under the terms of the trade embargo.*
See also **arrest, capture, grab, grasp, kidnap, possess**

seizure *See* **arrest, capture**

select
▷ VERB
1 to choose something: *They selected new members for the debating team.*
choose *St. John's was chosen as the site for the conference.*
decide on *I'm still trying to decide on an outfit for the wedding.*
opt for *You may wish to opt for the third choice.*
pick *He had picked ten people to interview for the jobs.*
settle on *They finally settled on the minivan because it was so roomy.*
single out *Her boss has singled her out for a special mission.*
take *"I'll take the grilled tuna," she told the waiter.*
▷ ADJECTIVE
2 of good quality: *a select group of top-ranked skiers*
choice *We use only the choicest ingredients.*
exclusive *the city's most exclusive club*
first-class *a first-class hotel*
first-rate *The first-rate cast includes many famous names.*
hand-picked *a hand-picked series of timeless classics*
prime *one of the city's prime locations with a view of the waterfront*
special *a special group of government officials*
superior *a superior range of products*
See also **choose, exclusive, nominate, pick, prime**

selection *See* **appointment, choice, range**

self-assurance *See* **confidence**

self-assured *See* **confident**

self-centred *See* **selfish**

self-conscious *See* **embarrassed, shy, uncomfortable**

self-consciousness *See* **embarrassment**

self-denial *See* **sacrifice**

self-evident *See* **obvious**

self-importance *See* **conceit**

self-important *See* **conceited**

selfish
▷ ADJECTIVE
caring only about yourself: *his greedy and selfish behaviour*
egoistic *or* **egoistical** *egoistic motives*
egotistic *or* **egotistical** *an intensely egotistic streak*
greedy *greedy bosses awarding themselves big bonuses*
self-centred *He was self-centred, but he wasn't cruel.*

self-possessed *See* **confident**

self-possession *See* **confidence**

self-propelled *See* **automatic**

self-satisfied *See* **smug**

self-sufficient *See* **independent**

sell
▷ VERB
to let someone have something in return for money: *a convenience store that sells stamps*
deal in *They deal in antiques.*
hawk *vendors hawking trinkets*
peddle *arrested for peddling drugs*
stock *The store stocks a variety of local crafts.*
trade in *They trade in spices and all kinds of grain.*
ANTONYM **buy**
See also **stock**

sell at *See* **cost**

selling price *See* **value**

semblance *See* **illusion, look, show**

send
▷ VERB
1 to arrange for something to be delivered: *She sent a basket of fruit and a card.*
dispatch *Police cars were dispatched to the house.*
forward *A letter was forwarded from my previous address.*

remit *We remit money to our family in Europe.*
2 to transmit a signal or message: *The pilot was trying to send a distress signal.*
broadcast *to broadcast a message to a large group of people at once*
transmit *the most efficient way to transmit data*

send in *See* submit

send out *See* emit

send to prison *See* imprison

senior
▷ *ADJECTIVE*
the highest and most important in an organization: *senior jobs*
better *After only three months, I was offered a better job.*
high-ranking *a high-ranking officer*
superior *negotiations between crew members and their superior officers*
ANTONYM **junior**
See also **superior**

sensation *See* feeling, success

sensational *See* incredible, melodramatic

sense
▷ *NOUN*
1 a feeling you have about something: *an overwhelming sense of guilt*
consciousness *a consciousness of tension*
feeling *It gave me a feeling of satisfaction.*
impression *The music creates an impression of magic.*
2 the ability to think and behave sensibly: *He had the good sense to call me at once.*
brains *At least I had the brains to keep quiet.*
common sense *completely lacking in common sense*
intelligence *He didn't have the intelligence to understand what was happening.*
judgment *I respect her judgment.*
reason *a conflict between emotion and reason*
wisdom *the wisdom that comes with old age*
▷ *VERB*
3 to become aware of something: *She sensed he wasn't telling her the whole story.*
be aware of *He was aware of her anger.*
feel *Suddenly, I felt that someone was behind me.*
get the impression *I get the impression he's lying.*
have a hunch *I have a hunch you're on to something.*
realize *We realized something was wrong.*
See also **feeling, impression,**

intelligence, meaning, reason

sense of duty *See* principle

sense of right and wrong *See* conscience

senseless *See* foolish, idiotic, unconscious, unwise

sensible
▷ *ADJECTIVE*
showing good sense and judgment: *a sensible, level-headed approach*
down-to-earth *the most down-to-earth person I've ever met*
judicious *the judicious use of discipline*
practical *practical suggestions*
prudent *It is prudent to start any exercise program gradually.*
rational *a rational decision*
sound *sound advice*
wise *a wise move*
ANTONYM **foolish**
See also **logical, practical, rational, realistic, reasonable, responsible, sane, sound, wise**

sensitive
▷ *ADJECTIVE*
easily upset about something: *He was sensitive about his height.*
easily offended *He's easily offended, so choose your words carefully.*
easily upset *He's easily upset, so break the news gently.*
thin-skinned *I'm too thin-skinned — I want everyone to like me.*
touchy *She is very touchy about her age.*
See also **fine, impressionable, sore, tactful, tender, touchy, tricky, understanding, vulnerable**

sensitivity *See* tact

sensual *See* sexy

sensuous *See* sexy

sentence *See* condemn, punish

sentiment *See* feeling

sentimental
▷ *ADJECTIVE*
expressing exaggerated sadness or tenderness: *sentimental love stories*
maudlin *He turned maudlin after an evening with his friends.*
mushy INFORMAL *I go completely mushy when I see a baby.*
nostalgic *nostalgic for the good old days*

S

sloppy INFORMAL *I hate sloppy, romantic films.*
See also **corny**

sentry *See* **guard**

separate

▷ ADJECTIVE
1 not connected to something else: *The question muddles up two separate issues.*
detached *a detached house*
disconnected *sequences of disconnected events*
discrete *two discrete components*
divorced *speculative theories divorced from reality*
isolated *He lives as if isolated from the rest of the world.*
unconnected *The two crimes are unconnected.*

▷ VERB
2 to end a connection between people or things: *We were separated from our friends when we changed schools.*
detach *Three of the cars on the train became detached.*
disconnect *Make sure the plug is disconnected from the outlet.*
divide *This was a plot to divide them.*
ANTONYM **connect**

3 to end a relationship or marriage: *Her parents separated when she was very young.*
break up *They broke up shortly before graduation.*
divorce *We divorced ten years ago.*
part *They are parting after only five months of marriage.*
split up *I split up with my boyfriend last year.*
See also **alone, different, divide, independent, individual, single, sort, split**

separation *See* **division**

sepulchre *See* **grave, tomb**

sequence

▷ NOUN
1 a number of events coming one after another: *an unbroken sequence of victories*
chain *the chain of events leading to the assassination*
course *a course of treatment*
cycle *the cycle of birth, growth, decay, and death*
progression *the progression of events as the tale unfolds*
series *a series of explosions*
string *a string of burglaries*

succession *a succession of jobs*
2 a particular order in which things are arranged: *the colour sequence: yellow, orange, purple, blue*
arrangement *a simple arrangement of coloured tiles*
order *I arranged my CDs in alphabetical order.*
pattern *a systematic pattern of behaviour*
progression *the natural progression of the seasons*
structure *the structure of a sentence*
See also **series**

serene *See* **cool, patient, peaceful, quiet, relaxed**

serenity *See* **calm, quiet**

series

▷ NOUN
a number of things coming one after the other: *a series of loud explosions*
chain *a bizarre chain of events*
run *The team is haunted by a run of errors.*
sequence *a sequence of novels*
string *a string of burglaries*
succession *a succession of jobs*
See also **range, sequence, set**

serious

▷ ADJECTIVE
1 very bad and worrying: *They survived their serious injuries.*
acute *an acute attack of appendicitis*
alarming *the alarming increase in crime*
bad *a bad bout of the flu*
critical *He remains in critical condition.*
dangerous *Her wound proved more dangerous than it seemed at first.*
extreme *the most extreme case doctors have ever seen*
grave *We are all in grave danger.*
grievous *grievous wounds*
grim *Our situation is grim indeed.*
intense *Intense fighting has broken out in the capital.*
precarious *He is in a very precarious position.*
severe *a severe shortage of drinking water*
worrying *It is a worrying situation.*
2 important and deserving careful thought: *I regard this as a serious matter.*
crucial *Negotiations were at a crucial stage.*
deep *This novel raises deep questions about the nature of faith.*
difficult *The government faces even more difficult problems.*
far-reaching *Their actions will have far-reaching consequences.*
grave *a grave situation*
important *We've got more important things*

to worry about now.

momentous *the momentous decision to go to war*

pressing *a pressing problem*

profound *someone who thinks about the more profound issues of life*

significant *the most significant question of all*

urgent *He is not equipped to deal with an urgent situation like this.*

weighty *a weighty problem*

ANTONYM **funny**

3 sincere about something: *I was not quite sure whether he was serious.*

earnest *It is my earnest hope that we can work things out.*

genuine *a genuine offer*

heartfelt *a full and heartfelt apology*

honest *She looked at me in honest surprise.*

in earnest *I can never tell if he's speaking in earnest or not.*

resolute *She was resolute about her ideals.*

resolved *They are quite resolved about their decision.*

sincere *He's sincere in his views.*

4 quiet and not laughing much: *She's quite a serious person.*

earnest *She looked up at me with an earnest expression.*

grave *He was looking unusually grave.*

humourless *a dour, humourless individual*

pensive *We're both in a pensive mood today.*

sober *sad, sober faces*

solemn *His solemn little face broke into a smile.*

staid *a staid country doctor*

stern *The principal was stern, but always fair.*

See also **acute, critical, deep, grave, heavy, important, severe, solemn**

sermon *See* **lecture, talk**

serrated *See* **jagged**

serve as *See* **form**

service *See* **ceremony, favour**

serving *See* **portion**

session *See* **round, term**

set

▷ NOUN

1 a group of things that belong together: *a set of tools*

batch *the latest batch of recruits*

kit *a first-aid kit*

outfit *She was wearing a brand new outfit.*

series *a series of books covering the history of aviation*

▷ VERB

2 to put or place something somewhere: *She set her briefcase down on the floor.*

deposit *Imagine if you were suddenly deposited on a desert island.*

lay *Lay a sheet of newspaper on the floor.*

locate *The restaurant is located near the school.*

place *She placed a hamburger in front of him.*

position *Plants were carefully positioned in the lobby.*

put *He put the photograph on the desk.*

rest *He rested one of his crutches against the rail.*

stick *Just stick your bag down anywhere.*

▷ ADJECTIVE

3 fixed and not varying: *a set charge*

arranged *We arrived at the arranged time.*

established *the established order*

firm *a firm booking*

fixed *a fixed rate of interest*

predetermined *Is your destiny predetermined from the moment of your birth?*

scheduled *The plane landed at the scheduled time.*

See also **bunch, category, class, firm, group, harden, insert, lay, lot, ready, rigid, thicken, time**

CONFUSABLES

Set means **put down**, and always takes an object.
Sit means **rest your rear end on something**, and usually does not take an object

set about *See* **begin, start**

set against one another *See* **divide**

set aside *See* **allow, reserve, save**

set back *See* **delay**

setback *See* **blow, delay, disappointment**

set down *See* **lay**

set free *See* **discharge, release**

set loose *See* **free**

set off *See* **explode, fire, flatter, go, provoke, sound**

set on

▷ ADJECTIVE

determined to do something: *She was set on going to Alberta.*

S

bent *He's bent on becoming a famous singer.*
determined *His enemies are determined to ruin him.*
intent *an actress who was intent on making a comeback*

set out *See* **lay**

setting *See* **scene, surroundings**

settle
▷ VERB
1 to put an end to an argument or problem: *The dispute has been settled.*
clear up *Eventually the confusion was cleared up.*
decide *None of the cases has been decided.*
dispose of *the way in which you disposed of that problem*
put an end to *I just want to put an end to this situation.*
reconcile *urging the two parties to reconcile their differences*
resolve *They hoped the crisis could be resolved peacefully.*
straighten out *doing their best to straighten out this confusion*
2 to decide or arrange something: *Let's settle where we're going tonight.*
agree *We haven't agreed on a date yet.*
arrange *Have you arranged our next appointment?*
decide on *They decided on an evening to meet.*
determine *The final wording had not yet been determined.*
fix *He's going to fix a time when I can see him.*
3 to make your home in a place: *My grandparents settled in Manitoba.*
make your home *those who had made their homes in the West*
move to *His family moved to New Zealand when he was 12.*
people *The plateau was peopled by nomadic tribes.*
populate *The island was populated by large turtles.*
See also **confirm, determine, lay, pay**

settle on *See* **pick, select**

settle up *See* **repay**

settled *See* **definite**

settlement *See* **agreement, colony**

set up
▷ VERB
to make arrangements for something: *setting up a system of communication*

arrange *We have arranged a series of interviews.*
establish *We have established links with clubs from around the world.*
install *We're having cable installed next week.*
institute *to institute better levels of quality control*
organize *a two-day meeting organized by the UN*
See also **organize, start**

set upon *See* **attack**

several
▷ ADJECTIVE
indicating a small number: *several boxes filled with CDs and DVDs*
assorted *a box of assorted chocolates*
some *some cheers from the audience*
sundry *He has won sundry music awards.*
various *a dozen trees of various sorts*
See also **numerous**

severe
▷ ADJECTIVE
1 extremely bad or unpleasant: *severe financial problems*
acute *an acute economic crisis*
critical *If the situation becomes critical, we will have to do something.*
deep *We will be in deep trouble if this goes on.*
dire *This would have dire consequences for the country.*
extreme *people living in extreme poverty*
grave *She said the situation was very grave.*
intense *A number of people collapsed in the intense heat.*
serious *The government faces very serious difficulties.*
terrible *terrible injuries*
ANTONYM **mild**
2 stern and harsh: *a severe sentence appropriate to the crime*
disapproving *I gave him a disapproving look.*
grim *Her expression was grim and unpleasant.*
hard *His grandfather was a hard man.*
harsh *the harsh treatment of the poor animals*
stern *He said stern measures would be taken.*
strict *My parents are very strict.*
See also **acute, drastic, extreme, grim, harsh, intense, serious, simple, violent**

severity *See* **violence**

sexism *See* **prejudice**

sexy

▷ ADJECTIVE

sexually attractive or exciting: *a sexy voice*
erotic *an erotic film*
seductive *a seductive smile*
sensual *a wide, sensual mouth*
sensuous *her sensuous appeal*
voluptuous *a voluptuous figure*

shabby

▷ ADJECTIVE

I ragged and worn in appearance: *a shabby overcoat*
dilapidated *a dilapidated old building*
ragged *dressed in a ragged coat*
scruffy *a scruffy appearance*
seedy *a seedy neighbourhood*
tatty *a tatty old sweater*
threadbare *a square of threadbare carpet*
worn *a worn corduroy jacket*
2 behaving meanly and unfairly: *shabby treatment*
contemptible *contemptible behaviour*
despicable *a despicable thing to do*
dirty *That was a dirty trick.*
mean *It was mean of you to hurt their feelings.*
rotten INFORMAL *That's a rotten thing to say!*
See also **scruffy**

shade See **colour, cover**

shadow See **blot out**

shadowy See **dark, dim**

shady See **corrupt, crooked, suspicious**

shaft See **bar**

shake

▷ VERB

I to move something from side to side or up and down: *You have to shake the bottle before use.*
agitate *Gently agitate the water.*
brandish *He appeared brandishing the missing keys.*
flourish *She flourished her glass to make the point.*
wave *The crowd was waving flags and cheering.*
2 to move from side to side or up and down: *The whole building shook with the force of the blast.*
jolt *The train jolted again.*
quake *The whole mountain quaked.*
quiver *My lower lip began to quiver.*
shiver *shivering with fear*
shudder *I shuddered with cold.*
tremble *The leaves trembled in the breeze.*

vibrate *The engine began to vibrate alarmingly.*
3 to shock and upset someone: *The news shook me quite a bit.*
distress *Her death has profoundly distressed me.*
disturb *dreams so vivid that they disturb me for days*
rattle *He was obviously rattled by the news.*
shock *Pictures of the emaciated prisoners shocked the world.*
unnerve *unnerved by the sight*
upset *I was too upset to speak.*
See also **disturb, shock, wave**

INFORMALLY SPEAKING

no great shakes: not unusual or important
shake down: cause to settle down or function normally

shaky

▷ ADJECTIVE

weak and unsteady: *threatening an already shaky economy*
rickety *They carefully climbed the rickety wooden stairway.*
tottering *the baby's first tottering steps*
trembling *a frail, trembling hand*
unstable *an unstable kitchen stool*
unsteady *His voice was unsteady.*
wobbly *This table's a bit wobbly.*
See also **unsteady**

sham See **fake, mock, phony**

shame

▷ NOUN

I a feeling of guilt or embarrassment: *She felt a deep sense of shame.*
embarrassment *He turned red with embarrassment.*
humiliation *the humiliation of being caught cheating*
ignominy *the ignominy of being defeated for the fourth straight year*
2 something that makes people lose respect for you: *I don't want to bring shame on the family.*
discredit *It was to his discredit that he did nothing to help.*
disgrace *She had to resign in disgrace.*
dishonour *his sense of dishonour at his brother's conduct*
scandal *The mayor resigned because of the scandal.*
▷ VERB
3 to make someone feel ashamed: *Her son's*

S

behaviour had shamed her.
disgrace *I have disgraced my school.*
embarrass *It embarrassed him that he had no idea of what was going on.*
humiliate *His coach continually humiliates him during practice.*
See also **disgrace, embarrass, embarrassment, humiliate, pity**

shameful *See* **disgraceful**

shameless
▷ ADJECTIVE
behaving badly without showing any shame: *shameless dishonesty*
barefaced *a barefaced lie*
brazen *a brazen theft*
flagrant *a flagrant violation of the rules*
unabashed *an unabashed liar*
unashamed *blatant, unashamed hypocrisy*

shampoo *See* **wash**

shape
▷ NOUN
1 the outline of something: *a round shape*
contours *the contours of the mountains*
figure *a trim figure*
form *the form of the human body*
lines *The belt spoiled the lines of her long dress.*
outline *the dim outline of a small boat*
▷ VERB
2 to make something in a particular form: *Shape the dough into a loaf.*
fashion *buttons fashioned from plastic*
form *Form the meat mixture into hamburgers.*
make *gold made into wedding rings*
model *She began modelling animals from clay.*
mould *Mould the clay into creations of your choice.*
See also **body, build, condition, design, determine, fashion, figure, form, health, model, outline, state**

share
▷ VERB
1 to divide something between two or more people: *We shared a pizza.*
divide *The prize money was divided between the two winners.*
split *We split the bill between us.*
▷ NOUN
2 a portion of something: *a share of the profits*
allotment *an allotment of three concert tickets per person*
portion *his portion of the lasagna*
quota *I met my daily quota of work.*

ration *their daily ration of water*
See also **proportion**

share out *See* **distribute**

shares *See* **stock**

shark *See* **crook**

sharp
▷ ADJECTIVE
1 having a fine cutting edge or point: *a sharp knife*
jagged *jagged rocks*
keen *a keen edge*
pointed *pointed teeth*
razor-sharp *the razor-sharp blade*
ANTONYM **blunt**
2 quick to notice or understand things: *a sharp intellect*
alert *At 85, she is alert and sprightly.*
astute *a series of astute business decisions*
bright *an exceptionally bright child*
observant *an observant eye*
perceptive *a perceptive gaze*
quick *Her quick mind soon grasped the situation.*
quick-witted *He is very alert and quick-witted.*
3 sudden and significant: *a sharp rise in prices*
abrupt *Her idyllic world came to an abrupt end.*
marked *a marked increase in crime*
sudden *a sudden change in course*
See also **acute, astute, bitter, brilliant, intelligent, perceptive, prompt, shrewd, shrill, sour**

shatter *See* **dash**

shattered *See* **broken**

shed *See* **discard**

sheen *See* **gloss**

sheepish *See* **ashamed, embarrassed**

sheer
▷ ADJECTIVE
1 complete and total: *scenes of sheer beauty*
absolute *I think it's absolute nonsense.*
complete *He shook his head in complete bewilderment.*
pure *To have an uninterrupted night's sleep was pure bliss.*
total *This is total madness!*
unqualified *The party was an unqualified disaster.*
utter *a look of utter confusion*
2 vertical: *There was a sheer drop just outside my window.*
perpendicular *the perpendicular wall of brick*

steep *a narrow valley with steep sides*
vertical *The climber inched up a vertical wall of rock.*

3 very light and delicate: *sheer curtains*
delicate *delicate fabric*
fine *a fine, pale grey material*
lightweight *We packed lightweight clothes for the canoe trip.*
thin *Watch out for the thin ice.*
ANTONYM **thick**
See also **absolute, fine, perfect, pure, rank, steep, transparent, utter**

sheet *See* **layer**

shell *See* **bomb, ruin**

shelter
▷ *NOUN*
I a place providing protection: *a bus shelter*
hostel *She spent two years living in a hostel.*
refuge *a mountain refuge*
sanctuary *a sanctuary for people fleeing the civil war*
2 protection from bad weather or danger: *During the flood, we took shelter in the school gym.*
asylum *refugees who sought political asylum*
cover *They ran for cover from the storm.*
harbour *The cove was a safe harbour for small boats.*
haven *The island is a haven for international criminals.*
protection *The officer's bulletproof vest provided her with some protection.*
refuge *They took refuge in an old barn.*
safety *the safety of one's own home*
sanctuary *Some of them sought sanctuary at the embassy.*
▷ *VERB*
3 to stay somewhere in order to be safe: *a man sheltering in a doorway*
hide *They hid behind a tree.*
huddle *They huddled under the awning.*
take cover *Shoppers took cover inside the store as the rain came pelting down.*
4 to hide or protect someone: *A neighbour sheltered the boy for seven days.*
harbour *They were accused of harbouring the prisoners.*
hide *They hid me until the coast was clear.*
protect *A purple scarf protected her against the wind.*
shield *He shielded his head from the sun with a baseball cap.*
See also **accommodate, defend, guard, protect, protection, refuge**

shelve *See* **delay, postpone**

shield *See* **defend, guard, protect, safeguard, shelter**

shielded *See* **secure**

shimmer *See* **shine, sparkle**

shimmering *See* **shining**

shine
▷ *VERB*
to give out a bright light: *The sun is shining.*
beam *The spotlight beamed down on the stage.*
gleam *The moonlight gleamed on the water.*
glow *The lantern glowed softly in the darkness.*
radiate *the amount of light radiated by an ordinary light bulb*
shimmer *The lake shimmered in the sunlight.*
sparkle *Diamonds sparkled on her wrist.*
See also **finish, gloss, glow, polish**

shining
▷ *ADJECTIVE*
giving out or reflecting light: *shining stainless steel*
bright *a bright star*
brilliant *brilliant sunshine*
gleaming *gleaming headlights*
luminous *the luminous dial on the clock*
radiant *He saw a figure surrounded by a radiant light.*
shimmering *a shimmering gold fabric*
sparkling *elegant cutlery and sparkling crystal*

shiny *See* **glossy**

ship *See* **transport**

shipment *See* **load, transport**

shirk *See* **avoid, dodge**

shiver *See* **shake**

shock
▷ *NOUN*
I a sudden upsetting experience: *The extent of the damage came as a shock.*
blow *It was a terrible blow when she was laid off.*
bombshell *Her departure was a bombshell for the team.*
distress *He wanted to save his parents all the distress he could.*
trauma *the trauma of losing a parent*
▷ *VERB*
2 to make you feel upset: *I was shocked by his appearance.*
numb *numbed by suffering*
paralyze *He stood paralyzed with horror.*
shake *The news of her death has shaken us all.*

S

stagger *The judge said he was staggered by the defendant's lack of remorse.*

stun *Audiences were stunned by the movie's violent ending.*

traumatize *We were both traumatized by the experience.*

3 to offend because of being rude or immoral: *She is very easily shocked.*

appal *I was appalled by her rudeness.*

disgust *He disgusted everyone with his boorish behaviour.*

offend *Many people are offended by certain words.*

outrage *They were outraged by his racist comments.*

See also **amaze, amazement, blow, horrify, scare, shake, surprise**

shocking *See* **disgraceful**

shoddy *See* **inferior, poor**

shoot *See* **fire, rush, tear**

shoot up *See* **explode**

shop *See* **store**

shoplifter *See* **thief**

shopper *See* **customer**

short
▷ ADJECTIVE
I not lasting very long: *a short break*
brief *a brief meeting*
fleeting *a fleeting glimpse*
momentary *a momentary lapse of concentration*
short-lived *a short-lived craze*
ANTONYM **long**

2 small in height: *a short, elderly man*
ANTONYM **tall**
See WORD STUDY **short**
3 not using many words: *a short speech*
brief *a brief description*
concise *a concise summary*
succinct *a succinct account*
terse *a terse comment*
See also **abrupt, brief, concise, deficient, inadequate, insufficient, low**

shortage
▷ NOUN
a lack of something: *a shortage of funds*
dearth *the dearth of good fiction by new Canadian writers*
deficiency *tests for vitamin deficiency*
lack *I was hampered by a lack of information.*
scarcity *a scarcity of water*
shortfall *a shortfall in income*
want *a want of good manners*
ANTONYM **abundance**
See also **lack, want**

shortcoming *See* **defect, failure**

shorten
▷ VERB
to make something shorter: *I had the pants shortened.*
abbreviate *The province of Nova Scotia is abbreviated N.S.*
cut *The movie was cut to two hours.*
trim *I need to get my hair trimmed.*
ANTONYM **lengthen**
See also **reduce**

shortfall *See* **shortage**

short-lived *See* **short**

shortly *See* **soon**

WORD STUDY: SHORT

Some words used to describe a person who is **short** can be more hurtful or insulting than others.

- A **little** or **small** person is not large in physical size.
She was too **little** to reach the books on the top shelf.
He is **small** for his age.

- A **diminutive** person is very small.
A **diminutive** figure stood in the doorway.

- If you describe a woman as **petite**, you are politely saying that she is small and slim. This is a complimentary word.
My mother is a **petite** blonde.

- A **tiny** person is extremely small.
Though she was **tiny**, she had a loud voice.

- If you describe someone as **dumpy**, you mean they are short and fat. This is an uncomplimentary word.
He was talking to a **dumpy** woman in a baggy tracksuit.

- If you describe someone as **squat**, you mean that they are short and thick, usually in an unattractive way.
He is a short, **squat** fellow, with a cheerful look on his face.

shot *See* **attempt, go, try**

shoulder *See* **assume, bear**

shoulder to shoulder *See* **together**

shout

▷ *NOUN*

1 a loud call or cry: *I heard a distant shout.*
bellow *a bellow of rage*
cry *She gave a cry of horror.*
roar *a roar of approval*
scream *screams of terror*
yell *He let out a yell of delight.*

▷ *VERB*

2 to call or cry loudly: *He shouted something to his brother.*
bawl *At the end of the movie, we were both bawling.*
bellow *He bellowed orders into the cellphone.*
call *He could hear them calling his name.*
cry *"You're under arrest!" he cried.*
roar *"I'll kill you for that!" he roared.*
scream *screaming at them to get out of my house*
yell *She yelled at the dog to go away.*
See also **call, cry, scream**

shove *See* **push, stick, stuff**

show

▷ *VERB*

1 to prove something: *Tests show that drinking impairs your ability to drive.*
demonstrate *The study demonstrated a link between pollution and respiratory problems.*
prove *History will prove her to be right.*
2 to do something in order to teach someone else: *I'll show you how to use this digital camera.*
demonstrate *She demonstrated how to make ice cream.*
instruct *He instructed us on how to give first aid.*
teach *She taught me how to ride a bike.*
3 to display a quality or characteristic: *Her sketches showed artistic promise.*
demonstrate *He has demonstrated his ability.*
display *She displayed remarkable courage.*
indicate *Her choice of words indicated her real feelings.*
manifest *Fear can manifest itself in many ways.*
reveal *His reaction revealed a lack of self-confidence.*

▷ *NOUN*

4 a public exhibition: *a fashion show*
display *a gymnastics display*
exhibition *an art exhibition*

presentation *her successful presentation to the committee*
5 a display of a feeling or quality: *a show of affection*
air *an air of indifference*
display *a display of remorse*
pose *a pose of injured innocence*
pretence *They have given up all pretence of neutrality.*
semblance *Maintain a semblance of order.*
See also **betray, expose, fair, front, indicate, play, program, represent**

INFORMALLY SPEAKING

get the show on the road: get started
run the show: be in charge

---

show signs of *See* **promise**

show up *See* **appear, come, expose, uncover**

shower *See* **hail, scatter**

showers *See* **rain**

showery *See* **wet**

show-off *See* **braggart**

showy *See* **flashy, gaudy, ostentatious**

shred *See* **tear**

shrewd

▷ *ADJECTIVE*

showing intelligence and good judgment: *a shrewd manager*
astute *an astute judge of character*
canny *She was far too canny to give herself away.*
crafty *He is clever and crafty.*
perceptive *a perceptive analysis of the situation*
sharp *She is very sharp, and a quick thinker.*
smart *a very smart move*
See also **acute, astute, clever, keen, smart, wise**

shriek *See* **scream**

shrill

▷ *ADJECTIVE*

high-pitched and piercing: *the shrill whistle of the engine*
penetrating *a penetrating voice*
piercing *a piercing squawk*
sharp *the sharp cry of a seagull*

shrink

▷ *VERB*

to become smaller: *My sweater shrank in the wash.*

S

contract *The rib cage expands and contracts as you breathe.*
diminish *The threat of nuclear war has diminished.*
dwindle *The factory's workforce has dwindled from 4000 to 200.*
get smaller *Electronic systems are getting smaller.*
narrow *The gap between the two political parties has narrowed.*
ANTONYM **grow**
See also **cower, decrease, diminish, flinch, lessen**

shrinkage *See* **decline**

shrivel *See* **burn, wither**

shroud *See* **obscure**

shudder *See* **shake**

shun *See* **avoid**

shunned *See* **unpopular**

shut
▷ VERB
I to close something: *Someone had forgotten to shut the door.*
close *If you are cold, get up and close the window.*
fasten *He fastened his seatbelt.*
slam *He slammed the gate shut behind him.*
ANTONYM **open**
▷ ADJECTIVE
2 closed or fastened: *An aroma of baking bread came from behind the shut door.*
closed *All the exits were closed.*
fastened *Is your bicycle helmet fastened?*
sealed *a sealed envelope*
ANTONYM **open**
See also **close**

shut up *See* **confine**

shy
▷ ADJECTIVE
nervous or timid in the company of other people: *a shy, quiet-spoken man*
bashful *Offstage, he is bashful and awkward.*
retiring *She was the quiet, retiring type.*
self-conscious *I felt a bit self-conscious in my bathing suit.*
timid *a timid little kitten*
ANTONYM **bold**
See also **timid**

sick
▷ ADJECTIVE
I unwell or ill: *The emergency room was full of very sick people.*
ailing *She tenderly nursed her ailing mother.*

under par *The flu has left me feeling under par.*
under the weather *Are you still a bit under the weather?*
unwell *He had been unwell for some time.*
ANTONYM **well**
2 feeling as if you are going to vomit: *The very thought of food made him sick.*
ill *The smell of bacon always makes me ill.*
nauseous *These drugs may make you feel nauseous.*
queasy *The motion of the ship was already making him queasy.*

sick of
▷ ADJECTIVE
tired of something: *I'm sick of your complaints.*
bored *I'm getting bored with this game.*
fed up *He is fed up with his summer job.*
tired *I am tired of this music.*
weary *He was weary of being alone.*
See also **ill, queasy, unhealthy, unwell**

sick person *See* **patient**

sicken *See* **disgust, horrify, repel**

sickening *See* **disgusting**

sickly *See* **puny, weak**

sickness *See* **illness**

side
▷ NOUN
I the edge of something: *Her legs hung over the side of the bed.*
edge *the edge of the balcony*
shoulder *He parked on the shoulder of the highway.*
2 one of two groups involved in a dispute or contest: *Both sides began to prepare for the debate.*
camp *Most of his supporters had now defected to the opposite camp.*
faction *leaders of the warring factions*
party *three major political parties*
team *Both teams played well.*
See also **aspect, bank, face, point, team**

side by side *See* **together**

sidestep *See* **avoid, dodge**

side with
▷ VERB
to support someone in an argument: *He always sided with his sister.*
agree with *He's bound to agree with his boss.*
stand up for *I was the one who always stood up for my younger brother.*
support *He supported me in the election.*
take the part of *Why do you always take his part?*
See also **support**

sidle *See* **edge, sneak**

sift *See* **investigate, search**

sight

▷ *NOUN*

1 the ability to see: *The singer lost his sight when he was a child.*

eyesight *He suffered from poor eyesight.*

visibility *Visibility was very poor.*

vision *That disease can cause blindness or serious loss of vision.*

2 something you see: *It was a ghastly sight.*

display *These flowers make a colourful display in spring.*

scene *a bizarre scene*

spectacle *an impressive spectacle*

▷ *VERB*

3 to see something or someone: *He had been sighted in the Maritimes.*

see *I saw a deer in the woods today.*

spot *I drove around till I spotted her.*

See also **see, spot**

CONFUSABLES

sight means **view** or **ability to see**
site means **area of ground** or **place for an activity**

sign

▷ *NOUN*

1 a mark or symbol: *The negative number is preceded by a minus sign.*

character *the characters used in typesetting*

emblem *The beaver is an official emblem of Canada.*

icon *desktop icons*

logo *the company's logo*

mark *Put a check mark against the statements you agree with.*

symbol *the chemical symbol for mercury*

2 a notice put up to give a warning or information: *a sign saying that the highway was closed*

board *Are any jobs posted on the notice board?*

notice *a notice saying "no entry"*

placard *The protesters sang songs and waved placards.*

3 evidence of something: *the first signs of recovery*

clue *the only real clue that something was wrong*

evidence *there has been no evidence of criminal activity*

hint *He showed only the slightest hint of emotion.*

indication *All the indications suggest that he is the culprit.*

symptom *typical symptoms of stress*

token *a token of goodwill*

trace *very few traces of evidence*

See also **indication, notice, omen, premonition, signal, symbol, trace**

sign up *See* **hire, join**

signal

▷ *NOUN*

1 something that is intended to give a message: *a distress signal*

beacon *an emergency beacon*

cue *The other actor gave me my cue to speak.*

gesture *She made a menacing gesture with her fist.*

sign *They gave him the thumbs-up sign.*

▷ *VERB*

2 to make a sign as a message to someone: *He was frantically signalling me to stop talking.*

beckon *I beckoned her over.*

gesticulate *He was gesticulating at me, but I didn't know what he wanted.*

gesture *I gestured toward the house, and he went in.*

motion *He motioned for me to join him at the table.*

nod *They nodded good night to the security guard.*

sign *She signed to me to come near.*

wave *He waved to me from across the room.*

See also **indicate, indication**

signal to *See* **hail**

significance *See* **meaning**

significant

▷ *ADJECTIVE*

large or important: *This drug seems to have a significant effect on the disease.*

considerable *Doing it properly makes considerable demands on our time.*

important *Canadian peacekeeping forces play an important role in international affairs.*

impressive *an impressive achievement*

marked *a marked improvement in the skater's technique*

notable *With a few notable exceptions, the cast was excellent.*

pronounced *The exhibition has a pronounced agricultural theme.*

striking *The most striking feature of these statistics is the rate of growth.*

ANTONYM **insignificant**

See also **important, major, serious, special**

S

signify See count, indicate, mean

silence

▷ NOUN

1 an absence of sound: *There was a momentary silence.*

calm *He liked the calm of the evening.*

hush *A hush fell over the crowd.*

lull *a lull in the conversation*

peace *I love the peace of the countryside.*

quiet *The quiet of the apartment was very soothing.*

stillness *An explosion shattered the stillness of the night air.*

ANTONYM **noise**

2 an inability or refusal to talk: *breaking his silence for the first time about the incident*

muteness *He retreated into a world of muteness.*

reticence *She didn't seem to notice my reticence.*

speechlessness *He was shy to the point of speechlessness.*

▷ VERB

3 to make someone or something quiet: *The shock silenced her completely.*

deaden *We hung up curtains to try and deaden the noise.*

gag *gagged with a towel*

muffle *You can muffle the sound with absorbent material.*

quiet *A look from her sister quieted her at once.*

stifle *He put his hand to his mouth to stifle a giggle.*

still *He raised a hand to still my protest.*

suppress *She barely suppressed a gasp.*

See also **peace, quiet**

silent

▷ ADJECTIVE

1 not saying anything: *The class fell silent as the teacher entered.*

dumb *We were all struck dumb for a moment.*

mute *a mute look of appeal*

speechless *speechless with rage*

taciturn *a taciturn man with a solemn expression*

wordless *They exchanged a wordless look of understanding.*

2 making no noise: *The room was silent except for the ticking of the clock.*

hushed *the vast, hushed space of the empty theatre*

quiet *a quiet engine*

soundless *My bare feet were soundless on the carpet.*

still *The room was suddenly still.*

ANTONYM **noisy**

See also **dumb, quiet**

silhouette See figure, outline

silky See smooth

silliness See stupidity

silly

▷ ADJECTIVE

foolish or ridiculous: *I know it's silly to get so upset.*

absurd *He found my theory absurd.*

foolish *It is foolish to risk injury.*

idiotic *What an idiotic thing to say!*

inane *He stood there with an inane grin on his face.*

ridiculous *a ridiculous suggestion*

stupid *a stupid mistake*

See also **foolish, frivolous, unwise**

similar

▷ ADJECTIVE

like something else: *a bike similar to mine*

alike *You two are very alike.*

analogous *Children playing is analogous to adults working.*

comparable *paying the same salary for work of comparable value*

like *They're as like as two peas in a pod.*

uniform *cookies of uniform size*

ANTONYM **different**

See also **alike, like**

similarity

▷ NOUN

the quality of being like something else: *the similarity of our backgrounds*

analogy *the analogy between poets and painters*

likeness *These myths have a startling likeness to one another.*

resemblance *I could see the resemblance to his grandfather.*

sameness *He grew bored by the sameness of the speeches.*

ANTONYM **difference**

See also **resemblance**

similarly See alike

simple

▷ ADJECTIVE

1 easy to understand or do: *a simple task*

easy *This ice cream maker is cheap and easy to use.*

elementary *elementary computer skills*

straightforward *It was a straightforward question.*

uncomplicated *an uncomplicated story*

understandable *He writes in a clear, understandable style.*

ANTONYM **complicated**

2 plain in style: *a simple but stylish outfit*
classic *classic designs that will fit in anywhere*
clean *the clean lines of Scandinavian furniture*
plain *The room was plain but tidy.*
severe *hair pulled back in a severe style*
ANTONYM **elaborate**
See also **crude, easy, humble, primitive, straightforward**

simplicity *See* **ease, innocence**

simplify

▷ VERB
to make something easier to do or understand: *measures intended to simplify the procedure*
make simpler *restructuring the rules to make them simpler*
streamline *an effort to cut costs and streamline operations*

simply *See* **only**

simulate *See* **fake, imitate**

simulated *See* **false**

simultaneously *See* **together**

sin

▷ NOUN
I immoral behaviour: *preaching against sin*
crime *a life of crime*
evil *You can't stop all the evil in the world.*
offence *an offence that carries a heavy penalty*
wickedness *a sign of human wickedness*
wrong *I intend to right that wrong.*
▷ VERB
2 to do something immoral: *I admit that I have sinned.*
do wrong *They have done wrong and they know it.*
See also **evil, wrong**

since *See* **because**

sincere

▷ ADJECTIVE
saying things that you really mean: *my sincere apologies*
genuine *a display of genuine emotion*
heartfelt *heartfelt sympathy*
real *the real affection between them*
wholehearted *a wholehearted and genuine response*
ANTONYM **insincere**
See also **real, serious**

sinful *See* **evil, wicked**

singe *See* **burn**

single

▷ ADJECTIVE
I only one and no more: *the beauty of a single rose*
lone *A lone police officer guarded the doors.*
one *I had just one slice of pizza.*
only *My only regret is that I never knew him.*
sole *the sole survivor of the accident*
solitary *There is not one solitary scrap of evidence.*
2 not married: *I'm surprised you're still single.*
unattached *He remained unattached for many years.*
unmarried *an unmarried woman*
3 for one person only: *a single room*
individual *an individual portion*
separate *separate rooms*
See also **alone, individual**

single out *See* **favour, select**

single-minded *See* **determined**

singular

▷ ADJECTIVE
unusual and remarkable: *a smile of singular sweetness*
exceptional *children with exceptional ability*
extraordinary *The task requires extraordinary patience and endurance.*
rare *a leader of rare strength and instinct*
remarkable *a remarkable achievement*
uncommon *She read the e-mail with uncommon interest.*
unique *a person of unique talent and determination*
unusual *He had an unusual aptitude for mathematics.*
See also **curious, extraordinary, odd, particular, weird**

sinister

▷ ADJECTIVE
seeming harmful or evil: *There was something cold and sinister about him.*
evil *an evil smile*
forbidding *a huge, forbidding building*
menacing *His dark eyebrows gave him a menacing look.*
ominous *An ominous figure stood in the doorway.*
threatening *her threatening appearance*
See also **creepy, ominous**

S

sink *See* **descend, drive, drop, fail**

sip *See* **drink, taste**

siren *See* **alarm**

sit down *See* **rest**

site *See* **location, place, scene, spot**

sited *See* **located**

situate *See* **place**

situated *See* **located**

situation

▷ NOUN

what is happening: *a serious situation*
case *a clear case of mistaken identity*
circumstances *I wish we could have met in happier circumstances.*
plight *the plight of the famine victims*
scenario *a nightmare scenario*
state of affairs *This state of affairs cannot continue.*
See also **affair, location, matter, state**

sixth sense *See* **instinct**

size

▷ NOUN

how big or small something is: *the size of the audience*
bulk *Despite his bulk, he moved gracefully.*
dimensions *She considered the dimensions of the problem.*
extent *the extent of the damage*
immensity *The immensity of the universe is impossible to grasp.*
proportions *In the tropics, plants grow to huge proportions.*
See also **area, capacity, extent, quantity**

sketch *See* **draw, outline, picture**

sketchy *See* **rough**

skilful

▷ ADJECTIVE

able to do something very well: *the NHL's most skilful player*
able *a very able manager*
accomplished *an accomplished pianist*
adept *an adept diplomat*
competent *a competent and careful driver*
expert *She is expert at handling complex negotiations.*
masterly *a masterly performance*
proficient *proficient with computers*
skilled *a skilled carpenter*
ANTONYM **incompetent**
See also **capable, expert, proficient, skilled**

skilfully *See* **well**

skill

▷ NOUN

the ability to do something well: *This task requires great skill.*
ability *a man of considerable abilities*
competence *her high professional competence*
dexterity *her dexterity on the guitar*
expertise *the expertise to deal with these problems*
facility *a facility for languages*
knack *the knack of getting along with people*
proficiency *basic proficiency in the language*
See also **ability, qualification**

skilled

▷ ADJECTIVE

having the knowledge to do something well: *skilled workers, such as plumbers*
able *an able technician*
accomplished *an accomplished pianist*
competent *a competent and careful driver*
experienced *lawyers who are experienced in these matters*
expert *It takes an expert eye to see the symptoms.*
masterly *the artist's masterly use of colour*
professional *professional people like doctors and engineers*
proficient *She is proficient in several foreign languages.*
skilful *the artist's skilful use of light and shade*
trained *Our workforce is highly trained.*
ANTONYM **incompetent**
See also **able, expert, perfect, practical, proficient, skilful**

skim *See* **glance**

skin *See* **coat, graze, hide, scrape**

skinny

▷ ADJECTIVE

extremely thin: *a skinny little boy*
bony *a long, bony finger*
emaciated *photographs of the emaciated prisoners*
lean *a tall, lean figure*
scrawny *the vulture's scrawny neck*
thin *tall and thin*
undernourished *undernourished children*
ANTONYM **plump**
See also **puny**

skip *See* **omit**

skirmish *See* **clash, fight**

slack *See* **flabby, lazy, limp, loose**

slacken *See* **ease, loosen**

slam *See* **bang, dash, shut**

slander

▷ NOUN

1 something untrue and malicious said

about someone: *He is now suing the company for slander.*
libel *defendants seeking damages for libel*
scandal *a magazine that spreads scandal*
slur *a vicious slur on my character*
smear *He called the allegation "an evil smear."*
▷ VERB
2 to say untrue and malicious things about someone: *He has been charged with slandering the mayor.*
libel *The newspaper that libelled her had to pay compensation.*
malign *She claims she is being unfairly maligned.*
smear *an attempt to smear their manager*

slant See **colour, slope, tilt**

slanted See **biased**

slap See **hit**

slash See **cut, lower**

slaughter See **kill, murder**

slave See **labour, work**

slay See **kill, murder**

slaying See **murder**

sleek See **glossy, smooth**

sleep
▷ NOUN
1 the natural state of rest in which you are unconscious: *They were exhausted from lack of sleep.*
doze *I had a doze after lunch.*
hibernation *Many animals go into hibernation during the winter.*
nap *I might take a nap for a while.*
slumber *He had fallen into exhausted slumber.*
snooze INFORMAL *a little snooze after dinner*
▷ VERB
2 to rest in a natural state of unconsciousness: *The baby slept during the car ride.*
doze *He dozed in an armchair.*
hibernate *Most bears hibernate from October to April or May.*
slumber *The girls were slumbering peacefully.*
snooze INFORMAL *He was snoozing in front of the television.*
take a nap *I try to take a nap every afternoon.*

sleepy
▷ ADJECTIVE
1 tired and ready to go to sleep: *Do you feel sleepy during the day?*

drowsy *This medicine may make you feel drowsy.*
lethargic *He felt too lethargic to get dressed.*
sluggish *I was still feeling sluggish after my nap.*
2 not having much activity or excitement: *a sleepy little village*
dull *a dull town*
quiet *a quiet street*
See also **tired**

slender
▷ ADJECTIVE
1 healthily thin: *a tall, slender woman*
lean *Like most athletes, she was lean and muscular.*
slight *She is small and slight.*
slim *a slim build*
2 small in amount or degree: *He won, but only by a slender majority.*
faint *They now have only a faint chance of survival.*
remote *a remote possibility*
slight *There is a slight improvement in his condition.*
slim *a slim hope*
small *a small chance of success*
See also **minute, narrow, remote**

slice See **piece**

slide See **flow**

slight
▷ ADJECTIVE
small in amount or degree: *a slight dent*
insignificant *an insignificant amount*
minor *a minor inconvenience*
negligible *The strike will have only a negligible impact.*
small *It only makes a small difference.*
trivial *trivial details*
ANTONYM **large**
See also **insult, light, minor, remote, scorn, slender, trivial, unimportant**

slightest See **least**

slightly See **rather**

slim See **narrow, remote, slender, thin**

sling See **throw**

slip
▷ VERB
1 to go somewhere quickly and quietly: *She slipped downstairs and out of the house.*
creep *I crept up to my room.*
sneak *Sometimes he would sneak out to see me.*
steal *They can steal away at night to join us.*

S

▷ *NOUN*

2 a mistake: *a slip of the tongue*
blunder *an embarrassing blunder*
error *a tactical error*
mistake *a spelling mistake*
slip-up *There must be no slip-ups.*
See also **error, mistake, sneak, steal**

INFORMALLY SPEAKING

give someone the slip: evade someone
let slip: tell without meaning to
slip one over on: get the advantage of, especially by trickery
slip up: make a mistake

---

slippery See **crafty, sneaky**

slit See **cut**

slog away See **work**

slogan
▷ *NOUN*
a short, easily remembered phrase: *Alberta's slogan is "Canada's Rocky Mountain Playground."*
jingle *a catchy advertising jingle*
motto *Canada's motto is "A mare usque ad mare" (From sea to sea).*

slope
▷ *NOUN*
I a flat surface, with one end higher than the other: *The street is on a slope.*
gradient *a steep gradient*
incline *The car was unable to negotiate the incline.*
ramp *There is a ramp allowing access for wheelchairs.*
▷ *VERB*
2 to be at an angle: *The bank sloped sharply down to the river.*
fall *The road fell steeply.*
rise *The climb is arduous, rising steeply through thick bush.*
slant *His handwriting slanted to the left.*
See also **tilt**

sloppy See **careless, inefficient, loose, sentimental**

slot See **opening**

slow
▷ *ADJECTIVE*
I moving or happening with little speed: *slow, regular breathing*
gradual *Losing weight is a gradual process.*
leisurely *He walked at a leisurely pace.*
lingering *a lingering death*

ponderous *Her steps were heavy and ponderous.*
sluggish *a sluggish stream*
unhurried *an unhurried way of life*
ANTONYM **fast**
2 not very bright: *I must be pretty slow if I didn't get that joke.*
dense *You're a bit dense this morning.*
dim *He is rather dim.*
obtuse *It should be obvious even to the most obtuse person.*
stupid *How stupid can you be?*
thick *I can't believe I've been so thick.*
See also **dim, gradual, reluctant**

slow (down)
▷ *VERB*
to go or cause to go more slowly: *The car slowed and then stopped.*
check *attempts to check the spread of flu*
decelerate *He decelerated when he saw the warning sign.*

slowly
▷ *ADVERB*
not quickly or hurriedly: *She turned and began to walk away slowly.*
by degrees *By degrees, the tension lessened.*
gradually *Their friendship gradually deepened.*
unhurriedly *The sailors drifted along unhurriedly.*
ANTONYM **quickly**

sluggish See **sleepy, slow**

slumber See **sleep**

slump See **decline, drop, fall, recession**

slur See **slander**

slushy See **sentimental**

sly
▷ *ADJECTIVE*
cunning and deceptive: *devious, sly, and manipulative*
crafty *a crafty mind*
cunning *Some of these kids can be very cunning.*
devious *an extremely dangerous, evil, and devious man*
scheming *You're a scheming little rat, aren't you?*
underhand *underhand tactics*
wily *wily behaviour*
See also **crafty, cunning, sneaky**

smack See **blow, hit**

small
▷ *ADJECTIVE*
I not large in size, number, or amount: *a small child*

2 not important or significant: *small changes*
See WORD STUDY **small**
See also **fine, low, minute, modest, remote, slender, slight**

smallest *See* **least**

small-minded *See* **petty**

smart
▷ ADJECTIVE
1 clean and neat in appearance: *a smart navy blue outfit*
chic *chic Parisian women*
elegant *She looked beautiful and elegant, as always.*
neat *a neat grey flannel suit*
spruce *He was looking spruce in his uniform.*
stylish *stylish shoes*
ANTONYM **scruffy**
2 clever and intelligent: *a smart idea*
astute *a series of astute business decisions*
bright *She is extremely bright.*
canny *He was far too canny to give himself away.*
clever *a very clever contestant*
ingenious *an ingenious plan*

intelligent *Dolphins are an intelligent species.*
shrewd *a shrewd manager*
ANTONYM **stupid**
See also **astute, bright, brilliant, clever, intelligent, neat, posh, shrewd**

smarting *See* **sore**

smash *See* **crash, dash**

smash into *See* **hit**

smashed *See* **broken**

smear *See* **slander, soil, spread**

smell
▷ NOUN
1 the quality of something that you sense through your nose: *a smell of damp wood*
aroma *the aroma of fresh bread*
fragrance *the fragrance of his cologne*
odour *a disagreeable odour*
perfume *enjoying the perfume of the apple blossoms*
reek *the reek of the skunk*
scent *flowers chosen for their scent*

WORD STUDY: SMALL

Depending on the sense of **small** that you mean, there are a number of words that you can use to vary your writing and make it more interesting.

• **of things, in size**
We sat around a **little** table.
I bought a **miniature** camera.
She's wearing a pair of **miniscule** shorts.
Only a **minute** amount is needed.
The living room is **tiny**.

• **in area**
It's only a **little** distance from the station.
The dog was trying to squeeze through a **narrow** gap in the fence.
Plants, like animals, often have a **restricted** habitat.

• **of a business**
He started with one **humble** corner shop.
The company grew from **modest** beginnings.
It began as a **small-scale** cheese factory.
It's an **unpretentious** restaurant, but the food's good.

• **of people, young**
This is my **baby** sister.
The pianist was an **infant** prodigy.

What did you look like when you were **little**?
Why, he's only a **young** child!

• **of people, in size**
See **short**

• **in importance**
At the time, it was a seemingly **inconsequential** event.
He was born in an **insignificant** village in the hills.
Fancy making such a fuss over such a **little** thing!
It's a **minor** detail which can be easily fixed.
The impact of the strike will be **negligible**.
Arguments would start over the most **petty** things.
It will only make a **slight** difference.
These are **trifling** objections.
Let's not get bogged down in **trivial** details.
The argument was a comparatively **unimportant** event.

S

stench *a foul stench*
stink *the stink of rotting vegetables*
▷ VERB
2 to have an unpleasant smell: *Do my feet smell?*
reek *The house reeks of garbage.*
stink *The house stinks of old fish.*
3 to become aware of the smell of something: *I could smell muffins baking in the oven.*
scent *The dog had scented something in the bushes.*
sniff *He opened his window and sniffed the air.*
See also **fragrance**

smelly
▷ ADJECTIVE
having a strong unpleasant smell: *smelly socks*
foul *His breath was foul.*
reeking *poisoning the air with their reeking cigars*
stinking *piles of stinking garbage*
ANTONYM **fragrant**

smile
▷ VERB
1 to move the corners of your mouth upward because you are pleased: *When he saw me, he smiled and waved.*
beam *She beamed at him in delight.*
grin *She grinned broadly.*
smirk *The mischievous children smirked at each other.*
▷ NOUN
2 the expression you have when you smile: *She gave me a big smile.*
beam *a strange beam of satisfaction on his face*
grin *She looked at me with a sheepish grin.*
smirk *a smirk of triumph*

smirk *See* **smile**

smitten *See* **crazy**

smooth
▷ ADJECTIVE
not rough or bumpy: *a smooth wooden surface*
glassy *glassy wet pebbles*
glossy *a glossy photograph*
polished *He slipped on the polished floor.*
silky *The dog's coat is silky in texture.*
sleek *her sleek, waist-length hair*
ANTONYM **rough**
See also **easy, even, flat, level**

smoothly *See* **well**

smother *See* **spread, suppress**

smoulder *See* **glow**

smudge *See* **mark, spot**

smug
▷ ADJECTIVE
pleased with yourself: *They looked at each other in smug satisfaction.*
complacent *an aggravating, complacent little smile*
conceited *They had grown too conceited and pleased with themselves.*
self-satisfied *a self-satisfied little snob*
superior *He stood there looking superior.*

smuggle *See* **sneak**

smugness *See* **pride**

snag
▷ NOUN
a small problem or disadvantage: *The snag was that he had no transportation.*
catch *It sounds too good to be true — what's the catch?*
difficulty *The only difficulty may be the price.*
disadvantage *The disadvantage is that this plant needs frequent watering.*
drawback *The apartment's only drawback was its small size.*
problem *The only problem about living here is the tourists.*
See also **catch, difficulty, drawback, stick**

snap *See* **crack**

snare *See* **catch, trap**

snatch *See* **extract, grab, grasp, seize**

snatch a glimpse *See* **peek**

sneak
▷ VERB
1 to go somewhere quietly: *Sometimes she would sneak out to see me.*
lurk *I saw someone lurking outside.*
sidle *He sidled into the room, trying to look inconspicuous.*
slip *He quietly slipped downstairs and out of the house.*
steal *They can steal out and join us later.*
2 to put or take something somewhere secretly: *He was caught trying to sneak the book out of the library.*
slip *He slipped me a note.*
smuggle *We smuggled a camera into the concert.*
spirit *treasures spirited away to foreign museums*
See also **slip, steal**

sneaky

▷ ADJECTIVE

doing things secretly or being done secretly: *He only won by using sneaky tactics.*

crafty *the crafty methods used by salespeople to get customers to sign up*

deceitful *They claimed the government had been deceitful.*

devious *He was devious, saying one thing to me and another to her.*

dishonest *It would be dishonest to mislead people in that way.*

mean *That was a mean trick.*

slippery *She's a slippery customer, and should be watched.*

sly *He's a sly one.*

untrustworthy *His opponents say he's untrustworthy.*

sneering See scornful

snide See spiteful

sniff See smell

snigger See laugh

snippet See extract

snobbery See pride

snobbish See haughty, pretentious, stuck-up, superior

snoop See pry

snooper See meddler

snooze See sleep

snub See insult

snug See cosy, tight

so See therefore

soak

▷ VERB

to make something very wet: *The water had soaked his jacket.*

bathe *Bathe the infected area in warm water.*

permeate *The heavy rain had permeated the soil.*

steep *tea leaves steeped in hot water*

wet *Wet the hair and work the shampoo through it.*

See also **steep, wet**

soak up See absorb

soaked See wet

soar See explode, fly

soaring See tall

sober See grave, realistic, reasonable, serious, solemn

sociable

▷ ADJECTIVE

enjoying the company of other people: *She's usually outgoing and sociable.*

friendly *The people here are very friendly.*

gregarious *I'm not a gregarious person.*

outgoing *He was shy, and she was very outgoing.*

socialist See left-wing

socialize See associate

society

▷ NOUN

1 the people in a particular country or region: *a major problem in society*

civilization *an ancient civilization*

culture *people from different cultures*

2 an organization for people with the same interest or aim: *the school debating society*

association *the photography association*

circle *a local painting circle*

club *He was at the youth club.*

group *an environmental group*

guild *the Screen Writers' Guild*

institute *the Art Institute*

league *the National Hockey League*

organization *student organizations*

union *the International Astronomical Union*

See also **association, body, club, fellowship, public**

sodden See damp, wet

soft

▷ ADJECTIVE

1 not hard, stiff, or firm: *a soft bed*

flexible *a flexible material*

pliable *a pliable dough*

squashy *a squashy tomato*

supple *supple leather*

yielding *yielding cushions*

ANTONYM **hard**

2 quiet and not harsh: *a soft tapping at my door*

gentle *a gentle voice*

low *She spoke in a low whisper.*

mellow *mellow background music*

muted *Their loud conversation became muted.*

quiet *He always spoke in a quiet tone to which everyone listened.*

subdued *His voice was more subdued than usual.*

3 not bright: *The soft lights made the room seem romantic.*

dim *The light was dim and eerie.*

faint *The stars cast a faint light.*

light *The walls were painted a light yellow.*

S

mellow *Their colour schemes tend towards rich, mellow shades.*
pale *dressed in pale pink*
pastel *delicate pastel hues*
subdued *subdued lighting*
ANTONYM **bright**
See also **gentle, limp, quiet**

soften *See* **moderate**

soggy *See* **damp**

soil

▷ NOUN
I the surface of the earth: *The soil is reasonably moist after the rain.*
clay *a thin layer of clay*
dirt *The bulldozers piled up huge mounds of dirt.*
earth *a huge pile of earth*
ground *a hole in the ground*
▷ VERB
2 to make something dirty: *He soiled his new white shirt.*
dirty *He was afraid the dog's hairs might dirty the seats.*
foul *The cage was fouled with droppings.*
pollute *chemicals that pollute rivers*
smear *The pillowcase was smeared with makeup.*
spatter *Her dress was spattered with mud.*
stain *Some foods can stain the teeth.*
ANTONYM **clean**
See also **dirt, earth, ground, stain**

soiled *See* **dirty**

soldier *See* **fighter**

sole *See* **only, single**

solely *See* **only**

solemn

▷ ADJECTIVE
not cheerful or humorous: *a taciturn man with a solemn expression*
earnest *an earnest woman who rarely smiled*
grave *He left the meeting looking unusually grave.*
serious *She looked at me with big, serious eyes.*
sober *sad, sober faces*
staid *He is boring, old fashioned, and staid.*
See also **grave, grim, heavy, serious**

solicitor *See* **lawyer**

solid

▷ ADJECTIVE
I hard and firm: *a block of ice*
firm *a firm mattress*

hard *The snow was hard and slippery.*
2 not likely to fall down: *a solid structure*
stable *stable foundations*
strong *a strong fence*
sturdy *The camera was mounted on a sturdy tripod.*
substantial *The posts are made of concrete and are fairly substantial.*
See also **firm, hard, rigid, secure, sound, stiff, stocky, sturdy, tough, trusty**

solitary *See* **single**

solitude

▷ NOUN
the state of being alone: *She went to the cottage for a few days of solitude.*
isolation *the isolation he endured while in captivity*
loneliness *I have a fear of loneliness.*
privacy *the privacy of my own room*
seclusion *They lived in seclusion and rarely went out.*

solution *See* **idea, liquid**

solve

▷ VERB
to find the answer to a problem or question: *attempts to solve the mystery*
clear up *During dinner, the confusion was cleared up.*
crack *He finally managed to crack the code.*
decipher *trying to decipher the hieroglyphics*
get to the bottom of *The police wanted to get to the bottom of the case.*
resolve *Scientists hope this will finally resolve the mystery.*
work out *I've worked out where I'm going wrong.*
See also **crack, resolve, work out**

sombre *See* **drab, dull, grave**

some *See* **several**

sometimes

▷ ADVERB
now and then: *People sometimes think I'm older than I am.*
at times *She can be a little opinionated at times.*
every now and then *He checks up on me every now and then.*
every so often *Every so often, he does something silly.*
from time to time *I go back to see my old friends from time to time.*
now and again *Now and again, I enjoy a silly movie.*
now and then *Every now and then, I visit him.*

occasionally *I know that I do put people down occasionally.*
once in a while *It does you good to get things off your chest once in a while.*

somewhat *See* **quite, rather**

soon
▷ ADVERB
in a very short time: *You'll be hearing from us very soon.*
any minute now *Any minute now, she's going to start laughing.*
before long *Your grades should improve before long.*
in a minute *I'll be with you in a minute.*
in the near future *The controversy is unlikely to be resolved in the near future.*
presently *I'll deal with you presently.*
shortly *The trial will begin shortly.*
ANTONYM **later**

sooner *See* **before**

soothe *See* **calm, comfort, pacify**

sophisticated
▷ ADJECTIVE
1 having refined tastes: *a charming, sophisticated companion*
cosmopolitan *His relatives are rich and extremely cosmopolitan.*
cultivated *an elegant and cultivated couple*
cultured *He is immensely cultured and well-read.*
refined *a woman of refined tastes*
urbane *a polished, urbane manner*
2 advanced and complicated: *a sophisticated piece of equipment*
advanced *the most advanced optical telescope in the world*
complex *complex machines*
complicated *a complicated voting system*
elaborate *an elaborate design*
intricate *intricate controls*
refined *a more refined engine*
ANTONYM **simple**
See also **polite**

sophistication *See* **style**

sorcery *See* **magic**

sore
▷ ADJECTIVE
causing pain and discomfort: *a sore throat*
inflamed *Her eyes were red and inflamed.*
painful *a painful bang on the knee*
raw *hands rubbed raw by the rope*
sensitive *the pain of sensitive teeth*
smarting *My eyes were smarting from the smoke.*
tender *My stomach feels very tender.*
See also **painful, tender**

soreness *See* **pain**

sorrow
▷ NOUN
1 deep sadness or regret: *a time of great sorrow*
grief *Their grief soon gave way to anger.*
heartache *suffering the heartache of a breakup*
melancholy *She has an air of melancholy.*
misery *All his money brought him nothing but misery.*
mourning *a day of mourning*
pain *My heart is full of pain.*
regret *She accepted his resignation with regret.*
sadness *It is with a mixture of sadness and joy that I say farewell.*
unhappiness *a lot of unhappiness in my childhood*
woe FORMAL *a tale of woe*
ANTONYM **joy**
2 things that cause deep sadness and regret: *the joys and sorrows of family life*
heartache *all the heartaches of parenthood*
hardship *One of the worst hardships is having so little time with my family.*
misfortune *She seems to enjoy the misfortunes of others.*
trouble *He told me all his troubles.*
woe FORMAL *He did not tell his friends about his woes.*
worry *a life with no worries*
ANTONYM **joy**
See also **distress, evil, grief, misery, regret**

sorry
▷ ADJECTIVE
1 feeling sadness or regret: *I'm terribly sorry to bother you.*
apologetic *"I'm afraid I can't help," she said, with an apologetic smile.*
penitent *He sat silent and penitent in a corner.*
regretful *Now I'm totally regretful that I did it.*
remorseful *He was genuinely remorseful.*
repentant *repentant sinners*
2 feeling sympathy for someone: *I was sorry to hear about your grandfather's death.*
moved *I'm moved by what you say.*
sympathetic *She gave me a sympathetic glance.*
3 in a bad condition: *He was in a pretty sorry state when we found him.*
deplorable *living in deplorable conditions*
miserable *a miserable existence*

S

pathetic *the pathetic sight of oil-covered seabirds*
pitiful *a pitiful creature*
poor *the poor condition of the baseball diamond*
sad *a sad state of affairs*
wretched *the wretched victims of the hurricane*
See also **ashamed, guilty, miserable, pathetic**

sort

▷ *NOUN*
1 one of the different kinds of something: *a dozen trees of various sorts*
brand *his favourite brand of soft drink*
category *The topics were divided into six categories.*
class *a better class of restaurant*
group *Meteorologists classify clouds into several different groups.*
kind *different kinds of roses*
make *a certain make of car*
species *About 400 species of fungi have been recorded.*
style *Several styles of shoes were available.*
type *What type of dog should we get?*
variety *many varieties of birds*
▷ *VERB*
2 to arrange things into different kinds: *He sorted the e-mails into three folders.*
arrange *Arrange the books in neat piles.*
categorize *ways to categorize information*
classify *Rocks can be classified according to origin.*
divide *Divide the pie into four pieces.*
grade *musical pieces graded according to difficulty*
group *The fact sheet is grouped into seven sections.*
separate *His work can be separated into three main categories.*
See also **arrange, category, class, classify, form, grade, group, kind, type, variety**

sort out *See* **resolve**

so-so *See* **tolerable**

sought-after *See* **popular**

soul *See* **essence, individual, person, spirit**

sound

▷ *NOUN*
1 something that can be heard: *the sounds of happy children*
din *make themselves heard over the din of the crowd*
hubbub *the hubbub of excited conversation*
noise *the noise of rush-hour traffic*
racket *the racket of drills and electric saws*
tone *the clear tone of the bell*
ANTONYM **silence**
▷ *VERB*
2 to produce or cause to produce a noise: *A young man sounded the bell.*
blow *The referee was blowing his whistle.*
chime *We heard the doorbell chime.*
clang *The school bell clanged.*
peal *Bells pealed at the stroke of midnight.*
ring *She heard the school bell ringing.*
set off *If you open the fire door, it will set off the alarm.*
toll *Bells tolled throughout the town.*
▷ *ADJECTIVE*
3 healthy, or in good condition: *His mind and body were still sound.*
all right *Does the roof seem all right?*
fine *The doctor said his hearing was perfectly fine.*
fit *Exercise is the first step to a fit body.*
healthy *His once healthy mind was deteriorating.*
in good condition *The old canoe is still in good condition.*
intact *The boat did not appear damaged and its equipment seemed intact.*
robust *He is in robust health for a man of his age.*
4 reliable and sensible: *a sound financial proposition*
down-to-earth *Their ideas seem very down-to-earth.*
good *Give me one good reason why I should tell you.*
reasonable *a perfectly reasonable decision*
reliable *It's difficult to give a reliable estimate.*
sensible *sensible advice*
solid *good solid information*
valid *Both sides made some valid points.*
See also **bay, logical, reasonable, reliable, responsible, sane, sensible, well**

soundless *See* **silent**

sour

▷ *ADJECTIVE*
1 having a sharp taste: *That apple is too sour for me.*
acid *That pineapple has an acid taste.*
bitter *a bitter drink*
pungent *a pungent sauce*
sharp *a clean, sharp flavour*
tart *the tart qualities of citrus fruit*
ANTONYM **sweet**
2 unpleasant in taste because no longer

fresh: *This cream's gone sour.*
curdled *curdled milk*
off *This meat's gone off.*
rancid *rancid butter*
3 bad-tempered and unfriendly: *a sour expression*
disagreeable *a shallow, disagreeable man*
embittered *She became embittered over her loss.*
jaundiced *a jaundiced attitude*
tart *a tart reply*
See also **bitter, rotten, stale**

source
▷ NOUN
the place where something comes from: *the source of his confidence*
beginning *the beginning of all the trouble*
cause *the cause of the problem*
derivation *The derivation of the name is obscure.*
origin *the origin of life*
originator *the originator of the theory*
See also **cause, head, origin**

souvenir
▷ NOUN
something you keep as a reminder: *a souvenir of our vacation*
keepsake *a cherished keepsake*
memento *a memento of the occasion*
relic *the threadbare teddy bear, a relic of childhood*
reminder *a permanent reminder of this historic event*

sovereign See **king, royal, ruler**

sovereignty See **power**

sow See **scatter**

space
▷ NOUN
1 an area that is empty or available: *a car with plenty of interior space*
accommodation *We have accommodation for six people.*
capacity *the capacity of the airplane*
room *no room to manoeuvre*
2 the gap between two things: *the space between the two tables*
blank *I've left a blank here for your signature.*
distance *the distance between the island and the mainland*
gap *a draft coming through gaps in the door frame*
interval *the intervals between periods of bad weather*
3 a period of time: *two incidents in the space of a week*
interval *a long interval of silence*

period *for a limited period only*
span *The batteries have a life span of six hours.*
time *I delivered pizzas for a short time.*
while *Sit down for a while.*
See also **capacity, gap, length, opening, room, stretch**

spacious
▷ ADJECTIVE
having or providing a lot of space: *a spacious lobby*
ample *There is ample parking behind the arena.*
broad *a broad expanse of green lawn*
expansive *an expansive play area*
extensive *the extensive grounds of the ranch*
huge *a huge apartment overlooking the park*
large *a large, detached house*
vast *the vast open spaces of the North*
See also **extensive**

span See **cross, length, space**

spare
▷ ADJECTIVE
1 in addition to what is needed: *Luckily I had a spare pair of glasses.*
extra *Allow yourself some extra time in case of emergencies.*
free *I'll do it as soon as I get some free time.*
superfluous *I got rid of all my superfluous belongings.*
surplus *surplus equipment sold at auction*
▷ VERB
2 to make something available: *Can you spare a loonie?*
afford *It's all I can afford to give you.*
give *It's good of you to give me some of your time.*
let someone have *I can let you have some milk and sugar.*
3 to save someone from an unpleasant experience: *I wanted to spare them that suffering.*
let off INFORMAL *I'll let you off this time.*
pardon *Relatives had begged the authorities to pardon him.*
relieve from *a machine that relieves you of the drudgery of housework*
save from *I was trying to save you from unnecessary worry.*
See also **extra**

sparkle
▷ VERB
to shine with small bright points of light: *Stars sparkled like diamonds.*

S

gleam *sunlight gleaming on the water*
glisten *The grass glistened with frost.*
glitter *A million stars glittered in the black sky.*
shimmer *In the distance, the lake shimmered.*
twinkle *The old man's eyes twinkled.*
See also **flash, shine**

sparkling *See* **brilliant, lively, shining, witty**

sparse *See* **few, meagre, rare, uncommon**

spartan *See* **bare, plain**

spate *See* **burst, flood, rash**

spatter *See* **soil**

speak
▷ *VERB*
to use your voice to say words: *She turned to look at the person who was speaking.*
See also **lecture**

speak out against *See* **oppose**

special
▷ *ADJECTIVE*
1 more important or better than others of its kind: *You are very special to me.*
exceptional *she gave an exceptional speech*
important *This is an important occasion.*
significant *of significant importance*
unique *a unique talent*
ANTONYM **ordinary**
2 relating to one person or group in particular: *the special needs of the chronically ill*
characteristic *a characteristic feature*
distinctive *the distinctive smell of chlorine*
individual *Each family needs individual attention.*
particular *This is a particular issue for northern countries.*
peculiar *This is not a problem peculiar to Canada.*
specific *the specific needs of the elderly*
ANTONYM **general**
See also **different, exceptional, individual, particular, peculiar, personal, private, select**

specialist *See* **expert**

speciality *See* **field**

species *See* **breed, kind, sort, type**

specific *See* **particular, precise, special**

specification *See* **requirement**

specify
▷ *VERB*
to state or describe something precisely: *Specify the size and colour you want.*
be specific about *She was never specific about her date of birth.*
indicate *Please indicate your preference below.*
name *The victims of the fire have been named.*
spell out *He spelled out the reasons why he was leaving.*
state *Please state your name.*
stipulate *His duties were stipulated in the contract.*
See also **state**

specimen *See* **example**

speck *See* **spot**

spectacle *See* **sight, view, wonder**

spectator
▷ *NOUN*
a person who watches something: *Spectators lined the route.*
bystander *an innocent bystander*
eyewitness *Eyewitnesses say the assailant fled on foot.*
observer *a disinterested observer*
onlooker *A small crowd of onlookers was there to greet her.*
witness *There were dozens of witnesses.*
See also **witness**

spectre *See* **ghost, spirit, vision**

speculate *See* **guess, wonder**

speculation *See* **guess**

speech
▷ *NOUN*
a formal talk given to an audience: *He delivered his speech in French.*
address *an address to the Canadian people*
discourse *a lengthy discourse on strategy*
lecture *a series of lectures on art*
talk *a talk on Canadian military history*
See also **lecture, talk**

speechless *See* **dumb, silent**

speechlessness *See* **silence**

speed
▷ *NOUN*
1 the rate at which something moves or happens: *a speed of 120 km/h*
haste *the old saying "more haste, less speed"*
hurry *the hurry and excitement of the city*
momentum *This campaign is gaining momentum.*
pace *He walked at a leisurely pace.*

rapidity *My moods change with alarming rapidity.*
swiftness *Time is passing with incredible swiftness.*
velocity *the velocity of light*
▷ VERB
2 to move quickly: *The pair sped off when the police arrived.*
career *His car careered into a river.*
flash *My life flashed past me.*
gallop *galloping along the path*
race *He raced across town.*
rush *He rushed off, closely followed by his assistant.*
tear *She tore off down the road.*
See also **fly, race, rate, tear**

speed up See **accelerate, hurry**

speedily See **quickly**

speedy See **fast, quick, swift**

spell See **influence, period, stretch, term, time**

spell out See **specify**

sphere See **ball**

spherical See **round**

spicy See **hot**

spill See **leak, upset**

spin
▷ VERB
to turn quickly around a central point: *as the earth spins on its axis*
pirouette *She pirouetted in front of the mirror.*
revolve *The satellite revolves around the planet.*
rotate *rotating propellers*
turn *a turning wheel*
whirl *The fallen leaves whirled around.*
See also **drive, turn**

spineless See **weak**

spiral See **coil**

spirit
▷ NOUN
I the part of you that is not physical: *They believed his spirit had left his body.*
life force *the life force of all animate things*
soul *praying for the soul of her dead father*
2 a ghost or supernatural being: *a protection against evil spirits*
apparition *an apparition of her dead friend*
ghost *the premise that ghosts exist*
phantom *People claim to have seen the phantom.*

spectre *a spectre from the other world*
sprite *a water sprite*
3 liveliness and energy: *They played with spirit.*
animation *They both spoke with animation.*
energy *At 80, her energy is amazing.*
enthusiasm *They seem to be lacking in enthusiasm.*
fire *His performance was full of fire.*
force *She expressed her feelings with force.*
vigour *We resumed the tennis game with renewed vigour.*
zest *He threw himself into the project with typical zest.*
See also **energy, essence, ghost, sneak**

spirited See **energetic, vital**

spirits See **alcohol, humour, mood**

spiritual See **religious**

in spite of
▷ PREPOSITION
even though something is the case: *In spite of all the rain, we drove to the campgrounds.*
although *Although it was cloudy, we went to the beach.*
despite *They manage to enjoy life despite adversity.*
even though *They did it even though I warned them not to.*
notwithstanding *Notwithstanding his age, he has an important job.*
regardless of *He led from the front, regardless of the danger.*
though *I enjoy painting, though I am not very good at it.*

spite
▷ NOUN
a desire to hurt someone: *He just did it out of spite.*
ill will *She didn't bear anyone any ill will.*
malevolence *a streak of malevolence*
malice *There was no malice in her voice.*
spitefulness *petty spitefulness*
venom *His wit had a touch of venom in it.*

spiteful
▷ ADJECTIVE
saying or doing unkind things to hurt people: *a stream of spiteful telephone calls*
catty INFORMAL *catty remarks*
cruel *They gave him a cruel nickname.*
malevolent *a malevolent stare*
malicious *spreading malicious gossip*
nasty *What nasty little snobs you all are.*
snide *He made a snide comment about my new hairstyle.*

S

venomous *a venomous attack*
vindictive *How can you be so vindictive?*
See also **malicious, unkind**

spitefulness *See* **spite**

spitting image *See* **look-alike**

splash *See* **dash, drip**

splendid
▷ ADJECTIVE
1 very good indeed: *I've had a splendid time.*
excellent *The quality of the DVD is excellent.*
fantastic INFORMAL *a fantastic combination of colours*
fine *a fine young man*
glorious *a glorious career*
great INFORMAL *a great bunch of guys*
marvellous *a marvellous thing to do*
wonderful *a wonderful movie*
2 beautiful and impressive: *a splendid old mansion*
gorgeous *a gorgeous designer outfit*
grand *a grand hotel*
imposing *imposing wrought-iron gates*
impressive *an impressive spectacle*
magnificent *magnificent views across the ravine*
superb *The hotel has a superb, isolated location.*
See also **fine, first-rate, grand, marvellous, superb**

splendidly *See* **well**

splendour *See* **glory**

split
▷ VERB
1 to divide into two or more parts: *The ship split in two.*
diverge *Their paths began to diverge.*
fork *Ahead of us, the road forked.*
part *For a moment the clouds parted.*
separate *Fluff the rice with a fork to separate the grains.*
2 to have a crack or tear: *His trousers split.*
burst *A water pipe has burst.*
come apart *My jacket's coming apart at the seams.*
crack *The glass pitcher cracked.*
rip *I felt the paper rip as we pulled in opposite directions.*
▷ NOUN
3 a crack or tear in something: *There's a split in my mattress.*
crack *The larvae burrow into cracks in the tree trunk.*

fissure *Water trickled out of fissures in the limestone.*
rip *the rip in her new dress*
tear *the ragged edges of a tear*
4 a division between two things: *the split between the two sides of the family*
breach *a serious breach in relations between the two countries*
breakup *the breakup of the Soviet Union in 1991*
divergence *a divergence between France and its allies*
division *the conventional division between "art" and "life"*
rift *There is a rift between us and the rest of the family.*
See also **breach, burst, divide, division, fissure, hole, share, tear**

split up *See* **divide, separate**

spoil
▷ VERB
1 to damage or destroy something: *Don't let it spoil your vacation.*
damage *This could damage our chances of winning.*
destroy *His criticism has destroyed my confidence.*
harm *This product harms the environment.*
impair *The flavour is impaired by overcooking.*
mar *The celebrations were marred by violence.*
mess up *He's messed up his life.*
ruin *My friend was ruining her health through worry.*
wreck *Injuries wrecked his career.*
2 to give someone everything he or she wants: *Grandparents often spoil their grandchildren.*
indulge *a heavily indulged youngest child*
pamper *pampered pets*
See also **rot, ruin**

spoils *See* **loot**

spoken *See* **oral**

spokesman *See* **representative**

spokeswoman *See* **representative**

sponge *See* **clean, scrounge**

sponsor *See* **supporter**

spoof *See* **parody**

spooky
▷ ADJECTIVE
eerie and frightening: *The whole place had a slightly spooky atmosphere.*
creepy *a place that is really creepy at night*
eerie *The wind made eerie noises in the trees.*

frightening *Whenever I fall asleep, I see these frightening faces.*

ghostly *The moon shed a ghostly light on the fields.*

haunted *a haunted house*

supernatural *The old building was bathed in a supernatural light.*

scary *a scary scene in the horror movie*

uncanny *The strange, uncanny feeling was creeping all over me.*

See also **creepy, scary**

sporadic *See* **occasional, rare**

sport *See* **wear**

spot
▷ NOUN

1 a small round mark on something: *a navy blue dress with white spots*

blemish *A small blemish spoiled the surface of the table.*

blot *an ink blot*

blotch *a small blotch on the skin*

mark *a little blue mark on your white shirt*

smudge *a fingerprint smudge on the paper*

speck *a speck of dirt*

2 a location or place: *an out-of-the-way spot*

location *The hotel is in a superb location.*

place *our favourite after-school place*

point *the point where the river had overflowed*

position *She moved the parcel to a position where it would not be seen.*

scene *He left a note at the scene of the crime.*

site *plans to construct a temple on the site*
▷ VERB

3 to see or notice something: *Her drama teacher spotted her ability.*

catch sight of *I caught sight of my cousin at the concert.*

detect *The test should enable doctors to detect the disease early.*

discern *I did not discern any change.*

observe *Can you observe any difference?*

see *I can see a resemblance between you.*

sight *A fleet of Portuguese ships was sighted off the coast of Labrador.*

See also **discern, location, notice, observe, place, random, recognize, scene, see, sight, stain**

INFORMALLY SPEAKING

hit the spot: be exactly what is required
in a spot: in a difficult situation

spotless *See* **clean, innocent, pure**

spotlight *See* **feature**

spouse *See* **partner**

spout *See* **pour**

sprain *See* **twist**

sprawl *See* **lie, spread**

spray *See* **bunch, wet**

spread
▷ VERB

1 to open out or extend over an area: *He spread his coat over the bed.*

extend *Nunavut extends over almost one-fifth of Canada.*

fan out *The dancer's skirt fanned out in a circle.*

open *She opened her arms and gave me a big hug.*

sprawl *The recreation area sprawls over 200 hectares.*

unfold *When the bird lifts off, its wings unfold to a 150-cm span.*

unfurl *We began to unfurl the sails.*

unroll *I unrolled my sleeping bag.*

2 to put a thin layer on a surface: *Spread the bread with the cream cheese.*

apply *Apply the preparation evenly over the wood's surface.*

coat *Coat the fish with crumbs.*

cover *I covered the table with a cloth.*

overlay *The floor was overlaid with rugs.*

slather *She slathered herself in lotion.*

smear *Smear a little oil over the inside of the bowl.*

smother *He likes to smother his fries with ketchup.*

3 to reach or affect more people gradually: *The sense of fear is spreading in the neighbourhood.*

circulate *Rumours were circulating that the project was to be abandoned.*

grow *Opposition grew, and the government agreed to negotiate.*

expand *The industry is looking for opportunities to expand into other countries.*

increase *The population continues to increase.*

proliferate *Internet services are proliferating across the world.*

travel *News of his work travelled all the way to Asia.*
▷ NOUN

4 the extent or growth of something: *the gradual spread of information*

diffusion *the development and diffusion of ideas*

expansion *the rapid expansion of new technologies*

extent *the growing extent of the problem*

S

growth the growth of organic farming
increase an increase of violence along the border
progression This drug slows the progression of HIV.
proliferation the proliferation of pesticide use
upsurge the upsurge of interest in these books
See also **circulate, communicate, distribute, lay, multiply, stretch**

spreading See **infectious**

sprightly See **active, agile, lively, vital**

spring See **develop, jump, leap**

sprinkle See **scatter**

sprinkling See **dash**

sprint See **dash, run**

sprite See **spirit**

sprout See **grow**

spruce See **neat, smart**

spruce up See **tidy**

spur See **drive, prompt**

spurn See **boycott, refuse, reject**

spurt See **gush**

squabble
▷ VERB
1 to quarrel about something trivial: His parents squabble all the time.
argue They continued arguing for the entire drive.
bicker The children bickered constantly.
feud feuding neighbours
fight Mostly, they fight about paying bills.
quarrel At one point, we quarrelled over something silly.
wrangle The two sides spend their time wrangling over procedural problems.
▷ NOUN
2 a quarrel: There have been minor squabbles about phone bills.
altercation an altercation with the referee
argument a heated argument
disagreement My instructor and I had a brief disagreement.
dispute a dispute over tariffs between Canada and the United States
fight He had a big fight with his older brother that night.
quarrel I had a terrible quarrel with my sister.
row There was a noisy row among the neighbours.

tiff She was walking home after a tiff with her boyfriend.
See also **argue, argument, clash, disagreement, fight, quarrel, row**

squad See **party, team**

squalid See **dirty**

squander See **waste**

squandering See **waste**

square See **agree**

squash See **crush**

squashy See **soft**

squat See **crouch, low**

squeal See **scream**

squeeze See **clasp, cram, ease, hug, press, stuff**

squirm See **fidget**

stab See **attempt, effort, go, poke**

stabilize See **balance, steady**

stable See **constant, secure, solid, steady**

stack See **heap, load, pile**

staff
▷ NOUN
the people who work for an organization: She made little effort to socialize with other staff members.
employees a temporary employee
human resources She's in charge of human resources at the company.
personnel An announcement was made to all personnel.
team The team worked well under his direction.
workers weekend and night-shift workers
workforce a resentful workforce

stage
▷ NOUN
1 a part of a process: the closing stages of the race
lap The first lap was clocked at under a minute.
period We went through a period of unprecedented change.
phase a passing phase
point a critical point in the campaign
step the next step in the process
▷ VERB
2 to organize something: Workers have staged a number of one-day strikes.
arrange We're arranging a surprise party for her.

engineer *She was the one who engineered the merger.*

mount *a security operation mounted by the army*

orchestrate *a carefully orchestrated campaign*

organize *a meeting organized by the UN*
See also **level, perform, round**

stagger *See* **amaze, shock, surprise**

staggering *See* **amazing**

stagnant *See* **stale**

staid *See* **serious, solemn, stuffy**

stain
▷ NOUN
1 a mark on something: *grass stains*
blot *an ink blot*
mark *I can't get this mark to come off.*
spot *The detergent left spots on the glasses.*
▷ VERB
2 to make a mark on something: *Some foods can stain the teeth.*
dirty *Her hands were dirtied from gardening.*
mark *the places where the boots had marked the wood*
soil *a soiled white shirt*
spot *Her coat was spotted with mud.*
See also **colour, mark, soil**

stake *See* **gamble**

stale
▷ ADJECTIVE
no longer fresh: *a slice of stale bread*
flat *flat beer*
old *mouldy old cheese*
sour *sour milk*
stagnant *stagnant water*
ANTONYM **fresh**
See also **corny, hackneyed, stuffy**

stalk *See* **follow**

stall *See* **jam**

stamina *See* **strength**

stamp out *See* **crush, eliminate, suppress**

stampede *See* **charge, dash, rush**

stance *See* **attitude**

stand *See* **base, endure, put up with, tolerate**

stand by *See* **wait**

stand for *See* **allow, put up with, represent**

stand up for *See* **side with**

stand up to *See* **brave**

standard
▷ NOUN
1 a particular level of quality or achievement: *There will be new standards of hospital cleanliness.*
calibre *the high calibre of these researchers*
criterion *What is the most important criterion in selecting a new coach?*
guideline *new guidelines for student council elections*
level *The exercises are marked according to their level of difficulty.*
norm *the commonly accepted norms of democracy*
quality *to improve one's quality of life*
requirement *These products meet all legal requirements.*
▷ ADJECTIVE
2 usual, normal, and correct: *It was standard practice for them to consult the parents.*
accepted *It is accepted wisdom that the state of your body affects the state of your mind.*
correct *the correct way to produce a crop of tomato plants*
customary *It is customary to offer a drink or a snack to guests.*
normal *Some stores were closed, but that's quite normal for this time of day.*
orthodox *orthodox police methods*
regular *This product looks and tastes like regular cheese.*
usual *It is usual to tip waiters.*
See also **average, common, conventional, ideal, level, normal, ordinary, routine, stock, typical, usual**

standards
▷ PLURAL NOUN
moral principles of behaviour: *My father has always had high moral standards.*
ethics *He questioned the ethics of the awards committee.*
ideals *The party has drifted too far from its environmental ideals.*
morals *He said he wouldn't compromise his morals.*
principles *He refused to do anything that went against his principles.*
rules *the rules of the road*
scruple *a man with no moral scruples*
values *the values of liberty and equality*

stand-in *See* **replacement**

standing *See* **rank, reputation, status**

standstill *See* **halt**

S

star

▷ *NOUN*

a famous person: *a movie star*
celebrity *Many celebrities attended the premiere.*
idol *Brazil's greatest soccer idol*
luminary *The event attracted an assortment of pop luminaries.*
See also **celebrity, feature, personality, success**

stare

▷ *VERB*

to look at something for a long time: *He stared at the floor, lost in meditation.*
gaze *gazing at himself in the mirror*
look *He looked at her with fascination.*
ogle *They were ogling the horses at the agricultural show.*

stark *See* plain

stark naked *See* naked

start

▷ *VERB*

1 to begin to take place: *School starts again next week.*
arise *A conflict is likely to arise.*
begin *A typical day begins at 8 a.m.*
come into being *The festival came into being in 1986.*
come into existence *a rock group that came into existence five years ago*
commence *The academic year commences in September.*
get under way *The game was just getting under way when the rain started.*
originate *The disease originated in Africa.*
ANTONYM **finish**

2 to begin to do something: *The child started to cry.*
begin *He began to groan with pain.*
commence *The Olympic Games commence on February 10.*
embark upon *He's embarking on a new career as a writer.*
proceed *He proceeded to tell us a long story.*
set about *How do you set about applying for a job?*
ANTONYM **stop**

3 to cause something to begin: *a good time to start a business*
begin *The United States is prepared to begin talks immediately.*
create *Criticism will only create feelings of failure.*
establish *The school was established in 1950.*

found *The National Hockey League was founded in 1917.*
get going *I've worked hard to get this business going.*
inaugurate *the company that inaugurated the first scheduled international flight*
initiate *They wanted to initiate a discussion.*
instigate *The violence was instigated by a few people.*
institute *We have instituted a number of measures.*
introduce *The government has introduced tax benefits.*
launch *The police have launched an investigation into the incident.*
open *We opened the meeting with an announcement.*
pioneer *the company that pioneered digital video recording*
set in motion *Several changes have already been set in motion.*
set up *A committee was set up to arbitrate in the dispute.*
trigger *Nuts can trigger an allergic reaction in some people.*
ANTONYM **stop**

▷ *NOUN*

4 the beginning of something: *His career had an auspicious start.*
beginning *the beginning of all the trouble*
birth *the birth of modern art*
commencement *the commencement of the school year*
dawn *the dawn of a new age*
foundation *the foundation of the Assembly of First Nations*
inauguration *the inauguration of Canada's national flag in 1965*
inception FORMAL *Since its inception, the company has produced a variety of software.*
initiation *There was a year between initiation and completion of the building project.*
onset *the onset of puberty*
opening *the opening of the trial*
outset *There were lots of problems from the outset.*
ANTONYM **finish**
See also **begin, beginning, flinch, head, opening, proceed, scare, surprise**

starter *See* beginner

startle *See* alarm, frighten, scare

startled *See* frightened

startling *See* amazing

starving *See* hungry

stash *See* hide, stockpile, store

state

▷ NOUN

1 the condition or circumstances of something: *the pathetic state of the roads*
circumstances *He's in desperate circumstances.*
condition *The patient remains in critical condition.*
plight *the plight of famine-stricken countries*
position *We are in a privileged position.*
predicament *the once great institution's current predicament*
shape *Her finances were in terrible shape.*
situation *a precarious situation*

2 a country: *the state of Denmark*
country *The country of Canada has ten provinces and three territories.*
kingdom *The kingdom's power declined.*
land *in that distant land*
nation *a leading nation in world politics*
republic *In 1918, Austria became a republic.*

▷ VERB

3 to say something, especially in a formal way: *Please state your occupation.*
affirm *a speech in which she affirmed her policies*
articulate *an attempt to articulate his feelings*
assert *He asserted his innocence.*
declare *She declared that she would fight on.*
express *He expressed regret that he had caused any offence.*
say *The police said he had no connection with the crime.*
specify *Please specify your preferences below.*
See also **condition, country, declare, observe, remark, report, specify, territory**

state of affairs See **situation**

state of mind See **mood**

statement

▷ NOUN

a short written or spoken piece giving information: *He was depressed when he made that statement.*
account *He gave a detailed account of what happened that night.*
announcement *She made her announcement after talks with the premier.*
bulletin *A bulletin was released announcing the decision.*
declaration *a public declaration of support*
explanation *They have given no public explanation for his dismissal.*
proclamation *The proclamation of independence was broadcast over the radio.*
report *A press report said that at least six*

people had died in the fire.
testimony *Her testimony was an important part of the prosecution's case.*
See also **announcement, bill, comment, declaration, remark, report, word**

station See **base, rank**

stationary See **still**

statistic See **figure**

stature See **reputation**

status

▷ NOUN

a person's social or professional position: *the status of children in society*
position *a privileged position*
prestige *to diminish the prestige of the British monarchy*
rank *He was stripped of his rank.*
standing *This has done nothing to improve her standing.*
See also **level, rank**

statute See **law**

staunch See **faithful, firm, loyal, reliable, steadfast, trusty**

stay

▷ VERB

to remain somewhere: *She stayed in bed till noon.*
hang around INFORMAL *I can't hang around here all day.*
linger *The humid weather will linger for a few more days.*
loiter *Don't loiter at the ATM.*
remain *You'll have to remain in hospital for the time being.*
tarry FORMAL *Don't tarry on the way.*
wait *I'll wait here till you come back.*
See also **live, remain, visit, wait**

stay afloat See **float**

stay behind See **remain**

steadfast

▷ ADJECTIVE

refusing to change or give up: *She remained steadfast in her belief.*
constant *They are constant companions.*
faithful *this party's most faithful voters*
firm *a firm belief in his team's chances*
immovable *On one issue, however, she was immovable.*
resolute *a decisive and resolute international leader*
staunch *a staunch supporter of these proposals*

S

steady *He was firm and steady, and I knew we could depend on him.*
unshakable *his unshakable belief in the project*

steady

▷ *ADJECTIVE*
1 continuing without interruptions: *a steady rise in profits*
consistent *consistent support*
constant *under constant pressure*
continuous *The patient is making continuous progress.*
even *an even level of sound*
non-stop *non-stop background music*
regular *a regular beat*
uninterrupted *28 years of uninterrupted growth*
2 not shaky or wobbling: *She held out a steady hand.*
firm *Make sure the tree is securely mounted on a firm base.*
secure *Check that the joints are secure and the wood is sound.*
stable *stable foundations*
▷ *VERB*
3 to prevent something from shaking or wobbling: *Two men were steadying a ladder.*
brace *The roof was braced with oak beams.*
secure *The frames are secured by metal bars.*
stabilize *Blocks should not be used to stabilize the foundation.*
support *Thick wooden posts support the ceiling.*
See also **balance, constant, even, gradual, reasonable, regular, steadfast**

steal

▷ *VERB*
1 to take something without permission: *He was accused of stealing a bicycle.*
appropriate *Several other companies have appropriated the idea.*
pilfer *The confidential files had been pilfered.*
swipe SLANG *Did you just swipe that book?*
take *The burglars took anything they could carry.*
2 to move somewhere quietly and secretly: *They can steal out and join us later.*
creep *We crept away under cover of darkness.*
slip *I wanted to duck down and slip past, but they saw me.*
sneak *Sometimes he would sneak out to see me.*

tiptoe *She slipped out of bed and tiptoed to the window.*
See also **slip, sneak**

steal from *See* **rob**

stealing *See* **theft**

steam *See* **cook**

steamy *See* **humid**

steep

▷ *ADJECTIVE*
1 rising sharply and abruptly: *a steep hill*
sheer *a sheer drop*
vertical *The slope was almost vertical.*
ANTONYM **gradual**
2 larger than is reasonable: *steep prices*
excessive *excessive charges*
exorbitant *an exorbitant rate of interest*
high *high loan rates*
unreasonable *unreasonable interest charges*
▷ *VERB*
3 to soak something in a liquid: *tea leaves steeped in hot water*
immerse *Immerse the vegetables in cold water and drain them.*
marinate *Marinate the chicken for at least four hours.*
soak *Soak the beans overnight.*
See also **sheer, soak**

steer *See* **drive, lead, manoeuvre**

steer clear of *See* **avoid**

stem *See* **result**

stench *See* **smell, stink**

stencil *See* **pattern**

step *See* **advance, measure, stage**

step down *See* **resign**

stereotyped *See* **corny, stock**

sterile

▷ *ADJECTIVE*
1 free from germs: *Protect the cut with a sterile dressing.*
antiseptic *an antiseptic hospital room*
germ-free *Keep your working surfaces germ-free.*
sterilized *a sterilized bottle for the baby's formula*
2 unable to produce: *He found out he was sterile.*
barren *a barren mare*
unproductive *thousands of hectares of unproductive land*
ANTONYM **fertile**
See also **barren**

sterilized *See* **clean, pure, sterile**

stern *See* **back, grim, harsh, serious, severe, strict**

stew *See* **cook**

stick

▷ NOUN

1 a long, thin piece of wood: *crowds armed with sticks and stones*
bat *a baseball bat*
cane *He wore a grey suit and leaned heavily on his cane.*
mace *a statue of a king holding a golden mace*
nightstick *the police officer's nightstick*
pole *a wooden ski pole*
rod *Hang your shirt on the rod in the closet.*
twig *the sound of a twig breaking underfoot*
wand *You can't wave a magic wand and make everything okay.*

▷ VERB

2 to thrust something somewhere: *They stuck a needle in my arm.*
dig *She dug her spoon into the pudding.*
insert *He inserted the key into the lock.*
jab *A needle was jabbed into my arm.*
poke *He poked his finger into the hole.*
push *I pushed my finger against the elevator button.*
put *She put the letter under my door.*
ram *He rammed the jacket under the seat.*
shove *We shoved a copy of the newsletter beneath their door.*
stuff *I stuffed my hands in my pockets.*
thrust *I thrust my arms in the air.*
3 to attach or become attached: *Stick down the tiles, following the instructions.*
adhere *The paper adhered to the wall.*
attach *The price tag was still attached to the present.*
bond *strips of wood bonded together*
cling *His sodden trousers were clinging to his legs.*
fix *Fix the photo to the card using double-sided tape.*
fuse *The flakes fuse together and produce ice crystals.*
glue *Glue the fabric in place.*
paste *The children were busy pasting stars on to a chart.*
4 to jam or become jammed: *The paper is stuck in the copier.*
catch *His ring caught on the sweater.*
jam *Every few moments the paper jammed in the printer.*
lodge *The car has a bullet lodged in the passenger door.*
snag *Their fishing nets kept snagging on the rocks.*
See also **club, fix, glue, jam, set**

INFORMALLY SPEAKING

stick around: wait nearby
stick in your throat: be hard for you to accept
stick it out: put up with unpleasant circumstances
stick it to someone: treat someone harshly
stick up for: support or defend someone

stick out *See* **bulge, extend**

stick up for *See* **champion, defend**

sticker *See* **label**

sticky

▷ ADJECTIVE

covered with a substance that sticks to other things: *a sticky smear of peanut butter.*
adhesive *adhesive tape*
tacky *covered with a tacky resin*
See also **humid**

stiff

▷ ADJECTIVE

1 firm and not easily bent: *stiff metal wires*
firm *a firm mattress*
hard *the hard wooden floor*
rigid *a rigid plastic container*
solid *a block of ice*
taut *They pulled the rope until it was taut.*
ANTONYM **limp**
2 not friendly or relaxed: *the rather stiff and formal surroundings of the official residence*
cold *My cousin was very cold with me.*
forced *a forced smile*
formal *His voice was grave and formal.*
stilted *Our conversation was stilted and polite.*
unnatural *a strained and unnatural atmosphere*
wooden *a wooden acting performance*
3 difficult or severe: *a stiff penalty*
arduous *an arduous undertaking*
difficult *a difficult job*
exacting *exacting standards*
formidable *a formidable task*
hard *a hard day's work*
rigorous *rigorous football training*
tough *a tough challenge*
See also **firm, formal, hard, rigid**

stiffen *See* **harden, strengthen**

stifle *See* **contain, silence, suppress**

stifling *See* **stuffy**

S

still

▷ ADJECTIVE

not moving: *The air was still.*
calm *the calm waters of the harbour*
inert *He covered the inert body with a blanket.*
motionless *He stood there, motionless.*
stationary *The train was stationary for 90 minutes.*
tranquil *a tranquil lake*
See also **calm, peaceful, silence, silent**

stillness See **calm, peace, quiet, silence**

stilted See **stiff**

stimulant See **drug**

stimulate See **interest, refresh**

stimulating See **exciting, interesting**

stimulus See **incentive**

stink

▷ VERB

1 to smell very bad: *Something in this kitchen stinks.*
reek *The whole house reeks of smoke.*
▷ NOUN

2 a very bad smell: *the stink of old fish*
stench *a foul stench*
See also **smell**

stinking See **smelly**

stint See **stretch**

stipulate See **specify**

stipulation See **condition, restriction**

stipulations See **terms**

stir See **fuss, touch, wake**

stir up See **excite**

stirring See **impressive, moving**

stock

▷ NOUN

1 shares bought in an investment company: *the buying of stocks*
bonds *the recent sharp decline in bond prices*
investments *Earn a rate of return of four percent on your investments.*
shares *He was eager to buy shares in the company.*
2 a supply of something: *The shoe store needs to add more stock.*
goods *Are all your goods on display?*
merchandise FORMAL *25 percent off selected merchandise*
reserve *65 percent of the world's oil reserves*

reservoir *the body's short-term reservoir of energy*
stockpile *treaties to cut stockpiles of chemical weapons*
store *my secret store of candy*
supply *What happens when food supplies run low?*
3 an animal's or person's ancestors: *He claims to be of Loyalist stock.*
ancestry *a family who can trace their ancestry back to the sixteenth century*
descent *All the contributors were of African descent.*
extraction *Her father was of Italian extraction.*
lineage *It's expensive to trace one's lineage.*
origin *people of Asian origin*
▷ VERB

4 to keep a supply of goods to sell: *The store stocks a wide range of paint.*
deal in *They deal in kitchen equipment.*
sell *It sells everything from CDs to souvenirs.*
supply *We supply office furniture for large companies.*
trade in *We have been trading in antique furniture for 25 years.*
▷ ADJECTIVE

5 commonly used: *National security is the stock excuse for government secrecy.*
hackneyed *It may be a hackneyed expression, but it's true.*
overused *an overused phrase*
routine *We've tried all the routine methods of persuasion.*
standard *the standard ending for a formal letter*
stereotyped *stereotyped ideas about people from small towns*
typical *the typical questions journalists ask celebrities*
usual *He came out with all the usual excuses.*
See also **bank, fill, origin, reserve, sell, stockpile, store, supply, typical**

stockpile

▷ VERB

1 to store large quantities of something: *People are stockpiling food for the winter.*
accumulate *Some people get rich by accumulating wealth very gradually.*
amass *It is best not to ask how he amassed his fortune.*
collect *Two young girls were collecting firewood.*
gather *We gathered enough wood to last the night.*
hoard *They've begun to hoard food and gasoline.*
save *Scraps of material were saved for quilts.*

stash *He had stashed money away in a secret account.*
store up *Investors were storing up cash in anticipation of disaster.*
▷ NOUN
2 a large store of something: *stockpiles of fuel*
arsenal *a formidable arsenal of guns*
cache *a cache of weapons and explosives*
hoard *a hoard of silver and jewels worth $40 million*
reserve *The country's reserves of food are running low.*
stash INFORMAL *a stash of pills*
stock *Stocks of canned goods were running low.*
store *his secret store of chocolates*
See also **gather, hoard, reserve, stock, store, supply**

stocky
▷ ADJECTIVE
short, but solid-looking: *a stocky, middle-aged man*
solid *a solid build*
sturdy *a short, sturdy woman*

stomach
▷ NOUN
the front part of the body below the waist: *Breathe in and flatten your stomach.*
belly *The puppy rested on its belly.*
paunch *That's quite a paunch you have.*
tummy INFORMAL *I'd like a flatter tummy.*
See also **bear, put up with**

stony See cold

stoop See bend

stop
▷ VERB
1 to cease doing something: *I stopped writing when the phone rang.*
cease *A small number of firms have ceased trading.*
cut out INFORMAL *Will you cut out that racket?*
desist *They have not desisted from commercial whaling.*
discontinue *Do not discontinue the treatment without seeing your doctor.*
end *public pressure to end the embargo*
quit *He's trying to quit smoking.*
ANTONYM **start**
2 to come to an end: *They waited for the blizzard to stop.*
cease *At one o'clock the rain ceased.*
come to an end *An hour later, the meeting came to an end.*
conclude *The evening concluded with dinner and speeches.*

end *The talks ended in disagreement.*
finish *The teaching day finishes at about 4 p.m.*
halt *Police halted the traffic.*
ANTONYM **start**
3 to prevent something: *measures to stop smuggling*
arrest *trying to arrest the bleeding*
check *a policy to check fast growth in large cities*
prevent *the most practical way of preventing crime*
See also **block, cease, check, end, halt, prevent, quit, suppress, visit**

stop working See fail

stoppage See blockage, halt, pause

stopper See plug, top

store
▷ NOUN
1 a supply kept for future use: *I have a store of food and water here.*
cache *The squirrel had a cache of nuts buried in our garden.*
fund *an extraordinary fund of energy*
hoard *a hoard of supplies*
reserve *the world's oil reserves*
reservoir *the body's short-term reservoir of energy*
stock *There's no paper. We're out of stock.*
stockpile *stockpiles of nuclear warheads*
supply *food supplies*
2 a place where things are sold: *I had to race around the stores in the mall.*
boutique *He owns a jewellery boutique.*
market *He sells fruit at the market.*
shop *a small beauty shop*
supermarket *Most of us do our food shopping at the supermarket.*
3 a place where things are kept: *a grain store*
depot *a food bank depot*
storeroom *a storeroom filled with furniture*
warehouse *a carpet warehouse*
▷ VERB
4 to keep something for future use: *The information is stored in the computer.*
hoard *They've begun to hoard food and gas.*
keep *Keep the book for as long as you need it.*
reserve *Grate the lemon zest and reserve it for later.*
save *He saved his allowance to buy me the present.*
stash *He had stashed money away in a secret account.*

S

stockpile *People are stockpiling wood for the coming winter.*
See also **bank, collection, fund, hoard, keep, reserve, stock, stockpile, supply, wealth**

store up *See* **stockpile**

WORDS FOR ... STORM	
blizzard	squall
hailstorm	tempest
snowstorm	thunderstorm

stormy *See* **wild**

story
▷ *NOUN*
a tale told or written to entertain people: *a science-fiction story*
account *a true account*
anecdote *colourful anecdotes about her experiences in the theatre*
legend *an old Inuit legend*
narrative *a fast-moving narrative*
tale *a fairy tale*
yarn *The story about giants is quite a yarn.*
See also **article, feature, plot**

CONFUSABLES
story means **narrative**
storey means **floor of a building**

storyline *See* **plot**

stout *See* **overweight, plump, sturdy**

straight
▷ *ADJECTIVE*
1 upright or level: *Keep your arms straight.*
erect *The upper back and neck are held in an erect position.*
even *an even line*
horizontal *a horizontal rule*
level *a completely level base*
perpendicular *The pole is perpendicular to the ground.*
upright *He sat upright in his chair.*
vertical *Keep the spine vertical.*
ANTONYM **crooked**
2 honest, frank, and direct: *They wouldn't give me a straight answer.*
blunt *She is blunt about her personal life.*
candid *I haven't been completely candid with you.*
forthright *a forthright reply*
frank *a frank discussion*
honest *Please be honest with me.*
outright *This was outright rejection.*
plain *plain talking*

point-blank *a point-blank refusal*
See also **direct, neat, straightforward**

straightaway *See* **immediately, now**

straighten *See* **stretch, tidy**

straighten out *See* **settle**

straightforward
▷ *ADJECTIVE*
1 easy and involving no problems: *The question seemed straightforward enough.*
basic *The movie's plot is pretty basic.*
easy *The shower is easy to install.*
elementary *elementary computer skills*
routine *a fairly routine procedure*
simple *simple advice on filling out your tax form*
uncomplicated *an uncomplicated solution to the problem*
ANTONYM **complicated**
2 honest, open, and frank: *I liked her straightforward, intelligent manner.*
candid *I haven't been completely candid with you.*
direct *He avoided giving a direct answer.*
forthright *He was known for his forthright manner.*
frank *They had a frank discussion about the issue.*
honest *I was totally honest about what I was doing.*
open *He had always been open with me.*
plain *I believe in plain talking.*
straight *He never gives a straight answer to a straight question.*
upfront *He was very upfront about his less-than-perfect job history.*
ANTONYM **devious**
See also **blunt, candid, direct, easy, frank, simple**

strain
▷ *NOUN*
1 worry and nervous tension: *the stresses and strains of a busy career*
anxiety *Her voice was full of anxiety.*
pressure *the pressure of work*
stress *the stress of finals*
tension *Laughing relieves tension and stress.*
▷ *VERB*
2 to make something do more than it is able to do: *You'll strain your eyes reading in this light.*
overwork *Too much food will overwork your digestive system.*
tax *He is beginning to tax my patience.*
See also **breed, burden, difficulty, stress, struggle, tax, variety**

strained *See* **tense**

strains *See* **tune**

straitlaced *See* **prim, stuffy**

straits *See* **distress**

strange

▷ ADJECTIVE

1 unusual or unexpected: *A strange thing happened.*
abnormal *an abnormal fear of spiders*
bizarre *a bizarre scene*
curious *a curious mixture of old and modern*
extraordinary *an extraordinary occurrence*
funny *a funny feeling*
odd *There was something odd about her.*
peculiar *It tasted very peculiar.*
uncommon *A 12-year lifespan is not uncommon for a dog.*
weird *He's a really weird guy.*
2 new or unfamiliar: *alone in a strange country*
alien *transplanted into an alien culture*
exotic *filmed in an exotic location*
foreign *This was a foreign country to him, so unlike his own.*
new *I'm always open to new experiences.*
novel *a novel idea*
unfamiliar *visiting an unfamiliar city*
See also **bizarre, curious, eccentric, extraordinary, funny, odd, peculiar, unfamiliar, weird**

strapping *See* **powerful**

strategy *See* **plan, procedure**

stratum *See* **layer**

stray *See* **ramble**

streak *See* **line, mark**

stream *See* **flood, flow, gush, pour**

streamline *See* **simplify**

street *See* **road**

strength

▷ NOUN

1 physical energy and power: *an astonishing display of physical strength*
brawn *He has plenty of brains as well as brawn.*
might *the full might of the army*
muscle *demonstrating both muscle and skill*
stamina *The race requires a lot of stamina.*
ANTONYM **weakness**
2 the degree of intensity: *the strength of his feelings for her*
force *the force of his argument*
intensity *the intensity of their emotions*
potency *the extraordinary potency of her personality*

power *the overwhelming power of love*
vehemence *I was surprised by the vehemence of his criticism.*
vigour *They resumed the game with renewed vigour.*
ANTONYM **weakness**
See also **character, energy, force, merit, power, virtue**

strengthen

▷ VERB

1 to give something more power: *This move will strengthen his political standing.*
consolidate *to consolidate an already dominant position*
encourage *encouraged by the shouts of their supporters*
harden *evidence that hardens suspicions about their involvement*
stiffen *This only stiffened my resolve to quit.*
toughen *They voted to toughen the rules.*
ANTONYM **weaken**
2 to support the structure of something: *The builders had to strengthen the joists with timber.*
bolster *steel beams bolstered the roof.*
brace *pillars braced by scaffolding*
fortify *citadels fortified by high stone walls*
reinforce *They had to reinforce the walls with exterior beams.*
support *the thick wooden posts that supported the ceiling*
ANTONYM **weaken**
See also **build, secure**

strenuous *See* **hard**

stress

▷ NOUN

1 worry and nervous tension: *the stresses and strains of a busy career*
anxiety *Her voice was full of anxiety.*
hassle INFORMAL *I don't think it's worth the money or the hassle.*
pressure *I felt the pressure of being the youngest person in the job.*
strain *He was tired and under great strain.*
tension *Laughing relieves tension.*
worry *It was a time of worry for us.*
▷ VERB
2 to emphasize something: *The leaders have stressed their commitment to the talks.*
accentuate *makeup that accentuates your best features*
emphasize *He waved his hand to emphasize the point.*
repeat *We are not, I repeat not, going to change the rules for you.*

S

underline *The report underlined their concern about falling standards.*
See also **beat, burden, care, emphasize, strain**

stressful *See* **tense**

stretch

▷ VERB

1 to extend over an area or time: *an artificial reef stretching the length of the coast*
continue *The road continued into the distance.*
cover *The oil slick covered a total area of 12 km.*
extend *The caves extend for some 18 km.*
go on *The dispute looks set to go on into the new year.*
hang *The branches hang right down to the ground.*
last *His difficulties are likely to last for a long time.*
reach *a trailer park that reached from one end of the bay to the other*
spread *The beach spreads as far as the eye can see.*
2 to reach out with part of your body: *She arched her back and stretched herself.*
extend *Stand straight with your arms extended.*
reach *He reached up for an apple on an overhanging branch.*
straighten *Point your toes and straighten both legs slowly.*
ANTONYM **bend**

▷ NOUN

3 an area of land or water: *It's a very dangerous stretch of road.*
area *extensive mountainous areas of Europe and South America*
expanse *a huge expanse of parkland*
extent *a vast extent of private property*
sweep *the full sweep of the shoreline*
tract *They cleared large tracts of forest for farming.*
4 a period of time: *She would study for eight-hour stretches.*
period *a long period of time*
run *The show will travel throughout Canada, following a long run in Toronto.*
space *They've come a long way in a short space of time.*
spell *a long spell of dry weather*
stint *He is coming home after a five-year stint overseas.*
term *the full term of her pregnancy*
time *doing very little exercise for several weeks at a time*

See also **extend, lengthen, period, range, tax, term, time**

strict

▷ ADJECTIVE

1 very firm in demanding obedience: *His parents are very strict.*
authoritarian *an authoritarian approach to parenthood*
firm *It's a firm rule, with no exceptions made.*
rigid *a rigid hospital routine*
rigorous *rigorous military training*
stern *Her uncle was stern and hard to please.*
stringent *stringent rules*
2 precise and accurate: *He has never been unemployed, in the strict sense of the word.*
accurate *an accurate record of events*
exact *I do not remember the exact words.*
meticulous *meticulous attention to detail*
particular *very particular dietary requirements*
precise *precise instructions*
true *a true account*
See also **accurate, faithful, right, rigid, severe**

stride *See* **walk**

strident *See* **loud, noisy**

strife *See* **conflict, riot, war**

strike *See* **beat, bump, occur**

striking *See* **bold, impressive, memorable, prominent, significant**

string *See* **sequence, series**

stringent *See* **rigid, strict**

stripe *See* **line**

stripped *See* **bare**

strive

▷ VERB

to make a great effort to achieve something: *She strives hard to keep herself fit.*
attempt *He attempted to smile, but found it difficult.*
do your best *I'll do my best to find out.*
do your utmost *She was certain he would do his utmost to help her.*
endeavour FORMAL *They are endeavouring to protect the local wildlife.*
make an effort *He made no effort to hide his disappointment.*
seek *We have never sought to impose our views.*
try *She tried to get me to change my mind.*
See also **aim, attempt, seek, struggle, try**

stroke *See* **feel, hit**

stroll *See* **ramble, walk, wander**

strong

▷ *ADJECTIVE*

1 having powerful muscles: *a strong, robust man*
ANTONYM **weak**

2 able to withstand rough treatment: *a strong material, which won't crack or chip*
ANTONYM **fragile**

3 great in degree or intensity: *Despite strong opposition, she was victorious.*
ANTONYM **faint**

See WORD STUDY **strong** *on next page*
See also **bold, fierce, hard, healthy, passionate, powerful, solid, sturdy, tough, violent, well**

strong point *See* **merit**

structure

▷ *NOUN*

1 the way something is made or organized: *the structure of this molecule*
arrangement *an intricate arrangement of mechanical parts*
construction *The chairs were light in construction but very strong.*
design *The shoes were of good design and good quality.*
makeup *the chemical makeup of the oceans and atmosphere*
organization *the organization of the economy*

2 something that has been built: *The museum is an impressive structure.*
building *an ugly modern building*
construction *an impressive steel and glass construction*
edifice *historic edifices in the area*
See also **building, form, sequence, system**

structuring *See* **organization**

struggle

▷ *VERB*

1 to try hard to do something: *They had to struggle to make ends meet.*
strain *straining to lift heavy weights*
strive *He strives hard to keep himself fit.*
toil *toiling to make up for lost time*
work *I had to work hard for everything I have.*

▷ *NOUN*

2 something that is hard to achieve: *Life became a struggle for survival.*
effort *It was an effort to finish in time.*
labour *weary from their labours*
toil *another day of toil and strife*
work *It's been hard work, but rewarding.*

See also **clash, competition, contest, effort, fight**

struggle against *See* **resist**

stubborn

▷ *ADJECTIVE*

determined not to change or give in: *a stubborn character who is used to getting her own way*
dogged *his dogged insistence on his rights*
inflexible *His opponents viewed him as dogmatic and inflexible.*
obstinate *a difficult and obstinate child*
tenacious *a tenacious and persistent interviewer*
wilful *a headstrong and wilful young employee*
See also **obstinate**

stuck-up

▷ *ADJECTIVE*

INFORMAL proud and conceited: *She was famous, but she wasn't a bit stuck-up.*
arrogant *He was so arrogant, he never even said hello to me.*
conceited *He's a very conceited young man.*
disdainful *She cast a disdainful glance at me.*
haughty *She looks haughty, but when you get to know her, she's very friendly.*
proud *He's too proud to use public transit.*
snobbish *I'd expected her to be snobbish, but she was warm and welcoming.*
See also **haughty, superior, vain**

student

▷ *NOUN*

a person taught at a school: *There are 30 students in my class.*
pupil *She's a model pupil.*
schoolchild *The bus was packed with schoolchildren.*

studied *See* **deliberate**

study

▷ *VERB*

1 to spend time learning about something: *He is studying history and economics.*
learn *I'm learning how to drive.*
read up *She spent a year reading up on farming techniques.*

2 to look at something carefully: *He studied the map in silence.*
contemplate *She contemplated her hands, frowning.*
examine *She examined my passport and stamped it.*

S

Strong is an overused word. Depending on what you are referring to, there are many substitutes that you can use in its place to add variety and interest to your writing.

• of a person, having powerful muscles
She was tall and **athletic**.
He's turned into a **brawny** hockey player.
My uncle is a big, **burly** man.
Like many female athletes, she was lean and **muscular**.
I'd like to be a **powerful** bodybuilder like you.
He was a bricklayer — a big, **strapping** fellow.
She's a fit, **well-built** runner.

• of a person, in good physical condition
She is positively **blooming** with health.
It won't be long till you're **fit** again.
He's in **good** condition.
She has always been a **healthy** child.
He was never a **robust** child.
You need to be in **sound** physical condition to play this sport.

• of a person, confident and courageous
You have to be **brave** for your own sake.
You are a **courageous** leader.
She's a **plucky** schoolgirl who battled leukemia.
You've always been **resilient** — I know you'll get over this.
He's attracted to **self-confident** women.
You have to be **tough** to survive in this business.

• of an object, able to withstand rough treatment
The toboggan is made of **durable** plastic.
I need **hard-wearing** cotton overalls.
She bought a **heavy-duty** canvas bag.
The bridge has **reinforced** concrete supports.
The camera must be mounted on a **sturdy** tripod.
We considered buying a **substantial** boat with a powerful motor.
It's a **tough** vehicle designed for all terrains.
You need a **well-built** fence all round the garden.

• of feelings, great in degree or intensity
As I walked into the room, I had an **acute** feeling of self-consciousness.
She's an **ardent** admirer of her own work!
He harboured a **deep** resentment of me.

It's my **fervent** hope that things will get better.
She inspires **fierce** loyalty in her friends.
I have an **intense** dislike of spiders.
He has a **keen** interest in hockey.
I'm a **passionate** believer in animal rights.
He had a **profound** distrust of their motives.
My announcement sparked off **vehement** criticism.
Her plans met with **violent** hostility.
His **zealous** regard for his family clouded his judgment.

• of an argument, convincing or supported by a lot of evidence
There is a **compelling** case for higher spending on education.
It is a **convincing** theory.
Industry has produced some **effective** arguments against the tax.
There are **persuasive** reasons justifying the move.
He made a **sound** case for using organically grown produce.
Her evidence provided the most **telling** condemnation of the system.

• of a smell, very noticeable
The young man wore an **overpowering** aftershave.
I noticed a **powerful** smell of ammonia.
We could smell the **pungent** aroma of coffee.

• of food or drink, having a powerful flavour
That's a delicious **hot** curry.
The food was spoiled by the **overpowering** taste of chili.
With fish, he liked a **piquant** sauce.
What's the name of the liqueur with a **powerful** aniseed flavour?
I love the **sharp** taste of pickles.
Avoid **spicy** foods and alcohol.

• of colours, very bright
She always dresses in **bold** colours.
The room was decorated in **bright** reds and blues.
Brilliant jewel colours are fashionable this season.
He wore a **glaring** red jacket.
I like shirts with **loud** patterns.

pore over *We spent hours poring over the websites.*

▷ NOUN

3 the activity of learning about a subject: *the serious study of architecture*
lessons *He was falling behind in his piano lessons.*
research *funds for medical research*
schoolwork *She buried herself in schoolwork.*
See also **consideration, examination, examine, investigate, observe, piece, read, research, review, scrutinize**

stuff

▷ NOUN

1 a substance or group of things: *"That's my stuff," he said, pointing to a bag.*
apparatus *all the apparatus you'll need for the job*
belongings *I collected my belongings and left.*
equipment *outdoor playing equipment*
gear *fishing gear*
kit *a first-aid kit*
material *organic material*
substance *An unknown substance was in the unlabelled jar.*
tackle *He kept his fishing tackle in his room.*
things *She told him to take all his things and not to return.*

▷ VERB

2 to push something somewhere quickly and roughly: *He stuffed all the paper into a recycling box.*
cram *I crammed everything into the drawer.*
force *I forced the key into the ignition.*
jam *He jammed his hands into his pockets.*
push *He pushed himself into the crowd.*
ram *He rammed his clothes into a drawer.*
shove *We shoved a flyer under their door.*
squeeze *I squeezed everything into my bag.*
thrust *She thrust a stack of photos into my hands.*

3 to fill something with a substance or objects: *He stood there, stuffing his mouth with popcorn.*
cram *I crammed my bag full of clothes and set off.*
fill *I filled the box with books.*
load *They loaded all their equipment into backpacks.*
pack *a truck packed with furniture*
See also **cram, equipment, fill, jam, material, matter, stick, substance, things**

stuffy

▷ ADJECTIVE

1 formal and old-fashioned: *his lack of stuffy formality*

dull *They are nice people but rather dull.*
formal *an austere and formal family*
old-fashioned *He was an old-fashioned type of person.*
staid *He is boring, old-fashioned, and staid.*
straitlaced *very straitlaced and narrow-minded*

2 not containing enough fresh air: *It was hot and stuffy in the classroom.*
close *The atmosphere was close.*
heavy *The air was heavy throughout much of the week.*
muggy *It was muggy and overcast.*
oppressive *The little room was windowless and oppressive.*
stale *A layer of smoke hung in the stale air.*
stifling *the stifling heat of the room*

stumble *See* **trip**

stumble on *See* **discover**

stump *See* **puzzle**

stun *See* **amaze, numb, shock, surprise**

stunned *See* **dazed, unconscious**

stunner *See* **beauty**

stunning *See* **amazing**

stunted *See* **low**

stupendous *See* **unbelievable**

stupid

▷ ADJECTIVE

lacking intelligence or good judgment: *How could I have been so stupid?*
absurd *absurd ideas*
dim *He is rather dim.*
foolish *It is foolish to risk injury.*
idiotic *What an idiotic thing to say!*
inane *She's always asking inane questions.*
obtuse *It should be obvious even to the most obtuse person.*
thick *I must have seemed incredibly thick.*
ANTONYM **smart**
See also **dim, idiotic, mad, silly, slow, unwise**

stupidity

▷ NOUN

lack of intelligence or good judgment: *I was astonished by his stupidity.*
absurdity *the absurdity of the suggestion*
folly *the danger and folly of going camping in that weather*
foolishness *He expressed remorse over his own foolishness.*
inanity *the inanity of the conversation*

S

silliness *She sounded quite exasperated by my silliness.*

sturdy

▷ ADJECTIVE

strong and unlikely to be damaged: *The camera was mounted on a sturdy tripod.*
durable *Fine china dishes are surprisingly durable.*
hardy *It's a hardy plant and should survive.*
robust *a robust mountain climber*
solid *The car feels very solid.*
substantial *The new model is a larger, more substantial car.*
stout *a stout oak door*
strong *strong material that shouldn't crack or chip*
well-built *He is well-built and of medium height.*
ANTONYM **fragile**
See also **powerful, solid, stocky, tough**

style

▷ NOUN

1 the way in which something is done: *a dictatorial management style*
approach *his blunt approach*
manner *a satire in the manner of Leacock*
method *a new method of education*
mode *a cheap and convenient mode of transportation*
technique *his driving technique*
way *He had a strange way of talking.*
2 smartness and elegance: *She has not lost her grace and style.*
chic *designer chic women's suits*
elegance *the actress's understated elegance*
flair *a flair for dressing fashionably*
sophistication *to add a touch of sophistication to any wardrobe*
taste *impeccable taste*
See also **design, fashion, language, manner, name, polish, sort, type, way**

stylish *See* **posh, smart, trendy**

subdue

▷ VERB

to bring people under control by force: *The government has not been able to subdue the rebels.*
crush *ruthless measures to crush the revolt*
defeat *an important role in defeating the rebellion*
overcome *working to overcome the enemy forces*
overpower *The police eventually overpowered him.*

quell *tough new measures to quell the disturbances*
vanquish *his vanquished foe*

subdued *See* **dull, soft**

subject

▷ NOUN

1 the thing or person being discussed: *They exchanged views on a wide range of subjects.*
issue *an issue that had worried him for some time*
matter *I don't want to discuss the matter.*
object *the object of much heated discussion*
point *There is another point to consider.*
question *the difficult question of unemployment*
theme *The book's central theme is power.*
topic *The weather is a constant topic of conversation.*
▷ VERB
2 to make someone experience something: *She was subjected to constant interruptions.*
expose *people exposed to high levels of radiation*
put through *The trainer put them through a series of exercises.*
submit *Don't submit to undue pressure to finish the project early.*
See also **affair, business, issue, matter, question**

submerge *See* **dive, flood**

submission *See* **surrender, tender**

submissive *See* **meek, obedient, passive**

submit

▷ VERB

1 to accept or agree to something unwillingly: *I submitted to their requests.*
agree *Management has agreed to the union's conditions.*
bow *Some stores are bowing to consumer pressure and stocking the product.*
capitulate *He capitulated to their ultimatum.*
comply *We complied with the new rules, though we weren't happy about it.*
give in *Officials say they won't give in to the workers' demands.*
surrender *We'll never surrender to these terrorists.*
yield *She yielded to her friend's pressure and took the child to a specialist.*
ANTONYM **resist**
2 to present a document or proposal formally: *The teachers submitted their reports to the principal.*
hand in *I'm supposed to hand in my essay on Friday.*

present *The group intends to present this petition to the mayor.*
propose *The Member of Parliament has proposed a bill to amend the Charter.*
put forward *She has put forward new peace proposals.*
send in *Applicants are asked to send in a résumé and covering letter.*
table *They've tabled a motion criticizing the government for its actions.*
tender *She tendered her resignation.*
ANTONYM **withdraw**
See also **give in, nominate, pose, subject, surrender**

subordinate *See* **inferior, junior**

subsequent *See* **next**

subsequently *See* **after, next**

subservient *See* **obedient**

subside *See* **abate, fall**

subsidize *See* **fund**

subsidy *See* **grant**

substance
▷ *NOUN*
a solid, powder, liquid, or gas: *Poisonous substances should be labelled as such.*
element *a chart of the chemical elements*
fabric *Chlorine will rot the fabric.*
material *resilient plastic material*
stuff *the stuff from which the universe is made*
See also **material, matter, stuff, wealth**

substantial *See* **solid, sturdy**

substantiate *See* **confirm**

substitute
▷ *VERB*
I to use one thing in place of another: *You can substitute honey for the sugar.*
exchange *exchanging one set of problems for another*
interchange *Turkey can be interchanged with beef in the meatloaf recipe.*
replace *We dug up the concrete and replaced it with grass.*
swap *Some hostages were swapped for convicted prisoners.*
switch *They switched the price tags on the printers.*
▷ *NOUN*
2 something used in place of another thing: *an artificial substitute for silk*
deputy *I can't make it, so I'll send my deputy.*
proxy *They must nominate a proxy to vote on their behalf.*
replacement *He has nominated his*

assistant as his replacement.
representative *Employees from each department elect a representative.*
surrogate *They had expected me to be a surrogate for my sister.*
See also **change, replacement**

subtle *See* **fine**

subtract
▷ *VERB*
to take one number away from another: *If you subtract 3 from 5 you get 2.*
deduct *Marks will be deducted for spelling mistakes.*
take away *Take away the number you first thought of.*
take from *Take the five percent discount from the total amount due.*
ANTONYM **add**

subvert *See* **undermine**

succeed
▷ *VERB*
I to achieve the result you intend: *To succeed, you must learn to overcome obstacles.*
be successful *Our figure skaters were successful at the Winter Olympics.*
do well *Their team did well.*
flourish *The business flourished.*
make it INFORMAL *It's a challenge for a Canadian actress to make it in Hollywood.*
prosper *His team has always prospered in regional competitions.*
thrive *The company has thrived by selling cheap, simple products.*
triumph *a symbol of good triumphing over evil*
work *The plan worked.*
ANTONYM **fail**
2 to be the next person to have someone's job: *She is almost certain to succeed me as president.*
replace *The coach who replaced her is another perfectionist.*
take over from *He took over from the company's founder as chief executive.*
See also **flourish, follow, pass, replace, triumph, win**

succeed in *See* **manage**

succeeding *See* **next**

success
▷ *NOUN*
I the achievement of a goal, fame, or wealth: *Do you believe that work is the key to success?*
celebrity *I never expected this kind of celebrity when I was writing my novel.*

S

eminence *a researcher who achieved eminence in the scientific world*
fame *her rise to fame as a dramatist*
prosperity *the country's economic prosperity*
triumph *last year's Conservative triumph in the elections*
victory *a victory in the battle over workplace rights*
wealth *Her hard work brought her wealth and respect.*
ANTONYM **failure**
2 a person or thing achieving popularity or greatness: *Everyone who knows her says she will be a huge success.*
celebrity *At the age of 12, she is already a celebrity.*
hit *The song became a huge hit.*
sensation *the movie that turned her into an overnight sensation*
star *I always knew he would be a star.*
triumph *a triumph of modern surgery*
winner *Selling was my game, and I intended to be a winner.*
ANTONYM **failure**
See also **triumph, victory, win**

successful
▷ ADJECTIVE
having achieved what you intended to do: *My mom is a highly successful computer analyst.*
flourishing *a flourishing business*
lucrative *a lucrative career*
profitable *a profitable exchange of ideas*
rewarding *a rewarding investment*
thriving *a thriving construction industry*
top *a top model*

successfully See **well**

succession See **sequence, series**

successor See **replacement**

succinct See **concise, short**

succumb See **develop, give in, surrender**

sudden
▷ ADJECTIVE
happening quickly and unexpectedly: *a sudden cry*
abrupt *His idyllic world came to an abrupt end when his family lost their business.*
hasty *his hasty departure*
quick *I had to make a quick decision.*
swift *a swift blow to the stomach*
unexpected *His death was totally unexpected.*

ANTONYM **gradual**
See also **abrupt, quick, sharp**

suffer
▷ VERB
to be affected by pain or something unpleasant: *I knew he was suffering some discomfort.*
bear *He bore his trials with dignity and grace.*
endure *The writer endured a harsh life.*
experience *She experienced many hardships over a long life.*
go through *I wouldn't like to go through that again.*
sustain *He had sustained massive injuries.*
undergo *He had to undergo a series of medical tests.*
See also **bear, endure, feel, receive, undergo**

sufferer See **patient**

suffering See **distress**

suffice See **do**

sufficient
▷ ADJECTIVE
being enough for a purpose: *He had sufficient time to prepare his speech.*
adequate *an adequate income*
ample *an ample supply of gasoline*
enough *enough cash to live on*
ANTONYM **insufficient**
See also **adequate, ample, satisfactory**

sugary See **sweet**

suggest
▷ VERB
1 to mention something as a possibility or recommendation: *My cousin suggested going out for dinner.*
advise *I advise you to keep quiet.*
advocate *Some members of the board advocated longer school days.*
propose *And where do you propose building such a huge thing?*
recommend *I have no qualms about recommending this approach.*
2 to hint that something is the case: *Reports suggested the factory would close.*
hint *The mayor hinted that she might make some changes.*
imply *The tone of the report implied that there would soon be a major shakeup.*
indicate *She has indicated that she may resign.*
insinuate *an article that insinuated he was lying*
intimate *He did intimate that he is seeking legal advice.*

See also **advise, hint, nominate, raise, vote**

suggestion

▷ NOUN

1 an idea mentioned as a possibility: *practical suggestions*
plan *The government is being asked to consider the plan.*
proposal *the proposal to do away with nuclear weapons*
proposition *a business proposition*
recommendation *a range of recommendations for change*
2 a slight indication of something: *a suggestion of dishonesty*
hint *He showed only the slightest hint of emotion.*
indication *She gave no indication of remorse.*
insinuation *The insinuation is that I have something to hide.*
intimation *He did not give any intimation that he was going to resign.*
trace *No traces of blood were found at the crime scene.*
See also **advice, hint, idea, indication, trace**

suit

▷ VERB

1 to be acceptable: *They will move only if it suits them.*
be acceptable to *The name chosen had to be acceptable to everyone.*
do *A holiday at home will do me just fine.*
please *I'll leave when it pleases me and not before.*
satisfy *Nothing you can do will satisfy him.*
2 to match something else: *The battery can be shaped to suit any device.*
agree *His statement agrees with those of the other witnesses.*
conform to *designed to conform to the new safety requirements*
correspond *a number that corresponds to a horse running in the race*
go with *Do these shoes go with this dress?*
match *tan slacks with a jacket to match*
See also **blend, flatter, match**

suitable

▷ ADJECTIVE

right or acceptable for a particular purpose: *Conditions were not suitable for the vegetation to flourish.*
acceptable *a mutually acceptable new contract*
appropriate *an appropriate outfit for the occasion*
apt *an apt name*

fit *the suggestion that they are not fit parents*
fitting *a fitting background for the wedding photos*
proper *It was once not thought proper for a woman to be on stage.*
right *He always said just the right thing.*
satisfactory *a satisfactory arrangement*
ANTONYM **unsuitable**
See also **appropriate, favourable, fitting, proper, right**

sulky

▷ ADJECTIVE

showing annoyance by being silent and moody: *a sulky adolescent*
huffy *What are you being so huffy about?*
moody *Her best friend had become withdrawn and moody.*
petulant *He's just being childish and petulant.*
resentful *a resentful teammate*
sullen *He lapsed into a sullen silence.*
See also **grumpy, moody**

sullen See **grumpy, moody, sulky**

sum See **count, quantity, total**

sum total See **whole**

summarize See **outline, sum up**

summary

▷ NOUN

a short account of something's main points: *a summary of the report*
outline *an outline of the proposal*
review *a book review*
rundown *Here's a rundown of the options.*
summation *The prosecution concluded its summation.*
synopsis *a brief synopsis of the book*
See also **outline**

summit See **peak, top**

sumptuous See **luxurious**

sumptuousness See **luxury**

sum up

▷ VERB

to describe briefly: *He summed up his weekend in one word: "Disastrous."*
recapitulate *Let's recapitulate just the essential points.*
summarize *The article can be summarized in three sentences.*

sundry See **several, various**

sunken See **low**

sunny See **cheery**

S

superb

▷ ADJECTIVE

very good indeed: *With superb skill, she managed to make a perfect landing.*
breathtaking *The house has breathtaking views.*
excellent *You've done an excellent job.*
exquisite *Her photography is exquisite.*
magnificent *a magnificent diamond necklace*
marvellous *He is a marvellous cook.*
outstanding *an outstanding performance*
splendid *a splendid Victorian mansion*
superior *a superior blend of the finest coffee beans*
unrivalled *He has an unrivalled knowledge of Canadian economics.*
wonderful *The sun setting over Lake Hudson was a wonderful sight.*
See also **brilliant, excellent, first-rate, marvellous, outstanding, splendid, wonderful**

supercilious See **scornful, superior**

superfluous See **excess, spare, waste**

superior

▷ ADJECTIVE

1 better than other similar things: *a superior brand of ice cream*
better *I'd like to move to a better area.*
choice *the choicest cuts of meat*
deluxe *a deluxe model*
exceptional *children with exceptional ability*
first-rate *a first-rate thriller*
surpassing *her surpassing achievements*
unrivalled *colour printing of unrivalled quality*
ANTONYM **inferior**
2 showing pride and self-importance: *He stood there looking superior.*
condescending *I'm fed up with your condescending attitude.*
disdainful *She shot a disdainful look in my direction.*
haughty *He spoke in a haughty tone.*
lofty *lofty disdain*
patronizing *his patronizing attitude to the homeless*
snobbish *a snobbish dislike of lighthearted movies*
stuck-up INFORMAL *She was a famous actress, but she wasn't a bit stuck-up.*
supercilious *His manner is supercilious and arrogant.*
▷ NOUN
3 a person in a higher position than you: *his immediate superior*

boss *Her boss was very supportive.*
manager *His plans found favour with his manager.*
senior *He was described by his seniors as a model officer.*
supervisor *Each student has a supervisor.*
ANTONYM **inferior**
See also **prime, select, senior, smug, superb**

superiority See **advantage, victory**

superlative See **incomparable**

supermarket See **store**

supernatural See **spooky**

supersede See **follow, replace**

superstar See **celebrity**

supervise

▷ VERB

to oversee a person or activity: *He supervised more than 400 volunteers.*
be in charge of *She is in charge of the whole project.*
direct *She will direct day-to-day operations.*
have charge of *He has charge of one group of tourists.*
keep an eye on *I told you to keep an eye on the children.*
manage *I manage a small team of workers.*
oversee *an architect to oversee the work*
run *Each teacher will run a different workshop.*
See also **administer, command, direct, guard, handle, lead, oversee**

supervision See **watch**

supervisor See **superior**

supplant See **replace**

supple See **agile, flexible, soft**

supplement

▷ VERB

1 to add to something to improve it: *I suggest supplementing your diet with vitamin A.*
add to *An eat-in kitchen adds to the value of any house.*
augment *a way to augment the family income*
complement *a benefit package that complements my salary*
reinforce *measures that will reinforce their current strengths*
top up *compulsory contributions to top up pension plans*
▷ NOUN
2 something added to something else: *a supplement to their basic pension*

addition *an addition to the chalet*
appendix *The report includes a six-page appendix.*
complement *The photographs are a perfect complement to the text.*
extra *an optional extra*
See also **add, addition, augment**

supplies
▷ PLURAL NOUN

food or equipment for a particular purpose: *I had only a litre of water in my emergency supplies.*
equipment *vital medical equipment*
provisions *provisions for two weeks*
rations *Officials said food rations had been distributed.*
stores *an important part of a ship's stores*

supply
▷ VERB

1 to provide someone with something: *an agreement not to supply chemical weapons*
equip *plans for equipping the island with water*
furnish *They'll be able to furnish you with the details.*
give *We'll give you all the information you need.*
provide *They'll provide all the equipment.*
▷ NOUN

2 an amount of something available for use: *a plentiful supply of vegetables*
cache *a cache of weapons and explosives*
fund *an extraordinary fund of energy*
hoard *a hoard of food and fuel*
reserve *the world's oil reserves*
stock *a fresh stock of new equipment*
stockpile *stockpiles of chemical weapons*
store *I have a store of food and water here.*
See also **equip, fund, give, hoard, issue, provide, reserve, stock, store**

support
▷ VERB

1 to agree with someone's ideas or aims: *We supported her political campaign.*
back *a new witness to back his claim*
champion *He passionately championed the cause.*
defend *He defended all of their decisions, right or wrong.*
promote *They continued to promote the idea of an elected Senate.*
second *The president of the board seconded the call for discipline.*
side with *accused of siding with terrorists*
uphold *We uphold the Canadian Charter of Rights and Freedoms.*
ANTONYM **oppose**
2 to help someone in difficulty: *Try to*

support each other when one of you is feeling down.
encourage *When things aren't going well, he encourages me.*
help *She'd do anything to help a friend.*
3 to hold something up from underneath: *Thick wooden posts support the deck.*
bolster *steel beams used to bolster the roof*
brace *Oak beams braced the roof.*
hold up *My legs wouldn't hold me up.*
prop up *Use sticks to prop the plants up.*
reinforce *They had to reinforce the walls with exterior beams.*
▷ NOUN

4 an object that holds something up: *the metal supports that hold up the canvas*
brace *He will have to wear a neck brace for several days.*
foundation *the foundation on which the bridge was built*
pillar *the pillars supporting the roof*
post *The device is fixed to a post.*
prop *a structural part such as a beam or prop*
See also **advocate, back, bear, blessing, champion, comfort, defend, encourage, favour, finance, fund, help, promote, sanction, side with, steady, strengthen**

supporter
▷ NOUN

a person who agrees with something or helps someone: *He is a strong supporter of the plan.*
adherent *The new political party was gaining adherents in the province.*
advocate *a strong advocate of free trade*
ally *a close friend and ally*
champion *a champion of equal rights*
fan *fans of this hockey team*
follower *followers of the Dalai Lama*
sponsor *The local pizza restaurant is a sponsor of our volleyball team.*
See also **defender, fan, follower, helper**

supportive See **helpful**

suppose
▷ VERB

to think that something is probably the case: *Where do you suppose he has gone?*
assume *I assume you have permission to be here?*
believe *We believe them to be hidden somewhere in the area.*
expect *I don't expect you've had much experience in the job yet.*
guess *I guess you're right.*

S

imagine *It is difficult to imagine what our ancestors were like.*

presume *I presume you're here on business.*

think *Do you think she was embarrassed?*
See also **assume, conclude, figure, guess, imagine, reckon, suspect**

supposed
▷ ADJECTIVE

1 planned, expected, or required to do something: *You're not supposed to leave the children on their own.*

expected *You were expected to arrive much earlier than this.*

meant *Parties are meant to be fun.*

obliged *He is legally obliged to declare his interests.*

required *Will I be required to come to every meeting?*

2 generally believed or thought to be the case: *What is his son supposed to have said?*

alleged *The accused is alleged to have killed a man.*

assumed *As usual, the mistakes were assumed to be my fault.*

believed *He is believed to have died in 1656.*

meant *They are meant to be one of the top teams in the world.*

presumed *This area is presumed to be safe.*

reputed *The creature Bigfoot is reputed to inhabit the Pacific Northwest.*

rumoured *They are rumoured to be on the verge of splitting up.*

supposition *See* **theory**

suppress
▷ VERB

1 to prevent people from doing something: *international attempts to suppress drug trafficking*

crush *a plan to crush the uprising*

quash *The announcement may help to quash these rumours.*

quell *The army moved in to quell the uprising.*

stamp out *steps to stamp out bullying in schools*

stop *measures to stop the trade in ivory*

2 to stop yourself from expressing a feeling or reaction: *She barely suppressed a gasp.*

conceal *He could not conceal his relief.*

contain *He could hardly contain his rage.*

curb *She curbed her temper.*

repress *people who repress their emotions*

restrain *unable to restrain her anger*

smother *I smothered a chuckle.*

stifle *He stifled a yawn and looked at his watch.*
See also **curb, silence**

suppressed *See* **pent-up**

suppression *See* **ban**

supremacy *See* **control, power**

supreme
▷ ADJECTIVE

of the highest degree or rank: *They conspired to seize supreme power.*

chief *his chief rival*

foremost *the world's foremost scientists*

greatest *Brazil's greatest soccer idol*

highest *the highest academic achievement*

leading *the world's leading basketball players*

paramount *a factor of paramount importance*

pre-eminent *a pre-eminent political figure*

principal *the principal reason*

top *the top student in the class*

ultimate *the ultimate international accolade, the Nobel Prize*
See also **absolute, ideal, incomparable, ultimate**

sure
▷ ADJECTIVE

1 having no doubts: *She was no longer sure how she felt about him.*

certain *certain of getting a place on the team*

clear *He is not clear on how he will go about it.*

convinced *She is convinced it's your fault.*

definite *a definite answer*

positive *I'm positive it will happen.*

satisfied *We must be satisfied that the treatment is safe.*

ANTONYM **unsure**

2 reliable or definite: *a sure sign that something is wrong*

definite *a definite advantage*

dependable *dependable information*

foolproof *a foolproof system*

infallible *an infallible eye for detail*

reliable *a reliable source*

trustworthy *trustworthy reports*

undeniable *a sad but undeniable fact*
See also **certain, confident, positive, reliable, yes**

INFORMALLY SPEAKING

for sure: without doubt
sure enough: definitely

surface *See* **appear, face, finish, outside**

surfeit *See* **excess**

surge *See* **burst, jump, rage, wave**

surly *See* **grumpy**

surmise *See* **conclude, theory**

surmount *See* **overcome**

surpass *See* **outdo, pass, top**

surpassing *See* **superior**

surplus *See* **excess, profit, rest, spare**

surprise
▷ *NOUN*
1 something unexpected: *The resignation came as a complete surprise.*
bombshell *His departure was a bombshell for the team.*
jolt *The entire team was jolted by the news.*
revelation *Tom Thomson's paintings had been a revelation to her.*
shock *I got a shock when I saw her.*
start *You gave me quite a start.*
2 the feeling caused by something unexpected: *an exclamation of surprise*
amazement *He stared in baffled amazement.*
astonishment *"What?" he asked in astonishment.*
incredulity *The announcement has been met with incredulity.*
wonder *The officer shook his head in wonder.*
▷ *VERB*
3 to give someone a feeling of surprise: *I was surprised by the vehemence of his criticism.*
amaze *Most of the cast members were amazed by the play's success.*
astonish *I was astonished to discover his true age.*
astound *He was astounded at the result.*
stagger *I was staggered by her reaction.*
stun *Audiences were stunned by the movie's tragic ending.*
take aback *I was taken aback when a man answered the phone.*
See also **amaze, amazement**

surprising *See* **amazing, extraordinary, unexpected**

surrender
▷ *VERB*
1 to agree that the other side has won: *We'll never surrender to terrorists.*
capitulate *They had no choice but to capitulate.*
give in *He gave in to them on everything.*
submit *I refuse to submit to their demands.*
succumb *The cabinet minister said her country would never succumb to pressure.*

yield *The government had to yield to local opinion.*
2 to give something up to someone else: *We have surrendered our political authority for economic gain.*
cede *After the war, Spain ceded the island to the United States.*
give up *She is loath to give up her hard-earned liberty.*
relinquish *She does not intend to relinquish power.*
renounce *He renounced his claim to the throne.*
yield *He was obliged to yield territory to France.*
▷ *NOUN*
3 a situation in which one side gives in to the other: *unconditional surrender*
capitulation *the German capitulation at the end of World War I*
submission *The army intends to force the city into submission.*
See also **give in, sacrifice, submit**

surrogate *See* **replacement, substitute**

surround
▷ *VERB*
to be all around a person or thing: *He was surrounded by bodyguards.*
encircle *A high concrete wall encircles the jail.*
enclose *The land was enclosed by a fence.*
encompass *the largest lake in Canada wholly encompassed by a town*
envelop *The rich smell of the forest enveloped us.*
hem in *a valley hemmed in by mountains*
See also **enclose**

surrounded by *See* **among**

surroundings
▷ *PLURAL NOUN*
the area and environment around a person or place: *He felt a longing for familiar surroundings.*
background *a plain background for the school photographs*
environment *a safe environment for marine mammals*
location *filmed in an exotic location*
neighbourhood *living in an affluent neighbourhood*
setting *Rome is the perfect setting for romance.*
See also **scenery**

surveillance *See* **watch**

S

survey *See* **inspect, measure, observe, review**

survive

▷ *VERB*

to live or exist in spite of difficulties: *companies that survived after the recession*
endure *Somehow their friendship endures.*
last *Nothing lasts forever.*
live *having lived through the war*
outlive *They have outlived the horror of the war.*
pull through *He should pull through without serious problems.*
See also **continue, endure, last, remain**

susceptible *See* **impressionable, prone, vulnerable**

suspect

▷ *VERB*

1 to think something is likely: *I suspect they are secretly planning to raise taxes.*
believe *Police believe the attacks were carried out by gangs.*
feel *I somehow feel he was involved.*
guess *As you probably guessed, I don't like him much.*
suppose *The problem is more complex than she supposes.*
2 to have doubts about something: *He suspected her motives.*
distrust *I don't have any particular reason to distrust them.*
doubt *Do you doubt my word?*
mistrust *He mistrusts all journalists.*
▷ *ADJECTIVE*
3 not to be trusted: *a rather suspect character*
doubtful *statistics of doubtful origin*
dubious *dubious practices*
fishy INFORMAL *There's something very fishy about it.*
questionable *the questionable motives of politicians*
shifty *shifty trading practices*
See also **dubious, guess, imagine, question, suspicious**

suspend *See* **cease, delay, hang, interrupt**

suspicion

▷ *NOUN*

1 a feeling of mistrust: *I was regarded with suspicion.*
distrust *an instinctive distrust of authority*
doubt *I have my doubts about his ability to govern.*
misgiving *Her first words filled us with misgiving.*

mistrust *a deep mistrust of banks*
scepticism *The report has been greeted with scepticism.*
2 a feeling that something is true: *I have a strong suspicion they are lying.*
hunch *The detective had a hunch she was on to something.*
idea *I had an idea that he joined the team later.*
impression *I get the impression he's hiding something.*
See also **idea, trace**

suspicious

▷ *ADJECTIVE*

1 feeling distrustful of someone or something: *She was rightly suspicious of their motives.*
apprehensive *She was apprehensive of strangers.*
distrustful *Voters are deeply distrustful of election promises.*
doubtful *At first I was doubtful about their authenticity.*
sceptical *Other archaeologists are sceptical about her findings.*
wary *Many people are wary of lawyers.*
2 causing feelings of distrust: *suspicious circumstances*
doubtful *selling something of doubtful quality*
dubious *This claim seems to us rather dubious.*
fishy INFORMAL *There's something fishy going on here.*
funny *There's something funny about him.*
questionable *There was something questionable about his behaviour.*
shady *shady deals*
shifty *a shifty business deal*
suspect *The whole affair has been highly suspect.*
See also **dubious, wary**

sustain *See* **have, receive, suffer**

sustained *See* **relentless**

swab *See* **clean**

swaggering *See* **boastful**

swallow *See* **believe**

swamp *See* **flood**

swap

▷ *VERB*

to replace one thing for another: *I swapped DVDs with my friend.*
barter *bartering wheat for cotton and timber*
exchange *exchanging one set of problems for another*

interchange *Meat can sometimes be interchanged with legumes as a source of protein.*
switch *They switched the tags on the boxes.*
trade *They traded books for CDs.*
See also **change, exchange, substitute**

swarm *See* **crawl, crowd**

swarthy *See* **dark**

sway *See* **hold, influence, persuade**

sweep *See* **blow, flourish, stretch**

sweep away *See* **wash**

sweeping *See* **broad, extensive**

sweet
▷ ADJECTIVE
1 containing a lot of sugar: *a cup of sweet tea*
cloying *a cloying apricot jam*
sugary *a sugary rhubarb crumble*
sweetened *sweetened iced tea*
ANTONYM **sour**
2 having a pleasant smell: *the sweet smell of roses*
aromatic *a plant with aromatic leaves*
fragrant *fragrant clover*
perfumed *perfumed soaps*
sweet-smelling *gardens filled with sweet-smelling flowers and herbs*
3 pleasant-sounding and tuneful: *the sweet sounds of children's singing*
harmonious *harmonious sounds*
mellow *mellow background music*
melodious *the melodious tones of the organ*
musical *He had a soft, musical voice.*
tuneful *The band was noted for its tuneful concerts.*
See also **lovable**

sweetened *See* **sweet**

sweet-smelling *See* **fragrant, sweet**

swell *See* **bulge, expand, increase, wave**

swelling *See* **boil, bulge, bump, lump**

swerve
▷ VERB
to change direction suddenly to avoid hitting something: *He swerved to avoid a truck.*
swing *The car swung off the road.*
turn *He turned sharply to the left.*
veer *The vehicle veered out of control.*
See also **curve, dodge**

swift
▷ ADJECTIVE
happening or moving very quickly: *Make a swift decision.*
brisk *walking at a brisk pace*
express *a special express service*

fast *The question is how fast the process will be.*
hurried *a hurried breakfast*
prompt *Prompt action is needed.*
quick *The company has been developing at a very quick pace.*
rapid *Will the bridge provide more rapid transportation than ferries?*
speedy *We wish you a speedy recovery.*
ANTONYM **slow**
See also **brief, fast, hasty, prompt, quick, sudden**

swiftly *See* **fast, quickly**

swiftness *See* **speed**

swig *See* **drink**

swindle *See* **cheat, con, rob**

swindler *See* **crook**

swine *See* **pig**

swing *See* **swerve**

swipe *See* **steal**

switch *See* **exchange, substitute, swap**

swivel *See* **turn**

swoon *See* **faint**

symbol
▷ NOUN
a design or idea used to represent something: *Hg is the chemical symbol for mercury.*
emblem *The beaver is an official emblem of Canada.*
figure *the figure of a five-pointed star*
icon *What does that desktop icon represent?*
logo *the company's logo*
mark *a mark of identification*
representation *Those stick figures are representations of a man and a woman.*
sign *a multiplication sign*
token *A ring is a token of love.*
See also **sign**

symbolize *See* **represent**

symmetry *See* **order**

sympathetic *See* **compassionate, favourable, sorry, understanding**

sympathize with *See* **pity**

sympathy
▷ NOUN
kindness and understanding toward someone in trouble: *My heartfelt sympathy goes out to all the relatives.*
compassion *I was impressed by the*

S

compassion he showed for a helpless old man.
empathy *They displayed an understanding
of the crime and empathy with the victim.*
pity *I feel a sense of pity for him.*
understanding *I'd like to thank you for
your patience and understanding.*
See also **pity**

symptom *See* **sign**

syndicate *See* **association, ring**

synopsis *See* **outline, summary**

system

▷ *NOUN*
1 an organized way of doing or arranging
something: *the advantages of the new system
over the old one*
arrangement *a well-designed floral
arrangement*
method *the methods employed in the study*
procedure *This is now the standard
procedure.*
routine *her daily routine*
structure *the structure of local government*
technique *a new technique for processing
sound*
See also **plan, procedure, process,
routine**

Tt

table   483   take care of

table *See* **submit**

taciturn *See* **silent**

tacky *See* **flashy, gaudy, sticky, tasteless**

tact
▷ NOUN
the ability not to offend people: *He has handled the incident with great tact.*
delicacy *Both countries are behaving with rare delicacy.*
diplomacy *It took all the director's diplomacy to get the star to return.*
discretion *I appreciate your discretion.*
sensitivity *The police treated the victims with great sensitivity.*
See also **consideration**

tactful
▷ ADJECTIVE
showing tact: *Sorry, that wasn't a very tactful question.*
diplomatic *She is very direct. I tend to be more diplomatic.*
discreet *They were gossipy and not always discreet.*
sensitive *his sensitive handling of the situation*
ANTONYM **tactless**

tactic *See* **manoeuvre**

tactless *See* **thoughtless**

tag *See* **label**

taint *See* **infect, pollute**

take
▷ VERB
1 to require something: *He takes three hours to get ready.*
demand *Training a puppy demands much patience.*
require *The race requires a lot of stamina.*
2 to carry something: *I'll take these papers home and read them.*
bring *He poured a cup of coffee and brought it to me.*
carry *She carried the packages from the car.*
convey *The shuttle bus conveyed us to the terminal.*
ferry *A plane ferries guests to the island.*
fetch *I fetched a towel from the washroom.*
transport *They use tankers to transport the oil from the drilling site.*
3 to lead someone somewhere: *She took me to a Mexican restaurant.*
bring *Come to my party and bring a friend with you.*

conduct *The usher offered to conduct us to our reserved seats.*
escort *I escorted him to the door.*
guide *a young Egyptologist who guided us through the pyramids*
lead *She led police to the crime scene.*
usher *I ushered him into the office.*
See also **accept, bear, bring, capture, carry, choose, demand, receive, select, steal**

INFORMALLY SPEAKING

on the take: accepting bribes
take five: take a break
take it out of: tire out
take lying down: accept something undesirable without a protest
take out: remove or get rid of

take aback *See* **surprise**

take advantage of *See* **impose on, profit**

take after *See* **resemble**

take away *See* **remove, subtract**

take care of
▷ VERB
1 to look after someone or something: *There was nobody to take care of the children.*
care for *They hired a nurse to care for her.*
look after *I love looking after the children.*
mind *He will mind the store while I'm away.*
nurse *His mother helped nurse him back to health.*
protect *He vowed to protect us forever.*
tend *He tends the flower beds that he has planted.*
watch *Parents are expected to watch their children 24 hours a day.*
ANTONYM **neglect**
2 to deal with a problem, task, or situation: *"Do you need clean sheets?" "No, your husband took care of that."*
attend to *We have business to attend to first.*
cope with *A new system has been designed to cope with the increased demand.*
deal with *the way my service provider deals with complaints*
handle *She handled the mayor's travel arrangements during the campaign.*
manage *He expects me to manage all the household expenses.*
see to *While my aunt saw to the luggage, my uncle took the children home.*
See also **deal, handle, look after, mind, process, tend, watch**

T

take down *See* **lower, write**

take for *See* **mistake**

take from *See* **subtract**

take in
▷ *VERB*
1 to deceive someone: *He was a real charmer who totally took me in.*
con *INFORMAL She was conned by the telemarketing scam.*
deceive *He has deceived us all.*
dupe *The e-mail seemed real enough to dupe them.*
fool *Dishonest antique dealers fool a lot of people.*
mislead *It appears we were misled by a professional con artist.*
trick *He'll be upset when he finds out how you tricked him.*
2 to understand something: *She seemed to take in all he said.*
absorb *It will take time for us to absorb the news.*
appreciate *She never really appreciated the bitterness of the conflict.*
assimilate *My mind could only assimilate one of those ideas at a time.*
comprehend *He failed to comprehend the significance of this remark.*
digest *They need time to digest the information they have learned.*
get *You just don't get what I'm saying, do you?*
grasp *The government has not yet grasped the seriousness of the crisis.*
understand *They are too young to understand what is going on.*
See also **absorb, admit, comprehend, deceive, grasp, involve, receive, trick, understand**

take into account *See* **consider**

take off *See* **remove**

take on *See* **assume, employ, play**

take out *See* **extract, remove, withdraw**

take over *See* **possess**

take over from *See* **replace, succeed**

take part *See* **participate, play**

take place *See* **come, happen, occur**

takeoff *See* **parody**

taking *See* **capture**

taking on *See* **employment**

takings *See* **income, profit**

tale *See* **story**

talent
▷ *NOUN*
a natural ability: *Both children have a talent for music.*
ability *Her drama teacher spotted her ability.*
aptitude *He has no aptitude for music.*
capacity *people's creative capacities*
flair *a musician with a flair for invention*
genius *his genius for chess*
gift *a gift for teaching*
knack *She has a knack for getting people to listen.*
See also **ability, gift**

talented *See* **able, exceptional**

talk
▷ *VERB*
1 to say things: *They were talking about environmental hazards.*
▷ *NOUN*
2 a conversation: *We had a long talk about her future.*
chat *I had a chat with him.*
chatter *idle chatter*
conversation *We had a long conversation.*
3 an informal speech: *a talk about career choices*
address *an address to the Canadian people*
discourse *a lengthy discourse on strategy*
lecture *a series of lectures*
sermon *a long sermon*
speech *He delivered his speech in French.*
See also **chat, discussion, lecture, speech, word**

INFORMALLY SPEAKING

look who's talking: the person criticizing is equally guilty
now you're talking: now you're saying what I want to hear
talk big: boast
you should talk: you are guilty of the thing you are criticizing

---

talk about *See* **discuss**

talk into *See* **coax, persuade**

talkative
▷ *ADJECTIVE*
talking a lot: *His eyes grew bright, and he suddenly became very talkative.*
chatty *She's quite a chatty person.*
communicative *She has become a lot more communicative.*
long-winded *I hope I'm not being too long-winded.*

tall

▷ ADJECTIVE

higher than average: *tall buildings*
high *a high wall*
lanky *He was 190 cm, all lanky and leggy.*
lofty *lofty ceilings*
soaring *the soaring spires of churches like St. Peter's in Rome*
towering *towering cliffs of black granite*
ANTONYM **short**

tally *See* **agree, correspond, count, match**

tamper *See* **interfere**

tang *See* **taste**

tangible *See* **real**

tangle

▷ NOUN

1 a mass of long things knotted together: *a tangle of wires*
jumble *a jumble of twisted tubes*
knot *The rope was full of knots.*
mass *a flailing mass of arms and legs*
mat *the thick mat of floating seaweed*
muddle *The back of the tapestry was a muddle of threads.*
web *a thick web of fibres*

▷ VERB

2 to twist together or catch someone or something: *Dolphins can get tangled in fishing nets and drown.*
catch *a fly caught in a spider's web*
jumble *The wires were all jumbled together and tied in a knot.*
knot *The kite strings had become knotted together.*
twist *strands twisted together into a rope*
See also **muddle**

tangled *See* **complex**

target *See* **aim, focus, goal**

tariff *See* **duty, rate, tax**

tarry *See* **stay**

tart *See* **bitter, sour**

task

▷ NOUN

a job that you have to do: *I had the task of breaking the bad news.*
assignment *written assignments and oral exams*
chore *household chores*
duty *I carried out my duties conscientiously.*
job *He was given the job of taking out the garbage.*
mission *a diplomatic mission to European capitals*

undertaking *Organizing the show has been a massive undertaking.*
See also **job, undertaking, work**

taste

▷ NOUN

1 the flavour of something: *I like the taste of this juice.*
flavour *a crumbly texture with a strong flavour*
tang *the tang of lemon*
2 a small amount of food or drink: *I'll have a taste of your dessert.*
bite *Chew each mouthful fully before the next bite.*
mouthful *She gulped down a mouthful of coffee.*
sip *a sip of water*
3 a liking for something: *a taste for adventure*
appetite *her appetite for success*
fondness *I've always had a fondness for jewels.*
liking *She had a liking for good clothes.*
penchant FORMAL *He had a penchant for playing jokes on people.*
See also **style**

tasteless

▷ ADJECTIVE

1 having little flavour: *The fish was overcooked and tasteless.*
bland *It tasted bland, like warmed cardboard.*
insipid *a rather insipid meal*
ANTONYM **tasty**
2 vulgar and unattractive: *a house crammed with tasteless ornaments*
flashy *a flashy sports car*
garish *garish bright red boots*
gaudy *his gaudy floral tie*
tacky INFORMAL *a collection of tacky souvenirs*
tawdry *tawdry jewellery*
vulgar *a vulgar display of dreadful paintings*
ANTONYM **tasteful**
See also **crude, flashy, vulgar**

tasty

▷ ADJECTIVE

having a pleasant flavour: *The food was very tasty.*
appetizing *a choice of appetizing dishes*
delicious *a wide selection of delicious desserts*
luscious *luscious fruit*
palatable *some very palatable wines*
ANTONYM **tasteless**
See also **delicious**

tattered *See* **worn out**

tattoo *See* **parade**

tatty *See* **scruffy, shabby**

taunt *See* **make fun of, tease**

taut *See* **stiff, tense, tight**

tawdry *See* **cheap, tasteless, vulgar**

tax

▷ NOUN

1 money paid to the government: *the tax on new cars*

duty *customs duties*

levy FORMAL *The local government may order a one-time levy to pay for the new sports facility.*

tariff *trade tariffs on cars*

▷ VERB

2 to make heavy demands on someone: *Those kids tax my patience.*

drain *conflicts that drain your energy*

exhaust *She exhausted my patience, and I lost my temper.*

sap *The illness sapped his strength.*

strain *The volume of flights is straining the air traffic control system.*

stretch *The drought is stretching the country's resources to their limits.*

See also **drain, duty, strain**

teach

▷ VERB

to instruct someone on how to do something: *She taught me to read.*

coach *He coached the basketball team.*

drill *He drills the choir to a high standard.*

educate *They were educated at the best schools.*

instruct *He instructed family members in first-aid techniques.*

school *She had been schooled to take over the family business.*

train *They train teachers in counselling skills.*

tutor *She was tutored at home by her parents.*

See also **instruct, lecture, show, train**

teacher

▷ NOUN

someone who teaches something: *a geography teacher*

coach *her drama coach*

guru *a spiritual guru*

instructor *a driving instructor*

lecturer *a lecturer in law*

professor *a professor of economics*

tutor *A tutor was hired to help him prepare for the exam.*

team

▷ NOUN

1 a group of people: *the football team*

band *a band of rebels*

crew *the ship's crew*

gang *a work gang*

group *The students work in groups.*

side *the opposing sides*

squad *the cheerleading squad*

troupe *troupes of travelling actors*

▷ VERB

2 to work together: *A friend suggested that we team up for a working vacation.*

collaborate *The two men met and agreed to collaborate.*

co-operate *Both countries are co-operating in the prevention of crime.*

join forces *The groups joined forces to fight against the ban.*

link up *the first time the two armies have linked up*

pair up *They paired up for the dance competition.*

unite *The two charities united their fundraising efforts.*

work together *We have always wanted to work together.*

See also **party, side, staff**

teammate *See* **partner**

tear

▷ NOUN

1 a hole or rip in something: *a tear in the curtains*

hole *the hole in my shoe*

rip *the rip in her new jacket*

rupture *a rupture in the valve*

scratch *I pointed to a number of scratches in the tile floor.*

split *the split in his trousers*

▷ VERB

2 to make a hole in something: *She nearly tore my jacket.*

rip *I tried not to rip the paper.*

rupture *a ruptured appendix*

scratch *Knives will scratch the surface of the counter.*

shred *They may be shredding documents.*

split *I split my trousers.*

▷ VERB

3 to go somewhere in a hurry: *He tore through busy streets in a high-speed chase.*

charge *He charged through the door.*

dart *She darted across the deserted street.*

dash *He dashed upstairs.*

fly *He flew to the store to get some dessert.*

race *He raced across town.*

shoot *The car shot out of the driveway.*
speed *The truck sped past several cars.*
zoom *We zoomed through the gallery.*
See also **dash, fly, hole, race, speed, split**

tease
▷ VERB
to make fun of someone: *He used to tease me about wanting to act.*
make fun of *He knows how to make fun of himself.*
mock *Don't mock me!*
needle INFORMAL *He used to enjoy needling people.*
taunt *They taunted him about his clothes.*
See also **bully, joke, pick on, provoke**

technique *See* **method, style, system, way**

tedious *See* **boring, dreary, dull**

tedium *See* **boredom**

teem *See* **crawl, rain**

tell
▷ VERB
1 to let someone know something: *They told us the dreadful news.*
advise *We advised them of our arrival time.*
inform *I was informed by e-mail that the job had been filled.*
notify *We have notified the police.*
2 to give someone an order: *A passerby told the driver to move his car.*
command *He commanded his troops to attack.*
direct *They have been directed to give special attention to the problem.*
instruct *The family has instructed their lawyer to sue the company.*
order *He ordered the soldiers to cease firing.*
3 to judge something correctly: *I could tell he was scared.*
discern *It was hard to discern why this was happening.*
see *I could see she was lonely.*
See also **announce, distinguish, inform, instruct, notify**

INFORMALLY SPEAKING

tell it like it is: tell the plain truth
tell me about it: I have experienced exactly what you mean
you're telling me: I agree completely

tell a lie *See* **lie**

tell apart *See* **distinguish**

tell off *See* **scold**

tell on *See* **inform on**

tell the difference *See* **distinguish**

telling *See* **convincing, powerful**

temper *See* **humour, moderate, mood**

temperament *See* **character**

temperamental *See* **moody**

temperate *See* **mild**

template *See* **pattern**

tempo *See* **rate, rhythm**

temporary
▷ ADJECTIVE
lasting a short time: *a temporary loss of memory*
ephemeral *summer's ephemeral pleasures*
fleeting *a fleeting glimpse*
interim *an interim measure*
momentary *a momentary lapse*
passing *a passing phase*
provisional *a provisional coalition government*
transient *the transient career of a pop singer*
transitory *the transitory nature of celebrity and fame*
ANTONYM **permanent**

tempt
▷ VERB
to persuade someone to do something: *Don't tempt me to eat anything else.*
entice *She resisted attempts to entice her into politics.*
lure *The company aims to lure travellers to the Amazon.*
seduce *We are seduced into buying all these items.*
See also **attract, lure**

temptation *See* **bait, lure**

tenacious *See* **determined, stubborn**

tenacity *See* **determination, resolve**

T

tend
▷ VERB
1 to happen usually or often: *I tend to forget things.*
be apt *She was apt to raise her voice.*
be inclined *He was inclined to self-pity.*
be liable *equipment that is liable to break*
be prone *He is prone to certain illnesses.*
have a tendency *Woollen sweaters have a tendency to be annoyingly itchy.*
2 to look after someone or something: *the way we tend our cattle*
care for *They hired a nurse to care for her.*

look after *I love looking after the children.*
nurse *They nursed me back to health.*
take care of *There was no one else to take care of the animals.*
See also **look after, take care of**

tendency

▷ *NOUN*
behaviour that happens very often: *a tendency to be critical*
inclination *his artistic inclinations*
leaning *their conservative leanings*
propensity *his propensity for getting into mischief*

tender

▷ *ADJECTIVE*
1 showing gentle and caring feelings: *tender loving care*
affectionate *She gave him an affectionate smile.*
caring *He is a lovely boy, and very caring.*
compassionate *a warm and compassionate person*
gentle *a voice that was gentle and consoling*
kind *She is warmhearted and kind to everyone and everything.*
loving *He was a most loving husband and father.*
sensitive *He was always so sensitive.*
warm *a very warm person*
ANTONYM **tough**
2 painful and sore: *My stomach felt very tender.*
aching *The weary hikers soothed their aching feet in the river.*
bruised *bruised legs*
inflamed *Her eyes were inflamed.*
painful *Her glands were swollen and painful.*
raw *His skin was raw from the rope burn.*
sensitive *Ouch! I'm sorry, my lip is still a bit sensitive.*
sore *My chest is still sore from the surgery.*
▷ *VERB*
3 to offer something, such as an apology or resignation: *She tendered her resignation from the job.*
hand in *All the committee members have handed in their resignation.*
offer *May I offer my sincere apologies?*
▷ *NOUN*
4 a proposal to provide something at a price: *Builders will be asked to submit a tender for the work.*
bid *London's successful bid for the 2012 Olympic Games*
estimate *The carpenter is preparing an estimate for the work.*

package *We opted for the package offered by our service provider.*
submission *A written submission has to be prepared.*
See also **affectionate, compassionate, gentle, loving, offer, painful, romantic, sore, submit**

tenet *See* **belief**

tense

▷ *ADJECTIVE*
1 nervous and unable to relax: *Never had she seen him so tense.*
anxious *She had become very anxious and alarmed.*
edgy *She was nervous and edgy, waiting for the phone call.*
jittery *Investors have become jittery about the country's economy.*
jumpy *I told myself not to be so jumpy.*
nervous *It has made me very nervous about going out.*
uptight INFORMAL *I never get uptight about exams.*
ANTONYM **calm**
2 causing anxiety: *the tense atmosphere during the last moments of the game*
anxious *They had to wait ten anxious days.*
nerve-racking *There's nothing more nerve-racking than the tryouts.*
stressful *a stressful job*
3 having tight muscles: *jaw muscles tense with anger*
rigid *He went rigid whenever he saw a dog.*
strained *His shoulders were strained with effort.*
taut *when muscles are taut or cold*
tight *It is better to stretch the tight muscles first.*
ANTONYM **relaxed**
See also **nervous, tight**

tension *See* **strain, stress**

tentative *See* **cautious**

tenure *See* **possession**

tepid *See* **warm**

term

▷ *NOUN*
1 a fixed period of time: *Her term as president of the student council was about to end.*
period *for a limited period only*
session *The parliamentary session was a success.*
spell *After a short spell in the Vancouver office, she returned home.*
stretch *He did an 18-month stretch in prison.*

time *He served the time of his contract and then left the company.*

2 a name or word for a particular thing: *the medical term for a heart attack*

designation *Code Blue is the hospital designation for an individual in need of emergency medical care.*

expression *She used some unusual expressions.*

name *The correct name for this condition is bovine spongiform encephalopathy.*

word *The word ginseng comes from the Chinese "Shen-seng."*

See also **expression, length, name, period, stretch**

terminal *See* **fatal**

terminate *See* **end, halt**

termination *See* **conclusion**

termination of employment *See* **sack**

terms
▷ *PLURAL NOUN*
conditions that have been agreed upon: *the terms of the agreement*

conditions *the conditions of their contract*

provisions *the provisions of the North American Free Trade Agreement*

proviso *In her will, she left me the house, with the proviso that it had to stay in the family.*

stipulations *He left, violating the stipulations of his parole.*

See also **condition**

terrain *See* **ground, scenery**

terrible
▷ *ADJECTIVE*
I serious and unpleasant: *a terrible illness*

appalling *an appalling headache*

awful *an awful crime*

desperate *a desperate situation*

dreadful *a dreadful mistake*

frightful *He got himself into a frightful situation.*

horrendous *horrendous injuries*

horrible *a horrible mess*

horrid *What a horrid smell!*

rotten *What rotten luck!*

2 of very poor quality: *That is a truly terrible haircut.*

abysmal *The standard of play was abysmal.*

appalling *Her singing is appalling.*

awful *Jeans look awful on me.*

dire *warnings of a dire situation this summer*

dreadful *My financial situation is dreadful.*

horrible *a horrible meal*

rotten *I think it's a rotten idea.*
ANTONYM **excellent**
See also **awful, dreadful, severe**

terribly *See* **really, very**

terrific *See* **grand**

terrified *See* **frightened**

terrify *See* **frighten, scare**

terrifying *See* **frightening, horrible, scary**

territory
▷ *NOUN*
the land that a person or country controls: *disputed territory*

area *They claim that the entire area belongs to them.*

country *She is an ambassador to a European country.*

district *The schools are in different districts.*

domain *He surveyed his domain from the roof of the castle.*

dominion *The dictator ruled the dominion with an iron hand.*

land *It is private land and does not belong to the government.*

nation *a border dispute between two nations*

province *an agreement between the provinces*

state *member states of the United Nations*

See also **colony, field, habitat, land, region**

terror *See* **fear, horror, panic**

terrorism *See* **violence**

terrorize *See* **frighten, scare**

terse *See* **abrupt, concise, short**

test
▷ *VERB*
I to find out what something is like: *The company is testing a new product.*

assess *The test was to assess aptitude rather than academic achievement.*

check *Check each item for possible damage.*

try *Try the cake.*

try out *The transit system hopes to try out the new buses in September.*

▷ *NOUN*
2 an attempt to test something: *the banning of nuclear tests*

assessment *an assessment of their language skills*

check *regular checks on his blood pressure*

trial *clinical trials*

See also **check, exam, examine, try**

T

testimony See **declaration, proof, statement, tribute**

tether See **tie**

textbook See **book**

textiles See **cloth**

texture
▷ NOUN
the way that something feels: *the bumpy texture of an orange*
consistency *Mix the dough to the right consistency.*
feel *The fabric has a papery feel.*
See also **finish**

thankful See **grateful**

thanks See **credit, gratitude**

thanks to See **by virtue of**

thaw See **melt, warm**

theatrical See **melodramatic**

theft
▷ NOUN
the crime of stealing: *the theft of classified documents*
robbery *The man was serving a sentence for robbery.*
stealing *She was jailed for six months for stealing.*

theme See **message, subject**

theological See **religious**

theory
▷ NOUN
an idea that explains something: *Darwin's theory of evolution*
conjecture *That was a conjecture, not a fact.*
hypothesis *Different hypotheses have been put forward.*
supposition *As with many such suppositions, no one had ever tested it.*

there See **present**

therefore
▷ ADVERB
as a result: *Muscles need lots of fuel and therefore burn lots of calories.*
as a result *I slept in, and, as a result, I was late for school.*
consequently *He's more experienced, and consequently earns a higher salary.*
for that reason *My opponent had never lost a match. For that reason, I was a little nervous.*
hence *These products are all natural, and hence, better for you.*
so *I was worried about her, so I phoned to check how she was.*
thus *They were getting tired, and thus, careless.*

thick
▷ ADJECTIVE
1 measuring a large distance from side to side: *a thick stone wall*
fat *a fat book*
wide *a desk that was almost as wide as the room*
ANTONYM **thin**
2 containing little water: *thick soup*
clotted *clotted blood*
concentrated *a can of concentrated orange juice*
condensed *cans of condensed milk*
ANTONYM **watery**
3 grouped closely together: *thick dark hair*
bristling *a bristling moustache*
dense *a large dense forest*
lush *the lush green meadows*
luxuriant *the luxuriant foliage of Algonquin Park*
ANTONYM **sparse**
See also **broad, dense, dim, slow, stupid**

thicken
▷ VERB
to become thicker: *The clouds thickened.*
clot *The patient's blood refused to clot.*
condense *Water vapour condenses to form clouds.*
congeal *The blood had started to congeal.*
set *as the gelatin starts to set*
ANTONYM **thin**

thief
▷ NOUN
someone who steals something: *a car thief*
burglar *Burglars broke into their home.*
crook *a petty crook*
mugger *after being threatened by a mugger*
pickpocket *Tourists should be wary of pickpockets.*
robber *armed robbers*
shoplifter *The guard followed the shoplifter out of the mall.*
See also **crook**

thin
▷ ADJECTIVE
1 measuring a small distance from side to side: *The material was too thin.*
fine *the fine hairs on your arms*
narrow *a narrow strip of land*
slim *a slim volume of poetry*
ANTONYM **thick**
2 not carrying a lot of fat: *a tall, thin man*
See WORD STUDY **thin**

WORD STUDY: THIN

Some words that you might use to describe someone who is **thin** are complimentary, some are neutral, and others are definitely uncomplimentary.

• A **slender** person is attractively thin and graceful.
He was standing beside a tall, **slender** woman in a straw hat.

• A **slim** person has an attractively thin and well-shaped body.
My sister is a pretty, **slim** girl with brown eyes.

• A **slight** person has a fairly thin and delicate-looking body.
He is a **slight** figure, and not very tall.

• A **light** person does not weigh very much.
You don't need to be **light** to be a good dancer.

• Someone who is **spare** is tall and not at all fat.
This is a literary word.
She was thin and **spare**, with a sharp, intelligent face.

• If you describe someone as **lean**, you mean that they he or she is thin but looks strong and healthy.
Like many athletes, she was **lean** and muscular.

• If you say someone is **lanky**, you mean

that he or she is tall and thin and moves rather awkwardly.
He had grown into a **lanky** teenager.

• A **skinny** person is extremely thin, in a way that you find unattractive.
This is an informal word.
I don't think these **skinny** supermodels are at all attractive.

• If you say a person is **scraggy** or **scrawny**, you mean that they look unattractive because they are so thin.
The salesperson was a **scraggy**, aggressive-looking woman.
He was a **scrawny** child when he was ten.

• People who are **bony** have very little flesh covering their bones.
A **bony** woman dressed in black sat beside us.

• If someone is **underweight**, they are too thin and therefore not healthy.
Nearly a third of the students were severely **underweight**.

• A person or animal that is **emaciated** is very thin and weak from illness or lack of food.
We watched horrific television pictures of **emaciated** prisoners.

---

3 containing a lot of water: *thin soup*
diluted *a diluted solution of bleach*
runny *a runny, soft cheese*
watery *watery beer*
weak *a cup of weak tea*
See also **narrow, sheer, skinny**

thing
▷ *NOUN*
a physical object: *What's that thing doing here?*
article *household articles*
object *everyday objects such as spoons*
See also **article, complex, item, object, obsession**

INFORMALLY SPEAKING

know a thing or two: be experienced
make a (big) thing (out) of: give too much importance to
make a good thing of: profit from

things
▷ *PLURAL NOUN*
someone's clothes or belongings: *She told him to take all his things with him.*
belongings *He was identified only by his personal belongings.*
effects *His daughters were collecting his effects.*
gear *They helped us put our gear back into the van.*
possessions *People had lost all their possessions.*
stuff *Where have you put all your stuff?*
See also **possessions, stuff**

think
▷ *VERB*
1 to consider something: *Let's think what we can do next.*
consider *The principal is being asked to consider the plan.*

T

contemplate *He spent part of the summer contemplating his future.*

deliberate *She deliberated over the decision for a good few weeks.*

meditate *He meditated on the problem.*

mull over *I'll leave you alone so you can mull it over.*

muse *Perhaps, he mused, he should follow my advice.*

ponder *I'm continually pondering how to improve the team.*

reflect *I reflected on the child's future.*

2 to believe something: *I think you're the best rower on the team.*

believe *Experts believe that the drought will be extensive.*

consider *She considers it the worst concert she ever attended.*

deem *All applicants deemed qualified will be interviewed for the job.*

hold *The theory holds that minor events are the trigger for larger events.*

imagine *I imagine he was just showing off.*

judge *She judged that this was the moment to say what had to be said.*

reckon *She reckoned that it must be about three o'clock.*

See also **assume, consider, expect, feel, guess, ponder, reckon, suppose**

think about *See* **consider, contemplate**

think of *See* **contemplate, regard**

thinking *See* **thought**

thin-skinned *See* **sensitive**

thirst *See* **longing, wish**

thorough
▷ ADJECTIVE
careful and complete: *a thorough examination*

complete *a complete overhaul of the car}s engine*

comprehensive *a comprehensive guide to the region*

exhaustive *exhaustive inquiries*

full *He gave a full account of the opening ceremony of the Assembly of First Nations.*

intensive *four weeks of intensive study*

meticulous *A successful school trip requires meticulous planning.*

painstaking *a painstaking search*

scrupulous *Observe scrupulous hygiene when preparing food.*

See also **absolute, careful, complete, full, utter**

thoroughly *See* **well**

though *See* **but, in spite of**

thought
▷ NOUN

1 an idea or opinion: *his thoughts on love*

idea *her ideas about democracy*

notion *We each have a notion of what kind of person we'd like to be.*

opinion *most of those who expressed an opinion*

view *I expressed my views in a letter to the editor.*

2 the activity of thinking: *After much thought I decided to become a teacher.*

consideration *There should be careful consideration of the CBC's future role in the country.*

contemplation *He was lost in contemplation of the landscape.*

deliberation *the result of lengthy deliberation*

meditation *He stared at the floor, lost in meditation.*

reflection *after days of reflection*

thinking *This is definitely a time for decisive action and quick thinking.*

See also **consideration**

thoughtful
▷ ADJECTIVE

1 quiet and serious: *She was looking very thoughtful.*

contemplative *a quiet, contemplative sort of chap*

pensive *He looked unusually pensive before the start of the race.*

reflective *I walked on in a reflective mood.*

2 showing consideration for others: *a thoughtful and caring man*

attentive *an attentive social worker*

caring *a caring son*

considerate *the most considerate person I've ever known*

kind *She is warmhearted and kind to everyone.*

ANTONYM **thoughtless**
See also **humane, kind**

thoughtless
▷ ADJECTIVE
showing a lack of consideration: *It was thoughtless of her to mention it.*

insensitive *My friend is surprisingly insensitive about my problem.*

tactless *a tactless remark*
See also **irresponsible, unkind**

thrash *See* **beat**

threadbare *See* **shabby, worn out**

threat

▷ NOUN

1 a statement that someone will harm you: *death threats*
menace *They were charged with demanding money with menace.*
threatening remark *He was overheard making threatening remarks to his neighbours.*
2 something that seems likely to harm you: *the threat of tropical storms*
hazard *a health hazard*
menace *a menace to the public*
risk *a fire risk*
See also **danger**

threaten

▷ VERB

1 to promise to do something bad: *He threatened to reveal the secret.*
make threats to *despite all the threats he'd made to harm them*
menace *prisoners being menaced with guard dogs*
2 to be likely to cause harm: *The new department store is threatening the business of the smaller shops.*
endanger *Toxic waste could endanger lives.*
jeopardize *He has jeopardized the future of our club.*
put at risk *putting patients at risk*
put in jeopardy *A series of setbacks has put the whole project in jeopardy.*
See also **endanger**

threatening See ominous, sinister

threatening remark See threat

thrift See economy

thrifty

▷ ADJECTIVE

careful not to waste money or resources: *thrifty shoppers*
careful *They are very careful with their money.*
economical *a very economical way to travel*
frugal *a frugal lifestyle*
prudent *the need for a much more prudent use of energy*
See also **economical**

thrill

▷ NOUN

1 a feeling of excitement: *the thrill of the game*
high INFORMAL *the high of a win and the low of a loss*
kick INFORMAL *I got a kick out of seeing my name in print.*

▷ VERB

2 to cause a feeling of excitement: *It thrilled me to see her looking so happy.*
excite *It's a project that really excites me.*
give a kick INFORMAL *It gave me a kick to actually meet her.*
See also **delight, excite, excitement**

thrilled See excited

thrilling See exciting

thrive

▷ VERB

to be successful: *His company continues to thrive.*
do well *They both did well at school.*
flourish *The plants are flourishing on the balcony.*
prosper *The business prospered, although the overall economy was poor.*
See also **flourish, succeed**

thriving See successful

throng See crowd, jam, mass

throw

▷ VERB

to make something move through the air: *throwing a tennis ball against a wall*
cast *He cast the stone away.*
chuck *He chucked the paper in the garbage.*
fling *She flung her shoes into the corner.*
hurl *children hurling snowballs*
lob *They lobbed a grenade in the direction of the enemy.*
pitch *She pitched the empty bottle into the car.*
sling *He took off his sweater and slung it into the back seat.*
toss *She tossed her suitcase onto the bed and kicked off her shoes.*

INFORMALLY SPEAKING

throw cold water on: discourage
throw in: add as a bonus
throw off: produce something in a casual way
throw up: vomit
throw yourself into: do enthusiastically

throw about See scatter

throw away See discard, dispose of, dump, waste

throw out See discard, dump

thrust See dig, drive, push, stick, stuff

thud See bump

thug

▷ *NOUN*

a very violent person: *a gang of armed thugs*
bandit *robberies carried out by bandits*
hoodlum *A bunch of hoodlums showed up in our quiet neighbourhood.*
hooligan *severe measures against soccer hooligans*
tough *The neighbourhood toughs beat them both up.*

thump *See* **bang, blow, bump**

thunderous *See* **loud**

thus *See* **therefore**

thwart *See* **block, dash, foil, frustrate, prevent**

ticket *See* **label, pass**

tide *See* **current, flow**

tidings *See* **news**

tidy

▷ *ADJECTIVE*

I arranged in an orderly way: *a tidy desk*
neat *She put her clothes in a neat pile.*
orderly *a beautiful, clean, and orderly city*
ANTONYM **untidy**

▷ *VERB*

2 to make something neat: *He tidied the garage.*
spruce up *Many buildings have been spruced up.*
straighten *straightening cushions and organizing magazines*
ANTONYM **mess up**
See also **neat, orderly**

tie

▷ *VERB*

I to fasten something: *They tied the ends of the bag securely.*
bind *Bind the twigs with twine.*
fasten *instructions on how to fasten the strap to the box*
knot *He knotted his tie.*
lash *The shelter is built by lashing poles together.*
rope *The climbers were roped together.*
secure *Secure the tent to the poles.*
tether *tethering his horse to a tree*
truss *He stuffed the turkey before trussing it.*
ANTONYM **untie**

▷ *NOUN*

2 a contest having the same score: *The game ended in a tie.*
dead heat *The two horses finished the race in a dead heat.*

deadlock *The game ended in a deadlock after being called on account of darkness.*
draw *It was the first time that a scoreless draw occurred.*
3 a connection with something: *I have very close ties with their family.*
affiliation *They asked what her political affiliations were.*
affinity *The photographer has a close affinity with the landscape.*
bond *The experience created a special bond between us.*
connection *The police say he had no connection with the crime.*
relationship *family relationships*
See also **association, attach, bond, fasten, join, link**

tie up *See* **secure**

tiff *See* **disagreement, squabble**

tight

▷ *ADJECTIVE*

I fitting closely: *The shoes are too tight.*
constricted *His throat began to feel swollen and constricted.*
cramped *families living in cramped conditions*
snug *a snug black T-shirt*
ANTONYM **loose**
2 firmly fastened: *a tight knot*
firm *He managed to get a firm grip on the slippery rope.*
secure *Check that your PC connection is secure.*
3 not slack or relaxed: *Pull the rope tight to make a knot.*
rigid *I went rigid with shock.*
taut *The clothesline is pulled taut and secured.*
tense *A bath can relax tense muscles.*
ANTONYM **slack**
See also **mean, secure, tense**

tight spot *See* **hole, predicament**

tightly *See* **fast**

till *See* **dig**

tilt

▷ *VERB*

I to raise one end of something: *He tilted his chair back on two legs.*
incline *She inclined her head.*
lean *Lean the plants against a wall.*
slant *The old floor slanted down to the right.*
slope *The path sloped down to the river.*
tip *She had to tip her head back to see him.*

▷ *NOUN*

2 a raised position: *the tilt of the earth's axis*
angle *The boat is now leaning at a*

dangerous angle.
gradient *a steep gradient*
incline *at the edge of a steep incline*
slant *The house is on a slant.*
slope *The room must have been on a slope.*

time
▷ *NOUN*
1 a particular period: *I enjoyed my time in New Brunswick.*
interval *a long interval of silence*
period *a period of calm*
spell *a brief spell teaching*
stretch *an 18-month stretch in the Canadian Forces*
while *They walked on in silence for a while.*
▷ *VERB*
2 to plan when something will happen: *We had timed our visit for the school break.*
schedule *The space shuttle had been scheduled to blast off at 04:38.*
set *A court hearing has been set for December 16.*
See also **beat, chance, life, moment, occasion, period, rhythm, space, stretch, term**

time off *See* **holiday, leave, leisure**

timely *See* **lucky**

timetable *See* **program**

timid
▷ *ADJECTIVE*
lacking courage or confidence: *a timid kitten*
bashful *Offstage, he is bashful and awkward.*
cowardly *I was too cowardly to complain.*
diffident *She was diffident and reserved.*
nervous *a very nervous person*
shy *a shy, quiet-spoken child*
ANTONYM **bold**
See also **meek, shy**

tinge *See* **trace**

tint *See* **colour**

tiny
▷ *ADJECTIVE*
very small: *The living room is tiny.*
diminutive *a diminutive figure standing at the entrance*
microscopic *a microscopic amount of the substance*
miniature *He looked like a miniature version of his older brother.*
minute *Only a minute amount is needed.*
negligible *The pay increase was negligible.*
ANTONYM **huge**
See also **minute**

tip *See* **hint, point, tilt**

tip over *See* **overturn**

tipple *See* **drink**

tipsy *See* **drunk**

tiptoe *See* **steal**

tire
▷ *VERB*
to use a lot of energy: *Early-morning practice sessions often tire me.*
drain *The events of the last few days have drained me.*
exhaust *Walking in the deep snow had exhausted her.*
fatigue *He is easily fatigued.*
See also **wear out**

tire out *See* **exhaust**

tired
▷ *ADJECTIVE*
having little energy: *I'm too tired to go out tonight.*
drained *I felt drained after last night's performance.*
drowsy *He felt pleasantly drowsy.*
exhausted *I was too exhausted and distressed to talk.*
fatigued *The humidity can leave you feeling fatigued.*
sleepy *I was beginning to feel sleepy.*
tuckered out INFORMAL *You must be tuckered out after that bus trip.*
weary *a weary traveller*
worn out *He's just worn out after the drive.*
See also **sick of, bored, hackneyed, weary, worn out**

tireless *See* **energetic, industrious**

tiresome *See* **boring**

titillate *See* **excite**

title *See* **book, name**

title holder *See* **champion**

titter *See* **laugh**

toast *See* **cook**

today's *See* **current**

toddler *See* **child**

to-do *See* **fuss**

together
▷ *ADVERB*
1 with other people: *We went on long bicycle rides together.*
collectively *The Cabinet is collectively responsible for government policy.*
en masse *The people marched en masse.*
in unison *My grandparents nodded in unison.*

T

jointly *an agency jointly run by the two provinces*

shoulder to shoulder *They fought shoulder to shoulder against a common enemy.*

side by side *They live side by side in harmony.*

2 at the same time: *Three horses crossed the finish line together.*

as one *The crowd of people in the stadium rose as one.*

at once *You can't do two things at once.*

concurrently *There were three races running concurrently.*

simultaneously *They arrived almost simultaneously.*

with one accord *With one accord, they turned and walked back.*

toil *See* **labour, struggle, work**

token *See* **sign, symbol**

tolerable

▷ *ADJECTIVE*

I able to be tolerated: *The pain was tolerable.*

acceptable *a mutually acceptable new contract*

bearable *A cool breeze made the heat bearable.*

ANTONYM **unbearable**

2 fairly satisfactory: *a tolerable salary*

acceptable *We've made an acceptable start.*

adequate *The level of service was adequate.*

OK INFORMAL *For a restaurant like this, the prices are OK.*

passable *passable Italian*

reasonable *able to make a reasonable living from his writing*

so-so *Their lunch was only so-so.*

See also **acceptable, decent**

tolerance *See* **patience**

tolerant

▷ *ADJECTIVE*

accepting of different views and behaviour: *a tolerant society*

broad-minded *a very fair and broad-minded person*

liberal *She is known to have liberal views on many subjects.*

open-minded *I am very open-minded about that question.*

understanding *Fortunately for him, he had an understanding family.*

ANTONYM **narrow-minded**

tolerate

▷ *VERB*

I to accept something you disagree with: *We will not tolerate such behaviour in our classroom.*

accept *Urban dwellers often accept noise as part of city life.*

put up with *You're late again and I won't put up with it.*

2 to accept something unpleasant: *She can no longer tolerate the position that she's in.*

bear *He can't bear to talk about it.*

endure *unable to endure the pain*

stand *He can't stand it when I talk so much.*

See also **allow, bear, put up with**

toll *See* **ring, sound**

tomb

▷ *NOUN*

a burial chamber: *Howard Carter discovered King Tut's tomb.*

grave *They visit the grave twice a year to put flowers on it.*

mausoleum *the elaborate mausoleums of the Paris cemetery*

sarcophagus *an Egyptian sarcophagus*

sepulchre *the ornate lid of the sepulchre*

vault *the family vault*

See also **grave**

tome *See* **book**

tone *See* **note, sound**

tone down *See* **moderate**

tongue *See* **language**

too

▷ *ADVERB*

I also or as well: *You were there too.*

as well *She published historical novels as well.*

besides *Besides, you get to take lots of samples home.*

in addition *There are, in addition, other objections to the plan.*

into the bargain *With a purchase, you also receive a $15 gift card into the bargain.*

likewise *She sat down, and after a moment he did likewise.*

moreover *He didn't know, and moreover, he didn't care.*

2 more than a desirable or acceptable amount: *You've had too many late nights.*

excessively *an excessively long practice session*

over- *I didn't want to seem overeager.*

overly *Most people consider him to be overly ambitious.*

unduly *She's unduly concerned with what people think of her.*

unreasonably *These prices seem unreasonably high to me.*

See also **also**

tool

▷ *NOUN*

a handheld instrument for doing a job: *The best tool for the purpose is a pair of shears.*

implement *knives and other implements*
instrument *instruments for cleaning and polishing teeth*
utensil *cooking utensils*
See also **gadget**

top

▷ *NOUN*

1 the highest part of something: *I waited at the top of the stairs.*
apex *at the very apex of the pyramid*
brow *the brow of the hill*
crest *the crest of the wave*
crown *the crown of the head*
culmination *the culmination of her career*
head *A different name was placed at the head of the chart.*
height *at the height of his success*
high point *the high point of her movie career*
peak *at the peak of the morning rush hour*
pinnacle *the pinnacle of the band's success*
ridge *the east ridge of Mount Logan*
summit *the summit of the mountain*
zenith *His career is now at its zenith.*
ANTONYM **bottom**

2 the lid of a container: *a bottle top*
cap *She unscrewed the cap of her water bottle.*
lid *the lid of the jar*
stopper *an antique crystal bottle stopper*

▷ *ADJECTIVE*

3 being the best of its kind: *She was the top student in physics.*
best *the best table tennis player in the school*
chief *one of the world's chief cancer researchers*
elite *the elite troops of the RCMP*
foremost *the foremost scientist of the century*
head *the head of the committee*
highest *She achieved one of the highest positions in the land.*
lead *She has landed the lead role in a major movie.*
leading *a leading member of the community*
pre-eminent *a pre-eminent political figure*
premier *the country's premier theatre company*
prime *The store will be built in a prime location.*
principal *the principal singer with the opera company*

▷ *VERB*

4 to be greater than something: *The temperature topped 23°C.*

cap *He capped his own record with another breathtaking performance.*
exceed *Its research budget exceeds $700 million a year.*
go beyond *This goes beyond anything I've ever attempted before.*
outstrip *Demand is outstripping supply.*
surpass *to surpass the achievements of previous generations*

5 to be better than someone or something: *You'll never manage to top that story.*
beat *Nothing beats a nice, long bath at the end of a day.*
better *As an account of adolescence, this novel cannot be bettered.*
eclipse *Nothing is going to eclipse winning the Olympic title.*
improve on *We need to improve on our performance against France.*
outdo *rivals trying to outdo each other*
surpass *He was determined to surpass the achievements of his brothers.*
See also **foremost, head, leading, maximum, outdo, peak, prize, successful, supreme**

INFORMALLY SPEAKING

from top to bottom: completely
off the top of your head: without preparation

top up *See* **augment, supplement**

topic *See* **issue, question, subject**

topple *See* **fall, overthrow, overturn**

torment *See* **bully, persecute, pick on**

torpedo *See* **bomb**

torrent *See* **burst, flood**

tortuous *See* **indirect**

torture *See* **ordeal, persecute**

toss *See* **throw**

tot *See* **child**

total

▷ *NOUN*

1 several things added together: *The companies have a total of 550 employees.*
aggregate *three successive defeats by an aggregate of 12 points*
sum *the sum of all the angles*
whole *taken as a percentage of the whole*

▷ *ADJECTIVE*

2 complete in all its parts: *a total failure*
absolute *absolute beginners*
complete *a complete mess*

T

out-and-out *an out-and-out lie*
outright *an outright rejection of the deal*
unconditional *unconditional surrender*
undivided *You have my undivided attention.*
unmitigated *an unmitigated failure*
unqualified *an unqualified success*
utter *utter nonsense*
▷ VERB
3 to reach the sum of: *Their debts totalled over a thousand dollars.*
add up to *Profits can add up to millions of dollars.*
amount to *Spending by tourists in the country amounted to over $45 billion.*
come to *That comes to over a thousand dollars.*
See also **absolute, add, complete, figure, sheer, utter, whole**

totally *See* **quite**

tottering *See* **shaky, unsteady**

touch
▷ VERB
1 to put your hand on something: *Don't touch the screen.*
feel *The doctor felt my head.*
finger *He fingered the few coins in his pocket.*
handle *Please handle the fruit carefully.*
2 to come into contact with: *I lowered my legs until my feet touched the floor.*
brush *Something brushed against her leg.*
graze *A bullet had grazed his arm.*
meet *when the wheels meet the ground*
3 to affect someone emotionally: *I was touched by his kindness.*
affect *I was badly affected by the defeat.*
move *These stories surprised and moved me.*
stir *The story stirred something very deep in me.*
See also **contact, feel, handle, move, note, reach, trace**

touch down *See* **land**

touch on *See* **mention**

touch upon *See* **mention**

touching
▷ ADJECTIVE
causing sadness or sympathy: *a touching tale*
affecting *an affecting memorial to Countess Rachel*
moving *It was a moving moment for all of us.*

poignant *a poignant love story*
See also **moving**

touchy
▷ ADJECTIVE
easily upset: *He's very touchy about that.*
easily offended *viewers who are easily offended*
sensitive *She's very sensitive about that subject.*
See also **sensitive**

tough
▷ ADJECTIVE
1 able to put up with hardship: *She is tough and ambitious.*
hardened *hardened criminals*
hardy *a group of hardy explorers*
resilient *He's resilient and will get over it soon.*
robust *She has an extremely robust constitution*
rugged *rugged individuals who went west searching for gold*
strong *a strong person and a survivor*
2 difficult to break or damage: *an apple with a rather tough skin*
durable *The inside of the computer case is lined in soft, durable material.*
hard-wearing *hard-wearing cotton shirts*
leathery *leathery skin*
resilient *made of resilient plastic material*
robust *very robust machinery*
rugged *You need a rugged, four-wheel-drive vehicle.*
solid *The car feels very solid.*
strong *a strong surface, which won't crack or chip*
sturdy *The camera was mounted on a sturdy tripod.*
ANTONYM **fragile**
3 full of hardship: *a tough childhood*
arduous *an arduous journey*
difficult *We're living in difficult times.*
exacting *an exacting task*
hard *a hard life*
ANTONYM **easy**
See also **hard, rough, stiff, thug**

toughen *See* **strengthen**

tour *See* **journey**

tournament *See* **competition, contest**

tow *See* **drag, pull**

towering *See* **tall**

town *See* **city**

toxic *See* **poisonous**

toxin *See* **poison**

trace

▷ VERB

1 to look for and find something: *Police are trying to trace the owner.*
locate *We've simply been unable to locate him.*
track down *I'm trying to track down that old CD.*

▷ NOUN

2 a sign of something: *No trace of him had been found.*
evidence *He'd seen no evidence of fraud.*
hint *I saw no hint of irony on her face.*
indication *He gave no indication of remorse.*
record *There's no record of any marriage or children.*
sign *I waited for any sign of illness.*
suggestion *a faint suggestion of a smile*
whiff *Not a whiff of scandal has ever tainted his private life.*
3 a small amount of something: *to write without a trace of sensationalism*
dash *a story with a dash of mystery*
drop *a drop of vanilla*
remnant *Beneath the present building were remnants of the original structure's flooring.*
suspicion *large blooms of white with a suspicion of pale pink*
tinge *Could there have been a slight tinge of envy in his voice?*
touch *a touch of the flu*
vestige *the last vestige of a UN force that once numbered 30 000*
See also **draw, lead, note, sign, suggestion**

track *See* **follow, line, path, road**

track down *See* **find, locate, trace**

track record *See* **record**

tract *See* **region, stretch**

trade

▷ NOUN

1 the buying and selling of goods: *foreign trade*
business *a career in business*
commerce *They have made their fortunes from industry and commerce.*
2 the kind of work someone does: *He learned his trade as an apprentice in the plumbing company.*
business *the music business*
line *Are you in the publishing line, too?*
line of work *In my line of work, I often get home late for dinner.*
occupation *her new occupation as an author*
profession *a teacher by profession*

▷ VERB

3 to buy and sell goods: *They had years of experience of trading with China.*
deal *They deal in antiques.*
do business *Don't do business with her.*
traffic *those who traffic in illegal drugs*
See also **business, change, exchange, job, swap**

trade in *See* **sell, stock**

trader

▷ NOUN

someone who trades in goods: *a timber trader*
broker *a financial broker*
dealer *dealers who specialize in sports cards*
merchant *a wine merchant*

trading *See* **business**

tradition

▷ NOUN

a long-standing custom: *the rich traditions of Afro-Cuban music*
convention *It's a social convention that men open doors for women.*
custom *A Canada Day picnic is a family custom.*
See also **convention, custom, habit**

traditional

▷ ADJECTIVE

existing for a long time: *traditional styles of dress*
conventional *conventional rules of grammar*
established *the established rules of the game*
ANTONYM **unconventional**
See also **conservative, conventional**

traffic *See* **trade**

tragedy *See* **disaster, play**

tragic

▷ ADJECTIVE

very sad: *a tragic accident*
distressing *distressing news*
heartbreaking *a heartbreaking succession of miscarriages*
heart-rending *heart-rending pictures of refugees*
See also **sad**

trail *See* **drag, lag, path**

train

▷ VERB

to teach someone how to do something: *We train them in bricklaying.*
coach *She coaches the basketball team.*

T

drill *He drills the band to a high standard.*
educate *I was educated in Ontario.*
instruct *All their members are instructed in first aid.*
school *They have been schooled to take over the family business.*
teach *This is something they teach us to do in our first year of high school.*
tutor *She tutored children at her home.*
See also **instruct, practise, teach**

trained *See* **skilled**

trainee *See* **beginner, recruit**

training *See* **education, exercise, experience, practice**

trait *See* **attribute, characteristic, point, property, quality**

trajectory *See* **course, curve, line**

trance *See* **dream**

tranquil *See* **calm, peaceful, quiet, still**

tranquility *See* **peace, quiet**

transaction *See* **business**

transfer *See* **transport**

transform
▷ VERB
to change something completely: *This technology has transformed our society.*
alter *New curtains can completely alter the look of a room.*
change *alchemists attempting to change base metals into gold*
convert *They have converted the factory into a restaurant.*
make over *I decided it was time to make over my room.*
reform *He was totally reformed by this experience.*
revolutionize *a device that will revolutionize the way you cook*
See also **change, turn**

transformation *See* **change**

transient *See* **temporary**

transitory *See* **temporary**

translucent *See* **clear, transparent**

transmit *See* **communicate, send**

transparent
▷ ADJECTIVE
able to be seen through: *a sheet of transparent plastic*
clear *a clear glass panel*
crystalline *crystalline lakes*

sheer *a sheer black shirt*
translucent *a translucent wall separating the dining room from the kitchen*
See also **clear**

transport
▷ NOUN
1 the moving of goods and people: *The prices quoted include transport.*
shipment *transported to the docks for shipment overseas*
transit *a good system of public transit*
transportation *the transportation of dangerous goods*
▷ VERB
2 to move people or goods somewhere: *They use tankers to transport the oil.*
carry *The ship could carry 70 passengers.*
convey *Ambulances conveyed them to the hospital.*
ship *the food being shipped overseas*
transfer *She was transferred to another hospital.*
See also **banish, bring, carry, take**

transportation *See* **transport**

trap
▷ NOUN
1 a device for catching animals: *a bear trap*
net *a fishing net*
snare *a snare for catching birds*
▷ VERB
2 to catch animals: *a more humane way to trap the creatures*
catch *an animal caught in a trap*
corner *like a cornered rat*
snare *He'd snared a rabbit earlier in the day.*
3 to trick someone: *Were you trying to trap her into making a confession?*
dupe *a plot to dupe them into buying fakes*
trick *He tricked me into going to that movie.*
See also **catch**

trapping *See* **capture**

trash
▷ NOUN
1 waste material: *They pick up the trash on Mondays.*
garbage *rotting piles of garbage*
refuse *a weekly collection of refuse*
rubbish *They had piled most of their rubbish into plastic containers.*
waste *a law that regulates the disposal of waste*
2 something of poor quality: *Don't read that awful trash.*
garbage INFORMAL *He spends his time watching garbage on TV.*
rubbish *She described her book as absolute rubbish.*

See also **garbage, junk, refuse, rubbish**

trauma *See* **shock**

traumatize *See* **shock**

travel
▷ VERB
to make a journey somewhere: *You had better travel to Ottawa tomorrow.*
go *We went to the Maritimes.*
journey *She intended to journey up the Amazon.*
make your way *He made his way home at last.*
take a trip *We intend to take a trip there sometime.*
See also **go, journey, proceed, spread**

traverse *See* **cross**

treacherous
▷ ADJECTIVE
I likely to betray someone: *He denounced the party's treacherous leaders.*
disloyal *disloyal members of the group*
unfaithful *an unfaithful spouse*
untrustworthy *He has tried to brand his opponents as untrustworthy.*
ANTONYM **loyal**
2 dangerous or unreliable: *treacherous mountain roads*
dangerous *a dangerous stretch of road*
hazardous *hazardous seas*
perilous *The roads grew even steeper and more perilous.*
See also **dangerous, two-faced**

treasure
▷ VERB
to consider something very precious: *We treasure our friendship.*
cherish *The previous owners had cherished the house.*
hold dear *forced to renounce everything he held most dear*
prize *He prizes the gifts his children made.*
value *if you value your health*
See also **appreciate, dear, prize, value**

treasured *See* **beloved, dear**

treasures *See* **valuables**

treat
▷ VERB
I to behave toward someone: *She treated most of us with indifference.*
act toward *the way you act toward other people*
behave toward *He always behaved toward me with great kindness.*
deal with *in dealing with troubled youngsters*

2 to give someone medical care: *the doctor who treated me*
care for *They hired a nurse to care for her.*
nurse *She nursed me back to health.*
See also **luxury**

treatment *See* **cure**

treaty *See* **agreement**

trek *See* **journey, walk**

tremble *See* **shake**

trembling *See* **shaky**

tremendous *See* **enormous, wonderful**

trend *See* **craze, fashion, wave**

trendy
▷ ADJECTIVE
fashionable: *a trendy night club*
fashionable *a very fashionable place to go on vacation*
in *what's in and what's not*
in fashion *That style is no longer in fashion this season.*
in vogue *I can't keep up with what's in vogue at the moment.*
latest *the latest thing in digital cameras*
stylish *This city has become a lot more stylish in recent years.*

trespass *See* **breach, intrude**

trial *See* **case, ordeal, test**

tribulation *See* **difficulty, ordeal**

tribunal *See* **court**

tribute
▷ NOUN
something that shows admiration: *Police paid tribute to her courage.*
accolade *To play for your country is the ultimate accolade.*
compliment *We consider it a compliment to be called "conservative."*
honour *Only two writers were granted the honour of lunch with the prime minister.*
praise *That is high praise indeed.*
testimony *a testimony to her dedication*
See also **honour, praise**

trice *See* **instant, minute**

trick
▷ NOUN
I something that deceives someone: *We are playing a trick on my little brother.*
con INFORMAL *Snacks that offer miraculous weight loss are a con.*
deception *the victim of a cruel deception*
hoax *a cruel hoax*

ploy *a cynical marketing ploy*
ruse *This was a ruse to divide them.*
▷ VERB
2 to deceive someone: *They tricked me into giving them all my money.*
con INFORMAL *We have been conned for 20 years.*
deceive *He deceived me into thinking the money was his.*
dupe *I was duped into letting them in.*
fool *They tried to fool you into coming after us.*
take in *I wasn't taken in for a minute.*
See also **con, deceive, dupe, fool, take in, trap**

INFORMALLY SPEAKING

How's tricks?: How are you?
not miss a trick: be very alert

---

trickery *See* **dishonesty, fraud**

trickle *See* **drip**

tricky
▷ ADJECTIVE
difficult to do or to deal with: *This could be a very tricky problem.*
complex *the whole complex issue of crime and punishment*
complicated *a complicated operation*
delicate *This brings us to the delicate question of his future.*
difficult *It was a difficult decision to make.*
hard *That's a hard question to answer.*
problematic *It's a very problematic piece of music to play.*
puzzling *a puzzling case to solve*
sensitive *The death penalty is a very sensitive issue.*

trifling *See* **insignificant, minor, petty, trivial, worthless**

trigger *See* **start**

trim *See* **border, fit, neat, shorten**

trinket *See* **ornament**

trip
▷ NOUN
1 a journey to a place: *a business trip*
excursion *a three-day excursion to the capital*
jaunt *a jaunt in the car*
journey *the journey to the remote mountain*
outing *a school outing*
voyage *Columbus's voyage to the West Indies*

▷ VERB
2 to fall over: *I tripped on the stairs.*
fall over *Plenty of top skiers fell over.*
lose your footing *He lost his footing and slid into the water.*
stumble *He stumbled and almost fell.*
See also **drive, fall, journey**

trite *See* **corny, hackneyed**

triumph
▷ NOUN
1 a great success: *The championships proved to be a personal triumph for the coach.*
success *The environmental program was a great success.*
victory *a victory for common sense*
ANTONYM **failure**
▷ VERB
2 to be successful: *a symbol of good triumphing over evil*
come out on top INFORMAL *The only way to come out on top is to adopt a different approach.*
prevail *I do hope my ideas will prevail over theirs.*
succeed *They succeeded beyond our expectations.*
win *The top four teams all won.*
ANTONYM **fail**
See also **succeed, success, victory, win**

triumph over *See* **overcome**

trivial
▷ ADJECTIVE
not important: *She doesn't concern herself with such trivial details.*
insignificant *The one criticism is insignificant compared with the movie's overall strengths.*
minor *a minor inconvenience*
negligible *The strike will have a negligible impact.*
paltry *They had no interest in paltry household concerns.*
petty *I wouldn't indulge in such petty and childish pranks.*
slight *It's only a slight problem.*
trifling *The amount involved was trifling.*
unimportant *Too much time is spent discussing unimportant matters.*
ANTONYM **important**
See also **insignificant, minor, petty, slight, unimportant, worthless**

trophy *See* **prize**

trouble
▷ NOUN
1 a difficulty or problem: *financial troubles*
bother *a minor bother, but an annoying one*
difficulty *economic difficulties*

hassle INFORMAL *There was a hassle over who was first in line.*

problem *The main problem is unemployment.*

▷ VERB

2 to make someone feel worried: *He was troubled by his brother's decision.*

agitate *The thought agitates her.*

bother *Is something bothering you?*

disturb *dreams so vivid that they disturb me for days*

worry *I didn't want to worry you.*

3 to cause someone inconvenience: *May I trouble you for some milk?*

bother *I don't know why he bothers me with such silly questions.*

disturb *a room where you won't be disturbed*

impose upon *I was afraid you'd feel we were imposing upon you.*

inconvenience *He promised to be quick so as not to inconvenience them further.*

put out *I've always put myself out for others.*
See also **agitate, bother, burden, care, concern, difficulty, distress, disturb, drawback, effort, hassle, jam, pain, problem, sorrow, worry**

troubled See **anxious, upset, worried**

troublesome See **difficult**

trounce See **defeat, vanquish**

trouncing See **defeat**

troupe See **band, company, team**

truce See **peace**

true

▷ ADJECTIVE

I not invented: *The movie is based on a true story.*

accurate *an accurate assessment of the situation*

correct *a correct diagnosis*

factual *a factual account of the Northwest Rebellion*

ANTONYM **inaccurate**

2 real or genuine: *She was a true friend.*

authentic *authentic Caribbean food*

bona fide *We are happy to donate to bona fide charities.*

genuine *a genuine signed autograph*

real *No, it wasn't a dream. It was real.*

ANTONYM **false**
See also **accurate, actual, authentic, correct, devoted, exact, faithful, loyal, real, realistic, reliable, right, strict, trusty**

truly See **really**

trunk See **box**

truss See **tie**

trust

▷ VERB

to believe that someone will do something: *He can be trusted to honour his promise.*

count on *I can always count on you to cheer me up.*

depend on *You can depend on me.*

have confidence in *We have the utmost confidence in your abilities.*

have faith in *I have no faith in him any more.*

place your trust in *I would never place my trust in someone so immature.*

rely upon *I know I can rely on you to sort it out.*
See also **belief, believe, confidence, depend, faith**

trusting See **gullible**

trustworthy See **honest, reliable, responsible, sure, trusty**

trusty

▷ ADJECTIVE

considered to be reliable: *a trusty member of the crew*

dependable *a dependable and steady worker*

faithful *his faithful black Labrador*

firm *She became a firm friend of the family.*

reliable *the problem of finding reliable staff*

solid *one of my most solid supporters*

staunch *He proved himself a staunch ally.*

true *a true friend*

trustworthy *trying to find a trustworthy adviser*
See also **loyal**

truth

▷ NOUN

the facts about something: *I'm keen to get to the truth of what happened.*

fact *How much was fact and how much was fiction no one knew.*

reality *Fiction and reality were increasingly blurred.*
See also **fact, reality**

truthful See **candid, honest**

try

▷ VERB

I to make an effort to do something: *I tried hard to persuade him to stay.*

attempt *He attempted to swim all the Great Lakes.*

endeavour FORMAL *I will endeavour to arrange it.*

make an attempt *She made three attempts to break the record.*

make an effort *He made no effort to hide his disappointment.*

seek *We have never sought to impose our views.*

strive *The school strives to treat students as individuals.*

2 to test the quality of something: *He wanted me to try the cake.*

check out INFORMAL *We went to the club to check it out.*

sample *We sampled a selection of different bottled waters.*

test *The lotion was tested on a group of volunteers.*

try out *The transit system hopes to try out the buses in September.*

▷ NOUN

3 an attempt to do something: *After a few tries he pressed the right button.*

attempt *He made a good attempt, but he was no stand-up comedian.*

effort *his efforts to improve*

endeavour *His first endeavours in photography were baby pictures.*

go INFORMAL *She won on her first go.*

shot *I had a shot at playing professional baseball.*

See also **attempt, go, seek, strive, test**

try out See **test, try**

try your hand at See **attempt**

trying See **difficult**

tryst See **meeting**

tuck See **fold**

tuckered out See **tired, weary**

tug
▷ VERB

1 to give something a quick, hard pull: *The puppy tugged at its leash.*

drag *We dragged the toboggan along.*

draw *I took his hand and drew him along.*

haul *I gripped the child's wrist and hauled him up.*

heave *They heaved the last bag into the trunk.*

jerk *He jerked his hand out of mine angrily.*

pluck *The little child plucked at my sleeve.*

pull *The cat pulled at the ball of yarn.*

wrench *The horse wrenched its head free.*

yank *He yanked me by the hand.*
▷ NOUN

2 a quick, hard pull: *He felt a tug at his arm.*

heave *With a mighty heave, she wrenched open the door.*

jerk *He gave a sudden jerk of the reins.*

pull *Give the cord three sharp pulls.*

wrench *He lowered the flag with a quick wrench.*

yank *He gave the wheel a yank to the right.*
See also **pull**

tuition See **education**

tumble See **drop**

tummy See **stomach**

tumour See **boil**

tumultuous See **noisy**

tune
▷ NOUN
a series of musical notes: *She was humming a merry little tune.*

melody *a beautiful melody*

strains *She could hear the strains of the chamber orchestra.*

tuneful See **sweet**

tunnel See **dig**

turbulent See **violent, wild**

turmoil See **disorder, mess**

turn
▷ VERB

1 to change the direction or position of something: *She had turned the chair to face the door.*

rotate *Take each foot in both your hands and rotate it.*

spin *He spun the wheel sharply and made a U-turn.*

swivel *She swivelled her chair around.*

twirl *I twirled the empty glass in my fingers.*

twist *She twisted her head sideways.*

2 to become or make something different: *A hobby can be turned into a career.*

change *She has changed into a self-confident woman.*

convert *a bed that converts into a sofa*

mutate *Overnight, the gossip begins to mutate into headlines.*

transform *the speed at which your body transforms food into energy*
▷ NOUN

3 someone's right or duty to do something: *Tonight it's my turn to cook.*

chance *All eligible people would get a chance to vote.*

go INFORMAL *Whose go is it?*

opportunity *Now is your opportunity to say what you've always wanted.*

See also **bend, curve, get, grow, spin, swerve**

turn back See **return**

turn down See **decline, refuse, reject**

turn out See **work out**

turn red See **blush**

turn under See **fold**

turn up See **appear, come, find**

tutor See **adviser, instruct, teach, teacher, train**

tutoring See **lesson**

twice See **double**

twig See **stick**

twin See **double**

twine See **coil, twist**

twinge See **pain**

twinkle See **flash, sparkle**

twirl See **turn**

twist
▷ *VERB*
1 to turn something around: *I twisted the light bulb into the socket.*
bend *Bend the bar into a horseshoe.*
curl *She sat with her legs curled under her.*
twine *She twined her arms around the child and helped him up.*
weave *He weaves his way through a crowd.*
wring out *Wring out the washcloth.*
2 to bend into a new shape: *The truck sat in the intersection with a broken headlight and a twisted fender.*
distort *A painter may exaggerate or distort shapes and forms.*
mangle *the mangled wreckage*
screw up *The child screwed up his face and began to cry.*
3 to injure a part of your body: *I've twisted my ankle.*
sprain *He fell and sprained his wrist.*
wrench *He had wrenched his back badly from the force of the fall.*
See also **bend, coil, misrepresent, tangle, turn**

twisted See **crooked**

twit See **idiot**

twitch See **fidget**

two-faced
▷ *ADJECTIVE*
not honest in dealing with other people: *a two-faced, manipulative person*
deceitful *a deceitful, conniving liar*
dishonest *She's been dishonest in her dealings with us both.*

disloyal *I can't stand people who are disloyal.*
false *He was betrayed by his false friends.*
hypocritical *a hypocritical and ambitious liar*
insincere *They are still widely seen as insincere and untrustworthy.*
treacherous *She has been consistently treacherous to both sides.*
See also **insincere**

twofold See **double**

two-timing See **unfaithful**

type
▷ *NOUN*
a group of things that have features in common: *There are various types of dogs suitable as pets.*
brand *his favourite brand of orange juice*
breed *a rare breed of cattle*
class *a better class of restaurant*
group *Weather forecasters classify clouds into several different groups.*
kind *I don't like that kind of movie.*
make *He'll drive only a certain make of car.*
sort *a dozen trees of various sorts*
species *a rare species of moth*
style *Several styles of hats were available.*
variety *Many varieties of birds live here.*
See also **breed, category, class, form, kind, sort, variety**

typical
▷ *ADJECTIVE*
having the usual characteristics of something: *a typical Winnipeg winter*
average *The average adult burns 100 calories while walking for 20 minutes.*
characteristic *a characteristic feature of the landscape*
normal *a normal day*
regular *He describes himself as just a regular guy.*
representative *fairly representative groups of adults*
standard *It was standard practice in cases like this.*
stock *She had a stock answer for all problems.*
usual *The buffet included all the usual dishes.*
ANTONYM **uncharacteristic**
See also **average, characteristic, natural, normal, regular, representative, routine, stock**

typically See **on average**

tyrannical See **absolute**

tyranny See **oppression**

T

Uu

ugly

▷ ADJECTIVE

having a very unattractive appearance: *an ugly expression on his face*

unattractive *painted in an unattractive shade of green*

unsightly *The view was spoiled by some unsightly houses.*

ANTONYM **beautiful**

ultimate

▷ ADJECTIVE

1 being the final one of a series: *It is not possible to predict the ultimate results.*

eventual *Winning the nationals is our eventual goal.*

final *the fifth and final day*

last *I'll give you one last chance.*

2 the most important or powerful: *the ultimate goal of any player*

greatest *Our greatest aim was to take the gold medal.*

paramount *His paramount ambition was to be an actor.*

supreme *the supreme test of her abilities*

utmost *This has to be our utmost priority.*

▷ NOUN

3 the finest example of something: *This hotel is the ultimate in luxury.*

epitome *She was the epitome of the successful executive.*

extreme *This was shyness taken to the extreme.*

height *the height of bad manners*

peak *roses at the peak of their perfection*

See also **extreme, final, last, limit, supreme**

umpire See **judge**

umpteen See **many**

unabashed See **shameless**

unable See **incompetent**

unacceptable See **unbearable, unsatisfactory, unsuitable**

unaccustomed See **inexperienced**

unadventurous See **conventional**

unaffected See **immune, natural, real**

unaided See **independent, on your own**

unappreciative See **ungrateful**

unashamed See **shameless**

unassuming See **humble, meek, modest**

unattached See **single**

unattractive See **ugly**

unavoidable See **necessary**

unaware

▷ ADJECTIVE

not knowing about something: *Many people are unaware of how much they eat.*

ignorant *They are completely ignorant of the relevant facts.*

oblivious *They appeared oblivious to their surroundings.*

unconscious *totally unconscious of my presence*

unsuspecting *The stolen bicycles were then sold to unsuspecting buyers.*

ANTONYM **aware**

See also **ignorant, unconscious**

unbearable

▷ ADJECTIVE

too unpleasant to be tolerated: *Life was unbearable for the victims of the earthquake.*

intolerable *The heat and humidity were intolerable.*

oppressive *An oppressive sadness weighed upon me.*

unacceptable *I left my job because of my boss's unacceptable behaviour.*

ANTONYM **tolerable**

unbeatable See **invincible**

unbelievable

▷ ADJECTIVE

1 extremely great or surprising: *He showed unbelievable courage.*

colossal *There has been a colossal mistake.*

incredible *You're always an incredible help on these occasions.*

stupendous *It cost a stupendous amount of money.*

2 so unlikely it cannot be believed: *He came up with some unbelievable story.*

implausible *a movie with an implausible ending*

improbable *highly improbable claims*

inconceivable *It was inconceivable that he'd hurt anyone.*

incredible *It seems incredible that anyone would want to do that.*

preposterous *The whole idea was preposterous.*

unconvincing *In response, he was given the usual unconvincing excuses.*

ANTONYM **believable**

See also **improbable, incredible, unlikely**

uncalled-for See **unnecessary**

uncanny *See* **spooky**

uncertain
▷ ADJECTIVE
I not knowing what to do: *For a moment he looked uncertain as to how to respond.*
doubtful *He was a bit doubtful about the weather.*
dubious *We were a bit dubious about the plan at first.*
unclear *I'm unclear about where to go.*
undecided *Even then, she was still undecided about her future plans.*
ANTONYM **certain**
2 not definite: *facing an uncertain future*
ambiguous *The wording of the contract was ambiguous.*
doubtful *The outcome of the game is still doubtful.*
indefinite *suspended for an indefinite period*
indeterminate *a man of indeterminate age*
ANTONYM **certain**
See also **doubtful, vague**

uncertainty *See* **doubt**

unchanging *See* **eternal**

unclean *See* **dirty**

unclear
▷ ADJECTIVE
confusing and not obvious: *It is unclear how much support they have.*
ambiguous *in order to clarify the earlier ambiguous statement*
confused *The situation remains confused, as no clear winner has emerged.*
vague *The description was pretty vague.*
ANTONYM **clear**
See also **uncertain, vague**

unclothed *See* **naked**

uncomfortable
▷ ADJECTIVE
I feeling or causing discomfort: *an uncomfortable bed*
awkward *Its shape made it awkward to carry.*
cramped *living in very cramped conditions*
disagreeable *designed to make flying a less disagreeable experience*
ill-fitting *Walking was difficult because of her ill-fitting shoes.*
painful *a painful back injury*
ANTONYM **comfortable**
2 not relaxed or confident: *Talking about money made her uncomfortable.*
awkward *Offstage, he is bashful and awkward.*
embarrassed *an embarrassed silence*

ill at ease *I always feel ill at ease in their company.*
self-conscious *She was always self-conscious about her height.*
uneasy *He looked uneasy and refused to answer any more questions.*
ANTONYM **comfortable**

uncommon
▷ ADJECTIVE
I not happening or seen often: *This type of weather is uncommon.*
exceptional *These are exceptional circumstances.*
extraordinary *an act of extraordinary generosity*
few *Genuine friends are few.*
infrequent *one of the infrequent visitors to the island*
out of the ordinary *My story is nothing out of the ordinary.*
scarce *places where jobs are scarce*
sparse *Traffic is sparse on this stretch of road.*
rare *a rare occurrence*
unusual *an unusual sight these days*
ANTONYM **common**
2 unusually great: *She had read his last e-mail with uncommon interest.*
acute *He has an acute dislike of animals.*
exceptional *a woman of exceptional beauty*
extraordinary *a young player of extraordinary energy*
extreme *regions suffering from extreme poverty*
great *They share a great love of Elton John's music.*
intense *intense heat*
remarkable *a musician of remarkable talent*
See also **particular, rare, scarce, singular, strange, unusual**

uncomplicated *See* **simple, straightforward**

unconcern *See* **neglect**

unconcerned *See* **uninterested**

unconditional *See* **total**

unconnected *See* **separate**

unconscious
▷ ADJECTIVE
I in a state similar to sleep: *By the time the ambulance arrived, he was unconscious.*
asleep *They were fast asleep in their beds.*
senseless *beaten senseless and robbed*
stunned *stunned by a blow to the head*

ANTONYM **conscious**

2 not aware of what is happening: *quite unconscious of their presence*
oblivious *She seemed oblivious of her surroundings.*
unaware *He was unaware of the chaos he was causing.*
unknowing *unknowing accomplices in his crimes*
unsuspecting *an unsuspecting victim of his deceit*
ANTONYM **aware**
See also **ignorant, unaware**

uncontaminated See **clean**

uncontrolled See **wild**

unconventional See **unusual**

unconvinced See **dubious**

unconvincing See **lame, unbelievable, unlikely**

uncoordinated See **clumsy**

uncouth See **vulgar**

uncover
▷ VERB
1 to find something out: *Teachers had uncovered evidence of cheating.*
bring to light *The truth is unlikely to be brought to light.*
expose *His lies were exposed in court.*
reveal *She will reveal the truth behind the scandal.*
show up *His true character has been shown up for what it is.*
unearth *determined to unearth the truth about him*
2 to remove the lid or cover from something: *Uncover the pot and drain the vegetables.*
expose *The wreck was exposed by the action of the tide.*
lay bare *Remains of an ancient building have been laid bare by archaeologists.*
open *I opened the jar of pickles.*
reveal *He revealed the contents of a mysterious box.*
unearth *Quarry workers have unearthed the skeleton of a mammoth.*
unveil *The statue will be unveiled next week.*
unwrap *unwrapping birthday presents*
See also **expose, open, reveal**

uncovered See **bare, open**

uncultivated See **wild**

uncut See **whole**

undecided See **dubious, uncertain**

undeniable See **certain, sure**

undeniably See **certainly**

under
▷ PREPOSITION
at a lower level than something: *a labyrinth of tunnels under the ground*
below *The sun had already sunk below the horizon.*
beneath *the frozen grass crunching beneath his feet*
underneath *Rescue crews freed the people trapped underneath the wreckage.*
ANTONYM **above**
See also **below**

under par See **sick**

under the weather See **sick**

undercover See **secret**

underfed See **skinny**

undergo
▷ VERB
to have something happen to you: *He had to undergo major surgery.*
be subjected to *She was subjected to constant interruptions.*
endure *The team endured a string of losses.*
experience *They seem to experience more problems than other people.*
go through *I wouldn't like to go through that again.*
suffer *The peace process had suffered a serious setback.*
See also **experience, feel, go through, have, receive, suffer**

underground See **secret**

underhand See **devious, sly**

underline See **emphasize, stress**

underling See **inferior**

undermine
▷ VERB
to make something less secure or strong: *You're trying to undermine my confidence again.*
impair *Their actions will impair the country's national interests.*
sap *The illness had sapped my strength.*
subvert *an attempt to subvert the law*
weaken *Her authority had been fatally weakened.*
ANTONYM **strengthen**
See also **weaken**

underneath See **below, under**

undernourished See **skinny**

understand

▷ VERB

1 to know what someone means: *Do you understand what I'm saying?*

catch on *I didn't catch on immediately to what he meant.*

comprehend *It was an interesting lecture, though I didn't comprehend it all.*

follow *I don't follow you at all.*

get *Did you get that joke?*

grasp *He instantly grasped that they were talking about him.*

see *"I see," she said at last.*

take in *too much to take in at once*

2 to know why or how something is happening: *too young to understand what was going on*

appreciate *You must appreciate how important this is.*

comprehend *I just cannot comprehend your viewpoint.*

fathom *His attitude was hard to fathom.*

grasp *We immediately grasped the seriousness of the crisis.*

realize *People just don't realize how serious it could be.*

3 to hear of something: *I understand she hasn't been well.*

believe *She's coming back tomorrow, I believe.*

gather *We gather the report is critical of the organization.*

hear *I hear you've been having some problems.*

learn *On learning who he was, I wanted to meet him.*

See also **appreciate, comprehend, gather, grasp, hear, know, learn, realize, see, take in**

understandable See **reasonable, simple**

understanding

▷ NOUN

1 a knowledge of something: *a basic understanding of computers*

appreciation *She has an appreciation of the problems that consumers face.*

comprehension *completely beyond our comprehension*

grasp *a good grasp of some other languages*

knowledge *I have no knowledge of her business affairs.*

perception *Her questions showed a shrewd perception.*

2 an informal agreement: *There was an understanding among the players.*

accord *trying to reach an accord*

agreement *A new union agreement was*

finally signed last month.

pact *The two friends made a secret pact.*

▷ ADJECTIVE

3 having a sympathetic nature: *Fortunately, he had an understanding family.*

compassionate *a deeply compassionate man*

considerate *They should be more considerate toward us.*

sensitive *He is always sensitive and caring.*

sympathetic *a sympathetic listener*

See also **experience, grasp, intelligence, pity, sympathy, tolerant**

undertake See **assume, do**

undertaking

▷ NOUN

a task that you have agreed to do: *Organizing the talent show has been a massive undertaking.*

affair *The surprise party is going to be a tricky affair to arrange.*

business *Livestock farming is an arduous and difficult business.*

endeavour *an endeavour that was bound to end in failure*

enterprise *It's a group enterprise.*

job *What made you decide to take this job on?*

operation *the person in charge of the entire operation*

project *I can't take responsibility for such a huge project.*

task *a task I do not feel equipped to take on*

venture *a venture that few were willing to take part in*

See also **act, enterprise, guarantee, promise, task**

undertow See **current**

undervalue See **belittle**

undesirable See **unpopular**

undivided See **complete, total, whole**

undo See **loosen, open, ruin**

undomesticated See **wild**

undone See **open**

undoubtedly See **certainly**

undressed See **bare, naked**

undue See **excessive**

unduly See **too**

unearth See **discover, expose, find, reveal, uncover**

unease See **anxiety, worry**

uneasy

▷ *ADJECTIVE*

worried that something may be wrong: *I was very uneasy about these developments.*
agitated *She seemed agitated about something.*
anxious *He admitted he was still anxious about the situation.*
nervous *He's a little nervous about his job.*
perturbed *I am not too perturbed at this setback.*
worried *If you're worried about it, just ask for more details.*
ANTONYM **comfortable**
See also **anxious, uncomfortable, worried**

uneconomical *See* **wasteful**

unemployed

▷ *ADJECTIVE*

not having a job: *an unemployed mechanic*
idle *He has been idle for almost a month.*
jobless *The country's jobless rate has decreased.*
laid off *Twenty workers were laid off yesterday.*
ANTONYM **employed**
See also **idle**

uneven

▷ *ADJECTIVE*

1 having an unlevel or rough surface: *I tripped and fell on the uneven pavement.*
bumpy *We bicycled along the bumpy road.*
not level *It was hard to walk because the road was not level.*
not smooth *The icing on the cake isn't smooth enough.*
rough *We hiked slowly across the rough ground.*
ANTONYM **level**
2 not the same or consistent: *six posts of uneven height*
fluctuating *a fluctuating temperature*
inconsistent *Their performance was inconsistent over the whole season.*
irregular *at irregular intervals*
patchy *Her career has been patchy.*
variable *The potassium content of food is very variable.*
ANTONYM **even**
See also **irregular, rough**

uneventful *See* **dreary**

unexpected

▷ *ADJECTIVE*

not considered likely to happen: *Their move was completely unexpected.*

astonishing *What an astonishing piece of good luck!*
chance *a chance meeting*
surprising *a most surprising turn of events*
unforeseen *The show was cancelled due to unforeseen circumstances.*
See also **abrupt, sudden**

unfair

▷ *ADJECTIVE*

without right or justice: *It's unfair that she had to miss the final game.*
unjust *an unjust decision*
wrong *It would be wrong to allow the trial to go any further.*
wrongful *his claim for wrongful dismissal*
ANTONYM **fair**
See also **wrong**

unfairness *See* **injustice**

unfaithful

▷ *ADJECTIVE*

not being faithful to your partner: *an unfaithful husband*
adulterous *an adulterous relationship*
two-timing INFORMAL *She called him a two-timing rat.*
ANTONYM **faithful**
See also **false, treacherous**

unfamiliar

▷ *ADJECTIVE*

not having been seen or heard of before: *She grew many plants that were unfamiliar to me.*
alien *transplanted into an alien environment*
exotic *filmed in an exotic location*
foreign *For me, it was a foreign experience.*
new *a new idea*
novel *having to cope with many novel situations*
strange *All these faces were strange to me.*
unknown *I'd discovered a writer quite unknown to me.*
See also **strange, unknown**

unfit *See* **inappropriate, unsuitable**

unflustered *See* **relaxed**

unfold *See* **spread**

unforeseeable *See* **unpredictable**

unforeseen *See* **abrupt, unexpected**

unforgettable *See* **memorable**

unfortunate *See* **unlucky**

unfriendly

▷ *ADJECTIVE*

not showing any warmth or kindness: *He can expect an unfriendly welcome.*
aloof *His manner was aloof.*

antagonistic *They were always antagonistic to newcomers.*

cold *She was a cold, unfeeling woman.*

disagreeable *He may be brilliant, but he's most disagreeable.*

hostile *The prisoner eyed him in hostile silence.*

unkind *There's no reason to be so unkind.*

ANTONYM **friendly**

See also **disagreeable, unpleasant**

unfurl *See* **spread**

unfurnished *See* **empty**

ungainliness *See* **clumsiness**

ungainly *See* **clumsy**

ungrateful

▷ ADJECTIVE

not appreciating the things you have: *the most miserable and ungrateful people on earth*

unappreciative *He was unappreciative of our efforts.*

unthankful *What an unthankful group!*

ANTONYM **grateful**

unhappiness *See* **grief, misery, sadness, sorrow**

unhappy

▷ ADJECTIVE

feeling sad or depressed: *He was a shy, sometimes unhappy man.*

depressed *She's depressed about this whole situation.*

despondent *He felt despondent after the job interview.*

down *They felt really down after they spoke to him.*

miserable *My job makes me really miserable sometimes.*

sad *I felt sad to leave our little house.*

ANTONYM **happy**

See also **miserable, sad, upset**

unhealthy

▷ ADJECTIVE

1 likely to cause illness: *an unhealthy lifestyle*

bad for you *the argument that eating meat is bad for you*

harmful *harmful to health*

noxious *factories belching out noxious fumes*

unwholesome *an epidemic originating from the unwholesome food they ate*

unsanitary *Unsanitary conditions contributed to his illness.*

ANTONYM **healthy**

2 not well: *an unhealthy-looking man*

ailing *The king is said to be ailing.*

ill *She didn't look at all ill when I last saw her.*

not well *When I'm not well, they take turns looking after me.*

sick *He's very sick and he needs treatment.*

unwell *an infection that could make you very unwell*

ANTONYM **healthy**

See also **ill, perverted**

unheard-of *See* **exceptional**

unhurried *See* **leisurely, slow**

unhurriedly *See* **slowly**

uniform *See* **constant, even, regular, similar**

uniformly *See* **alike**

unimaginable *See* **incredible**

unimportant

▷ ADJECTIVE

having little significance or importance: *The difference in their ages seemed unimportant at the time.*

insignificant *an insignificant amount of damage to the car*

minor *a minor inconvenience*

paltry *a paltry amount of money, not worth worrying about*

slight *We have a slight problem with our new software.*

trivial *She waved aside the trivial details.*

ANTONYM **important**

See also **insignificant, petty, trivial**

uninhabited *See* **empty, lonely**

unintelligent *See* **foolish**

unintelligible *See* **garbled**

uninterested

▷ ADJECTIVE

not interested in something: *I'm completely uninterested in anything you have to say.*

apathetic *apathetic about politics*

bored *She looked bored with the whole performance.*

impassive *She remained impassive while he ranted on.*

indifferent *He is totally indifferent to our problems.*

nonchalant *"Suit yourself," I said, trying to sound nonchalant.*

passive *That passive attitude of his drives me mad.*

unconcerned *She is unconcerned about anything except herself.*

U

ANTONYM **interested**
See also **apathetic, bored**

CONFUSABLES

uninterested means **having no interest in someone or something**
disinterested means **impartial**

---

uninteresting See **dull**

uninterrupted See **continual, continuous, direct, steady**

union
▷ NOUN
1 an organization of people or groups with mutual interests: *the Canadian Union of Public Employees*
association *a member of several different associations*
coalition *The country is governed by a coalition of three parties.*
confederation *the confederation of the provinces*
federation *a federation of six separate agencies*
league *The League of Nations came into being after World War I.*
2 the joining together of two or more things: *The majority voted for union with the larger organization.*
amalgamation *an amalgamation of two cities*
blend *a blend of traditional charm and modern comforts*
combination *the combination of science and art*
fusion *a fusion of the two music styles*
mixture *a mixture of nuts, raisins, and dried apricots*
See also **bond, club, society**

unique See **different, individual, peculiar, singular, special**

unit See **attachment, department, fitting, party**

unite
▷ VERB
to join together and act as a group: *We must unite to fight our common enemy.*
collaborate *They all collaborated on the project.*
combine *The companies have combined to form a multinational corporation.*
join *People of all kinds joined to make a dignified protest.*
join forces *The two political parties are joining forces.*

link up *Two media giants have linked up.*
merge *The publishing firm hopes to merge with its rival company.*
pull together *Staff and management are pulling together to save the company.*
work together *industry and government working together*
ANTONYM **divide**
See also **combine, team**

universal
▷ ADJECTIVE
relating to everyone or to the whole universe: *These programs have a universal appeal.*
common *The common view is that it is a good thing.*
general *This project should raise general awareness about the problem.*
unlimited *unlimited support*
widespread *Food shortages are widespread.*
worldwide *the fear of a worldwide epidemic*
See also **broad, common, general, mass, popular, public**

unjust See **unfair, wrong**

unkempt See **scruffy, untidy**

unkind
▷ ADJECTIVE
lacking in kindness and consideration: *It's very unkind to describe her in those terms.*
cruel *Children can be so cruel.*
malicious *spreading malicious gossip*
mean *I'd feel mean saying no.*
nasty *What nasty little brats you are!*
spiteful *How can you say such spiteful things about us?*
thoughtless *a small minority of thoughtless and inconsiderate people*
ANTONYM **kind**
See also **hostile, unfriendly**

unknowing See **unconscious**

unknown
▷ ADJECTIVE
not familiar or famous: *She was an unknown at that time.*
humble *From humble beginnings, she became president of the company.*
obscure *an obscure composer*
unfamiliar *There were several unfamiliar names on the list.*
unsung *the unsung heroes of our time*
ANTONYM **famous**
See also **obscure, unfamiliar**

unlawful See **criminal, illegal**

unlike
▷ ADJECTIVE
different from: *She was unlike her sister.*

different from *I've always felt different from most people.*

dissimilar to *a cultural background not dissimilar to our own*

distinct from *Their cuisines are quite distinct from each other.*

divergent from *That viewpoint is not much divergent from that of his predecessor.*

far from *Her politics are not all that far from mine.*

ANTONYM **like**

See also **different**

unlikely

▷ *ADJECTIVE*

probably not true or likely to happen: *A trophy seems unlikely.*

implausible *a movie with an implausible ending*

incredible *an incredible pack of lies*

unbelievable *I know it sounds unbelievable, but I wasn't there that day.*

unconvincing *He came up with a very unconvincing excuse.*

ANTONYM **likely**

See also **improbable**

unlimited *See* universal

unload *See* empty

unlock *See* open

unlocked *See* open

unlucky

▷ *ADJECTIVE*

having bad luck: *He was unlucky not to score during the first period.*

cursed *the most cursed family in history*

hapless *a hapless victim of chance*

luckless *the luckless owner of the worst car of the year*

unfortunate *Some unfortunate person nearby could be injured.*

wretched *the miserable existence of these poor wretched people*

ANTONYM **lucky**

unmarked *See* blank

unmarried *See* single

unmistakable *See* naked, noticeable, plain

unmitigated *See* perfect, pure, rank, total

unnatural *See* creepy, stiff

unnecessary

▷ *ADJECTIVE*

completely needless: *He frowns upon unnecessary expense.*

needless *causing needless panic*

pointless *pointless meetings*

uncalled-for *uncalled-for rudeness*

ANTONYM **necessary**

unnerve *See* alarm, frighten, scare, shake

unnerving *See* scary

unpaid *See* free, outstanding

unpalatable *See* unpleasant

unparalleled *See* incomparable

unpleasant

▷ *ADJECTIVE*

1 causing feelings of discomfort or dislike: *It has a very unpleasant smell.*

bad *I have some bad news.*

disagreeable *a disagreeable experience*

distasteful *I find gossip distasteful.*

nasty *This situation could turn nasty.*

repulsive *repulsive, fat, white slugs*

unpalatable *Only then did I learn the unpalatable truth.*

ANTONYM **pleasant**

2 rude or unfriendly: *a thoroughly unpleasant person*

disagreeable *She may be brilliant, but she's a very disagreeable woman.*

horrid *I must have been a horrid child.*

objectionable *His tone was highly objectionable.*

obnoxious *I see you've met my obnoxious cousin.*

rude *He is often rude to servers in restaurants.*

unfriendly *spoken in a rather unfriendly voice*

ANTONYM **pleasant**

See also **disagreeable, horrible, nasty, painful, rough, rude**

unpolluted *See* clean

unpopular

▷ *ADJECTIVE*

disliked by most people: *an unpopular idea*

detested *The rebels toppled the detested dictator.*

disliked *one of the most disliked members of the team*

shunned *the shunned former cabinet minister*

undesirable *all sorts of undesirable effects on health*

ANTONYM **popular**

unpredictable

▷ *ADJECTIVE*

unable to be foreseen: *England's notoriously*

U

unpredictable weather
chance *A chance meeting can change your life.*
doubtful *The outcome remains doubtful.*
hit or miss INFORMAL *Farming can be a very hit-or-miss business.*
unforeseeable *unforeseeable weather conditions*
ANTONYM **predictable**
See also **changeable**

unproductive See **sterile, useless, vain**

unprotected See **helpless**

unqualified See **sheer, total**

unquestionably See **certainly**

unreasonable See **excessive, extreme, steep**

unreasonably See **too**

unrelated See **independent**

unrelenting See **relentless**

unreliable See **deceptive, dubious**

unremitting See **relentless**

unrivalled See **incomparable, superb, superior**

unroll See **spread**

unruly See **rowdy**

unsafe See **unsteady**

unsatisfactory
▷ ADJECTIVE
not good enough: *His work was judged unsatisfactory.*
disappointing *The results were disappointing.*
inadequate *We received inadequate training for the job.*
mediocre *a mediocre string of performances*
poor *Her school record was poor at first.*
unacceptable *The quality of his work was unacceptable.*
ANTONYM **satisfactory**
See also **poor, rotten**

unscrupulous See **corrupt**

unsecured See **loose**

unseemly See **inappropriate**

unseen See **invisible**

unselfish See **kind**

unsettle See **disturb**

unsettled See **restless**

unshakable See **firm, steadfast**

unsharpened See **blunt**

unsightly See **ugly**

unsound See **faulty, irrational, wrong**

unstable See **changeable, shaky, unsteady**

unsteady
▷ ADJECTIVE
not held or fixed securely and likely to fall over: *a slightly unsteady item of furniture*
precarious *The beds are precarious-looking hammocks strung from the walls.*
rickety *She stood on a rickety old table.*
shaky *He climbed up the shaky ladder.*
tottering *a tottering pile of bricks*
unsafe *That bridge looks decidedly unsafe to me.*
unstable *the demolition of dangerously unstable buildings*
wobbly *wobbly chairs*
ANTONYM **steady**
See also **shaky**

unsuccessful See **futile, in vain**

unsuitable
▷ ADJECTIVE
not appropriate for a purpose: *Her shoes were unsuitable for walking any distance.*
improper *an improper diet*
inappropriate *inappropriate use of the Internet*
unacceptable *using completely unacceptable language*
unfit *unfit for human habitation*
ANTONYM **suitable**
See also **inappropriate, useless**

unsung See **unknown**

unsure See **dubious, hesitant**

unsuspecting See **unaware, unconscious**

untamed See **wild**

unthankful See **ungrateful**

unthinkable See **impossible, incredible**

untidy
▷ ADJECTIVE
not neatly arranged: *The place quickly became untidy.*
bedraggled *My hair was a bedraggled mess.*
chaotic *the chaotic mess of papers on his desk*
cluttered *There was no space on the cluttered counter.*
jumbled *We moved our supplies into a jumbled heap.*

messy *He was a good, if messy, cook.*
unkempt *the unkempt grass in front of the house*
ANTONYM **tidy**
See also **confused**

untie *See* **loosen**

untimely *See* **early, inappropriate**

untold *See* **countless, extensive, infinite**

untrue
▷ ADJECTIVE
not true: *The allegations were completely untrue.*
erroneous *an erroneous description*
false *He gave a false name and address.*
fictitious *fictitious rumours*
inaccurate *the passing on of inaccurate or misleading information*
incorrect *an incorrect account of the sequence of events*
misleading *It would be misleading to say we were friends.*
mistaken *I had a mistaken idea of what had happened.*
ANTONYM **true**
See also **false, wrong**

untrustworthy *See* **sneaky, treacherous**

untruthful *See* **lying**

unused *See* **waste**

unusual
▷ ADJECTIVE
not occurring very often: *many rare and unusual plants*
curious *a curious mixture of fashion trends*
exceptional *exceptional circumstances*
extraordinary *What an extraordinary thing to happen!*
rare *one of the rarest species in the world*
uncommon *It's a very uncommon name.*
unconventional *produced by an unconventional technique*
ANTONYM **common**
See also **curious, exceptional, extraordinary, funny, rare, scarce, singular, uncommon**

unveil *See* **reveal, uncover**

unwell
▷ ADJECTIVE
ill or sick: *He felt unwell and had to go home early.*
ailing *The king is said to be ailing.*
ill *He was seriously ill with pneumonia.*
queasy *I always feel queasy on boats.*
sick *Our teacher is sick today.*
ANTONYM **well**

See also **ill, queasy, sick, unhealthy**

unwholesome *See* **unhealthy**

unwilling
▷ ADJECTIVE
not wanting to do something: *an unwilling participant in school sports*
averse to *I'm not averse to going along with the suggestion.*
grudging *a grudging acceptance of the situation*
loath *She is loath to give up her coaching job.*
reluctant *They were reluctant to get involved at first.*
ANTONYM **willing**
See also **reluctant**

unwind *See* **relax**

unwise
▷ ADJECTIVE
foolish or not sensible: *It would be unwise to expect too much of him.*
foolish *It was foolish to risk injury like that.*
idiotic *What an idiotic thing to do!*
irresponsible *It would be irresponsible to quit your job now.*
rash *Don't panic or do anything rash.*
senseless *It would be senseless to try to stop him now.*
silly *You're not going to go and do something silly, are you?*
stupid *I've had enough of your stupid suggestions.*
ANTONYM **wise**
See also **foolish**

unwrap *See* **uncover**

up *See* **over**

up to *See* **equal to**

up-and-coming *See* **in the making**

upbeat *See* **cheery**

upbringing *See* **background**

upcoming *See* **near**

update *See* **revise**

upgrade *See* **improve, promote**

upheaval *See* **hassle**

uphill *See* **difficult**

uphold *See* **advocate, champion, defend, support**

upkeep
▷ NOUN
the process and cost of maintaining

something: *The money will be used for the upkeep of the grounds.*
keep *He does not contribute toward his keep.*
maintenance *the regular maintenance of condominium buildings*
overheads *If we don't cut our overheads, we may have to shut down.*
preservation *the preservation of historical sites*
running *The running of the business seems to take up all their time.*

upper limit *See* **maximum**

upright *See* **fair, noble, respectable, straight**

uprising *See* **rebellion**

uproar *See* **noise**

upscale *See* **exclusive, posh**

upset
▷ ADJECTIVE
1 feeling unhappy about something: *She was very upset when she heard the news.*
agitated *in an excited and agitated state*
distressed *The animals were distressed by the noise.*
frantic *frantic with worry*
hurt *I was very hurt when they refused to help me.*
troubled *He sounded deeply troubled by the news.*
unhappy *The entire experience made him very unhappy.*
▷ VERB
2 to make someone worried or unhappy: *The whole incident upset me terribly.*
agitate *The constant noise agitates her.*
bother *Don't let his manner bother you.*
distress *The whole thing really distressed him.*
disturb *These dreams disturb me for days afterwards.*
grieve *deeply grieved by their suffering*
ruffle *She doesn't get ruffled by anything.*
3 to turn something over accidentally: *Don't upset that pile of papers.*
capsize *He capsized the boat through his carelessness.*
knock over *The kitten knocked over the vase.*
overturn *I overturned my glass of water as I stood up.*
spill *The child spilled her juice.*
See also **agitate, blow, distress, disturb, grieve, hurt, overturn, shake**

upsetting *See* **sad**

upshot *See* **effect, result**

upsurge *See* **increase, rise, spread, wave**

uptight *See* **nervous, tense**

up-to-date *See* **modern, recent**

up-to-the-minute *See* **current, modern**

upturn *See* **improvement**

urbane *See* **polite, sophisticated**

urge
▷ NOUN
1 a strong wish to do something: *stifling the urge to scream*
compulsion *a compulsion to write*
desire *a strong desire to help and care for people*
drive *a strong drive to succeed*
impulse *She resisted an impulse to smile.*
longing *his longing to return home*
wish *She had a genuine wish to make amends.*
▷ VERB
2 to try hard to persuade someone: *He urged the referee to change her ruling.*
beg *I begged him to stop bothering me.*
beseech FORMAL *I beseech you to show mercy.*
implore *He left early, although they implored him to stay.*
plead *They pleaded not to have to leave.*
press *My friends are pressing me to visit.*
See also **advise, insist, instinct, press, push, whim, wish**

urgent
▷ ADJECTIVE
needing to be dealt with quickly: *an urgent need for food and water*
compelling *There are compelling reasons to act swiftly.*
immediate *The immediate problem is transportation.*
imperative *It is imperative we end up with a win.*
pressing *one of our most pressing problems*
See also **serious**

usage *See* **use**

use
▷ VERB
1 to perform a task with something: *Use a sharp knife to trim the edges.*
apply *Apply this technique when lifting heavy weights.*
employ *the building methods employed*
operate *Never let children operate a snowblower.*

utilize *The body utilizes many different minerals.*

▷ NOUN

2 the act of using something: *the use of force*
application *The application of his ideas isn't as simple as it seems.*
employment *the employment of completely new methods*
operation *the operation of the computer mouse*
usage *Parts of the motor wore out because of constant usage.*
3 the purpose for which something is utilized: *of no practical use whatsoever*
end *the use of public funds for political ends*
object *the object of the exercise*
point *I don't see the point of a gadget like that.*
purpose *It is wrong to use it for personal purposes.*
See also **impose on, benefit, employ, value, wear**

use up *See* **drain, exhaust**

used *See* **accustomed**

useful

▷ ADJECTIVE

helping to make things easier: *a great deal of useful information*
beneficial *It may be beneficial to study the guidelines.*
effective *Antibiotics are effective against this organism.*
helpful *a number of helpful brochures*
practical *practical suggestions for healthy eating*
valuable *Here are a few valuable tips to help you to succeed.*
worthwhile *a worthwhile source of information*
ANTONYM **useless**
See also **beneficial, convenient, handy, helpful, productive, valuable**

usefulness *See* **value**

useless

▷ ADJECTIVE

not suitable or useful: *We realized that our money was useless here.*
futile *It would be futile to make any further attempts.*
impractical *This software is impractical for home computers.*
unproductive *increasingly unproductive land*
unsuitable *This tool is completely unsuitable for use with metal.*
worthless *The old skills are worthless now.*
ANTONYM **useful**

See also **futile, hopeless, inadequate, incompetent, vain, worthless**

usher *See* **accompany, lead, take**

usual

▷ ADJECTIVE

done or happening most often: *sitting at his usual table*
accustomed *She approached the task with her accustomed creativity.*
common *the most common cause of computer problems*
customary *It's customary to bring a gift.*
habitual *His habitual lateness is becoming a problem.*
normal *That's quite normal for a Friday.*
regular *her regular seat in the restaurant*
standard *It was standard practice to remove our boots outside.*
See also **average, common, natural, normal, ordinary, regular, routine, standard, stock, typical**

usually *See* **as a rule, on average**

utensil *See* **tool**

utilize *See* **employ, use**

utmost *See* **limit, maximum, ultimate**

utter

▷ ADJECTIVE

complete or total: *scenes of utter chaos*
absolute *This is absolute madness!*
complete *a complete mess*
consummate *a consummate professional*
out-and-out *an out-and-out lie*
outright *an outright rejection of the deal*
perfect *a perfect stranger*
pure *She did it out of pure kindness.*
sheer *an act of sheer stupidity*
thorough *He is a thorough crook.*
total *a total failure*
See also **absolute, complete, emit, perfect, pure, rank, sheer, total**

utterance *See* **remark, word**

U

Vv

vacant *See* **bare, blank, empty**

vacation *See* **holiday, leave**

vague
▷ ADJECTIVE
not clearly expressed or clearly visible: *vague promises about a raise*
hazy *Many details remain hazy.*
indefinite *at some indefinite time in the future*
indistinct *The lettering on the page was indistinct.*
loose *a loose translation*
uncertain *Students are facing an uncertain future.*
unclear *The proposals were sketchy and unclear.*
ANTONYM **clear**
See also **broad, dim, faint, rough, unclear**

vain
▷ ADJECTIVE
1 very proud of your looks or qualities: *I think he is shallow and vain.*
conceited *They had grown too conceited and pleased with themselves.*
egotistical *an egotistical show-off*
ostentatious *They were generous with their money without being ostentatious.*
proud *She was said to be proud and arrogant.*
stuck-up INFORMAL *She was a famous actress, but she wasn't a bit stuck-up.*
2 not successful in achieving what was intended: *He made a vain effort to cheer her up.*
abortive *the abortive coup attempt*
fruitless *It was a fruitless search.*
futile *their futile attempts to avoid publicity*
unproductive *an unproductive strategy*
useless *There's a lot of useless information in that book.*
ANTONYM **successful**

in vain
▷ ADJECTIVE
unsuccessful in achieving what was intended: *Her complaints were in vain.*
fruitless *Four years of negotiation were fruitless.*
to no avail *His protests were to no avail.*
unsuccessful *Previous attempts have been unsuccessful.*
wasted *Their efforts were wasted.*
See also **conceited, fond, futile, hopeless**

valiant *See* **brave**

valid *See* **legal, logical, right, sound**

validate *See* **confirm**

TYPES OF ... *VALLEY*		
canyon	dell	gully
chasm	depression	hollow
coulee	glen	ravine
dale	gorge	vale
defile	gulch	

valour *See* **bravery, courage**

valuable
▷ ADJECTIVE
1 having great importance or usefulness: *The experience was very valuable.*
beneficial *the beneficial properties of protein*
helpful *a number of helpful booklets*
important *My family is the most important thing in my life.*
prized *one of the gallery's most prized paintings*
useful *a mine of useful information*
worthwhile *a worthwhile source of income*
ANTONYM **useless**
2 worth a lot of money: *valuable old baseball cards*
costly *a costly repair job*
expensive *expensive clothes*
precious *rings set with precious jewels*
ANTONYM **worthless**
See also **precious, productive, useful**

valuables
▷ PLURAL NOUN
the things you own that cost a lot of money: *Leave your valuables at home.*
heirlooms *family heirlooms passed down through the generations*
treasures *The house was full of art treasures.*

valuation *See* **estimate**

value
▷ NOUN
1 the importance or usefulness of something: *the value of a balanced diet*
advantage *the great advantage of this method*
benefit *They see no benefit in occasionally relaxing.*
effectiveness *the effectiveness of the new system*
importance *They have always placed great importance on live performances.*
merit *the artistic merit of their work*

use *This is of no use to anyone.*
usefulness *the usefulness of the Internet in disseminating new ideas*
virtue *the great virtue of modern technology*
worth *This system has already proved its worth.*
2 the amount of money that something is worth: *The value of their house has doubled.*
cost *the cost of a loaf of bread*
market price *buying shares of that stock at the current market price*
price *a sharp increase in the price of oil*
selling price *the average selling price of a new home*
worth *They sold the car for less than half its worth.*
▷ VERB
3 to appreciate something and think it is important: *Do you value your friends enough?*
appreciate *I would appreciate your advice.*
cherish *Cherish every moment you have with your friends.*
have a high opinion of *Your boss seems to have a high opinion of you.*
prize *These items are prized by collectors.*
rate highly *I rate her highly as a rower.*
respect *I respect his talent as a pianist.*
treasure *memories I will treasure for the rest of my life*
4 to decide how much money something is worth: *I have had my jewellery valued for insurance purposes.*
appraise *She was called in to appraise and sell the cottage.*
assess *Experts are now assessing the cost of the damage.*
cost *The building project was costed at about $400 million.*
estimate *a personal fortune estimated at more than $40 million*
evaluate *The company needs to evaluate the cost of leasing the building.*
price *The bicycle was priced at less than $200.*
See also **admire, appreciate, ideal, merit, price, prize, quality, treasure**

valueless *See* **worthless**

values *See* **standards**

vandal *See* **hoodlum**

vanish
▷ VERB
1 to disappear: *The moon vanished behind a cloud.*
become invisible *The plane became invisible in the clouds.*
be lost to view *They watched the ship until it was lost to view.*

disappear *The aircraft disappeared off the radar.*
fade *We watched the harbour fade into the mist.*
recede *Gradually their car receded into the distance.*
ANTONYM **appear**
2 to cease to exist: *Dinosaurs vanished from the earth millions of years ago.*
become extinct *Without help, these animals will become extinct.*
cease *At one o'clock, the rain ceased.*
cease to exist *Without trees, the world as we know it would cease to exist.*
die out *The dodo died out around 1690.*
dissolve *The crowds dissolved and we were alone.*
evaporate *All my pleasure evaporated when I saw him.*
fade away *His anxiety faded away.*
go away *All she wanted was for the pain to go away.*
melt away *All my cares melted away.*
pass *Breathe deeply and the panic attack will pass.*
See also **die out, disappear, melt**

vanished *See* **lost**

vanity *See* **conceit, pride**

vanquish
▷ VERB
to defeat someone completely: *a happy ending in which the hero vanquishes the villains*
beat *the team that beat us in the finals*
conquer *great warriors who conquer the enemies of their people*
crush *their bid to crush the rebels*
defeat *The enemy quickly defeated the soldiers.*
overcome *They overcame the opposition to win the Stanley Cup.*
rout *the battle at which the Norman army routed the English*
trounce *Australia trounced France by 60 points to 4.*
See also **beat, crush, defeat, overcome, subdue**

vapour *See* **cloud**

variable *See* **changeable, irregular, uneven**

variant *See* **form**

variation
▷ NOUN
a change from the normal or usual pattern: *a variation of the usual route*

alteration *some alterations in your diet*
change *a change of attitude*
departure *Her new novel is a departure from her previous work.*
deviation *Deviation from the norm is not tolerated.*
difference *a noticeable difference in his behaviour*
diversion *a welcome diversion from the daily grind*
See also **difference**

variety
▷ NOUN
1 a number of different kinds of things: *a wide variety of readers*
array *an attractive array of bright colours*
assortment *an assortment of pets*
collection *a huge collection of books*
medley *a medley of vegetables*
mixture *a mixture of desserts*
range *a range of skin-care products*
2 a particular type of something: *a new variety of celery*
category *There are three broad categories of soil.*
class *several classes of butterflies*
kind *different kinds of roses*
sort *several articles of this sort*
strain *a new strain of the virus*
type *What type of cameras were they?*
See also **breed, choice, form, kind, range, sort, type**

various
▷ ADJECTIVE
of several different types: *trees of various sorts*
assorted *bathing suits in assorted colours*
different *different brands of soft drinks*
disparate *the disparate cultures of India*
diverse *Society is more diverse than ever before.*
miscellaneous *a hoard of miscellaneous junk*
sundry *sundry journalists and other writers*
See also **several**

vary
▷ VERB
1 to change to something different: *weather patterns vary greatly*
alter *During the course of a day, the light alters constantly.*
alternate *My moods alternate with alarming speed.*
change *My feelings haven't changed.*
fluctuate *Weight may fluctuate markedly.*
2 to introduce changes in something: *Vary*

your routes as much as possible.
alternate *Alternate the chunks of fish with chunks of vegetables.*
diversify *They decided to diversify their products.*
modify *The government refuses to modify its position.*
See also **range**

vast
▷ ADJECTIVE
extremely large: *vast stretches of farmland*
colossal *a colossal statue*
enormous *The bedroom is enormous.*
giant *a giant meteorite heading for the earth*
gigantic *a gigantic shopping mall*
great *a great hall as long as a football field*
huge *a huge crowd*
immense *an immense castle*
massive *a massive theme park*
ANTONYM **tiny**
See also **broad, colossal, enormous, extensive, huge, immense, large, spacious**

vault *See* **jump, leap, tomb**

veer *See* **swerve**

vehemence *See* **heat, strength, violence**

vehement *See* **intense**

vehicle *See* **automobile, car, medium**

velocity *See* **rate, speed**

venerate *See* **respect, worship**

venerated *See* **holy**

vengeance *See* **revenge**

venom *See* **poison, spite**

venomous *See* **poisonous, spiteful**

vent *See* **opening**

venture *See* **dare, enterprise, undertaking**

verbal *See* **oral**

verdict
▷ NOUN
a decision or opinion on something: *The doctor's verdict is that I am fine.*
conclusion *I've come to the conclusion that she's the best skater in the country.*
decision *The editor's decision is final.*
finding *The court announced its findings.*
judgment *My judgment is that things are going to get worse.*
opinion *You should seek another medical opinion.*
See also **conclusion, decision, judgment**

verge *See* **side**

verification *See* **proof**

verified *See* **actual**

verify *See* **confirm, determine, prove**

vernacular *See* **language**

versed in *See* **familiar**

versus *See* **against**

vertical *See* **sheer, steep, straight**

very
▷ ADVERB
to a great degree: *very bad dreams*
deeply *I was deeply sorry to hear about your loss.*
extremely *My mobile phone is extremely useful.*
greatly *I was greatly relieved when he finally arrived.*
highly *a highly successful writer*
really *I know her really well.*
terribly *I'm terribly sorry to bother you.*
See also **precise, really**

very much *See* **far**

vessel *See* **container**

vestige *See* **trace**

vestiges *See* **remains**

veteran *See* **practical**

veto
▷ VERB
1 to forbid something: *They vetoed our plans for a party.*
ban *The authorities have banned the advertisement.*
forbid *Some airlines forbid the use of electronic devices during the flight.*
prohibit *The government intends to prohibit all trade with the country.*
▷ NOUN
2 the act of forbidding or power to forbid something: *The five permanent members of the UN Security Council have the power of veto.*
ban *a ban on tobacco advertising*
prohibition *a prohibition on nuclear testing*
See also **forbid**

vex *See* **annoy**

viable *See* **economic, possible**

vibrant *See* **colourful**

vibrate *See* **shake**

vice *See* **evil**

vicious *See* **cruel, malicious, savage, violent, wicked**

viciousness *See* **cruelty**

victor *See* **champion, winner**

victory
▷ NOUN
a success in a battle or competition: *the Canadiens' fourth consecutive victory*
laurels *A former champion took the laurels in this event.*
success *league and cup successes*
superiority *United Nations air forces won air superiority.*
triumph *last year's Liberal triumph in the provincial elections*
win *eight wins in nine games*
ANTONYM **defeat**
See also **success, triumph, win**

vie *See* **compete**

vie with *See* **play**

view
▷ NOUN
1 a personal opinion: *his political views*
attitude *other people's attitudes toward you*
belief *people's beliefs about crime*
conviction *a firm conviction that things have improved*
feeling *It is my feeling that your teacher is right.*
opinion *a favourable opinion of our neighbours*
point of view *an unusual point of view on the subject*
2 the things you can see from a particular place: *There was a beautiful view from the window.*
aspect *The surrounding hills give the cottage a lovely aspect.*
landscape *Saskatchewan's prairie landscape*
panorama *a panorama of fertile valleys*
perspective *an aerial perspective of the Rocky Mountains*
scene *The pilot surveyed the scene from high above the city.*
spectacle *a sweeping spectacle of rugged peaks*
▷ VERB
3 to think of something in a particular way: *They viewed me with contempt.*
consider *We consider them to be our friends.*
deem *His ideas were deemed unacceptable.*
judge *Her work was judged unsatisfactory.*
regard *They regard the tax as unfair.*
See also **belief, feeling, idea, judgment, observe, opinion, outlook, regard, scene, scenery, thought, watch**

viewpoint

▷ *NOUN*

an attitude toward something: *We all have our own personal viewpoints.*
attitude *other people's attitudes toward you*
belief *people's beliefs about the health-care system*
conviction *a personal conviction*
feeling *What are your feelings on this matter?*
opinion *a favourable opinion of our neighbours*
point of view *an unusual point of view on the subject*
See also **opinion**

vigilant See **alert, observant, wary**

vigorous See **energetic, powerful**

vigour See **drive, energy, power, spirit, strength**

vile See **disgusting, evil, nasty**

vilify See **attack**

villain See **criminal, crook**

vindicate See **justify**

vindictive See **spiteful**

violate See **break, disobey, intrude, invade**

violated See **broken**

violation See **breach, crime**

violence

▷ *NOUN*

I behaviour that is intended to hurt people: *Twenty people were injured in the violence.*
bloodshed *The government must avoid further bloodshed.*
brutality *the brutality of the war*
cruelty *human beings capable of such cruelty to each other*
force *We are against the use of force in such situations.*
savagery *acts of vicious savagery*
terrorism *horrific acts of terrorism*
2 force and energy: *She gestured with sudden violence.*
fervour *views he had put forward with fervour*
force *She expressed her feelings with unexpected force.*
harshness *the harshness of her words*
intensity *His voice became hoarse with intensity.*
severity *the severity of her scoldings*

vehemence *I was taken aback by my teacher's vehemence on the subject.*

violent

▷ *ADJECTIVE*

I intending to hurt or kill people: *violent criminals*
bloodthirsty *a bloodthirsty monster*
brutal *a brutal crime*
cruel *He is cruel toward animals.*
murderous *a murderous thief*
savage *savage warriors*
vicious *a cruel and vicious person*
ANTONYM **gentle**
2 happening unexpectedly and with great force: *violent storms*
powerful *a powerful hurricane*
raging *a raging flood*
rough *The ship sank in rough seas.*
strong *strong winds and rain*
turbulent *the turbulent events of the century*
wild *the wild gales sweeping up from the sea*
3 said, felt, or done with great force: *the violent reaction to his plans*
acute *pain that grew more and more acute*
furious *a furious argument*
intense *a look of intense dislike*
powerful *a powerful backlash against the government*
severe *a severe emotional shock*
strong *strong words*
See also **rude, savage, wild**

VIP See **celebrity**

virginal See **innocent**

virtually See **nearly**

virtue

▷ *NOUN*

I the quality of doing what is morally right: *a paragon of virtue*
goodness *I have faith in human goodness.*
integrity *She was praised for her fairness and integrity.*
morality *standards of morality and justice in society*
2 an advantage something has: *the virtue of neatness*
advantage *the advantages of the new system*
asset *Honesty is her greatest asset.*
attribute *a player with every attribute you could want*
merit *Each movie has its own merits.*
plus *The nutrients in milk have pluses and minuses.*
strength *the strengths and weaknesses of our position*

by virtue of

▷ PREPOSITION

because of: *The article stuck in my mind by virtue of one detail.*

as a result of *People will feel better as a result of their efforts.*

because of *She was promoted because of her experience.*

by dint of *He succeeds by dint of hard work.*

on account of *The city is popular with tourists on account of its many museums.*

thanks to *Thanks to recent research, new treatments are available.*

See also **merit, right, value**

virtuoso *See* **genius**

virtuous *See* **holy, honest, noble**

visibility *See* **sight**

visible

▷ ADJECTIVE

1 able to be seen: *The warning lights were clearly visible.*

clear *the clearest pictures ever of Pluto*

conspicuous *He felt more conspicuous than he'd have liked.*

distinguishable *colours that are distinguishable in the dark*

in sight *There wasn't a vehicle in sight.*

observable *the observable part of the universe*

perceptible *She gave a barely perceptible nod.*

ANTONYM **invisible**

2 noticeable or evident: *There was little visible excitement.*

apparent *There is no apparent reason for the delay.*

evident *He ate with evident enjoyment.*

manifest *his manifest enthusiasm*

noticeable *subtle but noticeable changes*

obvious *There are obvious dangers.*

plain *It is plain a mistake has been made.*

See also **evident**

vision

▷ NOUN

1 a mental picture in which you imagine things: *my vision of the future*

conception *my conception of a garden*

daydream *He learned to escape into daydreams.*

dream *her dream of becoming a pilot*

fantasy *fantasies of romance and true love*

ideal *your ideal of a vacation*

image *an image in your mind of what you are looking for*

2 the ability to imagine future developments: *a total lack of vision and imagination*

foresight *They had the foresight to invest in that company.*

imagination *He had the imagination to foresee dangers.*

insight *an insight into a person's character*

intuition *His intuition told him something was wrong.*

3 an experience in which you see things others cannot: *She was convinced her visions were real.*

apparition *One of the women in the room was the apparition he had seen.*

hallucination *The drug can cause hallucinations.*

illusion *Perhaps the footprint was an illusion.*

mirage *The lion was a mirage, created by his overactive imagination.*

phantom *People claimed to have seen the phantom.*

spectre *a spectre from the other world*

See also **dream, imagination, sight**

visit

▷ VERB

1 to go to see and spend time with someone: *He wanted to visit his brother in California.*

call on *Don't hesitate to call on me.*

go to see *I'll go to see her in the hospital.*

look up *She looked up friends she had not seen for a while.*

▷ NOUN

2 a trip to see a person or place: *They had recently paid him a visit.*

call *He decided to pay a call on his old friend.*

stay *An experienced guide is provided during your stay.*

stop *The last stop in the tour was Paris.*

See also **frequent**

visualize *See* **imagine, picture**

vital

▷ ADJECTIVE

1 necessary or very important: *a blockade that cut off vital fuel supplies*

central *He is central to the whole project.*

critical *This decision will be critical to our future.*

crucial *the diplomat who played a crucial role in the negotiations*

essential *It is essential that you see a doctor soon.*

important *the most important piece of evidence in the case*

indispensable *an indispensable piece of equipment*

necessary *the skills necessary for survival*

pivotal *He played a pivotal role in the tournament.*
2 energetic and full of life: *My grandparents remained active and vital.*
active *an active youngster*
dynamic *a dynamic and exciting place*
energetic *She became a shadow of her happy, energetic self.*
lively *a lively kitten*
spirited *a spirited performance*
sprightly *a sprightly old man*
vivacious *She is vivacious and charming.*
See also **basic, critical, crucial, essential, necessary**

vitality *See* **energy**

vivacious *See* **active, alive, lively, vital**

vivid *See* **bold, bright, brilliant, colourful**

vocabulary *See* **language**

vociferous *See* **noisy**

vogue *See* **craze, fashion**

voice *See* **express, say**

void *See* **abyss**

volatile *See* **changeable, moody**

volition *See* **will**

volley *See* **hail**

volume *See* **amount, book, capacity, quantity**

voluminous *See* **full**

voluptuous *See* **sexy**

vomit
▷ *VERB*
to have food and drink come back up through the mouth: *Any product made from milk made him vomit.*
be sick *She was sick in the washroom sink.*
bring up *Certain foods are difficult to bring up.*
heave *He gasped and heaved and vomited again.*
puke *INFORMAL They puked out of the window.*
regurgitate *swallowing and regurgitating large quantities of water*

vote
▷ *NOUN*
I a decision made by allowing people to state their preference: *Do you think we should have a vote on that?*

ballot *The result of the ballot will be known soon.*
plebiscite *the city's plebiscite on Sunday shopping*
polls *She was victorious at the polls.*
referendum *a referendum on sovereignty*
▷ *VERB*
2 to indicate a choice or opinion: *Many people will vote for the opposition.*
cast a vote *A large number of citizens did not cast a vote.*
go to the polls *Voters are due to go to the polls on Tuesday.*
opt *The majority opted for a new flag.*
return *Members will be asked to return a vote for or against the motion.*
3 to suggest that something should happen: *I vote that we all go to the mall.*
propose *I propose that we all try to get some sleep.*
recommend *I recommend that they practise a little harder.*
suggest *I suggest we go around the table and introduce ourselves.*
See also **say**

vow *See* **oath, promise**

voyage *See* **journey, trip**

vulgar
▷ *ADJECTIVE*
I socially unacceptable or offensive: *vulgar language*
coarse *coarse humour*
crude *crude pictures*
dirty *dirty jokes*
indecent *an indecent remark*
rude *a rude gesture*
uncouth *that oafish, uncouth person*
ANTONYM **refined**
2 showing a lack of taste or quality: *I think it's a very vulgar building.*
common *She could sometimes be a little common.*
flashy *flashy clothes*
garish *a garish outfit*
gaudy *a gaudy purple-and-orange hat*
tasteless *a house with tasteless decor*
tawdry *tawdry jewellery*
ANTONYM **sophisticated**
See also **common, crude, gaudy, indecent, low, naughty, tasteless**

vulnerability *See* **weakness**

vulnerable
▷ *ADJECTIVE*
weak and without protection: *vulnerable old people*
exposed *The village is exposed to Atlantic winds.*

sensitive *Most people are highly sensitive to criticism.*
susceptible *an area that is susceptible to attack*
weak *He spoke up for the weak and defenceless.*
See also **helpless, impressionable**

V

Ww

waffle *See* **nonsense**

waft *See* **blow**

wages *See* **income, pay, salary**

wail *See* **lament**

wait
▷ *VERB*
1 to spend time before something happens:
Wait until we get there.
linger *She lingered in front of the window before deciding to come into the store.*
pause *The crowd paused for a minute, wondering what to do next.*
remain *You'll have to remain in hospital for the time being.*
stand by *Helicopters are standing by to evacuate the people.*
stay *Stay here while I go for help.*
▷ *NOUN*
2 a period of time before something happens: *They faced a long wait for the ferry to Victoria.*
delay *The accident caused some delay.*
interval *a long interval when no one spoke*
pause *There was a pause before he replied.*
See also **pause, remain, stay**

wake
▷ *VERB*
to make or become conscious again after sleep: *It was still dark when he woke.*
awake *We were awoken by the doorbell.*
come to *When he came to, he found it was raining.*
rouse *We roused him at seven so he would be on time.*
stir *She shook him and he started to stir.*
waken *wakened by the thunder*

waken *See* **wake**

walk
▷ *VERB*
1 to go on foot: *I walked slowly along the road.*
See WORD STUDY **walk** on next page
▷ *NOUN*
2 a journey made by walking: *We'll have a quick walk before it gets dark.*
hike *a long hike in the country*
march *a protest march to the provincial capital*
ramble *They went for a ramble through the woods.*
stroll *After dinner, we took a stroll around the city.*
trek *He's on a trek to the Arctic.*

3 the way someone moves when walking:
Despite his gangling walk, he is a good dancer.
carriage *her regal carriage*
gait *an awkward gait*
pace *moving at a brisk pace down the road*
stride *He lengthened his stride to catch up with her.*
See also **ramble**

wall *See* **barrier**

wan *See* **pale**

wand *See* **stick**

wander
▷ *VERB*
to move about in a casual way: *They wandered aimlessly around the village.*
cruise *A police car cruised by.*
drift *The balloon drifted slowly over the countryside.*
ramble *to ramble through the woods*
range *Polar bears range widely in search of food.*
roam *Millions of buffalo once roamed the Prairies.*
stroll *We strolled down the street, looking in store windows.*
See also **ramble**

wandering *See* **indirect**

wane *See* **abate, fail, weaken**

want
▷ *VERB*
1 to feel a desire for something: *I want black running shoes for a change.*
covet *He coveted his boss's job.*
crave *Sometimes she still craved chocolate.*
desire *He could make them do whatever he desired.*
wish *I don't wish to know that.*
2 to need something: *My hair wants cutting.*
be deficient in *Their diet was deficient in vitamins.*
demand *Training to be a figure skater demands much sacrifice.*
lack *training to give him the skills he lacked*
need *My computer needs servicing.*
require *She knows exactly what is required of her.*
▷ *NOUN*
3 a lack of something: *becoming weak from want of rest*
absence *a complete absence of evidence*
deficiency *They did blood tests for signs of vitamin deficiency.*

There are a number of more interesting or creative words you can use in place of the basic verb **walk**, if you want to say something about the way in which a person walks.

- If you **step** in a particular direction, you move your foot in that direction.
I **stepped** carefully over the piles of garbage.

- If you **tread** in a particular way, you walk in that way.
This is rather a formal word.
She **trod** carefully across the grass.

- If you **amble**, **saunter**, or **stroll**, you walk in a slow, relaxed way.
We **ambled** along the beach hand in hand.
He was **sauntering** along as if he had all the time in the world.
They **strolled** down the street, looking in store windows.

- If you **wander**, you walk around in a casual way, often without intending to go anywhere in particular.
She was **wandering** aimlessly about in the garden.

- If you **tiptoe**, you walk very quietly without putting your heels on the ground, so as not to be heard.
I slipped out of bed and **tiptoed** to the window.

- If you **pace**, you walk up and down a small area, usually because you are anxious or impatient.
As he waited, he **paced** nervously around the room.

- If you **stride**, you walk with quick, long steps.
She turned abruptly and **strode** off down the corridor.

- If you **march**, you walk quickly and in a determined way, perhaps because you are angry.
He **marched** into the office and demanded to see the manager.

- If you **stamp**, or **stomp**, you put your feet down very hard when you walk, usually because you are angry.
"I'm leaving!" she shouted as she **stamped** out of the room.

- If you **stalk**, you walk in a stiff, proud, or angry way.
He **stalked** out of the meeting, slamming the door.

- If you **lurch**, you walk with sudden, jerky movements.
She **lurched** around the room, bumping into people.

- If you **stagger** or **totter**, you walk very unsteadily, often because you are ill or drunk.
He **staggered** to the side of the road and vomited.
I had to **totter** around on crutches for six weeks.

- If you **reel**, you walk about in an unsteady way as if you are going to fall.
She lost her balance and **reeled** back.

- If you **stumble**, you trip while you are walking and almost fall.
I **stumbled** into the room and collapsed on the nearest chair.

- If you **hike** or **ramble**, you walk some distance in the countryside for pleasure.
They **hiked** along a remote trail.
We had a relaxing holiday spent **rambling** in the foothills.

- If you **trek**, you make a journey across difficult country by walking.
This year we're going **trekking** in the Rockies.
You can also use **trek** to describe someone walking slowly and unwillingly, usually because of tiredness.
We **trekked** all round the mall looking for white shoes.

- If you **plod**, **tramp**, or **trudge**, you walk slowly, with heavy steps, often because you are tired.
He **plodded** about after me, looking bored.
They spent all day **tramping** through the snow.
We had to **trudge** all the way back up the hill.

lack *He got the job in spite of his lack of experience.*
scarcity *an increasing scarcity of water*
shortage *The drought has resulted in a water shortage.*
ANTONYM **abundance**
See also **deficiency, demand, desire, hardship, lack, need, poverty, require, shortage, wish**

wanting *See* **deficient**

wanton *See* **shameless**

war
▷ NOUN
1 a period of armed conflict between countries: *The war dragged on for five years.*
combat *those who died in combat*
conflict *The conflict is bound to intensify.*
fighting *He was wounded in the fighting that followed the treaty.*
hostilities *Be prepared in case hostilities break out.*
strife *The country was torn with strife.*
warfare *chemical warfare*
ANTONYM **peace**
▷ VERB
2 to fight against something: *The two countries had been warring with each other for years.*
battle *Rebels battled with the police.*
clash *The two armies clashed at dawn.*
combat *measures to combat smuggling*
fight *They fought against oppression.*
See also **conflict**

warden *See* **guard**

wardrobe *See* **clothes**

warehouse *See* **store**

warfare *See* **war**

warm
▷ ADJECTIVE
1 having some heat but not hot: *a warm spring day*
balmy *balmy summer evenings*
heated *a heated swimming pool*
lukewarm *Heat the milk until lukewarm.*
pleasant *After a chilly morning, the afternoon was very pleasant.*
tepid *a bath full of tepid water*
ANTONYM **cold**
2 friendly and affectionate: *a warm and likable personality*
affectionate *with an affectionate glance at her children*
amiable *He was very amiable company.*
cordial *We were given a cordial welcome.*

friendly *All her cousins were very friendly.*
genial *a warm-hearted friend and genial host*
loving *They are loving parents.*
ANTONYM **unfriendly**
▷ VERB
3 to heat something gently: *The sun came out and warmed the garden.*
heat *Heat the bread in the oven.*
heat up *The fire soon heated up the room.*
melt *He melted the butter in a small pan.*
thaw *Take the chicken from the freezer and thaw it completely.*
warm up *Gently warm up the muscles.*
ANTONYM **cool**
See also **cosy, hot, loving, tender**

warm up *See* **heat, warm**

warmth *See* **affection, enthusiasm, heat, passion**

warn
▷ VERB
to give advance notice of something unpleasant: *I warned her about the tires on her bike.*
alert *The siren alerted them to the danger.*
caution *Their reaction cautioned him against any further attempts.*
forewarn *We were forewarned of what to expect.*
notify *The weather forecast notified them of the coming storm.*
See also **alert, caution, notify**

warning
▷ NOUN
something that tells people of possible danger: *advance warning of the attack*
alarm *They heard the fire alarm and ran to safety.*
alert *a security alert*
caution *a note of caution*
notice *three months' notice*
premonition *He had a premonition of bad news.*
See also **alarm, indication, lecture, notice, omen**

warp *See* **bend**

warped *See* **crooked**

warrant *See* **deserve, justify, merit, permit**

warrior *See* **fighter**

wary
▷ ADJECTIVE
showing lack of trust in something: *She was wary of making a commitment.*
cautious *His experience has made him*

cautious *of playing with dogs.*
distrustful *Many voters are distrustful of politicians.*
guarded *She gave me a guarded look.*
suspicious *He was rightly suspicious of their motives.*
vigilant *She warned the public to be vigilant.*
See also **alert, cautious, suspicious**

wash
▷ VERB
1 to clean something with water: *He got a job washing dishes.*
bathe *She bathed her blistered feet.*
cleanse *the correct way to cleanse the skin*
launder *freshly laundered shirts*
rinse *Rinse several times in clear water.*
scrub *I scrubbed the bathroom floor.*
shampoo *We shampooed the dog in the bathtub.*
2 to carry something by the force of water: *washed ashore by the waves*
carry off *The debris was carried off on the tide.*
erode *Exposed soil is quickly eroded by wind and rain.*
sweep away *The floods swept away the cabins by the river.*
See also **clean**

wash away *See* **wear**

wash out *See* **fade**

washed *See* **clean**

waste
▷ VERB
1 to use too much of something unnecessarily: *I wouldn't waste my money on something like that.*
fritter away *He just fritters his time away.*
squander *She had squandered her chances of winning.*
throw away *You're throwing away a good opportunity.*
ANTONYM **save**
▷ NOUN
2 using something excessively or unnecessarily: *What a complete waste of money!*
extravagance *widespread tales of his extravagance*
misuse *This project is a misuse of public money.*
squandering *a squandering of his valuable time*
▷ ADJECTIVE
3 not needed or wanted: *waste paper*
leftover *leftover pieces of fabric*
superfluous *She got rid of many superfluous belongings.*

unused *spoiled or unused ballots*
See also **barren, garbage, refuse, rubbish, trash**

wasted *See* **in vain, weak**

wasteful
▷ ADJECTIVE
using something in a careless or extravagant way: *wasteful duplication of effort*
extravagant *an extravagant lifestyle*
uneconomical *the uneconomical duplication of jobs*
ANTONYM **thrifty**

watch
▷ NOUN
1 a period of time when a guard is kept on something: *Keep a close watch on the swimmers.*
observation *The patient will be under observation night and day.*
supervision *A toddler requires close supervision.*
surveillance *kept under constant surveillance*
▷ VERB
2 to look at something for some time: *I don't watch television very often.*
gaze at *gazing at herself in the mirror*
look at *They looked closely at the insects.*
observe *Researchers observed the behaviour of small children.*
pay attention *Pay attention or you won't know what to do.*
see *You have to see him in the school play.*
view *The police have viewed the video recording of the incident.*
3 to look after something: *Please watch the baby carefully.*
guard *They were guarded the whole time they were there.*
look after *I looked after her cat while she was away.*
mind *Can you mind the store for a couple of hours?*
take care of *Can you take care of the kids tonight?*
See also **look after, mind, observe, regard, take care of, witness**

watchful *See* **observant**

watch out
▷ VERB
to be careful or alert for something: *You have to watch out for snakes in the swamp.*
be alert *Be alert to e-mail attachments.*
be watchful *Be watchful for any warning signs.*

keep your eyes open *They kept their eyes open for any troublemakers.*
look out *What are the symptoms to look out for?*
See also **beware**

watch over *See* **guard**

water *See* **wet**

TYPES OF ... *WATERFALL*	
cascade	linn ✹
cataract	rapids
chute	torrent
falls	whitewater

waterlogged *See* **wet**

watery *See* **thin**

wave
▷ *VERB*
1 to move or flap to and fro: *The doctor waved a piece of paper at me.*
brandish *brandishing a knife*
flap *He flapped his hand and frowned at me to be quiet.*
flourish *She flourished her glass to emphasize the point.*
flutter *The flag fluttered in the breeze.*
shake *Shake the rugs well to air them.*
▷ *NOUN*
2 a ridge of water on the surface of a body of water: *the sound of the waves breaking on the shore*
breaker *The foaming breakers crashed onto the beach.*
ripple *gentle ripples on the surface of the lake*
swell *We bobbed gently on the swell of the incoming tide.*
3 an increase in a type of activity: *the heat wave*
flood *a flood of complaints about the program*
movement *a growing movement toward democracy*
rush *He felt a sudden rush of panic at the thought.*
surge *a surge of happiness*
trend *This is a growing trend.*
upsurge *an upsurge in criminal activities*
See also **flourish, rash, shake, signal**

wave down *See* **hail**

waver *See* **hesitate**

wavering *See* **hesitant**

wax *See* **polish**

way
▷ *NOUN*
1 a manner of doing something: *an excellent way of cooking meat*
approach *different approaches to gathering information*
manner *in a friendly manner*
means *a means to encourage recycling*
method *using the latest teaching methods*
procedure *Follow the correct procedure when applying for the job.*
technique *The tests were performed using a new technique.*
2 the customs or behaviour of a person or group: *Our neighbours' ways are certainly different from our own.*
conduct *People were impressed by her professional conduct.*
custom *The picnic is a Canada Day custom for our family.*
manner *His manner was rather abrupt.*
practice *a public inquiry into bank practices*
style *Behaving like that isn't his style.*
3 a route taken to a particular place: *I can't remember the way.*
course *The ship was on a course that followed the coastline.*
lane *the passing lane of the highway*
path *Lava covers everything in its path.*
road *the road into the village*
route *the most direct route to the school*
See also **course, direction, fashion, manner, method, passage, path, practice, route, style**

INFORMALLY SPEAKING

go out of your way: make a special effort
no way: absolutely not
under way: going on or in progress

way in *See* **entrance, entry**

ways *See* **conduct**

wayward *See* **naughty, wild**

weak
▷ *ADJECTIVE*
1 lacking in strength: *a weak heart*
delicate *a delicate child*
faint *I'm feeling faint.*
feeble *feeble and unable to walk far*
frail *in frail health*
puny *He was puny as a child but grew up to be a top athlete.*
sickly *a sickly baby*
wasted *muscles that were wasted through lack of use*
ANTONYM **strong**
2 likely to break or fail: *a weak economy*

deficient *The plane had a deficient landing system.*

faulty *The money will be used to repair faulty equipment.*

inadequate *inadequate safety measures*

3 easily influenced by other people: *He was a weak man who wouldn't stand up for himself.*

powerless *a powerless ruler governed by his advisers*

spineless *spineless politicians*

ANTONYM **resolute**

See also **flat, helpless, lame, mild, puny, thin, vulnerable**

weaken

▷ VERB

to make or become less strong: *Her authority was weakened by their actions.*

diminish *The strength of the storm eventually diminished.*

fail *His strength began to fail after a few hours.*

flag *Her enthusiasm was in no way flagging.*

lessen *The drugs lessen the risk of an epidemic.*

reduce *Reduced fan support forced the team to relocate.*

sap *I was afraid the illness had sapped my strength.*

undermine *They were accused of trying to undermine the government.*

wane *My interest in the theatre is beginning to wane.*

ANTONYM **strengthen**

See also **diminish, undermine**

weakness

▷ NOUN

1 a lack of physical or moral strength: *Extreme weakness caused him to collapse.*

defect *a serious character defect*

flaw *Her main flaw is her bad temper.*

fragility *the fragility of their bones*

frailty *the triumph of will over human frailty*

imperfection *He concedes that there are imperfections in the system.*

vulnerability *the extreme vulnerability of the young chicks*

ANTONYM **strength**

2 a great liking for something: *a weakness for chocolate*

fondness *a fondness for rich desserts*

liking *a liking for bacon and eggs*

passion *My other great passion is my motorbike.*

penchant *a penchant for designer jeans*

ANTONYM **dislike**

See also **defect, disadvantage, fault, love**

wealth

▷ NOUN

1 a large amount of money: *Wealth cannot buy happiness.*

affluence *an outward show of affluence*

fortune *She made a fortune in the stock market.*

means *a person of means*

money *All that money brought nothing but sadness and misery.*

prosperity *the country's economic prosperity*

riches *Her Olympic medal brought her fame and riches.*

substance *a person of substance*

2 a lot of something: *a wealth of information*

abundance *This area has an abundance of safe beaches.*

bounty *summer's bounty of fruits and vegetables*

plenty *He grew up in a time of plenty.*

store *She dipped into her store of theatrical anecdotes.*

ANTONYM **shortage**

See also **success**

wealthy

▷ ADJECTIVE

having plenty of money: *She came from a very wealthy background.*

affluent *living in an affluent neighbourhood*

comfortable *He's from a comfortable family.*

opulent *Most of the cash went into supporting his opulent lifestyle.*

prosperous *The place looks more prosperous than ever.*

rich *I'm going to be very rich one day.*

well-to-do *a rather well-to-do family in the shipping business*

ANTONYM **poor**

See also **rich**

wear

▷ VERB

1 to be dressed in something: *He was wearing a brown suit.*

be clothed in *She was clothed in a flowered dress.*

be dressed in *The women were dressed in their finest attire.*

don *The police responded by donning riot gear.*

have on *I had my new shoes on that night.*

put on *She had to put on her glasses to read the paper.*

sport *sporting a red tie*

2 to become worse in condition with use or

age: *The carpet is badly worn.*
corrode *The pipes were badly corroded.*
erode *Exposed rock is quickly eroded by wind and rain.*
fray *the tablecloth's fraying edges*
rub *Over the years, the inscription on my watch had been rubbed smooth.*
wash away *The topsoil had been washed away by the incessant rain.*
▷ *NOUN*

3 the type of use that causes something to be damaged: *The tires showed signs of wear.*
corrosion *Zinc is used to protect other metals from corrosion.*
deterioration *The building is already showing signs of deterioration.*
erosion *erosion of the river valleys*
use *The floors must be able to cope with heavy use.*
See also **clothes**

wear away *See* **eat away, erode**

wear down *See* **erode**

wearied *See* **bored**

weariness *See* **boredom**

wear out
▷ *VERB*
to make someone tired: *The past few days have really worn me out.*
exhaust *The long working day exhausted him.*
tire *Early-morning practice sessions sometimes tire me.*
weary *wearied by the constant demands on his time*
See also **exhaust**

weary
▷ *ADJECTIVE*
very tired: *I'm just too weary to walk another step.*
drained *He's always completely drained after a performance.*
exhausted *I was too exhausted and upset to talk.*
fatigued *This heat can leave you feeling fatigued.*
tired *I'm too tired to go out tonight.*
tuckered out INFORMAL *You must be tuckered out after that bus trip.*
worn out *She's just worn out after the long drive.*
See also **sick of, tired, wear out, worn out**

WORDS FOR ... THE WEATHER		
balmy	dull	rainy
blustery	fine	showery
breezy	foggy	snowy
clammy	hot	stormy
clear	humid	sultry
close	icy	sunny
cloudy	mild	thundery
cold	misty	wet
drizzly	muggy	windy
dry	overcast	

weave *See* **twist**

web *See* **tangle**

wedge *See* **lump**

wedlock *See* **marriage**

wee *See* **tiny**

weed out *See* **get rid of**

weep *See* **lament**

weigh *See* **compare, count**

weight *See* **burden, emphasis, influence**

weighted *See* **biased**

weighty *See* **heavy, important, serious**

weird
▷ *ADJECTIVE*
strange or odd: *I had such a weird dream last night.*
bizarre *his bizarre behaviour*
curious *What a curious thing to say!*
extraordinary *an extraordinary occurrence*
funny *There's something funny about them.*
odd *an odd coincidence*
singular FORMAL *I can't think where you got such a singular idea.*
strange *Didn't you notice anything strange about her?*
peculiar *It tasted very peculiar.*
ANTONYM **ordinary**
See also **bizarre, eccentric, odd, peculiar, strange**

welcome *See* **greet, receive**

welcoming *See* **favourable, friendly**

well
▷ *ADVERB*
l in a satisfactory way: *The interview went well.*
satisfactorily *The system should work satisfactorily.*
smoothly *So far, the rehearsals are going smoothly.*
splendidly *They have behaved splendidly, and we are very proud.*

successfully *The new system is working successfully.*
2 with skill and ability: *He draws well.*
ably *She was ably assisted by the other performer.*
admirably *dealing admirably with a difficult situation*
adequately *He speaks Spanish very adequately.*
competently *They handled the situation very competently.*
effectively *In the first period, she performed effectively at defence.*
efficiently *He works efficiently under pressure.*
expertly *He expertly arranged the flowers.*
professionally *These tickets have been forged very professionally.*
skilfully *He skilfully refinished the floors.*
ANTONYM **badly**
3 fully and with thoroughness: *The dishes should be well washed and well dried.*
amply *I was amply rewarded for my trouble.*
closely *He studied the documents closely.*
completely *Make sure you defrost the turkey completely.*
fully *The new system is now fully under way.*
highly *one of the most highly regarded authors*
meticulously *She had planned her trip meticulously.*
rigorously *Their duties have not been performed as rigorously as they might have been.*
thoroughly *Add the oil and mix thoroughly.*
4 in a kind way: *She treats her employees well.*
compassionately *He always acted compassionately toward them.*
considerately *I expect people to deal with me considerately and fairly.*
favourably *They treat some of their workers more favourably than others.*
humanely *They treat their livestock humanely.*
kindly *They treated the visiting team very kindly.*
with consideration *He was treated with consideration and kindness.*
▷ *ADJECTIVE*
5 having good health: *I'm not very well today.*
fit *She keeps herself really fit.*
healthy *Most people want to be healthy and happy.*
in good condition *He's in good condition for his age.*
in good health *She seemed to be in good health.*

robust *He's never been a very robust child.*
sound *a sound body*
strong *Eat well and you'll soon be strong again.*
ANTONYM **sick**
See also **fit, healthy**

well off *See* **rich**

well-behaved *See* **polite**

well-being *See* **comfort, health**

well-built *See* **sturdy**

well-known *See* **prominent**

well-liked *See* **popular**

well-mannered *See* **polite**

well-to-do *See* **wealthy**

well-versed *See* **experienced**

wet
▷ *ADJECTIVE*
1 covered in liquid: *Don't get your feet wet.*
damp *Her hair was still damp.*
drenched *getting drenched in the storm*
moist *The soil is reasonably moist after the September rain.*
saturated *The chips were saturated with grease.*
soaked *soaked to the skin*
sodden *We took off our sodden clothes.*
waterlogged *The game was called off because the grounds were waterlogged.*
ANTONYM **dry**
2 in rainy weather conditions: *It was a miserable, wet day.*
humid *hot and humid weather conditions*
misty *The air was cold and misty.*
rainy *Their rainy season starts in December.*
showery *The day had been showery with sunny breaks.*
ANTONYM **dry**
▷ *VERB*
3 to put liquid on to something: *Wet the edges and stick them together.*
dampen *Dampen the shirt before ironing it.*
irrigate *irrigated by a system of interconnected canals*
moisten *Take a sip of water to moisten your throat.*
soak *The water had soaked his jacket and shirt.*
spray *The mobile water tank can spray the whole field in half an hour.*
water *We have to water the plants when the weather is dry.*
ANTONYM **dry**
See also **damp, soak**

whack See **bang, blow**

whereabouts See **location, position**

wherewithal See **potential**

whiff See **trace**

while See **but, period, space, time**

whim
▷ NOUN
a sudden idea or wish to do something: *We decided to go there more or less on a whim.*
craze *the latest fitness craze*
fad *just a passing fad*
fancy *I had a fancy for some strawberries.*
impulse *Resist the impulse to smoke.*
urge *He had an urge to sing in public.*

whimsical See **eccentric**

whine See **complain, grumble, moan**

whip up See **incite**

whirl See **blow, spin**

whisper See **rumour**

SHADES OF ... *WHITE*	
cream	off-white
ivory	pearl
magnolia	snow-white

whole
▷ ADJECTIVE
1 indicating all of something: *We spent the whole summer away.*
complete *The list filled a complete page.*
entire *There are only ten of those stores in the entire country.*
full *a full week's notice*
total *The evening was a total disaster.*
uncut *the uncut version of the movie*
undivided *You have my undivided loyalty.*
▷ NOUN
2 the full amount of something: *the whole of Asia*
aggregate *the aggregate of the individual scores*
all *All is not lost.*
everything *Everything that happened is my fault.*
lot *I'm fed up with the lot of you.*
sum total *The small room contained the sum total of their possessions.*
total *The actual total was far higher.*
See also **complete, total**

wholehearted See **sincere**

wholesome See **beneficial, healthy, safe**

wicked
▷ ADJECTIVE
1 very bad or evil: *That was a wicked thing to do.*
atrocious *atrocious crimes against humanity*
bad *Please forgive our bad behaviour.*
depraved *the work of depraved criminals*
evil *the country's most evil terrorists*
sinful *"This is a sinful world," he said.*
vicious *a cruel and vicious dictator*
2 mischievous in an amusing or attractive way: *She always felt wicked when eating chocolate.*
impish *an impish sense of humour*
mischievous *like a mischievous child*
naughty *little boys using naughty words*
See also **evil**

wickedness See **evil, sin**

wide
▷ ADJECTIVE
1 measuring a large distance from side to side: *It should be wide enough to give plenty of working space.*
ANTONYM **narrow**
2 extensive in scope: *a wide range of colours*
ANTONYM **narrow**
▷ ADVERB
3 as far as possible: *Open wide!*
See WORD STUDY **wide** on next page
See also **broad, extensive, thick**

widen See **extend**

wide-ranging See **broad**

widespread
▷ ADJECTIVE
existing over a large area: *Food shortages are widespread.*
broad *The agreement won broad support.*
common *a common perception about teenagers*
extensive *extensive damage*
pervasive *the pervasive influence of technology in our lives*
prevalent *Computer viruses are prevalent on the Internet.*
rife *Bribery and corruption were rife.*
See also **common, extensive, general, mass, universal**

wife See **partner**

wild
▷ ADJECTIVE
1 not cultivated or domesticated: *a meadow of wild flowers*
fierce *Fierce hyenas scavenged for food after the kill.*
free *stunning pictures of wild and free animals*

There are a number of ways in which the word **wide** can be used, depending on what you are referring to. You can make your language more interesting by using one of the following instead.

- **measuring a large distance from side to side**

He was wearing ridiculously **baggy** trousers.

His shoulders were **broad** and his waist narrow.

The park has swings and an **expansive** play area.

The grounds were more **extensive** than the town itself.

She was wearing a dress with a **full** skirt.

The Great Lakes make up an **immense** body of water.

This fish lives mainly in **large** rivers and lakes.

I like **roomy** jackets with pockets.

The house has a **spacious** kitchen.

She pointed out the long **sweeping** curve of the bay.

The farmer owned **vast** stretches of land.

- **extensive in scope**

There is **ample** scope here for the imagination.

A **broad** range of issues was discussed.

He has very **catholic** tastes in music.

I want to buy a **comprehensive** guide to the region.

He has an **encyclopedic** knowledge of the subject.

The author's treatment of the topic is **exhaustive**.

The question has received **extensive** press coverage.

They voted for a plan to introduce **far-ranging** reforms.

The area provides an **immense** range of tourist activities.

The farmer's market offers a **large** selection of goods at reasonable prices.

The company makes a **vast** range of products.

The aims of the redesign are **wide-ranging** but simple.

- **as far as possible**

He opened the map out **completely** so we could see.

I could tell from his **dilated** pupils that he was terrified.

To get the best reception, extend the aerial **fully**.

His mouth was **fully open** in astonishment.

Spread the peanut butter **right out to** the crust.

---

natural *In the natural state, this animal is not ferocious.*

uncultivated *developed from an uncultivated type of grass*

undomesticated *These cats lived wild and were completely undomesticated.*

untamed *the untamed horses of Sable Island*

2 in stormy conditions: *They were not deterred by the wild weather.*

howling *a howling gale*

raging *We sought shelter from the raging torrent.*

rough *The two ships collided in rough seas.*

stormy *a dark and stormy night*

violent *That night they were hit by a violent storm.*

3 without control or restraint: *wild with excitement*

boisterous *Most of the children were noisy and boisterous.*

rowdy *the soccer fans' rowdy behaviour*

turbulent *five turbulent years of marriage*

uncontrolled *His uncontrolled behaviour disturbed the entire group.*

wayward *a group of wayward tourists*
See also **crazy, fanatical, irresponsible, on the rampage, rowdy, violent**

wildness *See* **abandon**

wilful *See* **obstinate, stubborn**

will

▷ *VERB*

1 to leave something to someone when you die: *He had willed his fortune to his children.*

bequeath *She bequeathed her collection to the local museum.*

leave *Everything was left to the housekeeper.*

pass on *He passed on much of his estate to charity.*

▷ *NOUN*

2 the strong determination to achieve something: *the will to win*

determination *Determination has always been a part of her make-up.*

purpose *They are enthusiastic and have a sense of purpose.*

resolution *He acted with resolution to clear his name.*

resolve *This will strengthen the public's resolve.*
willpower *succeeding by sheer willpower*
3 what someone wants: *the will of the people*
choice *It's your choice.*
inclination *She showed no inclination to go.*
mind *You can go if you have a mind to do so.*
volition *acting on my own volition*
wish *done against my wishes*

willing
▷ ADJECTIVE
ready and eager to do something: *a willing helper*
agreeable *We can go ahead if you are agreeable.*
eager *Children are eager to learn.*
game *He still had new ideas and was game to try them.*
happy *That's a risk I'm happy to take.*
prepared *I'm not prepared to take orders from you.*
ready *ready to take on last year's champions*
ANTONYM **unwilling**
See also **agreeable, ready**

willpower *See* **will**

wilt *See* **wither**

wily *See* **crafty, cunning, devious, sly**

wimp *See* **coward**

win
▷ VERB
I to defeat your opponents: *The top four teams all won.*
be victorious *Despite the strong opposition, she was victorious.*
come first *They unexpectedly came first this year.*
prevail *the votes he must win in order to prevail*
succeed *the skills and qualities needed to succeed*
triumph *a symbol of good triumphing over evil*
ANTONYM **lose**
2 to succeed in obtaining something: *trying to win the support of the community*
achieve *We have achieved our objective.*
attain *He recently attained his pilot's licence.*
gain *She finally gained a promotion.*
get *My entry got an honourable mention.*
secure *Her achievements helped secure her the job.*
▷ NOUN
3 a victory in a contest: *Last night's win was an important one.*

success *his success in the Tour de France*
triumph *their World Cup triumph*
victory *the 3-1 victory over Switzerland*
ANTONYM **defeat**
See also **earn, gain, triumph, victory**

win over *See* **persuade, reason**

wince *See* **flinch**

WORDS FOR ... WIND	
Alberta clipper ❆	hurricane
breeze	squall
Chinook ❆	tornado
cyclone	typhoon
gale	whirlwind
gust	wind

wind *See* **coil**

wind up *See* **conclude**

winner
▷ NOUN
a person who wins something: *The winners will be notified by mail.*
champion *a former Olympic champion*
conqueror *This time they easily overcame their former conquerors.*
victor *He emerged as the victor by the second day.*
ANTONYM **loser**
See also **champion, success**

wintry *See* **cold**

wipe *See* **clean**

wisdom
▷ NOUN
judgment used to make sensible decisions: *the wisdom that comes from experience*
discernment *Her keen discernment made her an excellent collector.*
insight *someone of considerable insight and diplomatic skills*
judgment *He respected our judgment on this matter.*
knowledge *the quest for scientific knowledge*
reason *a conflict between emotion and reason*
ANTONYM **foolishness**
See also **knowledge, sense**

wise
▷ ADJECTIVE
able to make use of experience and judgment: *a wise person*
informed *an informed guess at their wealth*
judicious *the judicious use of discipline*
perceptive *the words of a perceptive political commentator*
rational *You must look at both sides before*

you can reach a rational decision.
sensible *The sensible thing is to leave them alone.*
shrewd *a shrewd deduction about what was going on*
ANTONYM **foolish**
See also **logical, reasonable, sensible**

wisecrack *See* joke

wish
▷ NOUN
1 a desire for something: *She was sincere in her wish to make up with me.*
desire *his desire to play in a band*
hankering *She had always had a hankering to be an actress.*
hunger *a hunger for success*
longing *He felt a longing for familiar surroundings.*
urge *an urge to bicycle across the country*
want *Supermarkets respond to the wants of their customers.*
▷ VERB
2 to want something: *We wished to return.*
desire *He was bored and desired to go home.*
hunger *She hungered for adventure.*
long *I'm longing for the holidays.*
thirst *thirsting for knowledge*
want *people who know exactly what they want in life*
yearn *They yearned for a chance to win just one game.*
See also **desire, urge, want, will**

wistful *See* sad

wit *See* common sense, humour, intelligence

witchcraft *See* magic

withdraw
▷ VERB
1 to take something out: *I withdrew some money from the bank.*
draw out *I'll have to draw out some of my savings.*
extract *The dentist had to extract the tooth.*
remove *I removed the splinter from her finger.*
take out *They took out money from the account.*
2 to back out of an activity: *They withdrew from the conference.*
back out *He backed out of the agreement.*
leave *He left the game because of an injury.*
pull out *Their representative pulled out of the talks after two days.*
retire *The jury retired three hours ago.*
retreat *retreating from the harsh realities of life*
See also **leave, remove, retreat**

withdrawal *See* retreat

withdrawn *See* distant, remote

wither
▷ VERB
to become weaker and fade away: *Will the company flourish or wither?*
decline *My grandfather's health has declined.*
droop *plants drooping in the heat*
fade *Prospects for peace have already started to fade.*
shrivel *They watched their crops shrivel and die in the drought.*
wilt *The roses wilted the day after she bought them.*

withering *See* scornful

withhold *See* deny, refuse

without charge *See* free

without delay *See* now

without doubt *See* certainly

witness
▷ NOUN
1 someone who has seen something happen: *The police appealed for witnesses to come forward.*
bystander *An innocent bystander was slightly injured.*
eyewitness *Eyewitnesses described the crime they had witnessed.*
observer *A casual observer would not have noticed them.*
onlooker *a small crowd of onlookers*
spectator *carried out in full view of spectators*
▷ VERB
2 to see something happening: *Anyone who witnessed the attack should call the police.*
be present at *We were present at the opening of the new stadium.*
observe *We observed them training for the race.*
see *I saw him do it.*
watch *We watched them set up the display.*
See also **observe, spectator**

wits *See* head

witticism *See* joke

witty
▷ ADJECTIVE
amusing in a clever way: *He's so witty I could listen to him for hours.*
amusing *She provided an amusing commentary to the film.*

brilliant *a brilliant after-dinner speaker*
clever *The valedictorian had several clever lines.*
funny *a movie packed with incredibly funny dialogue*
humorous *a satirical and humorous parody*
sparkling *She's famous for her sparkling conversation.*
See also **funny**

wizard *See* **expert**

wobbly *See* **loose, shaky, unsteady**

woe *See* **care, misery, sorrow**

wolf *See* **gobble**

woman
▷ NOUN
an adult female human being: *The woman over there is my aunt.*
female *Females outnumber males in this group of students.*
lady *Ladies and gentlemen, may I please have your attention.*
See also **adult, female**

womanly *See* **female**

wonder
▷ VERB
1 to think about something with curiosity: *I wondered what that noise was.*
ask oneself *You have to ask yourself what this really means.*
ponder *pondering how to improve the team*
puzzle *Researchers continue to puzzle over the origins of the disease.*
speculate *He refused to speculate about the contents of the letter.*
2 to be surprised and amazed: *He wondered at their sudden change of plans.*
be amazed *Most of the cast was amazed by the play's success.*
be astonished *I was astonished to discover his true age.*
boggle *The mind boggles at what might be in store for us.*
marvel *We marvelled at her endless energy.*
▷ NOUN
3 something that amazes people: *one of the wonders of nature*
marvel *a marvel of high technology*
miracle *It's a miracle no one was killed.*
phenomenon *a well-known geographical phenomenon*
spectacle *a spectacle not to be missed*
See also **amazement, miracle, surprise**

wonderful
▷ ADJECTIVE
1 extremely good: *It's wonderful to see you.*
excellent *The recording quality is excellent.*
great INFORMAL *a great bunch of friends*
marvellous *What a marvellous time we had!*
superb *She gave a superb performance.*
tremendous *I thought it was a tremendous book.*
2 very impressive: *The sunset was a truly wonderful sight.*
amazing *containing some amazing special effects*
astounding *The results are quite astounding.*
incredible *The intensity of colour was incredible.*
magnificent *magnificent views across the valley*
remarkable *It was a remarkable achievement to complete the course.*
See also **brilliant, grand, marvellous, splendid, superb**

wont *See* **custom**

woo *See* **court**

wooden *See* **stiff**

wool *See* **coat**

word
▷ NOUN
1 a remark: *I'd like to say a word of thanks to everyone who helped me.*
comment *He left without any further comment.*
remark *Apart from that one remark, she stayed quiet all evening.*
statement *The singer issued a brief statement to the press.*
utterance *a crowd of admirers who hung on his every utterance*
2 a brief conversation: *May I please have a quick word with you?*
chat *We need to have a chat about the arrangements.*
conversation *He recalled his brief conversation with the writer.*
discussion *We had a very short discussion about what to do.*
talk *I bumped into her yesterday and we had a quick talk.*
3 a message: *Since then we've had no word from them.*
announcement *There has been no formal announcement from either government.*
bulletin *A spokesperson said no bulletin would be issued.*
communication *The ambassador brought a communication from the president.*
information *They will issue written*

information in due course.

intelligence *He wanted to convey the latest military intelligence.*

message *Did he leave any message for me?*

news *Is there any news from Parliament Hill?*

4 a promise or guarantee: *He gave me his word that he would be there.*

assurance *Do I have your assurance that you'll take responsibility?*

oath *She gave her solemn oath not to tell anyone.*

pledge *He gave his personal pledge that he would help.*

promise *I'll support you – you have my promise on that.*

word of honour *I want your word of honour that you'll respect my privacy.*

See also **bond, guarantee, information, message, news, put, remark, rumour, term**

word of honour *See* **word**

wording *See* **language**

wordless *See* **silent**

work

▷ VERB

I to do the tasks required of you: *I had to work ten hours a day.*

labour *labouring all day in the fields*

slave *slaving over my homework*

slog away *They are still slogging away at algebra.*

toil *millions of children toiling in factories around the world*

ANTONYM **laze**

▷ NOUN

2 someone's job: *She's trying to find work.*

business *We have business to attend to first.*

craft *She learned her craft from an expert.*

employment *unable to find employment*

job *I got a job as a gardener.*

livelihood *farmers who depend on the land for their livelihood*

occupation *Please state your occupation.*

profession *a dentist by profession*

3 the tasks that have to be done: *Sometimes he had to take work home.*

assignment *written assignments*

chore *We share the household chores.*

duty *My duty is to look after the animals.*

job *It turned out to be a bigger job than expected.*

task *catching up with administrative tasks*

See also **act, behave, book, drive, effort, exercise, fashion, function, go, labour, piece, struggle, succeed**

work together *See* **co-operate, team, unite**

workable *See* **possible**

worker

▷ NOUN

a person who works: *seeking a reliable research worker*

craftsperson *furniture made by local craftspeople*

employee *Many of its employees are university graduates.*

labourer *a farm labourer*

See also **employee**

workers *See* **labour, staff**

workforce *See* **labour, staff**

working *See* **busy**

workmate *See* **associate, colleague**

work out

▷ VERB

I to find the solution to something: *It took us some time to work out what was happening.*

calculate *First, calculate your weekly expenses.*

figure out *You don't need to be a detective to figure that one out.*

resolve *They hoped the crisis could be quickly resolved.*

solve *We'll solve the case ourselves and surprise everyone.*

2 to happen in a certain way: *Things didn't work out that way after all.*

develop *Wait and see how the situation develops.*

go *Did it all go well?*

happen *Things don't happen the way you want them to.*

turn out *Sometimes life doesn't turn out as we expect.*

See also **calculate, comprehend, crack, reckon, resolve, solve**

world *See* **earth, scene**

worldwide *See* **universal**

worn *See* **shabby, worn out**

worn out

▷ ADJECTIVE

I no longer usable because of extreme wear: *These shoes are worn out.*

broken-down *Broken-down cars lined the road.*

tattered *tattered clothes*

threadbare *threadbare carpet*

worn *Worn tires are very dangerous.*

2 extremely tired: *You must be worn out after the trip.*

exhausted *I'm too exhausted to do any more today.*

fatigued *The humidity can leave you feeling fatigued.*

prostrate *He lay prostrate with exhaustion.*

tired *I need to rest because I'm tired.*

weary *a weary traveller*

worried

▷ ADJECTIVE

being anxious about something: *I'm worried about our lost dog.*

anxious *I was very anxious about their safety.*

bothered *I'm not bothered about it at all.*

concerned *a phone call from a concerned neighbour*

nervous *They're nervous about driving in this weather.*

troubled *I was troubled by the news in their letter.*

uneasy *an uneasy feeling that everything was going wrong*

ANTONYM **unconcerned**

See also **anxious, nervous, uneasy**

worry

▷ VERB

I to feel anxious about something: *Don't worry, it's bound to arrive soon.*

be anxious *They admitted they were still anxious about the situation.*

brood *constantly brooding about his supposed bad luck*

feel uneasy *I felt very uneasy at the lack of response.*

fret *You mustn't fret about someone else's problems.*

2 to disturb someone with a problem: *I didn't want to worry the kids with this.*

bother *I hate to bother you again so soon.*

hassle INFORMAL *He was hassling me to get the work done.*

pester *I wish they'd stop pestering me for an answer.*

plague *I'm not going to plague you with more questions.*

trouble *Don't trouble me while I'm working.*

▷ NOUN

3 a feeling of anxiety: *a major source of worry*

anxiety *anxieties about money*

apprehension *real anger and apprehension about the future*

concern *growing concern for the environment*

fear *His fears might be groundless.*

misgiving *She had some misgivings about what she was about to do.*

unease *a deep sense of unease about the coming interview*

See also **agitate, anxiety, bother, burden, care, concern, distress, disturb, sorrow, stress, trouble**

worrying *See* **serious**

worsen

▷ VERB

to become more difficult: *Their relationship worsened.*

decline *Sales declined during the summer.*

degenerate *The whole tone of the election campaign began to degenerate.*

deteriorate *The weather conditions are deteriorating.*

go downhill *Things have gone steadily downhill since she left.*

ANTONYM **improve**

worship

▷ VERB

I to praise and revere something: *a place where people can worship*

honour *to honour those who defended us*

venerate *the most venerated religious figure in the country*

2 to love and admire someone or something: *She had worshipped him from afar for years.*

adore *an adoring parent*

idolize *She idolized her grandparents as she was growing up.*

love *They genuinely loved and cherished each other.*

ANTONYM **despise**

▷ NOUN

3 a feeling of love and admiration for

something: *Fans treated the home team with a respect close to worship.*
admiration *Her eyes widened in admiration.*
adoration *The new rock star wasn't used to such adoration.*
adulation *The book was received with adulation by the critics.*
devotion *the fans' devotion to the singer*
homage *pay homage to a sovereign*
praise *a poem in praise of their teacher*
See also **love**

PLACES OF ... WORSHIP	
cathedral	pagoda
chapel	shrine
church	sweat lodge ✤
gurdwara	synagogue
meeting house	tabernacle
mosque	temple

worth See **merit, quality, value**

worthless
  ▷ ADJECTIVE
having no real value or worth: *a worthless piece of junk*
meaningless *Your apology is meaningless to me.*
paltry *a paltry amount*
poor *a poor reward for his effort*
trifling *We were paid a trifling sum.*
trivial *She would go to the doctor for any trivial complaint.*
useless *I felt useless and a failure.*
valueless *The ring that I found turned out to be valueless.*
ANTONYM **valuable**
See also **empty, useless**

worthwhile See **productive, useful, valuable**

worthy See **noble, respectable**

would like See **fancy**

wound See **harm, hurt, injure, injury**

wounded See **hurt**

wrangle See **argue, clash, dispute, squabble**

wrap See **enclose**

wrapped up See **preoccupied**

wrapper See **cover**

wrath See **anger, rage**

wreak See **bring**

wreck See **crash, destroy, ruin, spoil**

wrench See **tug, twist**

wretched See **miserable, sorry, unlucky**

wring See **exact, twist**

wrinkle See **crumple, fold**

write
  ▷ VERB
to record something in writing: *Write your name and address on a piece of paper.*
compose *Calixa Lavallée composed the music for "O Canada."*
correspond *We corresponded by e-mail for several years.*
inscribe *Their names were inscribed on the front of the monument.*
record *He recorded his observations in his journal.*
take down *notes taken down at the meeting*
See also **compose**

write down See **record**

wrong
  ▷ ADJECTIVE
1 not correct or truthful: *That was the wrong answer.*
false *We don't know if the information is true or false.*
faulty *His diagnosis was faulty from the outset.*
incorrect *a decision based on figures that were incorrect*
mistaken *a mistaken view of the situation*
unsound *The thinking is well meaning, but the logic is unsound.*
untrue *The remarks were completely untrue.*
ANTONYM **right**
2 morally unacceptable: *It's wrong to hurt people.*
bad *He may be irresponsible, but he's not a bad person.*
crooked *crooked business deals*
evil *the country's most evil terrorists*
illegal *Identity theft is illegal.*
immoral *Many would consider such practices immoral.*
unfair *It was unfair that he should suffer so much.*
unjust *unjust treatment*
ANTONYM **right**
  ▷ NOUN
3 an unjust action: *the wrongs of our society*
abuse *human rights abuses*
crime *crimes against humanity*
grievance *He had a deep sense of grievance.*
injustice *A great injustice had been done to them.*
sin *He admitted the many sins of his past.*
See also **crime, injustice, sin, unfair**

wrongful See **unfair**

TYPES OF ... WRITING

autobiography
ballad
biography
column
dissertation
editorial
epitaph
essay
fable
feature
fiction
legend
letter
lyric
memoir
myth
narrative

nonfiction
novel
obituary
parable
play
poem
report
review
rhyme
riddle
script
story
thesis
verse

styles used in writing

alliteration
cliché

idiom
metaphor
narrative
parody
pun
satire
simile

features of writing

character
dialogue
imagery
motif
plot
setting
subplot
theme

Yy

yank *See* **pull, tug**

yarn *See* **story**

yawning *See* **deep**

yearn *See* **desire, long, wish**

yearn for *See* **be dying for, miss**

yearning *See* **desire, longing**

yell *See* **call, cry, scream, shout**

SHADES OF ... *YELLOW*	
amber	mustard
canary	primrose
champagne	saffron
citrus	sand
daffodil	straw
gold	topaz
lemon	

yelp *See* **bay**

yen *See* **desire**

yes
▷ *INTERJECTION*
an expression used to agree with something
or say it is true: *"Are you a friend of his?"*
"Yes."
okay *"Will we leave now?" "Okay, if you
like."*
sure *"Can I come too?" "Sure."*
ANTONYM **no**

yet *See* **but**

yield *See* **give, give in, submit,
surrender**

yielding *See* **soft**

young
▷ *ADJECTIVE*
1 not yet mature: *young people*
adolescent *adolescent years*
immature *an immature female whale*
infant *their infant daughter*
junior *a junior member of the family*
juvenile *the juvenile lead in the play*
little *What were you like when you were
little?*
youthful *the youthful stars of the movie*
ANTONYM **old**
▷ *PLURAL NOUN*
2 the babies an animal has: *The hen may not
be able to feed its young.*
babies *animals making nests for their babies*
brood *a hungry brood of fledglings*
family *a family of weasels*
litter *a litter of pups*

little ones *a family of elephants with their
little ones*
offspring *the rats' offspring*

youngster *See* **boy, child**

youth *See* **boy**

youthful *See* **young**

Zz

zany *See* **crazy**

zeal *See* **passion**

zealot *See* **fan, fanatic**

zealous *See* **fervent**

zenith *See* **peak, top**

zero
▷ *NOUN*
nothing or the number 0: *I will now count
from zero to ten.*
nil *They beat Argentina one-nil.*
nothing *Some weeks I earn nothing.*
nought *How many noughts are there in a
million?*

zest *See* **spirit**

zone *See* **area, region**

zoom *See* **tear**

X
Y
Z